# Family Property and Financial Provision

Tolley Publishing Company Limited

# Family Property and Financial Provision

by J G Miller, LLM, PhD,
*Solicitor, Professor of Law, University of East Anglia, Norwich*

Third Edition

Tolley Publishing Company Limited
A UNITED NEWSPAPERS PUBLICATION

ISBN 0 85459 750-6


First published 1974
Second edition 1983
Third edition 1993



Published by
Tolley Publishing Company Ltd
Tolley House
2 Addiscombe Road
Croydon
Surrey
CR9 5AF
081-686 9141

Typeset in Great Britain by
Kerrypress Ltd, Luton, Bedfordshire

Printed and bound by
BPCC Wheatons Ltd, Exeter

# Preface

It is ten years since the appearance of the last edition of this book. This interval is due in part to my commitments, particularly to university administration. Much has happened in the field of family property and financial provision during that period and extensive rewriting has been necessary. The original manuscript for this edition was completed in June 1992 but I had the opportunity of updating the text in March 1993. Material available to me between those two dates has been referred to and incorporated as far as possible. The section on the Child Support Act 1991 in Chapter 17 was written before publication of the voluminous regulations, but I have included reference to the relevant statutory instruments where appropriate.

The overall objective of the book remains the same. It is an attempt to examine the English law relating to family property and financial provision and the primary aim remains that of providing the practitioner with a guide to what still remains a complicated patchwork of legislation and case law. As in previous editions Chapter 1 traces the development of the law and summarises the overall context. In an area of rapid development it is important to try to provide such a wider view as well as attempting more detailed analysis and exposition. Some rationalisation has taken place as a result of legislation, for example, by the Children Act 1989 in relation to financial provision for children, but this is outweighed by the new approach of the Child Support Act 1991. The full impact of this new machinery has not yet been felt, but its effect will permeate many other areas considered in this book.

I am grateful for the support during the preparation of this edition of the staff of the publishers, originally Fourmat Ltd and subsequently Tolley Publishing Co Ltd of which Fourmat is now a part. Pauline Callow and Irene Kaplan were associated with the project from the start and I am very grateful to Alan Radford for his work on the manuscript. Tolley have also relieved me of the burden of preparing the Tables and Index. The patient forbearance and support of my family have, of course, been an essential precondition of such an undertaking as this.

*Gareth Miller*
*Norwich*
*September 1993*

# Contents

# Table of Statutes

xii

  Enforcement) Act............................389, 578
  s 2.................................................498, 576
    (5).....................................................577
    3(1)(2)..............................................401
    (4)-(6)...............................................401
    4(6) ...................................................404
    5.........................................................400
    (1)............................................403, 577
    (3) ...........................................404, 577
    (5) .....................................................403
    (6) .....................................................578
    6.........................................................576
    7.................................................401, 576
    9.................................................400, 575
    (1) .....................................................403
    (2)(3)(5)..........................................404
    12.......................................................401
    13, 14...............................................578
    21(1) .........................................401, 577
    22(2) .........................................400, 575
    26(1) .................................................402
    (2)(3)................................................402
    (4)(6)................................................402
    27A, 27B ..........................................402
    27C.....................................................403
    28.......................................................402
    28A(1)-(3) ........................................402
    32.......................................................403
    34(3) ..................................................404
    40..................400, 401, 403, 575, 576
    Part I..............400, 401, 564, 570, 573, 575
    Part II .......................................400, 564
1973 Administration of Justice Act
  s 8...............................................184, 185
1973 Domicile and Matrimonial Proceedings
  Act.....................................................354
    s 5(6) ................................................352
    (b)......................................................353
    6(1) ...................................................409
    Sch 1 para 8........................................351, 352
    para 9.................................352, 353
1973 Guardianship Act ....................5, 410, 564
  s 2(3)(4A).............................................570
1973 Matrimonial Causes Act .....7, 9, 10-12, 16,
    124,126, 148, 152, 154,
    157,158, 190, 206, 325,
    326, 340, 344, 353, 361,
    372, 375, 388, 410, 411,
    423, 425, 427, 428, 431,
    494, 497, 499, 514, 523,
    528, 535, 537, 547, 550,
    551, 576, 579
    s 1(1) ................................................207
    (2) .....................................................213
    (e)......................................................207
    (7) .....................................................262
    2(6) ...................................................397
    5........................210-212, 214, 215, 313
    (1) .....................................................207
    (f) ......................................................253
    (2) .....................................................207

    (3) .............................................208
    10(1) ..........................................213, 215
    (2) .....................................213, 215, 216
    (3) .....................................213, 214, 215
    (4) .....................................................214
    16.......................................................507
    18(2) ..................................................507
    22................................................216, 574
    23.........................54, 147, 195, 214, 215,
    219, 221, 229, 230, 241,
    242, 254, 258, 272, 291,
    341, 360, 362-364, 367,
    369, 377, 378, 390, 424
    (1) ...........................................348, 574
    (c)(f).................................................337
    (2) .........................237, 337, 413, 574
    (3) .............................................221, 412
    (a)(b).................................................216
    (4) .....................................................574
    (5) .............................................216, 237
    (6) .....................................................221
    24....................16, 60, 63, 68, 130, 147,
    150, 151, 153, 155, 163,
    170, 171, 178, 179, 187,
    214, 215, 225, 229-231,
    254, 258, 272, 291, 337-339,
    341, 362-364, 367-369,
    377, 412, 472
    (1) ...........................168, 169, 348, 378
    (a)..............................................226, 241
    (b).....................................230, 241, 417
    (c)(d).................................................227
    (3) .....................................................237
    (6) .....................................................349
    24A............147, 230, 231, 254, 255,
    258, 323, 363, 364
    (a)-(h)................................................255
    (1) .............................................229, 242, 348
    (2) .....................................................229
    (3)-(5)................................................230
    25........................213, 214, 217, 231, 232,
    249, 252, 254, 272, 274,
    280, 285, 286, 289, 290,
    291, 304, 316, 318, 338,
    360, 369, 392, 416, 468,
    534, 536
    (1) .....................10, 11, 253, 254, 258,
    308, 362, 393, 414
    (a)-(g)................................251, 255
    (2) .........................259, 405, 417, 533
    (a)..............224, 251, 255, 260, 283,
    327, 350, 414
    (b).....................251, 255, 260, 261,
    327, 350, 414
    (c)..............251, 255, 260, 327, 350,
    405, 406, 414
    (d).....................251, 327, 350, 532
    (e).....................251, 255, 260, 327,
    350, 414
    (f) ...........................54, 308, 327, 350
    (g).....................281, 310, 327, 350
    (h).....................................327, 350

# Table of Statutory Instruments

# Table of Cases

# Chapter 1

# Introduction

## 1. The economic aspects of the family

The family is a social institution of fundamental importance, but it is also an important economic unit. As an economic unit its successful functioning depends upon adequate financial resources, and involves the acquisition of assets of various kinds for the use of the family. A consideration of the principles relating to family property and financial provision for a family is dominated by the problems which arise on the break-up of a family unit based upon marriage, for generally it is only then that the law is called upon to play an active role in seeking to reconcile the conflicting financial and proprietary interests of its members. In the case of a family based upon a successful marriage these principles do not often have to be considered, for the law is rarely called upon to play an active role in regulating the management of its financial affairs and the allocation of its resources as between its members, except on the death of one of the spouses.

However, this is not invariably so, for it is not only the members of a family who are concerned with the allocation of its resources. The satisfaction of a family's needs will involve dealing with other persons so that, for example, the interests of creditors may have to be taken into account and reconciled with the interests of the members of the family even though the marriage has not failed. The State, too, is an interested party in the economic aspects of the family, not only for the purpose of collecting taxes, but also because it has increasingly taken upon itself the task of supplementing the resources of a family where these have proved deficient.

## 2. The family and the law of property

At common law a married woman was legally dependent upon her husband. On marriage he acquired the control and management of his wife's freehold property, and on her death before him, he took a life interest if there was a child of the marriage. He received the income from her leasehold property, and could dispose of it

1

*inter vivos*, though not by will. If she predeceased him, he took such property absolutely. Her personal chattels vested absolutely in the husband as did any such property acquired during the marriage.

The married woman's appalling position was to some extent alleviated by the intervention of equity, which allowed her to administer property given or conveyed for her separate use. Even this was designed not so much to protect the wife as her kinship group and was in reality of importance only in relation to investments. It had little relevance to the family as a unit, but it did serve as a model for the Married Women's Property Act 1882 which was the culmination of the efforts of the movement for reform over many years. The impetus for reform was the plight of the wage-earning wife which began to achieve publicity from about 1830 onwards. See Ulrich, *The Reform of Matrimonial Property Law in England during the Nineteenth Century* (1977) 9 Victoria University of Wellington L.R. 13.

The Married Women's Property Act of 1870 provided that a married woman's wages and earnings should be regarded as her separate property and gave her a power to maintain an action to recover them in her own name. The principle of separate property was extended by the Married Women's Property Act of 1882 which provided that:

"... a married woman shall be capable of acquiring, holding, disposing by will or otherwise, of any real or personal property as her separate property, in the same manner as if she were a *feme sole*, without the intervention of any trustee."

The difficulties which the reference to "separate property" caused in the fields of contract and tort were eventually removed by the Law Reform (Married Women and Tortfeasors) Act 1935. That Act abandoned the concept of the separate estate which had meant, for example, that a married woman's liability in contract was not personal but was limited to her separate estate. It provided that a married woman should be capable of holding and disposing of property in all respects as if she were a *feme sole*. Nevertheless the term "separation of property" has continued to be used to describe the system of matrimonial property established by the Married Women's Property Act of 1882 and consolidated by the Act of 1935, and to distinguish that system from systems of community of property found in other jurisdictions. The fundamental principle on which the system of separation of property is based is that each spouse may acquire and deal with his or her property as if he or she was not married.

The inadequacies of the system for which the reformers of the nineteenth century had struggled did not become apparent, or at least did not attract great attention, until well into the twentieth century. The rules of intestate succession were recast by the Administration of Estates Act 1925 which laid the foundation for the system which has eventually given the surviving spouse a dominant position, but only after amendments in 1952 and 1966. Following much discussion and several unsuccessful Bills, the Inheritance (Family Provision) Act 1938 enabled a surviving wife (or husband) to seek from the court reasonable maintenance out of a deceased spouse's estate. However, the inadequacies of the existing system on the breakdown of marriage and its termination by divorce as opposed to death, did not come to the forefront until the middle of the century.

The principle that each spouse can acquire and deal with his or her property as if he or she was not married takes no account of the family as a unit. While it may be adequate for property acquired as an investment, it ignores the fact that certain assets are acquired as family assets for the use of the family with little thought for the niceties of the law of property. The result was a considerable volume of litigation in which the courts were called upon to ascertain the ownership of such property as between the spouses, generally on the breakdown of marriage, but sometimes on the termination of a successful marriage by the death of one spouse. This revealed the further difficulty that the principle of separation of property also ignores the natural division of economic functions in many if not most families which makes the husband the breadwinner and deprives the wife, who devotes her time to looking after the family and the household, of an equal opportunity of acquiring property. Ownership must be ascertained according to the strict principles of the law of property, and unless a wife has made a financial contribution of some kind or its equivalent which entitles her to a share by virtue of those principles, she acquires no proprietary interest in the family assets. Thus while the employed wife who is able to make a financial contribution to family expenses was not without her problems, the courts were able to go a long way towards helping her. However, for the wife who remained at home the courts could do nothing, and it was probably this factor which gave the main impetus to reform in the mid-twentieth century, whereas it was the position of the employed wife which had provided the impetus for reform a century earlier.

The number of wage earning wives has increased markedly in the last decade or two and in 1978 Inland Revenue statistics indicated that there were more married women at work than at home (*Inland Revenue Statistics* 1977 H.M.S.O. (1978) p. 65). The increased employment of married women has important implications for the future development of matrimonial property rights and financial provision. A leading American commentator has noted that current English and American law reform efforts in the area of marital property were concentrating on the problem of mitigating the harsh effects of the traditional system of separate property in the situation of the housewife without property, through legal devices designed to recognise her contribution by giving her a share in the property acquired by the spouses during the marriage regardless of its source or how title is held. She asks: "Will the propertyless housewife still be around in significant numbers by the time her legal position has been improved? Will legal devices designed to introduce increased sharing of acquests into ... separate property systems be more compatible with current marriage behaviour ideologies than the highly individualistic system introduced by the Married Women's Property Acts in the latter part of the nineteenth century?" (Glendon, *Is there a future for Separate Property?* (1974) 8 Fam. L.Q. 315). This is an invaluable reminder that social conditions are changing and that legal responses must develop accordingly. In England and Wales at least, the housewife without property is still much in evidence and recent reported cases concerned with the economic consequences of divorce show that English law is not yet faced with the situation where husbands and wives have complete equality of opportunity of acquiring property, which is the real justification for a system of complete separation of property. Nevertheless, the increasing ability of married women to provide for themselves, and also perhaps to acquire capital in accordance with traditional property concepts, has important consequences not only in relation to property rights, but in relation to support rights and obligations.

### 3. Support rights and obligations – financial provision

*(a) The common law position*
The common law imposed a duty on a husband to maintain his wife in accordance with his means unless she forfeited her right to be maintained by her misconduct, but it provided her with slender means to enforce it as it merely enabled her to pledge his credit if he failed in his duty (see Chapter 16). It imposed no duty on a wife to maintain her husband, and probably imposed no duty on a parent to maintain a child, or at any rate provided no means by which any such duty might be enforced (see Chapter 17).

*(b) The development of statutory powers*
The power to order maintenance in a number of different circumstances has been conferred on the courts by statute. The Matrimonial Causes Act 1857, which introduced judicial divorce, also empowered the divorce court to order periodical payments by way of maintenance for a wife. The underlying concept in such proceedings was, until relatively recently, the maintenance of the wife and children by the husband, and the conduct of the parties to the marriage was important not only in establishing the right to the principal relief sought, but also when it came to considering the maintenance, if any, to be ordered in favour of the wife. Although since the Act of 1857 the court had had the power to order a settlement of a guilty wife's property for the benefit of her husband and the children of the marriage, it was not until the Matrimonial Causes Act 1937 that power was given to order a wife to pay maintenance to her husband. Even then this applied only when she obtained the decree of divorce on the ground of her husband's incurable insanity. Moreover, the concept of maintenance was reflected in the fact that until the introduction of the power to order a lump sum payment in 1963, the court could only order periodical payments or secured periodical payments. There was no power to order any capital payment or make any adjustment of property rights other than to vary an ante- or post-nuptial settlement. The whole basis of dealing with the financial position of the parties on divorce, nullity or judicial separation was recast by the Matrimonial Proceedings and Property Act 1970 following the reform of the law of divorce by the Divorce Reform Act 1969. The system introduced by the Act of 1970 places husband and wife on an equal footing so far as the powers of the court are concerned (see Chapters 10 and 11). It also gives the court wide powers to adjust the property rights of the parties and has shifted the emphasis from the maintenance of a wife by her husband, to a process of readjustment of the whole financial position of the spouses to meet the new situation brought about by the termination of marriage (see Chapter 11). The expression "maintenance" is replaced by the expression "financial provision", and the conduct of the parties has been reduced in importance, so that it is likely to be relevant only in the minority of cases.

Magistrates' courts obtained the power to order maintenance as part of their matrimonial jurisdiction the origin of which is to be found in the Matrimonial Causes Act 1878 (see Chapter 5 Part 10 and Chapter 16). This gave magistrates' courts power to order a husband convicted of aggravated assault upon his wife to pay maintenance to her in addition to the power to release her from the obligation to live with her husband. The grounds on which such an order might be made were gradually extended, and in the course of time the emphasis shifted from the protection of the wife by a non-cohabitation clause (which was in any event hardly an effective method of protection), to providing her with the financial means of living apart from her husband. It was not until 1937 that magistrates' courts were given a limited power to make an order against a wife in favour of her husband. When the jurisdiction was completely recast by the Domestic Proceedings and Magistrates' Courts Act 1978 the jurisdiction of the magistrates' courts to make orders for financial provision was separated from a new jurisdiction to make personal protection orders and exclusion orders designed to provide more effective protection for a spouse.

One of the grounds on which the magistrates' courts could make an order prior to the 1978 Act was the wilful neglect by one spouse to maintain the other or a child of the family. The concept of wilful neglect to maintain was made the basis of a separate jurisdiction when a wife was given a right to apply to the High Court (and later to a county court) for maintenance by the Law Reform (Miscellaneous Provisions) Act 1949. No such right was given to a husband until the Matrimonial Proceedings and Property Act 1970 effected a limited reform of such proceedings. The jurisdiction was eventually recast by the Domestic Proceedings and Magistrates' Courts Act 1978 which empowers either party to a marriage to apply to a divorce court for an order for financial provision on the ground that the other party to the marriage has failed to provide reasonable maintenance for the applicant or has failed to provide, or to make a proper contribution towards, reasonable maintenance for any child of the family (see Chapter 16).

The powers of the court to order financial provision in the three categories of matrimonial proceedings considered above extend to making provision for children of the family (see Chapter 17). However, in addition to these powers there were enacted a number of statutory provisions specifically concerned with financial provision for children. Thus, financial provision for children could be ordered in proceedings under the Guardianship of Minors Act 1971 and the Guardianship Act 1973 concerned with their custody. Most of these provisions have been replaced by the Children Act 1989, which is considered in Chapter 17. It may also be noted that a person may be ordered to reimburse the Department of Social Security at least part of the cost of assisting relatives whom he or she is liable to maintain under the Social Security Act 1986 (see Chapter 19).

## 4. The relationship between property rights and rights of support and protection

### (a) Occupation of the matrimonial home
The need to modify the exercise of property rights by one member of a family in order to provide support and sometimes protection for the other members of the

family has been evident a long time and has received growing recognition in the last two decades. A matrimonial home and its contents are acquired for the use of the family, and on the breakdown of marriage it is the occupation of the home which frequently becomes the first vital issue between the spouses. The rigour of the principles of separation of property has for some time been mitigated by the recognition that disputes as to occupation cannot be determined simply on the basis of property rights. The husband's property rights, at least, have been modified when necessary to give effect to his common law obligation to provide a home for his family. The Matrimonial Homes Act 1967 gave to a husband, as well as to a wife, statutory rights of occupation in a matrimonial home vested solely in the other spouse, and endeavoured to provide a means of protecting those rights against third parties dealing with the spouse who is the owner of the property (see Chapter 4). Increased public awareness of the problem of violence in the home provided the impetus for the Domestic Violence and Matrimonial Proceedings Act 1976 which sought to widen and improve the powers which had already emerged to regulate occupation of the home. The Domestic Proceedings and Magistrates' Courts Act 1978 added further powers (see Chapter 5).

The statutory provisions in this field have been described as "a hotchpot of enactments of limited scope passed into law to meet specified situations or to strengthen the powers of specified courts" (*per* Lord Scarman in *Richards* v *Richards* [1984] AC 174 at p. 206). In 1992 the Law Commission published a Report on *Domestic Violence and Occupation of the Family Home* (Law Com. No. 207) making recommendations for reform of the various discretionary remedies dealing with "two distinct but inseparable problems: providing protection for one member of a family against molestation or violence by another and regulating the occupation of the family home where the relationship has broken down whether temporarily or permanently" (para. 1.1). The recommendations have not yet been implemented.

*(b) Maintenance and property rights*
The interaction between property rights and the support of a family on the termination of a marriage by divorce also received increased acknowledgement during the sixties. Thus Lord Denning emphasised the importance of considering the position in relation to the matrimonial home when deciding the provision which ought to be made (*Button* v *Button* [1968] 1 WLR 457 at p. 462). If the wife was able to remain in the former matrimonial home or if she got part of the proceeds of sale, then her maintenance might be reduced on that account, whereas, if she had to leave and all the proceeds went to the husband, she would clearly need more. Yet, as has already been noted, the court's powers of property adjustment on the termination of marriage were very limited. On granting a decree of divorce or judicial separation the court was empowered to order a settlement of a guilty wife's property, and on granting a decree of divorce or nullity it had power to vary an ante- or post-nuptial settlement. Even allowing for the generous interpretation of the expression "ante- or post-nuptial", the limited powers of adjustment appeared quite inadequate a century after their introduction. The introduction of the power to award a lump sum payment by the Matrimonial Causes Act 1963 provided only limited relief, for it had to operate

within the system which was dominated by the idea of *maintenance* for an *innocent* wife by a *guilty* husband, and the courts hesitated to regard it as a method of property adjustment. This situation was rectified by the Matrimonial Proceedings and Property Act 1970 which conferred upon the court wide powers to order financial provision and property adjustment on or after the granting of a decree of divorce, nullity or judicial separation. These powers, which included the powers to order the transfer or settlement of property, are now contained in the Matrimonial Causes Act 1973.

*(c) The process of reform - the search for a concept of matrimonial property*

(i) The position during the lifetime of a spouse
The Law Commission in its Report on *Financial Provision in Matrimonial Proceedings* (Law Com. No. 25 para 67) which preceded the 1970 Act, after stating that the introduction of any concept of matrimonial or family property would require further consideration, said:
"If at a later date, a form of community of property is introduced, we do not envisage that the powers which we recommend in this Report will be rendered obsolete. The court's powers to review property rights will, we think, still be needed; the only difference will be that they will then deal with rights held in common instead of rights under the present system of individual ownership."
In due course the Law Commission produced its Working Paper on *Family Property* (Law Com. Working Paper No. 42) and again it pointed out that the scope of the 1970 Act was limited. The Act applied only on the breakdown of marriage, and:
"... it is not, strictly speaking, a property statute: it does not alter the legal rules which determine the ownership of property. For instance it does not declare that a wife's contribution by looking after the home confers upon her a right of property in the assets of the family: it is confined to empowering a court in certain circumstances to have regard to her contribution in deciding whether or not to transfer to her some or any part of her husband's property - or to make one or more of the financial orders available under the Act." (para 0.3).
The Working Paper then went on to consider whether a spouse or a child should enjoy rights of property in the assets of the family as distinct from being offered the opportunity to apply for an order of the court. It contained detailed proposals on, *inter alia*, (1) the introduction of a fixed principle of equal co-ownership of the matrimonial home; (2) a system of deferred community of property; (3) an extension of family provision legislation; and (4) fixed rights of inheritance.

While consultations on these suggestions were taking place Lord Denning delivered the now famous judgment of the Court of Appeal in *Wachtel* v *Wachtel* [1973] Fam 72. This made it clear that there was to be a new approach to financial provision on the dissolution of marriage unrestricted by the old concept of maintenance of an innocent wife by a guilty husband. On the dissolution of marriage the court was now able to deal with all the family assets, i.e. those of a capital nature such as the matrimonial home and the furniture in it, and those of a revenue producing nature, such as the earning power of the husband and wife. As might be expected there was a change in the pattern of litigation from proceedings designed only to ascertain the ownership of a matrimonial home to proceedings under the Act of 1970 for the adjustment of property rights. Moreover, in subsequent cases Lord Denning went further and said that it was unnecessary to decide the exact property rights of the spouses under s.17 of the Married Women's Property Act 1882 when all appropriate orders could be made under the 1970 Act (*Kowalczuk* v *Kowalczuk* [1973] 1 WLR 930 at p. 934. Contrast the view of the Law Commission in Law Com. No. 25, para 61).

In the meantime the Law Commission had reached certain conclusions which were set out in the *First Report on Family Property: A New Approach* (Law Com. No. 52). Consultations had revealed that there was wide support for the principle of co-ownership of the matrimonial home, both as the best means of reforming the law relating to the home, and as the main principle of family property law (para 21). The introduction of fixed property rights had been opposed by some who considered that the proper remedy was to allow the court to exercise its discretionary powers in matrimonial or family provision proceedings. The Law Commission acknowledged that recent cases had "shown that discretionary powers can be and are being exercised on a broad and generous basis which in many cases will lead to the decision that the spouses should have equal interests in the home" (para 26). However, it pointed out that:

"... those powers are essentially powers to adjust rather than to determine existing property rights, and can at present be exercised only where the parties are before the court in proceedings for divorce, nullity or judicial separation. Even if those powers could be exercised in cases where married persons were in dispute they would provide a most uncertain basis on which to decide rights of ownership, and it would still be necessary to go to court. If, as we believe, it would normally be fair and reasonable for the court to decide that a husband and wife should have equal interests in the matrimonial home, the interests of justice and certainty would best be served by applying this rule directly during the marriage without the need to resort to the court."

(ii) The position on the death of a spouse
On the other hand, the decision in *Wachtel* v *Wachtel* had shown that a divorced spouse was in a much better position than a surviving spouse who had not been adequately provided for by the deceased spouse, though on intestacy a surviving spouse was by now very generously treated (see Chapter 20). The Law Commission in Working Paper No. 42 had indicated that its tentative view was that the family provision jurisdiction should remain confined to its existing role of providing maintenance for certain dependants of the deceased. On this basis it could coexist with a system which recognised that certain persons, e.g. a wife, had fixed proprietary rights in the estate of the deceased which override any will he may have made. Furthermore, neither a community system nor a law which recognised co-ownership of the matrimonial home would replace the need for a family provision jurisdiction. A discretionary power to award maintenance to dependants would still be necessary, and family provision law should be "designed as a supplement to, but not as a substitute for, a reformed property law." (para 3.76).

However, the consultations carried out by the Law Commission revealed little enthusiasm for a system of legal rights of inheritance and the decision in *Wachtel* v *Wachtel* had revealed the potential of the wide powers conferred by the Act of 1970. In its *First Report on Family Property* (Law Com. No. 52 (para 41) the Law Commission indicated that it had changed its view, and that there should be a change in the objective of family provision law so far as the position of a surviving spouse is concerned. If the wider powers which the Working Paper had proposed for a court exercising family provision jurisdiction were applied in a manner similar to that applicable in divorce, then a surviving spouse who had not been adequately provided for could expect to be no less generously treated than a divorced spouse. Detailed proposals relating to family provision law were set out in the Law Commission's *Second Report on Family Property: Family Provision on Death* (Law Com. No. 61) published in 1974. The draft Bill contained in the Report became law, with only minor amendments, as the Inheritance (Provision for Family and Dependants) Act 1975 which applies to the estates of persons dying on or after 1 April 1976 (see Chapter 21). Among the matters to which the court is required to have regard in the case of an application by a surviving spouse is "the provision which the applicant might reasonably have expected to receive if on the day on which the deceased died the marriage, instead of being terminated by death, had been terminated by a decree of divorce" (s.3(2)).

*(d) The product - discretionary modification of separate property*
It can be seen, therefore, that the wide powers conferred by the Act of 1970, which are now contained in the Act of 1973, were not intended as the final remedy for the inadequacies of the law of property regarding ownership of the matrimonial home. They were certainly not envisaged as the basic principle of the new system of family property. Their role was to enable the court to adjust property rights in the light of changed conditions on divorce, nullity or judicial separation. In other words, they were intended to enable the court to deal with the situation where the family had split up and the matrimonial home could no longer provide a home for all the family, or, in broader terms, where the family assets could no longer be enjoyed by all the members of the family living together. The inadequacies of the law of family property, particularly in relation to the matrimonial home, were intended to be dealt with by one of the solutions canvassed in Working Paper No. 42 of the Law Commission. It subsequently emerged that the solution recommended by the Law Commission was co-ownership of the matrimonial home. However, in the absence of the introduction of such a principle it is not surprising that the powers conferred by the Act of 1970 have been used to remedy the inadequacies of the law of property in relation to the acquisition of an interest by one spouse in the matrimonial home vested in the name of the other spouse alone. It will be seen that in exercising those powers the court is required to take into account, *inter alia*, the contributions made by each of the parties to the welfare of the family, including any contribution made by looking after the home or caring for the family. This has played an important role in the court's efforts to help a "housewife" who has made no financial contribution (see para (f) of s.25(1) (Chapters 11 and 12) and the comments of Lord Denning in *Wachtel* v *Wachtel* [1973] Fam 72 at pp. 93-94).

Understandably this aspect has attracted a good deal of attention for it was the problem that gave the main impetus to reform. However the objective at which the court was required to aim by s.25(1) was to place the parties in the position in which they would have been if the marriage had not broken down and each had discharged his or her financial obligations and responsibilities towards the other. In seeking to achieve this objective the court was required to have regard to a number of factors of which the contributions of the parties to the welfare of the family was only one. These factors and the general objective made it clear that in exercising its powers the court was concerned not simply to adjust property rights to satisfy the contributions of the parties, but to balance their entitlement on that basis against their needs and other resources taking into account such matters as the ages of the parties and the duration of the marriage. This was recognised by Lord Denning in *Wachtel* v *Wachtel* in his justification for the so-called "one-third rule" instead of an equal division ([1973] Fam 72 at p. 95. See Chapter 11). Accordingly while separation of property of spouses remained the basis of English law the whole emphasis in the marriage breakdown situation had shifted to the process of reallocation on divorce. More accurately, perhaps, it was a process where ascertainment of vested rights and reallocation of those rights was not always, or even generally, distinguished. In any event it was a process of readjustment dominated by what may be called the "support" aspect, at least in the case of the small or modest estate.

In 1978 the Law Commission eventually published its *Third Report on Family Property: The Matrimonial Home (Co-ownership and Occupation Rights) and Household Goods* (Law Com. No. 86). Book 1 dealt with the detailed scheme for statutory co-ownership of the matrimonial home. Book 2 was concerned with rights of occupation of the home. Book 3 contained a scheme for protecting a wife or husband in the use and enjoyment of household goods. Some of the recommendations in Book 2 were implemented by the Housing Act 1980 (see Chapter 8) and the remainder by the Matrimonial Homes and Property Act 1981 (see Chapters 8 and 10). An attempt to implement the scheme of statutory co-ownership of the matrimonial home was made in 1981, but failed, so that the availability of the powers of the court under the Matrimonial Causes Act 1973 to readjust property rights remains of crucial importance in relation to the limitations of the principle of separate property.

*(e) Further reform*
In the meantime, however, the jurisdiction of the court under the 1973 Act had itself become a matter of debate. In 1980, the Law Commission reported that the law governing the financial consequences of divorce was the object of serious and sustained criticism (Fourteenth Annual Report, Law Com. No. 97 para 2.25). In the same year the Law Commission, while it took the view that it would not be appropriate for it to undertake a comprehensive review of this area of the law, published a Discussion Paper: *The Financial Consequences of Divorce: The Basic Policy* (Law Com. No. 103, Cmnd. 8041 (1980)). This contained a discussion of the fundamental ideas underlying the existing law and set out the main complaints about its operation in practice. It then examined some of the principles which might govern the formulation of any future law. In December 1981 it published a further report, *The Financial Consequences of Divorce* (Law Com. No. 112), dealing with the response

to the Discussion Paper and setting out its recommendations regarding the policy which it believed the law should follow.

The vast majority of those who commented on the Discussion Paper took the view that the policy incorporated in the statutory objective in s.25(1) was no longer appropriate. However, the response also indicated a substantial consensus that what was required was a change of attitude or emphasis in the law rather than a radical restructuring involving a wholly novel statutory framework. The material available to the Law Commission did not in its view justify radical change in the law, e.g. by abolishing altogether the power to order lifelong periodical payments for the divorced spouse (para 11). The Law Commission accepted the view that a change in the law should be evolutionary rather than revolutionary (para 23). The change would best be carried into effect by retaining the direction to the court to "have regard to all the circumstances of the case" (including certain specified matters), but adding certain provisions designed to give a clear indication of how the discretion - which should be retained as a central feature of the law - should be applied to the facts of individual cases.

The crucial recommendation was as follows:

"(5) The provisions of section 25 of the Matrimonial Causes Act 1973 should be amended in the following respects:

(i) To seek to place the parties in the financial position in which they would have been had the marriage not broken down should no longer be the statutory objective.

(ii) The guidelines contained in section 25(1) of the Matrimonial Causes Act 1973 should be revised, to give greater emphasis to the following matters:

(a) the provision of adequate support for children should be an overriding priority. (Administrative steps should also be taken to ensure that the courts have adequate and reliable information about the current cost of maintaining children);

(b) the importance of each party doing everything possible to become self-sufficient should be formulated in terms of a positive principle;

and weight should be given to the view that, in appropriate cases, periodical financial provision should be primarily concerned to secure a smooth transition from the status of marriage to the status of independence."

The recommendations of the Law Commission were carried into effect by Part II of the Matrimonial and Family Proceedings Act 1984 which amended the Matrimonial Causes Act 1973 with effect from September 1985.

## 5. Children

The welfare of the child, which was made a central feature of the reformulated provisions, was also the fundamental guiding principle of the Children Act 1989 which brought together the law relating to the physical care and upbringing of children. It also established a system of child maintenance to replace most of the statutory provisions, enabling financial provision to be ordered other than in matrimonial proceedings between their parents (see Chapter 17). In October 1990 the Government published a White Paper - *Children Come First* (Cm. 1264) which emphasised the responsibility of parents for their children even where the parents' own relationship has broken down. The payment of child maintenance was seen as one crucial way in which parents fulfilled that responsibility, but the existing system was unsatisfactory in several respects which are fully described in Chapter 1 of Volume 1 of the White Paper.

The White Paper therefore proposed an integrated package of measures (Chapter 2). First, it recommended the introduction of a clear and consistent formula by which maintenance assessments would be made, and rules by which those assessments would be reviewed to take account of changing circumstances. The key features of this formula were contained in the Child Support Act 1991 (operative from 1 April 1993). Secondly, it recommended the setting-up of a Child Support Agency, accountable through the Secretary of State for Social Security, to Parliament. This would bring together in one organisation all matters to do with the assessment, collection and enforcement of child maintenance in the majority of cases. There is no explicit reference to the Agency in the Child Support Act 1991, and its powers and duties are expressed as powers and duties of the Secretary of State. The Act provides for the appointment of Child Support Officers, Child Support Commissioners and the establishment of Child Support Appeal Tribunals. When this new system is fully in operation it will mean that child maintenance in the majority of cases will not be a matter for the courts, though questions relating to financial provision and property adjustment as between parents will continue to be determined by the courts under existing provisions. Concern has been expressed about the effect of the new approach to child maintenance on the policy of the "clean break" now embodied in the Matrimonial Causes Act 1973. The relationship between the new machinery and the courts is considered in Chapter 17.

The third element of the package envisaged in the White Paper is not dealt with in the Child Support Act. It comprised measures, to be introduced by the Secretary of State for Social Security, designed to make it easier to combine going to work with the responsibilities of looking after children. This involved a reduction in the number of hours of work which qualify for family credit and provision for the first £15 of maintenance paid to be left out of account for parents receiving family credit, housing benefit and certain other benefits and allowances.

## 6. Cohabitation

Although the legal basis of the typical family with which the law is concerned is marriage, it cannot ignore the fact that a family may come into existence without such a legal basis. That family may be a one parent family comprising a mother and her illegitimate child, or it may involve a man and a woman cohabiting as husband and wife without having gone through a ceremony of marriage. Cohabitation outside marriage has become increasingly common and the law has to cope with a variety of relationships. On the one hand it may be a relationship arising when a woman is "installed in a clandestine way by someone of substance normally married for his intermittent sexual enjoyment" (*per* Lord Kilbrandon in *Davis* v *Johnson* [1979] AC

264 at pp. 338-339. See e.g. *Horrocks* v *Forray* [1976] 1 WLR 230; *Malone* v *Harrison* [1979] 1 WLR 1353). On the other hand, it may comprise a man and a woman living together in a relationship identical to marriage. Such a relationship may precede legal marriage (see e.g. *Campbell* v *Campbell* [1976] Fam 347). It may arise because they are unable to marry or, as is probably increasingly the case today, because they choose not to marry. In between these extremes a variety of relationships will arise (see e.g *Helby* v *Rafferty* [1979] 1 WLR 13).

This diversity is more than matched by the diversity in terminology. The term "mistress" has been the term most commonly used by the judiciary to refer not only to the woman described by Lord Kilbrandon in *Davis* v *Johnson*, where it might be said to be accurate, but also to the woman living with a man as his wife (see e.g. *Cooke* v *Head* [1972] 1 WLR 518). It is only relatively recently that an attempt has been made to find alternative descriptions of which "cohabitees" seems most widespread despite its inelegance. The female partner is often called a "common law wife" but this is confusing and indeed inaccurate. (A "common law marriage" is exceptional, but is nevertheless a valid marriage: see *Wolfenden* v *Wolfenden* [1946] P 61.)

The parties to an unmarried relationship can, of course, seek to make use of general principles and doctrines of the law, such as contract, tort, property, trusts and restitution. (See particularly Chapters 2 and 5.) However the application of such principles and doctrines will not necessarily produce the same results when applied to cohabitees as distinct from spouses. Moreover, at least in the past, there was a very real danger that assistance would be refused by the courts because the arrangement between them was regarded as immoral and therefore contrary to public policy (see *Fender* v *St. John Mildmay* [1938] AC 1; *Diwell* v *Farnes* [1959] 2 All ER 379; Dwyer, *Immoral Contracts* (1977) 93 LQR 386). This danger is now clearly much reduced, but is still a potential pitfall especially in the field of contract.

The statutory right of the mother of an illegitimate child to seek maintenance through an affiliation order against the putative father was of long standing and is now replaced by provisions of the Children Act 1989. The provisions of the Rent Acts relating to the transmission of a tenancy on the death of a tenant to a member of his "family" have now been interpreted to extend to a cohabitee of the tenant in certain circumstances. More recently cohabitees have been given the benefit of certain specific statutory provisions. Thus a cohabitee may be able to apply for an order under s.2 of the Inheritance (Provision for Family and Dependants) Act 1975 for provision out of the estate of his or her deceased partner on the basis that immediately before the death of the deceased he or she was being maintained, either wholly or partly, by the deceased (see Chapter 21). This provision is not limited to "cohabitees", and not all "cohabitees" will be able to take advantage of it. Again, the provisions of ss.1 and 2 of the Domestic Violence and Matrimonial Proceedings Act 1976, designed to provide protection against domestic violence and harassment, apply not only as between husband and wife, but also to "a man and a woman who are living with each other in the same household as husband and wife" (see Chapter 5). There is also recognition of cohabitation in social security legislation, but although in some cases it results in an increase in benefit, it sometimes results in a decrease or even loss of benefit (see Chapter 19).

These developments are a recognition that where a man and a woman are living together, their needs and resources are in fact affected by their relationship and that where they have lived together for some time injustice would be caused if no remedy was available to deal with certain problems which arise on the breakdown of their relationship. However, while increased recognition of *de facto* marriage relationships by statute may seem the natural course of development, two arguments are made against such a development. First there is the long-standing view that recognition of unmarried cohabitation weakens the traditional concept of marriage (see the strong view of Sir George Baker P. in *Campbell* v *Campbell* [1976] Fam 347, at p. 352). Secondly, there is the more recent view that if parties have refrained from marrying because they do not wish to incur the legal and financial obligations of marriage, then the law should be slow to impose these obligations on them (see Deech, *The Case Against Legal Recognition of Cohabitation* (1980) 29 I.C.L.Q. 480. For further discussion see Freeman and Lyon, *Towards a Justification of Rights of Cohabitees* (1980) 130 NLJ 228).

# Chapter 2

# Ascertaining ownership

## 1. General principles

The principle of separate property remains the basis of the law of family property. Marriage does not directly change the ownership of property though it may affect its enjoyment (see Chapters 5 and 6). Property owned by one spouse before marriage remains the property of that spouse after marriage and the other spouse acquires no proprietary interest in that property unless there is some disposition in his or her favour, or an order of the court on or after the granting of a decree of divorce, nullity or judicial separation confers such an interest. Property acquired by one spouse during the marriage, whether by purchase or gift, remains the property of that spouse unless he or she makes some disposition thereof in favour of the other spouse, or an interest is conferred on the other spouse by an order of the court on or after the granting of a decree of divorce, nullity or judicial separation. The position is the same in relation to a spouse's share in property owned jointly with the other spouse. Although the basic principle is clear, the problem arises in its application. What is generally in dispute is whether a particular asset was in fact acquired by the husband, or the wife, or by both of them jointly. It is with this problem that this chapter is principally concerned.

Although the majority of reported cases concern ownership of the matrimonial home, the problem also arises in relation to other assets and between other members of a family. Indeed at present the problem is more likely to arise in relation to the home of an unmarried couple. The House of Lords has rejected any conception of "family assets" to which special principles apply, and it has been stated that disputes between husband and wife must be decided "by the principles of law applicable to the settlement of claims between those not so related, while making full allowance in view of that relationship" (*per* Lord Upjohn in *Pettitt* v *Pettitt* [1970] AC 777 at p. 813; *Gissing* v *Gissing* [1971] AC 886).

This statement will be examined later in this chapter when those "principles of law" are considered. They will be considered not only in relation to disputes between husband and wife but also in relation to disputes between persons who have been living together as husband and wife but who are not married to each other, for their application in the latter situation is of particular importance.

In relation to disputes between husband and wife, it was eventually made clear by the House of Lords that the "fact of breakdown of marriage is irrelevant in the determination of the question as to where ownership lay before breakdown" (*per* Lord Morris in *Pettitt* v *Pettitt* [1970] AC 777 at p. 813). The limited powers of the court to adjust property rights on breakdown of marriage before the coming into force of the Matrimonial Proceedings and Property Act 1970 made it particularly important for a spouse to establish, wherever possible, a beneficial interest in property such as the matrimonial home. Attempts to do justice in the different situations which frequently arose sometimes led to a blurring of the distinction between ascertaining and adjusting property rights especially in proceedings under s.17 of the Married Women's Property Act 1882. After the House of Lords had clearly emphasised the distinction between the two questions, the Matrimonial Proceedings and Property Act 1970 conferred upon the courts wide powers to adjust property rights on the granting of a decree of divorce, nullity or judicial separation. (See Chapters 10 and 11.)

The increased powers to adjust property rights reduced the relative importance of ascertaining ownership. The Law Commission, in Report No. 25, *Financial Provision in Matrimonial Proceedings* (1969) para 61, which preceded the 1970 Act expressed the view that "on a breakdown of marriage it will often be appropriate to invoke both sets of powers: those under the 1882 Act to determine the existing proprietary rights of the parties; those under an amended Matrimonial Causes Act to enable those rights to be altered to produce an equitable result in the light of the breakdown." In *Glenn* v *Glenn* [1973] 1 WLR 1016 a similar view was expressed by Dunn J, but a different view prevailed. This was expressed by Lord Denning MR in *Kowalczuk* v *Kowalczuk* [1973] 1 WLR 930 at p. 934 when he said:

"I hope that, in future, after there has been a divorce, the property rights of the parties may be adjusted by means of an application under section 4 of the Act of 1970. It is unnecessary to decide the exact property rights under section 17 of the 1882 Act when all appropriate orders can be made under the 1970 Act."

(Section 4 of the 1970 Act is now s.24 of the Matrimonial Causes Act 1973. See also *Hunter* v *Hunter* [1973] 1 WLR 958 at p. 961; *Griffiths* v *Griffiths* [1974] 1 WLR 1350 at pp. 1358-1359; *Suttill* v *Graham* [1977] 1 WLR 819; *Fielding* v *Fielding* [1977] 1 WLR 1146.)

Thus where the court is able to exercise its wide powers to order financial provision and adjust property rights under what is now the Matrimonial Causes Act 1973, there is generally no advantage in also commencing proceedings under s.17 of the Married Women's Property Act 1882. Moreover, in exercising its powers under the 1973 Act it does not, even in cases where existing property rights are in dispute, first embark on a precise determination of those rights before deciding what property adjustment order is appropriate. The court will proceed on a more general view of the position as indicated by Ormrod LJ in *P* v *P* [1978] 1 WLR 488 at p. 489 where reference had been made to the husband's "strict s.17 interests". He said:

"I do not find it particularly helpful to try to ascertain and quantify his so-called interests. It is useful to ascertain these interests in a broad way so that one can see the justice of each side's case, but I would prefer to avoid quantifying or seeking to quantify these rights in terms of figures ..."

## 2. The continuing relevance of ascertaining ownership

Although the whole emphasis has shifted to the powers of the court to adjust property rights there remain situations where it may still be necessary or desirable to determine existing property rights.

First, the determination of property rights as between spouses may become necessary where there is a claim by some third party, such as a creditor, against one of the spouses. Thus if a husband becomes bankrupt, his property will become vested in his trustee in bankruptcy, and if the wife claims an interest in any of that property which is vested in the husband's name alone, she will have to establish her rights according to traditional principles of property law. (See further Chapter 8.)

Secondly, an application for financial provision or property adjustment under the 1973 Act may not be possible because a party has remarried after dissolution or annulment of the marriage (Matrimonial Causes Act 1973, s.28(3). See e.g. *Suttill* v *Graham* [1977] 1 WLR 819; *Brykiert* v *Jones* (1981) 2 FLR 373).

Thirdly, one party may prefer to rely on a beneficial interest determined according to principles of property law where this is likely to be larger than the share he or she would obtain following an adjustment of property rights under the 1973 Act. However, in such a case it will be open to the other party to seek an adjustment of property rights under the 1973 Act unless prevented from making an application, e.g. by remarriage.

Fourthly, on the death of a party it may be necessary or desirable to establish the extent of the beneficial interest of that party in a particular item of property. It is, of course, possible for a surviving spouse to apply under the Inheritance (Provision for Family and Dependants) Act 1975 for reasonable financial provision out of the estate of the deceased spouse, and on such an application the court is required to have regard to the provision which the applicant might reasonably have expected to receive if on the day on which the deceased died the marriage, instead of being terminated by death, had been terminated by a decree of divorce. Generally, therefore, an application under the 1975 Act is likely to be preferable, but it must also be borne in mind that if a decree of judicial separation was in force at the date of the death of one party then the provision which the surviving party can obtain under the 1975 Act is limited to reasonable maintenance. (See Chapter 21.)

At the present time the situation in which the courts are most frequently called upon to establish existing property rights is on the termination of a relationship between parties who have been living together but have not been married to each other. The 1973 Act has no application and accordingly the only course open to a party to such a relationship is to seek to establish a beneficial interest in property vested in the name of the other. On the death of a party to such a relationship, an application for reasonable financial provision under the 1975 Act by the surviving party may be possible on the basis of dependency, but there are a number of hurdles to be surmounted and provision is limited to reasonable maintenance (see Chapter 21). The need to establish existing property rights may, of course, also arise in the case of disputes between other members of a family.

## 3. Procedure

### (a) Choice of procedure

The question of ownership of property as between members of a family may be brought before the court by a number of procedures. In *Gissing* v *Gissing* [1971] AC 886 the wife issued an ordinary originating summons in the Chancery Division seeking a declaration that she was entitled to a beneficial interest in the former matrimonial home. However, as between husband and wife, proceedings under s.17 of the Married Women's Property Act 1882 have proved particularly useful. The relevant part of this section provides that:

> "In any question between husband and wife as to the title to or possession of property, either party ... may apply, in a summary way to any judge of the High Court ... or ... of the county court ... and the judge ... may make such order with respect to the property in dispute ... as he thinks fit."

Several points call for comment in relation to the scope of this section.

### (b) Section 17 of the Married Women's Property Act 1882

(i) Availability of the procedure

The general principle is that the procedure is only applicable to disputes between spouses, but this is now subject to two qualifications.

First, an application may now be made under s.17 by either of the parties to a marriage notwithstanding that their marriage has been dissolved or annulled as long as the application is made within the period of three years beginning with the date on which the marriage was dissolved or annulled (Matrimonial Proceedings and Property Act 1970, s.39). This extension has no application when a marriage is terminated by the death of one spouse.

Secondly, where an agreement to marry is terminated, s.17 applies as if the parties were married, to any dispute between them or claim by one of them, in relation to property in which either or both had a beneficial interest while the agreement was in force (Law Reform (Miscellaneous Provisions) Act 1970, s.2(2). See *Marsh* v *Von Sternberg* [1986] 1 FLR 526 and Part 11, p. 60.) An application in these circumstances must, however, be made within three years of the determination of the agreement.

(ii) Permissible subject-matter

The courts have generally taken a broad view of the permissible subject-matter of an application under s.17. However, in *Tunstall* v *Tunstall* [1953] 1 WLR 770 the Court of Appeal took the view that there had to be specific property, or an identifiable fund, on which an order could operate, and there was no power to order the payment of money. The difficulties which would be caused by such a view, where money or property could be disposed of, or where the position was uncertain, were removed by the Matrimonial Causes (Property and Maintenance) Act 1958. Section 7 of that Act provides that applications can be made by either spouse in such circumstances, and the court can make orders for money payments in respect of the applicant's interest in the property or money disposed of, or with respect to property representing the property or money in question. Nevertheless, it appears that some identifiable asset must at any rate at one time have existed, though an order may be made even though the property was disposed of more than six years earlier (*Spoor* v *Spoor* [1966] 3 All ER 120; *Bothe* v *Amos* [1976] Fam 46). The procedure cannot be used in respect of a claim by one spouse against the other for repayment of money lent (*Crystall* v *Crystall* [1963] 1 WLR 574). An application under s.17 can, in certain circumstances, be made in respect of property outside England where the defendant spouse is present in England at the time of the proceedings, and a spouse cannot oust the jurisdiction of the court by removing the property in dispute from England (*Razelos* v *Razelos* [1970] 1 WLR 392).

Although the subject-matter of an application must be a question as to "title to or possession of" property, the court can order a sale (Matrimonial Causes (Property and Maintenance) Act, s.7). It may order payment of the appropriate sum of money out of the proceeds of sale (*Bothe* v *Amos*). However, if the sole question in issue is the question of sale, the proper course is to apply for an order for sale under s.30 of the Law of Property Act 1925 (*Rawlings* v *Rawlings* [1964] P 398. See Chapter 6).

(iii) The scope of the court's powers
There was formerly a considerable difference of judicial and other opinion as to the scope of the court's powers under s.17 in relation to disputes as to title. However, in *Pettitt* v *Pettitt* [1970] AC 777 all the members of the House of Lords were agreed that the section is purely procedural. The task of the court is to ascertain the rights of the parties and it has no power to vary established rights. The discretion it confers is limited to preventing such rights being fully enforced in appropriate circumstances. In the words of Lord Morris, the question is "Whose is this?" and not, "To whom shall this be given?" (*ibid.* at p.798. See, however, *Bothe* v *Amos* for the effect of the conduct of a party in disrupting a business when the court is assessing property rights in that business).

## 4. The family home

*(a) The vesting of the legal estate is not conclusive*
It is implicit in the views expressed by the House of Lords in *Pettitt* v *Pettitt* [1970] AC 777 and *Gissing* v *Gissing* [1971] AC 886 that the vesting of the legal estate in a property is not of itself to be regarded as conclusive so far as the beneficial interest in that property is concerned. Thus, the mere fact that property is vested in the name of one spouse alone will not prevent the other spouse from establishing a beneficial interest. Similarly, the mere fact that the legal estate is vested in the joint

names of the spouses will not prevent one spouse from establishing a share larger than one half or even entire beneficial ownership.

A claim to a beneficial interest in land by a person, whether spouse or stranger, in whom the legal estate is not vested, must be based on the proposition that the person in whom the legal estate is vested holds it as trustee to give effect to the beneficial interest of the claimant as *cestui que trust* (*Gissing* v *Gissing* [1971] AC 886 *per* Viscount Dilhorne at p. 900 and *per* Lord Diplock at p. 904). Such a trust may have been created expressly or it may have arisen as a resulting, implied or constructive trust. Where the legal estate is vested in the joint names of spouses or strangers, the beneficial interests will likewise depend on the trusts, express or implied, on which the property is held. This "applies to husband and wife, to engaged couples, and to a man and mistress, and maybe to other relationships too" (*per* Lord Denning MR in *Cooke* v *Head* [1972] 1 WLR 518 at p. 520).

### (b) The effect of an express declaration of trust

(i) Finding an express declaration of trust
An express declaration of trust respecting land or any interest therein must be manifested and proved by some writing signed by the creator of the trust (Law of Property Act 1925, s.53(1)(b) - contrast the position in relation to an oral trust of personalty such as a bank account: *Paul* v *Constance* [1977] 1 All ER 195). In the case of the matrimonial home such a declaration will generally be found, if at all, in the conveyance, lease or other document whereby the property was acquired from some third party. A conveyance or lease into the name of one spouse is unlikely to do more than vest the legal estate in that spouse and it will be most unusual to find an express declaration of trust. However, a conveyance or lease into the joint names of the spouses may go further and also declare the beneficial interests of the spouses. Where there is an express declaration of a trust for sale, there is almost invariably also a declaration that the spouses are beneficially entitled as joint tenants or as tenants in common, but even where there is no express trust for sale, the property may nevertheless be conveyed to the spouses as "beneficial joint tenants". It is submitted that what must be considered is not whether there is an express trust for sale, but whether there is an express declaration of the beneficial interests of the spouses (see Slade LJ in *Goodman* v *Gallant* [1986] 1 All ER 311 at p. 314). In *Re Gorman* [1990] 1 All ER 717 Vinelott J said that where a transfer of registered land into the joint names of the spouses declared not merely that they were entitled to the land for their own benefit, but went on to say that the survivor of them could give a valid receipt for capital moneys arising on a disposition of the land, this clearly and unequivocally pointed to a joint tenancy. It would only be on that footing that the survivor would be entitled to give a valid receipt. However, in *Harwood* v *Harwood* [1991] 2 FLR 274 where the transfer merely declared that the survivor could give a valid receipt for capital moneys but did not declare that they were entitled to the property for their own benefit, the Court of Appeal held that this did not amount to a declaration of the beneficial interests. Although it was entirely consistent with the existence of a beneficial joint tenancy, it was no less consistent with the spouses holding the property as trustees for a single third party. Slade LJ (at p. 288) said that

conveyancers who wished to avoid the risk of future misunderstanding or dispute would be well advised to insert in the relevant transfer the short form of addendum referred to in *Emmett on Title* (19th ed. para 10.37), i.e. "to hold unto themselves as joint tenants beneficially". (See further *Springette* v *Defoe* (1992) 24 HLR 552 and *Huntingford* v *Hobbs* (1992) 24 HLR 652.)

(ii) The effect of a declaration of trust
Before the decision of the House of Lords in *Pettitt* v *Pettitt* [1970] AC 777 a number of views were expressed as to the effect of an express declaration of trust (see (1970) 34 Conv. (NS) 156). In that case the property had been conveyed into the wife's name alone so that the question did not arise, but Lord Upjohn, who was the only member of the House of Lords to deal with the point, said (at p. 813):

"In the first place, the beneficial ownership of the property in question must depend upon the agreement of the parties determined at the time of its acquisition. If the property in question is land there must be some lease or conveyance which shows how it was acquired. If that document declares, not merely in whom the legal title is to vest but in whom the beneficial title is to vest that necessarily concludes the question of title as between the spouses for all time, and in the absence of fraud or mistake at the time of the transaction, the parties cannot go behind it at any time thereafter even on death or the break up of the marriage."

Although strictly *obiter*, this statement has been accepted and applied in subsequent cases such as *Re John's Assignment Trusts* [1970] 1 WLR 955, *Leake* v *Bruzzi* [1974] 1 WLR 1528 and *Brykiert* v *Jones* (1981) 2 FLR 373 and even where it was clear that one party had provided the whole of the purchase price as in *Boydell* v *Gillespie* (1971) 216 EG 1505. More recently in *Goodman* v *Gallant* [1986] 1 All ER 311 at p. 314 Slade LJ said that if "the relevant conveyance contains an express declaration of trust which comprehensively declares the beneficial interests in the property or its proceeds of sale, there is no room for the application of the doctrine of resulting implied or constructive trusts unless and until the conveyance is set aside or rectified; until that event the declaration in the document speaks for itself." In that case there was an express declaration of trust for the spouses as joint tenants so that when one of the spouses subsequently served a notice of severance on the other, they became entitled as tenants in common.

In *Re Gorman* [1990] 1 All ER 717 it was held that where a transfer of registered property into the joint names of the spouses provided in effect that they were to be beneficially entitled as joint tenants, this was evidence of the parties' intentions even though they had not signed the transfer. Moreover, in the circumstances of the case it was conclusive. Vinelott J noted that in the case of joint proprietors a restriction in Form 62 must be entered on the register unless the registrar is satisfied that the survivor will have power to give a valid receipt for the purchase price. He concluded that the registrar must have been satisfied that the declaration represented an agreement between the spouses and, in the absence of their signatures, he could only have been so satisfied if he had been informed by their solicitors that it reflected an agreement between them. This is likely to have been done in the form of an application for registration of the transfer. (Compare *Harwood* v *Harwood* [1991] 2 FLR 274 above, and *Huntingford* v *Hobbs* (1992) 24 HLR 652.)

The present position is therefore that an express declaration of trust is conclusive unless there has been (i) fraud, or (ii) a mistake. Where there has been no fraud or mistake it may nevertheless be possible to show that there has been a subsequent variation of the beneficial interests. In addition, a spouse may acquire an enlarged share under s.37 of the Matrimonial Proceedings and Property Act 1970 on the basis of a contribution in money or money's worth to the improvement of the property (see Part 6, page 53).

### (iii) Mistake

Where it is sought to go behind the express words of a conveyance on the basis of mistake, this involves something similar to an application for rectification of the conveyance (*Goodman* v *Gallant* [1986] 1 All ER 311 - but see the comments of Buckley LJ in *Pink* v *Lawrence* (1977) 36 P & CR 98 at p. 101 that the court may be able to grant relief without actually employing the machinery of rectification). The essence of rectification is that the parties must have reached a complete and definite agreement, but the instrument that records or carries that agreement into effect does not do so accurately. It is important, therefore, to establish what both parties agreed, and there can be no consideration of what the parties might have agreed if they had thought about it or indeed what one of them subsequently thinks about it. Where it is clear that both spouses were aware that the property was being conveyed into their joint names, a spouse seeking rectification will have to show that the agreement between them was that the other spouse was not to have a beneficial interest notwithstanding the words of the conveyance (see, e.g., *Wilson* v *Wilson* [1969] 1 WLR 1470). Moreover, where this is alleged there will have to be some explanation as to why the property was conveyed into their joint names. If that explanation reveals a motive which can only be fulfilled by transferring an interest to the other spouse it will be difficult, if not impossible, to deny that the other was to have some interest. In *Burgess* v *Rawnsley* [1975] Ch 429 it was said by the Court of Appeal that if the property was conveyed to two persons as beneficial joint tenants for a common purpose, such as marriage, which failed, for example because they changed their minds and did not get married, there would be a resulting trust for themselves as tenants in common in the proportions in which they had contributed the purchase money, notwithstanding the express declaration of trust. In that case the man alone had entered into the conveyance in contemplation of marriage and he had not communicated that purpose to the woman. The majority held that there was no common purpose which had failed and so no resulting trust arose. Lord Denning, however, said that where the parties contemplate different objects which *both* fail the position is the same as where their *common* object fails, and there is then a resulting trust according to their respective contributions.

### (iv) Variation of the beneficial interests

Where the parties to a conveyance containing an express declaration of trust subsequently agree on a variation of the beneficial interests, they must comply with the provisions of s.53(1)(c) of the Law of Property Act 1925 which requires a disposition of an equitable interest to be in writing and signed. A party who allows the other party to continue to occupy a home for many years without demanding any part of the rents and profits or demanding a sale does not thereby make a disposition of his or her interest or affect the existence of that interest. In *Brykiert* v *Jones* (1981) 2 FLR 373 the matrimonial home had been purchased in 1951 and vested in the joint names of the spouses upon trust for sale for themselves as joint tenants. Neither party sought a property adjustment order following their divorce in 1971 and both remarried. In 1979 the husband having paid off the mortgage sought an order for sale and a declaration that the former wife was only entitled to the deposit she had paid. The Court of Appeal held that as the parties had, by the terms of the conveyance, declared what their respective interests in the property should be, the wife at the time she left had a vested beneficial interest in the property. There had been no disposition of that interest within s.53(1)(c) and there was no need for her to justify any continuing claim. She was therefore entitled to a half share in the proceeds of sale of the property. She was prepared to give credit for the whole of the amount of the mortgage repaid by the husband. Beneficial interests may, however, be varied by an oral agreement of which specific performance will be granted (see *Sekhon* v *Alissa* [1989] 2 FLR 94 and the discussion in the next section).

### (c) Resulting, implied and constructive trusts

In the absence of an express declaration of trust, a claim to a beneficial interest by a person in whom the legal estate is not vested can only be established on the basis of a resulting, implied or constructive trust (*per* Lord Diplock in *Gissing* v *Gissing* [1971] AC 886 at pp. 904-905. See also Viscount Dilhorne at p. 900 and Lord Pearson at p. 902). The same applies to a claim to a beneficial interest larger than one half where the property is vested in the joint names of the parties and there is no express declaration of trust. Unfortunately, there does not seem to have been any general agreement as to the distinction between resulting, implied and constructive trusts, and in the present context the courts have in the past often not been concerned to draw any distinction and have sometimes used the expressions interchangeably (see the comments of Lord Diplock in *Gissing* v *Gissing* [1971] AC 886 at p. 905). However, the distinction between a resulting trust and a constructive trust has been more clearly drawn in recent cases and certain general principles may be noted.

### (d) The resulting trust

### (i) Basic principles

Where a person acquires the legal estate in a property, but has not provided the consideration, or the whole of the consideration, for its acquisition, then, unless a contrary intention is proved, the property will be held on a *resulting* trust for the benefit of the person providing the consideration to the extent of his or her contribution (*Dyer* v *Dyer* (1788) 2 Cox Eq. 92). Such a trust arises on the basis of the presumed intention of the person providing the consideration, rather than on his or her expressed intention, and for this reason is also an instance of an *implied* trust. The adjective "resulting" describes what happens to the property subject to the trust rather than the creation of the trust or the intention of the person providing the consideration. The adjective "implied" is concerned with the intention of that person.

More generally the term "implied trust" is used where the intention to create a trust is not clearly expressed but has to be found in the language used and all the relevant facts. It may also be used so as to include a constructive trust.

(ii) The presumption of advancement
In the case of certain special relationships between the person in whom the property is vested and the person who provided the consideration, there will be no presumption of a resulting trust in favour of the latter. On the contrary, there will be a presumption of advancement in favour of the former. Thus, where the legal estate in property is acquired in the name of a wife but the purchase price or part of it is provided by her husband, there has traditionally been a presumption that the husband intended to make a gift to his wife. The same would apply in relation to consideration provided by the husband where the legal estate is acquired in the joint names of the parties and there is no express declaration of trust (see e.g. *Silver* v *Silver* [1958] 1 WLR 257). The presumption arises even though a marriage is voidable (*Dunbar* v *Dunbar* [1909] 2 Ch 639), and also arises where a man purchases property in the name of his fiancée (*Moate* v *Moate* [1948] 2 All ER 486), and where a father purchases property in the name of his legitimate child (*Shephard* v *Cartwright* [1955] AC 431). In *Crisp* v *Mullings* (1974) 233 EG 511 Megarry J said that the presumption did not apply in favour of a woman living with a man as his wife but to whom she was not married. In *Cantor* v *Cox* (1975) 239 EG 121 Plowman V-C found it unnecessary to decide whether it should be extended to such a person in the light of changed social conditions.

The presumption of advancement may be rebutted by evidence that no gift was intended and that the beneficial interest was intended to be in the person providing the purchase money (*Loades-Carter* v *Loades-Carter* (1966) 110 SJ 51 and *Fennell* v *Fennell* (1966) 110 SJ 707). However, in a number of cases it has been held that a husband will not be permitted to rebut the presumption of advancement by adducing evidence that the property was vested in his wife's name for some purpose of an illegal or a fraudulent nature. Thus in *Gascoigne* v *Gascoigne* [1918] 1 KB 233 a wife was allowed to retain property purchased by her husband, but conveyed into her name with the fraudulent object of protecting it from his creditors, even though she was a party to the arrangement. In *Tinker* v *Tinker* [1970] P 136 this principle was applied even where the husband acted honestly and on the advice of his solicitors in conveying into his wife's name a property which was intended as a matrimonial home, in order to avoid it being claimed by creditors of his business if that should fail (but see *Tinsley* v *Milligan* [1992] Ch 310 (CA) and [1993] 3 WLR 126 (HL).

In the majority of disputes as to ownership of a matrimonial home that arise today, the presumption of advancement is unlikely to have any decisive effect and it has been the subject of much criticism (see, e.g., *Pettitt* v *Pettitt* [1970] AC 777 *per* Lord Reid at p. 793; *per* Lord Hodson at p. 811. But see *Harwood* v *Harwood* [1991] 2 FLR 274 at p. 294 where it was not displaced). Two criticisms may be noted. First, a presumption of fact is no more than a consensus of judicial opinion disclosed by reported cases as to the most likely inference of fact to be drawn in the absence of any evidence to the contrary (*per* Lord Diplock in *Pettitt* v *Pettitt* [1970] AC 777 at pp. 823 - 824). The presumption of advancement arose out of a series of cases in the nineteenth and early twentieth centuries, when social conditions were radically different from those which prevail today, when marriage is widely accepted as a partnership of equals (see Lord Denning in *Falconer* v *Falconer* [1970] 1 WLR 1333). Secondly, the application of the presumption of advancement, and indeed the presumption of resulting trust, presupposes the one fact which is often hotly disputed in this context. When is a spouse to be deemed to have acquired a property to put into his or her own name or into the name of his or her spouse or into their joint names? When will both spouses be deemed to have contributed to the acquisition of the property? In other words, the presumptions of advancement and resulting trust cannot be applied until it is established who has actually "purchased" or "contributed" to the purchase of the property (see (1970) 86 LQR 98).

(iii) Application of the principles
Where a property has been purchased outright without the aid of a mortgage advance, it will not generally be difficult to ascertain what part, if any, of the purchase price has been provided by each spouse or unmarried partner. If the property has been conveyed into the name of a spouse or unmarried partner who has not provided the whole of the purchase price, the sum contributed by the other party may be explicable as having been intended as (a) a gift, or (b) a loan, or (c) as consideration for a share in the beneficial interest in the property. In the absence of other evidence, the *prima facie* inference is that their common intention was that the contributing spouse should acquire a share in the beneficial interest in the property in the same proportion as the sum contributed bears to the total purchase price (*per* Lord Diplock in *Gissing* v *Gissing* [1971] AC 886 at p. 907. For a case where a contribution was found to be a loan, see *Re Sharpe* [1980] 1 WLR 219. See also *Risch* v *McFee* [1991] 1 FLR 105). More simply, and in traditional terms, the presumption of resulting trust will apply.

In the majority of cases, however, the matrimonial or family home will have been purchased with the assistance of a mortgage advance. The actual cash payment at the date of the conveyance is limited to little more than the deposit and the legal expenses, the balance being provided by a mortgage advance repayable over a period of up to twenty-five years or even thirty years. The fact that the mortgage instalments are repayable over such a period and under a variety of arrangements makes the application of traditional principles difficult as became apparent in the cases before *Pettitt* v *Pettitt* and *Gissing* v *Gissing* and, indeed, continued to be apparent after those decisions. The essential features of a claim based on a resulting trust are dealt with in the following paragraphs.

(iv) There must be a contribution to the acquisition of the property
The application of the presumption of resulting trust is only of assistance once it is established that there have been contributions of sufficient amount which can be linked with the acquisition of the property. Thus in *Burns* v *Burns* [1984] Ch 317 at pp. 328-329 Fox LJ said: "What is needed ... is evidence of a payment or payments by the plaintiff which it can be inferred was referable to the acquisition of the house". Accordingly, he said, "... if a payment cannot be said to be in a real sense referable to the acquisition of the house it is difficult to see how ... it can base a

claim for an interest in the house". The courts have not limited the concept of a "contribution" to direct payments towards the purchase price or mortgage instalments, but other payments or actions may be difficult to link to the acquisition of the home and hence to characterise as "contributions". Further consideration is given below to the possible different kinds of contributions. (See section (*f*), page 40.)

(v) The resulting trust is based on the presumed intention of the party making the contribution

As Bagnall J pointed out in *Cowcher* v *Cowcher* [1972] 1 WLR 425, strictly the relevant (contrary) intention is that of the party providing the purchase price or a proportion thereof. Thus did the wife, whose name was not on the legal title to the property, in making a contribution towards the purchase price intend that contribution to be a gift or a loan rather than payment for the acquisition of a beneficial interest in the property. However, during the last two decades the courts have frequently referred to the *common intention* of the parties. Thus in *Gissing* v *Gissing* [1971] AC 886 at p. 907 Lord Diplock said:

"If the land is conveyed into the name of a spouse who has not provided the whole of the purchase price, the sum contributed by the other spouse may be explicable as having been intended by both of them either as a gift or as a loan of money to the spouse to whom the land is conveyed or as consideration for a share in the beneficial interest in the land. In a dispute between living spouses the evidence will probably point to one of these explanations as being more probable than the others, but if the rest of the evidence is neutral the *prima facie* inference is that their common intention was that the contributing spouse should acquire a share in the beneficial interest in the land in the same proportion as the sum contributed bore to the total purchase price."

This reference to common intention does not seem to involve any departure from the traditional view, for the shares in the beneficial interest envisaged are proportionate to the contributions made and the "dispute" referred to appears to concern the inference to be drawn from the making of a contribution. In many cases the dispute will be as to whether the acts of the claimant party can be regarded as a contribution to the acquisition of the property. It seems that "common intention" has had a role to play in this respect.

In *Cowcher* v *Cowcher* [1972] 1 WLR 425 Bagnall J distinguished between an "interest consensus" and a "money consensus". By the former he meant a consensus as to what the beneficial interests are to be, irrespective of the source or sources of the purchase money. This is to move out of the sphere of the resulting trust and into the sphere of the express trust or, as will be seen below, the constructive trust. A "money consensus" he saw as a consensus as to the proportions in which the parties are to be taken as having provided the purchase money. In other words, this is an agreement that, irrespective of the actual payments to the vendor and the legal obligations to an outside mortgagee, as between themselves, A and B shall be treated as providing money (including being liable for mortgage repayments) in, say, equal shares. This would form the basis of the application of a resulting trust, with the parties entitled to the beneficial interest in proportion to their agreed contributions.

This was criticised by Goff J in *Re Densham* [1975] 1 WLR 1519 at p. 1525 who said that, in the vast majority of cases, parties do not direct their minds to treating money payments as notionally other than they are.

However, it is submitted that there have been cases where the court has found that the parties had a common intention that certain payments or acts were to be regarded as contributions to the acquisition of the property. This appears to have occurred mostly in cases where the property had been conveyed into the joint names of the parties but there had been no express declaration of the beneficial interest. In *Walker* v *Hall* (1983) 4 FLR 21 at p. 28 Dillon LJ said:

"Where, as here, the house has been conveyed into the joint names of the man and the woman, it is relatively easy to conclude ... that the reason why the house was acquired in joint names was that the parties intended that they should each have a beneficial interest in the house. To determine the extent of those beneficial interests - whether they are to be equal or not - is more difficult."

It is in determining the size of the beneficial interests in these circumstances that the common intention of the parties, that certain acts or payments should be regarded as contributions, has been crucial. Thus it may be inferred that the property was to belong to them in equal shares on the basis that they had assumed joint liability for the mortgage where the whole of the purchase price had been provided by the mortgage advance. (See *Walker* v *Hall; Bernard* v *Josephs* [1982] Ch 391; *Crisp* v *Mullings* (1976) 239 EG 119, but contrast *Young* v *Young* [1984] FLR 375. Consideration is given below to the question of "indirect contributions".)

In *Marsh* v *Von Sternberg* [1986] 1 FLR 526 an unmarried couple had purchased in their joint names a flat of which the woman had been a protected tenant and had accordingly been given an opportunity of buying at a price substantially below market value. Bush J inferred that as part of their agreement or arrangement the parties regarded the realisation of that financial benefit by way of discount as a contribution by the woman to the purchase of the flat. He also held that the man was entitled to credit for a sum representing his mortgage liability as opposed to his actual payments. It was inferred that the parties had agreed between themselves that they would service the mortgage 50 - 50 so that it followed that the man's "contribution at the time of the setting up of this trust was one half of the mortgage" (at p. 534). In *Passee* v *Passee* [1988] 1 FLR 263 the house had been purchased in the sole name of the plaintiff, but with initial contributions from his aunt and her daughter. They all lived there (though the daughter subsequently died) with other members of the family and made weekly contributions covering outgoings including repayment of the mortgage. In the Court of Appeal Nicholls LJ said that the inference to be drawn was that from the outset it was intended by the three of them that such contributions to the mortgage repayments should be taken into account in determining their respective beneficial interests. The liability for the mortgage of the plaintiff alone was not to be regarded as part of the initial contribution by the plaintiff.

A search for the common intention of the parties seems inevitable where there is a dispute as to whether a particular act or payment can be regarded as a contribution to the acquisition of the house. This may be more obvious and easier where it is clear from other evidence - e.g. a conveyance into joint names or an initial contribution - that the person doing the act or making the payment was intended to have some beneficial interest and the main point at issue is as to the extent of the interest. Even where there is no dispute that a claimant has provided funds for the acquisition of the home so as to give rise to a presumption of resulting trust in his or her favour, the court will in practice be concerned with the evidence of the intention of both parties in deciding whether that presumption has been rebutted. In other words it will be concerned not only with the intention of the party making the payment but also the extent to which that intention was shared by the party accepting the benefit of the payment, i.e. the basis on which it was accepted. Thus in *Sekhon* v *Alissa* [1989] 2 FLR 94 the house had been conveyed into the sole name of a daughter although her mother had contributed £22,500 towards the purchase price of £36,500. Hoffman J said that in these circumstances "the law presumes a resulting trust in her favour and *that presumption has to be rebutted by evidence that she intended a personal loan without acquiring any interest in the property*. I am not satisfied on the evidence that a loan was agreed" (p. 99. My italics). He had also concluded that "neither of the parties thought that the mother's contribution was really a gift" (at p. 98).

(vi) In the case of a resulting trust it is the intention of the parties at the time of the acquisition of the property which is relevant

The most commonly accepted method of reconciling this principle with the typical continuing acquisition arrangements encountered by the courts is to regard the contributions made after the date of the conveyance as evidence from which the common intention of the parties at the time of the conveyance can be inferred. Thus in *Bernard* v *Josephs* [1982] Ch 391 at p. 404 Griffiths LJ said that "in the absence of any special circumstances ... the time at which the beneficial interest crystallises is the time of the acquisition, but to ascertain this he must look at all the evidence including all the contributions made by the parties".

In *Burns* v *Burns* [1984] Ch 317 at p. 327 Fox LJ carried this further when he said that he agreed with the observations of Griffiths LJ but that did not "mean that for the purposes of determining the ultimate shares in the property one looks simply at the factual position as it was at the date of acquisition. It is necessary for the court to consider all the evidence, including the contributions of the parties, down to the date of separation (which in the case of a man and mistress will generally, though not always, be the relevant date). Thus the law proceeds on the basis that there is nothing inherently improbable in the parties acting on the understanding that the woman should be entitled to a share which was not to be quantified immediately on the acquisition of the home but should be left to be determined when the mortgage was repaid or the property disposed of, on the basis of what would be fair having regard to the total contributions, direct or indirect, which each spouse had made by that date." (See *Gissing* v *Gissing* [1971] AC 886 *per* Lord Diplock at p. 909 and Walton J in *Richards* v *Dove* [1974] 1 All ER 888.)

This approach was applied in *Passee* v *Passee* [1988] 1 FLR 263 where Nicholls LJ (at pp. 270-271) said:

"... the right inference to draw regarding the intentions of the plaintiff, the defendant and [the latter's daughter] who were three members of the same family is that at the outset they did not intend that the property would belong to them equally or in shares then defined in proportion to their initial contributions to the acquisition cost. Their approach was much less legalistic and less rigid. They intended, or are to be taken to have intended, that each would be entitled to a share to be determined when the property ceased to be theirs on the basis of what would be fair having regard to the contributions which in total each had by then made. Those contributions would include, in addition to the original contributions, sums contributed to the discharge of the initial mortgage and the cost of capital improvements."

It is, of course, open to a spouse or unmarried partner who claims a beneficial interest by virtue of some contribution made subsequent to the original conveyance of the legal estate in the property to the parties, or one of them, to show that notwithstanding that the beneficial interests were ascertained as at that date they have been varied by an agreement between them. Where there had been an express declaration of trust, this would be the only course open to a claimant. Such a variation involves a disposition of all or part of an equitable interest by one party to the other and so should be in writing to satisfy s.53(1)(c) of the Law of Property Act 1925. However, an oral agreement for valuable consideration to vary the trusts, of which equity would grant specific performance, is as valid as an assignment in writing for it operates as an agreement for the sale of an equitable interest, under which the "vendor" becomes a trustee for the "purchaser" subject only to the payment of the consideration (*per* Bagnall J in *Cowcher* v *Cowcher* [1972] 1 WLR 425 at p. 432).

Such an agreement will be difficult to establish. In *Cowcher* v *Cowcher* [1972] 1 WLR 425 at p. 432 Bagnall J expressed the opinion that "such an agreement, having terms of sufficient certainty, could be implied from conduct only in the most exceptional circumstances. In particular the mere payment by one beneficial owner of a mortgage instalment properly payable by the other could not alter the beneficial interests or ... imply an agreement to alter those interests". An agreement was found in *Sekhon* v *Alissa* [1989] 2 FLR 94 where a house had been purchased for £36,500 in the name of a daughter who obtained a mortgage advance of £15,000. The balance of the purchase price and costs (totalling some £22,500) was provided by her mother. Subsequently substantial improvements were made to the property including its conversion into two self-contained flats, to the cost of which the parties contributed more or less equally. Hoffman J concluded that the presumption of resulting trust in favour of the mother had not been rebutted and she had not intended to make a gift to her daughter of her initial contribution. He accepted that the extent of the mother's interest was governed by the presumption that the parties acquired the property in shares corresponding to the value of their contributions. Moreover, the equitable interests of the parties in those proportions would have come into existence at the time of the conveyance to the daughter and could not subsequently be varied except by a later transaction which would have been sufficient in itself to transfer a proprietary interest. The contributions to the improvements, being roughly of the same amount, did not have any effect on the beneficial ownership. However, there came a time, in 1984, after the conversion into two flats, when the parties agreed to treat the upstairs flat as belonging to the mother and the downstairs flat, into which the daughter and her husband moved, as belonging to the daughter. The mother could not thereafter, by virtue of the size of her original contribution, claim a larger interest than the value of the upstairs flat. In conveyancing terms her interest could be given effect by the grant to her of a leasehold interest in the upstairs flat.

In *Bernard* v *Josephs* [1982] Ch 391 at p. 404 Griffiths LJ thought that there might be exceptional circumstances in which it could be inferred that the parties agreed to alter their beneficial interests after a house was bought. He gave the example of a case where a man bought the house in the first place and the woman years later used a legacy to build an extra floor to make more room for the children. He said that in "such circumstances the obvious inference would be that the parties agreed that the woman should acquire a share in the greatly increased value of the house produced by her money. But this depends upon the court being able to infer an intention to alter the share in which the beneficial interest was previously held; the mere fact that one party has spent time and money on improving the property will not normally be sufficient to draw such an inference: see *Pettitt* v *Pettitt* [1970] AC 777."

(vii) Under a resulting trust a party is entitled to a share in the beneficial interest
    proportionate to his or her contribution
This principle is unlikely to cause difficulty where contributions are direct and easily identifiable. Where the contributions are indirect, it will be apparent from what has already been said that their identification and quantification will often be quite difficult. It has also been noted that it may be possible to infer that it was the common intention of the parties that particular acts or payments were to be regarded as contributions and hence can form the basis of a resulting trust. The shares which the parties are found to have in the property must be valued at the date of realisation and not at the date of any earlier separation of the parties (*per* Nourse LJ in *Turton* v *Turton* [1987] 2 All ER 641 at p. 648).

*(e) The constructive trust*

(i) General principles
A *constructive* trust arises when the court imposes a trust to enforce an obligation on one person to hold property for another or to transfer property to that other. It arises by operation of law and not necessarily by reason of the intentions of the parties express or implied, though it will be seen that a constructive trust can be imposed to give effect to the common intention of the parties that one of them should hold property as a trustee notwithstanding the absolute title vested in that party. A constructive trust will be imposed in a number of circumstances but only two instances seem relevant in this context.

(ii) Where a trustee obtains an advantage from the trust
A constructive trust will be imposed where a person who is already a trustee or otherwise clothed with a fiduciary character, seeks to retain an advantage from his trust. This principle was applied in *Protheroe* v *Protheroe* [1968] 1 WLR 519 in relation to the purchase of the freehold reversion of a matrimonial home. Although the leasehold interest was vested in the husband's name, it was accepted that it was held

in trust for himself and his wife in equal shares. After leaving the home the husband acquired the freehold reversion for £200, and while the value of the leasehold interest was £2,450, the property was worth £3,950 freehold. The Court of Appeal held that the freehold interest was held on the same trusts as the leasehold interest because, "being a trustee", the husband "had an especial advantage in getting in the freehold". The husband was, however, entitled to be reimbursed the purchase price of the freehold reversion and the expenses incurred in connection with the acquisition.

### (iii) To prevent fraudulent or unconscionable conduct

It has long been established that equity will not allow a statute to be used as a "cloak" or as an "engine" of fraud, and a constructive trust will be imposed to prevent a person "fraudulently" or "unconscionably" relying on the absence of written evidence required by s.53 (1) of the Law of Property Act 1925 to defeat the interest of another (see *Rochefoucauld* v *Boustead* [1897] 1 Ch 196). In *Bannister* v *Bannister* [1948] 2 All ER 133 at p. 136 this was explained by Scott LJ as follows:

"The fraud which brings the principle into play arises as soon as the absolute character of the conveyance is set up for the purpose of defeating the beneficial interest and that is the fraud to cover which the Statute of Frauds or the corresponding provisions of the Law of Property Act 1925, cannot be called in and cases in which no written evidence of the *real* bargain is available."

This line of cases would appear to underlie the more recent use of the constructive trust culminating in the decision of the Court of Appeal in *Grant* v *Edwards* [1986] 1 Ch 638 where Nourse LJ (at p. 646) said:

"In a case such as the present, where there has been no written declaration or agreement, nor any direct provision by the plaintiff of part of the purchase price so as to give rise to a resulting trust in her favour, she must establish a common intention between her and the defendant, acted on by her, that she should have a beneficial interest in the property. If she can do that, equity will not allow the defendant to deny that interest and will construct a trust to give effect to it."

It is essential to distinguish the constructive trust imposed to prevent inequitable conduct on this basis from the so-called "new model" constructive trust which Lord Denning sought to develop and impose "whenever justice and good conscience require it". (See *Eves* v *Eves* [1975] 1 WLR 1338 at p. 1341.) Both formulations refer to the speech of Lord Diplock in *Gissing* v *Gissing* [1971] AC 886. In particular Lord Diplock said (at p. 905):

"A resulting, implied or constructive trust - and it is unnecessary for present purposes to distinguish between these three classes of trust - is created by a transaction between the trustee and the *cestui que trust* in connection with the acquisition by the trustee of a legal estate in land whenever the trustee has so conducted himself that it would be inequitable to deny to the *cestui que trust* a beneficial interest in the land acquired. And he will be held so to have conducted himself if by his words or conduct he has induced the *cestui que trust* to act to his own detriment in the reasonable belief that by so acting he was acquiring a beneficial interest in the land."

The first part of this passage was used by Lord Denning to support the "new model" constructive trust which is evident in cases such as *Cooke* v *Head* [1972] 1 WLR 518 and *Eves* v *Eves* [1975] 1 WLR 1338 which were both concerned with unmarried couples. In *Eves* v *Eves* all members of the Court of Appeal were agreed that the plaintiff was entitled to a one-quarter share in the house vested in the name of her former cohabitee. She had made no financial contribution, but she had contributed in other ways in working on the home and garden. Lord Denning said that the law would "impute or impose a constructive trust by which he was to hold it in trust for them both" (at p. 1342). Moreover, he said that "a few years ago even equity would not have helped her. But things have altered now. Equity is not passed the age of child bearing. One of her latest progeny is a constructive trust of a new model. Lord Diplock brought it into the world and we have nourished it" (at p. 1341).

However, Browne LJ and Brightman J appear to base their decision on more traditional principles. They held that it could be inferred from the circumstances that there had been an arrangement between the parties whereby the plaintiff was to acquire a beneficial interest in the home in return for her labour in contributing to its repair and improvement (pp. 1343 and 1345). Hence her work in pursuance of this inferred arrangement gave her a beneficial interest in the house.

It is arguable that a constructive trust could have been imposed in *Eves* v *Eves* on the basis of an agreement between the parties that the property was to be vested in them jointly. The "trick" employed by the defendant to avoid this, coupled with the bargain, would clearly make it inequitable for him to complain of the lack of written evidence. Brightman J said (at p. 1345):

"The defendant clearly led the plaintiff to believe that she was to have some beneficial interest in the property, and that her name was omitted from the conveyance because of her age. This, of course, is not enough by itself to create a beneficial interest in her favour: there would at best be a mere voluntary declaration of trust which would be unenforceable for want of writing: *Gissing* v *Gissing*. If, however, it was part of the bargain between the parties, expressed or to be implied, that the plaintiff should contribute her labour towards the reparation of a house in which she was to have some beneficial interest, then I think that the arrangement becomes one to which the law can give effect. This seems to be consistent with the reasoning of the speeches in *Gissing* v *Gissing* [1971] AC 777 at pp. 790 and 995."

The wider concept of the constructive trust envisaged by Lord Denning was much criticised and can now be said to have been rejected. In *Grant* v *Edwards* [1986] Ch 638 Nourse LJ said that the ground relied on by Lord Denning MR in *Eves* v *Eves* "was at variance with the principles stated in *Gissing* v *Gissing* and by Browne LJ and by Brightman J" in *Eves* itself. It is now clear that a "common intention constructive trust" will be imposed on the basis explained by the members of the Court of Appeal in *Grant* v *Edwards*.

(iv) The requirements of the "common intention" constructive trust

In order to establish a constructive trust on the basis that it would be inequitable for the legal owner to claim sole beneficial ownership, two conditions must be satisfied:

- it must be shown that there was a common intention that both parties should have a beneficial interest; and

• it must be shown that the claimant has acted to his or her detriment on the basis of that common intention.

(Sir Nicolas Browne-Wilkinson V-C in *Grant* v *Edwards* [1986] Ch 638 at p. 654.) Thus, as Lord Diplock had made clear in *Gissing* v *Gissing* [1971] AC 886 at p. 905, mere common intention by itself is not enough. The claimant must also prove that he or she has acted to his or her detriment in the reasonable belief that by so acting he or she was acquiring a beneficial interest.

(v) Establishing a common intention

(1) Direct evidence
There may be direct evidence of a common intention that the party in whom the legal title is not vested is to have a beneficial interest in the property. In *Grant* v *Edwards* [1986] Ch 638 at p. 647 Nourse LJ said that there are some cases "where, although there has been no writing, the parties have orally declared themselves in such a way as to make their common intention plain". He regarded *Eves* v *Eves* as a clear example of this. The male defendant in that case had admitted in evidence that the female claimant's age had been used as an excuse for not putting the house into their joint names, and the Court of Appeal "inferred that there was an understanding between them, or a common intention, that the woman was to have some sort of proprietary interest in it; otherwise no excuse would have been needed" (*ibid.* at p. 647). In *Grant* v *Edwards* itself this was also the case. The legal title had been placed in the joint names of the male defendant and his brother. The former had told the plaintiff that her name was not going on to the title because it would cause some prejudice in the matrimonial proceedings between her and her husband. The defendant never had any real intention of replacing his brother with the plaintiff when those proceedings were at an end. Just as in *Eves* v *Eves* the facts raised "a clear inference that there was an understanding between the plaintiff and the defendant, or a common intention, that the plaintiff was to have some sort of proprietary interest in the house; otherwise no excuse for not putting her name on to the title would have been needed".

In *Midland Bank plc* v *Dobson* [1986] 1 FLR 171 a wife's claim to a beneficial interest in the house vested in her husband's name was made in response to a claim for possession by the mortgagee bank. The husband confirmed the wife's contention that the beneficial interest in the home was shared. Fox LJ (at p. 174) said that he thought that "assertions made by a husband and wife as to a common intention formed thirty years ago regarding joint ownership, of which there is no contemporary evidence and which happens to accommodate their current need to defeat the claims of a creditor, must be received with caution". Nevertheless, he did not feel able to accede to the bank's contention that the court should interfere with the judge's finding that there was a common intention of both Mr. and Mrs. Dobson from 1953 that they should share whatever beneficial interest Mr. Dobson had in the house. There was evidence on which the judge could so find, but, as will be seen, her claim failed because she could not show that she had acted to her detriment.

In *Lloyds Bank plc* v *Rosset* [1991] AC 107 at pp. 127-128 Lord Bridge said that the question which the judge had to determine was whether he could find that before the contract to acquire the property was concluded the parties "had entered into an agreement, made an arrangement, reached an understanding, or formed a common intention that the beneficial interest in the property would be jointly owned". He continued:

"I do not think it is of importance which of these alternative expressions one uses. Spouses living in amity will not normally think it necessary to formulate or define their respective interests in property in any precise way. The expectation of parties to every happy marriage is that they will share the practical benefits of occupying the matrimonial home whoever owns it. But this is something quite distinct from sharing the beneficial interest in the property asset which the matrimonial asset represents. These considerations give rise to special difficulties for judges who are called on to resolve a dispute between spouses who have parted and are at arm's length as to what their common intention or understanding with respect to interests in property was at a time when they were still living as a united family and acquiring a matrimonial home in expectation of living in it together indefinitely."

In that case the purchase price of the house, which was in a semi-derelict condition, and the cost of works of renovation were paid by the husband, with the assistance of funds from his family trust. Lord Bridge said that the wife faced formidable difficulties in trying to show an agreement that the property should be jointly owned. She needed to show that it had been the husband's intention to make an immediate gift to her of a half share in the equity of property purchased and improved at a cost of some £72,000 despite the fact that she knew that the trustees of the family trust had insisted in the property being in the husband's name alone. If they had ever thought about it they must have realised that the creation of a trust giving the wife a half share, or indeed any other substantial share in the property, would have been nothing less than a subterfuge to circumvent the stipulation of the trustees. The judge found that there was no evidence of an oral agreement.

In *Hammond* v *Mitchell* [1991] 1 WLR 1127 at p. 1137 Waite J found that in relation to the bungalow in which the parties had lived there had been express discussion on more than one occasion which, although not directed with any precision as to proprietary interests, was sufficient to amount to an understanding at least that the bungalow was to be shared beneficially.

Although Lord Diplock in *Gissing* v *Gissing* [1971] AC 886 at p. 906 referred to the formation of a common intention "at the time of acquisition" there is no reason in principle why a constructive trust should be imposed only on the basis of a common intention formed at the time of the first acquisition of the property. In *Grant* v *Edwards* [1986] Ch 638 at pp. 651-652 Mustill LJ said:

"In fact the event happening between the parties which, if followed by the relevant type of conduct on the part of the claimant, can lead to the creation of an interest in the claimant, may itself occur after acquisition. The beneficial interests may change in the course of the relationship."

This was approved by Lord Oliver in delivering the judgment of the Privy Council on an appeal from Australia in *Austin* v *Keele* (1987) 61 ALJR 605 at p. 609, though he acknowledged that it may be more difficult to prove the requisite intention in relation to property already held beneficially by the trustee. In *Hammond* v *Mitchell* [1991] 1 WLR 1127 Waite J was satisfied that the understanding reached by the parties as to the sharing of the beneficial interest in a bungalow applied also to extensions to that bungalow and adjoining land purchased subsequently. Whether an original common intention is to apply to additions to the original property in any given case is a question of fact which could, he said, be determined only on a review of the whole course of dealing between the parties (*ibid.* p. 1137. Contrast *Winkworth* v *Edward Baron Development Co Ltd* [1986] 1 WLR 1512 where property had been purchased by a company under the control of the spouses who occupied it as their matrimonial home. The House of Lords, reversing the Court of Appeal, refused to regard a subsequent payment by the wife of £8,600 into the company's bank account as giving her any beneficial interest in the property which was effective against a creditor of the company. It is not clear from the judgment of Lord Templeman whether the claim was based on a resulting trust or a constructive trust).

(2) Inferred common intention
Where, as is likely to be the situation in most cases, there is no direct evidence of the necessary common intention, that common intention may be inferred from the conduct of the parties. In *Gissing* v *Gissing* [1971] AC 886 at pp. 906-908 Lord Diplock said:
"But parties to a transaction in connection with the acquisition of land may well have formed a common intention that the beneficial interest in the land shall be vested in them jointly without having used express words to communicate this intention to one another; or their recollection of the words used may be imperfect or conflicting by the time the dispute arises. In such a case - a common one where the parties are spouses whose marriage has broken down - it may be possible to infer their common intention from their conduct."
He went on to say that "the relevant intention of each party is the intention which was reasonably understood by the other party to be manifested by that party's words or conduct notwithstanding that he did not consciously formulate that intention in his own mind or even acted with some different intention which he did not communicate to the other party". However, "he is not bound by any inference which the other party draws as to his intention unless that inference is one which can reasonably be drawn from his words or conduct". Lord Diplock's speech then considers the types of evidence from which the courts are most often asked to infer the necessary common intention, viz. contributions (direct or indirect) to the deposit, the mortgage instalments or general housekeeping expenses. (See *Springette* v *Defoe* (1992) 24 HLR 552 where Dillon LJ said that to establish a common intention it was not enough to show that each party had been thinking on the same lines if such thoughts were not communicated to the other party. There must be a shared common intention.)
In *Grant* v *Edwards* [1986] Ch 638 at p. 647 Nourse LJ noted that in most cases of this kind the difficulty was that the necessary common intention had to be inferred "almost always from the expenditure incurred by them respectively". He said that in "in this regard the court has to look for expenditure which is referable to the acquisition of the house ...". He did not find it necessary to decide whether, if

the common intention had not been orally made plain in the case before him, the expenditure of the wife would have been sufficient to justify inferring that common intention. However, so far as *Eves* v *Eves* was concerned, if the common intention had not been plain, the work done by the female claimant would not have been conduct from which the common intention could be inferred. He appeared to leave open the question whether the necessary common intention could be inferred from conduct other than the expenditure of money (at p. 650).

In *Lloyds Bank plc* v *Rosset* [1991] AC 107 at pp. 132-133 Lord Bridge said that where the court has to rely entirely on the conduct of the parties as the basis from which to infer a common intention to share the property beneficially "... direct contributions to the purchase price by the partner who is not the legal owner, whether initially or by payment of mortgage instalments, will readily justify the inference necessary to the creation of a constructive trust. But, as I read the authorities, it is *at least extremely doubtful whether anything less will do.*" (My italics. See the discussion of contributions in *(f)*, page 40.)

No common intention can be inferred where it is clear that the parties never had the necessary common intention. Thus in *Gissing* v *Gissing* [1971] AC 886 at p. 900 Viscount Dilhorne said: "One cannot counteract the absence of any common intention at the time of acquisition by conclusions as to what the parties would have done if they had thought about the matter". In other words, it seems that while it is permissible to infer from the conduct of the parties and the surrounding circumstances what the common intention of the parties must have been, it is not permissible to impute to them a common intention which they clearly did not have. This now seems to be clearly accepted although different views had been expressed by some members of the House of Lords in *Pettitt* v *Pettitt* [1970] AC 777. In *Grant* v *Edwards* [1986] Ch 638 at p. 652 Mustill LJ said that the court "must not impute to the parties a bargain which they never made or a common intention which they never possessed".

(vi) The detrimental act of the claimant
Proof of a common intention is by itself not enough. The claimant must also show that he or she has acted to his or her detriment on the basis of that common intention. What kind of conduct will satisfy this requirement?

(1) The acts relied upon as detriment must be referable to the common intention that the claimant was to have a beneficial interest in the property
In *Grant* v *Edwards* [1986] Ch 638 at p. 648 Nourse LJ referred to "conduct on which the woman could not reasonably have been expected to embark unless she was to have an interest in the house". Thus in *Eves* v *Eves* [1975] 1 WLR 1338 if the woman was not to have such an interest, she could, nevertheless, reasonably be expected to go and live with her lover, but not, for example, to wield a 14lb sledge hammer in the front garden. In adopting the latter kind of conduct she was seen to act to her detriment on the faith of the common intention. On the facts of *Grant* v *Edwards* itself Nourse LJ concluded (at p. 649) that the conduct of the claimant in making substantial contributions to housekeeping expenses, thereby assisting the defendant in paying off the mortgage, was conduct on which she could not reason-

ably have been expected to embark unless she was to have an interest in the house. She had, therefore, acted to her detriment. In *Hammond* v *Mitchell* [1991] 1 WLR 1127 at p. 1137 Waite J said that the female claimant, by her participation wholeheartedly in the commercial activities based on the home, not only acted consistently with their understanding as to the beneficial interest, but also acted to her detriment in that she gave her full support on two occasions to speculative ventures which, had they turned out unfavourably, might have involved the entire property being sold to repay indebtedness to the bank.

On the other hand, in *Midland Bank plc* v *Dobson* [1986] 1 FLR 171, while the claimant succeeded in showing that there was a common intention that she and her husband should share the beneficial interest in the house, she failed to "demonstrate that she was induced to act to her detriment upon the basis of" that common intention, or "that there was otherwise any nexus between the acquisition of the property and something provided or forgone by" her (*per* Fox LJ at p. 177). She made no direct contribution to the purchase price and there was never any agreement or understanding that she would do so. It was not until twelve years or so after the purchase that she earned any income of consequence and by then the amount outstanding on the mortgage was small and paid off within five years. She did use part of her earnings on household expenses but "it was not suggested that she did that in reliance upon any understanding as to joint ownership of the house. She did it, presumably, simply because she thought the expenditure appropriate and had the money. She also did some ordinary periodic decorating", but there was "no reason to suppose that was because of any arrangement that she would do so on account of a common intention as to joint ownership. It was the sort of work that members of a family do in a house" (*per* Fox LJ at pp. 176-177).

(2) The acts relied upon do not necessarily have to be referable to the house
It has already been noted that where the common intention has to be inferred from the conduct of the parties this will generally be from the expenditure incurred by the parties and it will need to be expenditure which is referable to the acquisition of the house. In *Grant* v *Edwards* [1986] Ch 638 at p. 647 Nourse LJ pointed out that: "If it is found to have been incurred, such expenditure will perform the two-fold function of establishing the common intention and showing that the claimant has acted on it". On the other hand, where the common intention is established by oral statements of the parties, so that the court is concerned only with conduct which amounts to acting on it by the claimant, then "although that conduct can undoubtedly be the incurring of expenditure which is referable to the acquisition of the house, it need not necessarily be so" (*ibid.*). Sir Nicolas Browne-Wilkinson V-C said (at p. 657): "As at present advised, once it has been shown that there was a common intention that the claimant should have an interest in the house, *any act* done by her to her detriment relating to the joint lives of the parties is, in my judgment, sufficient detriment to qualify. The acts do not have to be inherently referable to the house." (My italics.) He went on to say that:

"The holding out to the claimant that she had a beneficial interest in the house is an act of such a nature as to be part of the inducement to her to do the acts relied on. Accordingly, in the absence of evidence to the contrary, the right inference is that the claimant acted in reliance on such holding out and the burden lies on the legal owner to show that she did not do so: see *Greasley* v *Cooke* [1980] 1 WLR 1306."

He also referred to *Jones* v *Jones* [1977] 1 WLR 438 and *Pascoe* v *Turner* [1979] 1 WLR 431 which were also cases of estoppel, but although the analogy of propri- etary estoppel had been raised in argument it had not been fully argued and he did not therefore rest his judgment on that basis. (Proprietary estoppel is considered in Part 5, page 47.)

This broad approach to the question of what may be regarded as detrimental conduct for this purpose may be regarded as the most significant and encouraging feature of *Grant* v *Edwards*. (See Montgomery, [1987] Conv. 16.) It remains to be seen whether it is broad enough to include the contributions of a woman to the care of the family and house and the possible sacrifice of a career for those purposes. Sir Nicolas Browne-Wilkinson appears to say that the onus will be on the defendant to show that the acts relied upon were "not specifically referable to the claimant's belief that she has an interest in the house" - but "referable to the mutual love and affection of the parties" (at p. 657). (See also the conduct relied on in *Hammond* v *Mitchell* [1991] 1 WLR 1127.) It must, however, be remembered that any such lib- eral approach applies only to conduct relied on as a detriment and assumes that the common intention that the claimant shall have a beneficial interest has been clearly established. If it is necessary to infer such a common intention, then conduct must still be referable to the house.

**(3) It may be that the detrimental conduct relied upon must be such as was envis- aged by the common intention or bargain of the parties**

Support for this proposition may be found in the judgment of Mustill LJ in *Grant* v *Edwards* [1986] Ch 638 at p. 652 when he said :

"In order to decide whether the subsequent conduct of the claimant serves to complete the beneficial interest which has been explicitly or tacitly promised to her the court must decide whether the conduct is referable to the bargain, promise or intention. Whether the conduct satisfies this test will depend on the nature of the conduct and of the bargain, promise or intention."

Thus, if there was an express bargain whereby the defendant promised the claimant an interest in the property, in return for an explicit undertaking by the claimant to act in a certain way, the only question, in his view, is whether the claimant's con- duct is of the type explicitly promised. "It is immaterial whether it takes the shape of a contribution to the cost of acquiring the property or is of a quite different char- acter" (*ibid.*).

If there was an express but incomplete bargain whereby the defendant promised the claimant an interest in the property on the basis that the claimant would do something in return, but the parties did not make explicit what the claimant was to do, it will be for the court to infer what the *quid pro quo* was intended to have been. Mustill LJ said (at p. 652): "... no doubt it will often be easier in practice to infer that the *quid pro quo* was intended to take the shape of a financial or other contribu- tion to the cost of acquisition or improvement, but this need not always be so.

Whatever the court decides the *quid pro quo* to have been, it will suffice if the claimant has furnished it."

Mustill LJ left open the question (not considered by the other members of the court) whether an explicit promise by the proprietor that the claimant would have an interest in the property, unaccompanied by any express or tacit agreement as to a *quid pro quo*, could effectively confer an interest if the claimant relies on it by acting to her detriment. Although he thought it had not been directly addressed in *Gissing* v *Gissing* [1971] AC 886, he considered that the speech of Lord Diplock (at p. 905) supported an affirmative answer.

(vii) The size of the beneficial interests

Where the existence of some beneficial interest of the claimant has been shown, then *prima facie* the interest of the claimant will be that which the parties intended *(per* Sir Nicolas Browne-Wilkinson V-C in *Grant* v *Edwards* [1986] Ch 638 at p. 657, referring to the statement of Lord Diplock in *Gissing* v *Gissing* [1971] AC 886 at p. 908). If that intention has been made express then, in contrast to the position under a resulting trust, the beneficial interest acquired by the claimant need not be proportionate to his or her contributions. However, in many cases the parties will not have made express their common intention as to their respective beneficial interests. In *Stokes* v *Anderson* [1991] 1 FLR 391 at p. 400 Nourse LJ said that in that event "all payments made and acts done by the claimant are to be treated as illuminating the common intention as to the extent of the beneficial interest. Once you get to that stage, ... there is no practicable alternative to the determination of a fair share. The court must supply the common intention by reference to that which all the material circumstances had been shown to be fair." He referred to the view expressed by Lord Diplock in *Gissing* v *Gissing* [1971] AC 886 at p. 909:

"And there is nothing inherently improbable in their acting on the understanding that the wife should be entitled to a share which was not to be quantified immediately upon the acquisition of the home but should be left to be determined when the mortgage was repaid or the property disposed of, on the basis of what would be fair having regard to the total contributions, direct or indirect, which each spouse had made by that date. Where this was the most likely inference from their conduct it would be for the court to give effect to that common intention of the parties by determining what in all the circumstances of the case was a fair share."

Identifiable contributions to the purchase of the house will of course be an important factor in many cases, but in *Grant* v *Edwards* [1986] Ch 638 at pp. 657-658 Sir Nicolas Browne-Wilkinson V-C said that in other cases contributions by way of the labour or other unquantifiable action of the claimant will also be relevant.

In *Grant* v *Edwards* Sir Nicolas Browne-Wilkinson V-C said that taking into account the fact that the house was intended to be the joint property of the parties, the substantial contributions of the claimant to their common expenditure and the payment of surplus money received under a fire insurance policy into a joint bank account led him to conclude that she was entitled to a half share in the house *(ibid.* at p. 658. See also Nourse LJ at p. 650 and Mustill LJ at p. 654). In *Stokes* v *Anderson* the female plaintiff provided first the sum of £5,000, being the balance of

£45,000 which the male defendant had agreed to pay to his former wife in return for her half share in the former matrimonial home. She subsequently provided a further £7,000 which was used to reduce the mortgage on the property which had become the home of the plaintiff and the defendant. The judge at first instance had found that the two payments by the plaintiff were made pursuant to a common intention that she should have half the beneficial interest in the property and were not made as loans by her. However, in the Court of Appeal Nourse LJ pointed out that when the first payment of £5,000 was made, the male defendant was already entitled to half the beneficial interest in the property - it was only necessary to acquire the other half. Accordingly, the fair view of all the circumstances was that the female plaintiff was entitled to a beneficial interest equivalent to one half of the former wife's share, or one-quarter of the whole, subject to the mortgage. In *Hammond* v *Mitchell* [1991] 1 WLR 1127 at p. 1137 Waite J said that "This is not an area where the maxim that 'equality is equity' falls to be applied unthinkingly". Nevertheless, in that case when account had been taken of the claimant's contributions as mother, helper, unpaid assistant and at times financial supporter to the family prosperity generated by the defendant's dealing activities, he thought it right that her beneficial interest in the bungalow should be one half.

## *(f) Contributions*

### (i) The relevance of contributions

Contributions to the acquisition of a family home are crucial to the operation of a resulting trust. They are also likely to be of central importance in the operation of a constructive trust imposed to give effect to the common intention of the parties. In *Grant* v *Edwards* [1986] Ch 638 at p. 655 Sir Nicolas Browne-Wilkinson V-C suggested that, in the context of such a constructive trust, contributions made by a claimant may be relevant for four different purposes, namely:

(1) in the absence of direct evidence of intention, as evidence from which the parties' intentions can be inferred;
(2) as corroboration of direct evidence of intention;
(3) to show that the claimant has acted to his or her detriment in reliance on the common intention;
(4) to quantify the extent of the beneficial interest.

Where property is being acquired with the assistance of a mortgage repayable over a long period, or extensive work is done on the property, the concept of "contributions" gives rise to problems which are unlikely to be present in the case of a "once-and-for-all" purchase for cash. First, and most obviously, the task of ascertaining the contributions of the parties is more complicated and there may be a dispute as to whether certain acts do in fact amount to "contributions". Secondly, there is likely to be more difficulty in relation to the inferences to be drawn.

### (ii) Direct financial contributions

When a claimant has made a cash contribution to the deposit and legal costs on the purchase of the home with the assistance of a mortgage, this will generally give rise to the inference that it was the common intention of the parties that the claimant should share in the beneficial interest in the property. Where the claimant makes regular and substantial direct contributions to the mortgage instalments, this will generally lead to a similar inference even though there was no initial contribution to the cash deposit. This would seem to be in accord with the views expressed by the members of the House of Lords in *Pettitt* v *Pettitt* [1970] AC 777 and *Gissing* v *Gissing* [1971] AC 886 (see particularly Lord Diplock in *Gissing* at pp. 907-908). However, contributions to mortgage instalments must be regular and substantial so as to justify such an inference, and in *Gissing* Viscount Dilhorne sounded a note of caution when he said (at p. 900): "It would not, for instance, suffice if the wife just made a mortgage payment while her husband was abroad."

Clear direct financial contributions to the acquisition of property will give rise to a resulting trust of the beneficial interest proportionate to the contributions. Such contributions may also form the basis from which may be inferred a common intention justifying the imposition of a constructive trust as in *Grant* v *Edwards* [1986] Ch 638. The shares will then depend on the common intention of the parties and will not necessarily be proportionate to their respective contributions. If there is express oral evidence of a common intention to share beneficial ownership, then direct financial contributions will almost certainly be sufficient detriment to justify the imposition of a constructive trust.

It is essential to distinguish a direct cash contribution to the purchase price of a home from a loan, for if "moneys are advanced by way of loan there can be no question of the lender being entitled to an interest in the property under a resulting trust" (*per* Browne-Wilkinson J in *Re Sharpe* [1980] 1 WLR 219). That was the case of an aunt who had provided money towards the purchase price of property in which she was going to live. The judge held on the facts that it gave her a right to possession, but not to any proprietary interest.

However, in *Risch* v *McFee* [1991] 1 FLR 105 the Court of Appeal took the view that a payment of £1,700 by the claimant which had clearly started life as a loan could be taken into account as part of the claimant's contribution to the cost of acquiring the home. Balcombe LJ accepted that if the loan of £1,700 had stood by itself that could not have given the claimant an equitable interest in the house to the extent of that sum. The judge had found that there was a common intention that the female claimant should have a beneficial interest and that she had a beneficial interest at least to the extent of other payments of £2,250 and £800. Balcombe LJ (with Butler-Sloss LJ concurring) found that the claimant had clearly acted to her detriment as envisaged by the Court of Appeal in *Grant* v *Edwards* because after she had put in the further sums of money she never sought to recover the loan of £1,700 and at no time did she require interest on it. Accordingly, the judge was entitled on the facts, which differed from *Re Sharpe*, "to hold that although it may have started life as a loan, nevertheless, once it was established that the plaintiff had a beneficial interest in the house, to take into account that £1,700 as part of her contribution to the cost of acquiring the property; indeed that is what it had in fact become" (*per* Balcombe LJ at p. 110).

(iii) Indirect financial contributions
The extent to which payment of expenses not directly connected with the purchase of the family home, such as general household expenses, may be taken into account

remains a matter of some difficulty. The views expressed by the House of Lords in *Gissing* v *Gissing* [1971] AC 886 did not provide a clear statement of principle, but more recently attention has come to be focused on the judgment of Lord Diplock in that case, and this has become an essential starting point for a consideration of the question. He considered two possible situations at pp. 907-909. First:

"Where there has been an initial contribution by the wife to the cash deposit and legal charges which points to a common intention at the time of the conveyance that she should have a beneficial interest in the land conveyed to her husband, it would be unrealistic to attach significance to the wife's subsequent contributions to the mortgage instalments only where she pays them directly herself. It may be no more than a matter of convenience which spouse pays particular household accounts, particularly when both are earning, and if the wife goes out to work and devotes part of her earnings or uses her private income to meet joint expenses of the household which would otherwise be met by the husband, so as to enable him to pay the mortgage instalments out of his earnings, this would be consistent with and might be corroborative of an original intention that she should share in the beneficial interest in the matrimonial home and that her payments of other household expenses were intended by both spouses to be treated as including a contribution by the wife to the purchase of the matrimonial home."

Secondly,

"Where a wife has made no initial contribution to the cash deposit and legal charges and no direct contribution to the mortgage instalments, nor any adjustment to her contribution to other expenses of the household which it can be inferred was referable to the acquisition of the house, there is in the absence of an express agreement between the parties, no material to justify the court in inferring that it was the common intention of the parties that she should have any beneficial interest in a matrimonial home conveyed into the sole name of the husband, merely because she continued to contribute out of her earnings or private income to other expenses of the household. For such conduct is no less consistent with a common intention to share the day to day expenses of the household, while each spouse retains a separate interest in capital assets acquired with their own money or obtained by inheritance or gift. There is nothing here to rebut the *prima facie* inference that a purchaser of land who pays the purchase price and takes a conveyance and grants a mortgage in his own name intends to acquire the sole beneficial interest as well as the legal estate ...".

In order to give rise to a resulting trust it is essential that an act or payment can be related to the acquisition of the property so as to be regarded as a contribution thereto. The payment of household expenses by itself manifests no such relation and gives rise to no inference that a beneficial interest was to be acquired thereby. Where a claimant has also made a direct contribution to the initial costs of the home, this will almost certainly be sufficient to show an intention that he or she was to have a beneficial interest. It is also likely to make it easier to show that subsequent payment of household expenses should be regarded as a contribution to the acquisition cost (*Davis* v *Vale* [1971] 1 WLR 1202). Lord Diplock in the passage quoted above envisaged that this would be the case where this enabled the other party to pay the mortgage instalments. This factor may provide the link even where there is no initial contribution. Lord Pearson said (at p. 903):

"Contributions are not limited to those made directly in part payment of the price of the property or to those made at the time when the property is conveyed into the name of one of the spouses. For instance, there can be a contribution if *by arrangement* between the spouses, one of them by payment of the household expenses enables the other to pay the mortgage instalments." (My italics.)

In *Hargrave* v *Newton* [1971] 1 WLR 1611, where the wife had made no initial contribution to the purchase of the matrimonial home and no direct contribution to the mortgage instalments but had made substantial payments towards the household and family expenses, Lord Denning MR said:

"If her efforts or her contributions relieved him of other expenses which he would otherwise have had to bear - *so that he would not have been able to meet the mortgage instalments on the loan without her help* - then she does make an indirect contribution." (My italics.)

In the subsequent case of *Hazell* v *Hazell* [1972] 1 WLR 301 Lord Denning resiled from the restriction indicated by the italicised words, for the county court judge had not been satisfied that the husband could not have paid the mortgage instalments without the wife's contributions to the household expenses. He said:

"It is sufficient if the contributions made by the wife are such as to relieve the husband of expenditure which he would otherwise have had to bear. By so doing the wife helps him indirectly with the mortgage instalments because he has more money in his pocket with which to pay them. *It may be that he does not strictly need her help* - he may have enough money of his own without it - but, if he accepts it (and thus is enabled to save more of his own money), she becomes entitled to a share." (My italics.)

It may be that even this envisages some kind of arrangement between the parties whereby payment of the household expenses is accepted as a contribution to the mortgage repayments, thereby providing the necessary link with acquisition of the property. In the absence of some such arrangement, whether express or implied from the defendant's inability to pay the mortgage instalments without the claimant's contribution to household expenses, it is submitted that, where there has been no initial contribution, payment of household expenses cannot be said to be referable to the acquisition of the home and hence cannot give rise to a resulting trust.

If it can be shown that there was an express agreement between the parties that the beneficial interest was to be shared, or if such an agreement can be inferred from other evidence, then payment of household expenses may be sufficient detriment to justify imposition of a constructive trust. Thus in *Grant* v *Edwards* [1986] Ch 638 at p. 649 Nourse LJ concluded that "the very substantial contribution which the plaintiff made out of her earnings after August 1972 to the housekeeping and the feeding and to the bringing up of the children enabled the defendant to keep down the instalments payable under both mortgages out of his own income and, moreover, he could not have done that if he had had to bear the whole of the other expenses as well". He could not see that she could reasonably have been expected to give the defendant such substantial assistance in paying off mortgages on his house except on the basis that she was to have an interest in it. She had acted to her detriment on the faith of the common intention apparent from other evidence. However, it may be noted that he did not find it necessary to decide whether, if the common intention had not been made orally plain, the expenditure in the present case would have been such that a common intention could have been inferred.

Another form of indirect financial contribution was taken into account in *Marsh v Von Sternberg* [1986] FLR 526 where the property had been conveyed into the joint names of the parties but their beneficial interests had not been declared. In determining their respective shares, Bush J held that the discount available on the purchase price by virtue of one of the parties being a protected tenant of the property was a financial benefit for which that party was entitled to be credited. He said "... it is possible to infer ... that as part of the agreement or arrangement the parties regarded the realisation of that financial benefit by way of discount as a contribution by the respondent to the purchase of the flat" ( at p. 531). (See also *Springette v Defoe* (1992) 24 HLR 552 - discount under the "right to buy" scheme.)

(iv) Non-financial contributions
A significant number of reported cases concern claims based, at least in part, on work done by the claimant spouse or cohabitee to the property in question. These include three decisions of the House of Lords - *Pettitt v Pettitt* [1970] AC 777; *Gissing v Gissing* [1971] AC 886 and *Lloyds Bank plc v Rosset* [1991] AC 107 - in which such claims were unsuccessful, and two Court of Appeal decisions - *Cooke v Head* [1972] 1 WLR 518 and *Eves v Eves* [1975] 1 WLR 1338 - in which the claims were successful.

If there is other evidence of a common intention that the party carrying out work of improvement to the property was to have a share in the beneficial interest, then such work may amount to sufficient detriment to give rise to a constructive trust. The decision in *Eves v Eves* may be interpreted in this way and was so interpreted by the Court of Appeal in *Grant v Edwards* [1986] Ch 638 and by the House of Lords in *Lloyds Bank plc v Rosset*. There may be express evidence of the necessary common intention, but even where there is not, such intention may be inferred from other forms of contribution. Thus in *Smith v Baker* [1970] 1 WLR 1160 the wife's substantial help with the building of a bungalow on land purchased in the husband's name was not her sole contribution. She had provided most of the purchase price for the plot of land and it appears to have been common ground that some beneficial interest was to be acquired by the wife. The main question was the respective shares of the spouses. In *Cooke v Head,* where the female claimant may be regarded as having carried out work similar to that carried out by the claimant in *Eves v Eves,* and which was there regarded as insufficient to justify the inference of the necessary common intention, she had also contributed to a joint fund out of which the mortgage instalments were paid for some fifteen months, though she had not contributed anything in cash to the purchase price.

If there is no other evidence of a common intention it now seems unlikely, in the light of the views expressed in the House of Lords in *Lloyds Bank plc v Rosset,* that a common intention that a person carrying out such work on a property will have a beneficial interest in that property will be inferred solely from the fact that such work has been done. In that case the wife failed to establish any express agreement, arrangement or common intention that she should have a beneficial interest, but the judge was prepared to infer such a common intention from the wife's activities in connection with the renovation of the property which was a semi-derelict farmhouse. The wife, who was described as a skilled decorator and painter, carried out work on the farmhouse, obtained necessary materials, and generally urged on the builders who had been employed to work on the property. However, in the House of Lords Lord Bridge said that her activity in this regard could not possibly justify such an inference. He said (at p. 131):

"On any view the monetary value of Mrs. Rosset's work expressed as a contribution to a property acquired at a cost exceeding £70,000 must have been so trifling as to be almost *de minimis*."

Indeed, even if her husband's intention to make a gift to her of a share in the property had been clearly established, Lord Bridge had considerable doubt that the work was sufficient to support a claim for a constructive trust - presumably as an act of detriment.

It is not clear whether, if the wife's work had been more substantial, there might be circumstances in which an inference of an appropriate common intention might be drawn. Lord Bridge's comment (at p. 133), referred to on page 36, that he was extremely doubtful whether anything less than direct financial contributions to the purchase price would suffice, is hardly encouraging. He also emphasised (at p. 130) that neither a common intention by spouses that a house is to be regarded as a "joint venture" nor a common intention that the house is to be shared by parents and children as the family home throws any light on their intentions with respect to the beneficial ownership of the property. In *Thomas* v *Fuller-Brown* [1988] 1 FLR 237 the court refused to infer that it had been the common intention of an unmarried couple that the man, who had carried out substantial improvements to a house vested in the woman's name, should have a beneficial interest in that property. The man's submission that it was not realistic to suppose that he would have designed and constructed what he described as a valuable two-storey extension, and made major alterations and other improvements in return for meals, lodgings on site, pocket money and cohabitation, was rejected. Slade LJ said (at p. 247) "... this case illustrates, as many previous cases have done, that a man who does work by way of improvement to his cohabitee's property without a clear understanding as to the financial basis on which the work is to be done does so at his own risk". It was clear, too, that the woman had done nothing to lead the man to suppose that by carrying out the work he would acquire an interest. If she had, then a case of proprietary estoppel might have arisen (see page 47).

*(g) Resulting trusts and constructive trusts compared*

(i) Intention
A resulting trust is based upon the actual or presumed intention of a party to the purchase of property not to make a gift or loan of the contribution, but to acquire a beneficial interest proportionate to the contribution. The modern tendency is to refer to the common intention of two parties who have purchased a house in the name of one of them that the latter shall hold the property on a resulting trust for the other to

the extent of the latter's contribution. This appears to have developed in some cases to include an actual or inferred common intention of the parties that particular payments or acts are to constitute a contribution to the purchase of the property so as to give the party making those payments or doing those acts a proportionate beneficial interest. In this context a constructive trust is based upon the common intention of the legal owner and the claimant that they shall both have a beneficial interest in the property which it would be inequitable to permit the legal owner to repudiate.

### (ii) Time of intention
A resulting trust is based upon the intention of the parties at the time of the acquisition of the property. The relevant common intention which forms the basis of a constructive trust may and generally will also exist at the time of the acquisition of the property, but may come into existence subsequently.

### (iii) Relationship of contributions to the property
In the case of a resulting trust, payments and acts must be referable to the property if they are to be regarded as contributions to the acquisition of the property. In the case of a constructive trust, payments and acts will need to be referable to the property if they are to form the basis upon which the court infers a common intention that both parties are to have a beneficial interest in the property. However, if such a common intention is established by other evidence, then the detrimental conduct which a claimant must show may be conduct on the basis of which it would not be possible to infer the necessary common intention and probably need not be referable to the property.

### (iv) Size of the beneficial interests
Under a resulting trust the claimant is entitled to a share proportionate to his or her contribution to the purchase price of the property though the contributions may not be easily quantifiable. Where the court imposes a constructive trust because it would be inequitable to allow the person with legal title to claim sole beneficial ownership, the interest of the claimant will be that which the parties intended though their common intention may have to be inferred from conduct.

### (v) The position *vis-à-vis* creditors
A share to which a person is entitled under a resulting trust, being based upon the contribution of that person to the acquisition of the property, will be effective against the trustee in bankruptcy of the party in whom legal title is vested. However, where a constructive trust is imposed, the share of the claimant may be larger than the share which could be justified on the basis of his or her contributions. To the extent that it exceeds the share appropriate to those contributions it is vulnerable to attack by the trustee in bankruptcy of the other party under the Insolvency Act 1986 as a transaction at an undervalue. (See *Re Densham* [1975] 1 WLR 1519 and Chapter 8.)

### (vi) Nature of interest obtained
Under a resulting trust the equitable interest of the claimant will comprise a share of

the beneficial interest in the property. Where a constructive trust is imposed, the claimant may acquire some other form of interest such as a life interest (see e.g. *Bannister* v *Bannister* [1948] 2 All ER 133 and *Ungurian* v *Lesnoff* [1989] 3 WLR 840).

*(h) Unmarried couples*
It has already been noted that in *Pettitt* v *Pettitt* [1970] AC 777 at p. 813 Lord Upjohn said that "disputes between husband and wife must be decided by the principles of law applicable to the settlement of claims between those not so related" and that this was echoed by Lord Denning MR in *Cooke* v *Head* [1972] 1 WLR 518 at p. 520. However, Lord Upjohn added that full allowance should be made in view of the relationship of husband and wife, but did not indicate expressly what that allowance should be. In *Richards* v *Dove* [1974] 1 All ER 888 at p. 894 Walton J pointed out that it by no means followed that the application of the same principles would produce identical rights in the case of a wife and a mistress. It was impossible to leave out of the picture the fact that as between a husband and wife the husband had certain legal duties in relation to maintaining his wife whereas as between man and mistress the whole relationship was consensual with no legal obligation imposed (see also *Crisp* v *Mullings* (1974) 233 EG 511). This appears to mean that a wife would find it easier to show that she had made a contribution to the acquisition of property as she might have met expenses that would normally be the responsibility of the husband by virtue of his obligations to maintain her. An unmarried partner, on the other hand, making similar payments might be regarded as doing no more than discharging her share of the couple's joint expenses.

More relevant at the present time is the argument that where the parties are not married it is more difficult to infer an agreement because there is less evidence of a long-term joint commitment. This is supported by the view of Griffiths LJ in *Bernard* v *Josephs* [1982] Ch 391 that while the legal principles are the same whether the dispute is between married or unmarried couples, the nature of the relationship between the parties is a very important factor when considering what inferences should be drawn from the way they conducted their affairs. Only if the court was satisfied that the relationship was intended to involve the same degree of commitment as marriage would it be legitimate to regard an unmarried couple as no different from a married couple. In the same case Kerr LJ thought that cohabitation in marriage, in contrast to a less permanently intended relationship, might have an important bearing on the ascertainment of the parties' common intention and on the determination of an appropriate apportionment of their respective rights.

## 5. Proprietary estoppel

*(a) The scope of proprietary estoppel*
A claim to an interest in property the legal title to which is vested in another may be made on the basis of proprietary estoppel. Where a person has incurred expenditure or otherwise prejudiced himself in the belief or expectation, actively or passively encouraged by the owner of property, either that he already owns a sufficient inter-

est in the property to justify the expenditure or the prejudicial action, or that he would obtain such an interest, an estoppel arises against the owner of the property. Such an estoppel by encouragement or acquiescence gives rise to a cause of action in the other party which may be relied upon as a sword and not merely as a shield. It will be for the court to decide how the equity to which it gives rise is to be satisfied.

*(b) The circumstances in which estoppel may arise*

The belief or expectation may arise from a mistake on the part of one party who believes that he has an interest in the property of the other, and the latter, knowing of the former's mistake "abstain[s] from setting him right" and leaves him "to persevere in his error" (*per* Lord Cranworth LC in *Ramsden* v *Dyson* (1866) LR 1 HL 129 at p. 140). The belief or expectation may also arise where the party in whom the legal title is vested has made an "imperfect gift" of the property to the other party, i.e. has failed to observe the formalities appropriate to the property which is the subject-matter of the intended gift (see e.g. *Pascoe* v *Turner* [1979] 1 WLR 431; *Voyce* v *Voyce* (1991) 62 P & CR 290). Thirdly, and of particular importance in the present context, proprietary estoppel may operate where two persons have dealt with each other over a period of time in such a way as to lead one of them, with the knowledge and encouragement of the other, to act in reliance on a belief or assumption that he or she would acquire an interest of some kind in the property of the other (see e.g. *Inwards* v *Baker* [1965] 2 QB 29).

The classic statement of proprietary estoppel based on a promise or an expectation is to be found in the speech of Lord Kingsdown in *Ramsden* v *Dyson* (1866) LR 1 HL 129 at p. 170. In the same case Lord Cranworth LC (at p. 140) approached the matter in terms of unilateral mistake and in *Willmott* v *Barber* (1880) 15 Ch D 96 at p. 105 Fry J laid down five criteria that had to be established before estoppel could operate to deprive a person of his or her legal rights. Although these criteria were formulated in relation to cases of unilateral mistake - where the distinguishing feature was acquiescence on the part of the person with legal title - this formulation had a wider influence on the operation of estoppel. More recently in *Taylor Fashions Ltd* v *Liverpool Victoria Trustee Co Ltd* [1982] QB 133 at p. 147 Oliver J took a more general view which appears to have gained general acceptance. He thought that it might well be that the strict *Willmott* v *Barber* criteria remained a necessary requirement in those cases where all that has happened is that the party alleged to be estopped stood by without protest while his or her rights have been infringed - though even this must now be considered open to doubt. However, he concluded (at pp. 151-152) that "... the more recent cases indicate .... that the application of the *Ramsden* v *Dyson* principle (whether you call it proprietary estoppel, estoppel by acquiescence or estoppel by encouragement is really immaterial) requires a very much broader approach which is directed to ascertaining whether, in particular individual circumstances, it would be unconscionable for a party to be permitted to deny that which, knowingly or unknowingly, he has allowed or encouraged another to assume to his detriment rather than to inquiring whether the circumstances can be fitted within the confines of some preconceived formula serving as a universal yardstick for every form of unconscionable behaviour". On this basis knowledge of the true position by the party alleged to be estopped - the crucial issue in that case - became merely one of the relevant factors in the overall enquiry, though in certain cases it might be a determining factor.

At present it seems that three elements must be established in order to give rise to a proprietary estoppel.

### (c) Conditions to be satisfied

(i) Acquiescence, assurance or encouragement

There must be some form of acquiescence, assurance or encouragement by the party in whom the legal title is vested. Such acquiescence, assurance or encouragement must give rise to a belief or expectation in the other party that he or she has, or will have, an interest in the property concerned. Thus in *Pascoe* v *Turner* [1979] 1 WLR 431 the plaintiff had declared to the defendant not once, but on a number of occasions after he had left her, that "the house is yours and everything in it". This was in effect an imperfect gift. In *Voyce* v *Voyce* (1991) 62 P & CR 290 the claimant had been told by his mother that he could have a cottage situated on her farm if he renovated it to her satisfaction. In *Griffiths* v *Williams* (1978) 248 EG 947 a grand-daughter's expectation that she would be allowed to live in her grandmother's house for the whole of her life was raised by the grandmother's repeated assurances to her. In *Greasley* v *Cooke* [1980] 1 WLR 1306 Miss Cooke had been given assurances by the Greasley family that she could regard the property as her home for the rest of her life.

In *Re Basham deceased* [1986] 1 WLR 1498 the judge rejected the submission that the representation or belief on which a plaintiff relies must be related to an existing right. It was sufficient if the plaintiff had acted in the belief that future rights would be granted. Moreover, he held that proprietary estoppel need not be related to a particular property but can extend to property as indefinite and fluctuating as the whole of a deceased's estate. There appears to have been no reference to *Layton* v *Martin* [1986] 2 FLR 227, decided a few months earlier, where Scott J took the view that the question of proprietary estoppel "does not arise otherwise than in connection with some asset in respect of which it has been represented, or is alleged to have been represented, that the claimant is to have some interest". He said that a "representation that 'financial security' would be provided by the deceased to the plaintiff, and on which I will assume she acted, is not a representation that she is to have some equitable interest in any particular asset or assets" (at pp. 238-239). It is submitted that the two statements are not necessarily inconsistent and that an expectation of receiving the whole of a person's estate is sufficiently certain and, in this respect, different from a vague expectation of financial provision. In *Coombes* v *Smith* [1986] 1 WLR 808 the plaintiff and the child of which the defendant was the father moved into a house purchased by the defendant. The defendant did not himself move into the house and refused to vest it in their joint names. However, he did tell the defendant: "Don't worry. I have told you I'll always look after you". Jonathan Parker QC, sitting as a High Court judge, held that the plaintiff had wholly failed to establish that while her relationship with the defendant was continuing she acted under a mistaken belief that she was legally entitled to security of tenure which would continue notwithstanding the termination of that relationship. He said: "But a belief that the defendant would always provide her with a roof over her head is ... something quite different from a belief that she had a legal right to remain there against his wishes" (at p. 818).

### (ii) Reliance upon the acquiescence, assurance or encouragement

There must be reliance by the party claiming an interest upon the acquiescence, assurance or encouragement of the party in whom the legal title is vested. It is not, however, essential that the representation or encouragement was the sole reason for the claimant's conduct. In *Amalgamated Investment & Property Co Ltd* v *Texas Commerce International Bank Ltd* [1982] QB 84 at pp. 104-105 Goff J said:

"... the question is not whether the representee acted, or desisted from acting, solely in reliance on the encouragement or representation of the other party: the question is rather whether his conduct was so influenced by the encouragement or representation ... that it would be unconscionable for the representor thereafter to enforce his strict legal rights."

There have been conflicting views about the burden of proof which lies on the claimant to show that his or her action was sufficiently influenced by the assurance, acquiescence or encouragement. It now seems that a presumption may arise in his or her favour that he or she acted in reliance thereon (see *Greasley* v *Cooke* [1981] 1 WLR 1306 *per* Lord Denning MR at p. 1307 and *per* Oliver LJ in *Habib Bank Ltd* v *Habib Bank AG* [1981] 1 WLR 1265 at p. 1287 - in contrast to his comments in *Taylor Fashions Ltd* v *Liverpool Victoria Trustee Co Ltd* [1982] QB 133).

In *Coombes* v *Smith* [1986] 1 WLR 808 the court declined to accept that the claimant had acted in reliance on the defendant's assurances as described above. Thus it could not follow that she had allowed herself to become pregnant by the defendant and to have his child in reliance upon some mistaken belief as to her legal rights. She allowed herself to become pregnant because she wished to live with the defendant and to bear his child. Similarly she left her husband because she preferred to have a relationship with and a child by the defendant rather than continuing to live with her husband, and not because she relied on any assurance by the defendant that he would provide for her if and when their relationship came to an end. Again the acts of looking after the child and the house, and being ready for the defendant's visits, were done as occupier of the property and as the defendant's mistress and the child's mother.

### (iii) Detrimental conduct by the claimant

The party claiming an interest must have acted to his or her detriment on the faith of the acquiescence, assurance or encouragement of the other party. In many cases the detriment will take the form of carrying out or paying for work on the property concerned. However, such work or expenditure is not the only kind of detriment, as is shown by *Greasley* v *Cooke* and *Re Basham deceased*. In the former case Miss Cooke had devoted her life to looking after the Greasley family without payment. In the latter case the plaintiff and her family continued to live near her stepfather and they provided food for him, kept his garden in order, helped him with work about the home and bought carpets for his house. In *Jones* v *Jones* [1977] 1 WLR 438 the detriment consisted of a man giving up a job and going to live near the person by whom the assurances had been given. On the other hand, the various acts relied upon by the plaintiff in *Coombes* v *Smith* [1986] 1 WLR 808 as described above were held not to be detrimental for this purpose. In *Watts* v *Story* (1983) 14 July, Lexis, Enggen the claimant relied on the fact that he had given up a settled life and a protected tenancy in Leeds to move to his grandmother's house in Nottingham where he gave personal services to her and helped her pack her belongings and move to the Isle of Wight. He had also undertaken liability for the outgoings at the grandmother's house. The Court of Appeal held that the detriment suffered by the claimant was insufficient when compared with previous cases such as *Jones* v *Jones* and *Greasley* v *Cooke*. He had not shown that, when the benefits derived by him from his rent-free occupation of the property were set against any detriment suffered by him as a result of making the move from his flat in Leeds, he had on balance suffered any detriment in financial or material terms. Slade LJ said:

"I do not think it is possible, or even desirable, to attempt to define the nature and extent of the prejudice or detriment which has to be established, in a case such as the present, by a claimant who is relying on alleged detriment or prejudice other than the expenditure of money. All I would say is that, before allowing the claim in such a case, the court, in my opinion, has to be satisfied that, when all the circumstances are taken into account, the detriment or prejudice is such that it would be inequitable to allow the party who made the relevant representation to go back on it."

*(d) Satisfying the "equity"*

Proprietary estoppel gives rise to an equity in favour of the party who has acted to his or her detriment. It will be for the court to decide how the equity is to be satisfied. In deciding how the equity should be satisfied the court must consider all the circumstances and must decide what is the minimum equity necessary to do justice to the person entitled to it, having regard to the nature of the acquiescence, encouragement or representation and to the way in which, as a result, the claimant has changed his or her position for the worse.

In *Pascoe* v *Turner* [1979] 1 WLR 431 the court took the view that the equity could not be satisfied unless the fee simple was vested in the person entitled to the equity. This, unlike a licence to occupy for her lifetime, would ensure her security of tenure, quiet enjoyment and freedom of action in relation to repairs and improvements without interference from the plaintiff. (See also *Voyce* v *Voyce* (1991) 62 P & CR 290.) In *Re Basham* [1986] 1 WLR 1498 the plaintiff was successful in her claim to the whole estate of her stepfather. By way of contrast, in *Griffiths* v *Williams* (1977) 248 EG 947 and *Greasley* v *Cooke* [1980] 1 WLR 1306 more limited interests were found to be sufficient. In the former case the court directed the beneficiary under the grandmother's will to grant to the granddaughter a long lease determinable upon the latter's death at a nominal rent, since that would give her the right of occupation for her whole life but would not give her the statutory powers of the tenant for life under the Settled Land Act 1925. In *Greasley* v *Cooke* the court granted a declaration that the person entitled to the equity should be allowed to remain in the house for so long as she wished.

The way in which an equity should be satisfied may have to take a wholly different form from what had been intended when the parties were on good terms. Thus in *Burrows* v *Sharpe* (1989) 23 HLR 82 an elderly widow had entered into an agreement with a granddaughter and her husband whereby the widow was able to purchase at a discount the council house in which she lived. The granddaughter and her husband had agreed to pay the mortgage instalments on the understanding that they would inherit the property on the widow's death and make a home there for the latter's handicapped daughter. Subsequently, in view of the burden of the payments, the granddaughter and her family, by agreement, moved into the house but the parties later quarrelled. The Court of Appeal found that, in view of the relations between the parties, an order which allowed the granddaughter and her family to remain living in the house with the widow was unworkable although that had been the intention of the parties. The order therefore provided for the granddaughter and her family to give up possession but for them to receive compensation from the widow for the relevant expenditure. The relevant expenditure comprised the mortgage instalments paid in so far as they exceeded the rent of the granddaughter's previous flat, the conveyancing costs of the purchase of the house and certain other expenses relating to the house. (See also *Dodsworth* v *Dodsworth* (1973) 228 EG 1115.)

### (e) Proprietary estoppel and the constructive trust compared

(i) The similarities

In *Grant* v *Edwards* [1986] Ch 638 at p. 656 Sir Nicolas Browne-Wilkinson V-C noted that the principles underlying the law of proprietary estoppel are closely akin to those underlying the constructive trust laid down in *Gissing* v *Gissing* [1971] AC 886. He said:

> "In both, the claimant must to the knowledge of the legal owner have acted in the belief that the claimant has or will obtain an interest in the property. In both, the claimant must have acted to his or her detriment in reliance on such belief. In both, equity acts on the conscience of the legal owner to prevent him from acting in an unconscionable manner by defeating the common intention. The two principles have been developed separately without cross-fertilisation between them: but they rest on the same foundation and have on all other matters reached the same conclusions."

However, a number of differences remain between the operation of proprietary estoppel and that of the constructive trust as applied in *Grant* v *Edwards*.

(ii) The differences

(1) The basis upon which the party claiming an interest has acted to his or her detriment

A constructive trust is imposed in a situation such as that which arose in *Grant* v *Edwards* because the claimant has acted on the basis of a common intention or agreement that he or she will obtain an agreed share in the property in return for acting in a particular way. In contrast, proprietary estoppel is based on the fact that the claimant has acted on the basis of the acquiescence, assurance or encouragement of the party in whom the legal title is vested. In other words the basis of the constructive trust is the expressed or inferred common intention of the parties while the basis of proprietary estoppel may be the unilateral conduct of the party with legal title. Moreover, it has been said that proprietary estoppel "depends not on the actual intention of the representor but on the effect of his or her conduct or statements on a reasonable person in the position of the other" (*per* Cooke P in *Gillies* v *Keogh* [1989] 2 NZLR 327 at p. 333).

(2) The extent of the interest obtained by the claimant
Where a constructive trust is imposed on the basis of the common intention of the parties, the interest obtained by the claimant will be that which it was agreed that he or she should have. In the case of proprietary estoppel the interest obtained by the claimant will be that which the court considers appropriate in the circumstances of the case. This will normally be what the claimant was led to expect, i.e. an interest which is sufficient to satisfy the expectation raised in the mind of the claimant by the acquiescence, assurance or encouragement of the other party, but this may not always be appropriate and monetary compensation may be awarded by the court instead of an interest in the property concerned. It is for the court to determine the manner in which the equity to which proprietary estoppel gives rise will be satisfied, so that the court may take into account the nature and extent of the detriment resulting from the reliance of the claimant on the acquiescence, assurance or encouragement of the party with legal title. In contrast, if a claimant has acted to his or her detriment in pursuance of the express of inferred common intention of the parties, the extent of the interest obtained should not be affected by the nature or extent of the detriment provided that this was not inconsistent with the common intention of the parties. The interest should be that which was contemplated by the common intention.

(3) The nature of the interest obtained
Where a constructive trust is imposed on the basis of the common intention of the parties, the claimant will have an equitable interest independently of an order of the court. Such an equitable interest seems to arise as soon as he or she has acted to his or her detriment in pursuance of the common intention. In contrast, it may be that in the case of proprietary estoppel no equitable interest actually arises until the court has determined how the equity is to be satisfied. This might mean that until then the claimant may not have a sufficient interest to bind third parties, but *Inwards* v *Baker* [1965] 2 QB 29 and *Voyce* v *Voyce* (1991) 62 P & CR 290 provide support for the view that the claimant may have a sufficient interest at an earlier date.

## 6. Improvement of property

An attempt was made in the Matrimonial Proceedings and Property Act 1970 to remove the uncertainty which had arisen as to the circumstances in which a spouse who had paid for or carried out improvements on property vested in the other spouse alone or in the joint names of the spouses could acquire a beneficial interest or a larger beneficial interest in that property. Section 37 provides:

"It is hereby declared that where a husband or wife contributes in money or money's worth to the improvement of real or personal property in which or in the proceeds of sale of which either or both of them has or have a beneficial interest, the husband or wife so contributing shall, if the contribution is of a substantial nature and subject to any agreement between them to the contrary express or implied, be treated as having acquired by virtue of his or her contribution a share or an enlarged share, as the case may be, in that beneficial interest of such an extent as may have been then agreed or, in default of agreement, as may seem in all the circumstances just to any court before which the question of the existence or extent of the beneficial interest of the husband or wife arises (whether in proceedings between them or in any other proceedings)."

The section thus purports to be declaratory of the existing law and has been applied to improvements carried out before the commencement of the Act (*Davis* v *Vale* [1971] 1 WLR 1022). The intention behind the section was to apply to improvements the same principles as the courts had adopted in the case of contributions to the initial acquisition of property. However, it was thought better not to prescribe any rule that the share must be commensurate with or proportional to the cost or value of the improvements, but to allow the court, in the event of a dispute, to make such order as it thinks just in the circumstances (Law Com. No. 25 at pp. 29, 103 and 105). This reflects the fact that at that time it was the resulting trust with which the courts were principally concerned in disputes relating to ownership of the matrimonial home. The potential of the constructive trust had not then become apparent.

The section has been relied upon in a small number of cases (see *Davis* v *Vale; Re Nicholson deceased* [1974] 1 WLR 476; *Samuel's Trustee* v *Samuel* (1975) 233 EG 149 and *Griffiths* v *Griffiths* [1973] 1 WLR 1454). However, in the light of the powers of the court to order the adjustment of property rights on divorce under the Matrimonial Causes Act 1973 the section is now likely to be relied upon only rarely. In *Griffiths* v *Griffiths* Arnold J had awarded the husband £4,500 under s.37 and £7,000 by way of a lump sum under s.2 of the Matrimonial Proceedings and Property Act 1970, now s.23 of the Matrimonial Causes Act 1973. In the Court of Appeal Roskill LJ did not think it right, on the facts of the case, to split the matter up in this way. Where there are proceedings under the 1973 Act, effect can more easily be given to contributions under that Act, particularly having regard to s.25(2)(f), than under s.37. Section 37 has its own place in that residue of cases where it is necessary or advantageous to bring proceedings under s.17 of the Married Women's Property Act 1882.

In *Harwood* v *Harwood* [1991] 2 FLR 274, where s.37 was not considered, Slade LJ said (at p. 294) that "... the general rule is that monies voluntarily spent by one party on improving property beneficially owned by him and another will not increase the first party's proportionate beneficial interest in the property unless they specifically so agree, or (exceptionally) if such an agreement can be inferred" (referring to Griffiths LJ in *Bernard* v *Josephs* [1982] Ch 391 at p. 404). The difficulties facing a party seeking to establish a claim on the basis of improvements and alterations made to a property were apparent in *Thomas* v *Fuller-Brown* [1988] 1 FLR 237 where the parties were not married. (See also *Sekhon* v *Alissa* [1989] 2 FLR 94 where the parties were mother and daughter.)

## 7. Joint bank accounts

Where a bank account stands in the joint names of a husband and wife, both will generally be authorised to draw cheques upon that account without the concurrence of the other. In the event of a breakdown of the marriage, or on its termination on the death of one of the spouses, it may be necessary to determine (a) the ownership of property purchased with money drawn from the account by one spouse, and/or (b) the ownership of the balance remaining in the account.

*Prima facie*, all money paid into the account will be treated as belonging to them jointly so that each spouse can draw upon the account, not merely for the joint benefit of the spouses, but also for his or her own personal benefit (*Re Young* (1885) 28 Ch D 705; *Re Bishop* [1965] Ch 450. Approved by Lord Upjohn in *Pettitt* v *Pettitt* [1970] AC 777 at p. 815). If one spouse draws on the account to make a purchase in the joint names of the spouses, the property is *prima facie* joint property, but if one spouse draws on the account to purchase property for his or her own benefit, or to make an investment in his or her own name, then *prima facie* that property or investment belongs to the person in whose name it is purchased or invested. Thus in *Re Bishop*, Stamp J said (at p. 456):

"What is purchased is not to be regarded as purchased out of a fund belonging to the spouses in the proportions in which they contribute to the account or in equal proportions, but out of a pool or fund of which they were, at law and in equity, joint tenants."

On the death of one spouse, the survivor will be entitled to the balance of the account. When such an account is closed after breakdown of the marriage, the balance in the account belongs to the spouses in equal shares. In *Jones* v *Maynard* [1965] Ch 572 at p. 575 Vaisey J said:

"In my judgment, when there is a joint account between husband and wife and a common pool into which they put all their resources, it is not consistent with that conception that the account should thereafter (in this case in the event of a divorce) be picked apart, and divided up proportionately to the respective contributions of husband and wife, the husband being credited with the whole of his earnings and the wife with the whole of her dividends. I do not believe that, when once the joint pool has been formed, it ought to be, and can be dissected in any such manner. In my view a husband's earnings or salary, when spouses have a common purse and a pool of their resources, are earnings on behalf of both of them; and the idea that years afterwards the contents of the pool can be dissected by taking an elaborate account as to how much was paid in by the husband or the wife, is quite inconsistent with the original fundamental idea of a joint purse or a common pool. In my view the money which goes into the pool becomes the joint property."

Although money paid into a joint account is *prima facie* treated as belonging to the spouses jointly, the evidence may show a contrary intention. Thus, in the first place, the evidence may show that the spouses intended that investments purchased with money drawn from the account should be their savings so that they belong to the spouses in equal shares although purchased in the husband's name. This was the case in *Jones* v *Maynard* where accordingly, after dissolution of the marriage, the husband held the investments he had purchased with money from the account as trustee for the wife as to one half thereof.

Secondly, the evidence may show that a joint account was intended only to serve some specific and limited purpose. This is more likely to occur where a husband provides funds for an account in the names of himself and his wife. The presumption of advancement which arises can be rebutted by showing that the wife was given authority to draw upon the account only as a matter of convenience, so that the beneficial interest in the account is vested solely in the husband. Thus in *Marshal v Crutwell* (1875) LR 20 Eq 328 a husband who was in failing health transferred his banking account from his own name into the joint names of himself and his wife. He subsequently paid considerable sums into the account and all cheques were drawn by the wife at her husband's direction and the proceeds applied in payment of household and other expenses. It was held that the transfer of the account was not intended to be a provision for the plaintiff, but merely a mode of conveniently managing her husband's affairs. Accordingly, on her husband's death, the balance did not pass to her as survivor. (See also *Hoddinott v Hoddinott* [1971] 2 KB 406.) On the other hand, where the wife has never drawn on the account, or has done so only in exceptional circumstances, this is evidence of an intention to make provision for the wife, so that, if she survives her husband, she will be entitled to the balance of the account (see *Re Pattinson* (1885) 1 TLR 216 and *Re Harrison* (1920) 90 LJ Ch 186 where the wife was ignorant of the joint account and did not draw a cheque until informed about it by the bank manager shortly before her husband's death). In *Heseltine v Heseltine* [1971] 1 WLR 342 the wife provided the money for a joint account which was operated by the husband for convenience of administration for family purposes. It was held that property purchased in the husband's name with money from the account was held in trust for the wife. However, in *Re Figgis* [1969] 1 Ch 123 Megarry J expressed the view that even if convenience was the principal motive for opening a joint account the position may change. In that case, the joint account had been in existence for nearly 50 years and considerations of convenience had faded into insignificance. Long before the husband's death the main or only reason for the account standing in the joint names of the spouses was to benefit the wife. This view was strengthened rather than weakened by the fact that the husband had always used the account as if it were his own. In the case of a deposit account considerations of convenience are far less likely to have been relevant, and it will be difficult to rebut the presumption of advancement.

Even though the evidence shows an intention on the part of the husband in opening the joint account to make provision for his wife after his death, this does not necessarily mean that she acquires any interest before that time. It is also necessary to consider whether it was the husband's intention that his wife should operate the account only after his death, and if this is so, the beneficial interest in the account remains in the husband unless and until his wife survives him (*Thompson v Thompson* (1970) 114 SJ 455). Although the transaction then appears to be testamentary in character it has been held not to be invalid for non-compliance with s.9 of the Wills Act 1837: *Young v Sealey* [1949] 1 Ch 278.

## 8. Money and property derived from a housekeeping allowance

Before the Married Women's Property Act 1964, where a husband provided his wife with a housekeeping allowance, any savings which she was able to accumulate out of the allowance, and any property which she purchased with the allowance, were presumed to be the property of the husband (*Blackwell* v *Blackwell* [1943] 2 All ER 579 and *Hoddinott* v *Hoddinott* [1949] 2 KB 406). The Act sought to alleviate the injustice that might be suffered by a thrifty wife as a result of the application of this presumption. Section 1 provides:

"If any question arises as to the right of the husband or wife to money derived from any allowance made by the husband for the expenses of the matrimonial home or for similar purposes, or to any property acquired out of such money, the money or property shall, in the absence of any agreement between them to the contrary, be treated as belonging to the husband and wife in equal shares."

The provision thus applies only to money or property derived from an allowance provided by a *husband* and, where it applies, the money or property will be presumed to belong to the spouses in equal shares and not jointly. The whole beneficial interest will not, therefore, pass automatically to the survivor.

The scope of the Act is uncertain in two respects. First, it is uncertain whether or not the Act is retrospective in effect. In *Tymoszczuk* v *Tymoszczuk* (1964) 108 SJ 676 Master Jacob took the view that the provision was retrospective in its operation and applied to events which had taken place before its commencement on 25 March 1964. On the other hand in *Re John's Assignment Trusts* [1970] 1 WLR 955 Goff J, though finding it unnecessary to decide the point, stated that he felt some difficulty in applying the section retrospectively notwithstanding its wide terms. He inclined to the view that the relevant time is not when the question arises, but when the money which is under consideration, or which acquired the property, was in fact allowed by the husband to the wife, for otherwise there might be serious difficulties with regard to accrued titles.

Secondly, the Act applies only to money or property derived from an allowance made for "the expenses of the matrimonial home or for similar purposes". It is by no means clear what expenses fall within this description. In *Tymoszczuk* v *Tymoszczuk* it was necessary to consider whether the Act applied to mortgage repayments made by the wife out of her husband's earnings, which he gave to her for the management of the household. Master Jacob took the view that mortgage repayments were not "expenses of the matrimonial home", but were made in part purchase of the house and in part payment of interest on a loan. Accordingly, the wife was not entitled to be credited as having contributed any part of those mortgage repayments towards the purchase of the house. In *Re John's Assignment Trusts* Goff J again found it unnecessary to decide the point, but stated that he should not be taken as accepting the view that where the section does apply, moneys paid to discharge a mortgage on the matrimonial home are not expenses of the matrimonial home or expenses for similar purposes within the section.

The Law Commission in its report on *Matrimonial Property* published in 1988 (Law Com. No. 175) recommended that the 1964 Act be repealed, and that it should be replaced by two rules which would change the way in which the law treats the use of money within marriage and the effect of transfers of property (including money) between spouses. These rules, which would focus on the purpose for which property was purchased or transferred by one spouse to the other, would be as follows:

(i)  where money is spent to buy property, or property or money is transferred by one spouse to the other, for their joint use or benefit the property acquired or money transferred should be jointly owned;

(ii)  where money or property is transferred by one spouse to the other for any other purpose, it should be owned by that other.

These rules would give way to contrary intention on the part of the paying or transferring spouse, provided that the contrary intention was known to the other spouse.

## 9. Movable property

The principles relating to the ownership of movable property by members of a family are similar to those relating to the ownership of land. The beneficial interest will generally belong to the person who provided the purchase price so that where, for example, both spouses contribute to the purchase price, the ownership will be shared. The presumptions of resulting trust and advancement will be taken into account in appropriate circumstances and the constructive trust and proprietary estoppel may also be relevant. Section 37 of the Matrimonial Proceedings and Property Act 1970 applies to contributions to improvements of personal as well as real property. The principles relating to the ownership of property purchased from a joint bank account or from a housekeeping allowance as considered above are also applicable.

In practice, there will not often be a document vesting ownership, but movable property is generally more likely to be purchased for cash than land so that the problems of acquisition over a period of time are less likely to arise. (Special problems in relation to property being acquired on hire purchase were considered in Law Com. No. 86, para 3.135 *et seq*.) The most important items of movable property so far as the majority of families are concerned are the "household goods and furniture" even though their value may be small and in any event generally diminishing. The Law Commission in its First Report on *Family Property* (Law Com. No. 52) expressed the view that the problem of ownership was not so important as protection of their use and enjoyment. The existing power of the court to protect the use of furniture is uncertain. It seems that in proceedings under s.17 of the Married Women's Property Act 1882 the court may have some discretion to refuse an order so as to protect a wife who needs the furniture for her own use. This appears from *W v W* [1951] 2 TLR 1135 where a husband sought an order for delivery of furniture which was undoubtedly his property. The order was granted but Devlin J indicated that an order might be refused if the result would be to leave the wife "with nothing but bare boards, a mere empty shell ...", which was not the position in that case. It seems that such discretion would be of little assistance where it was the wife as non-owner who sought an order for the return of furniture which undoubtedly belonged to her husband. In view of this inadequate protection the Law Commission in its Third Report on *Family Property: The Matrimonial Home (Co-ownership and Occupation Rights) and Household Goods* (Law Com. No. 86, paras 3.31 and 3.144) recommended that at any time during the subsistence of a marriage (except while a decree of judicial separation is in force) the court should have power on the application of either spouse to make an order giving him or her the right, as against the other spouse, to use and enjoy the household goods or some of them. The power would not extend to household goods which are the subject of a hiring, hire purchase or conditional sale agreement. As noted in the previous section of this chapter, the Law Commission in its later Report on *Matrimonial Property* (Law Com. No. 175) published in 1988 recommended the introduction of two rules which would focus attention on the purpose for which property was acquired rather than on who paid for it, which is the case at present. Accordingly, if property (other than a life insurance policy or land) was purchased (or transferred) for their joint use or benefit it should belong to them jointly in the absence of a contrary intention. If such property was purchased for the sole use or benefit of one spouse, it should belong to that spouse in the absence of a contrary intention. This would make it much more likely than not that property acquired for the purpose of their life together would be co-owned although their freedom to determine ownership would remain. These recommendations have not been implemented.

In relation to unmarried couples Waite J in *Hammond* v *Mitchell* [1991] 1 WLR 1127 at p. 1138 said that he supported the comments of Millett J in *Windeler* v *Whitehall* [1990] FCR 268 at p. 279 to the effect that sorting out the ownership of chattels is something the parties should be expected to achieve by agreement without the necessity of a court hearing. He went on to say that while no one suggested that English law recognised or should develop a doctrine of community of property regarding the household goods of those who settle for an unmarried union, "the parties must expect the court in ordinary cases to adopt a robust allegiance to the maxim that 'equality is equity', if only in the interests of fulfilling the equally salutary maxim 'sit finis litis' ". If it is really necessary to bring before the court issues of disputed ownership of household chattels, the proper way of doing it is a claim for a declaration or inquiry as to the beneficial interest, supported with appropriate affidavit evidence, on the lines similar to the procedure for resolving disputes under s.17 of the Married Women's Property Act 1882. It is not normally appropriate to proceed by actions framed in conversion or detinue.

## 10. The ownership of gifts made to spouses

In determining whether a gift from a third party belongs to one spouse or to both of them, the court will endeavour to ascertain the donor's intention. This applies to wedding presents as to other gifts, and there is no principle of law that wedding presents are joint wedding presents to both spouses. Where there is evidence of intention on the part of the donor, it may well be that wedding presents may be found to have been given either to one spouse or the other, or to both (*Samson* v *Samson* [1960] 1 WLR 190. Contrast *Kelner* v *Kelner* [1930] P 411). If there is no evidence as to the donor's intention the inference may be drawn that gifts from relatives or friends of a spouse were gifts to that spouse. It may be, too, that the property that was given to one spouse may have become the property of both where by reason of the subsequent conduct of the spouses it can be regarded as having become mixed property (*Newgrosh* v *Newgrosh* (1950) 210 LTJ 108).

## 11. Property of engaged couples

*(a) Ownership of property generally*
An agreement between two persons to marry one another no longer has effect as a contract giving rise to legal rights, and no action lies for breach of such an agreement (Law Reform (Miscellaneous Provisions) Act 1970, s.1). Nevertheless, it has been recognised that since the parties to such an agreement will often have acquired property on the basis of their intended marriage, provision must be made for dealing with disputes relating to that property if the agreement is terminated (see *Moate* v *Moate* [1948] 2 All ER 486). In view of the similarity between the relationship of an engaged couple and the relationship of husband and wife in this respect, it is now provided by s.2(1) of the Law Reform (Miscellaneous Provisions) Act 1970 that:
"Where an agreement to marry is terminated, any rule of law relating to the rights of husbands and wives in relation to property in which either or both has or have a beneficial interest, including any such rule as explained in section 37 of the Matrimonial Proceedings and Property Act 1970, shall apply, in relation to any property in which either or both of the parties to the agreement had a beneficial interest while the agreement was in force, as it applies in relation to property in which a husband or wife has a beneficial interest."
Although an agreement to marry "no longer has effect as a contract giving rise to legal rights", the existence of such an agreement is a condition precedent to the application of this provision. An agreement may be found to exist for this purpose even though it was made at a time when one of the parties was married to a third party so that it would have been unenforceable at common law (*Shaw* v *Fitzgerald* [1992] 1 FLR 357). This provision applies only on the termination of the agreement, whether by repudiation, death or any other way and not, for example, on the bankruptcy of one of the parties. It also applies only in relation to interests acquired during the currency of the agreement.

In *Mossop* v *Mossop* [1988] 2 All ER 202 it was held that this provision did not confer on the court the power to make a transfer of property order under s.24 of the Matrimonial Causes Act 1973. It is a condition precedent to the exercise by the court of the discretionary powers contained in s.24 that a decree of divorce, nullity or judicial separation has been granted and by the very nature of things that cannot arise in the case of engaged couples who have not been married to each other (see Balcombe LJ at p. 205). While the court has no powers to vary the rights of the parties comparable to those applicable under the Matrimonial Causes Act 1973 on the termination of a marriage, the procedure under s.17 of the Married Women's Property Act 1882 is available where an agreement to marry is terminated, provided that proceedings are instituted within three years of the termination of the agreement (Law Reform (Miscellaneous Provisions) Act 1970, s.2(2)).

*(b) Ownership of gifts*
In addition to acquiring property for their future use for the purposes of their marriage, an engaged couple will generally have received gifts from third parties as well as having made gifts to each other.

Where gifts have been made to one or both of the engaged couple as such by third parties, they are presumed, in the absence of evidence to the contrary, to have been made conditional on the marriage taking place. Accordingly, if the marriage does not take place, for whatever reason, the gifts must be returned to the donors (*Jeffreys* v *Luck* (1922) 153 LTJ 139).

Where the parties to an agreement to marry make gifts to each other then, if the gifts are unconditional, they are not recoverable. However, if a gift was made in contemplation of marriage, then at common law it was regarded as conditional on the marriage taking place. Accordingly, if the agreement was broken by the recipient, such a gift could be recovered by the donor, but it could not be recovered by a donor who had broken the agreement (*Jacobs* v *Davis* [1917] 2 KB 532; *Cohen* v *Sellar* [1926] 1 KB 536). In accordance with the recommendation of the Law Commission designed to do away with inquiries into fault, it is now provided that a party to an agreement to marry who makes a gift of property to the other on the condition (express or implied) that it shall be returned if the agreement is terminated shall not be prevented from recovering the property by reason only of his having terminated the agreement (see Law Com. No. 26, para 45 and Law Reform (Miscellaneous Provisions) Act 1970, s.3(1)). Whether or not any particular gift is conditional is a question of fact. At common law, there was a presumption that the gift of an engagement ring was a conditional gift, but the Law Reform (Miscellaneous Provisions) Act 1970 s.3(2) provides that a gift of an engagement ring shall be presumed to be an absolute gift. This presumption may be rebutted by proving that the ring was given on the condition (express or implied) that it should be returned if the marriage did not take place for any reason. Thus, if a party succeeds in rebutting the presumption, it seems that he can recover the ring even though he terminated the agreement.

# Chapter 3

# The protection of beneficial interests

## 1. Where the legal estate is vested in two or more persons

*(a) General principles*
Where the legal estate in land is conveyed to a husband and wife or to any two or more members of a family who are together entitled to the beneficial interest, it will be held by them as joint tenants on trust for sale, express or implied (Law of Property Act 1925, ss.34 and 36). They may be entitled to the beneficial interest which exists behind the trust for sale either as joint tenants or as tenants in common. If the parties are beneficial joint tenants, then on the death of one of them his or her interest will accrue to the other. While they are both still alive either party may sever the joint tenancy, thus converting it into a beneficial tenancy in common. On the death of a tenant in common his interest passes under his will or on his intestacy. The joint tenancy of the legal estate cannot be severed.

*(b) Severance*
There are four ways in which a beneficial joint tenancy may be severed.

First, a joint tenancy may be severed by "an act of any one of the persons interested operating upon his own share" (*Williams* v *Hensman* (1861) 1 John & H 546 at p. 557). Thus if one joint tenant alienates his interest or mortgages his interest, this will effect a severance (*Goddard* v *Lewis* (1909) 101 LT 528; *First National Securities* v *Hegarty* [1985] QB 850; *Ahmed* v *Kendrick* [1988] 2 FLR 22). There are some statements supporting the view that an oral declaration of severance by one joint tenant to the other will now be sufficient to effect a severance (*Hawkseley* v *May* [1956] 1 QB 304 at p. 313; *Re Draper's Conveyance* [1969] 1 Ch 486), but this view has been criticised in *Nielson-Jones* v *Fedden* [1975] Ch 222 at p. 234, and it is difficult to reconcile with the statutory provision for written notice of severance described below. When a joint tenant becomes bankrupt, then under the Insolvency Act 1986 the joint tenancy will probably only be severed when the bankrupt's estate vests in his trustee in bankruptcy (s.306). For the position under the Bankruptcy Act 1914, see *Re Dennis* [1992] 3 WLR 204.

Secondly, severance may be effected by mutual agreement. It seems that the agreement need not be specifically enforceable and it does not matter if the parties subsequently decide not to carry out the agreement (*Burgess* v *Rawnsley* [1975] Ch 429). However, the parties must have reached an agreement (*Gore and Snell* v *Carpenter* (1990) 60 P & CR 456).

Thirdly, severance may be effected by "any course of dealing sufficient to intimate that the interests of all were mutually treated as constituting a tenancy in common" (*Williams* v *Hensman*). When severance depends upon an inference of this kind without any express act of severance, it will not suffice to rely on an intention, with respect to the particular share, declared only behind the backs of the other persons interested. There must be a course of dealing by which the shares of all the parties are affected (*ibid.*). In *Burgess* v *Rawnsley* [1975] Ch 429 at p. 447 Sir John Pennycuick thought that this covered only acts of the parties, including negotiations which, although not otherwise resulting in any agreement, indicate a common intention that the joint tenancy should be regarded as severed. There will be no severance unless the court is satisfied that the parties had that common intention. Thus in *Barton* v *Morris* [1985] 1 WLR 1257 a farmhouse, also used as a guesthouse, was conveyed into the joint names of an unmarried couple and there was an express declaration that they were entitled as beneficial joint tenants although the woman provided the larger share of the purchase price. Nicholls J refused to accept that the inclusion of the property in draft partnership accounts prepared by the woman, and the man's awareness of this, showed an intention on her part, let alone on the man's part, that thenceforth the property was to be held as tenants in common. On the death intestate of the woman her interest passed to the man by survivorship. (See also *Greenfield* v *Greenfield* (1979) 38 P & CR 570, *Gore and Snell* v *Carpenter* (1990) 60 P & CR 456, and *McDowall* v *Hirschfield, Lipson & Rumney* [1992] 2 FLR 126.)

Fourthly, severance may be effected by one party giving notice in writing to the other party under s.36(2) of the Law of Property Act 1925. In *Harris* v *Goddard* [1983] 1 WLR 1203 the Court of Appeal held that a prayer in a petition for divorce that such order might be made by way of transfer of property and/or settlement of property and/or variation of settlement in respect of the former matrimonial home as might be just did not operate as a notice in writing to sever the joint tenancy of that property. A notice must indicate an intention to sever the joint tenancy immediately. The prayer did no more than invite the court to consider at some future time whether to exercise its jurisdiction under s.24 of the Matrimonial Causes Act 1973 and, if it did, to do so in one or more of three different ways, two of which could bring co-ownership to an end by ways other than severance. However, the court did accept that severance could be effected by the commencement of legal proceedings as had been the case in *Re Draper's Conveyance* [1969] 1 Ch 486. In that case a wife, after decree nisi, but before decree absolute of divorce, issued a summons under s.17 of the Married Women's Property Act 1882 asking for an order that a house in the joint names of herself and her husband be sold and the proceeds of sale distributed in accordance with the parties' respective interests therein. Plowman J held that the summons and the affidavit in support together effected a severance during the lifetime of the husband. This decision was approved by the Court of

Appeal in *Harris* v *Goddard*, though Lawton LJ pointed out that it was not clear whether Plowman J regarded the summons *and* the filing of the affidavit or both as notices in writing or whether the service of the summons and the filing of the affidavit were acts which were effectual to sever the joint tenancy. Lawton LJ specifically stated that he did not share the doubts about the correctness of the decision expressed by Walton J in *Neilson-Jones* v *Fedden* [1975] Ch 222. In *Gore and Snell* v *Carpenter* (1990) 60 P & CR 456 a separation agreement proposed by the husband expressly referring to severance, but which was never accepted by the wife, was held not to amount to a notice under s.36(2).

## (c) Overreaching

### (i) General scope

A conveyance to a purchaser of a legal estate in land overreaches any equitable beneficial interest existing behind a trust for sale if it is made by at least two trustees for sale or a trust corporation (LPA 1925, s.2). Such a purchaser of a legal estate from trustees for sale is not concerned with the trusts affecting the proceeds of sale of land subject to a trust for sale (LPA 1925, s.27). A "conveyance" includes a "mortgage" for this purpose (s.205(1)(ii)). The beneficial interests - in the purchase money - are protected by the fundamental principle that a purchaser of the legal estate in the land must pay the purchase money to, and can only obtain a valid receipt from, at least two trustees or a trust corporation (LPA 1925, s.27(2); Trustee Act 1925, s.14(2)). This protection, however, is not without its limitations.

### (ii) Beneficial interests of persons who are not trustees

The protection will generally be quite adequate where the two trustees for sale in whom the legal estate is vested are also the only persons entitled to the beneficial interests behind the trust for sale. A purchaser or mortgagee will insist that both co-owners join in the conveyance or mortgage. However, the protection may be inadequate where the beneficial interest is shared between the trustees, be they spouses or not, and other members of the family. This was the case in *City of London Building Society* v *Flegg* [1988] AC 54 where a husband and wife purchased a house for £34,000 as a home for themselves and the wife's parents. The wife's parents contributed at least £18,000 towards the purchase price, but the property was conveyed to the husband and wife as beneficial joint tenants and they were registered as proprietors. Subsequently the husband and wife, without the knowledge of the parents, obtained a new mortgage to replace three existing charges on the property. When the husband and wife later defaulted under the mortgage it was held by the House of Lords that the interests of the parents as equitable tenants in common were overreached by the legal charge in favour of the building society executed by two trustees for sale.

While the decision was welcomed as affirming the effectiveness of the overreaching machinery of the trust for sale, it also drew attention to the limitations of the protection afforded by that machinery. In the first place the financial interests of the parents in the "purchase money" or mortgage advance were not in the circumstances adequately protected by payment to two trustees against the fraud or other wrongful conduct on the part of the co-owners who were trustees. Secondly, as the Law Commission has subsequently pointed out, "nowadays many beneficiaries may well feel defrauded, even if the trustees do not vanish with the money, through the very fact of losing their land" (Law Com. Working Paper No. 106, para 1.4). In *Flegg* the husband and wife no longer lived at the property but it remained the home of the wife's parents. Nevertheless, the House of Lords, reversing the Court of Appeal, held that the beneficial interests of the parents were overreached notwithstanding that they were in actual occupation.

(iii) Forgery by co-owner

The protection afforded by the requirement of two trustees to provide a valid receipt may be threatened where one co-owner forges the signature of the other co-owner on a conveyance or mortgage of the property. Where a husband forges his wife's signature on a conveyance of unregistered land the conveyance will not be effective to pass the legal estate and it will not operate to divest the wife of her beneficial interest in the property or its proceeds of sale (*Ahmed* v *Kendrick* [1988] 2 FLR 22). However, where the spouses are beneficial joint tenants the conveyance will operate to sever that beneficial joint tenancy. It will also pass to the purchaser all the interest which the husband had power to convey, i.e. his half share (*Ahmed* v *Kendrick*. The contrary view taken in *Cedar Holdings Ltd* v *Green* [1981] Ch 129 was disapproved by Lord Wilberforce in *Williams & Glyn's Bank Ltd* v *Boland* [1981] AC 487 at p. 507 and was not followed). The legal estate will then be held by the spouses on trust for sale for the wife and the purchaser - and the purchaser may then apply for an order for sale under s.30 of the Law of Property Act 1925.

Where the title to the property is registered, notwithstanding the forgery of the wife's signature the legal estate will pass to the purchaser on his being registered as proprietor. If the wife was in actual occupation of the property she will have an overriding interest which will be binding on the purchaser (see below). If the wife was not in actual occupation she will not have an overriding interest but she may apply for rectification of the register to give effect to her interest on the ground that the entry on the register was obtained by fraud (Land Registration Act 1925, s.82(1)(d)). Where the register is rectified, the proprietor of any registered land or charge claiming in good faith under a forged disposition is deemed to have suffered loss by reason of the rectification and is entitled to be indemnified under the Land Registration Act 1925 (s.83(4)). It should be noted that if the purchaser is in occupation, rectification can be ordered only in limited circumstances (s.82(3)). If the wife is unable to obtain rectification, she will be entitled to be indemnified under the Land Registration Act 1925, s.83(2).

The wife may discover the position before the purchaser becomes registered as proprietor, as in *Ahmed* v *Kendrick*. In that case the wife had left the matrimonial home which was registered in the joint names of herself and her husband. The husband forged his wife's signature on a transfer and the purchaser was allowed into possession. On learning of the transfer, the wife registered an inhibition against the property at the Land Registry precluding registration of the disposition. It was found that the wife, faced with a *fait accompli* of the unauthorised sale, had acquiesced in the existing mortgage being discharged out of the proceeds of sale. Slade LJ said that "the simple and correct analysis" of the legal position was that as soon as the wife had consented to the discharge of the existing mortgage the property was thereafter held by the husband and wife as joint proprietors of the legal estate upon trust for sale under which the purchaser was entitled to a payment of £31,779 - being the amount paid to redeem the mortgage - and subject to this prior interest the proceeds would be held in trust in equal shares for the wife and the purchaser (as assignee of the husband's beneficial interest). Since the wife had not consented to the original sale, she should not be deprived of any share of the benefit of the subsequent appreciation in value of the property. Accordingly, the amount to be paid by the purchaser to the wife for her beneficial interest was one half of the difference between the amount paid to redeem the mortgage and the present value of the property (£65,000) rather than the original purchase price (£40,500). The proceedings were conducted on the footing that practical effect should be given to the respective beneficial interests of the parties in the property by ordering a transfer of the wife's legal and beneficial interest to the purchaser at an appropriate price. If this had not been the case, then a sale of the property could have been sought under s.30 of the Law of Property Act 1925.

Where a husband forges his wife's signature on a mortgage, the charge affects only the husband's beneficial interest, but the mortgagee, seeking enforcement, will be able to take advantage of the Charging Orders Act 1979 (see Chapter 4).

*(d) The effect of undue influence and misrepresentation*
Where a disposition is made by two trustees it is essential that they are both free, willing and properly informed parties to the transaction. If one of them enters into a mortgage of the family home as a result of undue influence or misrepresentation, the mortgage may be voidable at the instance of that party. This is considered further in the last section of this chapter (see page 75).

*(e) Protection on the death of a trustee*
In the case of unregistered land a purchaser must investigate the vendor's title and such investigation should reveal the existence of any trust for sale. There will normally be a conveyance or other document vesting the legal estate in two or more trustees, so that anyone dealing with a sole surviving trustee will be able to recognise him or her as such. Where the conveyance shows that the co-owners held the beneficial interest as tenants in common, the purchaser will insist on the appointment of another trustee so as to ensure the application of the overreaching provisions. Where the conveyance shows that the co-owners held the beneficial interest as joint tenants, the same practice is followed because of the danger that the beneficial joint tenancy might have been severed. This may be avoided if the provisions of the Law of Property (Joint Tenants) Act 1964 are applicable. This provides that the survivor of two or more joint tenants shall, in favour of a purchaser of the legal estate, be deemed to be solely and beneficially interested if he conveys as beneficial owner, or the conveyance includes a statement that he is so interested, unless a memorandum of severance has been endorsed on or annexed to the conveyance by virtue of which the legal estate was vested in the joint tenants, or a bankruptcy order has been made against any of the joint tenants, or a petition for such an order has been registered under the Land Charges Act 1972 (s.1).

In the case of registered land the beneficial interests of tenants in common should be protected by the entry on the register of a restriction or caution. This is because in the absence of any caution, restriction or inhibition on the register, a purchaser is entitled to deal with a sole registered proprietor as if he or she were absolutely entitled and, at least where he or she is registered with absolute title, a purchaser is not concerned to enquire how or in what circumstances he or she became sole registered proprietor. However, actual occupation of the land by a person entitled to a beneficial interest will generally make the rights of that person an overriding interest and thus binding on a purchaser (LRA 1925, s.70(1)(g). See page 69).

## 2. Where the legal estate is vested in one person

*(a) General principles*
Where the legal estate is conveyed into the name of one person only, but another person claims, or is entitled to, a beneficial interest in the property, a number of difficulties arise. In relation to unregistered land the usual investigation of title reveals only the apparent sole beneficial owner in whom the legal estate is vested, and gives no indication as to the existence of a beneficial interest in any other person. Despite the theoretical difficulties involved in trying to fit this situation into the scheme of the 1925 property legislation, it has been stated on several occasions (e.g. *Bull* v *Bull* [1955] 1 QB 234; *Cook* v *Cook* [1962] P 235), and assumed on others (e.g. *Caunce* v *Caunce* [1969] 1 WLR 286), that it gives rise to a trust for sale (see (1963) 27 Conv. (NS) 51 for a full discussion). This now seems to be accepted as a correct statement of the position. It is therefore necessary to consider the effect of a sale, mortgage or other dealing with the legal estate by the apparent beneficial owner on the beneficial interest which exists only behind the trust for sale.

In relation to unregistered land it has been assumed that a purchaser from such a single trustee for sale will acquire a good title to the legal estate free from the claims of the person entitled under the trust for sale, provided he is a bona fide purchaser for value of the legal estate without notice (see e.g. *Caunce* v *Caunce*). On the other hand, there have been statements reiterating the general principle that a single trustee for sale cannot sell the property and give a good receipt for the proceeds without first appointing an additional trustee (*Waller* v *Waller* [1967] 1 WLR 451; *Taylor* v *Taylor* [1968] 1 WLR 387). However, these were cases in which no sale had been completed, and there was no consideration of the position of a bona fide purchaser for value of the legal estate without notice. The better view, therefore, appears to be that such a purchaser will acquire a good title free from the beneficial interest to which any other person may be entitled.

The person entitled only to a beneficial interest behind the trust for sale will accordingly be well advised to seek the appointment of another trustee as soon as possible. If the sole trustee refuses to co-operate, an application could be made to the court under s.41 of the Trustee Act 1925 for the appointment of another trustee and, if necessary, for a vesting order under s.44 of that Act. In as much as such an application relates to the legal estate in the land, there seems to be no reason why it should not be protected by the registration of a *lis pendens* under the Land Charges

Act 1972, s.5. If events have moved too quickly, and the sole trustee has already contracted to sell the property, then, on the authority of *Waller* v *Waller* [1967] 1 WLR 451, application could be made for an injunction restraining completion of the sale pending appointment of another trustee.

However, the extent, or even the very existence of the beneficial interest may be disputed by the person in whom the legal estate is vested. It may, therefore, be necessary for an application to be made, under s.17 of the Married Women's Property Act 1882 or otherwise, for a declaration as to the beneficial interests in the property. In *Taylor* v *Taylor* [1968] 1 WLR 387 it was held that such an application could not be protected by the registration of a *lis pendens* under the Land Charges Act. A pending action is defined in s.17(1) of the Land Charges Act 1972 as "any action ... pending ... relating to land or any interest in or charge of land ..." and it was pointed out that the applicant wife's interest was at the most a share in the proceeds of sale of the property, and she had no interest in the land having regard to the definition of land in s.20(6) of the Land Charges Act 1925, now s.17(1) of the Land Charges Act 1972. (It may be noted that an application for a property adjustment order under s.24 of the Matrimonial Causes Act 1973 is registrable as a pending land action (*Whittingham* v *Whittingham* [1979] Fam 9). See further Chapter 10.)

To some extent the provisions of the Matrimonial Homes Act 1967, at any rate as amended by s.38 of the Matrimonial Proceedings and Property Act 1970, have indirectly alleviated the position by allowing the registration of a class F land charge to protect the rights of occupation given by that Act. (See now s.1(11) of the Matrimonial Homes Act 1983. See further Chapter 5 and in particular *Barnett* v *Hassett* [1981] 1 WLR 1385 where the spouse seeking to rely on the protection afforded by registration had no intention of occupying the home.) This, of course, will be of no assistance where the parties are not husband and wife, and even where they are, the beneficiary may have no rights of occupation under the Act, or they may have been terminated.

*(b) The effect of occupation of the property*

(i) General effect

Even though the person entitled only to a beneficial interest has taken no steps to protect his or her interest, he or she may be protected if in occupation of the property. Thus in relation to unregistered land a purchaser will generally be deemed to have constructive notice of the beneficiary's rights under the principle in *Hunt* v *Luck* [1902] 1 Ch 428. In relation to registered land a purchaser takes subject not only to entries on the register, but also to overriding interests. Section 70(1)(g) of the Land Registration Act 1925 provides that the rights of a person in actual occupation of land amount to an overriding interest save where enquiry is made of such person and the rights are not disclosed. The significance of occupation is different in the two systems. In the case of unregistered land occupation may operate to give a purchaser or mortgagee notice that the person in occupation may have rights in relation to the land. In the case of registered land the fact of occupation makes the rights of the person in occupation an overriding interest. Unfortunately, a number of difficulties have arisen in relation to the application of these principles with regard to occupation.

(ii) Occupation with the title holder - who may occupy?
In relation to both unregistered and registered land difficulty has arisen where both the person in whom the legal estate is vested and the person entitled only to a beneficial interest are physically present on the property.

In *Caunce* v *Caunce* [1969] 1 WLR 286, which concerned unregistered land, both husband and wife were in occupation of the matrimonial home when the husband, in whom the legal estate was vested, mortgaged the property to a bank. Stamp J held that the bank was not affected with notice of the wife's beneficial interest merely because she was living in the home. He expressed the view that where a vendor is himself in occupation, a purchaser is not affected with notice of the equitable interest of any person who may reside there and whose presence is wholly consistent with the title offered. In *Hodgson* v *Marks* [1971] Ch 892, which concerned registered land, Russell LJ, who delivered the principal judgment in the Court of Appeal, cast doubt on this view. He did not consider it necessary to pronounce on the decision in *Caunce* v *Caunce*, for in any event the occupation of the wife may have been rightly taken not to be her occupation, but that of the husband. Nevertheless, he did say that in so far as "some phrases in the judgment might appear to lay down a general proposition that inquiry need not be made of any person on the premises if the proposed vendor himself appears to be in occupation I would not accept them" (at pp. 934-935). This criticism was approved by Lord Wilberforce in *Williams & Glyn's Bank Ltd* v *Boland* [1981] AC 487 at p. 505 which was also concerned with registered land. Also in that case Lord Scarman was "by no means certain that *Caunce* v *Caunce* was correctly decided", but since the case before him was concerned only with registered land, it was unnecessary to express a final opinion on the point (at p. 511).

An alternative basis for the decision in *Caunce* v *Caunce* was that the wife's occupation was nothing but the shadow of the husband's - a version of the doctrine of unity of husband and wife. This was also apparent in *Bird* v *Syme-Thomson* [1979] 1 WLR 440, but was described by Lord Wilberforce in *Boland* as "obsolete" (at p. 505). These criticisms were noted by the judge in *Kingsnorth Finance Co. Ltd* v *Tizard* [1986] 1 WLR 783 who held that the wife, who was entitled to a beneficial interest, was in occupation of the property notwithstanding that her husband, in whom the legal title was vested, was also living there.

In relation to registered land the position was clarified by the decision of the House of Lords in *Williams & Glyn's Bank Ltd* v *Boland* [1981] AC 487. The case was concerned with a house registered in the name of a husband alone although his wife had contributed a substantial sum of her own money towards the purchase and towards paying off a mortgage on it. Later the husband mortgaged the property to the bank which made no enquiries of the wife who was living with her husband in the house. When the husband defaulted under the mortgage the bank took proceedings for possession. The Court of Appeal reversed the decision of the judge who had made an order for possession. This was upheld by the House of Lords who held that the wife's interest in the property as an equitable tenant in common was binding on the bank as an overriding interest within s.70(1)(g) of the Land Registration Act 1925. Lord Wilberforce said (at p. 502) that "the presence of the vendor, with occupation, does not exclude the possibility of occupation by others". Occupation for the purposes of s.70(1)(g) need not be "apparently inconsistent with the title of the vendor". Lord Wilberforce rejected the suggestion that the wife of a husband-vendor was excluded because her apparent occupation would be satisfactorily accounted for by his. He concluded that "a spouse living in a house has an actual occupation capable of conferring protection, as an overriding interest, upon the rights of that spouse" (at p. 506). Moreover, this was not limited to cases involving husbands and wives. The better view now seems to be that this applies to unregistered land as well as to registered land. *Caunce* v *Caunce* is unlikely to be followed in so far as it takes a contrary view.

(iii) The effect of occupation

It is apparent from the decision of the House of Lords in *Williams & Glyn's Bank Ltd* v *Boland* that, in relation to registered land, the effect of occupation is automatically to convert what would otherwise be a minor interest into an overriding interest. Lord Wilberforce said that whether a particular interest is an overriding interest, and whether it affects a purchaser, is to be decided upon the terms of s.70 and other relevant provisions of the Land Registration Act 1925 and the law as to notice as it may affect purchasers of unregistered land has no application even by analogy to registered land. "In the case of registered land, it is the fact of occupation that matters. If there is actual occupation, and the occupant has rights, the purchaser takes subject to them. If not, he does not. No further element is material" ([1981] AC 487 at p. 504. See (iv) below for the meaning of occupation).

In relation to unregistered land, occupation is relevant in giving notice to a purchaser or mortgagee that the occupier may have rights in or over the property so that further inquiry is necessary to ascertain the extent of such rights, if any. Section 199 of the Law of Property Act 1925 provides that (apart from matters capable of registration under the Land Charges Act which have not been registered) a purchaser shall not be prejudicially affected by notice of -

"(ii) any other instrument or matter or any fact or thing unless -

    (a) it is within his own knowledge, or would have come to his knowledge if such inquiries and inspections had been made as ought reasonably to have been made by him; or

    (b) in the same transaction with respect to which a question of notice to the purchaser arises, it has come to the knowledge of his counsel, as such, or of his solicitor or other agent, as such, or would have come to the knowledge of his solicitor or other agent, as such, if such inquiries and inspections had been made as ought reasonably to have been made by the solicitor or other agent."

Thus if a purchaser or mortgagee carries out such inspections "as ought reasonably to be made" and does not find the person entitled to a beneficial interest in occupation, then (in the absence of other circumstances giving notice) the purchaser or mortgagee will not be fixed with notice of the claimant's rights. On the other hand, if a purchaser or mortgagee fails to make such inspections or inquiries he will be deemed to have notice of those rights and it is not open to him to say that if he had made a further inspection he would still not have found the claimant in occupation (see Judge Finlay in *Kingsnorth Finance Co Ltd* v *Tizard* [1986] 1 WLR 783 at p. 794).

It is therefore crucial to consider what inquiries and inspections "ought reasonably to be made". This will depend on all the circumstances of the case.

In *Kingsnorth Finance Co Ltd* v *Tizard* [1986] 1 WLR 783 at pp. 794-795 Judge Finlay went so far as to say that where the object of an inspection (or one of the objects) is to ascertain who is in occupation, an inspection at a time pre-arranged with the vendor will not necessarily attain that object. "Such a pre-arranged inspection may achieve no more than an inquiry of the vendor or mortgagor and his answer to it". In the circumstances of the case he was not satisfied that the pre-arranged inspection on a Sunday afternoon fell within the words of s.199. It is submitted that this puts too heavy an onus on a purchaser for it would seem to require a purchaser to make a "surprise" unannounced visit. Judge Finlay did acknowledge that in the case of residential property an appointment for inspection will, in most cases, be essential so far as an inspection of the interior is concerned.

A more satisfactory basis for the decision lies in the fact that whereas Mr. Tizard had described himself as "single" on the form of application for the mortgage, the mortgagees' agent who inspected the property was told by Mr. Tizard that he was married but his wife had moved out. The mortgagees were, therefore, prejudicially affected by the knowledge of their agent (LPA 1925, s.199(1)(b)). That put them on notice that further inquiries were necessary. The "inquiries which in these circumstances ought reasonably to have been made by the plaintiffs would ... have been such as to have apprised them of the fact that Mrs. Tizard claimed a beneficial interest in the property; and accordingly, they would have had notice of such equitable rights as she had and the mortgage in these circumstances takes effect subject to these rights: see s.199(1)(ii)(a) LPA 1925" ([1986] 1 WLR 783 at pp. 792-793).

(iv) What is occupation?

Occupation in this context means "presence on the land" and the phrase "actual occupation" in relation to registered land "merely emphasises that what is required is physical presence, not some entitlement in law" (*per* Lord Wilberforce in *Williams & Glyn's Bank Ltd* v *Boland* [1981] AC 487 at p. 505). "Physical presence" does not connote continuous and uninterrupted presence in a literal sense and is not necessarily negatived by regular and repeated absence (see *Kingsnorth Finance Co Ltd* v *Tizard* [1986] 1 WLR 783 at p. 788). Thus in *Kingsnorth Finance Co Ltd* v *Tizard*, following the breakdown of the marriage the wife did not sleep at the house in question unless the husband was away, but she was there virtually every day for some part of the day to care for the children. It was held that she did not cease to be in occupation despite the significant change in her living pattern whereby she slept elsewhere on numerous occasions. On the other hand, in *Abbey National Building Society* v *Cann* [1991] AC 56 at p. 93 Lord Oliver said that it does involve "some degree of permanence and continuity which would rule out mere fleeting presence". Thus a "prospective tenant or purchaser who is allowed, as a matter of indulgence, to go into property in order to plan decorations or measure for furnishings would not, in ordinary parlance, be said to be occupying it, even though he might be there for hours at a time". In that case, the claimant Mrs. Cann was on holiday but her son and brother-in-law moved in her belongings a short time before actual completion. Lord Oliver (at p. 94) was "unable to accept that acts of

71

this preparatory character carried out by courtesy of the vendor prior to completion" could constitute "actual occupation" for the purposes of s.70(1)(g).

The form of occupation will also depend upon the nature and state of the property in question. It need not take the form of residence in the ordinary sense. Thus in the case of a semi-derelict farmhouse, as in *Lloyds Bank plc v Rosset* [1989] Ch 350 (CA), [1991] AC 107 (HL) the Court of Appeal held that there was occupation whilst works of renovation proceeded and before anyone had started to live there. The wife was there almost every day during the hours her daughter was at school, generally assisting, keeping things moving and doing some work herself. Moreover, the physical presence of an employee or agent, such as the builder in that case, could be regarded as the presence of the employer or principal when determining whether the employer or principal was in occupation. In the view of the majority of the Court of Appeal (Nicholls and Purchas LJJ, with Mustill LJ dissenting) these factors taken together were sufficient to amount to actual occupation by the wife having regard to the actual state of the property. The House of Lords found that the wife had not acquired a beneficial interest in the property and thus found it unnecessary to consider the question of occupation. In *Abbey National Building Society v Cann* [1991] AC 56 at p. 93 Lord Oliver accepted that "actual occupation" does not necessarily involve the personal presence of the person claiming to occupy and that a caretaker could occupy on behalf of such a person.

(v) The date of occupation
In the case of registered land, completion of a transfer, in the traditional sense of the exchange of the transfer for the purchase price, must be followed by the making of an appropriate entry on the register - registration. There is inevitably an interval of time between completion and registration. In *Abbey National Building Society v Cann* [1991] AC 56 the House of Lords held that, while the relevant date for determining the existence of overriding interests which will affect the estate transferred or created is the date of registration, the relevant date for determining whether a claimant to a right is in actual occupation for the purposes of s.70(1)(g) is the date of completion. Accordingly, a claimant who enters into occupation of the property after completion, but before registration of a transfer or mortgage, will not have an overriding interest on the basis of that occupation.

*(c) Mortgage advances used to acquire the home*
The effect of the protection afforded by occupation of the home by the person entitled only to a beneficial interest in it, especially in relation to registered land following the decision of the House of Lords in *Williams & Glyn's Bank Ltd v Boland* [1981] AC 487, has been to cast a potentially heavy burden not only on a purchaser but also on a mortgagee. However, the position of a mortgagee who advances money for the acquisition of a property has been improved significantly in relation to unregistered land by the decision of the Court of Appeal in *Bristol & West Building Society v Henning* [1985] 1 WLR 778. The court there held that in the absence of any express declaration of trust or agreement relating to the beneficial interest in the property the occupier's right depended upon the imputed intention of the parties. Since the female cohabitee knew of and supported the obtaining of a

mortgage advance towards the purchase price of the property, it was "impossible" to impute to the parties any intention other than that she had authorised the man to raise the mortgage advance from the building society and that her rights were to be subject to the rights of the building society as mortgagee. This reasoning was applied in relation to registered land by the Court of Appeal in *Paddington Building Society* v *Mendelsohn* (1985) 50 P & CR 244. It was emphasised that if the rights of the person in actual occupation are not under the general law such as to give any priority over the holder of a registered estate, there is nothing in s.70 of the Land Registration Act 1925 which changes such rights into different and larger rights (see *National Provincial Bank Ltd* v *Ainsworth* [1965] AC 1175).

This approach will not assist a mortgagee where an advance is made after the purchase of the home and without the knowledge or consent of the occupying spouse or cohabitee, as was the case in *Williams & Glyn's Bank Ltd* v *Boland* [1981] AC 487. Indeed, it cannot apply where the mortgage advance was obtained at the time the property was being acquired if the occupying spouse or cohabitee was unaware that part of the purchase price was being provided by way of a loan. This is probably much less likely, though it was the case in *Lloyds Bank plc* v *Rosset* [1991] AC 107 where the reasoning in *Bristol & West Building Society* v *Henning* was approved by Nicholls LJ though not applied since the wife was unaware of the mortgage advance and believed that the whole of the purchase price was being made available to the husband by his family trust. In *Equity and Law Loans Ltd* v *Prestidge* [1992] 1 WLR 137 the Court of Appeal held that where an occupying cohabitee was aware of a mortgage advance at the time of the purchase of a property so that she was deemed to have consented to it, then consent to a re-mortgage of the property should also be imputed to her notwithstanding her lack of knowledge of it, but only up to the amount of the original loan. Thus the new mortgage had priority only to the extent of the original loan.

*(d) The effect of the trust for sale*
It has been held that where land is held on trust for sale the effect of the doctrine of conversion is that a beneficial interest subsists only in relation to the proceeds of sale and not in relation to the land. See *Irani Finance Ltd* v *Singh* [1971] Ch 59 where it was held that a charging order could not be made against the interest of a tenant in common under a trust for sale as he had no interest in the land as required by s.35 of the Administration of Justice Act 1956 (see now the Charging Orders Act 1979 considered in Chapter 8). However in *Williams & Glyn's Bank Ltd* v *Boland* [1981] AC 487 at p. 507 Lord Wilberforce agreed with Lord Denning MR that "to describe the interests of spouses in a house jointly bought to be lived in as a matrimonial home as merely an interest in the proceeds of sale, or rents and profits until sale, is just a little unreal ...". In his view the wife in that case had an equitable interest, "subsisting in reference to the land" and, while such an interest is generally a minor interest, if it is accompanied by actual occupation of the land, there is no reason why it should not acquire the status of an overriding interest.

Similarly, the doctrine of conversion should not affect the protection afforded by the doctrine of notice to a person entitled to a beneficial interest under a trust for sale of unregistered land. (See *Kingsnorth Finance Co Ltd* v *Tizard* [1986] 1 WLR

783, but contrast the position in relation to an attempt to obtain protection through registration of a *lis pendens* in *Taylor* v *Taylor* [1968] 1 WLR 387, considered above.)

More recently, in *City of London Building Society* v *Flegg* [1988] AC 54 Lord Oliver appeared to endorse the view taken in *Irani Finance Ltd* v *Singh*, but he did not appear to intend to disapprove of the decision in *Williams & Glyn's Bank Ltd* v *Boland*.

*(e) The consequences of Williams & Glyn's Bank Ltd v Boland*
The effect of the decision of the House of Lords in *Williams & Glyn's Bank Ltd* v *Boland* [1981] AC 487 was to strengthen the position of a spouse, and probably of a cohabitee, who is entitled to a beneficial interest in property the title to which is registered in the name of his or her spouse or partner alone. (It is, of course, of no assistance to a spouse or cohabitee who has left the property, even if forced to do so by the registered proprietor. In these circumstances protection by entry on the register is essential.) The disapproval by Lord Wilberforce of *Caunce* v *Caunce* [1969] 1 WLR 286 produced a similar though not identical position in relation to unregistered land where the person entitled to a beneficial interest is in occupation of the property (*Kingsnorth Finance Co Ltd* v *Tizard* [1986] 1 WLR 783).

On the other hand the decision in *Williams & Glyn's Bank Ltd* v *Boland* was criticised as imposing too heavy a burden on purchasers and mortgagees. However, Lord Wilberforce had pointed out that "... the extension of the risk area follows necessarily from the extension, beyond the paterfamilias, of rights of ownership, itself following from the diffusion of property and earning capacity". He went on to say (at p. 508) that:

"What is involved is a departure from an easy-going practice of dispensing with enquiries as to occupation beyond that of a vendor and accepting the risks of doing so. To substitute for this a practice of more careful enquiry as to the fact of occupation, and if necessary, as to the rights of occupiers cannot, in my view of the matter, be considered as unacceptable except at the price of overlooking the widespread development of shared interests of ownership."

Since the decision in *Williams & Glyn's Bank Ltd* v *Boland* it has become standard practice on the purchase of a dwelling-house to address an enquiry to the vendor before contract seeking the names of other adult occupants and inquiring whether any such person has a legal or equitable interest in the property. Occupiers who are thus disclosed may be required to consent in writing to a mortgage or may even be made a party to the mortgage. This seems to be preferred to embarking on a more sophisticated system of inspection and undertaking the task of determining whether a person found in occupation is in fact entitled to a beneficial interest. In *Lloyds Bank Ltd* v *Rosset* [1989] Ch 350 at p. 379 Nicholls LJ, in the Court of Appeal, noting that the mortgage was completed more than two years after the decision in *Williams & Glyn's Bank Ltd* v *Boland*, found "it surprising that the bank, knowing that this was to be the matrimonial home, did not seek the wife's written consent to the grant of the charge".

Such steps do not necessarily eliminate the risks. Thus a purchaser or mortgagee will not be protected against an occupier with an interest in the property if the vendor gives a negative response in good faith. Moreover, if an occupier does give consent or is made a party to a mortgage it is essential that such consent is freely given. Undue influence or fraudulent misrepresentation may vitiate the consent. This is considered further in the next section of this chapter.

The Law Commission in its *Report on The Implications of Williams & Glyn's Bank Ltd* v *Boland* (Law Com. No. 115 (1982)) sought to limit the protection afforded to occupiers as a result of the decision by the introduction of a registration requirement. It recommended "that co-ownership interests, whether in registered or unregistered land, should be registrable, and that purchasers should take subject to such an interest if, but only if, it has been registered" (para 83). However, it also recommended that for the protection of the matrimonial home, the rights of married co-owners should include a special consent requirement whereby no sale or other disposition of the home by one can be effective without the consent of the other or an order of the court (paras 95 and 97). In order to establish the existence and extent of co-ownership interests more effectively, it repeated its recommendation (made in Law Com. No. 86 (para 115)) for the introduction of a scheme of equal co-ownership of the matrimonial home .

An attempt to implement these recommendations failed when the Land Registration and Law of Property Bill was withdrawn in 1985 as a result of opposition. In its *Third Report on Land Registration* (Law Com. No. 158 (1987)) the Law Commission adopted a different view. In the interests of certainty and of simplifying conveyancing, the class of right which may bind a purchaser otherwise than as a result of an entry on the register should be as narrow as possible. However, "interests should be overriding where protection against purchasers is needed, yet it is not reasonable to expect or not sensible to require any entry on the register" (para 2.6). The rights of occupiers fall into that category. This was accompanied by a recommendation that where an overriding interest is asserted against a registered proprietor or chargee then he may apply for indemnity alone, but as a condition precedent to payment there might be rectification of the register. (See paras 2.10 - 2.14.)

### 3. Undue influence and misrepresentation

*(a) General principles*
Undue influence or fraudulent misrepresentation may affect the validity of a disposition in a number of situations considered in this chapter. Thus one co-owner may have been induced to enter into a mortgage to secure what is in reality a loan to the other co-owner. In some cases both co-owners may have been induced to enter into a mortgage to secure a loan to a third party, usually another member of the family or possibly a business associate. Such charges may be coupled with, or follow the signing of, a form of guarantee for a loan to the other co-owner or family member or business associate. Questions of undue influence or fraudulent misrepresentation may also arise where a lender takes the "precaution", which is common since *Williams & Glyn's Bank Ltd* v *Boland*, of seeking the consent of one co-owner (or

possible co-owner) to a mortgage by the other co-owner.

In order to establish a defence of undue influence when a mortgagee seeks to enforce a mortgage (or guarantee), a defendant must show that he or she was induced, or must be presumed to have been induced, to execute the mortgage (or guarantee) as a result of undue influence by the mortgagee directly or by the defendant's spouse or other relative in circumstances in which the mortgagee is treated as affected by the acts of that spouse or relative. Whether a person is relying on actual or presumed undue influence it must also be shown that the disposition has resulted in manifest disadvantage to him or her.

In order to establish fraudulent misrepresentation a person must show that he or she was induced to execute the mortgage (or guarantee) as a result of a false representation made knowingly, or without belief in its truth, or recklessly, without caring whether it was true or false, by the mortgagee directly or by the defendant's spouse or other relative in circumstances in which the mortgagee is affected by the acts of the spouse or other relative.

In the recent case of *Barclays Bank plc* v *O'Brien* [1992] 3 WLR 593, the Court of Appeal suggested another approach which involves developing a body of case law dating from the early years of this century. This is considered in (*d*) below.

*(b) Undue influence or misrepresentation by the mortgagee or other creditor*
It may be that a mortgagee or other creditor has exercised undue influence directly on the mortgagor or guarantor. The question has usually arisen in relation to mortgages or guarantees obtained by banks, though it is now well established that the relationship between banker and customer is not one which ordinarily gives rise to a presumption of undue influence (see Lord Scarman in *National Westminster Bank plc* v *Morgan* [1985] AC 686 at p. 707). In the ordinary course of banking business a banker can explain the nature of the proposed transaction without laying himself open to a charge of undue influence. However, where the bank goes further and advises on more general matters germane to the wisdom of the transaction, it may "cross the line" into an area where there is a conflict of interest between the bank and the customer to whom advice is being given and thus give rise to a presumption of undue influence (*ibid.* at pp. 708-709). This was found to be the case by the Court of Appeal in *Lloyds Bank Ltd* v *Bundy* [1975] QB 326 where an elderly farmer charged his farm as security for his son's indebtedness to the bank. This case may be regarded as exceptional in some respects, and the wider statements of Lord Denning MR in relation to undue influence being based on inequality of bargaining power were not approved by the House of Lords in *National Westminster Bank plc* v *Morgan*. However, in that case Lord Scarman said (at p. 708) that in considering the nature of the relationship necessary to give rise to the presumption of undue influence in the context of a banking transaction, Sir Eric Sachs in the Court of Appeal in *Lloyds Bank Ltd* v *Bundy* "got it absolutely right". In *National Westminster Bank plc* v *Morgan* the House of Lords held that a bank manager who had visited the wife in her home to seek her signature to a joint mortgage by her husband and herself to the bank had not "crossed the line" so as to impose a duty on the bank to ensure that she had independent advice.

*(c) Undue influence or misrepresentation by a third party*

There are two distinct grounds on which a mortgagee or other creditor may be affected by undue influence or fraudulent misrepresentation on the part of a spouse or other relative of the mortgagor or guarantor, or indeed on the part of any other third party.

(i) Agency

First, a mortgagee may be liable where the spouse, other relative or third party has acted as its agent. The mortgagee cannot be in any better position than the agent if, when that agent was acting on its behalf, he or she exerted or was presumed to have exerted undue influence. Since undue influence must have brought about the transaction before relief can be obtained, it would be inconsistent with the equitable nature of the relief for the mortgagee not to be affected by the undue influence exerted by its agent when the transaction would not exist but for the wrongful act of its agent (*per* Slade LJ in *Bank of Credit & Commerce International SA* v *Aboody* [1990] 1 QB 923).

The same applies in relation to fraudulent misrepresentation made by an agent in carrying out the specific instructions of his principal.

Whether in any particular case the person who exerts the undue influence or makes the fraudulent misrepresentation is the agent of the mortgagee is a question of fact. Thus in *Kings North Trust Co Ltd* v *Bell* [1986] 1 WLR 119 the mortgagee's solicitors had sent the documents to be executed to the husband's solicitors who entrusted to the husband the responsibility of procuring execution of the mortgage deed by the wife. The Court of Appeal found that the mortgagee was bound by the actions of the husband in inducing the wife to sign by his fraudulent misrepresentation as to the purpose of the advance. This might be interpreted as a finding that the husband had acted as the agent of the bank, and this appears to have been the view taken by the Court of Appeal in the *Aboody* case. In *Barclays Bank plc* v *O'Brien* [1992] 3 WLR 593, the Court of Appeal interpreted the decision differently (see (*d*) below). The same applies to *Avon Finance Co Ltd* v *Bridger* [1985] 2 All ER 281 where the majority of the Court of Appeal found that the finance company had chosen to appoint the son, who was the principal debtor, to procure from his parents the security which was needed to further the transaction between the son and the finance company. The person whom the company chose to appoint, being the son of the mortgagors, could be expected to have some influence over his elderly parents and that is something of which the finance company could or should have been aware. The son deceived his parents by telling them that the documents they were signing were connected with the building society mortgage with the aid of which the home was purchased. He took his parents to the offices of the solicitors for the finance company where the documents were put before them by a clerk and the parents signed them without reading them or receiving any explanation other than that provided by their son. The transaction was held to be voidable in equity at the instance of the parents. In *Bank of Credit & Commerce International SA* v *Aboody* [1990] 1 QB 923 the wife had executed several of the relevant documents at the premises of the bank and in these circumstances the husband could not be treated as the agent of the bank. However, it was accepted that, in respect of two guarantees, execution of the documents by the wife was procured by the husband as the bank's agent.

In *Barclays Bank plc* v *Kennedy* [1989] 1 FLR 356 Purchas LJ said that the real question was whether the bank was content to leave it to the husband to obtain his wife's signature upon the charge. In that case the mortgage of the matrimonial home to the bank secured all sums due from the spouses with particular reference to a guarantee by the husband in relation to credit afforded to a business associate of the husband. The mortgage having been executed by the husband as "proprietor", the manager left it to the husband to persuade the wife to call at the bank to sign the mortgage as "occupier". When she called at the bank a clerk presented her with the document for signature and there was no discussion. Purchas LJ said that the overwhelming inference was "that all had been agreed between the husband and the manager on the previous Friday and that the manager left it to the husband to persuade the wife to come to the bank on the Monday to execute the charge and sign the guarantee". He also took into account the fact that there was "a real incentive to the manager not only to disembarrass himself of a thoroughly unsatisfactory debtor by getting a guarantee secured by a charge on a registered property, but also of producing a satisfactory answer to the awkward interest being shown by Head Office". Again it might be argued that the husband had been acting as agent of the bank, although a different interpretation was given in *Barclays Bank plc* v *O'Brien* (see (*d*) below). In the event a retrial was ordered which was limited to the question of whether the husband had used undue influence or misrepresentation to obtain the wife's signature.

In *Coldunell Ltd* v *Gallon* [1986] QB 1184 the Court of Appeal found that neither the plaintiff finance company nor its solicitors had constituted a son as agent in relation to the execution of a mortgage by his parents to secure a loan which would be used for his benefit. The finance company had entrusted completion of the transaction to its solicitors who in turn had caused, or thought they had caused, the documents to be despatched direct to the parents with a covering letter to each parent specifically directing their attention to the desirability of obtaining independent advice. The letters were not received by the parents but the father executed the mortgage and the mother executed a form of consent in the presence of the son's solicitor who explained the consent form to the mother, but did not advise the parents as to the nature and effect of the transaction. The court said that although the son had exercised undue influence over the parents in obtaining their signatures to a transaction which was manifestly to their disadvantage, the mortgagee was not affected by this undue influence. The finance company had neither left to the son the task of obtaining his parents' signatures, nor in any other way had it accepted responsibility for or adopted the actions of the son.

A similar conclusion was reached in *Bank of Baroda* v *Shah* [1988] 3 All ER 24 where a husband and wife had charged their property to the bank to secure monies due to the bank from a company of which the wife's elder brother was a director. The brother had misrepresented the nature and amount of the charge and threatened that the husband would lose his job with the company. The company's solicitors described themselves as solicitors for the husband and wife though they had not been instructed by the spouses. The Court of Appeal held that neither the actions of the brother nor the company's solicitors could be attributed to the bank or its solicitors. The bank's solicitors had never intended to leave it to the brother to obtain the signatures of the husband and wife, and they were entitled to assume that the company's solicitors, who misrepresented that they acted for the spouses, would give them proper advice. In *Perry* v *Midland Bank plc* [1987] Fin LR 237 the Court of Appeal held that the fact that the husband had been asked by the bank manager to ascertain whether the wife was prepared to agree in principle to a charge on the home was not enough to constitute him as an agent. In *Midland Bank plc* v *Johns* 30 July 1987 CA Lexis Enggen, Croom-Johnson LJ said that the mere fact that the bank manager had said to the husband: "Will you please get your wife and bring her along because she will have to sign the mortgage document too" - was not enough to make the husband an agent of the bank. In *Lloyds Bank plc* v *Egremont* [1990] 2 FLR 351 the bank had sent the mortgage document for signature not to the husband but to the solicitor acting for him and, it seems, the wife. The document was executed in the office of the solicitor who added a note to the effect that he had explained the contents of the document to the wife. The Court of Appeal held that the bank had not left it to the husband to obtain his wife's signature and was entitled to assume that the solicitor had indeed given independent advice to the wife so that any misrepresentation by the husband did not affect the bank.

(ii) Notice

If a creditor has actual or constructive notice at the time of the execution of the charge or guarantee in question, that the charge or guarantee on which it relies has been procured by the exercise of undue influence or fraudulent misrepresentation, it will not be able to enforce the transaction. An equity is raised against the creditor irrespective of any question of agency (*Kempson* v *Ashbee* (1874) LR 10 Ch App. 15; *Bainbrigge* v *Broome* (1881) 18 Ch D 188). The necessary degree of notice will depend on the nature of the undue influence or misrepresentation alleged. Thus in a case of undue influence the creditor must have notice of the circumstances alleged to constitute the actual exercise of the undue influence. In a case where a presumption of undue influence is alleged to arise, the creditor must have notice of the circumstances from which the presumption is alleged to arise (*per* Slade LJ in *Bank of Credit & Commerce International SA* v *Aboody* [1990] 1 QB 923 at p. 973).

In *Avon Finance Co Ltd* v *Bridger* [1985] 2 All ER 281 the majority of the Court of Appeal (Brandon and Brightman LJJ) decided the case on a combination of the two grounds of agency and constructive notice. In *Bank of Credit & Commerce International SA* v *Aboody* the wife was persuaded by her husband to go to the bank to sign a charge on her property to secure loans to her husband's company. (This was one of several documents with which the court was concerned.) She saw a solicitor whom the bank had arranged to give her independent advice about the implications of the charge and to confirm that she understood its implications. While the solicitor was still attempting to advise her the husband burst into the room, and as a result of the distressing scene which followed, the wife signed. The Court of Appeal held that notwithstanding that the husband's company eventually paid the independent solicitor's fees, the solicitor was acting for the bank as well as the wife and his knowledge of the influence brought to bear on the wife by her husband in relation to the execution of the charge was imputed to the bank. The fact that disclosing these facts to the bank might have rendered him in breach of duty to his other client, Mrs. Aboody, did not alter that position. (See *Lancashire Loans Ltd v Black* [1934] 1 KB 380.)

In contrast, in *Perry* v *Midland Bank plc* [1987] Fin LR 237, the Court of Appeal found that the bank did not have notice of undue influence exercised over the wife by the husband (though the wife did have a remedy in negligence: see (*f*) below).

*(d) Special protection for wives and vulnerable persons*
In most of the cases mentioned in (*c*) reference had been made to two decisions dating from the early years of the century - *Turnbull & Co* v *Duval* [1902] AC 429 and *Chaplin & Co Ltd* v *Brammall* [1908] 1 KB 233. It was to this line of authority that the Court of Appeal turned in the recent case of *Barclays Bank plc* v *O'Brien* [1992] 3 WLR 593. Scott LJ concluded that those cases demonstrated a treatment of wives who have given security to support their husbands' debts more tender than that which would have been applied to other third party sureties. In the earlier cases the wife had lacked a full understanding of the security transaction into which she had entered and had had no independent advice. The security was unenforceable because (a) the security was given by the wife of the debtor, (b) the creditor knew of the relationship, (c) the creditor had done nothing to ensure that the wife understood the transaction, (d) the wife did not properly understand the transaction, and (e) she had had no independent advice. In those circumstances, equity did not permit the security to be enforced against the wife (*ibid.* at p. 609).

Reviewing the modern authorities, Scott LJ concluded that *Kings North Trust Ltd* v *Bell* [1986] 1 WLR 119 and *Barclays Bank plc* v *Kennedy* [1989] 1 FLR 356 were in line with the earlier authorities relied upon. In both, the court held that the creditor was not entitled to enforce the security against the wife. However, in neither case was there any explicit finding that the debtor husband had been acting as agent for the creditor, and such a finding would have been highly artificial. In both cases the creditor had left it to the debtor husband to deal with his wife as surety and had done nothing to satisfy itself that she understood what she was doing or to protect her from abuse by the debtor of the influence and reliance that would be likely to be present. The decision in *Avon Finance Co Ltd* v *Bridger* [1985] 2 All ER 281 was also in line with the earlier cases except that it extended the principle previously confined to husband and wife cases to a case of parents giving security for the debts of their son. On the other hand, *Midland Bank plc* v *Perry* [1987] FLR 237 did not recognise that wives who provide security for their husbands' debts should be treated any differently from sureties in general, and the decision was inconsistent with *Barclays Bank plc* v *Kennedy*. Again in *Bank of Credit & Commerce International SA* v *Aboody* [1990] 1 QB 923 the Court of Appeal had adopted the same view although this was immaterial on the facts.

In *Barclays Bank plc* v *O'Brien*, Scott LJ (at p. 618) concluded that the authorities left "the developing law, if not at the crossroads, at least at the junction of two diverging roads". "One road would treat the special protection previously provided by equity for married women who provide security for their husband's debts as now only of historical interest", and the matter would be determined on the basis of the analysis of Slade LJ in the *Aboody* case. A creditor would be affected by undue influence or misrepresentation by the debtor only if the creditor had knowledge of the relevant facts or if the debtor had been acting as the agent of the creditor in the true strict sense. Travellers along the other road would recognise that "equity has in the past treated married women differently and more tenderly than other third parties who provide security for the debts of others". They would notice, too, that the protected class had been extended to include vulnerable elderly parents who provide security for the debts of their adult son. Security given by a person within this protected class would in certain circumstances be unenforceable notwithstanding that the creditor might have no knowledge of, and not have been responsible for, the vitiating feature of the transaction. The security would be unenforceable if the following conditions were satisfied:

(i)   the relationship between the debtor and the surety, and the consequent likelihood of influence and reliance, was known to the creditor; and

(ii)  the surety's consent to the transaction was procured by undue influence or material misrepresentation on the part of the debtor *or the surety lacked an adequate understanding of the nature and effect of the transaction*; and

(iii) the creditor, whether by leaving it to the debtor to deal with the surety or otherwise, had failed to take reasonable steps to try and ensure that the surety entered into the transaction with an adequate understanding of the nature and effect of the transaction and that the surety's consent to the transaction was a true and informed one.

Authority could be found to justify taking either road. None of the modern authorities expressly overrules the earlier cases, but Scott LJ took the view that the choice should be made in favour of the second road on policy grounds.

The advantage of this approach is illustrated by the *O'Brien* case itself. Undue influence was not established since it was found that the wife had signed because she was persuaded that it was the right thing to do and not because her husband's pressure had deprived her consent of reality. There was misrepresentation by the husband but it was clear from the arrangements made by the bank for the signature of the documents that it had not appointed the husband to act as its agent in the strict sense. However, the bank had an obligation to take reasonable steps to see that the wife understood the transaction into which she was entering. This the bank had failed to do, but if the clerk in the sub-branch had carried out the manager's instructions the bank would then have discharged its obligation. In view of her misunderstanding of the transaction it was not enforceable against her beyond the sum represented to her by her husband as the limit of the security.

The extent of the protected class is not entirely certain. Scott LJ (at p. 610) said:
"... the class ought, logically, to include all cases in which the relationship between the surety and the debtor is one in which influence by the debtor over the surety and reliance by the surety on the debtor are natural and probable features of the relationship."

Purchas LJ (at p. 624) did not consider that the principle would be advanced by identifying specific categories such as husband and wife or elderly parents and adult children. He said "... the principle applies whenever a creditor knows or ought to have known that the relationship between debtor and surety gives rise to a real risk that the surety may not contract freely and with full appreciation of the nature of the obligation being assumed."

Finally, while each case within the protected class must depend on its own facts, Scott LJ said (at p. 620) that he "would regard a clear written recommendation to the surety to take independent advice before signing the security document as advisable in most cases".

### (e) Manifest disadvantage

A court will not grant relief to a party to a transaction on the ground of undue influence unless the transaction was manifestly disadvantageous to that party. In *Bank of Credit & Commerce International SA* v *Aboody* [1990] 1 QB 923 the Court of Appeal held that this applied not only where reliance is placed on the presumption of undue influence, but also where actual undue influence is established. Slade LJ said that "... the House of Lords, in referring in *National Westminster Bank plc* v *Morgan* [1985] AC 686 to disadvantage, was clearly not treating the overbearing of a person's will as being in itself a disadvantage in the relevant sense" (at p. 965).

In *Aboody* the wife had established that, as a result of undue influence by her husband, she had entered into a number of charges and guarantees affecting the matrimonial home, of which she was sole owner, to secure liabilities of the family company to the bank. However, the Court of Appeal found that, on balance, a manifest disadvantage had not been shown by the wife. Slade LJ said (at p. 965):

"Whenever a guarantee or charge is given, there is always the risk that the guarantee may be called in or the charge enforced. Therefore ... the question whether the assumption of such a risk is manifestly disadvantageous to the giver must depend on the balance of two factors, namely (a) the seriousness of the risk of enforcement to the giver, in practical terms, and (b) the benefits gained by the giver in accepting the risk."

In the circumstances of the case, while there were substantial liabilities and the risk of the loss of the family home to be put into the balance on the debit side, the company was the family business and the sole or principal means of support of the husband and wife. The company might have collapsed with or without the facilities covered by the various transactions, but at least these facilities gave it some hope of survival. If it had survived, the potential benefits to the wife would have been substantial.

In *Woodstead Finance Ltd* v *Petrou* [1986] Fin LR 158 an advance of £25,000 to the husband for six months at a rate of interest equivalent to 42 per cent was secured by a legal charge on the wife's property. It was held that even if undue influence had been established the transaction was not, on the evidence before the court, manifestly disadvantageous to the wife. The terms of the loan were the normal terms on which finance could be obtained given the acute financial stringency under which the spouses were labouring. The disadvantages were of a kind referable to the acute financial crisis of the spouses following possession proceedings commenced by a bank following default under a previous mortgage. The court also accepted that even if a chargor or guarantor is already subject to potential liabilities under previous transactions which expose him or her to the risk of penury or bankruptcy, the substantial increase of those liabilities is nevertheless capable of constituting a manifest disadvantage - though it will not necessarily do so. It depends on the circumstances of the case.

In *Aboody* Slade LJ accepted that the overall disadvantageous nature of a transaction cannot be said to be manifest if it emerges only after a fine and close evaluation of its various beneficial and detrimental features. It must be obvious. He also accepted that the nature of a transaction has to be judged in the circumstances subsisting at the date of the transaction, though subsequent events may conceivably throw light on what could reasonably have been foreseen at that date. In *Midland Bank plc* v *Phillips* [1986] The Times 28 March, Ralph Gibson LJ said that the court must look primarily at the terms of the transaction into which the parties have entered, but it also looks at what has happened as an example, if the result is shown fairly to flow from the transaction, of what might happen having made such an arrangement.

### (f) Negligence on the part of the mortgagee

A spouse who signs a mortgage or guarantee in favour of a bank may be able to recover damages if there was negligence on the part of the bank in relation to the execution of the document. It seems that a bank has no general obligation to explain the legal effect of a mortgage or guarantee to a non-customer who is asked to sign such a document (*O'Hara* v *Allied Irish Bank Ltd* [1985] BCLC 52). Whether a bank has such an obligation towards a customer seems uncertain, but it is clear that if a bank does explain to a customer the legal nature and effect of a mortgage or guarantee in favour of the bank the customer may be entitled to damages if the bank negligently misstates the effect of the mortgage (*Cornish* v *Midland Bank plc* [1985] 3 All ER 513). In *Cornish* v *Midland Bank plc* it was found that the bank's employees had failed to make clear to the wife that the mortgage was worded so as to secure any future borrowings that the bank might allow the husband. The statement that the mortgage was "just like a building society mortgage" was misleading for a wife who believed she was merely securing a temporary loan of up to £2,000 for renovation of the house which was vested in joint names. The mortgage was not set aside as there was no undue influence by or on behalf of the bank, but the wife recovered damages from the bank for the financial loss flowing from the negligent advice. In *Perry* v *Midland Bank plc* [1987] Fin LR 236 it was held that the bank manager had failed to explain adequately to a wife the effect of a charge and in particular did not make it clear to her that the charge attached to her beneficial interest in the property as well as to that of her husband. Again, the mortgage was not set aside as the husband had not acted as the agent of the bank and the bank had no notice of undue influence by him. Although the wife was thus entitled to damages the order for possession was upheld, notwithstanding that Fox LJ thought that the bank might be reluctant to enforce the order against the wife and daughter in view of the effect this would have on the damages recoverable.

In *Barclays Bank plc* v *O'Brien* [1992] 3 WLR 593 Scott LJ noted that a creditor will often find itself in a position of having to explain a mortgage transaction to a proposed surety if an unimpeachable security is to be obtained (see (*d*) above). He said (at p. 621):

"The creditor should not, in my opinion, be taken in so doing to have assumed a duty of care. If the surety is a customer or if the creditor assumes the role of adviser, it may be that the creditor will be found to have owed a contractual or tortious duty of care to the surety. *Midland Bank plc* v *Perry* ... is an example. But if there is no more than that the creditor, in an attempt to satisfy itself that the surety properly understands the proposed transaction and that the transaction will not subsequently be impeachable, offers an explanation of the transaction and of the security document, I do not think that the creditor should be taken to have assumed a tortious duty of care. If the explanation was inadequate, the security might not be enforceable but it would not follow that liability in damages would attach. As I have already observed, equity ought not to place creditors in the dilemma of having to choose between, on the one hand, risking the security being unenforceable, and, on the other hand, undertaking a duty of care."

### (g) Non-disclosure
A mortgagee such as a bank is under no general duty of disclosure except with regard to "anything that might not naturally be expected to take place between the parties ..." (*Hamilton* v *Watson* (1845) 12 C & F 109). In *Lloyds Bank plc* v *Egremont* [1990] 2 FLR 351 the wife had joined the husband in signing the bank's standard form of charge over the matrimonial home, which was in their joint names, for all monies due and owing from the husband as principal and surety. The Court of Appeal rejected the argument that the bank was under a duty to disclose to her the existence of a guarantee given by the husband to the bank in respect of a business overdraft, the fact that the charge was unlimited in scope and duration and would continue as security even after she and her husband had separated. There was nothing "in the least unusual about the transactions". On the contrary, they were "all transactions of the commonest business kind, in which there was nothing that [the wife] might not naturally expect" (*per* Lloyd LJ at p. 354).

## 4. The equity of exoneration
Where there is a charge on property jointly owned, to secure the debts of one only of the joint owners, the other joint owner, being in the position of a surety, is not only entitled to be indemnified by the debtor, but also to have the secured debt discharged as far as possible out of the equitable interest of the debtor to the exoneration of his or her own equitable interest. The effect of the equity of exoneration in such a case is to enhance the proprietary interest of the surety. This will be important where the debtor has become bankrupt - therefore the surety's personal right of indemnity is likely to be of limited value (see Scott J *In re Pittortou (A Bankrupt)* [1985] 1 WLR 58 at p. 61 and *In re A Debtor, ex p. Marley* v *Trustee of the Property of the Debtor* [1976] 2 All ER 1010). However, the equity of exoneration depends upon the presumed intention of the parties and will not apply if the circumstances of the case do not justify the inference that it was the joint intention of the mortgagors that the burden of the secured indebtedness should fall primarily on the share of the debtor. (See *In re Pittortou* and *In re Woodstock (A Bankrupt)* (unreported) 19 November 1979.)

# Chapter 4

# Occupation of the home

## 1. The matrimonial home

The term "matrimonial home" is used to refer to a dwelling-house or other accommodation which is or has been occupied by spouses jointly as their home. When accommodation occupied by one spouse has never been occupied by the other spouse, it is not to be regarded as a "matrimonial home". In such circumstances the occupying spouse is entitled to protection from incursion by the other into that accommodation: *Nanda* v *Nanda* [1967] 3 All ER 401. In *Syed* v *Syed* (1981) 1 FLR 129, French J held that a wife who, on returning from a visit to Pakistan, found her husband living with his Italian mistress in a house which he had bought during her absence, was not entitled to an order directing her husband to let her live in part of the house. The position might have been otherwise had the court been able to imply that she had an occupational licence granted by the husband. This was not possible on the evidence and, it is submitted, will generally be difficult to show. (For the position in relation to third parties, see *Jolliffe* v *Willmett & Co* [1971] 1 All ER 478.)

The basic function of a matrimonial home is to provide a place for the spouses and their family to live in, and the question of occupation is, therefore, of fundamental importance. This is not to underestimate the importance of such matters as ownership, or responsibility for the expenses of the home, which are, in any event, inextricably bound up with the question of occupation. However, the importance of occupation is such as to justify a modification of the general principles relating to such matters in certain circumstances.

Occupation of the matrimonial home has an "internal" and an "external" aspect. The "internal" aspect concerns the relationship between the spouses themselves, while the "external" aspect concerns the relationship between the spouses, or even one of them on the one hand, and some third party, such as a purchaser, mortgagee or other creditor on the other.

The "internal" aspect is unlikely to cause difficulty until the marriage itself has begun to run into difficulty. When that happens it may become impossible for the spouses to live together, and one of two main issues will generally emerge depending on the circumstances and, in particular, on the wishes of the parties. First, where both spouses wish to continue living in the matrimonial home the court may have to decide, in effect, which of the spouses shall be allowed exclusive occupation of the home unless the home is large enough to permit both to occupy separate parts. Secondly, where only one spouse wishes to continue living in the matrimonial home, the court may be called upon to decide in effect whether that person, who is generally in occupation, shall be protected, or a sale ordered at the instance of the other spouse.

Although these are generally the underlying issues they may arise in a variety of forms depending upon who is in occupation and in whom the ownership of the home is vested. Thus, where both spouses remain in occupation the court may be asked to order one of them to leave, thereby giving the other exclusive occupation. Where one spouse has been forced to leave the matrimonial home the court may be asked to restore that spouse to occupation which, if it is to be effective, means also ordering the other spouse to leave. Where a spouse has been forced to leave once, it is likely to happen again, so that in such circumstances exclusive possession is the only realistic possession. Where one spouse has left of his or her own accord the court may be asked to safeguard the occupation of the other spouse against the attempts of the former to return, but more often than not, against efforts to sell or otherwise deal with the property.

The "external" aspect of occupation may well involve problems even in the absence of marital difficulties when the family unit encounters economic difficulties such as arise in an extreme form on the bankruptcy of one of the spouses. However, not only are such difficulties more likely to arise on the breakdown of a marriage, but they are likely to arise in a more acute form, for they frequently raise difficult questions as to the extent to which third parties should be affected by the matrimonial difficulties of the parties. In such circumstances one spouse is particularly likely to default in the discharge of outgoings on the matrimonial home, thus making it necessary for the third parties to take steps to enforce payment, thereby placing occupation of the home in jeopardy.

In dealing with these problems it is necessary to consider the rights of occupation which may exist in relation to a matrimonial home and the different kinds of proceedings in which the problems may arise.

## 2. Rights of occupation

### (a) The different kinds of rights of occupation

Rights of occupation in relation to a matrimonial home fall into three categories. First, rights of occupation may exist as an incident of ownership of the matrimonial home or an interest in it, and may conveniently be referred to as proprietary rights of occupation. Secondly, personal rights of occupation may arise at common law from the status of marriage. Thirdly, statutory rights of occupation arise in certain circumstances under the Matrimonial Homes Act 1983. At any given time a spouse may have more than one kind of right of occupation of the matrimonial home.

*(b) Proprietary rights of occupation*
Ownership of the matrimonial home gives a spouse the same proprietary right of occupation as any other owner of property. In certain circumstances, however, such a proprietary right may be modified to give effect to a personal right of occupation arising from the status of marriage. Where the matrimonial home is owned jointly by the spouses they both have the same proprietary rights of occupation as any other co-owners. (See *Bull* v *Bull* [1955] 1 QB 234 approved in *Williams & Glyn's Bank Ltd* v *Boland* [1981] AC 487 *per* Lord Wilberforce at p. 507 and *per* Lord Scarman at p. 510; *Cobb* v *Cobb* [1955] 1 WLR 731; *Gurasz* v *Gurasz* [1970] P 11; *Barclay* v *Barclay* [1970] 2 QB 677.) Thus in such cases a proprietary right is not a right to exclusive possession, and neither can turn the other out. Where property is jointly owned it is held on trust for sale, and if there is no agreement as to occupation the property must generally be sold unless it was acquired for a specific purpose which can still be achieved, or, possibly, if one co-owner is acting in bad faith. However, the acquisition of a dwelling-house will generally be regarded as such a specific purpose, and its sale may be postponed to give effect to the personal right of occupation of one of the spouses (see Chapter 6). In such circumstances a spouse who remains in occupation will be enjoying both a proprietary right and a personal right of occupation while the proprietary right of the other spouse is to that extent modified.

A spouse entitled to a proprietary right of occupation is unlikely to have difficulty in enforcing that right against a third party where the legal estate is vested in that spouse either alone or jointly with the other spouse. Any dealing with the legal estate will have to be effected by that spouse or will require his or her concurrence. However, where the legal estate is not so vested, and the right of occupation arises merely from a beneficial interest, a spouse will be vulnerable to a dealing with the legal estate. The enforceability of the proprietary right of occupation will depend upon whether a third party is bound by the beneficial interest (see Chapter 3), though as will be seen it may be possible to rely on the statutory right of occupation (see Part 3, page 88).

*(c) Personal rights of occupation*
At common law two basic concepts flow from the status of marriage - (1) the right and duty of the spouses to live together, and (2) the duty of the husband to maintain his wife. Both concepts are of importance in relation to the occupation of the matrimonial home. The mutual obligation of the spouses to live together gives each spouse a personal right to share the occupation of the matrimonial home irrespective of ownership. This personal right will, however, be lost by misconduct which terminates the right to consortium. The discharge of the obligation to maintain involves the provision of a suitable home where the spouses will live together. A wife has no separate right to maintenance in a separate home unless she can justify living apart from her husband (see Chapter 16). Where the spouses have separated and the wife is left in occupation of the matrimonial home, she has a personal right to remain there, or to be provided with other accommodation, unless she has forfeited her right to be maintained by her misconduct. (See generally *National Provincial Bank Ltd* v *Ainsworth* [1965] AC 1175.) A husband, on the other hand, appears to have no

87

corresponding right against his wife (*Rawlings* v *Rawlings* [1964] P 398). But see *Bedson* v *Bedson* [1965] 2 QB 666, where a husband was protected. In *Morris* v *Tarrant* [1971] 2 QB 143 it was said that he is not a trespasser until the court has ordered him to go or until a decree absolute.

The wife's personal right of occupation does not generally entitle her to exclusive possession. The mere fact that a husband has deserted his wife will not entitle her to exclude him, for he is entitled to return at any time and terminate his desertion, though the position may be different after the wife has obtained a decree of judicial separation. This seems to have been envisaged by Lord Upjohn in *National Provincial Bank Ltd* v *Ainsworth* [1965] AC 1175 at p. 1232 when he said: "Furthermore (at all events until a decree of judicial separation) the wife's occupancy is not exclusive against the deserting husband for he can at any moment return and then resume the role of occupier without leave of the wife." On the other hand, where the husband has not merely deserted his wife, but has also committed adultery or treated her with cruelty, then she may be able to prevent his return as this may be essential to protect her right to remain in occupation and to protect the position of the children. This was envisaged by Lord Denning in *Bendall* v *MacWhirter* [1952] 2 QB 466 at p. 477 and there appears to be nothing inconsistent with this in the views of the House of Lords in *National Provincial Bank Ltd* v *Ainsworth*. Indeed in *Gurasz* v *Gurasz* [1970] P 11 the Court of Appeal, of which Lord Denning was a member, went so far as to exclude a husband who had not left the matrimonial home, and restored to occupation the wife who had left. Only Lord Denning elaborated on the court's powers at common law. He said (at p. 16):

"Some features of family life are elemental in our society. One is that it is the husband's duty to provide his wife with a roof over her head: and the children too. So long as the wife behaves herself she is entitled to remain in the matrimonial home. The husband is not at liberty to turn her out of it, neither by virtue of his command, nor by force of his conduct. If he should seek to get rid of her, the court will restrain him. If he should succeed in making her go the court will restore her. In an extreme case, if his conduct is so outrageous as to make it impossible for them to live together, the court will order him to go out and leave her there."

He went on to say that the court would protect the wife's personal right irrespective of whether the matrimonial home was in her name, her husband's name or their joint names.

Whatever the extent of the wife's personal right of occupation may be, it is not of unlimited duration. In *National Provincial Bank* v *Ainsworth* [1965] AC 1175 at p.1233 Lord Upjohn emphasised that "the right to remain may change overnight by the act or behaviour of either spouse". Lord Wilberforce said that the decision whether to give possession or not will be based on a consideration of what may be called the material circumstances. He said (at p. 1247):

"These include such matters as whether the husband can provide alternative accommodation, and, if so whether such accommodation is suitable having regard to the estate and condition of the spouses: whether the husband's conduct amounts to desertion, whether the conduct of the wife has been such as to deprive her of any of her rights against her husband. And the order to be made must be fashioned accordingly: it may be that the wife should leave immediately or after a certain period: it may be subject to revision on a change of circumstances."

He further emphasised that the rights are at no time definitive, but provisional, and subject to review at any time according to changes in the matrimonial circumstances and the conduct of the parties.

A wife will not be refused protection in appropriate cases even though she is receiving maintenance (see *Jones* v *Jones* [1971] 1 WLR 396) but, on the other hand, a wife will not continue to receive protection indefinitely merely because she is blameless. In any event it is frequently unrealistic to regard fault as one-sided, as was recognised by the Court of Appeal in *Jackson* v *Jackson* [1971] 1 WLR 1593. In that case Megaw LJ said (at pp. 1546-1547) that:

"... the husband's duty at common law is not in all circumstances inevitably and necessarily to provide the wife with a roof over her head, whether in the old matrimonial home or in some other building, in all cases where it can be said that the wife has behaved herself - in the sense that she has not been guilty of any matrimonial offence."

In his view,

"... that common law duty is one which is subject to limitation. It depends on the other facts of the individual case, not merely the way in which the wife has behaved. It depends upon what is equitable or reasonable in the circumstances of the particular case subject, it may be, to a general *prima facie* principle that the wife is entitled to remain in the matrimonial home."

Her right is in any event terminated on divorce (*Vaughan* v *Vaughan* [1953] 1 QB 762). Attempts were made from 1952 onwards to protect the deserted wife's right to remain in the matrimonial home against third parties, but in *National Provincial Bank Ltd* v *Ainsworth* [1965] AC 1175 the House of Lords held that the deserted wife's right was of a personal nature and not such as to bind third parties. As a result of that decision Parliament intervened in the shape of the Matrimonial Homes Act 1967. The Act has reduced the importance of the wife's personal right of occupation, for it became generally more advantageous to rely on the Act where this was possible in view of the greater protection afforded against third parties. However, the personal right of occupation still remains important in certain situations not covered by the Act.

*(d) Statutory rights of occupation*
Although the Matrimonial Homes Act 1967 was passed principally as a result of the situation revealed in *National Provincial Bank Ltd* v *Ainsworth*, it was not limited to the particular problem which provided the impetus for its enactment. The Act as amended has now been consolidated in the Matrimonial Homes Act 1983.

## 3. Rights of occupation under the Matrimonial Homes Act 1983

*(a) The circumstances in which the Act confers rights of occupation*
Where one spouse ("the entitled spouse") is entitled to occupy a dwelling-house by virtue of a beneficial estate or interest or contract, or by virtue of any enactment

giving him or her the right to remain in occupation, and the other spouse ("the non-entitled spouse") is not so entitled, the Act gives the latter certain "statutory rights of occupation" (s.1(1)). The Act confers no rights of occupation where both spouses already have proprietary rights of occupation arising from beneficial interests in the matrimonial home, and the legal estate in fee simple or a legal term of years absolute is vested in their joint names (*Gurasz* v *Gurasz* [1970] P 11). However, it is specifically provided that a spouse who has only an equitable interest in the home or in the proceeds of sale thereof, and in whom the legal estate is not vested, is to be treated as a "non-entitled spouse" even though the equitable interest gives rise to a right of occupation. (This provision was introduced by Matrimonial Proceedings and Property Act 1970, s.38.) Thus, where the legal estate in the home is vested in one spouse, the other will have statutory rights of occupation under the Act in addition to any right of occupation he or she may have arising from an equitable interest. Where the legal estate is held by trustees on trust for one spouse who is thus entitled to occupy only by virtue of his or her equitable beneficial interest, the other spouse is entitled to the statutory rights of occupation. (This was made clear by the amendments made by Matrimonial Homes and Property Act 1981. Where the legal estate is held by a spouse as a trustee or nominee with no beneficial interest, then no statutory rights of occupation are conferred on the other spouse thereby.)

The Act applies as between a husband and wife notwithstanding that the marriage in question was entered into under a law which permits polygamy, whether or not either party to the marriage in question has for the time being any spouse additional to the other party (s.10(2)).

The Act does not apply to a dwelling-house which has at no time been a matrimonial home of the spouses in question. (s.1(10). See *Whittingham* v *Whittingham* [1979] Fam 9). The expression "dwelling-house" includes any building or part of a building which is occupied as a dwelling, and any yard, garden, garage or outhouse belonging to the dwelling-house and occupied therewith (s.10(1)).

### (b) The statutory rights of occupation

Under s.1(1) the statutory rights of occupation given to the "non-entitled spouse" are:
  (a)  if in occupation, a right not to be evicted or excluded from the dwelling-house or any part thereof by the other spouse except with leave of the court given by an order under s.1 of the Act;
  (b)  if not in occupation, a right with the leave of the court so given to enter into and occupy the dwelling-house.

The court is the High Court or a county court, irrespective of the net annual value of the dwelling-house for rating (s.1(9)). In *Rutherford* v *Rutherford* [1970] 1 WLR 1479 Foster J took the view that a spouse who was not in occupation had no right of occupation under the Act unless and until leave of the court had been obtained. This view was overruled by the Court of Appeal in *Watts* v *Waller* [1973] 1 QB 153 where it was held that a non-entitled spouse out of occupation nevertheless has a conditional right of occupation which is capable of being protected in the manner prescribed by the Act and considered below, but which cannot be enforced until leave is obtained.

*(c) The duration of the rights of occupation*

The rights of occupation under the Act continue only so long as the marriage subsists, and so long as the entitled spouse remains entitled to occupy by virtue of an estate, interest, contract or enactment. Accordingly, they will come to an end on the death of the entitled spouse, or on the termination of the marriage by divorce or annulment unless in the event of a matrimonial dispute or estrangement the court sees fit to direct otherwise by an order under s.1 of the Act during the subsistence of the marriage (ss.1(10) and 2(4)). A spouse entitled to rights of occupation under the Act may by a release in writing release those rights, or release them as regards part only of the dwelling-house affected by them (s.6(1)).

So long as one spouse has rights of occupation under the Act, either of the spouses may apply to the court for an order (a) declaring, enforcing, restricting or terminating those rights, or (b) prohibiting, suspending or restricting the exercise by either spouse of the right to occupy the dwelling-house, or (c) requiring either spouse to permit the exercise by the other of that right (s.1(2)). On an application for any such order the court may make such order as it thinks just and reasonable having regard to the conduct of the spouses in relation to each other and otherwise, to their respective needs and financial resources, to the needs of any children and to all the circumstances of the case (s. 1(3). See further Chapter 5). In particular it may:

(a) except part of the dwelling-house from a spouse's rights of occupation (and in particular a part used wholly or mainly for or in connection with the trade, business or profession of the other spouse);

(b) order a spouse occupying the dwelling-house or any part thereof by virtue of the Act to make periodical payments to the other in respect of the occupation;

(c) impose on either spouse obligations as to the repair and maintenance of the dwelling-house or the discharge of any liabilities in respect of the dwelling-house.

In so far as an order has a continuing effect it may be limited so as to have effect for a period specified in the order or until further order (s.1(4)).

It is only the statutory rights of occupation conferred by the Act which can be declared, enforced, restricted or terminated. Orders declaring or enforcing rights of occupation will generally be sought by the non-entitled spouse, while orders restricting or terminating such rights are more likely to be sought by the entitled spouse. Originally the entitled spouse's proprietary rights of occupation could only be "regulated". In *Tarr* v *Tarr* [1973] AC 254 the House of Lords held that the word "regulate" was not apt to include a power to "prohibit" the exercise by the entitled spouse of his or her proprietary right of occupation. Accordingly it did not enable the court to give the non-entitled spouse exclusive occupation of the dwelling-house by excluding the entitled spouse even for a limited period. However, this can now be achieved as a result of s.3 of the Domestic Violence and Matrimonial Proceedings Act 1976 which replaced the power to "regulate" with the power of "prohibiting, suspending or restricting" the proprietary rights of occupation (see now s.1(2)). Thus where the beneficial interests in the home are jointly owned the court can by appropriate orders under s.1(2) give exclusive possession to one co-owner even though under the general principles of property law a co-owner has no right to exclusive possession. On the other hand, the court may also require the non-entitled spouse to allow the entitled spouse to exercise his or her proprietary right of occupation if this is more appropriate. This can be accompanied by an order restricting or terminating the statutory rights of occupation of the non-entitled spouse. (In *Kalsi* v *Kalsi* [1991] The Times 25 November the Court of Appeal held that it is not open to the court in proceedings under the 1983 Act to join other parties who were not affected by the Act, still less to grant relief against them when they were not parties.)

*(d) Protection of the statutory rights of occupation*
The protection of the statutory rights of occupation is dealt with in two stages. First, where one spouse is entitled to occupy a dwelling-house by virtue of a beneficial interest, then, by s.2(1), the other spouse's rights of occupation are declared to be a charge on that estate or interest having a like priority as if it were an equitable interest created at whichever is the latest of the following dates:
(a)   the date when the entitled spouse acquired the estate or interest;
(b)   the date of the marriage; and
(c)   the commencement of the 1967 Act, that is 1 January 1968.
If, at any time when a spouse's rights of occupation are a charge on an interest of the other spouse under a trust, there are apart from either of the spouses, no persons, living or unborn, who are or could become beneficiaries under the trust, then those rights are also a charge on the estate or interest of the trustees for the other spouse, having the like priority as if it were an equitable interest created (under powers overriding the trusts) on the date when it arises (s.2(2)).

Secondly, provision is made for a charge to be protected by registration in the method appropriate to unregistered and registered land as the case may be. Where the title to the legal estate in the matrimonial home is not registered, the non-entitled spouse's charge is registrable as a class F land charge, and will be void as against a purchaser of the land charged therewith or of any interest in such land unless so registered before the completion of the purchase (Land Charges Act 1972, ss.2(7) and 4(8)). Where the title to the legal estate in the matrimonial home is registered under the Land Registration Acts the statutory rights of occupation are not an overriding interest notwithstanding that the non-entitled spouse is in occupation. The charge must be protected by means of a notice (Matrimonial Homes Act 1983, s.2(8)).

It has been noted above that where the entitled spouse is entitled to occupy by virtue of a beneficial interest under a trust, the statutory rights of occupation of the non-entitled spouse are not only a charge on the beneficial interest of the entitled spouse, but also a charge on the estate or interest of the trustees (Matrimonial Homes Act 1983 s.2(2)). It is expressly provided that a charge is not registrable by notice or as a class F land charge unless it is a charge on a legal estate (s.2(11)). This means that where the legal estate in the matrimonial home is held by trustees on trust for the entitled spouse alone it is the charge on the legal estate which must be protected by entry of a class F land charge against the trustees or a notice on the title of which the trustees are the registered proprietors.

In order to obtain protection under these provisions it is essential to know whether or not the title to the matrimonial home is registered under the Land Registration Acts - if it is, the registration of a class F land charge will be ineffective. In cases of doubt where the co-operation of the entitled spouse (or the trustees) is not forthcoming, an application should be made to the Chief Land Registrar for an official search in the index map and parcels index. The certificate issued will state whether or not the title to the property is registered.

Where the title to the matrimonial home is not registered, a class F land charge must be registered in the proper names of the entitled spouse or the trustees as the case may be. If there is registration in "what may fairly be described as a version of the full names" of the estate owner, "albeit not a version which is bound to be discovered on a search in the correct full names" it is "not a nullity against someone who does not search at all, or who ... searches in the wrong name" (*per* Russell LJ in *Oak Co-operative Building Society* v *Blackburn* [1968] Ch 730 at p. 743). However, such a registration will be ineffective against a purchaser who applies for an official search in the correct names and obtains a nil certificate (Land Charges Act 1972, s.10(4). See *Diligent Finance Co Ltd* v *Alleyne* (1972) 23 P & CR 346). In the absence of any evidence to the contrary it may be assumed that the proper name of a person is that in which the conveyancing documents have been taken (*Diligent Finance Co Ltd* v *Alleyne*).

It has already been noted that it was held in *Watts* v *Waller* [1973] 1 QB 153 that a spouse who is not in occupation of the matrimonial home nevertheless has a conditional right of occupation which, although it cannot be enforced without leave of the court, is capable of protection by registration in the appropriate manner. In other words it is not necessary to obtain leave of the court before taking advantage of the prescribed methods of protection. However, in *Barnett* v *Hassett* [1981] 1 WLR 1385 it was held that where a husband had no intention of entering or occupying the matrimonial home it was a misuse of the Matrimonial Homes Act 1967 for him to register a class F land charge affecting the property in order to enable him to freeze the assets of his wife in pursuit of a claim against her for an alleged breach of contract. The registration was set aside.

Where a spouse is entitled to statutory rights of occupation in each of two or more dwelling-houses, only one of the charges to which that spouse is so entitled can be registered at any one time. If a second charge is registered, the Registrar must cancel the registration of the charge which was first registered (Matrimonial Homes Act 1983, s.3).

*(e) The effect of a protected charge*
Where statutory rights of occupation are a charge on the estate or interest of the entitled spouse or of the trustees for the entitled spouse, then s.2(5) provides that any order under s.1 of the Act declaring, enforcing, restricting or terminating those rights or prohibiting, suspending or restricting the exercise by either spouse of the right to occupy the dwelling-house has the same effect against persons deriving title under the entitled spouse or under the trustees and affected by the charge as it has against that spouse unless a contrary intention appears. Thus where the non-entitled spouse has obtained an order declaring his or her statutory right to occupy and prohibiting, suspending or restricting the exercise by the entitled spouse of his or her right to occupy, that order will be effective against a purchaser from the entitled spouse - though the purchaser will be entitled to apply for an order under s.1 termi-

nating the statutory rights of occupation and removing the prohibition, suspension or restriction previously imposed on the proprietary rights of occupation. Where no order under s.1 has been made before the disposition of the home by the entitled spouse to a purchaser on whom the statutory rights are binding, the non-entitled spouse may apply, as he or she could have done before the disposition, for an order under s.1. Thus in *Kaur* v *Gill* [1988] Fam 110 it was held that a non-entitled wife who was not in occupation of the former matrimonial home could apply under s.1 for an order declaring her right to occupy the property and for an order prohibiting the purchaser from exercising any rights to occupy the property until further order. It is, of course, equally open to the purchaser to apply at any time for an order determining the non-entitled spouse's statutory rights of occupation.

On an application for an order under s.1 after disposition of the home, the court must have regard to the factors set out in subsection (3), i.e. to the conduct of the spouses in relation to each other and otherwise, to their respective needs and financial resources, to the needs of any children and to all the circumstances of the case. In *Kaur* v *Gill* [1988] Fam 110 the majority of the Court of Appeal (Dillon and Bingham LJJ) held that the "circumstances of the case" included the circumstances of the purchaser as well as of the husband and wife. Bingham LJ thought that "one would not expect the husband to be able, by disposing of the property to a third party with notice, to weaken or undermine the rights or claims which the wife could assert against him if there had been no disposition" (at p. 117). However, the Act clearly contemplated application to the court by a purchaser for an order restricting or terminating a wife's rights of occupation. It also authorised the court to order a wife in occupation of the property to make payments to a purchaser and to allocate the burden of maintenance and repair between the wife and a third party. In making such order as it thought "just and reasonable" to govern these matters, the court must have regard to the respective ability of the parties, including the third party purchaser, to pay and to their respective needs. Moreover, the width of the language used - "all the circumstances of the case" - was such that the position and needs of the third party could not properly be put on one side as something which it was simply not permissible to consider. (Contrast *Kalsi* v *Kalsi* [1991] The Times 25 November where the husband's brothers were not affected by the provisions of the Act.)

On the other hand, Bingham LJ acknowledged that the claims of a third party buying with actual or constructive notice of a wife's rights will ordinarily carry little weight. Dillon LJ had "no doubt that the fact that a purchaser has constructive, or actual, notice of a wife's claim to rights of occupation and buys a property subject to that claim is, of itself, a highly material factor for the court to consider. Moreover, if the evidence was that the purchaser was buying by way of collusion with a husband to evict a wife, any other circumstances of merit on the purchaser's side might carry little weight in the balance" (at p. 116). In *Kaur* v *Gill* the purchaser was a blind man who bought the house so that he and his wife could live there as it was smaller and more convenient than his existing property. He did not have actual notice of the vendor's wife's rights. His solicitor had completed the purchase in reliance on a telephone search of the register immediately before the wife's application to register the notice against the title was received in the registry. This did not give the priority protection for the purchaser's registration which would have been obtained through an official certificate of search. The purchaser accordingly had constructive notice. It was accepted by the wife that if the judge had been entitled to take into account the purchaser's circumstances the judge's decision refusing the wife's application could not be challenged.

In his dissenting judgment, Sir Denys Buckley accepted that the effect of s.2(5)(b) of the Act was probably that a successor in title of the husband could apply for an order under s.1(2) against the wife. However, he suggested that it was directed to ensuring that on an application for an order under s.1 by a successor in title to a spouse who is not the spouse whose rights of occupation are protected under s.2(1), that successor shall be in neither a better nor a worse position than the spouse from whom he derives title would be in if he still owned the house. He said (at p. 121):

> "The wealth or impecuniosity of any purchaser for value or other disponee of the husband, or the state of the disponee's family and his domestic needs are, in my opinion, irrelevant to the considerations to which s.1(3) requires the court to pay regard. If this were not so, the husband could by means of a disposition of the house to a disponee with a much higher degree of economic and social need than the wife's drastically reduce the benefit secured to the wife by the charge, or even destroy it altogether. I cannot think that this would accord with intention of Parliament."

Where a leasehold estate which is subject to a charge under the Act is surrendered so as to merge in the freehold or superior leasehold reversion, then the surrender will take effect subject to the charge, provided that it has been protected in the appropriate manner, or where the surrender is not for value. This means that the person entitled to the superior interest will be bound by the statutory rights of occupation for so long as the surrendered interest would have endured but for the surrender unless, of course, they are determined under the provisions of the Act (s.2(4)).

Where the estate or interest of the entitled spouse (or of trustees for the entitled spouse) is subject to a mortgage made expressly for securing a current account or other further advances, the registration of a class F land charge will not of itself prevent subsequent further advances having priority. The mortgagee will be affected by the charge in relation to such further advances only if he actually makes a search in the land charges register or otherwise has notice of it. Where such a mortgage exists the non-entitled spouse may well be advised to give express notice to the mortgagee as well as registering a class F land charge (s.2(10) and see Law of Property Act 1925, s.94).

Under the Act in its original form a charge was void against the trustee in bankruptcy of the entitled spouse even though it was protected in the appropriate manner (s.2(7)). This was reversed by the Insolvency Act 1985, s.171(2). The present position is therefore that notwithstanding the bankruptcy of the "entitled spouse", the charge constituted by the statutory rights of occupation of the "non-entitled spouse" continues to subsist and, subject to the provisions of the Matrimonial Homes Act 1983, to bind the trustee of the bankrupt's estate and persons deriving title under the trustee. Accordingly, in order to obtain possession of the dwelling-house it will be necessary for the trustee to apply for an order under s.1(2) of the 1983 Act. This he is entitled to do by virtue of s.2(5)(b) of the Act which applies s.1(2) to any person deriving title under the entitled spouse. However, any application for an order under s.1 of the 1983 Act in this context must be made to the court having jurisdiction in relation to the bankruptcy (see Insolvency Act 1985, s.171(2) — now Insolvency Act 1986, s.336(2)). On such an application the court must make such order as it thinks just and reasonable having regard to the facts set out in s.336(4) of the Insolvency Act 1986 (see Chapter 8).

*(f) The "statutory rights" and purchasers*
The provisions of s.2(1) of the Act which make the charge of a non-entitled spouse an equitable interest are sufficient to secure priority for the charge over any interest, legal or equitable, subsequently acquired otherwise than for value. (See further *Wolstenholme & Cherry's Conveyancing Statutes* (13th ed) Vol. 2 p. 156). However, the provisions of s.2(8) of the Act and s.2 of the Land Charges Act 1972 are crucial in relation to priority over any interest, legal or equitable, subsequently acquired by a purchaser. In these circumstances the date of registration of a class F land charge, or the entry of a notice as appropriate, is of vital importance.

Where the statutory rights of occupation are a charge on the estate or interest of the entitled spouse or the trustees for the entitled spouse in the matrimonial home the title to which is not registered, then that charge will be void against a purchaser of the property or any interest therein unless protected by the registration of a class F land charge before completion of the purchase (Land Charges Act 1972, ss.2(7) and 4(8)). Moreover, a purchaser who has obtained an official certificate of search against the entitled spouse, or the trustees for the entitled spouse, will not be affected by the registration of a class F land charge after the date of the certificate, but before the date of the completion of the purchase, provided completion takes place before the end of the fifteenth working day after the date of the certificate (Land Charges Act 1972, s.11(5) - unless registered in pursuance of a priority notice).

Where the title to the estate of the entitled spouse (or of the trustees for the entitled spouse, as the case may be) in the matrimonial home is registered under the Land Registration Acts, a purchaser will not be bound by the charge arising from the statutory rights of occupation unless it is protected in the appropriate manner before the date of registration of the transfer (LRA 1925, ss.20(1) and 23(1)). A purchaser of registered land is also further protected by the provision that if he has obtained an official search certificate he will not be affected by any entry in the register made after the date of the certificate, but before the date of registration of the transfer, provided completion and registration are effected within 30 working days of the date of the search certificate (The Land Registration (Official Searches) Rules 1988, r.2(1)). (See *Watts* v *Waller* [1973] 1 QB 153 where the documents were not lodged within the priority period.)

Accordingly, in order to bind a purchaser the charge must be protected in the appropriate manner not only before the completion of the purchase, but also before the issue of an official search certificate to a purchaser who completes his purchase and, in the case of registered land, lodges the transfer for registration, within the period of protection afforded by that certificate. On the other hand, where a charge is protected in the appropriate manner before that time it will bind a purchaser unless it is released before completion of the purchase. The only exception to this appears to be in relation to unregistered land where, through an error, a search certificate fails to reveal the entry of a class F land charge. In that event, assuming that the purchaser has searched in the proper name of the entitled spouse, or the trustees for the entitled spouse, he will be entitled to rely on that certificate and the charge will not be binding on him if he completes the purchase within 15 working days (LCA 1972, s.10(4)). The spouse entitled to the charge will then be left with a claim for compensation against the Land Registry. In the case of registered land it seems that the entry of a notice will be effective even though, through error, it is not revealed in an official search certificate. In that event it is the purchaser, on whom the charge is binding, who is left to seek compensation from the Land Registry (*Parkash* v *Irani Finance Ltd* [1970] 1 Ch 101).

A conveyance or transfer of the legal estate in a dwelling-house is almost inevitably preceded by a contract whereby the purchaser acquires an equitable interest. There are, therefore, two situations which may need to be considered:

(a) where the charge of the non-entitled spouse is protected by registration before exchange of contracts for the sale of the property; and

(b) where the charge is protected after exchange of contracts, but before completion or the issue of a clear search certificate where appropriate.

Where the charge has been protected before exchange of contracts, it will clearly be effective as against a purchaser unless it is released or otherwise terminated under the Act. Where the charge is protected only after exchange of contracts it seems to have been assumed that this too will be effective unless the charge is released or otherwise terminated before completion of the purchase. Yet this is by no means clear, and no consideration appears to have been given to the possible argument in relation to unregistered land, that the charge will be void against the purchaser who has acquired an equitable interest by virtue of the contract. The charge arises when the entitled spouse acquires his or her estate or interest in the property or the date of the marriage, or the date of commencement of the 1967 Act, whichever is the latest, and not on the registration of a class F land charge or the entry of a notice or a caution (Matrimonial Homes Act 1983, s.2(1)). With regard to unregistered land the Land Charges Act 1972 provides that the charge shall be void against a purchaser of any interest in the land unless registered before completion of the purchase (s.4(8)). A purchaser is defined to mean "any person ... who for valuable consideration, takes any interest in land or in a charge of land" and "purchase" has a corresponding meaning (s.17(1)). If the charge is void against the equitable interest of a purchaser under a contract, it would be anomalous if the charge were held to be binding on him when he subsequently obtains the legal estate. A similar situation would arise in relation to an equitable mortgagee whose mortgage is not registrable and who subsequently obtains a legal mortgage after the registration of a class F land charge. There appears to be no authority directly in point, and it is submitted that the point should still be regarded as undecided.

On the basis that registration after the date of a contract for sale is effective it has been suggested that a purchaser should protect his interest by the registration of a class C(iv) land charge, and thereby preserve his priority. However, it is difficult to see how this could affect the position. Failure to register a C(iv) land charge will make the contract void against a purchaser of the legal estate for money or money's worth (Land Charges Act 1972, s.4(6)). The charge of the non-entitled spouse is only an equitable interest and will have arisen before the contract, generally when the entitled spouse acquired his or her interest in the property. In any event there is no provision that equitable interests are to rank in order of the date of registration except in relation to mortgages (see Law of Property Act 1925, s.97). Moreover, the general approach of the Land Charges Act is to reverse the principle that interests rank in order of their creation, and to lay down the principle that an earlier registrable interest is void against a purchaser of a subsequent interest if not registered before the creation of that interest.

In relation to registered land the charge of the non-entitled spouse is a minor interest as is the interest of a purchaser after exchange of contracts. A purchaser may protect his interest by the entry of a notice or caution, but this is not common practice. There is no provision in the Land Registration Acts comparable with that in the Land Charges Act which would make the charge of the non-entitled spouse void against a purchaser if not protected on the register before the date of the contract. If it is protected on the register after the date of the contract and before the issue of a clear search certificate to a purchaser, who completes the purchase and registers the transfer within the priority period, then it seems that generally this will be effective against the purchaser which, it is submitted, is in contrast to the position in relation to unregistered land.

There is no express provision dealing with priority as between competing minor interests. There is some support for the view that priority will depend upon the date of entries in the register protecting the competing interests. (See Lord Denning MR in *Re White Rose Cottage* [1965] Ch 940 at p. 949: "*Prima facie*, their priorities were governed by the order of the date of those entries.") On this basis a non-entitled spouse would lose priority if his or her charge was not protected by a notice before the purchaser protected his interest. However, since it is not usual to protect a contract in this way this would not often pose a threat to the non-entitled spouse. The better view at present seems to be that in the absence of express statutory provision (see e.g. the provision relating to liens created by deposit: Land Registration Act 1925 s.66, or relating to restrictive covenants: s.40) priority is governed by general equitable principles so that the order of creation of the equitable interests will *prima facie* govern priority (see Harman LJ in *Re White Rose Cottage* [1965] Ch 940 at p. 954 and Russell LJ in *Barclays Bank Ltd* v *Taylor* [1974] Ch 137). On this basis, even if the contract is protected on the register before the charge of the non-entitled spouse, the latter will have priority and bind the purchaser as it will have been created first in time. (It will have arisen at the date of purchase, the date of marriage or 1 January 1968, whichever is the latest.)

Although the Law Commission has recommended that minor interests should rank for priority according to the date of their entry on the register, it considers that rights arising under the Matrimonial Homes Act 1983 should be an exception and that the crucial date should be the date of the creation of the charge under the Act (Law Com. No. 158, *Third Report on Land Registration* (1987) paras. 4.94 – 4.99).

One qualification must be noted. An equitable interest loses its priority to a subsequent equitable interest if there is conduct on the part of the person entitled to it which amounts to fraud or negligence or raises an estoppel, such conduct being sufficient to induce the person entitled to the later equitable interest to act to his prejudice. It seems that mere failure by the non-entitled spouse to protect his or her charge by notice before a purchaser enters into a contract for the purchase of the home will not be enough to amount to such conduct so as to cause the non-entitled spouse to lose priority. However, it may be otherwise if there are additional factors. In *Wroth* v *Tyler* [1974] Ch 30 at p. 47 Megarry J referred to the possibility that the entitled spouse might be able to make out a case of estoppel against the non-entitled spouse, and said:

"If the protected spouse knowingly stands by or assists while the owning spouse contracts to sell the house with vacant possession, it may be that the protected spouse will thereafter be precluded from asserting his or her rights of occupation under the 1967 Act."

No allegation of estoppel was in fact made in that case, but might be made where the non-entitled spouse has acted in a positive manner in e.g. showing the purchasers around the home and generally acting towards them in a way that could be said to amount to a representation that she was concurring in the sale (*ibid.* at p. 47). The wife in *Wroth* v *Tyler* had not protected her charge until after her husband, the registered proprietor, had contracted to sell the home. The action between the husband and the purchaser proceeded on the basis that the wife's charge would bind the purchaser and it may be noted that on the facts it did not matter which of the two rules of priority mentioned above was applied.

*(g) The entitled spouse and a purchaser*

Where the charge of the non-entitled spouse has been effectively protected it is necessary to consider the position as between the entitled spouse as vendor and a purchaser. (The position of trustees for the entitled spouse will generally be the same.) It is provided by s.4 of the Act that it shall be a term of any contract for the sale by the entitled spouse of an estate or interest affected by a charge under the Act whereby he agrees to give vacant possession of the dwelling-house on completion, that he will before such completion procure the cancellation of the registration of the charge at his expense. (It is not necessary for the contract to contain an express provision for vacant possession, for in the absence of a contrary provision a vendor impliedly agrees to give vacant possession (see *Cook* v *Taylor* [1942] Ch 349).) This provision applies unless a contrary intention is expressed in the contract, and also applies to a contract for exchange, and, with the necessary modifications, to a contract for the grant of a lease or an under-lease of a dwelling-house (s.4(4) (5) and (6)). It does not apply to any such contract made by a vendor who is entitled to sell the estate or interest in the dwelling-house freed from any such charge (s.4(2)).

The entitled spouse as vendor will be deemed to have performed this term if he delivers to the purchaser or his solicitors an application by the spouse entitled to the charge for the cancellation of the charge, unless a contrary intention is expressed in the contract (s.4(3)). It is further provided (s.6(2)) that the rights of occupation constituting the charge shall be deemed to have been released on the occurrence of whichever of the following events first takes place:

(a) the delivery to the purchaser or his solicitor on completion of the contract of an application by the spouse entitled to the charge for the cancellation of the

registration of the charge; or
(b) the lodging of such an application at the Land Registry.
Where the entitled spouse is unable to fulfil his obligation to procure cancellation of the charge, he will be in breach of contract.

Once it is established that the vendor is in breach of contract he will be liable in damages. In *Wroth* v *Tyler* [1974] Ch 30 it was held that the rule in *Bain* v *Fothergill* (1874) LR 7 HL 158, which provided that where the vendor's failure to complete was due to a defect in his title the purchaser could recover only nominal damages, did not apply where the vendor's failure was due to his inability to procure cancellation of the registration of the non-entitled spouse's charge. That rule has in any event now been abolished by s.3 of the Law of Property (Miscellaneous Provisions) Act 1989. Accordingly the measure of damages will be such as will place the purchaser in the same position as if the contract had been performed, that is, generally, the amount necessary to enable him to purchase a comparable house. Moreover, in *Wroth* v *Tyler* it was held that damages should be assessed not at the date of the breach, but as at the date of the hearing.

If a purchaser seeks specific performance of the contract with vacant possession, the vendor would have to make an application to the court for an order under the Act terminating the non-entitled spouse's statutory rights of occupation unless he could obtain her consent to a release. In *Wroth* v *Tyler* Megarry J stated that the court would be slow to make a decree of specific performance against a vendor which would require him to undertake such litigation the outcome of which depended on disputed facts, difficult questions of law and, above all, on the exercise of discretionary jurisdiction ([1974] Ch 30 at p. 50).


## 4. Cohabitees

### *(a) Proprietary and personal rights*
Accommodation which is or has been occupied by a man and a woman who are or have been living together there as husband and wife, but who are not married, is obviously not a "matrimonial home", and neither party can take advantage of rights arising from the status of marriage. However, a cohabitee who has a freehold or leasehold interest in the home, or who is a tenant, has the "proprietary" right of occupation attaching to that interest (see section 2 (b), page 87). Lord Scarman pointed out in *Davis* v *Johnson* [1979] AC 264 at p. 348:

"The personal rights of an unmarried woman living with a man in the same household are very real. She has his licence to be in the home, a right which in appropriate cases the courts can and will protect ... She also has her fundamental right to the integrity and safety of her person. And the children living in the same household enjoy the same rights."

Nevertheless, the extent of such a licence and the enforcement of the right to the integrity and safety of the person have been problematical. Estoppel may also offer a measure of protection though probably the most immediately effective protection is likely to be under the Domestic Violence and Matrimonial Proceedings Act 1976 where this is applicable.

*(b) Rights in tort*
There is no doubt as to the existence of a cohabitee's personal right to the integrity and safety of his or her person and it seems clear that an injunction ancillary to proceedings in tort could restrain actions amounting to assault and/or battery of the applicant. However, it appears from the views expressed in the Court of Appeal in *Patel* v *Patel* [1988] 2 FLR 179 that a cohabitee has no right to obtain an injunction to restrain molestation which does not amount to an assault or battery or threat thereof. Waterhouse J said (at p. 182) that "in the present state of the law there is no tort of harassment". The proceedings in that case were commenced by a father-in-law of the defendant on the basis of trespass by the defendant in his father-in-law's home and the harassment was of the plaintiff in his own home. Nevertheless, the Court of Appeal held that the judge had rightly removed a provision restraining the defendant from approaching within fifty yards of the plaintiff's property (but see now the Court of Appeal decision in *Khorasandjian* v *Bush* [1993] 3 WLR 476). In contrast spouses have been able to obtain injunctions against molestation ancillary to divorce proceedings, originally, at least, on the basis that a spouse should be able to pursue his or her petition free from pressure which might lead to an abandonment of the proceedings. The position is considered further in Chapter 5. In any event it seems doubtful whether, in proceedings based on actual or threatened assault or battery to one cohabitee, an injunction could be made excluding the other cohabitee from the home of which the latter is owner or tenant.

*(c) The Domestic Violence and Matrimonial Proceedings Act 1976*
A cohabitee who comes within the Domestic Violence and Matrimonial Proceedings Act 1976 may obtain not only an injunction protecting his or her person from molestation, but also an injunction excluding the other cohabitee, at least for a limited term, from the home of which the latter is owner or tenant or part owner or joint tenant. To this extent this new remedy appears to give a new but limited right of occupation to the home (see further Chapter 5).

## 5. Rights of the homeless under the Housing Act 1985

*(a) Duties of housing authorities*
If a housing authority is satisfied that a person who has applied to it for accommodation or for assistance in obtaining accommodation is homeless or threatened with homelessness, ss.65 and 66 of the Housing Act 1985 (replacing the Housing (Homeless Persons) Act 1977) place the housing authority under a duty towards that person. The duty differs according to whether the person is actually homeless or only threatened with homelessness, whether the person has a priority need, and whether he became homeless intentionally. Where it is satisfied that he is homeless and has a priority need, but did not become homeless intentionally, its duty is to secure that accommodation becomes available for his occupation, i.e. it is subject to the "full" housing duty (Housing Act 1985, s.65(1) and (2)). Where it is satisfied that he is homeless and that he has a priority need but is also satisfied that he became homeless intentionally, it must ensure that accommodation is made avail-

able for his occupation for such period as it considers will give him a reasonable opportunity of himself securing accommodation for his occupation, i.e. a "temporary" housing duty. It must also furnish him with advice and such assistance as it considers appropriate in the circumstances in any attempts he may make to ensure that accommodation becomes available for his occupation (s.65(1)(3)). Where it is satisfied that he is homeless but is not satisfied that he has a priority need, duty is only to provide such advice and assistance (s.65(1) and (4)).

Where a housing authority is satisfied that a person is threatened with homelessness and he has a priority need, then if it is not satisfied that he became threatened with homelessness intentionally, it must take reasonable steps to secure that accommodation does not cease to be available for his occupation (s.66(1) and (2)). This does not affect any right of the local housing authority, whether by virtue of a contract, enactment or rule of law, to secure vacant possession of accommodation (s.66(4)). Where it is satisfied that a person is threatened with homelessness but is not satisfied that he has a priority need, or it is satisfied that he has a priority need but is also satisfied that he became threatened with homelessness intentionally, it must furnish him with advice and such assistance as it considers appropriate in the circumstances in any attempts he may make to secure that accommodation does not cease to be available for his occupation (s.66(1) and (3)).

A housing authority to which a person has applied for accommodation, or assistance in obtaining it, has two preliminary duties. First, if the authority has reason to believe that an applicant may be homeless or threatened with homelessness, it must make such inquiries as are necessary to satisfy itself as to whether he is homeless or threatened with homelessness, and, if so, whether he has a priority need and whether he became homeless or threatened with homelessness intentionally (s.66(1) and (2)). If it thinks fit, it may also make inquiries as to whether he has a local connection with the district of another local housing authority in England, Wales or Scotland. Secondly, if the authority has reason to believe that an applicant may be homeless and have a priority need, it must secure that accommodation is made available for his occupation and that of his family pending any decision it may make as a result of its inquiries (s.67(1)). This duty arises irrespective of any local connection which the applicant may have with the district of another local housing authority.

A housing authority to whom application has been made by a person who is homeless, has a priority need, and did not become homeless intentionally, i.e. to whom it owes the duty to secure permanent accommodation, may refer his application to another housing authority in England, Wales or Scotland in certain circumstances (s.67(1)). It may also do so if neither the applicant nor any person who might reasonably be expected to reside with him has a local connection with the district of that authority but the applicant or any such person does have a local connection with the district of the other authority. Moreover, there must be no risk, either to the applicant or to such person, of domestic violence in that other district (s.67(2)). See *R v Bristol City Council, ex p. Browne* [1979] 1 WLR 1437. For this purpose a person runs the risk of domestic violence (a) if he runs the risk of violence from any person with whom, but for the risk of violence, he might reasonably be expected to reside or from any person with whom he formerly resided, or (b) if he runs the risk of threats of violence from any such person which are likely to be carried out (s.67(3)).

A housing authority may perform any duty to secure that accommodation becomes available for the occupation of a person found to be homeless:
(a)  by making available suitable accommodation held by it; or
(b)  by securing that the applicant obtains suitable accommodation from some other person (s.69(1)); or
(c)  by giving him such advice and assistance as will secure that he obtains such suitable accommodation from some other person.

In *R* v *Bristol City Council, ex p. Browne* [1979] 1 WLR 1437 the applicant and her seven children had left the matrimonial home in the Republic of Ireland because of the husband's violence. In the circumstances of the case the Bristol housing authority was held to be able to fulfil its duty by advising and assisting the applicant to obtain accommodation from the welfare officer in her home town in Ireland.

*(b) Homelessness and threatened homelessness*
A person is homeless for the purposes of the Housing Act 1985 if he has no accommodation in England, Wales or Scotland (s.58(1)). A person is to be treated as having no accommodation if there is no accommodation which he, together with any other person who normally resides with him as a member of his family, is entitled to occupy by virtue of an interest in it or by virtue of an order of a court or which he has an express or implied licence to occupy. Moreover, he must not be occupying accommodation as a residence "by virtue of any enactment or rule of law giving him the right to remain in occupation or restricting the right of any other person to remain in occupation of it" (s.58(2)). This would include a statutory tenant and a wife living in the former matrimonial home owned by the husband. This definition of homelessness was amplified by amendments to s.58 introduced by s.14 of the Housing and Planning Act 1986 following the decision of the House of Lords in *R* v *Hillingdon LBC ex p. Puhlhofer* [1986] AC 484. It is now provided, first, that a person is not to be treated as having accommodation unless it is accommodation which it would be reasonable for him to continue to occupy (s.58(2A)). The authority is accordingly to be concerned not only with the rights of the person to occupy accommodation, but also with the quality of that accommodation. The test of reasonableness is the same as that applicable when the authority is considering whether homelessness is intentional, and reference may be made to the case law which has emerged in that context (see below). Thus it will not normally be reasonable for an applicant to remain in accommodation if there is a serious risk of domestic violence. In *R* v *Kensington & Chelsea LBC ex p. Hemmell* [1989] 2 FLR 223 a divorced woman with custody of her three children left council accommodation in Scotland because of the violence of her former husband who lived nearby. She moved to London and stayed with her sister but was asked to leave and applied to the housing authority for accommodation as a homeless person. The authority considered that she was not homeless because it was reasonable for her to return to the council accommodation in Scotland which was still available. The husband's violence had occurred outside the home and it was open to her to enforce an injunction. However, Parker LJ said (at p. 234) that since the position following the amendments made in

1986 is that the test is reasonableness of occupation, "it cannot be right in law to suggest, as the council appear to believe, that violence outside the home is not at least a very important factor going to the question of whether it is reasonable to occupy". (See also *R* v *Tynedale DC ex p. McCabe* (1992) 24 HLR 384.) On the other hand, the housing authority may be justified in concluding that an applicant is not homeless if as a result of enquiries there is insufficient evidence of a risk of violence (see *R* v *Purbeck DC, ex p. Cadney* [1986] 2 FLR 158 and *R* v *Islington Borough Council, ex p. Adigun* (1988) 20 HLR 600). Secondly, it is now provided that regard may be had, in determining whether it would be reasonable for a person to continue to occupy accommodation, to the general circumstances prevailing in relation to housing in the district of the local housing authority to which he has applied for accommodation or for assistance in obtaining accommodation (s.58(2B)). A person is also homeless if he has accommodation but, *inter alia*, it is probable that occupation of it will lead to violence from some other person residing in it or to threats of violence from some other person residing in it and likely to carry out the threats (s.58(3)).

A person is "threatened with homelessness" if it is likely that he will become homeless within twenty-eight days (s.58(4)).

### (c) Priority need

A homeless person or a person threatened with homelessness has a priority need for accommodation if, *inter alia*, he or she is a person with whom dependent children reside or might reasonably be expected to reside. A pregnant woman or a person with whom a pregnant woman resides or might reasonably be expected to reside also has a priority need (s.59(1). See further the *Code of Guidance for Local Authorities*, 3rd Edition (1991) para. 6.2). There is no definition of a dependent child, but the *Code of Guidance* (para. 6.3) urges local authorities to treat those under 16 and those under 19 who are either receiving full-time education or training, or are otherwise unable to support themselves, as dependants. They need not be the applicant's own children. A case should still be treated as within this category even if at the time of application the children are temporarily away from the applicant, e.g. with relatives (see *R* v *London Borough of Lewisham, ex p. Creppy* (1991) 24 HLR 121). However, a reservation is made in the case of children in care unless in the particular case it is reasonable that they should live with the applicant. In *R* v *Ealing LBC, ex p. Sidhu* (1982) 80 LGR 534 it was held that where a wife was residing with her dependent children in a women's refuge, the local authority was not entitled to require her to obtain a final custody order in respect of the children before treating her as a person in priority need of accommodation under the Act. For the position where a child has potentially two residences on the basis of spending a part of each week with each parent, see *R* v *Port Talbot BC, ex p. McCarthy* (1990) 23 HLR 207.

### (d) Intentional homelessness

(i) The meaning of intentional homelessness
A person becomes homeless intentionally for the purposes of the Act if he deliber-

ately does or fails to do anything in consequence of which he ceases to occupy accommodation which is available for his occupation and which it would have been reasonable for him to continue to occupy (s.60(1)). A person becomes threatened with homelessness intentionally if he deliberately does or fails to do anything the likely result of which is that he will be forced to leave accommodation which is available for his occupation and which it would have been reasonable for him to continue to occupy (s.60(2)). An act or omission in good faith on the part of a person who was unaware of any relevant fact is not to be treated as deliberate for these purposes (s.60(3). See *Robinson* v *Torbay BC* [1982] 1 All ER 726). In determining whether it would have been reasonable for a person to continue to occupy accommodation, regard may be had to the general circumstances prevailing in relation to housing in the district of the housing authority to which he or she applied for accommodation or assistance in obtaining accommodation (s.60(4)).

(ii) The responsibility of family members
Where a person has become homeless intentionally, whether as a result of non-payment of rent or mortgage instalments or for some other reason, the spouse or cohabitee of that person should not necessarily be regarded as intentionally homeless. Generally the Act does require consideration of the family unit as a whole, so that in the ordinary case where there is no material to indicate the contrary, the housing authority may properly assume that the conduct of one spouse or cohabitee is conduct to which the other spouse or cohabitee was a party. However, a wife's application for accommodation should be considered separately from her husband if there is material before the housing authority to suggest that she was not a party to, and had not acquiesced in, the acts or omissions of her husband which caused the homelessness (*R* v *North Devon DC, ex p. Lewis* [1981] 1 WLR 325). Thus in *R* v *Eastleigh BC, ex p. Beattie* (1985) 17 HLR 168 Webster J found that a wife had sworn an affidavit in earlier proceedings from which the housing authority should have gleaned that she was not a party to, and did not acquiesce in, her husband's failure to pay mortgage instalments. In *R* v *West Dorset DC, ex p Phillips* (1985) 17 HLR 336 Hodgson J found that the housing officers saw clear signs of non-acquiescence by the wife in that she actually physically attacked the husband when she learned of the debt involved. In *R* v *East Northamptonshire DC, ex p. Spruce* (1988) 20 HLR 508 Kennedy J found that there were clear indications which should have led the local authority positively to consider whether or not the wife had acquiesced in the creation of the homelessness. The wife became aware of the arrears of rent, but Kennedy J put forward the case of a wife who only finds out that her husband has failed to pay the rent or instalments of the mortgage at a time when the debt has become so substantial that the couple simply cannot cope with it. In that situation, he considered that "it would be very hard to say that simply because the wife was aware of the debt before the situation of homelessness arose, she was therefore acquiescing in the situation to such an extent that she should be regarded as being intentionally homeless". On the evidence it seemed that that might well have been the situation in the case before him. While generally the burden is on the housing authority to make the appropriate inquiries "what has to be raised by the wife in one way or another, is the issue as to whether or not she acquiesced in and was responsi-

ble for the state of affairs which led to the family becoming homeless" (*per* Kennedy J at pp. 516-517).

Where both parents of a young child have been found to be homeless intentionally, an application may not normally be made on behalf of that child (see *R* v *Oldham MBC ex p. G* (1992) 24 HLR 726, CA; [1993] 2 WLR 609 (HL)).

(iii) The effect of domestic violence

The second edition of the *Code of Guidance* issued in 1983 suggested that a battered woman who has left the matrimonial home should never be regarded as having become homeless intentionally because it would clearly not be reasonable for her to remain (para 2.16). This was reinforced in *R* v *Ealing LBC, ex p. Sidhu* (1982) 80 LGR 534 where the wife had been forced to leave the matrimonial home as a result of her husband's violence. Hodgson J held that there was no doubt that on the evidence and the surrounding circumstances, the applicant's case should have been considered separately from that of her husband, and no reasonable local authority could have come to any other conclusion but that she was not intentionally homeless. However, in *R* v *Wandsworth BC, ex p. Nimako-Boateng* (1984) 11 HLR 95 at p. 103 Woolf J said that a "local authority could perfectly properly in many cases in this country take the view that it would be reasonable for the wife to continue to occupy accommodation and to say to the wife ..." that she should go to a magistrates' court or to the Family Division and get protection against her husband. If she did not do so but chose to leave, the authority could then take the view that it was reasonable for her to have remained. It is submitted that this should not mean that such action on the part of the wife will always be considered appropriate, especially where such action has been ineffective in the past. In that case the accommodation was overseas and the question of violence was not a central feature of the case, but the same approach was taken in *R* v *Eastleigh BC, ex p. Evans* [1986] 2 FLR 195 where the matrimonial home took the form of RAF married quarters. The third edition of the *Code of Guidance,* issued in 1991, states:

> "7.11 It would not normally be reasonable for someone to continue to occupy accommodation if s/he:...(b) was a victim of domestic violence, or threats of violence from inside or outside the home. (Authorities should not automatically treat an applicant as intentionally homeless because s/he has failed to use legal remedies.)"

(iv) Available accommodation

Accommodation is only available for a person's occupation if it is available for occupation both by him and by any other person who might reasonably be expected to reside with him (s.75. See *R* v *Islam* [1983] AC 688; *R* v *Westminster CC, ex p. Ali* (1984) 11 HLR 83; *R* v *Peterborough CC, ex p. Carr* (1990) 22 HLR).

*(e) Enforcement*

The Act contains no enforcement provisions and there is no provision for appeal against the decisions of housing authorities. The appropriate remedy for an aggrieved applicant is to seek judicial review under Order 53 of the Rules of the Supreme Court. This does not enable the court to adjudicate on the merits of the case - the court will be concerned with whether the authority was justified in coming to its decision (see *Associated Provincial Picture Houses Ltd* v *Wednesbury Corporation* [1948] 1 KB 223 at p. 229 and *R* v *Hillingdon LBC, ex p. Puhlhofer* [1986] AC 484 at p. 518).

# Chapter 5

# Proceedings relating to occupation of the home

## 1. Introduction

The different forms in which disputes relating to occupation of the matrimonial or family home may arise were outlined at the beginning of Chapter 4. The most frequently sought orders are "commonly and not inappropriately described as 'ouster orders'" (*per* Lord Brandon in *Richards* v *Richards* [1984] AC 174 at p.214). Lord Brandon went on to say:

"Such an order takes the form of an injunction granted to one spouse (usually the wife) requiring the other spouse (usually the husband) to vacate the matrimonial home previously occupied by both and not to return to it until further order."

It may be sought not only where both parties continue to live in the home, but also by a spouse who has left the home but wishes to return after having obtained the order. The drastic effect of an ouster order has been emphasised on many occasions and was reiterated by Lord Brandon who said (at p. 215) that "... its effect upon the spouse against whom it is directed will often be extremely serious. This is because such an order involves turning such a spouse, usually at very short notice, out of what is in most cases the only home which he or she possesses, and leaving him or her to find, often with great difficulty, alternative accommodation in which to live."

An application for an "ouster order" is frequently coupled with an application for an order restraining the other spouse from "molesting" the applicant spouse and/or the children living in the home or with the applicant. "Molestation" may take a variety of forms and is not limited to physical violence. In the leading case of *Vaughan* v *Vaughan* [1973] 1 WLR 1159 the Court of Appeal was reluctant to define the expression too closely. Two members of the Court of Appeal referred to the Shorter Oxford English Dictionary which defines it as: "to cause trouble to: to vex, annoy, put to inconvenience". Stephenson LJ said that if he had to find one synonym for it, he would select "pester" (at p. 1165). In *Horner* v *Horner* [1982] Fam 90 at p. 93 Ormrod LJ said that he had no doubt that the word "molesting" in s.1(1)(a) of the Domestic Violence and Matrimonial Proceedings Act 1976 "does not imply necessarily either violence or threats of violence. It applies to any conduct which can properly be regarded as such a degree of harassment as to call for the intervention of the court". In that case the harassment of the wife by the husband had taken various forms including intercepting the wife on her way to work and sending her threatening letters. In *Johnson* v *Walton* [1990] 1 FLR 350 at p. 352 Lord Donaldson MR, noting the view expressed by Ormrod LJ, said that harassment "includes within it an element of intent to cause distress or harm". He took the view "that 'molestation' has that meaning whenever it is used, regardless of whether the particular proceedings are or are not brought under the [1976 Act]". In that case the defendant had sent a photograph of the plaintiff in a semi-nude state to a national newspaper with the intent of causing distress, and that could clearly come within the prohibition against molestation.

Clearly, there will be circumstances where an ouster order is insufficient and an order restraining molestation may be necessary if the ousted spouse continues to pester the applicant spouse. On the other hand, there may be cases where the situation may not justify an ouster order, but it is reasonable to provide protection from molestation. There are, of course, cases where there is no question of molestation and the sole dispute is as to who shall occupy their former joint home.

## 2. The choice of procedure

*(a) The position before Richards v Richards*
Before the decision of the House of Lords in *Richards* v *Richards* [1984] AC 174 there were in practice two ways in which a spouse might seek to obtain an ouster of the other spouse from the matrimonial home together, if appropriate, with a non-molestation order. First, he or she might seek an appropriate injunction as "ancillary relief" in proceedings for divorce, nullity or judicial separation. Secondly, he or she might apply for the appropriate orders under the Domestic Violence and Matrimonial Proceedings Act 1976 - a course which was also available in the case of certain unmarried couples.

The power of the court to grant injunctions, which at first sight is exceedingly broad, is subject to limitations which are considered in Part 6 of this chapter - see page 128.

Although the Matrimonial Homes Act 1967 gave the court power not only to determine the scope of the statutory rights of occupation which it created, but also the power to "regulate" the proprietary rights of occupation of a spouse, the latter power did not enable the court to give the other spouse exclusive occupation (see the decision of the House of Lords in *Tarr* v *Tarr* [1973] AC 254). Accordingly ouster orders continued to be sought as ancillary relief in divorce proceedings. The disadvantage of this was that it frequently meant that in order to obtain an immediate remedy, even in cases of violence, it was necessary to file a petition for divorce or judicial separation. This was altered in relation to county courts by s.1 of the Domestic Violence and Matrimonial Proceedings Act 1976 which enables ouster and non-molestation orders to be obtained even though no other relief is sought. (The position in relation to the High Court is considered later in the chapter.)

The 1976 Act therefore provided spouses with an element of choice in relation to proceedings for obtaining an ouster or non-molestation order. It also contained two important provisions relating to the Matrimonial Homes Act. First, it replaced the power of the court to "regulate" the proprietary rights of occupation of the entitled spouse with the power of "prohibiting, suspending or restricting" those rights, thereby reversing the decision in *Tarr* v *Tarr* [1973] AC 254 (see s.3). Secondly, where the matrimonial home was vested in the joint names of the spouses so that the original main scheme of the Act did not apply, it enabled one spouse to obtain an order excluding the other spouse in the same way as if the home was vested in the latter's name alone (s.4. See now Matrimonial Homes Act 1983, s.9). Neither change had any immediate impact on the practice of seeking ouster orders ancillary to divorce proceedings, though s.1 of the Act had provided an alternative procedure.

*(b) The circumstances in which an order would be made*
Attention was focused on the circumstances in which a non-molestation order and, in particular, an ouster order would and should be granted. The Domestic Violence and Matrimonial Proceedings Act 1976 does not specify the factors which the court is required to take into account in exercising the power to grant injunctions conferred by s.1 of the Act. The Select Committee on Violence in Marriage, on whose recommendation the provision was based, had approved the approach adopted by the Court of Appeal in *Bassett* v *Bassett* [1975] Fam 76 in upholding the grant of an injunction excluding a husband from the matrimonial home in an application ancillary to proceedings for divorce. This left it open to the courts in applications under s.1 of the Act to apply the same principles as were applied in ancillary applications for injunctions (Report of the Select Committee on Violence in Marriage, Session 1974-75, Vol.1, para 50). The better view seems to be that, despite the title of the Act, it is not necessary to show violence on the part of the respondent in order to obtain an injunction under s.1, although there are *dicta* suggesting the contrary. The point is given further consideration later in this chapter.

The principles applicable to the grant of ancillary injunctions had undoubtedly developed over the previous two decades. This is understandable and appropriate in the light of the great changes that have taken place in the law and in the attitudes relating to divorce, and especially in relation to the disposition of the matrimonial home on divorce. Unfortunately a difference of opinion emerged which manifested itself in conflicting views being expressed in decisions of the Court of Appeal. In general terms it can be said that on one view the decisive factor would often be the need to provide a home for the children of the family. Where the children of the family were living in unsatisfactory accommodation, such as a women's refuge or hostel, or in overcrowded accommodation with relatives, the court would almost certainly conclude that they should return to live in the matrimonial home. The question then became: "Who is going to look after them?". In the majority of cases it would be the mother so that unless the court concluded that it was reasonable for both spouses to live in the home, it followed that the husband must be excluded. On this basis, the conduct of the husband, or indeed of the wife, was not often a decisive factor. The high water mark for this view was *Samson* v *Samson* [1982] 1 All ER 780.

The other view stressed the importance of considering whether it was really necessary for anyone to go. It was not sufficient that the wife, who might be the most obvious person to care for the children, made it clear that she would not return to the matrimonial home until the husband left. The court had to consider whether there were reasonable grounds for her to be unwilling to do so. (See *Elsworth* v *Elsworth* (1981) 1 FLR 245; *Myers* v *Myers* [1982] 1 WLR 247.)

*(c) The decision in Richards v Richards*
The question was eventually considered by the House of Lords in *Richards* v *Richards* [1984] AC 174. In this case the wife had left the husband in the matrimonial home, taking the children with her. Having filed a petition for divorce the wife sought an injunction excluding the husband from the home. The judge found that her allegations about the husband's behaviour were "flimsy", and that she had no reasonable grounds for refusing to return to live in the same house as him. However, in the interests of the children (and following *Samson* v *Samson*) he made an ouster order. This was upheld by the Court of Appeal which followed *Samson*, and disapproved of *Elsworth* v *Elsworth* and *Myers* v *Myers* and treated the children's needs as paramount.

The House of Lords adopted a different approach and (Lord Scarman dissenting) held that applications of the kind under consideration should be dealt with under s.1 of the Matrimonial Homes Act and determined on the basis of the matters specified in s.1(3). Lord Hailsham LC (at p. 202) said that the effect of s.1 of the 1967 Act, which was in no way referred to in argument in the Court of Appeal or, it seems, in any of the reported cases cited, was "to codify and spell out where it is applicable the jurisdiction of the High Court and county court in ouster injunctions between spouses whether in pending proceedings or by way of originating applications and the criteria to be applied are those referred to in subsection (3) and not any other criteria sometimes treated as paramount by reported decisions of the court." In particular, the language of s.1 of the Matrimonial Homes Act was to be contrasted with the language of s.1 of the Guardianship of Minors Act 1971 whereby the welfare of a minor was to be the first and paramount consideration in any proceedings relating to the custody or upbringing of the minor. In the Matrimonial Homes Act "'the needs of [the] children' are an important and specified, but not in every case first or paramount, consideration to be applied" (*ibid.* at p. 203). The criterion in s.1 of the Guardianship of Minors Act 1971 is to be applied only in the proceedings of the type specified in the section, and not in cases to which s.1(3) of the Matrimonial Homes Act is to be applied even though in the latter cases the interests of the children are directly or indirectly affected. On the facts the appeal of the husband was unanimously allowed. Lord Brandon (with whom Lord Diplock and Lord Bridge agreed) said that the judge, by applying *Samson* rather than *Myers*, "failed to have regard to one of the matters which s.1(3) of the Matrimonial Homes Act required him to have regard to, namely the conduct of the wife in refusing to return to the matrimonial home when there were, as he had found on the evidence before him, no reasonable grounds for such a refusal" (*ibid.* at p. 223). Lord Hailsham said that the wife had "never made out a case for excluding the husband from the home" (at p. 178). He accepted the reasoning of Lord Scarman in this respect that "it was neither just ... nor reasonable nor necessary to oust the father ... The evidence did not justify the making of the order. The needs of the children did not on the judge's findings, require the protection of an ouster order." (*Ibid.* at p. 192.) The Court of Appeal has recently held that the decision in *Richards* v *Richards* has not been affected by the Children Act 1989 (*Gibson* v *Austin* [1992] 2 FLR 437).

### 3. The effect of *Richards* v *Richards*

*(a) Choice of procedure*

The view of the majority of the House of Lords in *Richards* v *Richards* [1984] AC 174 was that a spouse seeking an ouster order should do so under s.1 of the Matrimonial Homes Act when the application will be governed by the criteria in subs.(3) of that section. Thus, as noted above, Lord Hailsham (at p. 202) said:

". . . in my view the effect of section 1 of the Matrimonial Homes Act ... is to codify and spell out where it is applicable the jurisdiction of the High Court and county court in ouster injunctions between spouses whether in pending proceedings or by way of originating applications and the criteria to be applied are those referred to in subsection (3) . . ."

Later Lord Brandon (at p. 221) said:

"I conclude that it was the intention of the legislature, in passing and later amending and extending the scope of the Act of 1967, and in passing the Act of 1976, that the power of the High Court to make, during the subsistence of a marriage, orders relating to the occupation of a matrimonial home, including in particular an ouster order, which had previously been derived from section 45(1) of the Act of 1925, should for the future be derived from, and exercised in accordance with, section 1 of the Act of 1967."

He went on to say (at p. 222) that:

"I reach a similar conclusion with regard to ouster orders made in a county court, namely that it was the intention of the legislature that the power of a county court to make ouster orders, which had been previously derived from the very general provisions of section 74 of the County Courts Act 1959, should for the future be derived from, and exercised in accordance with, the provisions of the Act of 1967."

Although it seemed clear that a spouse should seek an ouster order under the Matrimonial Homes Act rather than as ancillary relief in divorce proceedings in reliance on s.37 of the Supreme Court Act 1981, it was not clear whether the Matrimonial Homes Act was also required to be used in preference to an application under the Domestic Violence and Matrimonial Proceedings Act 1976. Lord Brandon did go on to say (at p. 222) that:

"County courts were given an additional power to make ouster orders by section 1 of the Act of 1976, but it seems to me to be a necessary inference that the legislature intended such additional power to be exercised in accordance with the principles laid down in the Act of 1967."

This could at least be said to assume that applications for ouster orders would continue to be made under the 1976 Act as well as under the Matrimonial Homes Act (though the same criteria should be applied in both cases). Applications by spouses for ouster orders under the 1976 Act have come before the Court of Appeal in a number of subsequent cases without any objection being taken to the procedure adopted (*Lee* v *Lee* [1984] FLR 243; *Thurley* v *Smith* [1984] FLR 875; *Galan* v *Galan* [1985] FLR 905; *Wiseman* v *Simpson* [1988] 1 WLR 35). The position that emerged, therefore, was that an application by a spouse for an ouster order should in general be made under the Matrimonial Homes Act 1983 unless the behaviour of the respondent was such as to make an application under the Domestic Violence and Matrimonial Proceedings Act 1976 appropriate. (For a comparison, see below.) However, in 1984 the County Court Rules were amended so as to enable, as a matter of convenience, an application for an ouster order to be made by notice in divorce proceedings (CCR Ord. 47, r. 4 inserted by the County Court (Amendment) Rules 1984, r. 10). In effect the range of choice available before the decision in *Richards* v *Richards* was restored but with applications under the Matrimonial Homes Act 1983 (and the factors set out in s.1(3) of the Act) now occupying a much more significant position. A non-molestation order cannot be made under the Matrimonial Homes Act and application must therefore be made under the 1976 Act or ancillary to proceedings for divorce.

Where the parties have not been married, the Matrimonial Homes Act does not apply and application will have to be made under the Domestic Violence and Matrimonial Proceedings Act 1976 if the necessary conditions are satisfied (see Part 5, page 119). A further option is available to married persons who may apply to a magistrates' court under the Domestic Proceedings and Magistrates' Courts Act 1978 for a "personal protection order" and/or an "exclusion order" (see Part 10, page 141 *et seq.*).

There will be a residue of cases where none of the statutory procedures is applicable. It is then necessary to explore the possibility of proceedings in tort or in reliance on the powers of the court under s.37 of the Supreme Court Act 1981 or the inherent jurisdiction of the court either generally or with particular reference to the protection of children.

*(b) Criteria for granting an order*
Where an ouster order is sought under the Matrimonial Homes Act the applicable criteria are expressly set out in s.1(3) of the 1983 Act (see below). If, as now seems to be accepted, an ouster order may also be sought by a spouse under the Domestic Violence and Matrimonial Proceedings Act 1976, the same citeria will also be applicable. This is in accord with the view expressed by Lord Brandon in *Richards* v *Richards* [1984] AC 174 at p. 222 and referred to above.

It is arguable that this fails to take account of the different objectives of the two Acts. The 1976 Act, in conferring the "additional power" on county courts by s.1, makes no reference to the criteria in s.1(3) of the Matrimonial Homes Act, though a later section reformulates the power of the court to deal with the proprietary rights of occupation (s.3). This is consistent with the view that the two procedures were seen as dealing with two different situations. The Matrimonial Homes Act was a response to the problems of the deserted wife and was passed before the reform of divorce law and the introduction of wide powers of property adjustment. Machinery was provided for the protection of the statutory rights of occupation against third parties, and while those rights would come to an end on divorce, the protection afforded could be seen as dealing with the question of occupation on a "medium term" basis, at least pending divorce. On the other hand, the 1976 Act was a response to the problems of the battered and molested spouse. It was perceived as a means of obtaining short term but immediate relief for an intolerable situation. This view is apparent in *Davis* v *Johnson* [1979] AC 264 where, for example, Lord Salmon (at p. 343) said that he believed that "the major object which the Act sought to achieve [was] first aid but not intensive care for 'battered wives'". It was, he said, concerned not with proprietary rights but with providing "protection to 'battered wives' by giving them the chance of finding fresh accommodation in safety when the husband or paramour had made life in the matrimonial home intolerable, impossible or dangerous." Again Viscount Dilhorne (at p. 335) said that the purpose of s.1 of the 1976 Act was "the provision of immediate relief not permanent resolution of the situation arising on the break-up of a marriage or an association where the parties though unmarried had been living as if they were." He envisaged that in the case of spouses an injunction under the 1976 Act might be followed by an application under the Matrimonial Homes Act.

There are a number of differences between the two procedures which can be said to reflect their different objectives.

First, the need for a speedy procedure to deal with an immediate problem is reflected in the fact that under the 1976 Act only two clear days' notice of proceedings is required whereas twenty-one days' notice is normally required in relation to applications under the Matrimonial Homes Act. (Family Proceedings Rules 1991, rr. 3.8 and 3.9, and CCR Ord. 47 r. 8(3) as amended in 1991.)

Secondly, under the 1976 Act the court may exclude a party not only from the home, but also from the "vicinity" of the home. Under the Matrimonial Homes Act the court may exclude a party only from the home, but may alternatively exclude a spouse from part of a matrimonial home (s.1(1)(c) and s.1(3) respectively).

Thirdly, no order against molestation may be made under the Matrimonial Homes Act, so that a spouse will have to rely on the 1976 Act for such an order unless it can be obtained by an ancillary application in divorce proceedings.

*(c) The significance and timing of an ouster order*

There are many judicial reminders that an ouster order is a very serious order which should only be made in cases of real necessity. It must not be allowed to become a routine stepping-stone on the road to divorce on the ground that the marriage has already broken down and that the atmosphere in the home is one of tension. However, when an ouster order is justified, it should normally take effect within a week or two, as soon as the party ordered to vacate the matrimonial home can make alternative arrangements. It should not be left as something hanging over a man's head. It should not be used as a threat to bring him to his senses, or, as the judge said in *Burke* v *Burke* [1987] 2 FLR 71, "as a dose of cold water". In that case Lloyd LJ (at p. 73) said that the courts should not countenance any such creature as an ouster order nisi. Having come to the conclusion that the husband should vacate the matrimonial home, the question for the judge is: "What is the reasonable time, in all the circumstances of the case, for this husband to obtain some alternative accommodation?" (*Chadda* v *Chadda* (1981) 11 Fam Law 142). In *Dunsire* v *Dunsire* [1991] 2 FLR 314 at p. 317 Butler-Sloss LJ said that the time allowed should be that which would permit someone to move out with some degree of urgency, two to three weeks at the outside.

## 4. Applications under the Matrimonial Homes Act 1983

*(a) The court's powers*

(i) Where the legal estate is vested in one spouse alone
Where the legal estate in the matrimonial home is vested in the name of one spouse alone then so long as the other spouse has rights of occupation in relation to that home under the Act, either of the spouses may apply to the court for an order (a) declaring, enforcing, restricting or terminating those rights, or (b) prohibiting, suspending, or restricting the exercise by either spouse of the right to occupy arising from entitlement to a beneficial interest the home (s.1(2)).

(ii) Where the legal estate is vested in the joint names of the spouse
Where each of two spouses is entitled, by virtue of a legal estate vested in them jointly, to occupy a dwelling-house in which they have or at any time have had a matrimonial home, either of them may apply to the court, with respect to the exercise during the subsistence of the marriage of the right to occupy the dwelling-house, for an order prohibiting, suspending or restricting its exercise by the other or requiring the other to permit its exercise by the applicant (s.9(1)). This also applies in the same way where each of two spouses is entitled to occupy a dwelling-house by virtue of a contract, or by virtue of any enactment giving them the right to remain in occupation (s.9(3)).

*(b) The exercise of the powers*
On an application for an order under s.1 or s.9 the court may make such order as it thinks just and reasonable having regard to the conduct of the spouses in relation to each other and otherwise, to their respective needs and financial resources, to the needs of any children and to all the circumstances of the case. In particular, the court may (a) except part of the dwelling-house from a spouse's rights of occupation (and in particular a part used wholly or mainly for or in connection with the trade, business or profession of the other spouse); (b) order a spouse occupying the dwelling-house or any part thereof by virtue of the Act to make periodical payments to the other in respect of the occupation; and (c) impose on either spouse obligations as to the repair and maintenance of the dwelling-house or the discharge of any liabilities in respect of the dwelling-house (s.1(3) and s.9(2)).

*(c) The criteria applied*

(i) The conduct of the spouses in relation to each other and otherwise
The conduct of both spouses must be considered in relation to each other. In

*Richards* v *Richards* [1984] AC 174 at p. 224 Lord Brandon laid stress on the reasonableness of the applicant's attitude in declining to live with the respondent. He said:

"The conduct of the wife who has no reasonable grounds for refusing to return to the matrimonial home so long as her husband remains in it but nevertheless asserts that she will not do so, is clearly 'conduct of a spouse in relation to each other and otherwise' within the meaning of that expression as used in s.1(3) ... It follows that the court, when adjudicating on the wife's application for an order under s.1 of that Act, must have regard to her conduct in this respect, and is not entitled to treat it as irrelevant to the decision which has to be made."

He did not go so far as to say that the conduct of an applicant wife in this respect was necessarily in all cases decisive against her, but it was an important factor to be weighed in the scales with the other factors in s.1(3). He did think that in a substantial number of cases it would be a factor of such weight as to lead to the court concluding that it would not be just or reasonable to allow her application. He thought that *Elsworth* v *Elsworth* and *Myers* v *Myers* came into that category. In *Richards* this factor had not been taken into account.

The reasonableness of the applicant wife's attitude will generally depend very much on the conduct of the respondent husband. It is not necessary to show violence on his part. Indeed in *Wiseman* v *Simpson* [1988] 1 WLR 35 at p. 41 Ralph Gibson LJ in dealing with an application under s.1(1)(c) of the Domestic Violence and Matrimonial Proceedings Act 1976 rejected as unsustainable the contention that no ouster order could be made without proof of violence or serious molestation. He considered that the views to that effect expressed by the Court of Appeal in *Spindlow* v *Spindlow* [1979] Fam 52 had not been affected by the decision in *Richards* v *Richards*. He referred to *Summers* v *Summers* [1986] 1 FLR 343 where there was no violence but repeated loud quarrels between a young couple who were equally to blame for those quarrels. The Court of Appeal in setting aside the ouster order did not dismiss the application, but concluded that there was a *prima facie* case which had to be considered in a new trial. However, since the decision in *Richards* v *Richards* the general view appears to be that violence or serious misbehaviour on the part of the respondent must be shown. An exception to this is the recent case of *Scott* v *Scott* [1992] 1 FLR 529 where the allegation against the husband was that he could not accept the breakdown of his marriage and constantly begged his wife for a reconciliation. He was in breach of an earlier non-molestation undertaking and a non-molestation order and there was concern about the effect on the younger daughter of further breaches which were likely to occur if an ouster order was not made. There was no immediate problem about accommodation for the husband as the parties had available a home owned by the husband's company as well as the jointly owned matrimonial home.

Where there is evidence of violence by both parties it is essential that responsibility for that violence is clearly established. In *Blackstock* v *Blackstock* [1991] 2 FLR 308 the main issue was the effect of one very serious incident in the course of which the spouses inflicted on each other injuries of considerable severity. The judge had been unable to make a finding on culpability and concluded that the wife would be adequately protected by a non-molestation undertaking by the husband

and refused to make an ouster order. The Court of Appeal dismissed the wife's appeal stating that the source of the violence could not be ignored and that the husband had not been found to be culpable. It seems that Butler-Sloss LJ (at p. 311) would probably have made an ouster order not only if the husband had been found to blame but also if the spouses had been found equally to blame. However, on the facts there was a real possibility that the wife herself might have been the instigator of the violence to which the husband responded. She said: "In exercising the discretion to make an order which the court thinks just and reasonable, and with the duty to have regard to conduct, it would be manifestly unjust in a case of violence to oust him if she created the situation. The unsatisfactory accommodation of the children in itself would not on these facts have been the deciding factor (see *Richards* v *Richards* [1984] AC 174) ... The court has always to remember the draconian nature of the order and the effect upon the party ordered to leave." The inability of the judge to make a finding on culpability showed that the wife had not satisfied him that the husband had resorted to any violence against her save by way of reasonable self-defence.

Where the affidavits of the parties make cross-allegations, it will not normally be appropriate to proceed without an oral hearing to permit cross-examination. Thus in *Shipp* v *Shipp* [1988] 1 FLR 345 at p. 347 Nourse LJ said that it was impracticable to have proper regard to the conduct of the spouses in relation to each other on the contradictory and untested affidavit evidence which was before the court. Although there might be cases where an interim ouster order might be made on the basis only of affidavit evidence, arrangements should have been made for the application to be heard effectively with oral evidence as soon as practicable. There had been only one serious incident and it was hotly disputed which of the two spouses was responsible for it. (See also *Whitlock* v *Whitlock* [1989] 1 FLR 208; *Harris* v *Harris* [1986] 1 FLR 12; *Tubb* v *Nicholls* [1989] 1 FLR 283.)

(ii) The respective needs and financial resources of the spouses
The spouse who has care of the children is likely to have the greater need for the accommodation provided by the matrimonial home, but this is only one factor to be taken into account. In *Wiseman* v *Simpson* [1988] 1 WLR 35 at p. 40 Ralph Gibson LJ acknowledged that the exclusion of the man would appear to most people to be fair and sensible if the task of the court was to decide who, in fairness, between the man who is going to work and the woman who has the care of the child, should have the flat to live in. However, the court did not have power to decide the case simply as a matter of housing policy and it was not appropriate to make an order excluding the male respondent (who had done no wrong) merely because of the greater need of the applicant for the accommodation.

On the other hand, where the husband's conduct is such as to make it not unreasonable for the wife to live apart from him the court will have regard to his housing need and the resources available to him to meet it. Thus in *Baggott* v *Baggott* [1986] 1 FLR 377, in contrast to *Richards* v *Richards*, the wife's allegations about the husband's behaviour were not flimsy in that he had threatened to kill her. The court concluded that it could not be said that the husband had no means of finding anywhere to live temporarily until the property interests of the parties had been determined in the pending divorce proceedings. Sir Roger Ormrod (at p. 380) said that it could not be suggested that the husband could not find himself a home or somewhere to live because he had offered to raise a further sum on the matrimonial home to provide a fund to enable one of them to live elsewhere. (See also *Scott* v *Scott* [1992] 1 FLR 529.)

In *Thurley* v *Smith* [1984] FLR 875 at p. 878 Sir John Arnold P said that one of the factors to be taken into account in relation to the needs of the parties is the duty of the local authority in relation to homeless persons under what is now the Housing Act 1985. (See also *Wootton* v *Wootton* [1984] FLR 871 and Chapter 4 Part 5.) However, not only does this raise the question of the relationship between the powers of the court and the housing policy of the local authority, but it is the party with care of the children who is more likely to be rehoused because of her priority need.

### (iii) The needs of any children

The interests of the children are not the paramount consideration when it comes to regulating occupation of the matrimonial home (see *Richards* v *Richards* [1984] AC 174). Nevertheless, the housing needs of the children (and caring parent) are an important factor to be taken into account. The weight to be given to that factor is a matter for the discretion of the judge. In some cases it will be given greater weight than the conduct of the parties (see Dunn LJ in *Lee* v *Lee* [1984] FLR 243 at p. 248). In *Anderson* v *Anderson* [1984] FLR 566 the wife had left the home and was living in a hostel for battered wives with her two year old son. She was expecting a further child a month later. The Court of Appeal held that the Recorder had not taken proper account of the impact which the birth of the child would have on life within the restricted accommodation of the matrimonial home if she had to return there while the husband remained. It had been a very short and turbulent marriage and the husband's right of occupation was accordingly withdrawn. On the other hand, in *Richards* v *Richards* [1984] AC 174 at p. 205 Lord Hailsham said that the court ought not confine itself to consideration of purely material requirements or immediate comforts. He continued:

"These may have to be given priority in a given case either owing to their urgency or the seriousness of denying them. But it is not necessarily for the interests of the children that either parent should be allowed to get away and be seen to get away with capricious, arbitrary, autocratic, or merely eccentric behaviour. It may well be difficult for a court to exercise control. But the difficulty is not rendered less if it is prepared to throw its hand in so readily."

### (iv) All the circumstances of the case

In *Anderson* v *Anderson* [1984] FLR 566 it appears that Purchas LJ considered that the court should have due regard to the fact that there had been repeated breakdowns of the relationship in the past when reconciliations were attempted in a marriage of extremely short duration. In *Summers* v *Summers* [1986] 1 FLR 343 at p. 347 May LJ said that if the view that the judge had taken and the reason why he made an ouster order was "to allow the dust to settle for a time, which might perhaps then lead to a fresh reconciliation as there had been only two months earlier ..." that was not the approach which the statute required the court to take. Moreover, "the judge failed to include in the balance of the exercise of his discretion what in this and many cases is an important consideration, namely the draconian nature of an ouster order and the effect that it has upon the party against whom it is made."

### 5. Applications under s.1 Domestic Violence and Matrimonial Proceedings Act 1976

*(a) Jurisdiction*

Section 1 of the Domestic Violence and Matrimonial Proceedings Act 1976 expressly confers jurisdiction only on county courts, but is also expressed to be without prejudice to the jurisdiction of the High Court. Since the jurisdiction of county courts is entirely statutory it was clear that any amendment could only be accomplished by legislation. The position in the High Court could be altered by an amendment to the Rules of Court and after some delay the Rules were amended. Order 90 r. 30 now provides that:

"(1) An application to the High Court by a party to a marriage within the meaning of section 1(1) of the Domestic Violence and Matrimonial Proceedings Act 1976 for an injunction containing one or more of the provisions mentioned in that subsection shall, if no other relief is sought in the proceedings, be made by originating summons issued out of the principal registry or out of a district registry as defined by the matrimonial causes rules."

*(b) The power to grant an injunction*

On an application by a party to a marriage a county court has jurisdiction under s.1(1) to grant an injunction containing one or more of the following provisions, namely:

(a) a provision restraining the other party to the marriage from molesting the applicant;

(b) a provision restraining the other party from molesting a child living with the applicant;

(c) a provision excluding the other party to the marriage from the matrimonial home or a part of the matrimonial home or from a specified area in which the matrimonial home is included;

(d) a provision requiring the other party to the marriage to permit the applicant to enter and remain in the matrimonial home or a part of the matrimonial home,

whether or not any other relief is sought in the proceedings. The effect of this provision was to make it no longer necessary to commence proceedings for divorce or judicial separation in order to obtain an injunction against molestation or an injunction excluding the other spouse from the matrimonial home. Inasmuch as "molestation" includes conduct which does not amount to violent behaviour, an injunction against molestation under s.1 can afford wider protection than that afforded by a "personal protection order" made by a magistrates' court under s.16 of the Domestic Proceedings and Magistrates' Courts Act 1978. (See *Horner* v *Horner* [1982] Fam 90 and Part 10 below, page 141.)

The expression "child living with the applicant" is not defined in the Act. This was considered unnecessary, indeed undesirable, for the provision is concerned with the factual situation of domestic upheaval in which the relationship of the two parties to the child is not really important. The point is that the children who are living in the house must not be made to suffer, and protection must be given to any such child, whether a child of one party or the other party, or of both, or of neither, such as a foster child living with the applicant at the time.

*(c) Unmarried couples*

Section 1 also applies to a man and a woman who are living with each other in the same household as husband and wife even though they are not married, and any reference to the matrimonial home is to be construed accordingly (s.1(2)). Sir George Baker P in *Davis* v *Johnson* [1979] AC 264 at p. 285 said that this is a much more restricted status than that of cohabitee, and whether the requirements are satisfied will be a question of fact in each individual case. The wording was intended to exclude casual relationships and to indicate a continuing state of affairs where a common household is maintained. The phrase "as husband and wife" would also exclude relationships such as housekeeper and employer or brother and sister (Standing Committee F. 30 June, 1976, at p. 9).

On the literal meaning of the words used it would be necessary for the man and the woman to be still living with each other at the time when one of them applies to the court. However, it has been recognised that in most cases an application is likely to be made by a woman who has left the home and that the scope of the section would be greatly reduced if relief was not available where the conduct of one cohabitee had forced the applicant to leave the home. In *Davis* v *Johnson* [1979] AC 264 at p. 275 Lord Denning MR, noting that the literal meaning would deprive the subsection of much of its effect, said:

"To my mind these words do not present any difficulty. They are used to denote the relationship between the parties before the incident which gives rise to the application. If they were then living together in the same household as husband and wife, that is enough."

This point was not specifically dealt with in the House of Lords in that case, but in subsequent cases the Court of Appeal has adopted the approach of Lord Denning (*McLean* v *Nugent* (1980)1 FLR 26; *McLean* v *Burke* (1982) 3 FLR 70; *O'Neill* v *Williams* [1984] FLR 1). In *O'Neill* v *Williams* (at p. 6) Cumming-Bruce LJ reviewed the cases and said that the approach of the courts had been "to inquire whether it was proved that at the date of the violence complained of the parties were then fulfilling the condition of living together in one household as husband and wife." He rejected as inconvenient and probably impracticable the alternative approach which would involve an "assessment of questions of fact and degree in order to explain the circumstances excusing, if it could be excused, the interval between the ouster and the date of the originating summons." (*Ibid.* at pp. 8-9.)

Nevertheless, the reference to the "violence" complained of is too narrow. In *Davis* v *Johnson* [1979] AC 264 at p. 334 Viscount Dilhorne clearly believed that the protection of the Act was not limited to cases where the applicant had left as a result of violence or molestation. Thus the man may suddenly tell her to leave which she does. Indeed "[h]e may not say anything but just change the locks on the house when she is out and refuse to admit her." This was in fact the "incident" giving rise to the application in *McLean* v *Burke* (1982) 3 FLR 70. The proper approach, therefore, appears to be to consider whether the parties were living with each other in the same household as husband and wife immediately before the incident giving rise to the application, rather than to circumstances surrounding the period after they ceased to live together and up until an application was made. Delay in seeking relief is not relevant in relation to jurisdiction though it will be a very relevant consideration in the decision of the judge whether or not to exercise the discretion. Thus in *O'Neill* v *Williams* [1984] FLR 1 at p. 10 Cumming-Bruce LJ said that "the longer the time elapses the less and less likely it will become that any judge would, or could, find it right to grant the remedy afforded by the 1976 Act, because that is an Act which deals with short-term relief, not with long-term solution of conflicts in matters of property." In that case there was a delay of some six months between the end of cohabitation and the commencement of proceedings. The Court of Appeal held that there was jurisdiction to make an order under s.1 but it was inappropriate for an ouster order to be made.

The reference to an incident giving rise to an application is not, however, without difficulty as was acknowledged by Ormrod LJ in *McLean* v *Nugent*. Where the departure of the applicant spouse is the consequence of a course of conduct on the part of the other spouse the precipitating event may not be easy to identify. Is it really necessary to go beyond a requirement that the parties were living together in the same household as husband and wife immediately before the separation? See the comments of Lord Donaldson MR in *Pidduck* v *Molloy* [1992] 2 FLR 202 at p. 206 and in *Duo* v *Osborne* [1992] 2 FLR 425 at p. 434 criticising the restricted scope of the 1976 Act.

Where the parties have continued to live under the same roof they will not necessarily be living with each other in the same household if they are able to lead completely separate lives in a large house. However, the fact that they are living at arm's length in small accommodation from which they may not be able to escape by reason of housing difficulties, will not take them outside the subsection. Thus in *Adeoso* v *Adeoso* [1980] 1 WLR 1535 a man and a woman were joint tenants of a two-roomed council flat. For some 18 months there had been no sexual intercourse between them and for some 12 months they had been sleeping in separate rooms which were kept locked. The woman stopped cooking for the man and washing his clothes and they did not speak to each other though she continued to share the outgoings on the flat. At first instance the judge accepted a submission that they could not be living with each other in the same household. The Court of Appeal disagreed and said that too much importance had been attached to the old cases about desertion which held that it was possible for a spouse to desert the other while living in closest possible contiguity and so on. Those cases had no application to the situation before the court and in practical terms for present purposes "one cannot live in a two roomed flat with another person without living in the same household." (*Ibid.* *per* Ormrod LJ at p. 1539.)

## (d) Exercising the powers

### (i) General principles

The Act does not specify the factors which the court should take into account in exercising its powers under s.1(1), but leaves it to the courts to determine the circumstances in which one of the specified injunctions is appropriate. Before the decision of the House of Lords in *Richards* v *Richards* [1984] AC 174 the courts applied the principles evolved in the considerable number of reported cases concerned with the grant of injunctions ancillary to proceedings for divorce or judicial separation, so far as married persons were concerned. In *Davis* v *Johnson* [1979] AC 264 at pp. 330, 333, 339, 341 and 349 it was accepted that s.1(1) effected no change in the substantive law relating to husbands and wives but merely gave them a quicker and cheaper method of protection. Those principles have subsequently developed in both groups of cases until the decision in *Richards* v *Richards*. It has already been noted above that, following that decision, applications under the 1976 Act, whether by a spouse or a cohabitee, must be determined on the basis of the criteria set out in s.1(3) of the Matrimonial Homes Act 1983. However, two matters merit special consideration.

### (ii) Violence is not essential

First, the better view is that violence is not an essential precondition for an injunction under s.1 though the provisions of s.2 (considered below) are expressly qualified by reference to violence. This view was taken in the early decision of *Spindlow* v *Spindlow* [1979] Fam 52 and was reiterated more recently in *Galan* v *Galan* [1985] FLR 905 at p. 914 where Purchas LJ said:

"The heading of the Act, of course, is 'Domestic Violence and Matrimonial Proceedings Act 1976'; but there is no specific mention of violence or injury as a qualifying factor enabling the court to exercise its power. In my judgment it is a reasonable inference, by comparison with the powers in section 2, that something short of actual violence may be sufficient to give the court the powers provided under s.1. For my part, construing this Act, and in particular sections 1 and 2 as a whole, I would hold the view that the real threat of violence, or disturbance, to the other party to the marriage, or a child living with that party, would be sufficient to give the court jurisdiction to make any one or more of the orders provided for in section 1 of the Act."

In that case there was no recent evidence of violence, though there had been violence in the past. Nevertheless, the risk of disturbance and violence if the husband was permitted to return to the matrimonial home was sufficient to enable the court to make any order it considered appropriate in its discretion under s.1. The Court of Appeal upheld an exclusion order.

This approach is consistent with the views expressed in *Davis* v *Johnson* and *Richards* v *Richards*. Thus in *Davis* v *Johnson* [1979] AC 264 at p. 335 Viscount Dilhorne said that "the purpose of the Act was to give protection from domestic violence and from eviction". Lord Salmon (at pp. 341-342) said: "I do not think that a county court judge could properly exclude the paramour from his home or its environs under s.1(1)(c) unless he had been guilty of serious molestation likely to expose the so-called common law wife or her children to serious danger or intolerable conditions while he remained there." Lord Scarman (at p. 348) said:

"I conclude that the mischief against which Parliament has legislated by s.1 of the Act may be described in these terms: conduct by a family partner which puts at risk the security, or sense of security, of the other partner in the home. Physical violence, or the threat of it, is clearly within the mischief. But there is much more to it than that. Homelessness can be as great a threat as physical violence to the security of a woman (or man) and her children. Eviction - actual, attempted or threatened - is therefore within the mischief: likewise, conduct which makes it impossible or intolerable, as in the present case, for the other partner, or the children, to remain at home."

In *Richards* v *Richards* [1984] AC 174 at p. 208 Lord Scarman said:

"It must be unlikely that the section, though it offers no express guidance, can be applicable unless there be shown violence, or the threat of it, or a reasonable apprehension that the presence of the man (or the woman) in the house constitutes a danger to the physical or emotional health or well-being of the woman (or man) and the children."

To require evidence of violence would, moreover, be incompatible with the view adopted since *Richards* v *Richards* that applications should be determined on the basis of the criteria in s.1(3).

(iii) An order may be made notwithstanding any proprietary interest of the excluded party

Secondly, an ouster order may be made under s.1 notwithstanding any property interest of the excluded party in the home. As between husband and wife it was clearly established that on an application ancillary to divorce proceedings an injunction excluding one spouse from the matrimonial home could be granted irrespective of the property rights in the home. (See e.g. *Jones* v *Jones* [1971] 1 WLR 396.) Thus a husband could be excluded from the matrimonial home even though he was its owner or tenant, or a joint tenant with his wife. Accordingly, all that s.1 did for spouses was to provide them with a "simpler, speedier, more widely available and more effective remedy for threatened violation of legal rights ..." (*per* Lord Diplock in *Davis* v *Johnson* [1979] AC 264 at p. 330). In the case of a man and a woman living together within the terms of subs.(2) the section clearly gave the woman who was sole owner of their home a more effective remedy. (See *Hills* v *Bushby* (1978) 8 Fam Law 77.) However, if the section was held to enable a county court judge to exclude a man from a home of which he was sole owner or tenant, this would go further and give his female cohabitee a right she did not have before the Act. In *B* v *B* [1978] Fam 26 the Court of Appeal declined to construe the section in this way and held it to be merely procedural. In *Cantliff* v *Jenkins* [1978] Fam 47 a differently constituted Court of Appeal took the same view where the parties were joint tenants of the home.

In *Davis* v *Johnson* [1979] AC 264 a specially constituted five-judge bench of the Court of Appeal rejected by a majority of four to one the interpretation in *B* v *B* and *Cantliff* v *Jenkins*, and held that s.1 gave a county court jurisdiction to exclude a cohabitee from a home he had shared with the other cohabitee irrespective of any right of property vested in the person excluded, whether as owner, tenant or joint tenant. This construction was upheld by the House of Lords (Lord Diplock dissenting). Viscount Dilhorne (at p. 334) said:

"To hold that protection can only be given if she has property rights is to differentiate between married women and unmarried women to whom subsection (1) is intended to apply and would in my opinion frustrate the intention of Parliament."

Lord Scarman (at p. 349) explained that:

"First, the purpose of the section is not to create rights but to strengthen remedies. Subsection (2) does, however, confer on the unmarried woman with no property in the home a new right. Though enjoying no property rights to possession of the family home, she can apply to the county court for an order restricting or suspending for a time her family partner's right to possession of the premises and conferring on her a limited right of occupancy."

### (e) The duration of an order

#### (i) Immediate relief, not permanent resolution

In *Davis* v *Johnson* [1979] AC 264 the majority of the House of Lords made it clear that the purpose of s.1 was "the provision of immediate relief, not permanent resolution of the situation arising on the breakdown of a marriage or an association where the parties though unmarried had been living together as if they were" (*per* Viscount Dilhorne at p. 335). An injunction granted under s.1 could interfere with the enjoyment of property rights, but did not otherwise affect them. It was a short-term remedy giving protection from domestic violence and from eviction. Where the parties are married to each other and divorce proceedings are imminent or pending, then the longer term position is likely to receive attention from the court on applications for financial provision and property adjustment under the Matrimonial Causes Act 1973. However, if there is no immediate likelihood of a divorce or a decree of judicial separation there is a danger, as Ormrod LJ pointed out in *Hopper* v *Hopper* [1978] 1 WLR 1342 at p. 1345, that the injunction will operate as the equivalent of a property adjustment order under the 1973 Act. Where the parties are not married to each other, the danger of the injunction having more permanent effect is even greater. This is particularly so where the property is held on a tenancy so that the interests of the parties will not even be considered in proceedings under s.30 of the Law of Property Act 1925 for an order for sale. In *Davis* v *Johnson* [1979] AC 264 at p. 342 Lord Salmon expressed regret that the Act did not regulate the period for which a man could be deprived of occupation and his former mistress allowed to enjoy it. The object should be to provide protection for a reasonable time. A reasonable time in the case of a married woman "being enough to enable [her] to make other arrangements for her accommodation or to take steps ... to get her matrimonial status clarified, and to enable the court to exercise its powers to make property adjustment orders" (*per* Ormrod LJ in *Hopper* v *Hopper* [1978] 1 WLR 1342 at p. 1345). In the case of unmarried persons it should be such as "to enable both parties to regulate their affairs" (*per* Viscount Dilhorne in *Davis* v *Johnson* [1979] AC 264 at p. 336).

Thus in *Davis* v *Johnson,* where the home in question was a council flat, Viscount Dilhorne noted that the council had granted the tenancy on the basis of the housing needs of the woman and her child and that she and the man became joint tenants of it at his insistence and after she and the child had been living there without him for some three months. He thought that in view of what had happened the council might now be disposed to terminate the joint tenancy and give her the sole tenancy. He added that "the county court judge may think that the injunction should only continue until the council has dealt with the matter". (*Ibid.* at p. 336. The "ability" of the council to deal with the matter was drastically reduced by the introduction of secure tenancies by the Housing Act 1980. For the scope for terminating a secure joint tenancy with a view to the grant of a new tenancy to one party, see Chapter 7.)

In *Freeman* v *Collins* (1983) 4 FLR 649 the Court of Appeal set aside an order excluding a man from a council house of which he was tenant "until further order". The court limited the order to one month which would give the housing authority sufficient time to consider the application for housing of the female cohabitee. She and her three children had moved into the house which the man had already been occupying as tenant. Dunn LJ saw the ultimate responsibility for rehousing the woman and her children as being on the local housing authority, and all the court could do was to give a breathing space so as to enable the woman and the children to live unmolested while the council decided the long-term future. The court had no jurisdiction to transfer any interest to her, and, he said (at p. 653):

"In my view, this Act should not be used as a device whereby unmarried persons can acquire interests in property which they have occupied, maybe for only a short period of time, as licensees of the true owner or tenant. The right to occupy in circumstances such as we have before us in this case, is a strictly limited one, to give the respondent enough time to find alternative accommodation."

(Contrast cases where the parties have cohabited for many years, e.g. *Wooton* v *Wooton* [1984] FLR 871.)

(ii) A short fixed period is generally appropriate

It is important, therefore, that the temporary nature of the protection should be made clear to the applicant. In order to secure uniformity a direction was issued in 1978 which, while recognising the discretion of the court, said that "whenever an injunction is granted excluding one of the parties from the matrimonial home (or part thereof or a specified area), consideration should be given to imposing a time limit on the operation of the injunction. In most cases a period of up to three months is likely to suffice in the first instance. It will be open to the respondent in any event to apply for the discharge of the injunction before the expiry of the period fixed, for instance on the ground of reconciliation, and to the applicant to apply for an extension." (Practice Direction (Injunctions: Domestic Violence) [1978] 1 WLR 1123.)

Generally, therefore, an ouster order for a short fixed period will be the appropriate order (if any) for the court to make, and an order of indefinite duration, which may be expressed to endure until further order, will not be appropriate. A short fixed period should normally enable the parties, either by negotiation or by recourse to the courts, to determine their rights either at common law or under other statutes (*per* Slade LJ in *Galan* v *Galan* [1985] FLR 905 at p. 919). In the case of married couples resort may be had to the Matrimonial Causes Act 1973 or the Matrimonial Homes Act 1983. In the case of unmarried couples resort may be had to s.30 of the Law of Property Act 1925 where the parties are joint owners of the property.

(iii) Exceptional cases
However, such other proceedings may not be open to the parties either in the short term or, indeed, at all. In these circumstances it may be appropriate to make an injunction until further order, i.e. one which is intended to be of indefinite duration. This was the position in *Galan* v *Galan* where the parties had arrived at stalemate. On the one hand, the judge had found that it was impossible for the wife to come into direct face-to-face contact with the husband. On the other hand, the wife had failed in her divorce petition relying on paragraph (b) of s.1(1), and the husband would not consent to a divorce on the basis of paragraph (d). The wife had no remedy until she was able to present a petition relying on five years' separation within paragraph (e). In these circumstances the Court of Appeal approved an ouster order "until further order of the court". Even so, Purchas LJ strongly encouraged the wife to apply under the Matrimonial Homes Act and indicated that it was inappropriate for the ouster order under the Domestic Violence Act to last until the hearing of the divorce petition based on five years' separation.

More difficult is the case of *Spencer* v *Comacho* (1983) 4 FLR 662 where the man and the woman held a tenancy of the home in their joint names. The court had previously made an exclusion order for a period of three months following the respondent's violence, and this order had been extended for a further period of three months and subsequently for a period of six months. The Court of Appeal held that in the circumstances the court could make an injunction until further order. This would have the advantage of making it unnecessary for the applicant to come back to the court at all as long as the injunction was in force. If after a sufficient period of time had elapsed the respondent was advised that it would be appropriate for him to apply to bring the injunction to an end, it was always open to him to do so. However, unless the parties became reconciled it is difficult to see what would justify a discharge of the order on the application of the man. As Sir David Cairns pointed out (at p. 667), in the particular case there was no statute open to them, and in these circumstances the ouster order begins to take on the appearance of a property adjustment order. It is true that the parties were joint tenants in contrast to the position in, for example, *Freeman* v *Collins* (1983) 4 FLR 649 where the ouster order was sought against the sole tenant. However, this in itself would seem to make no difference to the applicability of the general principle that orders are intended only to provide breathing space. The position of parties who are joint tenants of a house and the steps open to them to resolve the dispute as to occupation of it were considered by Ralph Gibson LJ in the later case of *Wiseman* v *Simpson* [1988] 1 WLR 35 at pp. 42-43. He pointed out that as joint tenants each has the right to occupy and neither can lawfully exclude the other. If the woman truly found it intolerable to remain in the flat while the man was there and the man had infringed no right of the woman, then she had no remedy at law and could do nothing but leave the flat. The man infringed no right of the woman merely because, knowing that she found it intolerable to remain in the flat while he was there, he nevertheless remained there hoping that she would be thus forced to go. If the parties as joint tenants own some sellable interest in the flat then the woman, unable to reside in the flat because of the presence of the man, could apply to the court for an order that the flat be sold with vacant possession. (See *Jackson* v *Jackson* [1971] 1 WLR 1539 and Chapter 6.) However, the parties in that case, as joint tenants of a council flat on a weekly or monthly tenancy, had no ordinarily sellable interest. Ralph Gibson LJ noted that when the 1976 Act was passed, tenants of council houses generally had no security of tenure and the council could recover possession on lawful termination of the tenancy. Accordingly, upon the breakdown of the relationship between the occupants of a council flat, "the question as to whether either party should remain in occupation, and if so which, could be decided by the council in accordance with their housing policy." As a result of the Housing Act 1980 the position had changed, but there was no new provision for dealing with the breakdown of the relationship of unmarried joint tenants of such property. Ralph Gibson LJ went on to point out that one joint tenant could by notice bring such a periodic tenancy to an end, and this could provide the council with an opportunity of reallocating the accommodation. (See Chapter 7.)

It would seem, therefore, that at least where the tenancy is held jointly, an ouster order for a short fixed period will in general provide sufficient breathing space for a party to seek the assistance of the council and, if appropriate, to terminate the joint tenancy by notice. An ouster order until further order, as in *Spencer* v *Comacho*, will generally be unnecessary. As was acknowledged by Ralph Gibson LJ in *Wiseman* v *Simpson* [1988] 1 WLR 35 at p. 43 it is, no doubt, often difficult for a housing authority to make an arrangement with one joint tenant to the detriment of the other when the council is unable with confidence to determine who, if anyone, is to blame for the breakdown of the relationship and what are the respective needs and resources of the parties. This is particularly so where, as in that case, there was nothing in the conduct of the party remaining in occupation to justify the refusal of the other to return home while he was there. Moreover, it places the responsibility on the housing authority rather than on the courts, which was the general policy of the Housing Act 1980 in relation to spouses. (See Chapter 7.)

Where a tenancy is in the sole name of a man against whom an ouster order is sought, then there appears to be no means whereby the tenancy can be terminated or transferred against his will. This should make no difference in principle though a woman who is unable to show a priority need may find herself in a difficult position. (See Chapter 4.) This may perhaps explain the extreme course taken in *Fairweather* v *Kolosine* (1982) 11 HLR 61 where the Court of Appeal upheld an order ousting a man who was sole tenant of a council house until the youngest of the woman's children attained the age of 16. Postponement for a period of some five years produced a result akin to that of a Mesher order and seems difficult to justify in principle. (See *Mesher* v *Mesher* [1980] 1 All ER 126, considered in Chapter 12.)

## 6. Injunctions under the general power of the court

*(a) The power to grant an injunction*
The power of the High Court to grant injunctions is at first sight exceedingly broad. Section 37 of the Supreme Court Act 1981 (replacing s.45 of the Supreme Court of Judicature (Consolidation) Act 1925) provides that the High Court "may by order (whether interlocutory or final) grant injunctions ... in all cases in which it appears to the court to be just and convenient to do so." In *Richards* v *Richards* it was unnecessary for the House of Lords to consider whether the court had any inherent jurisdiction apart from the section. Lord Hailsham said that if it has, it is indistinguishable in its application to the jurisdiction conferred by the section. He preferred (at p. 199) "to say that any inherent jurisdiction is absorbed by the section". The power of a county court to grant an injunction is derived from s.38 of the County Courts Act 1984 (replacing s.74 of the County Courts Act 1959). It has been noted above that as a result of the view of the majority of the House of Lords in *Richards* v *Richards* a spouse seeking an ouster order must now proceed under the Matrimonial Homes Act 1983 and not rely on the general power of the court to grant injunctions. However, Lord Hailsham emphasised that s.37 is still in force, and is still there "in reserve where the special legislation does not apply ...".

There are in fact a number of situations where the Matrimonial Homes Act 1983, the Domestic Violence and Matrimonial Proceedings Act 1976 and the Domestic Proceedings and Magistrates' Courts Act 1978 will not be available. This will be the case once spouses are divorced. The 1976 Act will no longer be available where an unmarried couple are no longer "living with each other in the same household as husband and wife". Nevertheless, the power of the court to grant an injunction in such situations under its apparently wide general power is restricted by certain well established principles.

First, the injunction sought must be ancillary to the substantive relief sought in the cause or matter in which the application is made. Secondly, it is well established that an injunction will only be granted to support a legal or an equitable right.

*(b) An injunction must be ancillary to the substantive relief*
The grant of an injunction must be ancillary to, and comprised within the scope of, the substantive relief sought in the cause or matter in which the application is made. Thus in *Des Salles d'Epinoix* v *Des Salles d'Epinoix* [1967] 1 WLR 553, where the wife had issued an originating summons seeking maintenance under s.22 of the Matrimonial Causes Act 1965 on the ground of wilful neglect to maintain, an application by the husband for an injunction against the wife restraining her from preventing him from returning to the matrimonial home, was refused because it did not arise out of, and was not incidental to, the wife's cause of action for maintenance. In *Lucas* v *Lucas* [1992] Fam Law 100 Balcombe LJ accepted that it would be quite inappropriate if, long after a marriage had been dissolved by decree absolute and where there were no other relevant interests to be protected, divorce proceedings should be used as a vehicle for the purpose of making a claim to an injunction which could be made in fresh proceedings launched for the purpose. However, in that case the decree absolute had been granted only 2 months before the wife issued

her application for an injunction and she was sole tenant of the former matrimonial home. (See also *Andrew* v *Andrew* [1990] 2 FLR 376.)

*(c) An injunction will only be granted to support a legal right*

(i) Proprietary rights
A party with a proprietary right in the former matrimonial or family home may seek to protect that right by injunction. Thus where the applicant is entitled to the whole beneficial interest in the property, he or she may obtain an injunction to restrain a trespass by the other. Where both parties have proprietary rights in the property it seems that one party cannot justify keeping the other out of the property on this basis. Thus in *Ainsbury* v *Millington* [1986] 1 All ER 73 the parties had obtained a joint tenancy of a council house at a time when they were cohabiting. When the man was imprisoned the woman married another man and lived in the house until her former cohabitee was released from prison. The woman and her husband and child then left the house but she sought to exclude the former cohabitee from the property. The Court of Appeal held that there was no power to make an injunction, and Dillon LJ said:

"Has she then any legal right on which she can rely to claim that relief? She is one of the joint tenants of the property. Each of the tenants has an equal right to occupy the property, but neither has a right to occupy the property to the exclusion of the other. Ordinarily, as between co-owners, for one to oust the other would be an actionable wrong."

He contrasted the position with that in *Re W (a minor)* [1981] 3 All ER 401 where the flat concerned was the sole property of the applicant, "who had therefore a proprietary interest in the flat capable of supporting her application for an injunction".

(ii) The right not to be assaulted or molested
Every person has a right not to be assaulted and there is no doubt that this is a right which can be enforced by an injunction restraining another from assaulting or threatening to assault the applicant. This is a right which exists irrespective of whether or not the parties are married to each other. There must, however, be evidence that the respondent or defendant has assaulted or threatened to assault the applicant. Assaults on children can also be restrained in this way.

In *Wilde* v *Wilde* [1988] 2 FLR 83 at p. 92 Bingham LJ said that the same applied to molestation for "everyone has a right not to be molested". However, this statement was *obiter* because there was no evidence of molestation in that case. Moreover, it conflicts with the views expressed in *Patel* v *Patel* [1988] 2 FLR 179 that there is no tort of molestation. (See further Chapter 4.) The strict view applied by many judges now appears to be that while there is power to grant an injunction restraining assault, there is no power to grant an injunction against molestation except pursuant to one of the statutory provisions considered earlier in this chapter (but see now the decision of the Court of Appeal in *Kharasandjian* v *Bush* [1993] 3 WLR 476).

(iii) Rights in relation to pending proceedings
It was well established that while divorce proceedings were pending a spouse had a right to pursue his or her remedies in court free from pressure or threats of pressure to abandon or modify his or her claim. (See e.g. Pearce J in *Silverstone* v *Silverstone* [1953] P 174 at p. 177, and Ormrod J in *Montgomery* v *Montgomery* [1965] P 46 at p. 51.) Even though a marriage has been dissolved by a decree absolute there may still be pending proceedings under s.24 of the Matrimonial Causes Act 1973 or s.17 of the Married Women's Property Act 1882, or there may continue to exist a caution placed upon the matrimonial home under the Matrimonial Homes Act 1983. In *Wilde* v *Wilde* [1988] 2 FLR 83 at p. 91 Purchas LJ noted that in *Stewart* v *Stewart* [1973] Fam 21 Sir George Baker P discarded these sources of jurisdiction in favour of a general inherent jurisdiction. It might be inferred that, had it been necessary, the President would have used these considerations to support the exercise of jurisdiction. In *Wilde* v *Wilde* both parties had a joint interest in the matrimonial home and clearly this could be protected if either party threatened to take steps which would prejudice the fair disposal of those interests. The court had jurisdiction to act under s.17 of the 1882 Act or s.24 of the 1973 Act but none of these considerations arose. He questioned the validity of using these interests as affording a continuing jurisdiction to grant injunctions which are really for the purpose of protecting the interests of the children. (See also *Lucas* v *Lucas* [1992] Fam Law 100.)

*(d) Protecting the interests of the children*
It is possible that even in the absence of any infringement or threatened infringement of a legal right of the applicant, the court may have jurisdiction to grant an injunction to protect the interests of the children in the care of the applicant. Unfortunately some of the views expressed in the Court of Appeal are difficult to reconcile.

In *Wilde* v *Wilde* [1988] 2 FLR 83 at p. 87 Purchas LJ said that there was "powerful authority for the proposition that an inherent jurisdiction exists where the welfare of the children is involved". Having considered the earlier cases, he came to the decision of the Court of Appeal in *Quinn* v *Quinn* (1983) 4 FLR 394 which he regarded as binding on the court. In that case, following divorce, the parties and their children continued to live at the former matrimonial home. Subsequently, the court, having granted custody of the younger children to the wife, ordered that the husband should leave the matrimonial home within four weeks. Purchas LJ said that the order had been made "for the protection of the children and for the preservation of a peaceful home for them". Bingham LJ (at p. 92) said that apart from that authority he would have doubted "whether there was an inherent jurisdiction in the court to ensure the protection of the children's interests unless there were some infringement or threatened infringement of the legal rights of the wife or the children". However, he accepted that the principle expressed in *Quinn* "justified the grant of an injunction to exclude one parent from the matrimonial home 'no matter what the proceedings if that was desirable in the interests of the children', apparently without reference to any infringement or threatened infringement of a legal right."

Even the absence of such a general jurisdiction would not in the view of

Bingham LJ necessarily have deprived the wife of the injunction granted by the judge since the court's order had given care and control of the children to her. It had thereby imposed duties upon her and the court should recognise and enforce her right to perform her duties in an appropriate manner. It could be said that the husband's conduct had prevented her doing so, but the question whether the reasonable protection of the wife's right would have justified the exclusion of the husband from the home of which he was joint owner pending an early decision on the disposition of that property did not in his view fall for determination.

On the other hand, in *Ainsbury* v *Millington* [1986] 1 All ER 73 the Court of Appeal took the view that an ouster order could not be made in proceedings under the Guardianship of Minors Act 1971 simply on the basis of the requirements of the welfare of a child. Dillon LJ (at p. 75) said that an "ouster application can only be made consistently with the decision of the House of Lords in *Richards* v *Richards* if, in a case where the Matrimonial Homes Act 1983 and the Domestic Violence and Matrimonial Proceedings Act 1976 are not appropriate, the applicant can make out a legal right which entitles her to the injunction under the terms of the Supreme Court Act 1981". This was followed in *M* v *M (Custody Application)* [1988] 1 FLR 225.

It is arguable that the decision in *Ainsbury* v *Millington* does no more than make it clear that the legal right necessary to support an injunction under the Supreme Court Act 1981 cannot be found merely in the fact that the applicant for an injunction has applied for or obtained custody or care or control of a child living with him or her. This conflicts with the view expressed by Purchas LJ in *Wilde* v *Wilde* [1988] 2 FLR 83 at p. 91, but the jurisdiction principally relied upon in *Quinn* v *Quinn* and *Wilde* v *Wilde* was not that based on the existence of a legal right in the applicant requiring protection. An injunction was granted on the basis of a general jurisdiction to protect children. An injunction on this basis can be justified only if there is a real need for protection in the short term. In *Wilde* v *Wilde* Purchas LJ traced the references to the "inherent jurisdiction to ensure protection of the children", starting with the decision in *Stewart* v *Stewart* [1973] Fam 21. He concluded that the assumption of such an inherent jurisdiction seemed "almost certainly to have been based upon the view of the judges originally exercising wardship jurisdiction in the Chancery Division". Such jurisdiction was unaffected by s.37 of the 1981 Act, but it appears that the nature and extent of the jurisdiction had not been argued before the court and he was content to proceed on the basis that the decision in *Quinn* v *Quinn* was binding on the court.

In *Wilde* v *Wilde* the judge had found that in the light of what had happened it was impossible for the wife to return to the home while the husband remained there. It was not acceptable that the children should return to the house to live with their father on his suggestion of shared care with the mother as she came and went while living a considerable distance away with her mother. It was in the interests of the children to return home and the mother, who did not work, should return to look after them (see also *Beard* v *Beard* [1981] 1 WLR 369). In contrast in *Ainsbury* v *Millington* the applicant was seeking to oust the respondent from the home of which they were joint tenants and to take up occupation with her husband whom she had married while the respondent was in prison. Dillon LJ said: "True it is that she would be doing so with [the child] also and as having the custody of [the child], or at any rate interim custody, but it seems to me that that is very drastic relief way outside anything contemplated by the Guardianship of Minors Act 1971." In other words the focus of the application was not on the protection of the children, and reliance was not placed, or at least could not properly be placed, on the same general jurisdiction as in *Wilde* but on the jurisdiction contained in s.37 of the Supreme Court Act 1981.

The present uncertain position is unsatisfactory. On the one hand it is desirable that courts should have power to exclude a party from the family home where this is necessary to protect the interests of the children of the family and there is no other basis on which this can be done. On the other hand, if such jurisdiction is not narrowly confined there is a danger that it would come into conflict with the principles laid down by the House of Lords in *Richards* v *Richards* that in considering applications for injunctions the interest of a child is not the paramount consideration but one of the factors to be taken into account in the balancing exercise required by s.1(3) of the Matrimonial Homes Act 1983. In that context it has been made clear that there are cases in which the interest of a child will be the factor carrying most weight. It is important that the exercise of the inherent jurisdiction under consideration should be consistent with this approach.

It seems that occupation of the family home may be regulated by the making of residence and contact orders under s.8 of the Children Act 1989. A "residence order" is an order settling the arrangements to be made as to the person with whom a child is to live. A "contact order" is an order requiring the person with whom a child lives, or is to live, to allow the child to visit or stay with the person named in the order, or for that person and the child otherwise to have contact with each other. In *Nottingham County Council* v *P* [1993] 3 WLR 406 Ward J made a residence order in respect of two children in favour of their mother. He further directed that the children should live with their mother at the address which was their home, and that the father, who was found to have abused another child, should not enter or attempt to enter that property and was to have no contact with either child except under the supervision of the local authority. He rejected the submission that, where no contact is being allowed, it follows that there is no contact order. In the circumstances it was inappropriate and unnecessary to make a "prohibited steps order" under s.8.

## 7. *Ex parte* applications for injunctions

Generally, notice of an application for an injunction must be served on the other party together with affidavit evidence. The period of notice is 21 days under the Matrimonial Homes Act 1983, 2 days under the Domestic Violence and Matrimonial Proceedings Act 1976 and 2 days if the application is made ancillary to divorce proceedings (CCR, Ord. 7, r. 10(5); FPR 1991, rr. 3.8 and 3.9; and CCR, Ord. 13 r. 1(2)). However, the court has power to intervene immediately without such notice on an *ex parte* application if this is justified in the circumstances.

In *Ansah* v *Ansah* [1977] Fam 138 at pp. 142-143 Ormrod LJ emphasised that:
"... this power must be used with great caution and only in circumstances in

which it is really necessary to act immediately. Such circumstances do undoubtedly tend to occur more frequently in family disputes than in other types of litigation because the parties are often still in close contact with one another and, particularly when a marriage is breaking up, in a state of high emotional tension; but even in such cases the court should only act *ex parte* in an emergency when the interests of justice or the protection of the applicant or a child clearly demands immediate intervention by the court. Such cases should be extremely rare, since any urgent application can be heard *inter partes* on two days' notice to the other side: ... circumstances, of course, may arise when prior notice cannot be given to the other side; for example, cases where one parent has disappeared with the children, or a spouse, usually the wife, is so frightened of the other spouse that some protection must be provided against a violent response to service of proceedings, but the court must be fully satisfied that such protection is necessary."

This was echoed in a Practice Direction [1978] 1 WLR 925 issued by the President of the Family Division in which concern was expressed at the increasing number of applications being made *ex parte*.

If an order is to be made *ex parte*, it should be strictly limited in time if the risk of causing serious injustice is to be avoided. The time is to be measured in days, i.e. the shortest period which must elapse before a preliminary hearing *inter partes* can be arranged, and the order must specify the date on which it expires (*per* Ormrod LJ in *Ansah* v *Ansah* [1977] Fam 138 at p. 143). In *Masich* v *Masich* (1977) 7 Fam Law 245 Ormrod LJ went so far as to say that an application by a spouse seeking an injunction to exclude the other spouse from the matrimonial home should never be made *ex parte*. Such an application should be on notice and it was desirable that both parties should be present at the hearing. *Ex parte* applications should be confined to injunctions against molestation. Certainly, the circumstances will need to be truly exceptional in order to justify an *ex parte* application for an ouster order.

## 8. Enforcing injunctions

### (a) Committal

(i) The court's powers
Where there is a breach of an injunction in this context the conventional remedy for this contempt of court is committal to prison. In the High Court this is governed by RSC Ord. 45, r. 5. A county court is given similar jurisdiction by the County Courts Act 1984, s.38(1), and the procedure is governed by the County Court Rules 1981, Ord. 29. Strict conditions must be satisfied before an injunction can be enforced by an order of committal.

(ii) Notice
In the case of a mandatory injunction, such as an injunction ordering a husband to vacate the matrimonial home by a specified time, it is essential that the respondent

has been served personally with a copy of the injunction before the expiration of the time within which he was required to act (RSC Ord. 45, r. 7(2); CCR 1981, Ord. 29, r. 1). In the case of a prohibitory injunction, such as an injunction restraining a husband from molesting his wife, it will be sufficient if the respondent was present in court when the injunction was granted, or if the respondent has been notified of the terms of the injunction whether by telephone, telegram or otherwise (RSC Ord. 45, r. 7(6); CCR 1981 Ord. 29, r. 1(6)). The court has power to dispense with these requirements (RSC Ord. 45, r. 7(7); CCR 1981, Ord. 29, r. 1(7); see *Hussain* v *Hussain* [1986] Fam. 134).

(iii) The penal notice
It is essential that the copy of the injunction served on the respondent was endorsed with the requisite penal notice, i.e. a notice informing him that disobedience to the injunction will render him liable to be committed to prison (RSC Ord. 45, r. 7(4); CCR 1981 Ord. 29, r. 1(3); *Williams* v *Fawcett* [1985] 1 WLR 501).

(iv) Application for committal
If the above requirements have been satisfied and there has been a breach of the injunction, the next stage is to apply for an order for committal. The respondent must be given notice calling on him to show cause why a committal order should not be made against him. The notice must make clear to the respondent what he is alleged to have done and that it is a breach (RSC Ord. 52, r. 4; CCR 1981, Ord. 29, r. 1)). In *Harmsworth* v *Harmsworth* [1988] 1 FLR 349 at p. 354 Nicholls LJ said that the proper test is whether the notice gives the person alleged to be in contempt enough information to enable him to meet the charge. In satisfying this test it is clear that, if lengthy particulars are needed, they may be included in a schedule or other addendum either at the foot of the notice or attached to the notice so as to form part of the notice rather than being set out in the body of the notice itself. However, a reference in the notice to a wholly separate document, such as the wife's affidavit in support of her application, for particulars that ought to be in the notice was, he thought, a different matter. Such a reference cannot cure what otherwise would be a deficiency in the notice. (See now CCR Ord. 29, r. 1(4A).) The notice must be served personally on the defendant/respondent and at least two clear working days' notice of the hearing must be given. The court may dispense with service of the summons if it thinks it just to do so, but it will allow what is in effect an *ex parte* application for a committal order to be made only in exceptional circumstances (RSC Ord. 45, r. 7(7); CCR Ord. 29, r. 1(7)). In *Wright* v *Jess* [1987] 1 WLR 1076 at p. 1081 Sir John Donaldson MR emphasised "that this is a wholly exceptional course to take and one which can only be justified if no other course is open in order either to uphold the authority of the court or to protect the applicant." Such a course was justified in that case on both grounds. The appellant had already served three sentences of imprisonment for breach of the injunction and had been warned of the dire consequences which would be likely to ensue if there was any further breach. (See also *Lamb* v *Lamb* [1984] FLR 278; *Benesch* v *Newman* [1987] 1 FLR 262; *Wright* v *Jess* [1987] 1 WLR 1076.)

(v) Courses of action open to the court
Applications in the High Court or in a county court must be made to a judge. A number of courses are open to the judge.

First, the judge may adjourn the application after issuing a warning. This may be used where the judge wishes to give the respondent a last chance to be of good behaviour. (See *George* v *George* [1986] 2 FLR 347.)

Secondly, the judge may make a suspended committal order. The effect is similar to an adjournment except that a definite period of imprisonment is being held in abeyance. It means that the applicant will have to refer the matter back to the court before committal can take place. (See *Ansah* v *Ansah* [1977] Fam 138; *Linkleter* v *Linkleter* [1988] 1 FLR 360 and *Goff* v *Goff* [1989] 1 FLR 492.)

Thirdly, the judge may make a committal order. Committal must be for a fixed term not exceeding 2 years (Contempt of Court Act 1981, s.14, as amended by the County Court (Penalties for Contempt) Act 1983 and County Courts Act 1984, s.38(1)).

(vi) The approach of the courts
Although committal to prison is the conventional remedy for breach of an injunction it may not be the most appropriate course of action in the family context. In *Ansah* v *Ansah* [1977] Fam 138, where an *ex parte* injunction had been granted to the husband restraining the wife from returning to the home and molesting the husband, the wife had returned there on a few occasions to look after her father who was staying on a visit from Ghana and had also been there to collect the children who had been wrongfully taken there. Even assuming the injunction to have been properly made, Ormrod LJ said (at pp. 143-144): "Such a breach or breaches, of an injunction in the circumstances of such a case as this do not justify the making of a committal order, suspended or otherwise." He went on to say that "... the real purpose of bringing the matter back to the court, in most cases is not so much to punish the disobedience, as to secure compliance with the injunction in the future. It will often be wiser to bring the matter before the court again for further directions before applying for a committal order. Committal orders are remedies of last resort; in family cases they should be the very last resort. They are likely to damage complainant spouses almost as much as offending spouses, for example, by alienating the children. Such orders should be made very reluctantly and only when every other effort to bring the situation under control has failed or is almost certain to fail. In most cases, stern warnings combined with investigation and an attempt to alleviate the offending spouse's underlying grievances or an adjournment to allow tempers to cool will resolve the problem. In some cases the assistance of the court welfare officer may help to remove some of the tension." (See also *Patterson* v *Walcott* [1984] FLR 408; *Thomason* v *Thomason* [1985] FLR 214; *Smith* v *Smith* [1988] 1 FLR 179; *Goff* v *Goff* [1989] 1 FLR 436.)

In *Smith* v *Smith* [1988] 1 FLR 179 at p. 181 Sir John Donaldson MR said that it was wrong to assume that a breach of an order or of an undertaking automatically or normally leads to imprisonment. While orders of the court must and will be maintained there is nothing automatic about committal to prison. It must depend upon all the circumstances, and if the judge is to be in a position to determine the appropriate penalty he has to know the full background. He cannot take account of any matter which has not been put to the defendant and the defendant given an opportunity of dealing with it. If it is disputed by the defendant, he must either accept the defendant's denial or he must give the plaintiff an opportunity of proving it and the defendant an opportunity of probing that evidence.

The court will take into account the nature and seriousness of the breach. The breach may have been of a very minor character such as where the defendant had been found within half a mile of the plaintiff's house having undertaken not to go within one mile thereof. Such a breach would not justify committal to prison unless it could be shown to be an act preparatory to some form of molestation (*per* Sir John Donaldson MR in *Smith* v *Smith* [1988] 1 FLR 179 at p. 181). In *Smith* v *Smith* the defendant had entered the plaintiff's garden and waved papers at her and was drunk. The Court of Appeal found that committal for 28 days was excessive and it was reduced to 7 days, enabling him to be released immediately. In *George* v *George* [1986] 2 FLR 347 the Court of Appeal found committal for 28 days to be justified where the husband, as well as writing to the wife, had "yelled and screamed at her and used abusive language" when she was collecting the children following access by the husband. At the other extreme are cases where the defendant has assaulted the plaintiff occasioning her actual bodily harm. In *Juby* v *Miller* [1991] 1 FLR 133 at p. 135 Lord Donaldson MR said that "... it cannot be too widely known that the court will regard as being in a wholly special category cases in which people commit criminal offences which constitute a breach of the court's orders." In that case the Court of Appeal dismissed an appeal against committal to prison for 8 months in respect of each of two offences with the two sentences to run consecutively. In *Mason* v *Lawton* [1991] 2 FLR 50 there had also been serious breaches of the court's order, but Lord Donaldson MR (at p. 52) said that while a custodial sentence was fully justified and, indeed, was required if the authority of the court was to be upheld, it had to be borne in mind that the maximum period of committal is limited to 2 years. He said that: "Serious though the contempts were, they would have been even more serious if, in addition, the applicant or her children had suffered actual physical violence." In all the circumstances the committal for 2 years was excessive and the appropriate period was 9 months. (See also *Benesch* v *Newman* [1987] 1 FLR 262.)

Even though a contempt is viewed as serious the court will have regard to the fact that it is the first occasion on which there has been a breach. (See *Re H (A Minor) (Injunction: Breach)* [1986] 1 FLR 558 *per* Fox LJ at p. 562.) On the other hand, where there have been repeated breaches of an order, particularly where there have been previous committals, then any further breach is likely to attract a severe sentence and possibly the maximum sentence. (See *Wright* v *Jess* [1987] 2 FLR 373 and *Mesham* v *Clark* [1989] 1 FLR 370.)

A defendant's attitude, when brought before the court for what is a defiance of the court's order, is also a relevant factor. In *Brewer* v *Brewer* [1989] 2 FLR 251 stress was laid on the fact that the husband, far from adopting an attitude of contrition before the court, had adopted an attitude of aggression in the form of perjurious evidence of a particularly unattractive kind, namely a false allegation of yielding to sexual intercourse by the wife which she had strenuously denied. In *Roberts* v

*Roberts* [1990] 2 FLR 111 at p. 113 Butler-Sloss LJ said: "A total absence of apology is not the way to appear before a court when you are in danger of being committed to prison for a serious breach of an undertaking ...". Where there has been a change of attitude the court may subsequently reconsider the matter. In *Mason* v *Lawton* [1991] 2 FLR 50 at p. 54 Lord Donaldson MR noted that s.14(1) of the Contempt of Court Act 1981 had preserved the ancient power of the court to order the release of a contemnor earlier than at the end of the fixed term of detention required by that section. It is a power which is appropriately used where the contemnor seeks to purge his contempt and the court is convinced of his sincerity. In that case the Court of Appeal concluded that there was some evidence that the defendant had indeed learned his lesson.

(vii) The committal order

If a committal order is made it must be for the issue of a warrant of committal, and a copy of the order must be served on the person to be committed either before or at the time of the execution or within 36 hours of the execution of the warrant (CCR Ord 29, r. 1(5) as amended with effect from 1 May 1991. See *B* v *B* *(Contempt: Committal)* [1991] 2 FLR 588 and the note thereto). The prescribed forms are N79 and N80. It is essential that the order of committal sets out the court's findings - otherwise the contemnor does not have any basis upon which to challenge them (*per* Farquharson LJ in *Clarke* v *Clarke* [1990] 2 FLR 115 at p. 117. See also *Nguyen* v *Phung* (1984) 5 FLR 773). Applications for discharge from prison are governed by CCR Ord. 29, r. 3). The committal order must contain a statement reminding the contemnor that he can apply to the court to purge his contempt and ask for release (*B* v *B* *(Contempt: Committal)* [1991] 2 FLR 588).

*(b) Attaching a power of arrest*

(i) Circumstances in which a power of arrest may be attached

The enforcement of an injunction in the conventional way, by seeking committal of the respondent, may involve delay at a time when the applicant seeking protection is vulnerable to further attacks. With a view to providing a quicker and probably more effective enforcement of injunctions in this area, the Domestic Violence and Matrimonial Proceedings Act 1976 enables a power of arrest exercisable by the police to be attached to certain injunctions at the time they are granted.

Section 2(1) of the Act empowers a judge to attach a power of arrest to an injunction granted on the application of a party to a marriage if it contains a provision, in whatever terms,

(a) restraining the other party to the marriage from using violence against the applicant, or

(b) restraining the other party from using violence against a child living with the applicant, or

(c) excluding the other party from the matrimonial home or from a specified area in which the matrimonial home is included.

He may do so only if he is satisfied (1) that the other party has caused actual bodily harm to the applicant, or, as the case may be, to the child concerned, and (2) considers that he is likely to do so again.

The provision applies to injunctions granted in the High Court as well as to injunctions granted in a county court. Moreover, the power is not confined to injunctions granted under s.1 of the 1976 Act, but extends to all injunctions containing provisions within paragraphs (a), (b) or (c) of s.2(1). Thus a power of arrest can be attached to an injunction granted in the course of divorce proceedings. It also applies to the case of a man and a woman who are living with each other in the same household as husband and wife even though they are not married to each other. However, if the 1976 Act is no longer applicable because they are no longer "living together" then no power of arrest can be attached to an injunction granted ancillary to an action in tort or for the protection of the children (*R* v *S* [1988] 2 FLR 339). A court cannot attach a power of arrest to an injunction against a former spouse, i.e. after the date on which the marriage has been dissolved by a decree absolute, unless the parties are still living together as husband and wife (*Harrison* v *Lewis* [1988] 2 FLR 339. See also *White* v *White* [1983] 2 All ER 51 where an injunction had been granted excluding the former husband from the former matrimonial home which had been vested in the former wife's sole name). A power of arrest cannot be founded upon an undertaking but must be attached to an appropriate injunction (*Carpenter* v *Carpenter* [1988] 1 FLR 121).

It must be emphasised that a power of arrest can be attached only to certain injunctions and then only if the judge is satisfied that actual bodily harm has been caused to the applicant or to a child living with the applicant. (See *McClaren* v *McClaren* (1980) 1 FLR 85 where the Court of Appeal held that a power of arrest had been wrongly attached to an injunction not to interfere with or contact the three children of the family since there was no evidence of any violence towards the children.) The provisions of s.2 are, therefore, limited to cases of violence, and do not extend to other forms of conduct which might come within the expression "molestation". In this respect the scope of s.2 is narrower than the scope of s.1. In order to establish actual bodily harm in the absence of any evidence of physical injury there must be clear evidence that the person assaulted has suffered real psychological damage as a result of physical battery (Glidewell LJ in *Kendrick* v *Kendrick* [1990] 2 FLR 107 at p. 110). In that case the only evidence was that the wife was afraid that the husband would return to the home and was therefore so afraid that she felt she could not herself return there. In the opinion of Glidewell LJ that was not enough to establish a sufficient degree of psychological harm to come within the definition of the words "actual bodily harm" for the purposes of s.2.

Even if there is evidence of violence in the past, it is also necessary for the judge to be satisfied that the respondent is likely to act in this way again. Thus in *Lewis* v *Lewis* [1978] Fam 60 the Court of Appeal noted that the judge at first instance had virtually no evidence before him to enable him to make a finding on this second requirement, and apparent peace had existed for some six weeks. The case was remitted to him for rehearing. In that case it was also emphasised by both members of the court that the power to attach a power of arrest was not for general and indiscriminate use. It was not to be regarded as a routine addition to an order or injunction.

A Practice Note (Domestic Violence: Power of Arrest) [1981] 1 WLR 27 suggested that judges should consider the period of time for which a sanction was required and, unless a judge is satisfied that a longer period is necessary in a particular case, the period should not exceed three months. In those few cases where danger to the applicant is still reasonably apprehended towards the expiry of that period, application can be made to the court to extend the duration of the injunction. In *Carpenter* v *Carpenter* [1988] 1 FLR 121 at p. 125 Glidewell LJ left open the question whether there was power to extend a power of arrest which had already been added to an existing injunction. However, if there was power, it could only be exercised (1) if the injunction continues (though he thought it would be sufficient if it has been replaced by an undertaking, as in that case), (2) if the court exercising the power to extend the power of arrest finds that there has been a later incident in which it finds proved an assault upon the complainant occasioning actual bodily harm and further specifically finds that there is a likelihood of the husband committing further breaches of the injunction.

It was also said in *Lewis* v *Lewis* [1978] Fam 60 that notice should be given to the other party, in an application for an injunction, that it is proposed to ask the court to attach a power of arrest. This means that a power of arrest should not be attached to an *ex parte* injunction, though this has been criticised on the basis that it is the most exceptional cases which result in *ex parte* applications.

(ii) The effect of attaching a power of arrest

If a power of arrest is attached to an injunction, then a police constable may arrest without warrant a person whom he has reasonable cause for suspecting of being in breach of a provision in that injunction within (a), (b) or (c) of subs.(1) by reason of that person's use of violence or, as the case may be, of his entry into any premises or area (s.2(3)). Where the person to whom the injunction is addressed is so arrested, then he must be brought before a judge within the period of 24 hours beginning with the time of his arrest. He must not be released within that period except on the direction of the judge, but s.2 does not authorise his detention at any time after the expiry of that period (s.2(4)). Where the arrest takes place at a time when the period of 24 hours will expire before a courtroom is normally available, the appropriate procedure is described in Practice Direction (Domestic Violence: Procedure on Arrest) [1991] 1 WLR 278.

The Act is silent as to the powers of the judge when the arrested person is brought before him by the police officer pursuant to subs.(4). To close the lacuna, orders have been made in the High Court and the county courts by the relevant Rules Committees (RSC Ord. 90, r. 30(4); CCR Ord. 47, r. 8). The effect of these orders has now been held to be the same. The judge can exercise his power to punish the arrested person for disobedience to the injunction notwithstanding that no copy of the injunction has been served upon him and that no formal application for an order for committal has been made by the applicant. However, in *Boylan* v *Boylan* (1981) 11 Fam Law 76 it was emphasised that the fact that all the conventional protection previously given to persons liable to be committed to prison for contempt of court, and all the procedural hurdles had been swept away and the judges given a completely free hand means "that they must use these draconian powers with great care, otherwise the risk of producing a grave injustice is very real". In particular there is "no necessity to commit people to prison for breaching an order simply to show that orders are not to be broken" (*ibid.* at p. 77). The whole of the facts of the domestic situation must be looked at as well as the merits of the case. Moreover, as a matter of good practice, it is very doubtful whether a judge will feel justified in sending a husband to prison for breach of an injunction without at least finding out what the wife's view is. In that case the most that the husband had done was to decline to go when first requested to do so by the police. That technical contempt was amply punished by his overnight stay in custody and the matter should have been left the following day by the judge simply giving the husband a warning if, on the particular facts of the case, a warning was necessary.

Where the judge needs to find out the attitude of the wife, or any other matter necessary to enable what is in effect an application for committal to be dealt with, and in particular where the arrested person wishes to call witnesses who may possibly corroborate part of his evidence and cast a less serious light on some of the matters that appear to have been done in breach of the order, or which may affect the penalty, the proper course is to adjourn the application to a convenient date within a short time (CCR Ord. 47, r. 8(7A) now provides for an adjournment and for the arrested person to be dealt with within 14 days of the day on which he was arrested). The wife may be protected in the meantime by a continuation of the injunction with the power of arrest attached. In some cases it may be appropriate to make an immediate committal order before there can be a full hearing, if that appears to be the only way in which the wife can be protected. This should be on the clear and explicit condition that the alleged contemnor should be at liberty to apply to set aside the committal order when a full hearing is possible. There is no power to release the arrested person on bail or to remand him in custody because the time of any period in custody pursuant to the arrest, as opposed to the time pursuant to a subsequent order for committal, is strictly limited by the section itself to 24 hours. (See *Roberts* v *Roberts* 1991] 1 FLR 294.)

Where a committal is made after the contemnor has been brought before the court under the exercise of a power of arrest, Form 111 must be used.

## 9. Undertakings

An undertaking may be accepted from the respondent, e.g. not to molest the applicant, in lieu of an injunction. This is generally equivalent to an injunction in the same terms. A breach of it will be a contempt of court and can be enforced in the same way as an injunction (*Hussain* v *Hussain* [1986] Fam 134. See CCR Ord. 29, r. 1A). However, the power of arrest under s.2 of the Domestic Violence and Matrimonial Proceedings Act 1976 can only be attached to an injunction (*Carpenter* v *Carpenter* [1988] 1 FLR 121). An undertaking to the court, including its duration, should be recorded in the prescribed form which states that the meaning of the undertaking was explained to the person giving it by the judge (Form N117). Where the person giving the undertaking was not present in court the most convenient procedure is to record the undertaking in an order of the court which will usually be necessary if only to record that "no order" was made on the application. That order should then be served on the party giving the undertaking. It is also desirable that the order should contain some notice drawing his attention to the consequences of a breach of the undertaking although it must be drawn in terms which show that it applies to the undertaking as distinct from the order. (See Sir John Donaldson MR in *Hussain* v *Hussain* [1986] Fam 134 at p. 140.) An undertaking is binding on the person giving it as soon as it is accepted by the court and personal service of the record of an undertaking is not necessary. In relation to a county court Ord. 29, r. 1A now provides that a copy of the document recording the undertaking must be delivered by the proper officer of the court to the party giving the undertaking (a) by handing a copy to him before he leaves the court building, or (b) where his place of residence is known, by posting a copy to him at his place of residence, or (c) through his solicitor. Where delivery cannot be effected in this way, the court must deliver a copy to the party for whose benefit the undertaking was given and that party must cause the document to be served personally as soon as is practicable.

The use of undertakings has sometimes been criticised (*McConnell* v *McConnell* (1980) 10 Fam Law 214). On the other hand an undertaking does not require the party giving it to admit that he or she has in the past assaulted or molested the applicant, and further bitterness and expense may be avoided. Moreover, it is often thought that the respondent is more likely to comply with an undertaking given voluntarily than with a court order. Where the facts are disputed it may be appropriate for each party to give an undertaking not to molest the other. Where a husband offers an undertaking not to molest or assault the wife and children on an application by the wife for an order requiring the husband to vacate the home, the court must consider whether the wife will be sufficiently protected by the undertaking. It must be satisfied that it is unnecessary to make an order excluding the husband from the matrimonial home (*Dirir* v *Dirir* (1981) 1 Fam Law 8).

A party who has given an undertaking to the court may apply, on notice, for it to be discharged or for the terms to be varied, on good grounds, provided that there has not been a disposal of the application which gave rise to the giving of the undertaking (*Butt* v *Butt* [1987] The Times, 27 June).

## 10.  Orders under s.16 Domestic Proceedings and Magistrates' Courts Act 1978

*(a) Background and scope*
The matrimonial jurisdiction of magistrates' courts originated in the Matrimonial Causes Act 1878 which attempted to provide a remedy for ill-treated wives who did not have the financial means to obtain protection from the divorce court. It had come to be realised that punishment of the husband through the criminal law was not the answer since the husband would return home more brutalised and infuriated than ever. The method adopted was to empower a magistrates' court to order a husband to pay maintenance to his assaulted wife who would thus have the financial means to live apart from him which was the only real protection in many cases (see McGregor, Blom-Cooper and Gibson, *Separated Spouses* (1970) p. 10 *et seq.*). The inadequacy of this approach became apparent in the course of time as did the limita-

tions of the non-cohabitation clause which a magistrates' court was empowered to include in a matrimonial order on the application of a wife. The effect of such a clause was merely to declare that the applicant wife was no longer bound to cohabit with her husband. It did nothing to remove the husband from the matrimonial home which was the only effective answer in many cases. The non-cohabitation clause was abolished by the Domestic Proceedings and Magistrates' Courts Act 1978 which gave the magistrates' courts power to make what are generally referred to as "personal protection orders" and "exclusion orders". (See Law Com. No. 77, *Report on Matrimonial Proceedings in Magistrates' Courts* (1976) particularly paras. 3.1 - 3.48. These terms are used in para. 3.13 but not in the Act.)

It should be noted that unlike ss.1 and 2 of the Domestic Violence and Matrimonial Proceedings Act 1976, s.16 of the 1978 Act applies only to married couples and affords no protection to a person living with another in an unmarried state. Applications under s.16 are "family proceedings" for the purposes of the Magistrates' Courts Act 1980 (s.65), and a magistrates' court sitting for the purposes of hearing family proceedings is known as the "family proceedings court" (Children Act 1989, s.92(1)).

## *(b) Personal protection orders*

On the application of either party to a marriage a magistrates' court may, under s.16, and whether or not an application is made under s.2 of the Act for an order for financial provision, make one or both of the following orders:

(a) an order that the respondent shall not use, or threaten to use, violence against the person of the applicant;

(b) an order that the respondent shall not use, or threaten to use, violence against the person of any child of the family.

(For the meaning of "child of the family" see s.88(1) and Chapter 17, Part 5.) The court may include provision that the respondent shall not incite or assist any other person to use, or threaten to use, violence against the person of the applicant, or as the case may be, the child of the family (s.16(10)).

Before making an order the court must be satisfied:

(i) that the respondent has used, or threatened to use, violence against the person of the applicant or a child of the family, and

(ii) that it is necessary for the protection of the applicant or a child of the family that an order should be made.

A "personal protection order" thus provides protection from violence or threatened violence but not against other forms of harassment which would amount to "molestation". The protection is in this respect more limited than that afforded by an injunction against molestation under s.1 of the Domestic Violence and Matrimonial Proceedings Act 1976 or ancillary to proceedings for divorce. (See *Horner* v *Horner* [1982] Fam 90 where a wife having obtained a "personal protection order" found it necessary to seek an injunction against molestation). Violence or the threat of violence against the applicant or a child of the family is also a necessary precondition to the making of an order. There will be no ground for making a personal protection order if the only complaint against the husband is that he uses or threatens violence outside his home and family circle, e.g. that he is given to violent or threatening behaviour when attending a football match. However, evidence of violent behaviour outside the home and family circle should be relevant to the making of an exclusion order (Law Com. No.77, para. 3.20).

### (c) Exclusion orders

On an application for an order under s.16, a magistrates' court is given the power under subs. (3) to make one or both of the following "exclusion orders":
(a) an order requiring the respondent to leave the matrimonial home;
(b) an order prohibiting the respondent from entering the matrimonial home.
In this event the court may, if it thinks fit, make a further order requiring the respondent to permit the applicant to enter and remain in the matrimonial home (s.16(4)). This may be necessary to stop a violent spouse who is excluded from the home from taking steps, such as changing the locks, to prevent the other party who has fled the home from re-entering and occupying it.

An exclusion order can only be made if the court is satisfied:
(1) that:
    (a) the respondent has used violence against the person of the applicant or a child of the family, or
    (b) the respondent has threatened to use violence against the person of the applicant or a child of the family and has used violence against some other person, or
    (c) the respondent has in contravention of a personal protection order made under s.16(2) threatened to use violence against the person of the applicant or a child of the family; and
(2) that the applicant or a child of the family is in danger of being physically injured by the respondent (or would be in such danger if the applicant or child were to enter the matrimonial home).

In relation to the second requirement Sir George Baker P said in *McCartney* v *McCartney* [1981] Fam 59 at p. 63 that the "danger" must be an objectively observable danger, one which the justices believe to exist and not merely one which the complainant believes to exist. Subjective belief by a complainant is not the requirement. He also said that it was an error to regard "danger" as having to be "immediate" danger in order to satisfy the requirements of s.16(3). The subsection itself uses the word "danger" without any qualification and Ewbank J thought it a mistake to add other words to the terms of the subsection (*ibid.* at p. 62. Compare s.16(6), authorising expedited orders, which refers to "imminent danger"). It has been suggested that this broadens the scope of the provision, but merely because the danger need not be immediate does not mean that the justices need not base their decision on the prospect of violence (see Gypps (1980) 144 JPN 468).

### (d) Contents of an order

An order under s.16 may be made subject to such exceptions or conditions as may be specified in the order, and may be made for such term as may be so specified (s.16(9) - subject to the limits in subs.(8) in relation to "expedited orders"). This enables effect to be given to the recommendation of the Law Commission that the court should have power to authorise entry into the home for a temporary or limited purpose, e.g. to enable a husband to collect his clothes or other personal belongings (Law Com. No. 77, paras. 3.25(b) and 3.40(d)). It is doubtful whether this enables the court to exclude the respondent from *part* of the matrimonial home, in contrast to the position under the Domestic Violence and Matrimonial Proceedings Act 1976. An unsuccessful attempt was made in Parliament to introduce a reference to part of the home, and while a magistrates' court may not often be concerned with a house large enough for completely separate occupation by two people, the omission is, it is submitted, unfortunate.

It is specifically provided that, except so far as the exercise by the respondent of a right to occupy the matrimonial home is suspended or restricted by an exclusion order, an order under s.16 is not to affect any estate or interest in the matrimonial home of the respondent or any other person (s.17(4)).

*(e) Expedited orders and hearings*

Where on an application for an order under s.16 the court is satisfied that there is imminent danger of physical injury to the applicant or a child of the family, the court may make a personal protection order notwithstanding -

(a) that the summons has not been served on the respondent or has not been served on the respondent within a reasonable time before the hearing of the application, or

(b) that the summons requires the respondent to appear at some other time or place.

Any order made in these circumstances is referred to as an "expedited order" (s.16(6)). It is important to note that this procedure does not apply to the making of an exclusion order.

The power of the court to make an expedited order may be exercised by a single justice as well as by a full bench (s.16(7)). Where on an application for a personal protection order or an exclusion order the court considers that it is essential that the application should be heard without delay, the court may hear the application notwithstanding:

(a) that the court does not include both a man and a woman;

(b) that any member of the court is not a member of a domestic court panel;

(c) that the proceedings on the application are not separated from the hearing and determination of proceedings which are not domestic proceedings.

(s.16(5). See Magistrates' Courts Act 1980, ss.65-69.)

An expedited order does not take effect until the date on which notice of the making of the order is served on the respondent in the prescribed manner or any later date specified by the court as the date on which the order is to take effect (s.16(8)). An expedited order ceases to have effect on whichever of the following dates occurs first:

(a) the date of the expiration of the period of 28 days beginning with the date of the making of the order (i.e. not from the date when it takes effect); or

(b) the date of the commencement of the hearing, in accordance with the provisions of Part II of the Magistrates' Courts Act 1980, of the application for an order under s.16.

(s.16(8)).

The expiry of an expedited order does not prejudice the making of a further expedited order.

*(f) The power of arrest*
A court may attach a power of arrest to an order under s.16 if the order provides that the respondent:
(a)  shall not use violence against the person of the applicant, or
(b)  shall not use violence against a child of the family, or
(c)  shall not enter the matrimonial home.
(s.18(1)).
Accordingly no such power may be attached to an order requiring the respondent to leave the matrimonial home. Such a power may be attached only if the court is satisfied (1) that the respondent has physically injured the applicant or a child of the family, and (2) considers that he is likely to do so again (s.18(1)). The attachment of a power of arrest should never become a routine matter. Justices can avoid any suggestion that the power of arrest is being attached indiscriminately by stating at the time why they thought it necessary to attach a power of arrest *(per* Sir John Arnold P in *Widdowson* v *Widdowson* (1983) 4 FLR 121 at p. 125).

Where a power of arrest has been attached to an order, a constable may arrest without warrant a person whom he has reasonable cause for suspecting of being in breach of any such provision of the order within (a), (b) or (c) above by reason of that person's use of violence or, as the case may be, his entry into the matrimonial home. Where a person is so arrested he must be brought before a justice of the peace within a period of 24 hours beginning at the time of his arrest, and the justice of the peace before whom he is brought may remand him (s.18(3) and (4)).

Where a court has made an order under s.16 but has not attached to the order a power of arrest, then if at any time the applicant considers that the other party to the marriage has disobeyed the order, he may apply to a justice of the peace for the commission area in which either party ordinarily resides for the issue of a warrant for the arrest of that other party. A justice of the peace must not issue a warrant on such an application unless:
(a)  the application is substantiated on oath, and
(b)  the justice has reasonable grounds for believing that the other party to the marriage has disobeyed the order.
(s.18(4)).
This method of enforcement is thus available in respect of any kind of order made under s.16. Thus while a power of arrest cannot be attached to an order requiring the respondent to leave the matrimonial home, the applicant can apply for the issue of a warrant under this provision if the respondent does not leave the home. The magistrates' court before whom any person is brought by virtue of such a warrant may remand him (s.18(5)).

*(g) Variation*
A magistrates' court has power by order to vary or revoke any order made under s.16 on an application by either party to the marriage (s.17(1)).

# Chapter 6

# Sale of the home

## 1. Sale by a spouse who is sole owner

Where the matrimonial home is the sole property of one spouse in whom the legal estate is vested, then he or she will be able to sell or otherwise dispose of the property without the concurrence of the other spouse. However, the other spouse will have the statutory rights of occupation given by the Matrimonial Homes Act 1983 which can be protected by registration in the appropriate manner (see Chapter 4). If they have been so protected, then a sale with vacant possession and free from those rights can only be effected if they are released or terminated in accordance with the provisions of the Act.

## 2. Sale where spouses are co-owners

Where spouses are co-owners of the matrimonial home it is necessary to distinguish two situations, namely (a) where the legal estate is vested in both spouses, and (b) where the legal estate is vested in only one spouse.

### (a) Where the legal estate is vested in both spouses

Where the legal estate in the matrimonial home is vested in both spouses it will be held on trust for sale, express or implied, and one spouse will not be able to deal with that estate without the concurrence of the other. (See Chapter 3. In *Watts* v *Spence* [1976] Ch 165 the husband entered into a contract to sell the matrimonial home without the authority of his wife as co-owner. Specific performance of the contract against them was refused, but the husband was held liable in damages assessed under s.2(1) of the Misrepresentation Act 1967 as if his misrepresentation had been fraudulent. He was liable for the purchaser's loss of bargain.) Accordingly, where the spouses no longer agree on the enjoyment and retention of the property, a spouse who wishes the property sold will have to apply to the court for an order for sale. The spouse who opposes the sale will almost invariably do so because he or she wishes to remain in occupation of the property. In deciding whether an order for sale is appropriate the court will, therefore, be concerned with the extent to which the spouse who opposes the sale should be allowed to continue to enjoy the joint asset, and the circumstances in which the other spouse, who will usually have left the property, should be entitled to realise his or her share by insisting on a sale. An order for sale may be made in proceedings under s.30 of the Law of Property Act 1925, or s.17 of the Married Women's Property Act 1882. No statutory rights of occupation under the Matrimonial Homes Act 1983 arise in this situation. Where there are proceedings for divorce, nullity or judicial separation the court may make an order for sale under s.24A of the Matrimonial Causes Act 1973 (see Chapter 10).

*(b) Where the legal estate is vested in one spouse only*
Where the legal estate in the matrimonial home is vested in one spouse, but both spouses have a beneficial interest in the property the general view is that a trust for sale is created. The spouse in whom the legal estate is vested is, therefore, in effect a single trustee for sale, and before effecting any sale he or she should appoint another trustee so that a valid receipt can be given for the proceeds of sale. Once this has been done the position is the same as in (a) above, but unless and until it has been done, the spouse who has the legal estate will appear to be a sole beneficial owner, and will be able to pass a good title free from the equitable interest of the other spouse to a bona fide purchaser for value of the legal estate without notice. The problems relating to the protection of an equitable interest in these circumstances have been considered in Chapter 3, and apply equally to any right of occupation arising from that interest. In as much as occupation of the matrimonial home by the spouse entitled only to an equitable interest may amount to constructive notice of that interest, or may make it an overriding interest, it may be necessary for the spouse who has the legal estate to seek the assistance of the court in effecting a sale. The position of a spouse entitled only to an equitable interest has been strengthened by the provision that for the purposes of the Matrimonial Homes Act 1983 he or she is to be treated as not entitled to occupy the matrimonial home by virtue of that interest. Accordingly, he or she will have the statutory rights of occupation conferred by that Act, and the question of occupation may therefore now be dealt with in proceedings under that Act.

However, it is not necessarily the spouse who has the legal estate who wishes the matrimonial home sold, and where it is the other spouse who desires a sale, an application to the court for an order for sale will be necessary. An application to the court may in any event be necessary to establish the existence of a beneficial interest in the property where this is disputed by the spouse who has the legal estate, and an order for sale may be sought in such proceedings. Again where there are proceedings for divorce, nullity or judicial separation the court may make an order for sale under s.24A of the Matrimonial Causes Act 1973 where orders are made by the court under s.23 or s.24 of the Act.

## 3. Orders for sale of jointly owned property

*(a) Procedure*

Where the parties are married, an order for sale may be sought in proceedings under s.30 of the Law of Property Act 1925, or s.17 of the Married Women's Property Act 1882. It was pointed out in *Rawlings* v *Rawlings* [1964] P 398, *per* Willmer LJ at p. 409; *per* Harman LJ at p. 414 and *per* Salmon LJ at p. 417 that where the sole question arising is that of sale, then proceedings should be brought under s.30. However, s.17 will generally be used where the court is also called upon to decide whether the property is in fact jointly owned. Both sections empower the court to make such an order as it thinks fit, and despite earlier doubts it now seems established that in deciding whether or not to order a sale the court will take into account the same factors irrespective of the section under which the proceedings are brought. Moreover, the same factors are relevant whenever the beneficial interest is jointly owned, whether or not the legal estate is also vested in the joint names of the parties. Where the parties are married, the question of sale is now more likely to arise in the context of an application for financial provision and property adjustment ancillary to proceedings for divorce under the Matrimonial Causes Act 1973. The position in relation to an order for sale under that Act is considered in Chapter 12, but it is necessary to consider in this chapter the relationship between applications for orders for sale under s.30 or s.17 and applications for property adjustment. Recent cases have shown that the problems described in the preceding sections of this chapter may also arise in relation to a home which has been occupied by two persons living with each other as husband and wife but who have not been married to each other. In that event, s.17 of the Married Women's Property Act 1882 is not applicable and an application for an order for sale will have to be made under s.30 of the Law of Property Act 1925. The position as between cohabitees is also dealt with in this section.

*(b) General principles*

It is well established that a trust for sale is mandatory unless all the trustees agree to exercise the power to postpone sale (*Re Mayo* [1943] Ch 302). However, if the property was acquired for some special purpose the court will not allow that purpose to be defeated by strict enforcement of the trust for sale (*Re Buchanan-Wollaston's Conveyance* [1939] Ch 738). If that purpose, such as the provision of a matrimonial home, can still be achieved, then a sale will not be enforced. In *Jones* v *Challenger* [1961] 1 QB 176 the Court of Appeal took the view that once a marriage has been terminated by divorce, the purpose of a matrimonial home has clearly come to an end. In *Rawlings* v *Rawlings* [1964] P 398 the court took the view that the purpose was likewise at an end when a marriage was at an end in fact, though not in law. In both cases a sale was ordered. If the purpose of the matrimonial home is to provide a home for the spouses, this approach affords limited scope for allowing one spouse alone to occupy the home, though in *Bedson* v *Bedson* [1965] 2 QB 666 a wife was refused an order for sale. An important factor was that the property was not merely the home, but also the business premises of the husband, so that a sale would have destroyed his means of livelihood and of support of his family.

In all these cases the application for sale had been made by the wife who had left the property. (In *Re Solomon* [1967] Ch 573 the application was made by the husband's trustee in bankruptcy. This raises different considerations: see Chapter 8.) The first reported application by a husband who had left his wife in occupation of the matrimonial home was *Re Hardy* (1970) 114 SJ 864. The husband was refused an order for sale under s.30 by Stamp J who said that, as he understood the speeches in *National Provincial Bank Ltd* v *Ainsworth* [1965] AC 1175, the wife had a right to have a roof over her head provided by the husband. That being so, unless the husband provided some alternative accommodation, he could not get a sale. On the other hand, in *Jackson* v *Jackson* [1971] 1 WLR 1539 the Court of Appeal made it clear that the husband's obligation, whatever its extent (see Chapter 4), was only one factor to be taken into account. Other factors were also relevant. Megaw LJ said (at p. 1547) "It depends upon what is equitable or reasonable in the circumstances of the particular case, subject, it may be, to a general *prima facie* principle that the wife is entitled to remain in the matrimonial home." In the particular circumstances of the case the Court of Appeal upheld an order for sale taking into account also the fact that apart from conduct the house was too large for one person and the accommodation far larger than the wife could possibly require. Clearly, therefore, the nature of the property and the needs and financial circumstances of the parties are relevant circumstances.

### (c) The effect of the presence of children

In *Rawlings* v *Rawlings* [1964] P 398 at p. 419 Salmon LJ expressed the view, *obiter*, that the presence of children for whom the property might continue to provide a home, might justify the postponement of a sale. He said:

"If there were young children the position would be different. One of the purposes of the trust would no doubt have been to provide a home for them, and whilst the purpose still existed a sale would not generally be ordered. But when these children are grown up and the marriage is dead, the purposes of the trust have failed."

On the other hand, in *Burke* v *Burke* [1974] 1 WLR 1063 the Court of Appeal appeared, at first sight at least, to take a narrower view of the purpose of a matrimonial home. In that case Buckley LJ acknowledged that in considering whether or not to postpone sale the court must have regard to the situation of both beneficial owners and personal problems affecting those beneficiaries relevant to that question. The interests of the children in that case were only incidentally to be taken into consideration, namely only in so far as they affected the equities of the matter between the two spouses as beneficial owners. It will be seen that this view must now be read with caution in the light of subsequent cases.

### (d) The possibility of future variation of property rights in divorce proceedings

The disposition of the matrimonial home on the breakdown of a marriage will frequently be the dominating factor in the financial arrangements to be made. A point which seemed to remain open after *Jackson* v *Jackson* was the extent to which it was permissible for the court to take into account the possibility of a variation of property rights on a subsequent divorce in deciding whether or not to order a sale.

Judicial opinion differed as to the relevance of the possible exercise of the court's limited power of property adjustment before the Matrimonial Proceedings and Property Act 1970, i.e. the power to vary an ante- or post-nuptial settlement (see *Rawlings* v *Rawlings* [1964] P 348 at p. 415 where Harman LJ thought it was not relevant. Contrast Lord Denning and Russell LJ in *Bedson* v *Bedson* [1965] 2 QB 666 at pp. 679 and 697 respectively). The desirability of maintaining the status quo until the whole financial position of the parties can be considered, at least when proceedings are pending, was recognised by the Law Commission in Working Paper No. 42 on Family Property.

The point became of greater significance when the courts acquired much wider powers of property adjustment on divorce, nullity and judicial separation. In *Brown* v *Brown* (1975) 5 Fam Law 51 Lord Denning emphasised that it was now undesirable that an application for sale should be dealt with under s.17 alone. Such an application ought to be heard together with applications under s.4 of the Matrimonial Proceedings and Property Act 1970 (now s.24 Matrimonial Causes Act 1973) whereby the court could deal with the whole matter and make any order for transfer of property, payment of money or for securing any payment which might be just in all the circumstances. In *Williams* v *Williams* [1976] Ch 278 the Court of Appeal took the same view in relation to applications under s.30. Lord Denning said that the applications should be made to the Family Division under the relevant provision. If taken out in another Division, they should be transferred to a judge of the Family Division. In *Williams* v *Williams* it was some time after the marriage of the parties had been terminated by a decree absolute of divorce that the former husband applied in the Chancery Division under s.30 for an order that the wife should concur in the sale of the former matrimonial home which was vested in their joint names and was occupied by the former wife and four sons of the marriage. Foster J rejected the wife's argument that sale should be postponed so that, in particular, the youngest son could remain in the same area until he had finished his schooling. He ordered a sale so that the husband should have his money even though it meant that the wife would have to leave.

In the Court of Appeal Lord Denning described the approach exemplified by *Jones* v *Challenger* and *Burke* v *Burke* as outdated, and said (at p. 285):

"When judges are dealing with the matrimonial home, they nowadays have great regard to the fact that the house is bought as a home in which the family is to be brought up. It is not treated as property to be sold nor as an investment to be realised for cash. That was emphasised by this court in the recent case of *Browne (formerly Pritchard)* v *Pritchard* [1975] 1 WLR 1366 [which was concerned with an application for a property adjustment order under the Matrimonial Causes Act 1973]. The court, in executing the trust should regard the primary object as being to provide a home and not a sale. Steps should be taken to preserve it as a home for the remaining partner and children, but giving the outgoing partner such compensation, by way of a charge or being bought out, as is reasonable in the circumstances."

He considered that it would not be proper at this stage to order the sale of the house unless it were shown that alternative accommodation could be provided at a cheaper rate and some capital released. That had not been done. The order for sale was set aside and the matter remitted for further consideration by a judge of the Family Division when an application had been taken out under "the matrimonial property legislation" (*sic*).

*(e) Some conclusions from the cases*

(i) Where divorce proceedings have been commenced
If divorce proceedings have already been commenced the position is covered by the statements in *Williams* v *Williams,* and the disposition of the matrimonial home should not be considered in proceedings under s.17 or s.30 alone, but in conjunction with applications under the Matrimonial Causes Act 1973.

It is wrong in principle not to deal with property matters in full under the Matrimonial Causes Act 1973. Thus in *Rushton* v *Rushton* (1981) 1 FLR 195 the former matrimonial home had, by agreement, been transferred by the husband into the joint names of the parties. However, the judge decided to make no provision as to the right of occupation but to leave the parties to their rights under s.30. This deprived the court of its discretionary powers under the 1973 Act and was described by Ormrod LJ as "an extremely unsatisfactory situation" (at p. 197). It would mean further proceedings in the Chancery Division with great doubt as to the proper way of approaching it. The court gave leave to appeal and made a Mesher order (see Chapter 12).

If a party has remarried after divorce without making an application under s.24 of the Matrimonial Causes Act, then no application by that party under that section will be possible. If no application is possible under the Matrimonial Causes Act for this or any other reason, then obviously the disposition of the former matrimonial home will have to be dealt with under s.30 alone. Section 17 of the Married Women's Property Act 1882 remains available to former spouses for three years after dissolution of their marriage (Matrimonial Proceedings and Property Act 1970, s.39).

(ii) Where there are no imminent divorce proceedings
If no basis for proceedings for divorce or judicial separation yet exists, or if the immediate possibility of divorce is uncertain, the court should, in proceedings under s.17 or s.30 bear in mind the possibility of the court exercising its powers under the Matrimonial Causes Act in favour of a party or the children in due course.

If an adjustment of property rights which would safeguard occupation of the former home is likely, then disturbance of the status quo would not seem justified simply to give effect to existing strict property rights. Two factors may be relevant in this context. First, in cases like *Bigg* v *Bigg* (1976) 6 Fam Law 56 where the parties are not young, it is in any event by no means certain that divorce proceedings will be started at all or at any rate in the immediate future. This is obviously something that has to be taken into account for if there is no real prospect of the court being able to consider the disposition of the matrimonial home under the Matrimonial Causes Act then it will have to deal with the matter under s.17 or s.30. A second factor, however, is the extent to which protection seems called for in any event. An important, perhaps crucial, factor in *Bigg* v *Bigg* seems to have been that even under the Matrimonial Causes Act it was unlikely that the trust for sale would have been postponed so as to allow the husband to remain in occupation. It was not necessary for the husband (who was well over 60) to stay in the house in order to keep a roof over his head. He would have sufficient capital and income to be able to find a niche somewhere and would be able to move his driving school which he had carried on from the house. There was no reason why the wife should not have her small amount of capital released. Accordingly, unless one party and/or the children seem to merit protection which might be more effectively provided in proceedings under the Matrimonial Causes Act there is no reason why the court should not deal with the matter under s.17 or s.30 and, if appropriate, order a sale.

### (iii) Sale under s.17 or s.30

The question of sale may have to be dealt with solely in proceedings under s.17 or s.30. This may occur where no divorce proceedings are likely, or where no application is made before remarriage following divorce, or because the parties have never been married. In this event family considerations are nevertheless relevant though there is some conflict in the cases as to the manner in which and the extent to which such considerations operate.

In *Williams* v *Williams* [1976] Ch 278 at pp. 285-286 Lord Denning MR said:

"The truth is that the approach to these cases has been transformed since the Matrimonial Proceedings and Property Act 1970 and the Matrimonial Causes Act 1973 which have given the power to the court after a divorce to order the transfer of property. In exercising any discretion under section 30 of the Law of Property Act 1925, those Acts must be taken into account. The discretion should be exercised on the principles stated by this court in *Jackson* v *Jackson* [1971] 1 WLR 1538, 1534."

In *Jackson* v *Jackson* the court was concerned with the position where there had been no divorce and there seemed little prospect of one. It had regard to conduct and to the duty of the husband to provide a home for his wife, though it was concerned to reduce their importance to being merely two of the matters to be taken into account by the court in exercising its discretion. Lord Denning there stated that "in all these cases when the husband or the wife has an equitable interest in a dwelling-house or in the proceeds of sale thereof, the court will make such order about the occupation as it thinks just and reasonable having regard to the conduct of the parties and the circumstances of the case" (at p. 1543).

Once there has been a divorce it is impossible to justify the occupation of a spouse alone on the basis of a matrimonial obligation, so the position of the children becomes crucial. In *Brown* v *Brown* (1975) 5 Fam Law 51, where the decree nisi had been made absolute, Lord Denning said, in relation to an application for sale under s.17, that the interests of the children as well as of the husband and wife had to be taken into account. *Burke* v *Burke* [1974] 1 WLR 1963 had not, he claimed, laid down anything to the contrary. The right approach was that of Lawton LJ in *Burke* v *Burke* when he said (at p. 1068):

"If the circumstances are such that the parents buy a house in which to accommodate themselves and any children of the marriage ... I cannot see why the children should not be beneficiaries under any implied trust which may come into existence on the purchase of the house; and if that is the position ... then it may well be that the position of the children has to be considered."

Lawton LJ had concurred in the order for sale made in *Burke* on the basis that such an implied trust had not been established on the facts of the case, for the registrar had simply declared that the property was held in trust for the husband and wife in equal shares. It is of interest to note that he was also a member of the Court of Appeal in *Brown* v *Brown* and concurred in the judgment of Lord Denning. On the other hand, in *Burke* the reasoning of Buckley LJ with whom Davies LJ concurred, was not so limited. Moreover, any express declaration of trust which the parties may have made, e.g. in the conveyance to themselves, is likely to be in the same terms as the registrar's declaration in *Burke* and is unlikely to refer to the children. The approach of Lawton LJ is therefore of limited assistance.

In *Re Holliday* [1981] Ch 405 Goff LJ acknowledged that while there may be cases in which the children are beneficiaries, "normally that will not be so". Where that was not the case he preferred the view of Buckley LJ in *Burke* to that of Salmon LJ in *Rawlings* [1964] P 398. However, both he and Buckley LJ in *Re Holliday* considered that *Jones* v *Challenger* [1961] 1 QB 176 and *Burke* on the one hand were distinguishable from *Williams* v *Williams* [1976] Ch 278 on the other. When *Jones* v *Challenger* was decided neither the Matrimonial Proceedings and Property Act 1970 nor the Matrimonial Causes Act 1973 had been enacted and no court had such a power to adjust the property rights of the parties to a dissolved marriage as was conferred by those Acts. In *Burke* no recourse was sought to the power to adjust property rights under the 1973 Act. In *Williams* the powers existed and the opportunity to use them was still open ([1981] Ch 405 at p. 418). This appears to imply that the preservation of a home for children in the manner envisaged by Lord Denning in *Williams* is something that can generally be achieved only in proceedings under s.24 of the Matrimonial Causes Act 1973 and not where the court only had before it an application under s.17 or s.30.

However, it is doubtful whether Lord Denning in *Williams* intended to take such a restricted view. No doubt he certainly regarded it as preferable to have an application under s.24 as well as under s.17 or s.30 for the court's powers are wider. It can order a transfer or a settlement of property rather than simply refuse an order for sale. Nevertheless in proceedings under s.30 the court has a discretion to be exercised by taking into account the factors mentioned in *Jackson* v *Jackson*. Moreover, in *Brown* v *Brown* the only application before the court was under s.17 and despite the absence of any application under s.24 the court preserved the property concerned as a home for the former husband and his mistress and the son of the marriage. The Court of Appeal held that the judge had correctly exercised his discretion in declining to order a sale on the ground that there would be a real risk, if the home were sold, that the son would have to leave the district where his school and friends were, whereas the wife and daughter of the marriage were accommodated in a flat. (See also *Smith* v *Smith* (1977) 74 Law Soc. Gaz. 187.) In *Re Holliday* [1981] Ch 405 Goff LJ left the matter open. He said (at p. 419): "I need not consider how the matter will stand if a party applies in the Chancery Division for a sale and the other does not seek ancillary relief, since the wife has done so".

In the more recent case of *Chhokar* v *Chhokar* [1984] FLR 313 Cumming-Bruce

LJ said that it was established that the court had regard to the underlying purpose of a trust and will not order a sale which will prevent the beneficiaries or one of them occupying the home as a matrimonial and/or family home unless there are unusual circumstances or some special considerations. He continued (at p. 327):

"Where there are children of the family they are not themselves beneficiaries under the trust, but the existence of the children is a factor to be taken into account and, as a matter of common sense, the arrangements made by the court should take proper account of the need of the children for accommodation."

*(f) Unmarried couples*

More recently the courts have been concerned with applications under s.30 by cohabitees where there can be no question of the Matrimonial Causes Act 1973 applying. In *Re Evers' Trust* [1980] 1 WLR 1327 the plaintiff father and the defendant mother had begun to live together in August 1979 in the father's former matrimonial home. In 1976 a child was born and at about that time the mother's two children by her dissolved marriage came to live with them. In 1978 the parties acquired a new property for £13,950 of which £10,000 was raised jointly on mortgage. The balance was provided as to £2,400 by the mother and as to £1,050 plus expenses by the father. The property was conveyed into their joint names on trust for sale with power to postpone sale in trust for themselves as joint tenants. Ormrod LJ said (at p. 1333):

"The irresistible inference from these facts is that, as the judge found, they purchased this property as a family home for themselves and the three children. It is difficult to imagine that the mother, then wholly responsible for two children and partly for the third, would have invested nearly all her capital in the purchase of this property if it was not to be available to her as a home for the children for the indefinite future. It is inconceivable that the father, when he agreed to this joint adventure, could have thought otherwise or contemplated the possibility of an early sale without the consent of the mother. The underlying purpose of the trust was, therefore, to provide a home for all five of them for the indefinite future."

The Court of Appeal held that a sale was not justified at the present time as it would put the mother into a very difficult position because she could not raise the finance to re-house herself or meet the cost of borrowing money at present rates. Moreover, the father had a secure home with his mother and there was no evidence that he had any need to realise his investment which was in any event smaller than the mother's investment amounting arguably to less than one-fifth of the purchase price.

Ormrod LJ noted that in *Burke* v *Burke* [1974] 1 WLR 1063 the court was not referred to *Re Buchanan-Wollaston* [1939] Ch 738 so that Buckley LJ did not "seem to have considered in so many words, whether or not the primary purpose of the trust, i.e. for sale, 'the letter of the trust' in the words of Devlin LJ in *Jones* v *Challenger* [1961] 1 QB 178 at p. 181, ... had been affected by the underlying purpose, quoting Devlin LJ again, 'written or unwritten' of providing a home, not only for the parents but also for the children." He considered that the *dictum* of Salmon LJ in *Rawlings* v *Rawlings* [1964] P 398 at p. 419 appeared therefore to be more in line with the judgments of the Court of Appeal in the *Buchanan-Wollaston* case and in *Jones* v *Challenger*. Moreover, it was now supported by a *dictum* of Lord Denning MR in *Williams* v *Williams* [1976] Ch 278 at p. 285, that "the court, in executing the trust, should regard the primary object as being to provide a home and not a sale". He concluded ([1980] 1 WLR 1327 at pp. 1332-1333):

"This approach to the exercise of the discretion given by section 30 has considerable advantages in these 'family cases'. It enables the court to deal with substance (that is, reality) rather than form (that is, convenience of conveyancing); it brings the exercise of the discretion under this section, so far as possible, into line with the exercise of the discretion given by section 24 of the Matrimonial Causes Act 1973; and it goes some way to eliminating differences between legitimate and illegitimate children in accordance with present legislative policy (see for example the Family Law Reform Act 1969, Part II)."

This was followed in *Dennis* v *McDonald* [1981] 1 WLR which had originally been commenced in the Chancery Division. It was transferred to the Family Division to enable the matter to be considered by the judge who considered an application under the Guardianship of Minors Act 1971 which had been made in relation to the five children involved. Three of the children lived with the father in the property concerned and the plaintiff mother was accommodated in a council house with the two youngest children. (See also *Cousins* v *Dzosens* [1981] The Times 12 December and *Bernard* v *Josephs* [1982] Ch 391.)

It can be said, therefore, that in order for the occupation of a family home by children to be protected it is not necessary for them to be beneficiaries under the trust of the property in the sense of having beneficial interests in the proceeds of sale of the home. Indeed this would be unusual. The beneficial interests in that sense are clearly vested in their parents. However, where it can be said that the purpose in acquiring the property was to provide a home for the children as well as for the parents, neither parent should generally be able to insist on a sale which would frustrate that purpose. This does not, on the other hand, mean that there can never be an order for sale where there are children.

The absence of children for whom the property can continue to provide a home does not mean that an immediate order for sale will necessarily be made, but it will be difficult to resist an order for sale where only one partner wishes to continue living in the property. This is apparent from the views of the majority in *Bernard* v *Josephs* [1982] Ch 391. In that case Mr Josephs and Miss Bernard had purchased a home in their joint names, but following the breakdown of their relationship Miss Bernard left the property. By the time the application came before the Court of Appeal Mr Josephs and his new wife had been living in the house for three years and Miss Bernard had not lived in it for five years. Lord Denning MR thought it would be unduly harsh to turn Mr Josephs and his wife out of the house simply in order to provide funds for Miss Bernard (at p. 401). Griffiths LJ said: (at p. 405):

"The court should look at the purpose for which the house was bought in joint names and which resulted in it being held on trust for sale. If the purpose of the trust is exhausted, then the Court of Appeal should make an order directing a sale of the house. This house was bought to provide a home in which Miss Bernard and Mr. Josephs could live together. Now that they have separated, the purpose of the trust has been exhausted and if Miss Bernard insisted upon a sale

I can see no legitimate ground upon which the court could refuse an order for sale although it could, of course, postpone sale for a few months to give Mr. Josephs a reasonable chance to make other arrangements for his accommodation."

Kerr LJ agreed that the purpose for which the house was bought came to an end when Miss Bernard moved out. He said (at pp. 409-410):

"She could obviously never have intended that it should continue to provide a home for Mr Josephs with his new wife. Nor could it be said ever to have been their common intention that, if their relationship should break down and one of them should move out, let alone unwillingly, the house should remain available as a home for the other. Accordingly, decisions such as *In re Evers' Trust*, have no application ..."

It was held that the judge had been justified in ordering a sale subject to a postponement of four months, but a provision was added whereby the order for sale was not to be enforced if Mr Josephs paid Miss Bernard the sum of £6,000 within four months. In effect, therefore, Mr Josephs was given the opportunity of buying out Miss Bernard.

Kerr LJ said that the threat of making an order for sale under s.30 can be used against the occupant in order to seek to compel him to make an equitable financial adjustment in favour of the party who is out of occupation if the latter does not insist on a sale *(ibid.* at p. 410, approving the reasoning of Purchas J in *Dennis* v *McDonald* [1982] Fam 63 in relation to charging the occupier an occupation rent). However, he concluded that it was not possible to use the threat of refusing to make an order for sale, or postponing a sale indefinitely, as a means of forcing the non-occupant to agree to allow his interest in the property to be bought out on reasonable terms. Once the purpose of the trust has come to an end, a sale can be insisted upon by any of the beneficiaries unless the court considers that it is inequitable for him to want to realise his investment.

## (g) Third parties

Where a family home has been purchased by a husband and wife or by an unmarried couple, an order for sale under s.30 may be sought by a third party. The most likely instance of this is where an order for sale is sought by a creditor of one or both parties seeking payment of the debt or by the trustee in bankruptcy of one party for the benefit of creditors generally. The principles to be taken into account in such circumstances are considered in Chapter 8. The court may also have to consider an application under s.30 by a person who has acquired, or acquired a charge over, the interest of only one spouse or unmarried partner or has purchased the property from one co-owner only to find that he is bound by the rights of the other co-owner. In *Chhokar* v *Chhokar* [1984] FLR 313 at p. 327 Cumming-Bruce LJ said that in such a situation the court must consider the voice of each party and give proper weight to what those voices say. The question is: "Whose voice should in equity prevail?". In that case the matrimonial home was in the husband's name alone, but the wife had a beneficial interest in it. The husband sold the property at an undervalue to a purchaser. Cumming-Bruce LJ said:

"... this is a case in which there is no problem for a court of equity to consider. It is manifestly obvious that the voice of the innocent tenant in common in equity should prevail over the voice of the scoundrel who, as an accomplice [of the husband] attempted by fraud and diverse devices to frustrate and destroy the wife's overriding interest."

Looking at the situation of the wife he was quite unable to see any reason for holding that there was anything wrong in her continuing to occupy the house for as long as she wished to enjoy it.

### (h) The form of an order

When considering an application under s.30 of the Law of Property Act or s.17 of the Married Women's Property Act 1882 a court does not have the wide range of powers available to it when acting under the Matrimonial Causes Act 1973. Under s.30 the court can order a sale of the property and, if appropriate, impose terms, or it can decline to make an order, leaving the property unsold unless and until the trustees reach agreement or the court makes an order at some future date. Thus in *Re Evers' Trust* [1980] 1 WLR 1327 the court concluded that it would probably be wiser simply to dismiss the application while indicating the sort of circumstances which would justify a further application. Thus it might not be appropriate to order a sale when the child reached 16 years, a purely arbitrary date, or it might become appropriate to do so much sooner, e.g. on the mother's remarriage or on it becoming financially possible for her to buy the father out. The uncertainty was unfortunate, but the court had no power to adjust property rights or redraft the terms of the trust.

Where no order for sale is made, the court may order the party remaining in occupation to pay an occupation rent. Generally one tenant in common in sole occupation of premises is not liable to pay an occupation rent where the other tenant in common voluntarily chooses not to exercise a right of occupation. However, if the non-occupying tenant has been excluded from the premises the court will order payment of an occupation rent if it is necessary to do justice between the parties. This was the view taken by Purchas J in *Dennis* v *McDonald* [1982] Fam 63 where he held it was unreasonable to expect the plaintiff mother to exercise her right of occupation as she had done before the breakdown of her relationship with the defendant. She was, for practical purposes, excluded from occupation and prevented from enjoying her rights as tenant in common. Thus, although s.30 did not confer any power on the court to make orders where no order for sale was made, on general principles it was open to the court to make an order for payment of an occupation rent. In any event, he pointed out that it was open to the court to indicate that unless an undertaking to pay an occupation rent was forthcoming from the defendant then an order for sale would be made. The order for payment of rent in the circumstances of the case was not contested in the Court of Appeal which was principally concerned with the method of assessing such a payment. (See also *Bernard* v *Josephs* [1982] Ch 391.) It was held that the proper approach was to require the occupying party to pay to the other one half of such sum as represented a fair rent as assessed under s.70(1) and (2) of the Rent Act 1977, but without regard to any other provisions of the Act. Since the defendant occupied the property by virtue of being a tenant in common, it was not appropriate to take into account such extra payment as a tenant would have to make by reason of the scarcity of relevant accommodation in the market (*ibid.* at p. 82).

In *Re Evers' Trust* [1980] 1 WLR 1327 the terms upon which the court declined to make an order for sale included an undertaking by the defendant mother who was occupying the premises to discharge the liability under the mortgage. This included not only capital but also the interest element, and, therefore, in effect required her to pay an occupation rent for the privilege of continuing to occupy as a tenant in common the whole property adversely to the father.

In *Leake* v *Bruzzi* [1974] 1 WLR 1528, an application under s.17 of the Married Women's Property Act 1882, the Court of Appeal held that a husband who had remained in sole occupation of the matrimonial home and made the mortgage repayments after his wife left should be allowed credit for his wife's share only in respect of the capital element of the repayments. In effect, by depriving him of relief in respect of the wife's liability for the interest element of the mortgage repayments, the court was charging him indirectly with an occupation rent. In *Suttill* v *Graham* [1977] 1 WLR 819, also an application under s.17, the husband had continued to live in the former matrimonial home after divorce and the remarriage of both parties. The Court of Appeal held that if he sought to charge his co-beneficiary trustee, i.e. his former wife, with half of the mortgage interest, he should be charged with half the occupation rent in respect of his occupation of the property. Since he was not willing to submit to being charged an occupation rent, he was not entitled to charge the wife with half the mortgage interest payments. The effect of the order made by the court was that the husband should buy the wife's interest. There was no application under the Matrimonial Causes Act 1973 before the court.

In *Chhokar* v *Chhokar* [1984] FLR 313 the Court of Appeal deleted a provision in the order made by the judge that the wife pay an occupation rent to the husband's accomplice who had purchased the property from the husband but was bound by the wife's interest. Cumming-Bruce LJ said that for this purpose the purchaser stood "in the shoes of the original holder of the legal interest in the house and it would not be fair to require the wife to pay an occupation rent to the purchaser, although she was required to account for half the rent received from a former tenant of rooms at the property." He also said (at p. 332) that although the purchaser was a tenant in common in equity with the wife (Mrs Chhokar) no court would allow him to try to occupy the matrimonial home in common with Mrs Chhokar.

# Chapter 7

# Occupation of the tenanted home

## 1. Rights of occupation in tenanted property and their protection

Where the matrimonial home consists of accommodation held on a tenancy by one or both of the spouses, then the general principles relating to the duration and extent of the proprietary, personal and statutory rights of occupation considered in Chapter 4 apply. However, the protection of those rights raises different problems in view of the more limited interest held in the home. Thus where one spouse has an estate or interest in the matrimonial home which is capable of being dealt with or disposed of for value, then the other spouse needs protection against persons who might acquire an interest in the home such as a purchaser or a mortgagee. Accordingly, the Matrimonial Homes Act 1983 provides protection for the non-entitled spouse's rights of occupation in such property by making them a charge on the estate or interest of the entitled spouse, and by enabling that charge to be protected by registration in the manner considered in Chapter 4. Even in that situation those provisions will not protect the statutory rights of occupation where the entitled spouse's estate or interest is long leasehold if that estate is terminated by the lessor, e.g. by forfeiture. Where one spouse is merely a periodic or short-term tenant of the matrimonial home, the principal danger to the other spouse's occupation lies in the termination of the tenancy and not in any assignment or mortgage of the tenancy. Indeed, where the home is held on a statutory tenancy, no assignment of his interest is possible. Moreover, if the tenant himself is unable, or does not wish to occupy the home, its lack of realisable value gives him little inducement to preserve it merely for the benefit of the other spouse. At the same time an arrangement terminating the tenancy might also be attractive to the private landlord of premises within the Rent Act 1977. In these circumstances, protection of the statutory rights of occupation by making them a charge on the interest of the entitled spouse is irrelevant and the Matrimonial Homes Act 1983 makes no such provision. Some protection for the wife of a tenant was, however, evolved by the courts and this has been reinforced by the Matrimonial Homes Act 1967 and subsequent amendments. These provisions are now contained in the Matrimonial Homes Act 1983.

## 2. Common law and statutory protection of non-tenant spouse

*(a) Statutory tenancies*

In a series of cases before the Matrimonial Homes Act 1967, which were approved by the House of Lords in *National Provincial Bank Ltd* v *Ainsworth* [1965] AC 1175 (*per* Lord Hodson at p. 1227 and *per* Lord Upjohn at p. 1231), the deserted wife of a statutory tenant was given the benefit of her husband's statutory protection under the Rent Acts by treating her occupation of the premises as occupation by the husband (*Brown* v *Draper* [1944] KB 309; *Old Gate Estates* v *Alexander* [1950] 1 KB 311; *Middleton* v *Baldock* [1950] 1 KB 657). Since the husband, as tenant, could not contract out of his rights under the Rent Acts, no order for possession could be made against him or his wife except on the grounds specified in the Acts. Thus in *Middleton* v *Baldock,* where a husband who had deserted his wife offered to give possession, the landlord brought an action against the husband claiming possession merely on the ground that the contractual tenancy had come to an end, and not on any ground specified in the Acts. The Court of Appeal held that an order for possession was wrongly made. The husband's admission was futile, and his offer to give possession was one that he was unable to perform. The only way he could give possession, apart from physically removing his wife, was to get a court of competent jurisdiction in matrimonial matters to order his wife out, which presumably it would be unlikely to do unless and until he provided alternative accommodation (see Lord Evershed MR at p. 662).

The protection afforded by *Middleton* v *Baldock* applies equally against an attempted surrender by the tenant husband as in *Hoggett* v *Hoggett* (1980) 39 P & CR 121. There had been no express surrender, and a surrender by operation of law requires delivery of possession by the tenant or action by him equivalent thereto. This was not possible where the tenant's wife remained in occupation.

The common law protection developed from the duty of the husband towards his wife, and hence no similar protection was developed for a husband where his wife was tenant. In *Metropolitan Properties Co Ltd* v *Cronan* (1982) 44 P & CR 1 the Court of Appeal refused to accept that there could be representative occupation by a child of the tenant.

The Matrimonial Homes Act 1967, which introduced the provision that either spouse may have statutory rights of occupation in a home of which the other is tenant, went on to introduce a form of statutory representative occupation. This is now contained in the Matrimonial Homes Act 1983 which provides that a non-entitled spouse's occupation of the matrimonial home by virtue of s.1 of the Act is to be treated for the purposes of the Rent Act 1977 as possession by the other spouse (s.1(6)).

*(b) Secure tenancies*

Tenancies granted by various public authorities, and in particular by local authorities, have always been excluded from the Rent Acts. This meant that before 1980 tenants of such authorities had no real protection against termination of their tenancies so that representative occupation by the wives of such tenants was not an issue. As from 3 October 1980 the Housing Act 1980 conferred on most public authority tenants security of tenure similar to, but by no means identical with, that enjoyed by private sector tenants under the Rent Act 1977. Such secure tenants were then included in the statutory protection introduced for private sector tenants by the Matrimonial Homes Act 1967 and now contained in the Act of 1983. Secure tenancies are now governed by the Housing Act 1985.

*(c) Assured tenancies*
Generally a tenancy of a dwelling-house created on or after the Housing Act 1988 came into force on 15 January 1989 will be an assured tenancy or an assured short-hold tenancy. With only limited exceptions, a tenancy entered into on or after that date cannot be a protected tenancy (Housing Act 1988, s.34), though existing protected and statutory tenancies will remain a significant feature of the housing scene for some time to come. The Housing Act 1988 applies to assured tenancies the provisions of the Matrimonial Homes Act 1983 relating to representative occupation (Sched. 17, para. 33).

## 3. Extent of the protection of the tenant's spouse

*(a) The matrimonial home*
A wife's occupation of premises will be deemed at common law to be that of the husband only if she is in occupation of what was or, before the husband moved out, had been the matrimonial home (*Hall* v *King* (1987) 283 EG 1400). It is also specifically provided that the Matrimonial Homes Act 1983 does not apply to a dwelling-house which has at no time been a matrimonial home of the spouse (s.1(10)). Thus where a husband took a tenancy of a cottage within the Rent Act limits in order to provide accommodation for his wife and son, but never occupied it himself as his residence, the wife was merely his licensee. She was not occupying the cottage on his behalf so as to enable him to claim the protection of the Rent Act, and her own occupation was accordingly unprotected (*Hall* v *King* (1987) EG 1400. It might have been possible to argue that the husband was a mere nominee and that the wife was the real tenant: see *Firstcross Ltd* v *East West Ltd* (1980) 41 P & CR 145).

*(b) Occupation of the non-tenant spouse*
A wife will be able to take advantage of the protection afforded by the common law and the 1983 Act through the concept of representative occupation only if she is in fact in occupation of the home. However, in certain circumstances a wife will be deemed to be in occupation for this purpose even though she is physically absent from the house. In *Hoggett* v *Hoggett* (1980) 39 P & CR 121 at p. 127, Sir David Cairns, in considering the position of a wife who is forced to leave the matrimonial home by her husband's conduct, said:

"In my view the question whether an evicted wife is still in occupation in law depends on the same sort of considerations as apply in cases where a statutory tenant has left the house, but asserts a continuing right to occupation: that is to say, whether he has had a continuing intention to return and whether there remain at the premises some person or goods constituting the corpus of occupation: see e.g. *Brown* v *Brash* [1948] 2 KB 247."

Thus if a wife goes to hospital for a few days this could not be regarded as going out of occupation, any more than if the wife had gone on a weekend visit to a friend, or, indeed, gone out shopping for a few hours. Where the wife has been evicted by the tenant husband who has treated her with violence, her intention to return will not be destroyed because it is subject to the condition of not having to live in the same house as the husband. This was the position in *Hoggett* v *Hoggett* where the wife had demonstrated her desire to get back into the house by taking proceedings under the Domestic Violence and Matrimonial Proceedings Act 1976, seeking an injunction excluding the husband from the house so that she could return with her son. The fact that she refused a request to remove her furniture was further evidence of her intention, and the presence of that furniture provided the "corpus" of occupation. The position may be otherwise if the wife has left voluntarily even if she later wishes to return, and possibly where she has been evicted and shows no intention of returning for some time.

### (c) Termination of the marriage

The representative character of a wife's occupation at common law and of a non-entitled spouse under the 1983 Act can continue only so long as the parties are married to each other. Once the marriage is terminated by a decree absolute of divorce or nullity, the protection afforded at common law and under the Act is accordingly terminated (*Robson* v *Headland* (1948) 64 TLR 596; *Metropolitan Properties Co Ltd* v *Cronan* (1982) 44 P & CR 1).

### (d) Termination of the tenancy

(i) Effect on the position of the tenant's spouse

The protection afforded to the wife of a tenant at common law would be destroyed if the tenancy was terminated as a result of an order for possession under the Rent Acts obtained by the landlord. The statutory rights of occupation will come to an end when the entitled spouse ceases to be entitled to occupy the home, and they are equally vulnerable to a valid order for possession under the Rent Act 1977, the Housing Act 1985 or the Housing Act 1988. Thus if a husband tenant should cease to pay the rent, this will provide the landlord with a ground for seeking possession under the Rent Act 1977 (Sched. 15, Pt. I, Ground 1), the Housing Act 1985 (s.84, Sched. 2, Pt. I, Ground 1) and the Housing Act 1988 (s.7, Sched. 2, Pt. II, Ground 10). The occupying wife's protection will be destroyed unless she can herself remedy the situation by paying the rent. There is now no doubt that she can pay the current rent and arrears. The Matrimonial Homes Act 1983, s.1(5), provides that where a spouse is entitled by virtue of s.1 of the Act to occupy a dwelling-house, any payment or tender made by that spouse in respect of rent shall be as good as if made by the other spouse.

More difficulty arises in relation to the opportunity to be afforded to a non-entitled spouse to take advantage of the right to pay or tender the rent and, if appropriate, to seek a transfer of the tenancy.

(ii) Statutory tenancies

In relation to a home which is within the Rent Act 1977 it is established that proceedings by the landlord must be brought against the entitled spouse as tenant and not merely against the non-entitled spouse as the person in occupation (*Brown* v *Draper* [1944] KB 309), and the same must be true in relation to secured tenancies and assured tenancies. Since the decision in *Middleton* v *Baldock* [1950] 1 KB 657 the normal practice has been to take proceedings not only against the tenant but also against the tenant's spouse who has been left in occupation of the home. (See now Megarry, *Rent Acts* 11th ed. Vol 1 at p. 293). This practice was followed by the landlord's solicitors in *Penn* v *Dunn* [1970] 2 QB 686 where the tenant had deserted, leaving his wife and children in occupation of the matrimonial home. He subsequently informed the landlord that he did not intend to pay any further rent, and that in future it would be paid by the wife. In fact the wife did not pay the rent and the landlord brought proceedings against both spouses. Neither spouse appeared in the county court, and an order for possession in twenty-eight days was made against the husband, but no order was made against the wife. Subsequently the landlord brought fresh proceedings for possession against the wife as trespasser. The wife, presumably seeing that she had no defence to the second action, applied to have the judgment against the husband set aside, and when this was refused, she applied, after the twenty-eight days had expired, for a suspension of the order for possession under s.11(2) of the Rent Act 1968 - now s.100 of the Rent Act 1977. This, too, was refused.

Upholding this decision, the Court of Appeal held that once an order for possession had been lawfully made, or at any rate once the date for giving possession had passed, the tenant was no longer a statutory tenant (*American Economic Laundry Ltd* v *Little* [1951] 1 KB 400. It should be noted that the order in *Penn* v *Dunn* was a final order. It seems that a conditional order leaves the statutory tenancy still in being: *Sherrin* v *Brand* [1956] 1 QB 403. See the discussion of the difficulties in Pettit, *Private Sector Tenancies* (2nd ed.) p. 227). Since the husband had lost the right to occupy, his wife also lost her rights under the Matrimonial Homes Act. Thereafter only the former tenant had the right to apply for a suspension or postponement of the order. This was reversed by s.75 of the Housing Act 1980 which extended the provisions of s.100 of the Rent Act 1977 (see s.100 (4A) and (4B)). The present position is that where a tenancy is terminated in proceedings for possession of a dwelling-house occupied by the tenant's spouse or former spouse, having rights of occupation under the Matrimonial Homes Act, the spouse or former spouse has the same rights to apply for an adjournment or a stay, suspension or postponement, as if his or her rights of occupation were not affected by the termination of the tenancy (s.100(1) and (2). The same applies to tenancies under the Rent (Agriculture) Act 1976).

Although the tenant's spouse may now apply for a suspension of an order for possession, his or her position is not necessarily as satisfactory as it would be if an order for possession had not been made in the first place. Thus once a statutory tenancy has been terminated, presumably there is nothing the court can transfer under s.7 of the Matrimonial Homes Act 1983 or s.24 of the Matrimonial Causes Act 1973, and there can be no transmission on the death of the former tenant (see Parts 4

163

and 5 below for the provisions relating to transfer and transmission respectively). It is, therefore, advisable for the spouse of a tenant to intervene at an early stage to prevent an order being made.

If the non-entitled spouse is not made a party to proceedings against the entitled spouse, and hears of the proceedings only after an order for possession has been made, then he or she can apply to be made a party to the proceedings against the tenant spouse and seek leave to appeal against the order for possession made against the tenant, as in *Middleton* v *Baldock* [1950] 1 KB 657. Assuming she can pay the rent she can then keep the tenancy in existence, rather than perhaps merely seeking a suspension of the order for possession under s.100. If the non-entitled spouse is at the outset made a party to the proceedings against the tenant spouse, then she should take advantage of her rights under the 1983 Act and an order for possession should not be made, in the light of *Middleton* v *Baldock,* if she is in occupation and in a position to tender the rent. If for some reason an order for possession is made against the tenant, and, as Brightman LJ said in *Grange Lane South Flats Ltd* v *Cook* (1983) 1 FLR 177 at p. 178, it may well be that this should now only occur by mistake, application should be made, if necessary, for leave to appeal out of time. This was the situation in *Grange Lane South Flats Ltd* v *Cook* where an order for possession was made against the tenant husband by the registrar on a successful application by the landlord that the defence of the husband be struck out. The wife's solicitors were present, but no reference was made at that stage to the implications of *Penn* v *Dunn.* The implications of that case seem to have become apparent only when the action came on for trial against the wife some eight months later when what appears to have been her first line of defence, namely that she had become a contractual tenant, failed. The Court of Appeal held that she should have been given leave to appeal out of time to enable her to argue her defence under the Matrimonial Homes Act 1967. It was a strong case in that the landlord's solicitors were apparently aware all along of the decision in *Penn* v *Dunn* (if not of its implications), and it was their duty to bring the case to the attention of the registrar. If this had been done, the order for possession against the husband would never have been made. Moreover, while cogent reasons are required to justify an appeal out of time, the interlocutory order had been made not against the intending appellant, but against a co-defendant and only affected the intending appellant by a side wind. After the order the action was intended to continue against the wife on the basis of the pleadings, which included the wife's defence under the Matrimonial Homes Act 1967. There was no injustice to the landlord in allowing the appeal and thus enabling the wife to argue that defence on its merits.

(iii) Secure tenancies

The Housing Act 1985, s.85 confers upon the court in relation to secure tenancies powers similar to those conferred by s.100 of the Rent Act 1977 in relation to statutory tenancies. Thus proceedings for possession on certain grounds may be adjourned for such period or periods as the court thinks fit, and on the making of an order for possession on any of these grounds, or at any time before the execution of the order, the court may (a) stay or suspend the execution of the order, or (b) postpone the date of possession, for such period or periods as the court thinks fit.

Moreover, the spouse or former spouse of a secure tenant can take advantage of these powers on the same basis as the spouse of a statutory tenant (s.85(5)). The more satisfactory course in the long term is to seek a transfer of the tenancy but, as in the case of a statutory tenancy, this will only be possible if the tenancy still subsists.

In this respect it seems from the decision of the Court of Appeal in *Thompson* v *Elmbridge Borough Council* [1987] 1 WLR 1425 that a secure tenant will be in a worse position than the spouse of a statutory tenant. Thus it appears that a statutory tenancy continues to subsist until possession is obtained where a conditional, rather than an absolute or unconditional, order for possession is made. In relation to secure tenancies s.82(2) provides that where a landlord obtains an order for possession of a dwelling-house, the tenancy ends on the date on which the tenant is to give up possession in pursuance of the order. In *Thompson* v *Elmbridge Borough Council* this meant that in the case of a suspended order for possession, once the defendant had ceased to comply with the conditions of the order, namely the punctual payment of the current rent and arrears, and there was a breach of the terms of the order, the tenancy came to an end at that moment. There was therefore nothing to transfer. In this situation the spouse or former spouse should seek to be made a party to the proceedings against the original tenant and then apply to have the original order varied or set aside so as to revive the secure tenancy (see *Governors of Peabody Donation Fund* v *Hay* (1987) 19 HLR 145 where the Court of Appeal upheld the exercise of discretion by a county court judge to set aside or suspend a possession order notwithstanding that a warrant for possession had been issued and executed).

(iv) Assured tenancies

In relation to assured tenancies, the Housing Act 1988 also confers powers similar to s.100 of the Rent Act 1977. It is provided that in any case where (a) at a time when proceedings are brought for possession of a dwelling-house let on an assured tenancy, the tenant's spouse or former spouse, having rights of occupation under the Matrimonial Homes Act 1983, is in occupation of the dwelling-house, and (b) the assured tenancy is terminated as a result of those proceedings, then the spouse or former spouse, so long as he or she remains in occupation, has the same rights in relation to, or in connection with, any such adjournment or any such stay, suspension or postponement referred to in s.9 as he or she would have if those rights of occupation were not affected by the termination of the tenancy (s.9(5)).

*(e) Suitable alternative accommodation*

A court may make an order for possession of a dwelling-house under s.98 of the Rent Act 1977 if it is satisfied that suitable alternative accommodation is available for the tenant or will be available when the order takes effect. Such alternative accommodation must be reasonably suitable to the needs of the tenant and his family (Rent Act 1977, Sched. 15, Pt. IV, para 5). "Family" for this purpose has the same meaning as in the provisions of the Act relating to the transmission of a tenancy on the death of a tenant. (See Part 5 below, and *Standingford* v *Probert* [1950] 1 KB 377 and *Kavanagh* v *Lyroudias* [1985] 1 All ER 560.)

Under s.84 of the Housing Act 1985 the court must not make an order for possession on the grounds set out in Parts II and III of Schedule 2 of the Act unless suitable alternative accommodation will be available for the tenant when the order takes effect. Again the court must be satisfied that the accommodation is reasonably suitable to the needs of the tenant and his family, taking into account the matters set out in the Act (see Sched. 4, Pt. II). Accordingly, every member of the tenant's family living in the premises is a person with a potential interest in any possession proceedings. Any such person who considers that the accommodation is unsuitable because it is too far from his place of work, or too far from some other members of the family to whom it is essential he should live in close proximity, may raise the matter even if the tenant does not wish to do so. He or she should therefore be allowed to be joined as a party for this purpose (see Parker LJ in *Wandsworth London Borough Council* v *Fadayomi* [1987] 1 WLR 1473 at p. 1478). In that case the tenant's wife was held to be entitled to be made a party to proceedings for possession so that she could present her case in relation to alternative accommodation where the marriage had broken down and separate accommodation was desired by the spouses.

A court may make an order for possession of a dwelling-house let on an assured tenancy if suitable alternative accommodation is available for the tenant or will be available for him when the order for possession takes effect (Housing Act 1988, s.7 and Sched. 2 Pt. II, Ground 9). The accommodation must be reasonably suitable to the needs of the tenant and his family (Pt. III). A member of the tenant's family can therefore require to be made a party to the proceedings.

## 4. Transfer of tenancies

### (a) The desirability of obtaining a transfer

The statutory rights of occupation of the non-entitled spouse in relation to tenanted property will come to an end in accordance with the general principles of the Matrimonial Homes Act 1983 on the termination of the marriage by a decree absolute of divorce or nullity unless extended under the provisions of s.2(4) of the Act. Such an order does not appear to be common and it seems preferable to procure a transfer of the tenancy. There are two statutory provisions under which a court may order the transfer of a tenancy from the entitled spouse to the non-entitled spouse or from the joint names of the spouses into the name of one spouse alone. It is essential that such a transfer is obtained while the tenancy still subsists. Once the tenancy has been terminated as a result of an order for possession or because the tenant is no longer occupying the property as his residence either personally or through the representative occupation of his or her spouse, there will be nothing to transfer. In this respect it has already been noted that representative occupation by a spouse is terminated by a decree absolute of divorce or nullity so that the existence of a tenancy thereafter may depend on occupation by the tenant personally. (It is arguable that the inclusion of the expression "former spouse" as well as "spouse" in s.100 of the Rent Act 1977 as amended by the Housing Act 1980, s.75, and in s.85 of the Housing Act 1985 and s.9(5) of the Housing Act 1988, may have been intended to extend the concept of representative occupation to a former spouse, but it would be unwise to rely on this.)

## (b) Matrimonial Homes Act 1983, s.7 and Schedule 1

The relevant provisions of the 1967 Act originally applied only to protected and statutory tenancies but their application has been extended so that the 1983 Act now also applies to secure tenancies and assured tenancies. An order can be made not only where one spouse is entitled to occupy as sole tenant, but also where both spouses are tenants and thus jointly entitled to occupy the home. An order under these provisions can now be made on the granting of a decree of divorce or nullity (whether before or after the decree is made absolute) or a decree of judicial separation, or at any time thereafter by the court by which the decree is granted. The original provisions did not apply to judicial separation, and only empowered the court to make an order after decree nisi of divorce or nullity and before the decree was made absolute - to become effective on decree absolute. In *Lewis* v *Lewis* [1985] AC 459 it was held that the removal of the latter restriction by s.6 of the Matrimonial Homes and Property Act 1981 was not retrospective and did not enable the court to revive a statutory tenancy which had ceased to exist before the application for transfer had been made. It must be borne in mind that although a transfer may now be ordered after termination of a marriage by divorce, the representative occupation of the tenant's spouse will also be terminated by the divorce and thus the tenancy will come to an end (*Metropolitan Properties Co Ltd* v *Cronan* (1982) 44 P & CR 1). It therefore seems that an application by a former spouse after termination of the marriage will only be possible in the less common situation where the tenant is still personally in residence. In any event, a former spouse who remarries is no longer entitled to apply for an order (Sched. 1, para. 7). In the case of divorce or nullity of marriage the date specified in an order as the date on which it is to take effect must not be earlier than the date on which the decree is made absolute (Sched. 1, para. 6).

Where a spouse is entitled to occupy the dwelling-house by virtue of a protected tenancy, a secure tenancy, or an assured tenancy, the court may by order direct that, as from such date as may be specified in the order, the estate or interest which the spouse so entitled had in the dwelling-house before that date by virtue of the lease or agreement creating the tenancy and any assignment of that lease or agreement, shall be transferred to, and vested in, the other spouse *without further assurance* (Sched. 1 para. 2). The estate or interest is vested with the benefit of all rights, privileges and appurtenances attaching to that estate or interest but subject to all covenants, obligations, liabilities and incumbrances to which it is subject. There will also be vested in the transferee spouse the liability of the other spouse under any express or implied covenant of indemnity by the latter spouse as an assignee of the lease or agreement. However, no liability or obligation under any covenant having reference to the dwelling-house in the lease or agreement falling due to be discharged or performed on or after the date of the transfer can be enforced against the spouse in whom the tenancy is no longer vested. The transferee spouse or former spouse will be deemed to be a "successor" within the meaning of the Housing Act 1985 or the Housing Act 1988 if the other spouse or former spouse was "successor" to the tenancy. This means that, in that event, on the death of the transferee there can be no further transmission of the tenancy under s.89 of the Housing Act 1985 in the case of a secure tenancy or under s.17 of the Housing Act 1988 in the case of an assured tenancy.

Where the spouse is entitled to occupy the dwelling-house by virtue of a statutory tenancy within the Rent Act 1977, the court may by order direct that, as from such date as may be specified in the order, that spouse shall cease to be entitled to occupy the dwelling-house and that the other spouse shall be deemed to be the tenant, or as the case may be, the sole tenant under that statutory tenancy (Sched. 1, para. 3). The extent to which the provisions of the Rent Act 1977, relating to succession to a statutory tenancy by the surviving spouse of a deceased tenant or by a member of the deceased tenant's family, can take effect will depend upon whether the transferor was a first or second "successor". The transferee spouse steps into the transferor's shoes for this purpose so that if the transferor spouse was already a "second successor" there can be no further succession on the death of the transferee spouse.

Where the court makes an order under the above provisions it may also by order direct that both spouses shall be jointly and severally liable to discharge or perform any or all of the liabilities and obligations in respect of the dwelling-house (whether arising under the tenancy or otherwise) which have at the date of the the order fallen due to be discharged or performed by only one of the spouses or which, but for the direction, would fall due to be discharged or performed by one only of them before the date specified as the date on which the order is to take effect. Where the court gives such a direction it may further direct that either spouse shall be liable to indemnify the other in whole or in part against any payment made or expenses incurred by the other in discharging or performing any such liability or obligation (Sched. 1, para. 5).

It will be noted that in each case the transfer is effected by the order itself without any further action on the part of either of the spouses (contrast s.24 of the 1973 Act, considered below). Provision is made for the landlord of the dwelling-house to be given an opportunity of being heard in relation to the application. It seems, however, that the landlord's objections to a proposed transfer will not necessarily prevent an order being made (see *Buckingham* v *Buckingham & London Brick Co* (1978) unreported, but discussed at (1979) 129 NLJ 52). The position may be otherwise where the tenancy contains an absolute prohibition against assignment or a qualified covenant and the landlord refuses his consent on reasonable grounds (Landlord and Tenant Act 1927, s.19(1). Contrast the position under s.24 of the 1973 Act, considered below).

### (c) Matrimonial Causes Act 1973, s.24

On granting a decree of divorce, a decree of nullity of marriage or a decree of judicial separation or at any time thereafter (whether, in the case of a decree of divorce or of nullity, before or after the decree is made absolute), the court may make an order that a party to the marriage shall transfer to the other party, to any child of the family or to such person as may be specified in the order for the benefit of such child, such property as may be so specified, being property to which the first-mentioned party is entitled, either in possession or reversion (s.24(1) Matrimonial Causes Act 1973. See Chapter 10).

It should be noted that in contrast to s.7 of the Matrimonial Homes Act 1983 which provides that the tenancy is transferred "by virtue of the order and without further assurance", s.24 merely empowers the court to order a party to transfer property which might consist of a tenancy. It is essential that a transfer in appropriate form is effected. In *Crago* v *Julian* [1992] FLR 475 the Court of Appeal held that a deed was necessary to transfer an oral weekly tenancy. Although no order had been been made under s.24 the husband had undertaken to do all acts necessary to transfer the tenancy to the wife. However he had failed to do so, and the landlords refused a transfer and were able to terminate the tenancy which was still vested in the husband who was no longer entitled to statutory protection as he was not in possession. Again in contrast to s.7, there is no specific provision requiring notice of an application for a transfer of property order affecting a tenancy to be given to the landlord, though the court will almost certainly wish to know the attitude of the landlord - particularly if the landlord is a public authority.

In *Hale* v *Hale* [1975] 1 WLR 931 the Court of Appeal held that a weekly tenancy was "property" for this purpose and that in the absence of any contractual or statutory prohibition preventing it being transferred by the tenant himself, the court had power in an appropriate case to exercise its power under s.24(1) to make an order for its transfer. The court thought that different considerations might apply where there was a contractual prohibition or restriction on the right of assignment, or in relation to a statutory tenancy which is not assignable (*ibid.* at pp. 936 and 937).

In *Thompson* v *Thompson* [1976] Fam 25 the Court of Appeal held that a council tenancy was "as much a form of property as any other tenancy ..." (*per* Buckley LJ at p. 29). In that case there was no covenant against assignment, despite the requirement to that effect in s.113(5) of the Housing Act 1957, and in the circumstances the court saw no reason why it should not have jurisdiction to order a transfer of the tenancy under s.24. Sir John Pennycuick (at p. 32) doubted if the absence of such a covenant was a consideration of much importance, bearing in mind that in the event of an assignment by the tenant to someone who was unwelcome to the council, the council could determine the tenancy at short notice. In the later case of *Hutchings* v *Hutchings* (1975) 237 EG 571 the Court of Appeal was concerned with a council tenancy which by its terms was subject to a covenant not to assign. However, Cairns LJ pointed out that there was no obligation on the part of the local authority as landlords to insist upon that covenant. The tenancy could not be assigned without its consent, but if it had consented, the tenancy became assignable. In cases decided before the Housing Act 1980 the attitude of the local authority was crucial. Thus in *Regan* v *Regan* [1977] 1 WLR 84 the local authority was not prepared to consent to a transfer of the tenancy from the husband to his wife (whom it was prepared to house elsewhere) and the Court of Appeal held that in these circumstances the court should not make an order under s.24 in respect of the tenancy. Sir George Baker said at p. 87: "Housing is a matter for the local authority." This attitude was not surprising, for at that time it was, of course, open to a local authority to terminate a tenancy after it had been transferred even if there was no covenant against assignment. The Housing Act 1980 introduced the secure tenancy, and, moreover, sought to give full recognition to the power of the divorce court to order a transfer of a tenancy. Thus while a secure tenancy, which is assigned will generally cease to be a be a secure tenancy, it is specifically provided that this will not be the case if an assignment is made in pursuance of an order under s.24 of the 1973 Act. (See now s.91(2) and (3)(b) of the Housing Act 1985.) It is also provided that a secure tenancy will remain a secure tenancy if it is assigned to a person in whom the tenancy would or might have vested under the succession provisions of what is now the Housing Act 1985 (Housing Act 1985, s.91(2) and (3)(c). See Part 5 below). Accordingly, if an order for the transfer of a secure tenancy is made under s.7 of the Matrimonial Homes Act 1983 it will not cease to be a secure tenancy provided that the transferee is a person qualified to succeed, though not necessarily the person who would have succeeded, to the tenancy under the 1985 Act.

The Housing Act 1980 also repealed s.113(5) of the Housing Act 1957 so that a local authority is no longer obliged to include in a tenancy agreement a prohibition against assignment (s.35(4)). Nevertheless, there will remain a large number of tenancies which do contain a covenant against assignment and where an element of uncertainty continues to exist. In this situation it is arguable that there can be no order, or at any rate no effective order, without the local authority's consent. Thus in *Waugh* v *Waugh* and *Bardsell* v *Bardsell* (1982) 3 FLR 375 at p. 376, Ormrod LJ said:

> "As in so many local authority and indeed other tenancy agreements, there is an absolute prohibition against assignment. In those circumstances, there is no property upon which the property adjustment order can operate."

In *Waugh* an order for the transfer of the tenancy from the husband to the wife was subject to the consent of the local authority which was in fact refused. In *Bardsell* the local authority refused to consent to the transfer of the tenancy as ordered by the court. However, the consolidated judgment of the Court of Appeal in these cases was not directly concerned with the question of a transfer of the tenancies but with applications for ouster orders. It has since been held that an assignment of a secure tenancy without the required consent of the landlord will pass the secure tenancy to an assignee who is a person who would have been qualified to claim succession to the tenancy under the 1980 Act (*Governors of the Peabody Donation Fund* v *Higgins* [1983] 1 WLR 1091). Nevertheless, the court did point out that the assignee was at risk that the landlord would seek possession on the basis of the assignor's breach of covenant by taking appropriate steps under s.33 of the 1980 Act (see now s.84 and Sched. 2 of the Housing Act 1985). It is arguable that only a voluntary assignment will amount to a breach of such a covenant and that an assignment pursuant to an order of the court under s.24 is not a voluntary assignment so that a local authority would not be entitled to seek possession on this basis. This argument would be even stronger if the tenancy was transferred by virtue of an order of the court under s.7 of the Matrimonial Homes Act 1983. Moreover, under s.84 of the Housing Act 1985 the court must not make an order for possession on the basis of a breach of an obligation of the tenancy unless it considers it reasonable to make the order. It might not be easy to persuade a court to make an order on the basis of the transfer of the tenancy made in pursuance of an order which another court considered appropriate to make under s.24.

*(d) Other methods of effecting a transfer*

Some of the cases before 1980 show that where a local authority was the landlord of the home, it was prepared to transfer a tenancy from one spouse to the other on breakdown of a marriage, though it might insist on the non-tenant spouse obtaining a court order of some kind, such as an injunction excluding the tenant spouse (see *Thompson* v *Thompson* [1976] Fam 25; *Hutchings* v *Hutchings* (1975) 237 EG 571). Similarly, where one cohabitee was able to obtain an injunction under the Domestic Violence and Matrimonial Proceedings Act 1976 excluding the tenant cohabitee, a local authority might transfer the tenancy from the excluded cohabitee to the other. The ability of a local authority to effect a *"de facto* property adjustment" of this kind depended on the fact that local authority tenancies were not protected under the Rent Acts. Since October 1980 council tenants have been protected as secure tenants. In relation to spouses a transfer of a tenancy can be obtained under s.7 of the Matrimonial Homes Act 1983 or s.24 of the Matrimonial Causes Act 1973. Indeed, as noted above, the policy of the 1980 Act was to make the transfer of a tenancy on the breakdown of a marriage a matter for the court. On the breakdown of an unmarried relationship there is no statutory power to transfer a tenancy from one cohabitee to the other.

There seems to be no entirely satisfactory way of dealing with this problem unless the parties can reach agreement. A tenant may assign the tenancy to his or her cohabitee and it will generally remain a secure tenancy since a person living with another "as husband and wife" will qualify as a "successor" for the purposes of s.91 of the Housing Act 1985 (see Part 5, page 171). If the tenant cohabitee has been forced to leave the home by an ouster order it might be argued that the parties are no longer living together as husband and wife. However, it would seem appropriate to adopt the same approach as that adopted in relation to similar wording in s.1 of the Domestic Violence and Matrimonial Proceedings Act 1976. Under that provision the courts have exercised jurisdiction to make an order notwithstanding that the parties are no longer living together as husband and wife because the applicant has left as a result of the conduct of the tenant spouse (see Chapter 5). If the tenancy contains a covenant against assignment, the assignee will of course be vulnerable to an action for possession on the basis of a breach of covenant as suggested in *Governors of the Peabody Foundation Fund* v *Higgins* [1983] 1 WLR 1091. If the tenant cohabitee is prepared to surrender his or her tenancy, then the local authority will be in a position to grant a new tenancy to the other tenant if this is appropriate, e.g. in view of the presence of children.

In the absence of agreement it is arguable that where the tenant cohabitee has been excluded from the home by a court order, e.g. under the Domestic Violence and Matrimonial Proceedings Act 1976, he no longer occupies the home as his only or principal home and has thus lost his secure status (see Housing Act 1985, s.81). This would enable the local authority to obtain possession and grant a new tenancy to the other cohabitee as it might have done before 3 October 1980. This seems open to strong objection. The tenant is only out of occupation in compliance with a court order, and it is clear that an order under s.1 of the 1976 Act is to be regarded as a temporary measure to procure a period of stability until some further step can be taken (see *Davis* v *Johnson* [1979] AC 264; *Hopper* v *Hopper* [1978] 1 WLR

1342; Practice Direction [1978] 1 WLR 1123). In *Freeman* v *Collins* (1983) 4 FLR 649 the Court of Appeal held that where a woman had no legal or equitable interest in the home (a council house of which her former partner was tenant) and the court had no jurisdiction to transfer any interest to her, an order under s.1 of the 1976 Act should not be used as a device whereby she could acquire such rights. Generally, it was said, the judge should limit the period of an order excluding the man as owner or tenant and giving the woman a right of occupation. In that case the order was limited to one month which was thought to give the housing authority sufficient time to deal with the woman's application for rehousing. On the other hand, in *Spencer* v *Comacho* (1983) 4 FLR 662, while it was recognised that an order under s.1 was generally designed only to provide short-term relief, it was also recognised that there might be exceptional circumstances in which it was appropriate to make an order "until further order" (see Chapter 5). Although the circumstances of the case may have been unusual it is significant that Sir David Cairns noted that where the parties are not married "the only Act which can be looked to to deal with the situation is the Act of 1976" (*ibid.* at p. 667). Where an indefinite exclusion order can be obtained by a cohabitee there is perhaps greater force in the argument that the other cohabitee is no longer occupying the premises as his or her home. If the cohabitee is a sole secure tenant then he would lose his security of tenure and the way would be open for the local authority to terminate the tenancy. Nevertheless, it is hardly satisfactory to have to rely on such reasoning (see the full discussion in Williams, *Ouster Orders, Property Adjustment and Council Housing* [1988] Fam Law 438).

This argument will, of course, be of no assistance where the cohabitees are joint tenants of the home, since security will be retained so long as one joint tenant is in occupation. However, in this situation there is another way in which the tenancy can be terminated so as to give the local authority the opportunity of granting a new sole secure tenancy to one cohabitee. Where the tenancy is periodic it was recognised by the Court of Appeal in *Greenwich London Borough Council* v *McGrady* (1982) 46 P & CR 223 that one joint tenant may give notice to quit on the landlord which will effectively terminate the joint tenancy. That case concerned former spouses, but the same reasoning applies to a joint tenancy held by cohabitees. That case was approved by the House of Lords in *Hammersmith and Fulham London Borough Council* v *Monk* [1992] AC 478. The cohabitee giving notice would no doubt do so only upon the understanding that the local authority would grant to him or her a new sole secure tenancy. These decisions have gone some way towards restoring the *de facto* power of local authorities to "transfer" a tenancy following breakdown of a family relationship, and this is obviously more important in the case of cohabitees than in the case of spouses (see Ralph Gibson LJ in *Wiseman* v *Simpson* [1988] 1 WLR 35 at p. 43). Nevertheless, it is of assistance only in relation to joint tenancies, and the principle applies only to periodic tenancies. If the tenancy is for a fixed term, then both tenants will have to act together to terminate the tenancy. (See Luba, *Domestic Violence and Secure Council Tenants*, LAG Bulletin, February 1983, p. 26. Williams in [1988] Fam Law 438 at p. 442 refers to the possible argument that the surrender would amount to a breach of trust and that any new sole tenancy granted in consequence might be held on a constructive trust.)

## 5. Transmission of tenancies

*(a) Statutory tenancies*

(i) The statutory provisions
A statutory tenancy is a purely personal right which cannot be disposed of by will and does not vest in the tenant's personal representatives (*Lovibond & Sons Ltd* v *Vincent* [1929] 1 KB 687). However, the Rent Act 1977 (following previous legislation) provides, in certain circumstances, for a transmission of the statutory tenancy to the surviving spouse of the tenant or to some other member of the tenant's family (s.2 and Sched. 1 as amended by the Housing Acts 1980 and 1988).

A protected tenancy may be disposed of by will and does vest in the tenant's personal representatives. Nevertheless, on the death of the protected tenant, his or her surviving spouse or some other member of his or her family may become a statutory tenant by succession. This is so even though the original tenant bequeathed the contractual tenancy to someone else, but while there is a statutory tenancy in existence the contractual tenancy is in abeyance (*Moodie* v *Hosegood* [1952] AC 61).

In both situations, on the death of the statutory tenant by succession (the "first successor"), one further transmission may take place.

This system was modified in several important respects by the Housing Act 1988, s.39 where the original tenant (i.e. a protected tenant of the dwelling-house or the statutory tenant of it by virtue of his or her previous protected tenancy) dies after the commencement of that Act on 15 January 1989. (This is subject to the operation of transitional provisions: see Sched. 4 Pt. 1.)

On the death of the original tenant his or her surviving spouse, if residing in the dwelling-house immediately before the death of the original tenant, will become (as before) the statutory tenant if and so long as he or she occupies the dwelling-house as his or her residence. It is now provided that for this purpose a person who was living with the original tenant as his or her wife or husband is to be treated as the spouse of the original tenant. If more than one person fulfils the qualifying condition then such one of them as may be decided by agreement, or in default of agreement by the county court, is to be treated as the tenant's spouse for the purposes of succession. On the death of the successor surviving spouse (or cohabitee), a person who (a) was a member of the original tenant's family immediately before that tenant's death, and (b) was a member of the first successor's family immediately before the first successor's death will be entitled to an assured tenancy of the dwelling-house by succession if he or she satisfies the residence qualification. This requires residence in the dwelling-house with the first successor at the time of, and for the period of two years immediately before, the first successor's death. If there is more than one such person the successor will be such one of them as may be decided by agreement or, in default of agreement, by the county court. There can be no succession to that assured tenancy (see below).

If, on the death of the original tenant, there is no surviving spouse (or cohabitee), but a person who was a member of the original tenant's family was residing in the dwelling-house at the time of, and for the period of two years immediately before, his or her death, then that person is entitled to an assured tenancy of the dwelling-house by succession. On the death of that successor there can be no succession to that assured tenancy (see Rent Act 1977, Sched. 1, Pt. 1 as amended by the Housing Act 1988, s.39 and Sched. 4, Pt. 1).

Since the Housing Act 1988 increased the qualifying period of residence for succession by persons other than a surviving spouse or cohabitee (for whom there is no qualifying period as long as there is residence immediately before the tenant's death) from six months to two years, transitional provisions seek to safeguard succession rights which had accrued at the date of the commencement of the Act. Thus if the original tenant or first successor died within eighteen months of the commencement of the Act, a person who was residing in the dwelling-house with the tenant or the successor at the time of the tenant's death or the successor's death, is to be taken to have been residing with the original tenant or the successor, as the case may be, for the period of two years immediately before his death. The requirement of residence in the dwelling-house (rather than simply with the deceased tenant) is in contrast to the position in relation to secure tenancies (see *Waltham Forest LBC* v *Thomas* [1992] 2 AC 198, considered below).

Where a successor becomes entitled to an assured tenancy by succession, that tenancy will be a periodic tenancy taking effect in possession immediately after the death of the protected or statutory tenant on whose death the successor became so entitled (see further s.39 of the Housing Act 1988).

(ii) The tenant's spouse and family
The legislation continues to require a successor to be either the spouse of the tenant or a member of the tenant's family. There has been no statutory definition of "family" for this purpose and none was introduced by the Housing Act 1988. In *Brock* v *Wollams* [1949] 2 KB 388, in which it was held that a person adopted *de facto*, but not legally, by the tenant was a member of his family, Cohen LJ said that the proper question was: "Would an ordinary man, addressing his mind to the question whether Mrs Wollams was a member of the family or not, have answered 'Yes' or 'No'?" (*Ibid.* at p. 394.) Although this test has generally been accepted, its application has not always been easy especially in relation to a cohabitee or *de facto* spouse (see *Gammans* v *Elkins* [1950] 2 KB 328; *Hawes* v *Evenden* [1953] 1 WLR 1169; *Dyson Holdings Ltd* v *Fox* [1976] QB 503). In relation to cohabitees it seemed that the crucial factor was the degree of stability and permanence of the relationship that existed. The absence of children did not prevent the relationship being regarded as a family, but the presence of children indicated permanence and strengthened the presumption that there was a family.

The Housing Act 1988 now expressly provides that a person who was living with the original tenant as his or her wife or husband is to be treated as the spouse of the original tenant for this purpose (Sched. 4, Pt. 1, para. 2). The position of the cohabitee is undoubtedly improved by this provision. There is no requirement of any particular period of residence with the tenant before his or her death. If they were living together as husband and wife then the degree of permanence or stability of their relationship may be thought to be less important than was the case hitherto. However, the relevance of permanence and stability was in determining the nature of the relationship so that this factor may still have some relevance when the court is determining whether a couple were living together "as husband and wife". That phrase can be interpreted to mean "living in the same manner as if they were husband and wife", but it can be more narrowly construed to mean "regarding themselves or holding themselves out as husband and wife". On either approach there seems little doubt that *Gammans* v *Elkins*, where a man had cohabited with the female tenant for some twenty years and had posed as her husband, would now be regarded as satisfying the statutory requirement and would be decided differently. On the other hand, *Helby* v *Rafferty* [1979] 1 WLR 13 presents more difficulty. In that case the male defendant had lived with the female tenant for some five years before her death, but they had had no intention of getting married and did not hold themselves out as married. The tenant had wished to retain her independence and the court concluded that their relationship did not have a sufficient degree of permanence and stability. Could it now be said that they were living together as husband and wife? Again in *Chios Property Investment Co Ltd* v *Lopez* (1987) 20 HLR 120 the defendant had moved into the deceased tenant's flat some two years before the latter's death with the intention of marrying him when their financial circumstances permitted. The Court of Appeal concluded that there was a sufficient degree of permanence and stability in their relationship to make the defendant a member of the tenant's family. It would be unfortunate if their deferred intention of getting married would now prevent their being regarded as living together as husband and wife even though in the narrower sense they did not consider themselves to be married.

In *Watson* v *Lucas* [1980] 1 WLR 1493 the majority of the Court of Appeal held that the fact that a man had remained married to his wife during the whole of the nineteen years he had lived with the deceased female tenant, and the fact that he and the deceased had continued to use their own names, was not sufficient to contradict the evidence that there was a lasting relationship between them. The man was held to have been a member of the deceased tenant's family. In view of the fact that it is now not uncommon for married women to continue to use their own names, such conduct on the part of a cohabitee should not be considered significant in this context unless there is other evidence of an intention to retain their independence. It is submitted, too, that the fact that one cohabitee remains married to a third person should not matter if the parties have regarded themselves as husband and wife. If the evidence shows that a man and a woman have set up home together and have a common household in the same way as a husband and wife, then they should be so regarded for this purpose. (Compare *Adeoso* v *Adeoso* [1980] 1 WLR 1535 - a decision under the Domestic Violence and Matrimonial Proceedings Act 1976 where, following a period when the parties had undoubtedly lived together as husband and wife, they had attempted for over a year to lead separate lives in a two-bedroomed flat: see Chapter 5. For the significance of the intentions of the parties as demonstrated by their conduct, see *City of Westminster* v *Peart* (1992) 24 HLR 389 where the Court of Appeal was concerned with a secure tenancy.) A homosexual or lesbian relationship would not be recognised for this purpose. (See *Harrogate Borough Council* v *Simpson* [1986] 2 FLR 91 in relation to secure tenancies.)

The concept of the tenant's "family" for this purpose has not been limited to cases of strict legal familial status, but the courts have, in the words of Russell LJ in

*Ross* v *Collins* [1964] 1 All ER 861 at p. 866, required "at least a broadly recognisable *de facto* familial status". He went on to say:
"This may be capable of being found and recognised as such by the ordinary man - where the link would be strictly familial had there been a marriage or where the link is through adoption of a minor, *de jure* or *de facto*, or where the link is 'step', or where the link is 'in law' or by marriage. But two strangers cannot ... ever establish artificially for the purposes of this section a familial nexus by acting as brothers and sisters, even if they call each other such and consider their relationship to be tantamount to that."
In that case the claimant, who had regarded the deceased tenant as a sort of elderly relative, partly as her father, partly as her elder brother, was held not to have been a member of his family for this purpose (see also *Carega Properties S.A.* v *Sharratt* [1979] 2 All ER 1084 - *de facto* nephew and aunt relationship, and *Sefton Holdings* v *Cairns* (1988) 14 EG 58 - *de facto* brother/sister relationship extending over 45 years held to be insufficient). The *de facto* adoption of a minor has been held to be sufficient (*Brock* v *Wollams* [1949] 2 KB 388).

(iii) "Residence"
In order to succeed to a tenancy on the death of the tenant, his or her spouse must have been residing in the premises immediately before the death of the tenant. It is not necessary for such residence to have been for any particular period and (since 1980) the spouse need not have been residing with the tenant (though in order to be treated as a spouse, a cohabitee must have been living with the tenant as his or her wife or husband).

In contrast, if a member of the tenant's family is to succeed, he or she must not only have been residing in the premises, but also have been residing with the tenant for the period of two years immediately preceding the death of the tenant (see Housing Act 1988, s.39 and Sched. 4, Pt. I, para. 3). Whether a person is residing with the tenant for this purpose is a question of fact and degree. One approach of the courts has been to consider whether the dwelling-house has become the home of the person claiming to succeed to the tenancy. Thus in *Morgan* v *Murch* [1970] 1 WLR 778 a son who had deserted his wife, leaving her in occupation of the matrimonial home of which he was tenant, was held to be residing with his mother with whom he went to live more than six months before her death (see also *Collier* v *Stoneman* [1957] 1 WLR 1108). Another approach has been to consider whether the person claiming to succeed had become part of the tenant's household before the tenant's death. Thus in *Foreman* v *Beagley* [1969] 1 WLR 1387 at p. 1392, Sachs LJ said that "the words 'residing with' import some measure of actual community of family living and companionship", and later that "'residing with' is something more than 'living at'". (See also *Edmunds* v *Jones* [1957] 1 WLR 1118 where a subtenant was held not to be "residing with" a tenant even though some accommodation was shared.) In the more recent case of *Swanbrae Ltd* v *Elliott* (1986) 19 HLR 86 both tests were referred to by the Court of Appeal. In that case the daughter, who claimed a tenancy by succession, had cared for her elderly mother during the latter's final illness, and for the six months preceding the mother's death the daughter had slept in a spare room at the premises for three or four nights each week rather than at her home some two miles away. In rejecting her claim, Swinton Thomas J said that the words "residing with" had "the connotation of having a settled home" though a person may have more than one home. In his view the person claiming to succeed to the tenancy had to show that he or she had made a home at the premises and had "become in the true sense a part of the household". Kerr LJ also accepted that the fact that the daughter had a home of her own was not necessarily fatal to her claim, but the existence and continued availability of that home was bound to render it more difficult to satisfy the requirement of having resided with the tenant at the same time. "The reason is that 'residence' must connote more than physical presence during the required period, albeit as a member of the household." (*Ibid.* at p. 96).

This case was distinguished by the Court of Appeal in *Hildebrand* v *Moon* [1989] 37 EG 123 where a daughter who had acquired a flat of her own some years previously, moved back to the premises of which her mother was tenant in order to nurse her mother. For more than six months before her mother's death the daughter slept there and spent much of each day there. She lived with her mother as one household. She was contemplating selling her own flat and it was accepted that all objective indicia were that the daughter had made her home with her mother. She was entitled to succeed to the tenancy of her mother's home. In *Hedgedale Ltd* v *Hards* (1991) 23 HLR 158 a 19 year old grandson was held by the Court of Appeal to be entitled to succeed to his grandmother's tenancy when he had had his permanent home in the premises during the relevant period before death, even though the grandmother herself was not living there for the whole of that period. When he moved in, his grandmother was living with her daughter, because she had broken her arm. Although she returned to the property before her death she died before she and the grandson had resided there for the requisite period. His right to succeed was not affected by the temporary absence of his grandmother who had intended to return to live there with him as a family unit.

*(b) Succession to secure tenancies*
Where a secure tenancy is a periodic tenancy and, on the death of the tenant there is a person qualified to succeed him, the tenancy will vest in that person by virtue of s.89 of the Housing Act 1985 unless the deceased was himself a successor. It will remain a secure tenancy. A person is qualified to succeed the tenant for this purpose if (1) he or she occupied the dwelling-house as his or her only or principal home at the time of the tenant's death, and (2) either (a) he or she is the tenant's spouse, or (b) he or she is another member of the tenant's family, and has resided with the tenant throughout the period of twelve months ending with the tenant's death (s.87).

A person is a member of another's family for this purpose if he or she is his or her spouse, parent, grandparent, child, grandchild, brother, sister, uncle, aunt, nephew or niece, or if they live together as husband and wife (s.113). Thus, while a spouse must have occupied the dwelling-house as his or her only or principal home at the time of the tenant's death, it is not necessary for him or her to have resided with the tenant throughout the period of twelve months ending with the tenant's death. A widow may therefore succeed to the tenancy of a dwelling-house which she has continued to occupy after her husband deserted her or was excluded by an order of the court. However, a female cohabitee will have to show that she resided with the tenant throughout the period of twelve months ending with his death. Moreover, where the tenant's spouse is qualified to succeed, he or she is entitled to be preferred to another member of the tenant's family who is also qualified to succeed. As between two or more other members of the tenant's family, the successor will be such one of them as may be agreed between them or, in default of agreement, as is selected by the landlord (Housing Act 1985, s.89(2). Contrast the position under the Rent Act 1977 where determination is by the county court). It has been held that the expression "living together as husband and wife" is not apt to include a homosexual relationship. The essential characteristic of living together as husband and wife "... is that there should be a man and a woman and that they should be living together in the same household." (*per* Ewbank J in *Harrogate Borough Council* v *Simpson* [1986] 2 FLR 91 at p. 95).

The requirement of residence with the tenant "throughout the period of 12 months ending with the tenant's death" does not mean that such residence must have been at the premises in which the tenant resided at the time of his death throughout that period (*Waltham Forest LBC* v *Thomas* [1992] 2 AC 198 overruling the earlier decision of the Court of Appeal in *South Northamptonshire DC* v *Power* [1987] 1 WLR 1433). Thus in *Waltham Forest LBC* v *Thomas,* a tenant's brother who had resided with the deceased for the requisite period but at two different properties was entitled to succeed to the tenancy of the property occupied at the time of the tenant's death. (Contrast the position in relation to statutory tenancies - see above.)

There can be no succession under s.89 if the deceased tenant was himself a "successor" - there can only be one statutory succession. The tenant will obviously be a successor if the tenancy vested in him by virtue of s.89. He will also be a successor if (1) he had been a joint tenant and had become sole tenant, (2) his periodic tenancy is one which arose automatically under s.86 of the Housing Act 1985 and the prior fixed term was granted to some other person or to the present tenant together with another person, or (3) he became tenant on the tenancy being assigned to him or on it being vested in him on the death of the previous tenant. However, if the tenancy was assigned to him in pursuance of an order under s.24 of the Matrimonial Causes Act 1973, he is a successor only if the other party to the marriage was himself or herself a successor (s.88). The deceased will not have been a successor if the local authority had granted him or her a new tenancy on the earlier death of his or her spouse. Thus in *Epping Forest DC* v *Pomphrett* (1990) 22 HLR 475 the local authority had agreed on the death of a tenant husband to transfer the tenancy to his widow. The Court of Appeal found that the effect of the agreement was to create a new tenancy in the widow so that she was not a successor and one or both of her children could succeed to that new secure tenancy on her death. In *Bassetlaw DC* v *Renshaw* [1992] 1 All ER 925 a joint tenancy of a council house held by a husband and wife had been terminated by the husband, and the council had entered into a new tenancy with the wife. The Court of Appeal held that she was not a successor to the joint tenancy so that her son was entitled to succeed to the new tenancy on her death. Fox LJ emphasised that it was important not to confuse the property with the tenancy. The widow "was successively a joint tenant and then a single tenant of the property. But she was never both a joint tenant and a single tenant under one tenancy". (*Ibid.* at p. 928.)

If there is no statutory succession to a periodic tenancy under s.89 (because there is no qualified successor or the deceased tenant was himself or herself a successor) then the tenancy will devolve in accordance with the general law of succession and will cease to be a secure tenancy (s.89(3)). It may then be determined in accordance with the terms of the contract.

Where a secure tenancy is a tenancy for a term certain, then on the death of the tenant the tenancy will remain a secure tenancy if it is vested or otherwise disposed of in the course of administration of the tenant's estate either (a) to a person qualified within s.87 to succeed the tenant, or (b) in pursuance of a property adjustment order made under s.24 of the Matrimonial Causes Act 1973. If it is not vested in such a person or disposed of in pursuance of such an order, it ceases to be a secure tenancy and it is determinable in accordance with the terms of the contract of tenancy (Housing Act 1985, s.90).

*(c) Succession to assured periodic tenancies*

Where the sole tenant under an assured periodic tenancy dies and, immediately before the death, the tenant's spouse was occupying the dwelling-house as his or her only or principal home, then, if the tenant was not himself or herself a successor, the tenancy vests on the death in the spouse and does not devolve under the tenant's will or intestacy (Housing Act 1988, s.17(1)). The right of succession thus has no application to a joint tenancy and applies only where the tenant was not a successor, so that there can only be one succession. A tenant is a successor in relation to a tenancy for this purpose if (a) the tenancy became vested in him or her either by virtue of s.17 or under the will or intestacy of a previous tenant; or (b) at some time before the tenant's death the tenancy was a joint tenancy held by himself or herself and one or more other persons and, prior to his or her death, he or she became the sole tenant by survivorship; or (c) he or she became entitled to the tenancy as a successor to a statutory tenancy or a periodic tenancy as provided in s.39(5) (s.17(2)). A tenant is also treated as a successor where he or she became a tenant by the grant of a new tenancy of a dwelling-house which is the same or substantially the same as the dwelling-house comprised in an earlier tenancy in relation to which he or she was a successor (s.17(3)). Where the tenancy was transferred from one spouse or former spouse to the other spouse or former spouse by an order under the Matrimonial Homes Act 1983, then if the spouse or former spouse from whom it was transferred was a successor for this purpose then the spouse or former spouse to whom the tenancy was transferred is also deemed to be a successor for this purpose (Matrimonial Homes Act 1983, Sched.1 Pt II as amended by the Housing Act 1988, Sched. 17, para. 34).

The right of succession is limited to a periodic tenancy. A tenancy for a fixed term will devolve according to the will or intestacy of the tenant. The successor will be entitled to an assured tenancy but will be a successor so that no further succession can take place on his or her death.

Only a surviving spouse is eligible to succeed to an assured periodic tenancy, but a person who was living with the tenant as his or her wife or husband is to be treated as the tenant's spouse (s.17(4)). If more than one person fulfils the qualifying condition then such one of them as may be decided by agreement or, in default of agreement, by the county court is to be treated as the tenant's spouse for the purpose of succession (s.17(5)).

# Chapter 8

# Creditors and the family home

## 1. Introduction

The ability of a husband and wife to continue to live in the matrimonial home may be affected by the claims of their creditors. This may happen even though there is no dispute between the spouses, though in practice financial problems will often accompany a breakdown of the marriage relationship. The most direct threat to the home is likely to be action by the mortgagee following default in payments due in respect of the mortgage. However, an unsecured creditor may seek a charging order in relation to a party's beneficial interest in the home with a view to seeking an order for sale. The financial problems may lead to the bankruptcy of one of the spouses, usually the husband, whereupon his property vests in his trustee in bankruptcy whose duty it is to realise it for the benefit of the creditors. This may lead to an application for sale which not only threatens occupation of the home, but may cast upon the non-bankrupt spouse or partner the burden of establishing a beneficial interest in the home. Even if there is no doubt about the entitlement of the other party to a beneficial interest, it may be vulnerable to attack by the trustee in bankruptcy if it was derived from the bankrupt. Bankruptcy of a husband may also threaten a property adjustment order being sought, or which has been obtained by the wife in divorce proceedings.

## 2. Claims by mortgagees

*(a) Mortgagees and rights of occupation of the mortgagor's spouse*
Where the matrimonial home is vested in the name of one spouse only, any personal right of occupation to which the other spouse may be entitled will not bind a mortgagee of the property (*National Provincial Bank Ltd* v *Ainsworth* [1965] AC 1175). Where a spouse has a beneficial interest in the home the legal estate in which is vested in the other spouse alone, proprietary rights of occupation will exist. The main problem is likely to be whether the beneficial interest is binding on third par-

ties such as mortgagees by virtue of occupation of the property (see Chapter 3). The statutory rights of occupation under the Matrimonial Homes Act 1983 will, however, bind any subsequent mortgagee if they have been protected in the appropriate manner (see Chapter 4). In practice it is unlikely that a mortgagee would complete an advance unless his mortgage was given priority over the charge of the non-entitled spouse. The more common situation is where the mortgage is created at the same time as the property is acquired as the matrimonial home, so that the non-entitled spouse will have no real opportunity of protecting the statutory rights of occupation before the completion of the mortgage. Such a mortgage will, therefore, have priority over the statutory rights of occupation. In the event of default by the entitled spouse as mortgagor, the mortgagee will be entitled to the usual remedies in accordance with the terms of the mortgage, and will, for example, be entitled, in exercise of any power of sale, to convey the property to a purchaser free from the statutory rights of occupation. In practice the mortgagee is likely to seek possession of the property with a view to a sale with vacant possession, and the entitled spouse may have little inclination to oppose the application or to remedy the situation. In these circumstances, the position of the non-entitled spouse who remains in occupation of the property, but whose statutory rights of occupation are not binding on the mortgagee, gives rise to several problems.

*(b) The position of the mortgagor's spouse with no binding rights of occupation*

(i) The right to make mortgage payments
The first problem is whether the non-entitled spouse, assuming he or she is aware of the position, can pay the amount due under the mortgage so as to safeguard his or her occupation. It seems doubtful whether anyone not entitled to an equity of redemption could make a good tender of sums due under a mortgage, but the Matrimonial Homes Act 1983 provides that, where a spouse has rights of occupation under s.1, any payment or tender by him or her of, *inter alia*, mortgage payments, shall, whether or not done in pursuance of an order under s.1, be as good as if made by the entitled spouse (s.1(5). See further Chapter 4).

(ii) Time for payment
The second problem concerns the opportunity to be afforded to a non-entitled spouse to take advantage of the right to make payments due under the mortgage. The non-entitled spouse may be unable to pay the instalments due, at any rate immediately, and may need time to obtain assistance, or to bring pressure to bear on the entitled spouse to pay the arrears, or to obtain maintenance or increased maintenance to cover the instalments. (It is possible that assistance may be obtained from the Department of Social Security to cover interest: see Chapter 19 and the Social Security (Mortgage Interest Payments) Act 1992.) Clearly if arrears accumulate, the chances of the non-entitled spouse having, or obtaining, the necessary funds are diminished. The position becomes even more serious when the whole capital sum becomes due, as will generally be the case when several instalments are outstanding. The non-entitled spouse's ability to pay is therefore likely to be prejudicially affected if he or she does not become aware of the default at an early stage.

Moreover, it was arguable that once an order for possession had been made against the entitled spouse, the statutory rights of the non-entitled spouse were terminated because the entitled spouse had ceased to be entitled to occupy the property. This danger was removed by the Matrimonial Homes and Property Act 1981 (s.2). It is now provided that in determining for the purposes of the 1983 Act whether a spouse or former spouse is entitled to occupy a dwelling-house by virtue of an estate or interest, any right to possession of the dwelling-house conferred on a mortgagee of the dwelling-house under or by virtue of the mortgage is to be disregarded, whether the mortgagee is in possession or not. However, the non-entitled spouse is not to have any larger right against the mortgagee to occupy the dwelling-house by virtue of his or her statutory rights than the entitled spouse has by virtue of his or her estate or interest and of any contract with the mortgagee, unless the statutory rights are, by virtue of protection under s.2, a charge on the estate or interest affecting the mortgagee (s.8(1)).

There appears to be no provision which ensures that the non-entitled spouse is appraised of the fact of default at an early stage, but as a result of the Matrimonial Homes and Property Act 1981 his or her position has been materially improved in relation to proceedings commenced by the mortgagee. Where a mortgagee of land which consists or substantially consists of a dwelling-house brings an action for the enforcement of his security, he must serve notice of the action on the non-entitled spouse if the latter has registered a Class F land charge against the entitled spouse or other estate owner in the case of unregistered land, or entered a notice under s. 2(8) of the 1983 Act in the case of registered land (s.8(3) of the 1983 Act). In *Hastings and Thanet Building Society* v *Goddard* [1970] 1 WLR 1242 at p.1245, Foster J at first instance took the view that the building society "... had notice because of the Class F Land Charge when they started the proceedings for possession that there was a deserted wife in the premises ...". As the Court of Appeal pointed out, registration was at the time irrelevant since the building society was a prior mortgagee, which on general principles was unaffected by the registration of a Class F land charge after the creation of the mortgage ([1970] 1 WLR 1533. The property was also registered land). The effect of the 1981 Act was therefore to add another dimension to registration of such a land charge or the entry of the equivalent notice. The subsequent registration of a Class F land charge will not make the non-entitled spouse's statutory rights of occupation binding on the mortgagee, but merely requires the mortgagee to serve notice of proceedings where the statutory rights have been protected at the relevant time.

*(c) The non-entitled spouse and proceedings for possession*

(i) The right to be made a party to proceedings
When a non-entitled spouse receives notice of proceedings from the mortgagee or otherwise learns of them, he or she will usually wish to be made a party to the proceedings. In *Hastings and Thanet Building Society* v *Goddard* [1970] 1 WLR 1544 the Court of Appeal thought that this course should be taken only where there was a real prospect in the very near future of her being able to redeem the property. It is now provided that where a mortgagee of land which consists of or includes a dwelling-house brings an action in any court for the enforcement of his security, a

spouse who is not a party to the action and who is enabled by s.1(5) or (8) of the 1983 Act to meet the mortgagor's liabilities under the mortgage, on applying to the court at any time before the action is finally disposed of in that court, is entitled to be made a party to the action if two conditions are satisfied (s.8(2)). First, the court must not see any special reason against such a course. Secondly, the court must be satisfied that the applicant may be expected to make such payments or do such things in or towards satisfaction of the mortgagor's liabilities or obligations as might affect the outcome of the proceedings, or that the expectation of it should be considered under s.36 of the Administration of Justice Act 1970.

(ii) The power to allow time to pay

The second condition means that in considering the non-entitled spouse's application to be made a party, the court must have regard to the possibility of him or her being able to utilise s.36 of the Administration of Justice Act 1970. That section provides that where the mortgagee under a mortgage of land which consists of, or includes, a dwelling-house brings an action in which he claims possession of the mortgaged property the court (a) may adjourn the proceedings, or (b) on giving judgment, or making an order for delivery of possession of the mortgaged property, or at any time before the execution of the judgment or order, may (i) stay or suspend execution of the judgment or order, or (ii) postpone the date for delivery of possession, for such period or periods as the court thinks reasonable. Any such adjournment, stay, suspension or postponement may be made subject to such conditions with regard to payment by the mortgagor of any sum secured by the mortgage or the remedying of any default as the court thinks fit.

However, the court can exercise these powers only if it appears to the court that in the event of their exercise the mortgagor is likely to be able within a reasonable period to pay any sums due under the mortgage or to remedy any other default (s.36(1)). Thus, although the mortgagor's spouse is able to take advantage of these provisions by virtue of s.1(5) of the Act of 1983, this will not improve her position unless this condition is satisfied. In *Halifax Building Society* v *Clark* [1973] Ch 307 it was held that the condition would be satisfied only if there was a prospect of all the sums then due under the mortgage being paid within a reasonable period, so that if the principal sum secured by the mortgage had become due on default, it was the amount necessary to redeem the mortgage which had to be considered and not merely the arrears. In that case there was no such prospect. (In *First Middlesbrough Trading and Mortgage Co Ltd* v *Cunningham* (1974) 28 P & CR 69 the Court of Appeal accepted the argument that the entire original mortgage term was the reasonable period for the purposes of s.36. See also Smith, *The Mortgagee's Right to Possession - The Modern Law* [1979] Conv. 266.) The position of the mortgagor, and hence of his spouse, had meanwhile been improved by the Administration of Justice Act 1973, s.8. This provides that where a mortgagor is entitled or permitted to pay the principal sum by instalments or otherwise to defer payment of it in whole or in part, but provision is also made for earlier payment in the event of any default by the mortgagor or of a demand by the mortgagee or otherwise, then for the purposes of s.36 of the 1970 Act, a court may treat as due under the mortgage only such amounts as the mortgagor would have expected to be required to pay if there had been no such provision for earlier payment. A court must not exercise its powers under s.36 on this basis unless it appears that the mortgagor is likely to be able to pay within a reasonable period not only the amounts regarded as due by virtue of this provision, i.e. the arrears, but also any further amounts that he would have expected to pay during that period if there had been no default, i.e. further instalments becoming due. In *First National Bank plc* v *Syed* [1991] 2 All ER 250 at p. 255, Dillon LJ said:

"It cannot be proper, with a view ostensibly to clearing the arrears within a reasonable period, to make an order for payments which the defendants cannot afford and have no reasonable prospects of being able to afford within a reasonable time. Equally it cannot be proper, under these sections, to make an order for payments which the defendants can afford if those will not be enough to pay off the arrears within a reasonable period and also to cover the current instalments."

Two conditions must be satisfied before s.8 is applicable. First, there must be a provision whereby the mortgagor is entitled or permitted to pay the principal sum by instalments or otherwise to defer payment thereof. Second, there must be a provision for earlier payment in the event of any default by the mortgagor or of a demand by the mortgagee or otherwise. Such provisions must be in the mortgage or in the agreement between the parties. The traditional building society mortgage where the loan is repayable by regular instalments, each including an element of principal in addition to the interest due, clearly falls within the section. In *Bank of Scotland* v *Grimes* [1985] QB 1179 the Court of Appeal held that an endowment mortgage fell within the provisions of the Act. In *Centrax Trustees Ltd* v *Ross* [1979] 2 All ER 952 Goulding J held that the section applied to a mortgage which provided for repayment on a date six months after the date of the mortgage because it was apparent from other provisions in the mortgage, in particular the provision for payment of interest, that the mortgagor would be entitled to defer payment of the principal indefinitely beyond the fixed date so long as interest was paid. However, in *Habib Bank Ltd* v *Tailor* [1982] 1 WLR 1218 the section was held to be inapplicable to a charge securing an ordinary banking overdraft whereby payment of the principal sum was not due from the borrower until a demand for payment was made. Accordingly, until that time there was no due date from which deferment of payment could be made. Moreover, the charge did not provide for the mortgagor to defer payments of the principal after demand had been made and there was no provision in the charge for payment to be made earlier than the date of demand in the event of default. An order for possession was upheld. It has been suggested that the decision may be restricted to mortgages securing straight overdrafts and may be distinguished where the overdraft is granted for the purpose of house purchase. In that case the facility letter from the bank is likely to specify the period over which it is intended that the loan is to be repaid, and a demand could be seen as a demand for early repayment. (See Tromans, *Mortgages: Possession by Default* [1984] Conv. 91.)

### (d) The Consumer Credit Act 1974

If the loan was made under a regulated agreement within the Consumer Credit Act 1974 the court has a discretion to order payment by instalments which are reasonable having regard to the means of the debtor - a "time order" (s.129). It will be a regulated agreement if the land does not exceed £15,000 in value and the lender is not a local authority, building society or other body exempted under s.16 of the Act (s.8). The court can only exercise its power under s.129 if it appears just to do so. In *First National Bank plc* v *Syed* [1991] 2 All ER 250 at p. 256 Dillon LJ said that consideration of what is just does not exclude consideration of the creditor's position. In that case he did not think it just in the circumstances, including the fairly long history of default, to require the plaintiff to accept the instalments the defendants could afford when those would be too little even to keep down the accruing interest on the defendant's account.

## 3. Charging orders

### (a) The scope of the Charging Orders Act 1979

The Charging Orders Act 1979 enables a creditor who has obtained a judgment or order of the High court or a county court requiring payment of a sum of money to him by the debtor to apply to the court for a charging order. This is an order imposing on such property of the debtor as may be specified in the order a charge for securing the payment of any money due or to become due under the judgment or order (s.1(1)).

A charge may be imposed by a charging order on any interest held by the debtor beneficially (a) in land or certain kinds of securities specified in s.2(2), or (b) under any trust. Thus, by virtue of (b) a charge may now be imposed on the beneficial interest of a joint owner under a trust for sale (*National Westminster Bank Ltd* v *Stockman* [1981] 1 WLR 67. This reverses the decision in *Irani Finance Ltd* v *Singh* [1971] Ch 59). A charge may also be made against any interest held by a person as trustee if the interest is in such an asset and the whole beneficial interest under the trust is held by the debtor unencumbered and for his own benefit, or where there are two or more debtors, all of whom are liable to the creditor for the same debt, and they together hold the whole beneficial interest under the trust unencumbered and for their own benefit. Thus where co-owners are liable to the creditor for the same debt, a charging order may be imposed on the legal estate held by them as trustees for sale for their own benefit.

An application for a charging order may be made *ex parte* and the court will first make an order nisi. The judgment debtor will then be required to show cause why the order should not be made absolute. In deciding whether to make a charging order the court must consider all the circumstances of the case and, in particular, that evidence before it as to (a) the personal circumstances of the debtor, and (b) whether any creditor of the debtor would be likely to be unduly prejudiced by making the order (s.1(5)). A charging order may be made subject to conditions as to the time when the charge is to become enforceable, or as to other matters (s.3(1)).

### (b) The effect of a charging order

The effect of a charging order is to make the judgment creditor a secured creditor. A charge imposed by a charging order has the like effect and is enforceable in the same courts and in the same manner as an equitable charge created by the debtor by writing under his hand (s.3(4)). A receiver may be appointed to collect the debtor's share of the income, or an application can be made to the court for an order for sale of the beneficial interest on which the charge has been imposed. Where a charging order has been imposed upon the beneficial interest of one co-owner, the more effective course of action is likely to be an application to the court under s.30 of the Law of Property Act 1925 for an order for sale of the jointly owned property so as to enable the charge to be satisfied out of the debtor's share of the proceeds. A judgment creditor is a "person interested" within s.30 even though the charging order has been imposed on the share of one co-owner (*Midland Bank plc v Pike* [1988] 2 All ER 434. It has been held that a receiver is not a "person interested" for this purpose: *Stevens v Hutchinson* [1953] Ch 299, but see the comments of Balcombe J in *Levermore v Levermore* [1980] 1 All ER 1 at p. 4).

Although a charging order can now be made on the beneficial interest of one co-owner by virtue of its being held under a trust, such an interest is not an interest in land under the Land Charges Act 1972. Accordingly it cannot be protected by registration as a "writ or order affecting land" against the debtor. Thus in *Perry v Phoenix Assurance plc* [1988] 1 WLR 940 an attempt to register a charging order on such a share was ineffective and the charge did not have priority over a subsequent legal mortgage. Some protection may be obtained by giving notice to the trustees - this will give priority over a purchaser of the equitable interest of the debtor. However, the charge will be overreached by a sale of the legal estate and will attach to the proceeds of sale which may not be satisfactory where the charge is on the interest of both co-owners who are the trustees or where the debtor is one of the trustees and forges the signature of the other trustee/co-owner.

*(c) Balancing the interests of the creditor and the debtor's spouse*

It will be obvious that a conflict may arise between the interests of a judgment creditor who has obtained a charging order against the beneficial interest of one spouse in a jointly owned matrimonial home and the interests of the debtor's spouse. This may arise when the judgment creditor seeks an order for sale of the matrimonial home under s.30 of the Law of Property Act 1925 which is resisted by the debtor's spouse. (The debtor's spouse can apply under s.3(5) of the Act for variation or discharge of the order: *Harman v Glencross* [1986] Fam 81.) Moreover, where the marriage of the co-owners has broken down, the debtor's spouse may petition for divorce and seek a property adjustment order in respect of the matrimonial home under s.24 of the Matrimonial Causes Act 1973. Such an order may affect the enforceability of a charging order and, if it takes the form of a transfer of the debtor's beneficial interest in the home to his or her spouse, would destroy the subject matter of the charge.

On the other hand, as between creditor and debtor spouse, the creditor, though not entitled to a charging order as of right, is normally justified in expecting that an order will in fact be made (see *Roberts Petroleum Ltd v Bernard Kenny Ltd* [1983] 2 AC 192 and *First National Securities Ltd v Hegarty* [1985] QB 850 at p. 867). Accordingly, a balance needs to be struck between the normal expectation of the creditor and the hardship to the wife and children of the debtor if an order is made.

In *Harman* v *Glencross* [1986] Fam 81 at pp. 99 -100 Balcombe LJ set out how he thought the court should deal with the problem.

(1) "Where a judgment creditor has obtained a charging order nisi on the husband's share in the matrimonial home and his application to have that order made absolute is heard before the wife has started divorce proceedings, there is, of course, no other court to which the application for the charging order absolute can be transferred, the wife having no competing claim to the husband's share. In these circumstances it is difficult to see why the court should refuse to make the charging order absolute, and the wife's right of occupation should be adequately protected under s.30 of the Law of Property Act 1925: see the analysis of Goff LJ in *Re Holliday* [1981] Ch 405 at p. 415." In *Lloyds Bank plc* v *Byrne* (1991) 23 HLR 472 the Court of Appeal held that in considering whether a sale of a jointly owned matrimonial home should be ordered under s.30 the test to be applied was the same as that applicable when a sale was sought by a trustee in bankruptcy. It will be seen that the protection afforded to the wife and children of a debtor in proceedings under s.30 is very limited. In *Re Holliday* the court declined to order a sale on the application of the husband's trustee in bankruptcy. In *Re Lowrie* [1981] 3 All ER 353 it was described as "exceptional" and the only other reported case in which a sale was deferred was *Re Gorman* [1990] 1 All ER 717. (See Part 5, below.)

(2) "Where a charging order nisi has been made after the wife's petition, then on the application for a charging order absolute the court should consider whether the circumstances are such that it is proper to make the charging order absolute even before the wife's application for ancillary relief has been heard by the Family Division." Balcombe LJ considered that there would be cases (such as *Llewellyn* v *Llewellyn* - unreported but heard immediately after *Harman* v *Glencross* and referred to in the report) where the figures are such that, even if the charging order is made absolute and then the charge is realised by a sale of the house, the resultant proceeds of sale (including any balance of the husband's share after the judgment debt has been paid) will be clearly sufficient to provide adequate alternative accommodation for the wife and children.

(3) "Unless it appears to the court hearing the application for the charging order absolute that the circumstances are so clear that it is proper to make the order there and then, the usual practice should be to transfer the application to the Family Division so that it may come on with the wife's application for ancillary relief and one court can then be in a position to consider all the circumstances of the case."

(4) "Once the charging order absolute has been made, it would normally require some special circumstance, e.g. where ... the wife had no proper opportunity to put the case before the court, for the charging order to be set aside under s.3(5) of the 1979 Act and thereby deprive the judgment creditor of his vested right." This was the case in *Harman* v *Glencross* itself where the creditor had obtained a charging order absolute on the husband's interest in the matrimonial home without serving the application on the wife or giving her notice of it. The wife had already petitioned for divorce and commenced proceedings for

ancillary relief. In *Austin-Fell* v *Austin-Fell* [1989] 2 FLR 497 the creditor had already obtained a charging order against the husband's half-share of the matrimonial home before the wife petitioned for divorce and sought a discharge of the charging order. The application for discharge and the application for ancillary relief in divorce proceedings were heard at the same time in the Family Division.

The purpose of a transfer to the Family Division of an application for a charging order (or for the discharge of such an order) is simply to ensure that the court is fully appraised of the circumstances of the case so far as the debtor and his family are concerned. It is not to be treated as if it were a wife's application under the matrimonial jurisdiction for the disposition of the husband's property for the benefit of the wife and children (*per* Fox LJ in *Harman* v *Glencross* [1986] Fam 81 at p. 105). When considering the circumstances, the court should bear in mind the statement of Sir Denys Buckley in *First National Securities Ltd* v *Hegerty* [1985] QB 850 that a judgment creditor is justified in expecting that a charging order over the husband's beneficial interest in the matrimonial home will be made in his favour (*per* Balcombe LJ [1986] Fam 81 at p. 99).

The court should first consider whether the value of the equity in the home is sufficient to enable the charging order to be made absolute (or to stand) and be realised at once even though that may result in the wife and children being housed at a lower standard than they might reasonably have expected had only the husband's interests been taken into account against them. Failing that, the court should make only such an order as may be necessary to protect the wife's right of occupation (with the children where appropriate) bearing in mind that the court is holding the balance, not between the wife and the husband, but between the wife and the judgment creditor. If the judgment creditor asks, even in the alternative to his claim to an immediate order, for a Mesher type of order (see Chapter 12), then exceptional circumstances should be required before the court should make an order for the outright transfer of the husband's share in the house to the wife, thereby leaving nothing on which the judgment creditor's charging order can bite, even in the future (*per* Waite J in *Austin-Fell* v *Austin-Fell* [1989] 2 FLR 497 at p. 505). In *Harman* v *Glencross* such an order had been made by Ewbank J at first instance and the Court of Appeal had refused to interfere with his exercise of his discretion though clearly regarding it as an exceptional case. This was emphasised by Waite J in the subsequent case of *Austin-Fell* v *Austin-Fell* [1989] 2 FLR 497 where again a balance had to be struck between the family security claimed by the wife and children in matrimonial proceedings and the commercial security claimed by the husband's business creditor in charging order proceedings. However, Waite J noted two significant differences between the case before him and *Harman* v *Glencross*.

First, the judgment debt in *Harman* v *Glencross* represented a very much higher proportion, when measured against the total value of the beneficial interest in the property, than in the case before him. The equity in the property in the former case was £22,400 so that a charge on the husband's half-interest for the debt of £13,000 would have exhausted that interest entirely. In *Austin-Fell* the equity was worth £60,000 and the judgment debt was £10,000. Secondly, in *Harman* v *Glencross* the judgment creditor adopted an "all or nothing" approach to the enforcement of his security, seeking only an immediate charge. He did not ask for the alternative option of postponement to be considered and, although Fox LJ indicated that postponement was the solution he would personally have favoured, the Court of Appeal did not criticise the decision of Ewbank J to treat that option as not being open to the court in that case because it had not been requested by the judgment creditor. This was not the case in *Austin-Fell.*

In the latter case an immediate sale and payment of the judgment creditor would leave insufficient to give the wife any prospect of being re-housed in the area of the present home in accommodation suitable to herself and the girls. "It would be unfairly harsh to the wife and unduly favourable to the judgment creditor to force her at this stage to move to another area, or to a different part of the country altogether in search of cheaper housing and to leave behind her mother, her pupils and the school which have become familiar to the girls, all for the sake of ensuring immediate payment of the bank's debt" (*per* Waite J at p. 505). The necessity of paying off the bank's debt in ten years' time with the interest that had accumulated in the meantime might no doubt be expected to involve the wife in a degree of hardship, just as the necessity of waiting ten years for its money might be expected to involve a degree of hardship for the bank. Nevertheless, a postponed enforcement order represented the fairest balance between the competing claims of wife and creditor.

It should be noted that in *First National Securities Ltd* v *Hegerty* [1985] QB 850 the Court of Appeal had held that there were no sufficient grounds for holding that Bingham J at first instance had wrongly exercised his discretion to make a charging order absolute notwithstanding that the creditor's wife had commenced divorce proceedings and applied for ancillary relief after the charging order nisi had been made. The court preferred not to comment on the correctness of the decision of Ewbank J in *Harman* v *Glencross* in view of the pending appeal in that case. The Court of Appeal in *Harman* v *Glencross,* in affirming the decision of Ewbank J, pointed out that the court in *Hegerty* was not concerned with the exercise of powers under the Matrimonial Causes Act 1973 but with the exercise of the court's discretion under the Charging Orders Act 1979. It did not therefore regard itself as bound by the decision in *Hegerty* (*per* Balcombe LJ at p. 522, *per* Fox LJ at p. 561).

## 4. Statutory provisions designed to protect creditors

*(a) The background*
A transfer of property from one member of a family to another may prejudice the transferor's creditors by depriving them of recourse to that property while at the same time enabling the transferor, or at any rate his family, to continue to enjoy the benefit of that property. There were two statutory provisions under which such transfers could be set aside in certain circumstances. Both were replaced by provisions in the Insolvency Act 1985 and now contained in the Insolvency Act 1986.

The first provision replaced was s.172 of the Law of Property Act 1925. This provided that a conveyance of property with intent to defraud creditors was voidable at the instance of any person thereby prejudiced. This did not apply where property was conveyed: "(1) for valuable consideration and in good faith or upon good consideration and in good faith", and "(2) to any person not having, at the time of the conveyance, notice of the intent to defraud creditors".

Secondly, s.42 of the Bankruptcy Act 1914 provided that a settlement of property was voidable by the settlor's trustee in bankruptcy within the period of two years after the date of the settlement. If the settlor became bankrupt more than two years after the date of the settlement but within ten years thereof, the settlement was voidable unless the parties claiming under the settlement could prove that the settlor was, at the time the settlement was made, able to pay all his debts without the aid of the property comprised in the settlement, and the interest in the property of the settlor passed to the trustee of the settlement immediately. A "settlement" for this purpose included any conveyance or transfer of property and the fact that it had to be made in order to comply with a property adjustment order in proceedings for divorce, nullity or judicial separation did not prevent that settlement or transfer from being a settlement for this purpose (s.39 Matrimonial Causes Act 1973, but see *Re Abbott* [1983] Ch 45). Certain settlements were specifically excluded from the ambit of the section. These included any settlement made before and in consideration of marriage and any settlement made in favour of a purchaser or incumbrancer in good faith and for valuable consideration.

*(b) Transactions defrauding creditors*

Section 172 of the Law of Property Act 1925 has been replaced by ss.423-425 of the Insolvency Act 1986. Where a person (the "debtor") has entered into a transaction at an undervalue the court may make such order as it thinks fit for:

(a) restoring the position to what it would have been if the transaction had not been entered into, and

(b) protecting the interests of persons who are the victims of the transaction.

A person enters into a "transaction at an undervalue" with another person if:

(i)   he makes a gift to another person or he otherwise enters into a transaction with the other on terms that provide for him to receive no consideration;

(ii)  he enters into a transaction with the other in consideration of marriage; or

(iii) he enters into a transaction with the other for a consideration the value of which, in money or money's worth, is significantly less than the value, in money or money's worth, of the consideration provided by himself.

(s.423(1) and (2). A "transaction" includes a gift, agreement or arrangement: s.436.)

Thus, no order can be made under s.423 unless the transaction is at an undervalue. Under the replaced s.172 a transaction could be set aside even though it was for full value if the transferee had notice of the intent to defraud. This occurred in *Lloyds Bank Ltd* v *Marcan* [1973] 1 WLR 1387 where the conveyance took the form of a lease of a house and land at full rent by the debtor to his wife with the object of preventing mortgagees obtaining vacant possession. No order could now be made under s.423 in these circumstances. On the other hand a transaction in consideration of marriage is a transaction at an undervalue, whereas under s.172 a conveyance could not be set aside if made in consideration of marriage to a person without notice of the intent to defraud.

An order must only be made if the court is satisfied that the person who entered into the transaction did so for the purpose -

(a) of putting assets beyond the reach of a person who is making, or may at some time make, a claim against him, or

(b) of otherwise prejudicing the interests of such a person in relation to the claim which he is making or may make.

(s.423(3).)

In *Chohan* v *Saggar* [1991] The Times 16 October it was held that a transaction at an undervalue will be within s.423 as long as the dominant purpose of a debtor in entering into that transaction was to place assets beyond the reach of a creditor despite the possible existence of other motives for the transaction.

Generally an application can only be made by a "victim" of the transaction, i.e. a person who is, or is capable of being, prejudiced by the transaction (s.423(5) and s.424(1)). Thus an applicant need not be an existing creditor. Where the debtor has been adjudged bankrupt an application can only be made by the Official Receiver or by the trustee of the bankrupt's estate or, with leave of the court, by a victim of the transaction. Where the victim of a transaction is bound by a voluntary arrangement approved under Part I or Part VIII of the Insolvency Act 1986, application can be made by the supervisor of the arrangement or by any person who (whether or not so bound) is a victim of the transaction. In all cases an application is to be treated as made on behalf of every victim of the transaction (s.424(2)).

An order under s.423 in relation to a transaction may in particular:

(a) require any property transferred as part of the transaction to be vested in any person, either absolutely or for the benefit of all the persons on whose behalf the application for the order is treated as made;

(b) require any property to be so vested if it represents, in any person's hands, the application either of the proceeds of sale of property so transferred or of money so transferred;

(c) release or discharge (in whole or in part) any security given by the debtor;

(d) require any person to pay to any other person in respect of benefits received from the debtor such sums as the court may direct;

(e) provide for any surety or guarantor, whose obligations to any person were released or discharged (in whole or in part) under the transaction, to be under such new and revived obligations as the court thinks appropriate;

(f) provide for security to be provided for the discharge of any obligation imposed by or arising under the order, for such an obligation to be charged on any property and for such security or charge to have the same priority as a security or charge released or discharged (in whole or in part) under the transaction.

(s.425(1). See *Chohan* v *Saggar* [1993] BCLC 661.)

An order under s.423 may affect the property of, or impose any obligation on, any person whether or not he is the person with whom the debtor entered into the transaction. However, such an order must not prejudice any interest in property which was acquired from a person other than the debtor and was acquired in good faith, for value and without notice of the relevant circumstances, or prejudice any interest deriving from such an interest. Further, it must not require a person who received a benefit from the transaction in good faith, for value and without notice of the relevant circumstances to pay any sum unless he was a party to the transaction (s.425(2)). The "relevant circumstances" for this purpose are the circumstances by virtue of which an order under s.423 may be made in respect of the transaction (s.425(3)).

## *(c) Transactions at an undervalue*

(i) Orders in respect of transactions at an undervalue
Where an individual is adjudged bankrupt and has, within the period of five years ending with the day of the presentation of the bankruptcy petition on which the individual is adjudged bankrupt, entered into a transaction at an undervalue, the trustee of the bankrupt's estate may apply to the court for an order under s.339 of the Insolvency Act 1986 with respect to that transaction. On such an application the court must make such order as it thinks fit for restoring the position to what it would have been if the bankrupt had not entered into that transaction. However, where the individual entered into the transaction at an undervalue more than two years before the end of the five-year period, the court cannot make an order unless the individual (a) was insolvent at the time of the transaction, or (b) became insolvent in consequence of the transaction (s.341(2)).

An individual is insolvent for this purpose if (a) he is unable to pay his debts as they fall due, or (b) the value of his assets is less than the amount of his liabilities, taking into account his contingent and prospective liabilities (s.341(3)). This requirement will be presumed to be satisfied, unless the contrary is shown, in relation to any transaction at an undervalue which is entered into by an individual with a person who is an associate of his (otherwise than by reason only of his being an employee) (s.341(2)). A lengthy definition of "associate" is to be found in s.435 of the Act. In particular, it should be noted that a person is an associate of an individual if that person is the individual's husband or wife - or is a relative, or the husband or wife of a relative, of the individual or of the individual's husband or wife (s.435(2); a "relative" is defined in subs.(8)).

(ii) Meaning of "transaction at an undervalue"
An individual enters into a transaction with a person at an undervalue for this purpose in three circumstances.

(1) If he makes a gift to that person or he otherwise enters into a transaction with that person on terms that provide for him to receive no consideration. This clearly covers the case where a spouse who is sole owner of the home transfers that property, or a share in it, to the other spouse. It will also cover the situation where the matrimonial home is purchased in the name of one spouse, but the purchase money has been provided by the bankrupt spouse (see *Re a Debtor, ex p. the Official Receiver, Trustee of the Property of the Debtor* v *Morrison* [1965] 1 WLR 1498). The expression "enters into a transaction" suggests a positive act rather than negative or acquiescent behaviour. It has been suggested that it could include the provision of services for no consideration

such as building a house or extension, but not day-to-day domestic or informal arrangements (Muir Hunter, *Personal Insolvency* para. 3.295).

This paragraph does not apply if some consideration, though not full consideration, was received. Reference must then be made to paragraph (3) below. There is no provision exempting "small transactions and ordinary gifts made out of income" as recommended by the Insolvency Law Reform Committee (the "Cork Committee" - para. 1234) and as contained in the EEC Draft Bankruptcy Convention, but it will be for a trustee to decide when to make an application under the section.

(2) If he enters into a transaction with that person in consideration of marriage. This removes one of the exceptions that applied under the Bankruptcy Act 1914, i.e. where the bankrupt made a marriage settlement in relation to his or her marriage and in consideration thereof. This was of no assistance where the matrimonial home was purchased after marriage.

(3) If he enters into a transaction with that person for a consideration the value of which in money or money's worth is significantly less than the value in money or money's worth of the consideration provided by the individual bankrupt. There was no doubt that a disposition for merely nominal consideration was caught by s.42 of the Bankruptcy Act 1914 (*Walker* v *Burrows* (1745) 1 Atk. 93). However, where there was clearly more than nominal consideration, but something less than full consideration, the position was not free from doubt, though the Cork Committee (para. 1226) considered that all dispositions for valuable consideration were outside s.42 even when the consideration represented a gross undervalue unless such disposition for valuable consideration was not made in good faith. On this view, if a husband transferred property worth £3,000 to his wife who paid him £2,000 for it, then the wife would be a purchaser for valuable consideration and the transfer could not be attacked under s.42 unless the parties were acting in bad faith. However, it was arguable that the wife was merely a purchaser of a two-thirds share in the property so that the husband had settled on her a one-third share which could be reached under s.42. This view was taken by Goff J in *Re Densham* [1975] 1 WLR 1519 where the wife's contribution to the joint purchase of the matrimonial home was such as would, apart from the agreement between them that it should be owned equally, have entitled her only to a one-ninth share. Goff J held that what was settled was not her whole share in the property (one half) but so much as exceeded her contribution (one-ninth), and she could not be regarded as a purchaser of that (one-third). (This argument is perhaps less justifiable where there is a clear transfer from the bankrupt to another rather than a joint purchase by the bankrupt and another.) On the other hand, in *Re Densham*, Goff J commenting on *Re Pope* [1908] 2 KB 169 rejected an argument on behalf of the trustee in bankruptcy that consideration received by the bankrupt had to equal the value of the property transferred if the settlement was to be immune from attack under s.42. In *Re Abbott* [1983] Ch 45 an application for a property adjustment order in relation to the jointly owned matrimonial home, following divorce, provided for the sale of the house and for the wife to be paid out of the proceeds the sum of £18,000 and

one half of any excess. On the subsequent bankruptcy of the husband his trustee argued that there had been a settlement of £9,000 on the wife within s.42. It was held that the wife was a purchaser for valuable consideration and there was no need for the consideration moving from the "purchaser" to replace in the hands of the debtor the consideration moving from the debtor. Section 39 of the Matrimonial Causes Act 1973 provided that the fact that a settlement or transfer of property had to be made in order to comply with a property adjustment order did not prevent an order setting it aside being made under s.42 of the Bankruptcy Act 1914. If therefore the claim had not been compromised, but an order had been made in the same terms by the court, it seems the wife could not have been described as a purchaser for valuable consideration and would have been worse off.

The new provision makes it clear that inequality in consideration will not necessarily enable an order to be made under s.339. The consideration provided by the two parties to the transaction must be assessed in monetary terms, and only if that provided by the other party was significantly less than that provided by the bankrupt can an order be made under s.339. There remains an element of uncertainty in the meaning of the term "significant undervalue". It seems clear that if a house is purchased for £50,000 and vested in the joint names of the spouses by a conveyance expressly declaring that they are entitled to the beneficial interest in equal shares, then if the wife provided only £5,000 of the purchase price this would be a transaction at a significant undervalue so far as the husband is concerned. However, if she had contributed £24,000 towards the purchase price would the undervalue still be regarded as significant? If not, where would the line be drawn? In practice the position is likely to be less clear cut. The home is unlikely to have been acquired outright for cash, but to have been purchased with the aid of a mortgage repayable over a period of years. In these circumstances it is, as seen in Chapter 2, frequently difficult to arrive at the respective shares of the parties, and, as a result, there is some flexibility even though the court is strictly concerned with identifying the actual contributions of the bankrupt spouse.

In view of the emphasis on consideration in money or money's worth there is also uncertainty regarding the significance of non-monetary consideration. The new statutory provisions leave the authority of *Re Abbott* uncertain. Section 39 of the Matrimonial Causes Act 1973 as amended now provides that the fact that a settlement or transfer of property had to be made in order to comply with a property adjustment order shall not prevent that settlement or transfer from being a transaction in respect of which an order may be made under s.339 or s.340 of the Insolvency Act 1986. Where a "clean break" is agreed or ordered (see Chapters 10 and 11) it may be difficult for the trustee to argue that termination of the wife's rights to periodical payments is consideration that is significantly less than the value of the share of the former matrimonial home provided by the husband. It should be noted that s.39 applies only to "property adjustment orders" and not to the provision of security for periodical payments or payment of a lump sum pursuant to a court order under s.23 of the Matrimonial Causes Act 1973 (see *Platt* v *Platt* (1976) 120 SJ 199 and Steiner, *Trustees in Bankruptcy and Matrimonial Proceedings* (1976) 120 SJ 459).

In *Re Kumar (A Bankrupt)* [1993] 1 WLR 224 a husband had transferred his half share in the matrimonial home to his wife some seven months before a decree nisi of divorce was made in respect of their marriage. Some three months later a consent order provided that in consideration of that transfer the wife's claim for capital provision was dismissed. Following the husband's subsequent bankruptcy the transfer was set aside under s.339. Ferris J held that the wife had provided no consideration other than the assumption of sole liability in respect of the mortgage on the home. As the mortgage "stood at only £30,000 at the time of the transfer and there was clearly an equity of redemption of very considerable value, the value of such consideration was, clearly, significantly less that the value of the consideration provided by" the husband (*ibid.* at p. 240). The transfer was therefore a transaction at an undervalue for the purposes of s.339.

### (iii) Contents and effect of an order under s.339

It may be that, apart from any flexibility arising from the concept of "significant undervalue", s.339 gives a degree of flexibility more directly than s.42 of the 1914 Act. Whereas a settlement which fell within s.42 was void (or at least voidable on the application of the trustee), if a transaction is within s.339 then the court is required to make such order as it thinks fit for restoring the position to what it would have been if the bankrupt had not entered into that transaction. Section 342(1) specifies (without prejudice to the generality of s.339(2)) a number of provisions that may be included in an order under s.339. Thus the court may require any property transferred as part of the transaction to be vested in the trustee of the bankrupt's estate as part of that estate. It may require any property to be so vested if it represents in any person's hands the application either of the proceeds of sale of property so transferred or of money so transferred. The order may require any person to pay, in respect of benefits received by him from the bankrupt, such sums to the trustee as the court may direct.

An order under s.339 may affect the property of, or impose any obligation on, any person whether or not he is the person with whom the bankrupt entered into the transaction. However, such an order must not prejudice any interest in property which was acquired from a person other than the bankrupt and was acquired in good faith, for value and without notice of the relevant circumstances, or prejudice any interest deriving from such an interest. Such an order must also not require a person who received a benefit from the transaction in good faith, for value and without notice of the relevant circumstances to pay a sum to the trustee of the bankrupt's estate, except where he was a party to the transaction (s.342(2)). The "relevant circumstances" for this purpose are the circumstances by virtue of which an order under s.339 could be made in respect of the transaction if the individual in question were adjudged bankrupt within a particular period after the transaction is entered into and, if that period has expired, the fact that individual has been adjudged bankrupt within that period (s.342(4)).

### (d) Dispositions after presentation of a petition

Where a person is adjudged bankrupt, any disposition of property by that person in the period beginning with the day of the presentation of the petition for the bankruptcy order and ending with the vesting of the bankrupt's estate in a trustee, is void except to the extent that it is or was made with the consent of the court, or is or was subsequently ratified by the court (Insolvency Act 1986, s.284. See *Re Flint (A Bankrupt)* [1993] 1 FLR 763).

## 5. Occupation of the family home

### (a) Where the bankrupt was sole owner of the home

Where the matrimonial home is in the sole ownership of the bankrupt spouse, the court had no discretion to allow the other spouse or the children to remain in possession. In *National Provincial Bank Ltd* v *Ainsworth* [1965] AC 1175 the House of Lords, overruling *Bendall* v *MacWhirter* [1952] 2 QB 466, finally decided that a deserted wife's right to remain in occupation of the matrimonial home was purely personal against her husband and did not bind his trustee in bankruptcy or other successors in title. Lord Wilberforce pointed out at p.1256 that:

"... our law does not, as does the law in many places (particularly in the U.S.A. and Canada), recognise a 'homestead' right of the wife, nor does it give the wife of a bankrupt any preference or priority - perhaps it ought to do so - but in fact the wife of a bankrupt is left to depend upon the share of his future earnings."

The statutory rights of occupation conferred by the Matrimonial Homes Act 1967 (and subsequently the Matrimonial Homes Act 1983) on a "non-entitled spouse", even though protected by registration in the appropriate manner (see Chapter 4), were void against the trustee in bankruptcy of the "entitled spouse" or the trustees under a conveyance or assignment of his or her property for the benefit of his or her creditors generally (s.2(7)). The position was reversed by the Insolvency Act 1985, the relevant provisions of which are now contained in the Insolvency Act 1986, s.336(2). This means that notwithstanding the bankruptcy of the "entitled spouse", the charge constituted by the statutory rights of occupation of the "non-entitled spouse" continues to subsist and, subject to the provisions of the 1983 Act, bind the trustee of the bankrupt's estate and persons deriving title under the trustee. Therefore, in order to obtain possession of the dwelling-house it is necessary for the trustee to apply for an order under s.1(2) of the 1983 Act. (He is entitled to do this by virtue of s.2(5)(b) which applies s.1(2) to any person deriving title under the entitled spouse.) Under s.1(2) the order of the court may, *inter alia*, "declare, enforce, restrict or terminate" the statutory rights of occupation of the "non-entitled spouse". However, s.336(2) provides that any application for an order under s.1 of the 1983 Act in this context must be made to the court having jurisdiction in relation to the bankruptcy. On such an application the court must make such order as it thinks just and reasonable having regard to the facts set out in subsection (4) of the section. This is considered below.

### (b) The jointly owned home

Where the non-bankrupt spouse is entitled to a beneficial interest in the matrimonial home, he or she will generally be entitled to receive the appropriate share of the proceeds of sale when the home is sold on the initiative of the trustee in bankruptcy of the bankrupt spouse - subject to an application by the trustee under s.339 of the

Insolvency Act 1986 (see above). However, apart from the disruption involved in a sale, the non-bankrupt spouse's share may, by itself, be insufficient to purchase alternative accommodation. The non-bankrupt spouse may not therefore be prepared to concur in a sale and, in that event, the trustee in bankruptcy may seek an order for sale under s.30 of the Law of Property Act 1925.

On such an application, the court has a discretion whether or not to order a sale. In exercising that discretion the guiding principle which emerged before the Insolvency Act 1986 was not whether the trustee or the wife was being reasonable, but in all the circumstances of the case whose voice in equity ought to prevail (see Goff J in *Re Solomon* [1967] Ch 573 at p. 588 and *Re Turner* [1974] 1 WLR 1556 at p. 1558). In a series of cases the courts clearly distinguished between cases where an order for sale was sought by the husband's trustee in bankruptcy and those cases where such an order was sought by the husband himself. Where the application was made by the trustee, then the husband's obligation to provide for his wife and children would not by itself be enough to prevent a sale. The same was true of the rights a wife might have by virtue of being entitled to a beneficial interest in the home. To prevent an order for sale it was necessary to show special circumstances producing a case of substantial hardship on the part of the family. Such hardship then had to be balanced against the claim of the trustee and the hardship which the creditors would suffer if a sale was not ordered. The only reported case in which a sale had been refused was *Re Holliday* [1981] Ch 405 which was regarded as exceptional in *Re Lowrie* [1981] 3 All ER 353 and in *Re Citro (A Bankrupt)* [1991] Ch 142. In the latter case Nourse LJ (at p. 157) summarised the broad effect of the earlier authorities as follows:

"Where a spouse who has a beneficial interest in the matrimonial home has become bankrupt under debts which cannot be paid without the realisation of that interest, the voice of the creditors will usually prevail over the voice of the other spouse and a sale of the property ordered within a short period. The voice of the other spouse will only prevail in exceptional circumstances. No distinction is to be made between a case where the property is still being enjoyed as the matrimonial home and one where it is not."

The Insolvency Act 1986, s.336(3) (replacing s.171(3) of the Insolvency Act 1985) now provides that any application by a trustee in bankruptcy for an order under s.30 of the Law of Property Act 1925 must be made to the court having jurisdiction in relation to the bankruptcy. In exercising its discretion to make such order as it thinks just and reasonable, the court is required to have regard to the factors set out in subs.(4) as explained by subs.(5) of s.336.

*(c) Factors to be taken into account by the court*

(i) The statutory provisions
The factors to be taken into account by the court in considering applications by a trustee in bankruptcy under s.1 of the Matrimonial Homes Act 1983 and s.30 of the Law of Property Act 1925 are thus set out in s.336(4) of the Insolvency Act 1986. The factors are:
  (a) the interests of the bankrupt's creditors;

(b) the conduct of the spouse or former spouse so far as contributing to the bankruptcy;

(c) the needs and financial resources of the spouse or former spouse;

(d) the needs of any children; and

(e) all the circumstances of the case other than the needs of the bankrupt.

Earlier decisions will be referred to in considering how these factors may operate. In *Re Citro* [1991] Ch 142, in which the 1986 Act was not applicable, Nourse LJ (at p.159) said that he had no doubt that s.336(5) was intended to apply the same test as that which had been evolved in previous bankruptcy decisions. This was satisfactory because s.336(5) applies only to the rights of occupation of those who are or have been married. The case law will continue to apply to unmarried couples "who nowadays set up house together in steadily increasing numbers". A difference in the basic tests applicable to the two classes of case would have been most undesirable.

(ii) The interests of the bankrupt's creditors

Under paragraph (a) the court may consider the impact on the creditors of any delay in the realisation of the property. Thus delay may be particularly serious for a small business creditor whereas different considerations may apply to a bank (see *Re Holliday* [1980] Ch 405). In *Re Bailey* [1977] 1 WLR 278 at p. 282 it was said that it was relevant to consider what the creditors may have to pay by way of interest for any borrowing they themselves have to make to fill the gap until they are paid. In *Re Gorman* [1990] 1 All ER 717 Vinelott J was concerned with the fact that the creditors had already been kept out of their money for very many years during a period of high interest rates and, regretfully, inflation, and could look to nothing except the proceeds of sale of the property to pay a dividend on their debts. In *Re Citro* [1991] Ch 142 at p. 157 Nourse LJ regarded *Re Holliday* as exceptional because it was highly unlikely that postponement of payment of the debts would cause any great hardship to any of the creditors.

(iii) The conduct of the spouse or former spouse so far as contributing to the bankruptcy

If the bankrupt's spouse has been guilty of reckless expenditure and obviously knowingly benefited from the bankrupt's financial mismanagement, then this is likely to be taken into account under paragraph (b) as a factor militating against postponement. (In *Re Densham* [1975] 1 WLR 1519 the bankruptcy had resulted from stealing, and the principal creditor was the bankrupt's employer from whom the money had been stolen.)

(iv) The needs and financial resources of the spouse or former spouse

The availability of alternative accommodation for the bankrupt's spouse and children is obviously a relevant consideration under paragraphs (c) and (d). In *Re Citro* [1991] Ch 142 at p. 157 Nourse LJ acknowledged that it was not uncommon for a wife with young children to be faced with eviction in circumstances where the realisation of her beneficial interest will not produce enough to buy a comparable home in the same neighbourhood, or indeed elsewhere. If she has to move elsewhere there may be problems over schooling. Although such circumstances may engender a natural sympathy in all who hear of them, they could not, in his view, be described as exceptional. If alternative accommodation cannot be provided out of the spouse's share of proceeds or her other assets, it will be necessary to consider the availability of rented accommodation, particularly local authority housing in the light of the provisions of the Housing Act 1985. A person with whom dependent children reside or might be expected to reside has a priority need for accommodation under s.59, though the provisions of s.60 relating to intentional homelessness must be borne in mind. In *Re Densham* a factor of no small importance was that the local authority was trying to find alternative accommodation for the family (contrast *Re Holliday*).

(v) The needs of any children

The needs of the children under paragraph (d) may be crucial so far as the implications of a move are concerned and particularly in relation to the suitability of alternative accommodation. However, it is clear from *Re Citro* [1991] Ch 142 that only in exceptional circumstances are the educational needs of the children likely to justify postponement of a sale for any significant period. In that case, two brothers had been adjudicated bankrupt. Each brother had three children living in the relevant home, the youngest in one case being ten and, in the other case, twelve. At first instance, Hoffman J had made orders for possession and sale, but after considering the accommodation and educational problems which would be encountered, he provided for postponement until the youngest child in each case attained the age of sixteen. The Court of Appeal did not regard the problems that might arise as in any way "exceptional" or "special". They were "the melancholy consequences of debt and improvidence with which every civilised society has been familiar" (*per* Nourse LJ at p. 157). The provisos for postponement were deleted and in each case the Court of Appeal substituted a short period of postponement not exceeding six months.

In *Re Holliday* the court had also been influenced by the fact that it would be difficult, if not impossible, for the wife to obtain suitable accommodation in or near the area in which the three children attended schools. It would be upsetting for their education if they had to move away from their existing schools even if it was practicable, having regard to the wife's means, to find an alternative home at some distant place. In *Re Citro* the court did not regard this aspect of *Re Holliday* as in any way exceptional or as justifying by itself any lengthy postponement (*per* Nourse LJ at p. 157).

Apart from the possible effect on a child's education there may be other special factors relating to a child or indeed a spouse which might justify a postponement. In *Re Bailey* [1977] 1 WLR 278, where the evidence about the interference with the educational prospects of the child involved was said to be very slight and did not justify a postponement, Walton J referred to the example of a home specially adapted to suit the needs of a handicapped child where there were obviously special circumstances, "so special that undoubtedly this court would hesitate long before making an immediate order for sale" (at p. 284). In *Re Densham* [1975] 1 WLR 1519 a postponement was sought on the basis of the nervous illness which all the troubles had brought upon the wife as well as the possible harmful effects of a sale on the children. It was clear that what was being sought was an indefinite adjournment to soften the blow of losing the home, and a postponement was rejected. However, it seems that the court might have been more sympathetic if the object had been "to achieve some particular remedial purpose, such as to enable a course of treatment to be completed ..."(*ibid.* at p. 1531).

**(vi) All the circumstances of the case other than the needs of the bankrupt**
Under paragraph (e) it might be relevant to take into account the conduct of the bankrupt's spouse more generally. Thus some regard may be had to the fact that the bankrupt's wife may have struggled to maintain the home in the face of the bankrupt's irresponsible behaviour. In those cases where the bankrupt's spouse has contributed the whole or a substantial part of the purchase price of the home which has been vested in the joint names of the spouses, the non-bankrupt spouse will not be able to go behind the express declaration of beneficial interests (*Boydell* v *Gillespie* (1971) 216 EG 1505 and *Re Gorman* [1990] 1 All ER 717), but it would seem fair to take this fact into account in determining the timing of a sale. However, this did not carry much weight in *Re Gorman* where the wife had provided £2,000 of the purchase price of £5,800 and costs. The balance had been provided by a mortgage advance but Vinelott J said that it was immaterial that she had paid all the mortgage instalments - that was a matter to be dealt with on taking an account following sale. Nevertheless, a sale was deferred until the determination of the wife's claim for damages against her former solicitors on the basis of their negligence in failing to advise her to make an application for a property adjustment order in respect of the house. If that claim was successful then she would probably have been in a position to purchase the trustee's share in the property. In the event of the wife wishing to purchase at that time, the price would have been a sum equal to the trustee's share of the market value of the property together with interest calculated at market rates for the period between the date of judgment and the date when the calculation fell to be made.

The conduct of the creditors might very occasionally be relevant under paragraph (e) in so far as it is not covered by paragraph (a). It is arguable that the irresponsible granting of credit should be taken into account. Some weight may have been given in *Re Holliday* to the fact that the bankrupt filed his own petition and that the creditors had not themselves seen fit to take action, though this may simply have been a matter of timing and of little significance. In *Re Citro* Nourse LJ commenting on *Re Holliday* said (at p. 157) that he would not have regarded it as an exceptional circumstance that the husband had presented his own petition, even as a "tactical move".

*(d) Weighing the factors*
The crucial question is how the factors are to be weighed, for the section appears to give the court a wide discretion. This was seen by the Cork Committee as necessary in view of the wide variety of circumstances which the court would have to consider. Indeed it thought that "[s]uch guidelines as can be given must of necessity be in the most general terms and, indeed, little more than an indication of the factors for consideration" (para. 1123).

The objective of the Committee was limited to delaying enforcement of the creditors' rights. It thought that "while the court will first consider the dependants - and the greater their vulnerability the greater will be the protection needed - creditors' rights should be postponed only in order to prevent injury to the welfare of those dependants; not to preserve for them any particular standard of life" (para. 1122). Moreover, the extent of the delay envisaged by the Committee was limited. Some members of the Committee considered that there should be a statutory limit on the length of time for which a postponement could be ordered. All were agreed that, in practice, any very lengthy postponement should be rare. The majority concluded that the court's powers should not be limited in duration (para. 1123).

In the result the Act does not impose an absolute time limit to the period of postponement, but provides in s.336(5) that:

"Where an application is made after the end of the period of one year beginning with the first vesting ... of the bankrupt's estate in a trustee, the court shall assume, unless the circumstances of the case are exceptional, that the interests of the bankrupt's creditors outweigh all other considerations."

The intention was that the court should regard the period of one year as the normal maximum breathing space to be allowed to the members of the family under normal circumstances, to enable them to adjust to their changed circumstances and either to seek alternative accommodation or arrange the buying out of the bankrupt's estate (see HC Vol. 83, Col. 547 where it was said that: "The court may, of course, allow only a shorter period, or no period at all, if circumstances warrant it"). However, the provision is not happily drafted to give effect to this intention as it is expressed to apply only to applications made after the expiry of the specified twelve-month period. Where an application is made before the expiration of that period, the court is not strictly required to assume that the interests of the creditors will outweigh other considerations once the twelve-month period has expired. In practice it seems unlikely that the inappropriate wording will prevent effect being given to the underlying intention, particularly in view of the wide discretion given to the court.

If application is made after the expiration of the twelve-month period, the way is left open for an argument on behalf of the spouse and children to be advanced for a longer period of postponement on the basis of exceptional hardship or inconvenience which would be occasioned by a sale of the home within one year. Thus the postponement allowed in *Re Holliday* would still be possible, but it is doubtful whether it would be more likely.

### (e) The "family"

In conferring the modest protection outlined above, the Act adopts a restricted view of the family. The Cork Committee had expressed the view that the terms "husband" and "wife" should include persons of the opposite sex living as husband and wife (para. 1125). On the other hand, in the Department of Trade and Industry Consultation Paper it was said that it might be difficult to give effect to such a concept, and in addition the Government took the view that any innovation in the law in that area should take place as part of a comprehensive review of the subject generally (para. 2.4). The courts have already had to consider the question of sale of the family home under s.30 as between cohabitees. In both *Re Evers' Trust* [1980] 1 WLR 1327 and *Dennis v Macdonald* [1981] 1 WLR 810 the court was prepared to take into account the "family" interest as between cohabitees and in effect to postpone a sale. There has been no reported case in which a trustee in bankruptcy has sought to enforce a sale against the bankrupt's cohabitee, but it is not an unlikely situation and it is unfortunate that the modest protection of the Insolvency Act was not extended expressly to this situation. The interests of cohabitees may be taken into account under paragraph (e) - all the circumstances of the case. The same probably applies to the interests of "any adult members of the family who are ailing or elderly" which also fail to receive any express mention despite the recommendation of the Cork Committee (para. 1120). In view of the increasing incidence of elderly relatives now living with younger members of their family, an express recognition of their interests would have been desirable.

### (f) The bankrupt caring for children

In some cases the bankrupt has no spouse entitled or willing to occupy the family home but is responsible for the upbringing of children. Section 337 is designed to apply to a limited extent the principles of s.336 to this situation. It applies where:

(i)     a person who is entitled to occupy a dwelling-house by virtue of a beneficial estate or interest is adjudged bankrupt; and

(ii)    any persons under the age of eighteen with whom that person had at some time occupied that dwelling-house and who had their home with that person at the time when the bankruptcy petition was presented and at the commencement of the bankruptcy.

If these conditions are satisfied, then whether or not the bankrupt's spouse (if any) has rights of occupation under the Matrimonial Homes Act 1983, the bankrupt is given rights of occupation as against the trustee of his estate. These are the same as the statutory rights of occupation conferred on a non-entitled spouse by the 1983 Act (see Chapter 4). They have effect as if they were rights under the 1983 Act and an application for leave to enter and occupy is to be treated as an application for an order under s.1 of that Act (s.337(3)). The statutory rights of occupation constitute a charge on so much of the bankrupt's estate or interest in the dwelling-house as vests in the trustee, having the like priority as an equitable interest created immediately before the commencement of the bankruptcy (s.337(2)). The 1983 Act has effect, with necessary modifications, as if the charge on the estate or interest of the trustee were a charge under that Act on the estate or interest of a spouse (s.337(3)).

The effect, therefore, is that in order to obtain possession of the home it will be necessary for the trustee to apply for an order under s.1(2) of the 1983 Act. On such an application the court must make such order under s.1 of the 1983 Act as it thinks just and reasonable having regard to:

(a)    the interests of the creditors;

(b)    the bankrupt's financial resources;

(c)    the needs of the children; and

(d)    all the circumstances of the case other than the needs of the bankrupt.

(s.337(5).)

Again, where such an application is made after the end of the period of one year beginning with the first vesting under the Act of the bankrupt's estate in a trustee, the court must assume, unless the circumstances of the case are exceptional, that the interests of the bankrupt's creditors outweigh all other considerations (s.337(6)).

*(f) Provisions applicable where sale is postponed*

(i) Charge on the dwelling-house
The provisions of ss.336 and 337 mean that the rights of occupation of the bankrupt's spouse or former spouse, or indeed, of the bankrupt himself, may outweigh for a time the interests of the bankrupt's creditors in relation to the family home. Two provisions may then become relevant. In the first place, where any property consisting of an interest in a dwelling-house which is occupied by the bankrupt, or by the bankrupt's spouse or former spouse, is comprised in the bankrupt's estate, and the trustee is for any reason unable for the time being to realise that property, the trustee may apply to the court for an order imposing a charge on the property for the benefit of the bankrupt's estate (s.313(1)). If the court imposes such a charge on any property the benefit of that charge is comprised in the bankrupt's estate. It is enforceable up to the value from time to time of the property secured, for the payment of any amount which is payable otherwise than to the bankrupt out of the bankrupt's estate (and of interest on that amount at the prescribed rate) (s.313(2)). Such an order made in respect of property vested in the trustee must provide, in accordance with the rules, for the property to cease to be comprised in the bankrupt's estate and to vest in the bankrupt, subject to the charge and any prior charge (s.313(3)). Certain supplemental provisions of the Charging Orders Act 1979 are applied to orders under s.313 (s.313(4)).

The importance of a charge (or an application for a charge) under s.313 is in relation to the release of the trustee in bankruptcy. Where it appears to a trustee that the administration of the bankrupt's estate is for practical purposes complete, he will need to summon a final general meeting of the bankrupt's creditors with a view to obtaining his release (unless the trustee is the Official Receiver). Generally, a trustee must not summon such a meeting where he has been unable to realise property comprised in the estate consisting of an interest in a dwelling-house which is occupied by the bankrupt or by the bankrupt's spouse or former spouse. However, a trustee will be able to call a meeting and obtain his release if the court has made an order under s.313 or has declined to make an order on the trustee's application under s.313 (s.332).

(ii) Payments
Where any premises comprised in the bankrupt's estate are occupied by him (whether by virtue of s.337 or otherwise) on condition that he makes payments towards satisfying any liability arising under the mortgage of the premises or otherwise towards the outgoings of the premises, the bankrupt does not, by virtue of those payments, acquire any interest in the premises (s.338). This preserves the existing position. (For provisions relating to income payment orders, see s.310.)

*(h) The court*
It will be noted that once a spouse has been adjudged bankrupt any application for an order under s.1 of the Matrimonial Homes Act 1983 and any application for an

order for sale under s.30 of the Law of Property Act 1925 must be made to the court having jurisdiction in relation to the insolvency (see s.336(2) and (3) and s.337(4)). This will be the High Court in relation to proceedings which, in accordance with the rules, are allocated to the London insolvency district, and otherwise each county court in relation to the proceedings which are so allocated to the insolvency district of that court. (See further s.373.)

# Chapter 9

# Financial provision on divorce, nullity and judicial separation – preliminary considerations

## 1. General principles

The powers of the court to order financial provision in proceedings for divorce, nullity and judicial separation were rationalised and extended by the Matrimonial Proceedings and Property Act 1970. This Act removed not only the confusing terminology which existed, but also the unjustifiable differences of substance. The powers of the court formerly varied according to the principal relief sought, and husband and wife were not on an equal footing. The Act introduced a uniform set of powers applicable in suits for divorce, nullity and judicial separation and drew no distinction between husband and wife, or between petitioner and respondent. It will be seen, however, that account has had to be taken in some provisions of the fact that a decree of judicial separation does not terminate a marriage in law. In as much as such a decree does signify the end of a marriage in fact, it was thought appropriate that the court should have available the same wide powers as were made available in suits for divorce or nullity. (See Law Com. No. 25, para 65.)

The importance of proper financial provision on dissolution of marriage was recognised to the extent that the commencement of the Divorce Reform Act 1969 was postponed until 1 January 1971 so that the Act of 1970 could be brought into operation at the same time. Moreover, the Divorce Reform Act itself recognised that the effect of the dissolution of a marriage on the financial position of a spouse is a factor which may need to be considered before a decree is granted. Indeed it recognised that in certain circumstances it is a factor which should be taken into account in deciding whether or not a marriage should be dissolved. It also recognised that there are circumstances in which final dissolution of a marriage should be delayed until satisfactory financial arrangements have been made.

The Divorce Reform Act 1969 and the relevant provisions of the Act of 1970 have been consolidated in the Matrimonial Causes Act 1973 to which significant amendments were made by the Matrimonial and Family Proceedings Act 1984. This chapter first examines the provisions of the Act which require the court in certain circumstances to consider, prior to the grant of a decree nisi or prior to that decree being made absolute, the effect of dissolution of the marriage on the financial position of the respondent spouse. Secondly, consideration will be given to financial provisions which can be made pending the outcome of the principal suit, which the Act distinguishes from financial provision made on or after the grant of a decree (see Chapter 10). The provision which may be ordered pending suit is known as "maintenance pending suit" and is limited to periodical payments in favour of a spouse.

## 2. Proceedings for divorce

A petition for divorce may be presented to the court by either party to a marriage on the ground that the marriage has broken down irretrievably (Matrimonial Causes Act 1973, s.1(1)). However, the court cannot hold a marriage to have broken down irretrievably unless the petitioner satisfies the court of one or more of the following facts:
(a) that the respondent has committed adultery and the petitioner finds it intolerable with the respondent;
(b) that the respondent has behaved in such a way that the petitioner cannot reasonably be expected to live with the respondent;
(c) that the respondent has deserted the petitioner for a continuous period of at least two years immediately preceding the presentation of the petition;
(d) that the parties to the marriage have lived apart for a continuous period of at least two years immediately preceding the presentation of the petition and the respondent consents to a decree being granted;
(e) that the parties to the marriage have lived apart for a continuous period of at least five years immediately preceding the presentation of the petition.
(*Ibid.* s.1(2).)

## 3. Refusal of a decree on the ground of hardship

*(a) The Matrimonial Causes Act 1973, s.5*
Where a petition is presented alleging that a marriage has broken down irretrievably on the basis of s.1(2)(e), the respondent may oppose the grant of a decree nisi on the ground that the dissolution of the marriage will result in grave financial or other hardship to him or her and that it would in all the circumstances be wrong to dissolve the marriage (s.5(1)).

If a decree is opposed on this ground the court must first be satisfied that (a) the petitioner is entitled to rely in support of his petition on the fact of five years' separation and makes no such finding as to any other fact mentioned in s.1(2), and (b) apart from s.5 it would grant a decree (s.5(2)). If these conditions are satisfied then the court must consider all the circumstances, including the conduct of the parties to the marriage and the interests of those parties and of any children or other persons concerned, and, if the court is of opinion that the dissolution of the marriage will result in grave financial or other hardship to the respondent and that it would in all the circumstances be wrong to dissolve the marriage, it must dismiss the petition. There are, therefore, two matters on which the court must be satisfied before a petition will be dismissed under this provision:

(1) that dissolution of the marriage will result in grave financial or other hardship to the respondent; and

(2) that in all the circumstances it would be wrong to dissolve the marriage.

In respect of the first matter, attention will be confined to financial hardship.

*(b) Grave financial hardship*

(i) The hardship must be such as would result from the dissolution of the marriage

Generally much of the hardship suffered will already have been caused by the breakdown of the marriage and dissolution will result in no further hardship (*Talbot v Talbot* [1971] The Times 19 October). It is true that if a marriage is dissolved the petitioner will be free to remarry and thereby undertake further commitments. But even if the marriage is not dissolved he may form another association with consequent commitments and in many cases may already have done so. A husband's obligations to his mistress and their children may take second place to those owed to his wife and the children of the family, but they are not entirely disregarded when considering his ability to make financial provision (see *Roberts* v *Roberts* [1970] P 1). In *Dorrell* v *Dorrell* [1972] 1 WLR 1087 at p. 1092 Sir George Baker P went so far as to say that "Remarriage and new commitments are now accepted as irrelevant".

It is specifically provided that "for the purpose of this section, hardship shall include the loss of the chance of acquiring any benefit which the respondent might acquire if the marriage were not dissolved" (s.5(3)). The benefit which is most likely to be lost by dissolution of a marriage is the right to receive a widow's pension from the petitioner's employers in the event of the respondent surviving the petitioner. Dissolution of a marriage may also affect benefits and liabilities under the national insurance scheme (see Chapter 19).

(ii) The relevance of what is practicable

In deciding whether dissolution of the marriage will result in grave financial hardship to the respondent the court will need to consider what will be possible by way of financial provision if the decree is granted. Although this inquiry will not have to anticipate the actual determination of the orders that the court will subsequently make if the decree is pronounced, it does involve an inquiry to the point of appreciating the limits within which the court will have the opportunity of arriving at a determination on or after the granting of a decree (*per* Cumming-Bruce J in *Parker* v *Parker* [1972] Fam 116 at p. 119). In some cases an analysis of what will be practicable by way of financial provision (in accordance with the principles considered in Chapter 11) will show not only that there will be a diminution in the standard of living of both parties, but that the respondent will suffer grave financial hardship. On the other hand, in other cases it may become apparent that the petitioner's available resources are sufficient to compensate for a contingent loss so that dissolution of itself will not result in grave financial hardship (as in *Parker* v *Parker* [1972] Fam 116. In *Dorrell* v *Dorrell* [1972] 1 WLR 1087 the petition was adjourned so as to give the petitioner an opportunity of putting forward proposals to offset the potential loss of a pension. See also *Le Marchant* v *Le Marchant* [1977] 1 WLR 559).

(iii) Subjective test of hardship

Grave financial hardship must be considered subjectively in relation to the particular marriage and the circumstances in which the parties lived while it subsisted (*per* Dunn J in *Talbot* v *Talbot* [1971] The Times 19 October. Approved by Karminski LJ in *Mathias* v *Mathias* [1972] Fam 287 at p. 293). Thus a prospective financial loss may be a grave hardship to a wife who is elderly or middle-aged or in bad health and incapable of supporting herself, while it may be no more than the inevitable consequence of the breakdown of the marriage of a wife who is young and healthy and capable of earning her own living. In *Parker* v *Parker* [1972] Fam 116 the wife of a police officer who was in her late forties, and who had been married for over 20 years, opposed the granting of a decree principally on the ground that she would thereby lose her right to a police widow's pension, though her state retirement pension would also be affected. Cumming-Bruce J said (at p. 123):

"Though the loss of the police widow's pension is contingent upon her surviving him, and though the contingency may be regarded, on a scrutiny of actual averages, as remote in time, her loss of possible future security after the death of her husband, at a time when she will most need it, is a grave hardship when considered in the light of her probable financial stringency after the age of 60, that is in 13 years' time."

In contrast, in *Talbot* v *Talbot* and *Mathias* v *Mathias* the court was concerned with wives who were comparatively young and capable of working and supporting themselves, at least in part. In *Mathias* v *Mathias*, Stephenson LJ said in relation to the corresponding provisions of the Act of 1969 (at p. 301):

"It is also reasonable to believe that the main, although not the only, purpose of section 4 was to protect respondent wives, especially those who had reached middle age, from losing the security, especially the financial security, of being married, and the chance of the benefits which a continuation of the married state would bring them, especially by way of a widow's pension rights on their husbands predeceasing them at not too remote a date. I am not saying that no young, able-bodied wife can hope to succeed in resisting a section 2(1)(e) petition by relying on section 4, or that the loss of the chance of obtaining a state pension, or an army pension, without any adequately compensating provision by the husband, can never be a grave financial hardship to a wife resulting from the dissolution of the marriage which would in all the circumstances be wrong. But it must usually be harder for her than for a wife of the age of Mrs Parker or Mrs Talbot, or, it seems, Mrs Parkes (see *Parkes* v *Parkes* [1971] 1 WLR 148) to make out the statutory defence ..."

However, even in the case of the older woman the potential loss may be considered too remote to amount to grave financial hardship. This was the case in *Reiterbund* v *Reiterbund* [1975] Fam 99 where a 52 year old wife complained that divorce would deprive her of a widow's pension. That pension would only have been payable if her 54 year old husband predeceased her before the age of 60 at which age she would in any event have been entitled to a retirement pension.

It will also be apparent that the effect of a prospective financial loss will depend very much on the means of the particular respondent. Thus in *Dorrell* v *Dorrell* [1972] 1 WLR 1087 at p. 1093 Sir George Baker P, rejecting an argument that it was impossible to regard a prospective loss of £2 per week as grave financial hardship, pointed out that "When a woman is living on £6 or £8 a week, £2 a week is a third or a quarter of her income. It is as important to her as £100,000 may be to a millionaire, indeed more important." In that case the pension of approximately £2 a week which the wife would lose if the marriage was dissolved would have been of no direct benefit to her for it would have passed to the Department of Health and Social Security in discharge of the benefit paid to her. Nevertheless, the fact that social security benefit was available to a wife did not relieve a husband of his obligation, and the loss of the pension was held to amount to a grave financial hardship.

This does not mean that the availability of income support to a divorced wife cannot be taken into account in considering whether she will suffer grave financial hardship. In *Reiterbund* v *Reiterbund* [1975] Fam 99, while a divorce would have deprived the wife (who was living on supplementary benefit) of a widow's pension during the following eight years if her husband predeceased her during that period, she would suffer no loss of income because she would continue to receive supplementary benefit. Nevertheless, the Court of Appeal emphasised that each case must depend on its own facts and it would not necessarily be appropriate in all cases under s.5 to take into account the wife's potential social security benefits. It would be inappropriate to take the availability of such benefits into account where the wife was working, or capable of working, and her entitlement to supplementary benefit would be affected, whereas the widow's pension might not be affected, or affected to the same extent, by her earnings (a similar position might arise if the wife had capital and/or investment income). Again it would be inappropriate if the potential widow's pension was greater in amount than the potential supplementary benefit (*per* Ormrod LJ at p. 112; and Megaw LJ at p. 109). If the husband (unlike the husband in *Reiterbund*) can make financial provision for the loss of a chance of the widow's pension the court may require him to do so, without taking into account the fact that supplementary benefit is available as a longstop to protect the wife from destitution.

(iv) The onus of proof

The onus of proving grave financial hardship lies on the respondent, and she should, by pleading, set forth the facts relied upon (*per* Cumming-Bruce J in *Parker* v *Parker* [1972] Fam 116 at pp. 119-120). If the answer sets up a *prima facie* case of financial hardship the onus is then on the petitioner to put forward a proposal which is acceptable to the court as reasonable in all the circumstances and sufficient to remove the element of grave financial hardship which otherwise would lead to the dismissal of the petition. In *Le Marchant* v *Le Marchant* [1977] 1 WLR 559 the wife had established a *prima facie* case of grave financial hardship on the basis that divorce would terminate her contingent entitlement to a widow's index-linked post-office pension of some £1,300 per annum if she survived her husband. The Court of Appeal held that as the husband had failed to make any realistic proposal his petition should have been dismissed or at any rate adjourned so that the husband could make sensible proposals to deal with the hardship. However, in the Court of Appeal the husband made acceptable proposals and the decree was allowed to stand. The proposals were (a) an outright transfer to the wife of the matrimonial home; (b) a cash payment to the wife of £5,000 when the husband received the capital sum payable under his pension scheme; and (c) the effecting by the husband of a policy of insurance on his own life in the sum of £5,000 payable to the wife in the event of her surviving him, otherwise to be disposed of as he wished. Thus while the wife would lose the index-linked pension she would, if she survived her husband, have £10,000 available for investment.

In contrast, in *Julian* v *Julian* (1972) 116 SJ 763 the husband was unable to make satisfactory proposals. The parties had married in 1939 and the husband, a senior police officer, left the matrimonial home in 1965 with the intention of marrying a younger woman. In 1971 the husband, then aged 61, retired and in bad health, petitioned for divorce relying on the fact of separation for five years. The wife, then aged 58 and also in poor health, alleged that the loss of the right to a police widow's pension of £790 per annum would result in grave financial hardship. The husband offered to increase periodical payments from £65 to £81 per month (which would be possible in view of his prospective wife's earnings) and to pay a lump sum of £2,000 - worth some £215 in the form of an annuity. However, Cusack J said that there would still be a very substantial monetary gap between this provision and the financial benefit she would receive if the marriage was not dissolved. The petition was dismissed, and this appears to be the only reported case in which the defence under s.5 has succeeded. In *Lee* v *Lee* the wife succeeded at first instance ((1974) 4 Fam Law 114) but failed in the Court of Appeal ((1975) 5 Fam Law 48). There had, however, been an important change in the circumstances between the two hearings.

### (c) It would be "wrong" to dissolve the marriage

In *Talbot* v *Talbot* [1971] The Times 19 October Dunn J pointed out that words like "wrong" or "right" are unusual in a statute. He considered that, in construing "wrong", regard had to be had to the circumstances of the persons involved, including the children, but also to the balance which had to be maintained between upholding the sanctity of the marriage, and the desirability of ending "empty" ties. It must also be remembered that the court is required to take into account the interests not only of the parties and any children, but also of any person involved. This will include the interest of a woman with whom the husband is living or whom he desires to marry. Where the parties are young the dissolution of the marriage may not only enable the petitioner to marry, but also the respondent. This view was taken by the Court of Appeal in *Mathias* v *Mathias* [1972] Fam 287 at p. 300 where Karminski LJ said:

"So far as the wife is concerned, the fact that the husband has left her for many years and desires to set up a home married to another woman is bound to cause her, having regard to their respective means, some degree of financial hardship. But on the other hand what this court has to consider ... is whether in all the circumstances it would be wrong to dissolve this marriage ... One has to consider the broader aspect: whether a marriage which has so hopelessly broken down for so long should be preserved or whether it is not right in the public interest to put an end to it. I remind myself that after all the wife is still a young woman who may find a happy future with another man as a husband. Having regard to all the circumstances of this case, I have come to the conclusion, bearing in mind also the position of the husband ... that this is a case where the public interest requires ... that this marriage should be dissolved."

In *Lee* v *Lee* (1974) 4 Fam Law 114, Stirling J treated the 42 year old married son of the parties as a person concerned in the circumstances which he had to consider. The husband's financial proposals, though not "ungenerous", were not enough to enable the wife to retain accommodation in the same area as her sick son whom she nursed while his wife went out to work. Divorce would cause hardship, whether it was called financial or other hardship, not only to the wife but to the son and his wife. By the time the matter came before the Court of Appeal ((1975) 5 Fam Law 48) the son had died and the appeal was not fully argued. Scarman LJ said that it was not necessary for the court to take any view as to whether Stirling J was right to take account of such circumstances, but personally he thought he was right to do so, for s.5 was so drawn that the whole family picture might be reviewed by the court.

The court is also required to take into account the conduct of the parties. In *Dorrell* v *Dorrell* [1972] 1 WLR 1087 at p. 1092 Sir George Baker P accepted the argument that "conduct" could not mean conduct in the sense of the old matrimonial offence; because if it did, "then it would be impossible to carry out one express purpose of the Act, namely, divorce after living apart continuously for five years". However, in *Brickell* v *Brickell* [1974] Fam 31 Davies LJ disagreed with this view. He considered that "conduct" in this context was not confined to conduct in the sense of the old matrimonial offences, but must clearly include it, and if it were established it was one of the matters to be taken into account. In that case the court was satisfied that the wife would suffer grave financial hardship as a result of the divorce but held that in the light of her conduct it would not be wrong to dissolve the marriage.

The conduct of the respondent in relation to financial matters is clearly a factor which may influence the court. Thus in *Mathias* v *Mathias* [1972] Fam 287 although the wife had experience of several jobs, she had done very little work of any kind since her husband left her in 1964. She took the view that the proper course was to look after the children of the marriage. Karminski LJ noted that her conduct had not been impugned in any way so far as the break-up of the marriage was concerned, and he said later (at p. 298):

"It is possible to observe that a great many mothers in this unhappy position do manage to do a part-time job without prejudicing in any way the welfare and interests of their children. But in this particular case the wife takes a different view and has, as a matter of considered policy, decided not to work. So to that extent she has suffered financially through her own choice in the sense of abstaining from working for the reasons that she gave and I have recited."

If either party intends to rely on any matter of misconduct of the other party, or any other particular circumstance which is alleged to be relevant to the court's consideration, the other party should be given notice thereof in sufficient time to enable the allegation to be investigated and rebutted.

## 4. Power to rescind decree nisi

Where the court has granted a decree of divorce on the basis of a finding that the petitioner was entitled to rely in support of his petition on the fact of two years' separation coupled with the respondent's consent to a decree being granted, and has made no such finding as to any other fact mentioned in s.1(2), the court may, on an application made by the respondent at any time before the decree is made absolute, rescind the decree if it is satisfied that the petitioner misled the respondent (whether intentionally or unintentionally) about any matter which the respondent took into account in deciding to give consent (Matrimonial Causes Act 1973, s.10(1)).

## 5. Special protection for respondent in separation cases

*(a) Matrimonial Causes Act 1973, s.10(3)*
The respondent to a petition for divorce in which the petitioner alleged two years' or five years' separation coupled, in the former case, with the respondent's consent to a decree being granted, may apply to the court for consideration under s.10(3) of his or her financial position after the divorce. Such an application may be heard only when the court has granted a decree on the petition on the basis of a finding that the petitioner was entitled to rely in support of his petition on the fact of two years' or five years' separation (as the case may be), and has made no such findings as to any other fact mentioned in s.1(2) (s.10(2)).

On hearing any such application the court must, under s.10(3), consider all the circumstances, including the age, health, conduct, earning capacity, financial resources and financial obligations of each of the parties, and the financial position of the respondent as, having regard to the divorce, it is likely to be after the death of the petitioner should the petitioner die first, and must not make absolute the decree of divorce unless it is satisfied:
(a) that the petitioner should not be required to make any financial provision for the respondent; or
(b) that the financial provision made by the petitioner for the respondent is reasonable and fair or the best that can be made in the circumstances.
The circumstances in which a petitioner should not be required to make any financial provision for the respondent are illustrated by *Krystman* v *Krystman* [1973] 1 WLR 927.

*(b) Reasonable and fair financial provision*
In determining what financial provision is "reasonable and fair" for this purpose the court applies the same approach as in an application for financial provision where s.25 applies (*Lombardi* v *Lombardi* [1973] 1 WLR 1276; *Krystman* v *Krystman*). The words "the best that can be made in the circumstances" are "intended to cover

the case where the husband's means are so slight that it would be impracticable to make what would otherwise be a reasonable and fair order" (*per* Cairns LJ in *Lombardi* v *Lombardi* [1973] 1 WLR 1276 at p. 1280).

There is an obvious contrast between the language of s.10(3) and the language of s.5. Under s.5 the court must dismiss a petition if it is of opinion that the dissolution of the marriage will result in grave financial or other hardship and that it would be wrong to dissolve the marriage. Under s.10(3) a respondent cannot prevent a decree nisi from being made absolute if the court is satisfied that the financial provision is reasonable and fair or the best that can be made in the circumstances even though grave financial or other hardship will result (see *Parker* v *Parker* [1972] Fam 116 at p. 118). However, in *Hardy* v *Hardy* (1981) 2 FLR 321 at p. 328 Ormrod LJ said that there are cases where the court is entitled to say that the best order it can make under s.23 or s.24 of the 1973 Act is not adequate to protect the wife, bearing in mind that she is being divorced against her will. It will then be for the husband to put forward proposals and implement them before the decree is made absolute. "What those proposals are will vary ... from case to case but they would not necessarily be within the four corners of the court's jurisdiction under ss.23, 24 and 25 because the sanction is that the decree will not be made absolute." This might be appropriate in a situation such as that which arose in *Hardy* where the husband was employed by his father and was receiving an artificially low salary, but enjoying a standard of living much higher than that salary would indicate. There were also prospects of succession to the family business at some uncertain time in the future. In these circumstances it was not unreasonable for the court to apply s.10 so as to protect the wife, especially where the husband was adopting a formalistic position regarding his artificial financial resources. Although there might be many cases where it was convenient for an application under s.10 and applications under ss.23 and 24 to be dealt with together, it was wrong to require a wife to make applications under ss.23 and 24 at the same time as she applied under s.10: *per* Ormrod LJ in *Hardy* v *Hardy* (1982) 2 FLR 321 at p. 327.

In *Wilson* v *Wilson* [1973] 1 WLR 555 the Court of Appeal pointed out the danger of relying on mere proposals by a petitioner to make financial provision. If a respondent relies on s.10(3), reasonable and fair financial provision should actually have been made before the decree is made absolute, for otherwise it would be open to a petitioner to resile from mere proposals leaving the respondent without protection.

*(c) Undertakings to make financial provision*
Under s.10(4) the court may, if it thinks fit, proceed to make the decree absolute without observing the above requirements if:
(a) it appears that there are circumstances making it desirable that the decree should be made absolute without delay; and
(b) the court has obtained a satisfactory undertaking from the petitioner that he will make such financial provision for the respondent as the court may approve.
In *Grigson* v *Grigson* [1974] 1 WLR 228 the Court of Appeal held that before a judge is asked to exercise this jurisdiction the husband ought to put before the court

an outline of what he thinks he will be able to carry out and what he is proposing to do. An undertaking should then be taken from him on the basis of those proposals if they are approved by the court at that time and not at some later, unspecified time. In other words, the approval of the court, in outline at least, should be asked for and given at that date, and not at some vague unspecified time in the future. In that case the husband had not formulated any proposals but proffered an undertaking to make such financial provision for the wife as the court might approve. The Court of Appeal held that this was insufficient and leave to make the decree nisi absolute was refused.

*(d) The use of s.10(3)*
Where a respondent has consented to the grant of a decree and the petitioner has accordingly proceeded in reliance on paragraph (d), it should not normally be necessary to rely on s.10(3), for the respondent may be expected to have approved the proposed financial provision prior to consenting. Moreover, if the respondent has been misled, application can be made under s.10(1) of the Act to rescind the decree nisi.

Where a respondent has been induced not to oppose the grant of a decree under s.5, if it transpires that he or she has been mistaken or misled, or that the petitioner has failed to make a full and frank disclosure, then an application under s.10(2) may be desirable and, if appropriate, for the decree nisi to be set aside on the ground of mistake (as in *Parkes* v *Parkes* [1971] 1 WLR 1481). If the respondent opposes the grant of a decree under s.5 but the court decides that no grave financial or other hardship would result from dissolution of the marriage, or if it decides that despite such hardship it would not be wrong to dissolve the marriage, it has been said that a notice under s.10(2) may be desirable as the best practicable way of safeguarding the financial future of the respondent (see Cumming-Bruce J in *Parker* v *Parker* [1972] Fam 287 at p. 301).

More recently, however, the value of an application under s.10(2), where it is joined with an application for financial provision under ss.23 and 24 of the Act, has been doubted. Thus in *Robertson* v *Robertson* (1983) 4 FLR 387 at p. 393 Balcombe J said that it was almost inevitable in the ordinary case where the court makes an order for financial provision, that "the court could hardly be other than satisfied that the provision it has made is reasonable and fair, otherwise it would not be making it." He referred to the comments of Ormrod LJ in *Cumbers* v *Cumbers* [1974] 1 WLR 1331 at p. 1334 where he pointed out that s.6 of the Divorce Reform Act 1969, from which s.10(2) and (3) are derived, was inserted at a time when the court's powers to order financial provision were much more restricted than they were before the enactment of ss.23 and 24. In *Garcia* v *Garcia* [1991] 3 All ER 451 at p. 457 Butler-Sloss LJ thought that s.10(2) would be unlikely to be frequently used. Ralph Gibson LJ (at p. 460) said:

"I would expect that normally the court would decline to apply its jurisdiction under s.10 if the financial provision which is sought, and which the respondent contends should be required, can and should be dealt with, both conveniently and appropriately, under an ordinary application for financial provision upon the making of the decree."

Nevertheless, there remain cases where it may be appropriate to use s.10(2). That was so in *Garcia* v *Garcia* where the wife was not making an application for financial provision, but sought to delay the making of the decree absolute until the husband had fulfilled his obligations to their child under an agreement ratified under Spanish law some years before. The procedure had served to bring what the wife said was an injustice to the attention of the court and it might prove to be a convenient way of disposing of the whole issue between the parties in a sensible and expeditious way. The Court of Appeal also took the view that s.10 was not solely concerned with future financial provision, but enabled the court to look to past obligations which are unfulfilled. See also *Griffiths* v *Dawson & Co* [1993] Fam Law 476.


## 6. Maintenance pending suit

### (a) The court's powers

On a petition for divorce, nullity of marriage or judicial separation the court may make an order for maintenance pending suit, i.e. an order requiring either party to the marriage to make to the other such periodical payments for his or her maintenance and for such term, being a term beginning not earlier than the date of the presentation of the petition and ending with the date of the determination of the suit, as the court thinks reasonable (Matrimonial Causes Act 1973, s.22).

No order can be made before a petition is filed, and generally application must be made in the petition or answer, as the case may be (s.26 and Family Proceedings Rules 1991, r. 2.53). Provision is limited to periodical payments, which may be ordered to be paid as from the presentation of the petition up until final determination of the suit as the court thinks reasonable. In proceedings for divorce or nullity of marriage the suit is determined not on the grant of a decree nisi, but when the decree is made absolute. Proceedings for judicial separation are determined on the grant of a decree. The suit may also be determined by dismissal of the petition or it may be abated by the death of either party. If there is an appeal the court may order the maintenance pending suit to be continued if it is fair and reasonable to do so (*Corbett* v *Corbett (No. 2)* [1971] P 110 at p. 113). It will be seen in Chapter 10 that in the case of proceedings for divorce or nullity, while financial provision in favour of a spouse may be ordered on or after the grant of a decree nisi, it will take effect only from the date of the decree absolute (s.23(5)). Up until that date a spouse can only obtain the benefit of maintenance pending suit, though this limitation does not apply to financial provision for children of the family (s.29(2)). However, orders for periodical payments, secured or unsecured granted on or after a decree which became effective on final determination of the suit, may provide for the payments to be made as from the date of the making of the application for such orders (s.28(1)). Moreover, orders for lump sum payments may be made on or after the grant of a decree to cover liabilities and expenses incurred prior to the making of an application for financial provision (s.23(3)(a) and (b)). See further Chapter 10. It should also be noted that on an application for an order under s.1 of the Matrimonial Homes Act 1983 the court on making an order may impose on either spouse obligations as to the repair and maintenance of the dwelling-house or the discharge of any liabilities in respect of the dwelling-house: s.1(3)(c). See Chapter 4. In *Barry* v *Barry* [1992] 2 WLR 799 Waite J held that although the court does not have power to order an interim capital payment, it does have an administrative power of appropriation of assets which enabled him to authorise the release of substantial funds for the purchase of a house for the wife subject to appropriate undertakings.

*(b) The object of maintenance pending suit*
The object of maintenance pending suit is to provide for the immediate needs of a spouse pending the outcome of the proceedings. The Act of 1973 contains no description of the matters which the court is to take into account in deciding whether or not to order maintenance, or in fixing the amount. The court is required only to make such order as it "thinks reasonable" and it has been said that the section "gives the court as wide and unfettered discretion as can well be imagined" (*per* French J in *Offord* v *Offord* (1982) 3 FLR 309 at p. 312). In *F* v *F* (1983) 4 FLR 382 at p. 385 Balcombe J considered the approach which the court should take, now that divorce was no longer based on the idea of matrimonial fault. He said:

"Clearly there must be an empirical approach, since on an application for maintenance pending suit it is quite impossible practically to go into all the kinds of detail that the court can go into when dealing with the full hearing of an application for financial relief, and in the ordinary sort of case the registrars who deal with these applications will have to take a broad view of means on the one hand and income on the other and come to a rough and ready conclusion."

However, in individual cases "administrative expediency, even if it promotes justice for the great bulk of litigants in this type of case, cannot be allowed to work injustice ..." (*ibid.*). The court may take into account other relevant circumstances in addition to the means and needs of the parties (see French J in *Offord* v *Offord* (1982) 3 FLR 309 at p. 312). Moreover, the fact that s.25 of the Act makes no reference to s.22 does not prevent the court taking into account the matters set out in s.25 (*per* Balcombe J in *F* v *F* (1983) 4 FLR 382 at pp. 384-385).

In *F* v *F* Balcombe J took into account three matters, apart from the means and needs of the parties, in coming to the conclusion that no order for maintenance should be made. First, he was concerned with an extremely short marriage. It had lasted for only a few days, though the parties had a sexual relationship for about a year before the marriage. Secondly, an important factor was that the wife's financial position did not appear to have been affected in any way by the marriage. She had given up her work as a model in order to be an art student before their cohabitation started, well before the marriage. She had also retained her own flat and she did not need support for any period of adjustment. Thirdly, it seems that he took some account of the fact that there was evidence that the wife had brought the marriage to an end by resuming a relationship with a former boyfriend. He was not prepared to make a finding in relation to that allegation relating to the wife's conduct, but if it was established in due course the husband would have little prospect of recovering payments made in the meantime.

Where the wife is in receipt of state benefits so that she is unlikely to benefit personally from an order for maintenance pending suit, the principles upon which the court should act "... must be the same for applications pending suit and interim periodical payments as they are for what are called final orders, that is full periodical payments orders either for a spouse or for children" (*per* Booth J in *Peacock* v *Peacock* [1984] 1 WLR 532 at p. 534. See Chapter 19, Part 6).

*(c) Maintenance pending suit and matrimonial orders*
In many cases when a petition for divorce or nullity is presented there may already exist a matrimonial order made by a magistrates' court. The existing order is not affected. Indeed such an order is not automatically terminated on decree absolute (see *Bragg* v *Bragg* [1925] P 20; *Wood* v *Wood* [1957] P 254 and Chapter 16). However while an application for maintenance pending suit may still be made, it is unlikely that an order will be made while the matrimonial order remains in force (*Kilford* v *Kilford* [1947] P 100; *Pooley* v *Pooley* [1952] P 65). It is now provided that where after the making of an order for financial provision by a magistrates' court proceedings between, and relating to the marriage of, the parties are commenced in the High Court or a county court, the High Court or county court may, if it thinks fit, direct that the order made by the magistrates' court shall cease to have effect on such date as the court may specify (Domestic Proceedings and Magistrates' Courts Act 1978, s.28(1)). This does not apply to an order for payment of a lump sum by a magistrates' court. This means that if an order in the High Court or county court is thought to be more convenient or desirable, there will be no need to make a separate application to the magistrates' court for revocation of the existing order.

In other cases an application may have been made to a magistrates' court by one spouse, generally the wife, but no order may yet have been made at the time when the other spouse presents a petition for divorce or nullity. In these circumstances the magistrates' court may proceed to deal with the application and make an order if appropriate, but normally it ought not to do so. The application should be adjourned by the magistrates' court and the wife should seek maintenance pending suit in the High Court or county court (*Kaye* v *Kaye* [1965] P 100). In practice this may cause hardship to a wife in need of immediate assistance, for her application for maintenance pending suit may not be dealt with as quickly as her application to the magistrates' court. Accordingly, it is recognised that there are circumstances in which it is proper for a magistrates' court to make an order. (See *Lanitis* v *Lanitis* [1970] 1 All ER 466, especially at p. 472.)

# Chapter 10

# Financial provision orders and property adjustment orders

## 1. Orders that may be made

On granting a decree of divorce, a decree of nullity of marriage or a decree of judicial separation or at any time thereafter (whether, in the case of a decree of divorce or nullity of marriage, before or after the decree is made absolute), the court may, under the Matrimonial Causes Act 1973, make orders for financial provision, orders adjusting property rights and orders for the sale of property. These powers are exercisable only if a decree had been granted by a court in England and Wales, but similar powers are now exercisable under Part III of the Matrimonial and Family Proceedings Act 1984 where a decree has been granted by a court outside England and Wales. (See Chapter 14.)

## 2. Financial provision orders

*(a) The court's powers*
Under s.23 of the Matrimonial Causes Act 1973 the court may make one or more of the following orders:
  (a) that either party to the marriage shall make to the other such periodical payments, for such term, as may be specified in the order;
  (b) that either party to the marriage shall secure to the other to the satisfaction of the court such periodical payments, for such term, as may be specified in the order;
  (c) that either party to the marriage shall pay to the other such lump sum or sums as may be so specified;
  (d) that a party to the marriage shall make to such person as may be specified in the order for the benefit of a child of the family, or to such child, such periodical payments, for such term, as may be so specified;
  (e) that a party to the marriage shall secure to such person as may be specified in

the order for the benefit of a child of the family, or to such a child, to the satisfaction of the court, such periodical payments, for such a term, as may be so specified;

(f) that a party to the marriage shall pay to such person as may be specified in the order for the benefit of a child of the family, or to such child, such lump sum as may be so specified.

## *(b) Orders for periodical payments*

An order for periodical payments may take several forms (see Ormrod LJ in *Dipper* v *Dipper* [1981] Fam 31 at p. 47).

First, the court may make an order for periodical payments unlimited as to time which may be either:

(i) a substantive order, i.e. an order for the amount considered appropriate at the time or;

(ii) a nominal order, e.g. 50p per annum, "the purpose of which is to enable the party obtaining it to take advantage of the variation section without difficulty" (*per* Ormrod LJ in *Dipper* v *Dipper* at p. 47).

In *Freeman* v *Swatridge* [1984] FLR 762 at p. 763 Wood J said that an "order of 50p per week is not a nominal order: a nominal order is now virtually a term of art and represents 50p or £1 a year". Dunn LJ at p. 767 described the order of 50p per week as "perhaps no more than a token of his obligation to maintain his own children".

Secondly, the court may make a substantive order for periodical payments for a limited term, and:

(i) make no provision for the period after the expiration of that term; or

(ii) may provide for periodical payments at a nominal rate thereafter (see e.g. *Robertson* v *Robertson* (1983) 4 FLR 387); and

(iii) may (in the case of (i)) give a direction under s.28(1A) that no application for an extension of the term shall be made.

In the case of (i) the person in whose favour the order is made may apply for an extension of the term before that term has expired, but not thereafter. Thus in *T* v *T* *(Financial Provision)* [1988] 1 FLR 480 the order provided for periodical payments to be made to the wife until such date as she remarried or until the husband retired from his employment with the John Lewis Partnership, or further order. Butler-Sloss LJ held that once the husband had so retired no application for variation of the order could be made, for by then there was no order, "not even a nominal order, upon which to hang an application to vary" (at p. 483). Moreover, once the order had been terminated by the occurrence of one of the specified events, the words "until further order" were of no assistance to the wife. Unless there was some clear context to the contrary, these words were to be construed as "further order in the meantime". In the case of (ii) the recipient is protected by being able to apply for a variation of the nominal order. However, if the court has given a direction as in (iii) then it has ensured a deferred "clean break" at the end of the limited term.

Thirdly, the court may dismiss the application with a direction that the applicant shall not be entitled to make any further application in relation to that marriage for an order for periodical payments (s.25A(3), reversing the view taken by the Court of

Appeal in *Dipper* v *Dipper* [1981] Fam 31). The court can thus impose an immediate "clean break". In *Thompson* v *Thompson* [1988] 2 All ER 376 Ewbank J held that the court has power to dismiss the claim of one party for financial provision by consent and, at the same time, make an order for financial relief in favour of the other party. In that case the parties had negotiated an agreement whereby the husband undertook, *inter alia*, to transfer the former matrimonial home, to pay a lump sum and to make periodical payments to the wife, and he agreed that his claim for maintenance pending suit, periodical payments and secured periodical payments should be dismissed and that he should not be entitled to make any further application in relation to the marriage for an order under s.23. Moreover, having regard to s.25A, Ewbank J said he could envisage circumstances when it would be possible to do the same thing without the consent of the party concerned.

Fourthly, the court may "adjourn the application generally if the court does not wish to make any order at that time". It is not appropriate for a court to make an "order" in the terms: "No order as to periodical payments", because of the difficulty of interpretation which may subsequently arise. (See *Carter* v *Carter* [1980] 1 WLR 390 at p. 395 and *Dipper* v *Dipper* [1981] Fam 31 at pp. 48 and 50.)

Where the court makes an order for periodical payments against a party who is ordinarily resident in England and Wales (a "qualifying periodical maintenance order") it may make an order as to the method of payment (a "means of payment order") under s.1 of the Maintenance Enforcement Act 1991. (See Chapter 22.)

*(c) Orders for lump sum payments*
An order for the payment of a lump sum to a party to a marriage may be made for the purpose of enabling that party to meet any liabilities or expenses reasonably incurred by him or her in maintaining himself or herself or any child of the family before the making of an application for a financial provision order. Similarly, an order for the payment of a lump sum to or for the benefit of a child of the family may be made for the purpose of meeting any liabilities or expenses reasonably incurred by or for the benefit of that child before an application for a financial provision order was made (s.23(3)).

An order for the payment of a lump sum may provide for the payment of that sum by instalments of such amount as may be specified in the order, and may require the payment of the instalments to be secured to the satisfaction of the court (s.23(3)). Where the court makes an order for the payment of a lump sum and directs that (1) payment of that sum or any part of it is to be deferred, or (2) that sum or any part of it is to be paid by instalments, the court may order that the amount deferred or the instalments are to carry interest at such rate as may be specified in the order from such date, not earlier than the date of the order, as may be specified in the order, until the date when payment of it is due (s.23(6), inserted by Administration of Justice Act 1982, s.16. See *Gregory* v *Wainwright* (1984) 14 Fam Law 86 where Sheldon J ordered a husband to pay interest at 12 per cent on the amount of a lump sum when there was delay in payment under the terms of a consent order). Where the court makes an order for the payment of a lump sum by instalments which are to be secured, it may direct that the matter be referred to one of the conveyancing counsel of the court for him to settle a proper instrument to be executed by all necessary parties. If it thinks fit the court may defer the grant of the decree in question until the instrument has been duly executed (s.30).

Although it is provided that the court may order payment to a party to a marriage of such *lump sum or sums* as may be specified in the order, it was held in *Coleman v Coleman* [1973] Fam 10 that this does not enable the court to make a second lump sum order. Sir George Baker P took the view that the purpose of the italicised words was to enable the court to provide for more than one lump sum payment in one order. Thus in the subsequent case of *Dopson* v *Cherry* (1975) 5 Fam Law 57 the court ordered the husband to make an immediate lump sum payment of £3,000 to the wife and to pay a further lump sum of £2,000 to be raised on the security of the former matrimonial home. In *Banyard* v *Banyard* (1984) 5 FLR 643, a consent order made in 1976 provided, *inter alia*, that the husband should transfer to the wife his interest in the matrimonial home which was subject to a mortgage secured by an endowment policy on the life of the husband. The order provided that when the policy matured in 1992, the husband was to pay to the wife, if she survived, a sum to discharge the amount of the mortgage. If the property was sold before the policy matured, the husband was to pay to the wife the surrender value of the policy without such profits as may have accumulated. The latter provision was held to be a provision for a lump sum at a future date, thereby precluding any further application for a lump sum. Such a lump sum order was the only way in which the husband could be ordered in effect to pay off the mortgage on the house for the benefit of the wife. (See also *Sandford* v *Sandford* [1985] FLR 1056.)

A difficult problem may arise where the existing assets of a party are too limited to enable him or her to make a lump sum payment, or to make more than a very small lump sum payment, but it is probable that he or she will acquire capital assets in the future. This is particularly likely to arise in relation to capital sums which may become payable on retirement under occupational pension schemes or by way of terminal gratuities, but it may also involve the possibility of a party receiving property by way of gift or inheritance from his or her family. There are two approaches which the court may adopt.

First, the court may make a contingent lump sum order. Thus in *Milne* v *Milne* (1981) 2 FLR 286 the Court of Appeal made an order that if the wife was alive at the material time, i.e. the husband's retirement, or his earlier death, she should receive a sum equal to half the amount to which the husband or his estate would be entitled from his occupational pension scheme. This followed *Priest* v *Priest* (1981) 1 FLR 189 where the order was made in two parts. It provided first that the husband should pay to the wife half the cash he then had in hand. Secondly, it provided that the husband, if and when he received from the Crown his gratuity pay on retirement from the Royal Marines, should pay a proportion of it, namely one-third, to his former wife. While this form of order may be appropriate in relation to terminal payments and gratuities generally, there is a special difficulty in relation to payments that may be made to servicemen. The court in *Priest* v *Priest* was not referred to the statutory provisions in s.203 of the Army Act 1955 and s.203 of the Air Force Act 1955 which (a) render void every assignment of or charge on any pay, grant, pension or allowance payable to any person in respect of his or any other person's service in Her Majesty's forces, and (b) provide that no court shall make any order the effect of which would be to restrain any person from receiving any such sum and directing payment thereof to another person. The second restriction clearly prevents a court making an order directing payment in the future of a proportion of the gratuity of a soldier or airman to his wife or former wife (as was the case in *Priest* v *Priest* and *Roberts* v *Roberts* [1986] 1 WLR 437). In *Walker* v *Walker* [1983] Fam 68 the Court of Appeal held that it also prevented an order directing the Paymaster-General to pay such sum into court - otherwise the protection afforded by the statutory restriction would be meaningless. However, the court did uphold an order directing the husband on receipt of the gratuity from the Paymaster-General to pay the money into court, though this did not meet the concern that the husband might dissipate the gratuity before doing so. In *Ranson* v *Ranson* [1988] 1 WLR 183 the Court of Appeal held that an order, that the husband pay the wife a lump sum equal to twenty per cent of the terminal gratuity received by the husband on his discharge from the Air Force, contravened the statutory restrictions. Although in a literal sense this was not a direction to pay part of the gratuity to another person or a charge on the gratuity, adopting a purposive construction it was contrary to the spirit of the statutory restrictions in that, despite its form, it "had the effect of directing payment of twenty per cent of the husband's terminal gratuity to another person, to wit his wife" (*ibid. per* May LJ at p. 189). It was acknowledged that once a gratuity has been received and assimilated into the capital of an ex-serving airman, the court can take account of its existence and make whatever order it thinks appropriate having regard to the capital and income assets of the husband. However, May LJ said that in considering all the circumstances of the case, it would be right for the court (even then) at least to bear in mind the source from which that particular capital had come and the statutory provisions which would have been applicable to it (*ibid.* at p. 188). In *Happe* v *Happe* [1990] 2 FLR 212 the husband had already received his gratuity and the Court of Appeal held that, once the pensioner has safely received the sum of money to which he is entitled under the pension arrangements to which the statutory restrictions relate, the court is in no way inhibited by the statutory restrictions in exercising its power to order a lump sum payment. The position is different in relation to gratuities payable to members of the Royal Navy. In *Cotgrave* v *Cotgrave* [1991] 4 All ER 537 it was noted by the Court of Appeal that s.4 of the Naval and Marine Pay and Pensions Act 1865, while prohibiting an assignment by the seaman himself, contains no restriction on the power of a court to make an order directing payment of the gratuity to be made to another person.

The second course of action which the court may take is to adjourn the application to await the date of the receipt of the capital asset. This may be the only course open where the restrictions of the Army Act and the Air Force Act apply. It may also be appropriate where there is uncertainty about the receipt of the assets. In *Hardy* v *Hardy* (1981) 2 FLR 321 the husband, aged 28, was employed by his wealthy father at a modest wage. It was probable that on the father's retirement the son would take over the running of the business, but this might not happen for perhaps ten to fifteen years. Even then there was no certainty that the business would vest in the son in such a way as would enable him to make a lump sum payment. At first instance the judge refused to adjourn the wife's application for a lump sum payment as a way of keeping the option open for the wife to see if something turned up. However, the Court of Appeal allowed the adjournment, but indicated that in such a situation the wife might have been advised not to make the application for the lump sum at that stage. She had not filed an answer and so would not have needed leave to make an application at a later date, though if a long period elapsed before it was made the merits of her claim would be weaker. (See Part 5 below for the circumstances in which leave to apply is necessary.)

It has become clear that adjournment to an uncertain future date is inappropriate. In *Morris* v *Morris* (1977) 7 Fam Law 244 an adjournment was granted where the payment of a gratuity on completion of service was only some two or three years ahead. In *Davies* v *Davies* [1986] 1 FLR 497 the Court of Appeal upheld the adjournment of the wife's application for a lump sum payment in view of the possibility that the husband's farming partnership would be dissolved, thereby releasing capital. Ackner LJ (at p. 501) said:

"Bearing in mind that it is a once-for-all application, it seems to me that the judge in that sort of situation was perfectly entitled, having resolved that there was no valid basis for an immediate order for a lump sum payment, to adjourn the application in order to see whether the event that he thought might well occur fairly soon, did in fact occur. That is not the same position as if the judge, anxious to preserve the wife's entitlement, should order an adjournment merely because the future might in some way or another throw up a possible fund of capital, in regard to which the wife could make an application. It would not, in my judgment, be proper for him in this case to have said for example:

'Well, the husband, true, is 48 years of age and has an expectation of life of perhaps another thirty years, but we all know that accidents can occur in farming and, if there was a fatal accident, there might well be an asset of value which the wife could ask to be considered in an application for a lump sum payment ...'

or make some other attempt to provide for a vague contingency in order to keep open the wife's application.

This is not such a case. It seems to me to be closely analogous to the *Morris* case, where there was no capital locked in, as in this case, but there was capital which was very likely to become available for consideration within a matter of two or three years."

In contrast, the period involved before the sum fell due in *Milne* v *Milne* (1981) 2 FLR 286 was some ten years, and an adjournment was held to be inappropriate. As already noted the court in that case made a contingent lump sum order. In *Roberts* v *Roberts* [1986] 1 WLR 437 where such a course was not open to the court in view of the provisions of the Army Act, it would be at least six years, and might even be much longer, before the husband would be likely to receive the gratuity. An adjournment was held to be inappropriate and, as there was no other capital out of which a lump sum might be ordered, the wife's application was dismissed. Wood J (at p. 442) commenting on *Milne* v *Milne* said that the longest period that the Court of Appeal seemed to have in mind was some four to five years and that in his view that was about the longest period that would be appropriate.

It must also be borne in mind that neither a contingent lump sum order nor an adjournment is open to the court unless the prospective asset falls within s.25(2)(a) as being property which a party to the marriage is likely to have in the foreseeable future. Thus in *Michael* v *Michael* [1986] 2 FLR 389 the Court of Appeal concluded that it could not be said that there was any real possibility of the wife inheriting from her mother an interest in the property in which she lived. The judge should, therefore, have dismissed the husband's application rather than adjourn it.

Where there is a real possibility that a party will receive capital assets at some time in the future it may be appropriate to consider the advice of the Court of Appeal in *Hardy* v *Hardy* (1981) 2 FLR 286 and not make an immediate application for a lump sum payment. However, the disadvantage of this course of action is that (1) it may be necessary to obtain leave to make the application, (2) the merits may be more debatable especially if a large part of the assets will have been built up after the breakdown of the marriage, and (3) the right to apply will be lost on remarriage. (See the interpretation of *Hardy* by Nourse LJ in *Michael* v *Michael* [1986] 2 FLR 389 at pp. 395-396.)

An attempt to create a lump sum payable at a future date, namely the husband's retirement, failed in *Milne* v *Milne* (1981) 1 FLR 286 where it was held that the court could not order one party to take out, keep up, and assign the benefit of a life assurance policy to the other.

## 3. Property adjustment orders

*(a) The court's powers*

Under s.24 of the Matrimonial Causes Act 1973 the court may make one or more of the following property adjustment orders:

(a) an order that a party to the marriage shall transfer to the other party, to any child of the family or to such persons as may be specified in the order for the benefit of such a child such property as may be so specified to which the party first mentioned is entitled either in possession or reversion;

(b) an order that a settlement of such property as may be so specified being property to which a party to the marriage is so entitled, be made to the satisfaction of the court for the benefit of the other party to the marriage and of the children of the family or either or any of them;

(c) an order varying for the benefit of the parties to the marriage and of the children of the family or either or any of them any ante-nuptial or post-nuptial settlement (including such a settlement made by will or codicil) made on the parties to the marriage;

(d) an order extinguishing or reducing the interest of either of the parties to the marriage under such a settlement.

The court may make an order varying a settlement under (c) notwithstanding that there are no children of the family. The power to make an order under (d) is designed to make it clear that the court has power to extinguish the interest of a spouse under any ante-nuptial or post-nuptial settlement notwithstanding that this does not benefit the other spouse or children.

There are restrictions on the making of a transfer of property order in favour of a child who has attained the age of 18 (see s.29(1) and Chapter 17).

Where a court decides to make one or more of the above orders it may direct that the matter be referred to one or more of the conveyancing counsel of the court for him to settle a proper instrument to be executed by all necessary parties. If it thinks fit, the court may defer the grant of the decree in question until the instrument has been duly executed (s.30).

*(b) Property*

On an application by a spouse under s.24 for a transfer of property order it is fundamental that the judge should know over what property he is entitled to exercise his discretion. Accordingly, if there is a dispute between the respondent spouse and a third party as to the ownership of a particular item of property which stands in the respondent's name, that dispute must be resolved before the judge can make an effective final order under s.24. There are two ways of resolving the dispute. First, the application under s.24 may be adjourned pending the trial of the claim in other proceedings. Secondly, the third party can be allowed to intervene in the proceedings under s.24 when the court has jurisdiction to determine not only the rights and interests of the spouses in the property, but also the rights and interests of the third party (*Tebbutt* v *Haynes* [1981] 2 All ER 238). In *Harwood* v *Harwood* [1991] 2 FLR 274, where the partnership of which the husband had been a member had an interest in the matrimonial home, the Court of Appeal rejected an adjournment not only because of the further expense and delay involved, but also because the court considered it was in a position to adjudicate on the beneficial ownership of the house to the extent necessary to deal with the wife's application for ancillary relief.

The court only has power to order a transfer of existing property (*Banyard* v *Banyard* (1984) 5 FLR 643). Thus where a home is subject to a mortgage, it can order one party to transfer his or her interest in the equity of the home, but it cannot order that the property be transferred to the other spouse free from incumbrances. The only way in which provision can be made for repayment of the mortgage in the future is by means of an order for payment of a lump sum (see *Banyard* v *Banyard*).

The court can only make an order in respect of property in which, or in the proceeds of sale of which, either or both of the parties to the marriage has or have a beneficial interest. Thus while it can make an order in respect of shares owned by a spouse in his or her own right, it cannot make an order for the transfer of the assets of a company in which a spouse has shares or an order which will have have the effect of forcing the company to sell assets vested in it. However, in *Nicholas* v *Nicholas* [1984] FLR 285 the Court of Appeal took the view that where the shareholding is such that the minority interests can for practical purposes be disregarded, the court can pierce the corporate veil and make an order which has the same effect as an order that would be made if the property was vested in the majority shareholder. In that case the house in which the wife was living was vested in a company in which the husband had a majority holding, but it was clear that the minority interests, amounting to some 29 per cent of the shares, were real interests that could not be disregarded. It was not, therefore, possible to make an order which would have the effect of forcing the company to sell the house to the wife who would have the necessary funds through a lump sum payment from the husband.

A contractual weekly tenancy is "property" for the purposes of s.24(1)(a) and the court may order the transfer of such a tenancy if the tenant is free himself to transfer it (*Hale* v *Hale* [1975] 1 WLR 931). The position is the same where the tenancy has been granted by a local authority (*Thompson* v *Thompson* [1976] Fam 25. See further Chapter 7).

### (c) Ante- and post-nuptial settlements

(i) The scope of the powers
The powers of the court to make orders under s.24(1)(c) and (d) can only be exercised in relation to an "ante-nuptial" or "post-nuptial" settlement, an expression on which the Law Commission felt unable to improve, though in accordance with its recommendation it is now made clear that the expression includes settlements made by will as well as *inter vivos* settlements (Law Com. No. 25, para. 66). The Law Commission considered that the existing expression was "familiar to lawyers and the courts, hallowed by long usage and, in meaning, now reasonably definite; to change it would be likely to do more harm than good." (*Ibid.*) Nevertheless, the exact scope of the expression has caused difficulty in the past, due in some measure to the liberal interpretation frequently adopted to overcome the court's lack of general power to adjust property rights on the termination of a marriage. In view of the court's present power to transfer property it is now unnecessary to resort to the powers of variation as often as in the past. But see *B* v *B* (1993) The Times 5 May.

To constitute an "ante-nuptial or post-nuptial settlement" two conditions must be satisfied. First, there must be a "settlement", and secondly, the settlement must have the requisite nuptial element.

(ii) There must be a settlement
A settlement in the traditional form familiar to conveyancers is clearly within the scope of these provisions, provided that the requisite nuptial element is present. It does not matter whether it was created by one spouse or by both spouses or by some third person for the benefit of one or both of them. The courts have, however, given the term "settlement" a much wider meaning in this context. It has been held to comprise a variety of other documents by which provision is made for one or both spouses. The test to be applied was indicated by Hill J in *Prinsep* v *Prinsep* [1926] P 225 at p. 232:

> "Is it upon the husband in the character of husband or on the wife in the character of wife, or upon both in the character of husband and wife? If it is, it is a settlement on the parties within the meaning of the section. The particular form of it does not matter. It may be a settlement in the strictest sense of the term, it may be a covenant to pay by one spouse to the other, or by a third person to a spouse. What does matter is that it should provide for the financial benefit of one or other of the spouses as spouses and with reference to their married state."

A settlement has been held to include:
(a) a covenant by one spouse to pay a yearly sum to the other (*Dormer* v *Ward* [1901] P 157; *Bosworthick* v *Bosworthick* [1927] P 64);
(b) a separation agreement (*Tomkins* v *Tomkins* [1948] 1 All ER 237; *Jeffrey* v *Jeffrey (No.2)* [1952] P 122);

(c) an insurance policy effected by one spouse under which the other spouse obtains an interest (*Gulbenkian* v *Gulbenkian* [1927] P 237; *Gunner* v *Gunner and Stirling* [1948] 2 All ER 771; *Bown* v *Bown* [1948] 2 All ER 778);

(d) a conveyance of the matrimonial home to a husband and wife whether as joint tenants or as tenants in common (*Brown* v *Brown* [1959] P 86; *Ulrich* v *Ulrich and Fenton* [1968] 1 WLR 180; *Meldrum* v *Meldrum* [1970] 3 All ER 1084).

It has also been held that a settlement in this context may come into existence orally or may arise by operation of law. (See *Cook* v *Cook* [1962] P 235 where the matrimonial home had been conveyed into the husband's name though both spouses had contributed to its acquisition.)

On the other hand, not all dispositions made by one spouse in favour of the other, or by a third party in favour of a spouse, can be regarded as a settlement, but the distinction which must be drawn is not between a gift and a settlement, for a settlement is normally in the nature of a gift even if made in consideration of marriage (*Prescott* v *Fellowes* [1958] P 260). The distinction is between a disposition which takes the form of an absolute, unqualified and immediate transfer of property on the one hand, and a disposition which makes provision for one or both spouses without making an absolute, unqualified and immediate transfer of the property affected to either or both of them on the other hand. In the latter case the property has been settled so as to make provision for one or both of the spouses, and it is therefore appropriate for the court to consider whether that provision should continue in view of the dissolution of the marriage. In the former case the property has simply been transferred or "given" to the spouse so that it has become the absolute property of that spouse and if it is to be reconsidered on termination of the marriage it can only be on the basis that it has become the absolute property of the beneficiary. In practical terms the distinction is now of less importance in view of the court's power to order a transfer or settlement of property, but it will still be necessary for the court to decide the appropriate form of order.

(iii) The requisite "nuptial" element must be present

The settlement must have been made "in contemplation of or because of marriage and with reference to the interests of married people or their children" (*per* Hill J in *Hargreaves* v *Hargreaves* [1926] P 42 at p. 45). In the case of an ante-nuptial settlement it is essential that it was made in contemplation of the particular marriage which is the subject of the decree. The powers to vary do not apply to settlements made before marriage without reference to any particular marriage (*Hargreaves* v *Hargreaves*; *Burnett* v *Burnett* [1936] P 1). Where a settlement is made after a marriage there will generally be little difficulty in showing that it was made in relation to that marriage. Indeed, it has been said that a court "would have great difficulty in saying that any deed which is a settlement of property made after marriage, and on the parties to the marriage, is not a post-nuptial settlement" (*per* the Judge Ordinary in *Worsley* v *Worsley* (1869) LR 1 P & D 648 at p. 651).

It is, however, essential that a settlement made after marriage is made on the basis that the marriage is to continue. If it is made only on the basis that the marriage is to be dissolved or annulled then it is not a post-nuptial settlement. (See *Young* v *Young* [1962] P 27. Contrast *Melvill* v *Melvill* [1930] P 159.)

## 4. Orders for the sale of property

*(a) The power to order a sale*
The extensive powers of the court under the Matrimonial Causes Act 1973 did not include an express power to order a sale of property. Such a power is now to be found in s.24A which was inserted into the 1973 Act by the Matrimonial Homes and Property Act 1981 (s.7. See Law Com. No. 99, *Orders for the sale of property under the Matrimonial Causes Act 1973* for the background). The power is exercisable where the court makes, under s.23 or s.24 of the Act, (a) a secured periodical payments order, (b) an order for the payment of a lump sum, or (c) a property adjustment order. On making any such order, or at any time thereafter, the court may make a further order for the sale of such property as may be specified in the order being property in which, or in the proceeds of sale of which, either or both of the parties to the marriage has or have a beneficial interest, either in possession or reversion. Thus the power enables the court to order a sale of property in which the applicant had, as a matter of property law, no claim to a beneficial interest. (Contrast s.17 Married Women's Property Act 1882 and s.30 Law of Property Act 1925.) It is available whenever the court makes an order which involves capital assets, but its usefulness will no doubt mostly be in connection with orders for payment of lump sums (Law Com. No. 99, paras. 8-12).

*(b) Consequential and supplementary provisions*
An order for sale under s.24A(1) may contain such consequential or supplementary provisions as the court thinks fit. In particular it may include (a) a provision requiring the making of a payment out of the proceeds of sale of the property to which the order relates, and (b) a provision requiring any such property to be offered for sale to a person, or class of persons, specified in the order (subs.(2)).

This does not confer a jurisdiction upon the court to make orders for payments to creditors unconnected with an interest in the property which is the subject matter of the order (*per* Butler-Sloss J in *Burton* v *Burton* [1986] 2 FLR 419 at p. 423. In particular it does not overrule *Mullard* v *Mullard* (1982) 3 FLR 330). An order may contain directions relating to the method of sale, costs of sale and payments to third parties having a beneficial interest in the property. While the court may not order that certain debts, unconnected with the property, be paid out of the proceeds of sale, it may be possible to achieve this objective by the use of undertakings or phrases such as "on the basis of" or "it being agreed that", or such other similar way of expressing the intention of the basis upon which the order is to be made. However, it was pointed out by Butler-Sloss J in *Burton* v *Burton* that there are dangers of injustice in attempts to exercise "a bankruptcy type of jurisdiction by the back door" if it is done without proper disclosure by both parties of the debts of the family.

The Law Commission envisaged that a provision such as that described above in (b) might be useful where, for example, the property available for transfer is the husband's shareholding in his family company and, though it might be appropriate that the wife should have the benefit of the value of the shareholding, it was highly undesirable that she should be able to exercise the voting rights which she would have if the shares were transferred to her and she was permitted to retain them. In such a case the court can order the husband to transfer his shareholding (or part of it) to the wife, but also order that the holding be sold. In effect the court would have the power to order the transfer of the proceeds of sale. Moreover, the court could also require the shares to be offered to a specified person, or class of persons such as the family of the husband (Law Com. No. 99, para. 9).

In *Crosthwaite* v *Crosthwaite* [1989] 2 FLR 86 it was held that the subsection does not enable a court to make a possession order against a wife who is in possession of the matrimonial home and who has an equitable interest in that property, even though such an order was a means of enabling the husband to effect a sale with vacant possession with a view to a division of the proceeds between the spouses. An appropriate way of proceeding would have been to have made an order requiring the wife to transfer her interest in the property to the husband, thereby enabling him as sole owner to obtain possession.

*(c) Effect of an order for sale*

Where an order for sale is made on or after the grant of a decree of divorce or nullity, the order will not take effect unless the decree has been made absolute (s.24A(3)). The court may also direct that the order, or such provision thereof as the court may specify, shall not take effect until the occurrence of an event specified by the court or the expiration of a specified period (s.24A(4)). Where an order for sale contains a provision requiring the proceeds of sale of the property to which it relates to be used to secure periodical payments to a party to the marriage, the order ceases to have effect on the death or remarriage of that person (s.24A(5)). An order may also be varied or discharged under s.31 of the Matrimonial Causes Act 1973.

Where the court has made an order conferring rights of occupation on a party to a marriage so as to create a settlement of property within s.24(1)(b), the court has jurisdiction to hear an application for sale under s.24A even though this determines the rights of occupation. Thus where the court has made a Mesher order postponing sale until certain specified events or "further order", the court does have power to order an early sale. However, the power to order a sale under s.24A is ancillary to orders under ss.23 and 24 and is not a power to vary such orders. Accordingly, an order for sale must be a "working out" of the original order for a settlement rather than a variation of it. This was the case in *Thompson* v *Thompson* [1986] Fam 38 where it was the wife, who was in actual occupation of the home subject to a Mesher order, who desired a sale as she wished to move to another area during the period of postponement though neither contingency triggering a sale under the original order had occurred. (The husband appears to have been opposed to a sale because the wife's move to another area would result in a change in the children's schooling arrangements and affect the practicability of his having regular access to them. Mesher orders are considered in Chapter 12.) On the other hand, an application by a husband, not in occupation of the property, at a time when the property was still required by the wife and children as a residence, merely for the purpose of obtaining an early realisation of his share would be regarded as tantamount to an application to vary. (See *Taylor* v *Taylor* [1987] 1 FLR 142 where the matter was remitted to the county court to be considered afresh. See also *Norman* v *Norman*

[1983] 1 WLR 295.) Thus the discretion of the court to order a sale under s.24A "will not be exercised if the consequences would be to displace vested rights - that is to say, rights vested under the order previously made" (*ibid. per* Ralph Gibson LJ at p. 147).

One disadvantage of an order for sale under s.24A as compared with a property adjustment order was highlighted in *R* v *Rushmoor Borough Council, ex p. Barrett* [1988] 2 All ER 268. Thus where a matrimonial home was purchased at a discount from the local authority in exercise of the "right to buy" granted to council tenants by the Housing Act 1985, the local authority will generally be entitled to payment of the discount or a proportion thereof if the property is disposed of within three years (formerly five years) of the purchase. A disposition of the home in pursuance of a property adjustment order under s.24 will be exempt from this requirement (Housing Act 1985, s.160) but the exemption does not apply where a sale is ordered under s.24A.

*(d) Factors to be taken into account*
In deciding whether or not to exercise the power to order a sale the court must have regard to the matters specified in s.25 of the Act of 1973. Where some third party has a beneficial interest in the property concerned, then before deciding whether or not to make an order for sale, the court must give that third party an opportunity to make representations (see, for example, *Levermore* v *Levermore* [1979] 1 WLR 1277). Any representations made by that third party are included among the circumstances to which the court is required to have regard (s.25(4)). The problems which might thus arise would be similar to those arising in applications under s.30 of the Law of Property Act 1925. (See Law Com. No. 99, para. 15. See Chapter 6 for a consideration of s.30.) The Law Commission emphasised that the fact that the court would have power, if need be, to order a sale should not affect the general principle that a party ordered to provide capital should be permitted to make his own proposals as to the methods by which it is to be provided (see *O'D* v *O'D* [1970] Fam 83 *per* Ormrod LJ at p. 92). If a party did consider that the discretion to order a sale had been exercised unnecessarily or inappropriately in the light of the statutory guidelines an appeal would lie in the usual way (Law Com. No. 99, para. 13).

## 5. Applications

*(a) Time and manner of applications*
An application for a financial provision order or a property adjustment order by a petitioner or by a respondent who files an answer claiming relief should be made in the petition or the answer as the case may be. An application may subsequently be made only by leave of the court unless the parties are agreed upon the terms of the proposed order (Matrimonial Causes Act 1973, s.26; Family Proceedings Rules 1991, r. 2.53). A petitioner or respondent who intends to proceed with an application made in the petition or the answer as the case may be, must in due course give notice of his intention to do so (FPR 1991, r. 2.58; Form 13). Where no application

has been included in the petition or answer, then, after leave of the court has been obtained where necessary, application may be made by notice or at the trial (*ibid.* r. 2.53; Form 11). Where a respondent has not filed an answer, or an answer claiming relief, the proper procedure is to give notice of intention to apply, and this is also the case where application in respect of a child of the family is to be made by some person or body other than a spouse (*ibid.* r .2.54; Form 11).

The powers of the court to make property adjustment orders introduced by the Matrimonial Proceedings and Property Act 1970 as from 1 January 1971 are retrospective in the sense that applications for such orders can be made in cases where a decree was pronounced before that date when such applications could not have been made (*Williams* v *Williams* [1971] P 271). In such cases it will be necessary to obtain leave of the court and this provides "an effective brake on, or filter for applications in such cases" (*per* Brandon J in *Powys* v *Powys* [1971] P 340 at p. 351).

The broad intention of the requirement that leave of the court must be obtained to make an application which should have been made in the petition or answer is clear. It is intended to protect a party from being unjustly harassed or put to expense in resisting claims for financial or other provision put forward long after the divorce and the consequent financial arrangements have been apparently settled, and to enable the court to hold the balance of justice between the parties (*per* Ormrod LJ in *Chaterjee* v *Chaterjee* [1976] Fam 199 at p. 207). However, to secure the right to apply for ancillary relief of all kinds, at any time, it is only necessary to include appropriate words in the petition or answer, if any, e.g. a reference to financial provision and/or a property adjustment order. (This would be crucial if the applicant has remarried. But see the note of caution by Dunn LJ in *Hardy* v *Hardy* (1981) 2 FLR 321.) No time limits are prescribed, so a party whose pleading is in order is free to activate an application at any time, whereas a party whose pleading is defective requires leave to apply at all times. Moreover, a party who allows the suit to go through undefended is free of constraint at all times though delay in making an application may affect the likelihood of an order being made or the extent of any provision ordered. (See *Pearce* v *Pearce* (1981) 1 FLR 261; *Fraser* v *Fraser* (1982) 3 FLR 98.)

In the light of this, the Court of Appeal in *Chaterjee* v *Chaterjee* [1976] Fam 199 held that the court ought not to refuse leave to apply in any case in which on the evidence the applicant has or appears to have reasonable prospects of obtaining the relief claimed, i.e. has a seriously arguable case. It will not be enough to demonstrate that on the one-third yardstick the applicant can make a case on the figures. To assess the prospects of success all the facts referred to in s.25 of the 1973 Act, including, in particular, practicability and conduct, in the sense of the way in which the parties have conducted themselves and their affairs up to the time of the application, must be considered. Delay which prejudices the other party and any conduct which has the effect of "lulling" the other party into the belief that all claims have already been dealt with are important considerations. Similarly it may be unjust to interfere with property rights after a lapse of time during which the other party has ordered his or her affairs in a reasonable or proper manner in the belief that the financial consequences of the divorce have been settled (*ibid. per* Ormrod LJ at p. 208). Thus in *Marsden* v *Marsden* [1973] 1 WLR 620 a husband was refused leave to apply for a transfer of property order or a variation of settlement order since he had given no reasonable excuse or explanation for the absence of such applications in the petition, and there was no prospect that the order would be made. The husband's silence as to his intentions had resulted in the wife failing to make any application for a property adjustment order before she remarried. Thereafter, no application by her was possible by virtue of s.28(3), and she had also acted to her detriment in other respects. (See also *McKay* v *Chapman* [1978] 1 WLR 620 where a wife was refused leave to apply for a lump sum payment for the children.) In *Chaterjee* v *Chaterjee*, on the other hand, leave was granted. The facts were in one sense exceptional in that the parties had lived together for 12 or 13 years after the divorce and their only child was born during that period. However, there had been no delay in any relevant sense in seeking to make the application and the parties had not concluded their affairs in any meaningful sense. (See also *S* v *S* [1973] The Times 4 December.)

This was followed in *Pearce* v *Pearce* (1981) 1 FLR 261 where the parties had been divorced in 1969. At the time the husband had been an undischarged bankrupt and only a nominal order for periodical payments was possible. In 1978, following his discharge from bankruptcy, he inherited his father's house and some £15,000 in cash. The Court of Appeal held that the wife, who had struggled to bring up three children on social security without any contribution from the husband, had a strong case which outweighed the lapse of time.

In *Twiname* v *Twiname* [1992] 1 FLR 29 at p. 38 Purchas LJ said that "there is no mandate for the court arbitrarily to restrict the wide ambit of discretion given by Parliament to the court to deal with these cases, even if there are long periods of delay". At the time of the hearing of the case the husband was aged 73 and the wife aged 70. The marriage had broken down in 1967 and had been dissolved in 1971 when the wife had obtained an order for periodical payments. In 1989, on hearing that the husband's business had been sold for a very substantial amount she sought a lump sum payment. Emphasising that the court was at that stage concerned only with jurisdiction, Purchas LJ said that the purpose of the legislation was furthered by retaining in the hands of the court unlimited discretion. Thus the court hearing the substantive application could take into account all the circumstances of the case and exercise its discretion in the light of the very considerable delay. In addition, instead of increasing the periodical payments it would be open to the court on hearing the application to achieve a clean break by means of a lump sum payment.

In view of the express prohibition in s.31(5) on the making of a lump sum order or a transfer of property order on the application to vary an order for periodical payments or an order for secured provision, it has been said that the court will not allow the declared policy of the Acts of 1970 and 1973 to be undermined or outflanked by making a lump sum order or a transfer of property order on an original application made many years after an order for periodical payments or secured provision (*per* Brandon J in *Powys* v *Powys* [1971] P 340 at p. 355). However, in *Chaterjee* v *Chaterjee* [1976] Fam 199 at p. 207 Ormrod LJ did not think that the discretion of the court should be circumscribed in this way, not only because the subsection is limited to applications to vary when it could very easily have been made to refer to fresh applications if that was the intention, but also because the Law Commission itself envisaged that original and fresh applications for lump sums might be made (Law Com. No. 25, *Report on Financial Provision in Matrimonial Proceedings*, para. 90). Nevertheless, in considering whether leave should be granted, he suggested that it was probably wise to draw a distinction between cases which involve retroactive use of the powers in the 1973 Act and those in which the decree was granted after the new legislation came into force. This was not so much because there is a difference in principle between the two classes, but because the factors to be taken into account may have to be weighed differently if justice is to be done to both parties.

### (b) Applicants

An application for ancillary relief can be made by either spouse and is not restricted to a spouse seeking the benefit of the ancillary relief. The court has jurisdiction to hear the application of a husband who genuinely and for good reason wishes to obtain an order against himself. In *Simister* v *Simister* [1986] 1 WLR 1463 at p. 1467 Waite J said that such a spouse may not indeed be such a maverick figure as at first sight appears. There may be sound fiscal reasons for the order sought (though the significance of this has been reduced as a result of the changes made in the Finance Act 1988 (see Chapter 18)), or there may be family reasons, such as the fact that the maintained spouse is under a disability. In *Simister* the circumstances were quite unusual. Under a maintenance agreement the husband was liable to pay the wife a sum equivalent to one-third of his income from all sources however derived and regardless of any income to which the wife herself might become entitled. The husband's earnings had increased dramatically as a result of changes of employment. His liability was expressed to continue until the death or remarriage of the wife or the making of a court order against him in favour of the wife. An order in his favour therefore replaced his liability under the agreement.

### (c) The effect of remarriage

If after the grant of a decree dissolving or annulling a marriage either party to that marriage remarries, that party is not entitled to apply, by reference to the grant of that decree, for a financial provision order in his or her favour, or for a property adjustment order against the other party (MCA 1973, s.28(3)). An application is made for this purpose when it is initiated and not when it is heard. Accordingly where, as will usually be the case, an application is made in the petition or answer, the court will have jurisdiction even though it is not heard before the applicant remarries after decree absolute (*Jackson* v *Jackson* [1973] Fam 99). A respondent's affirmative replies to questions relating to ancillary relief in the Acknowledgment of Service have been held to be merely an indication of an intention to apply for such relief at a future date and not an application for ancillary relief in substance or in form (*Hargood* v *Jenkins* [1978] Fam 148). If a wife has never made an application on her own behalf, she cannot make such an application after her remarriage simply because she has previously made an application on behalf of the children (*Nixon* v *Fox* [1978] Fam 173). However, if she has made an application under one section for one kind of provision, she may be entitled if there has been an oversight, to amend her application so as to bring it within another section allowing another kind of provision. Thus in *Doherty* v *Doherty* [1976] Fam 71 the wife had, before her remarriage, applied for a transfer of property order and for periodical payments, but not for a lump sum. The Court of Appeal held that the original notice of application seeking a transfer of property order in respect of the matrimonial home was sufficient to include an order in respect of the proceeds of sale of the matrimonial home out of which a lump sum could be paid. It was pointed out that there was no question of the husband having been misled, and from the beginning everybody concerned knew that what the wife was seeking was her share in the former matrimonial home in the form of a cash payment. (Compare *Wilson* v *Wilson* [1976] Fam 142.)

The courts have stressed on a number of occasions the importance of ensuring that all necessary applications for ancillary relief in the form of lump sum orders and property adjustment orders have been made before a party remarries (*Doherty* v *Doherty*; *Hargood* v *Jenkins* [1978] Fam 148 at p. 156; *Fielding* v *Fielding* [1977] 1 WLR 1146). The practice has developed of making an application for ancillary relief in the form of an omnibus claim for periodical payments, a lump sum payment and property adjustment. While this might be generally convenient and advisable it was suggested by Ormrod LJ in *Hardy* v *Hardy* (1981) 2 FLR 321 at pp. 326-327 that in some cases more discrimination is advisable. Thus in that case it might have been reasonable for the wife to have limited her claim to periodical payments as there was no immediate prospect of a lump sum payment. This would have enabled the wife to apply for a lump sum payment when the husband's means justified it rather than risk dismissal of the application at that stage. Once an application for a lump sum had been dismissed there could be no further application. If a long period elapsed before an application was made for a lump sum order she might, in addition to seeking leave where appropriate, have to meet the argument that the situation had entirely changed and her husband's then successful and affluent position would have nothing to do with her. (But see *Pearce* v *Pearce* (1981) 1 FLR 261.) Such an application would, of course, have had to be made before remarriage.

*(d) Death of an applicant*

Where one of the parties to a divorce suit dies, there is no general rule that the suit abates. Whether further proceedings in the suit can or cannot be taken depends first on the nature of the proceedings sought to be taken and, secondly, on the true construction of the relevant statutory provision or provisions, or of a particular order made under them, or both. It may also depend on the applicability of s.1(1) of the Law Reform (Miscellaneous Provisions) Act 1934 (*per* Lord Brandon in *Barder* v *Caluori* [1988] AC 20 at p. 37).

Thus in *Barder* v *Caluori* the House of Lords held that the jurisdiction of a judge to entertain an appeal out of time by one party to a divorce suit against an order or decision made or given by a registrar did not lapse on the death of the other party. Lord Brandon said (at p. 38) that "the purpose of the statutory right of appeal is to enable decisions of a county court which are unjust to be set aside or varied by the Court of Appeal. The fulfilment of that purpose is not made any the less necessary or desirable by the death of one of the parties to the cause in which the decision was made." In that case the order concerned was a transfer of property order relating to the former matrimonial home. Lord Brandon also doubted the view expressed by Ormrod LJ in *Purse* v *Purse* [1981] Fam 143 that there could be no appeal against an order for periodical payments after the death of one party. He said (at p. 38) that "If the order was unjust over the period during which it operated, in that it required the party paying under it to pay more than it was just to make him pay", then his provisional view was "that subject to any question of leave to appeal out of time, an appeal would lie". However, it was not necessary to decide any such question and he expressed no conclusive opinion on it.

On the other hand, it has been held that where an applicant dies before an application for a property adjustment order has been heard, the court has no jurisdiction to entertain an application which the deceased's representatives seek to continue (*D'Este* v *D'Este* [1973] Fam 55). The same seems to apply where the respondent to an application for a property adjustment order dies before the application is heard. The representatives of the deceased spouse may seek to establish that the deceased was entitled to a beneficial interest in property vested in the other spouse. (See Chapter 2 and *Re Cummins* [1972] Ch 62.)

*(e) Protection of applications*
An application of a spouse for a property adjustment order should be protected by registration as a pending land action (Land Charges Act 1925, s.5. It is, of course, also possible under the Matrimonial Homes Act 1983 to protect statutory rights of occupation in property which has been the matrimonial home and which is vested in the name of the other spouse alone by registration of a class F land charge or entry of the appropriate notice on the register if the title is registered). In *Perez-Adamson* v *Perez-Rivas* [1987] Fam 89 the Court of Appeal held that it was not necessary for the petition to particularise the property that might be affected by the application, and it was sufficient for the petition to make a general claim to a property adjustment order in respect of any property the respondent husband might own. Particularisation of the property, however, is necessary for the protection of those dealing with the owner of the property and it is sufficient if there is registration in respect of a particular property. It does not matter that the applicant has no existing proprietary right in the property until the property adjustment order is made (*Whittingham* v *Whittingham* [1979] Fam 9).

Where the applicant spouse has protected his or her application by registration it will have priority over all other subsequent conveyances or mortgages executed by the respondent in respect of the property. (In the case of unregistered land, registration constitutes actual notice of the proceedings to all persons and for all purposes connected with the land affected: s.198(1) Law of Property Act 1925, *per* Nicholls LJ in *Perez-Adamson* v *Perez-Rivas* [1988] Fam 89 at p. 97.) Thus in *Perez-Adamson* v *Perez-Rivas* the mortgage executed by the husband in favour of a bank after the wife had protected her application by registration was set aside, and an order transferring the proceeds of sale of the mortgaged property to the wife was upheld by the Court of Appeal. Where an applicant has failed to protect the application by registration, the application will not be binding on a subsequent purchaser or mortgagee. The applicant is then "placed in the unenviable position of having to establish that a transaction which subsequently takes place by way of sale or mortgage is a reviewable disposition within s.37 involving litigation in which the good faith of the purchaser or mortgagee and the question of whether he had notice of the wife's intention fall to be considered" (*per* Stamp LJ in *Whittingham* v *Whittingham* [1979] Fam 9 at p. 21). It may, of course, be possible to assert a claim to a beneficial interest in the property which may bind a third party if it is, for example, an overriding interest. (See Chapter 3.)

## 6. Commencement of orders

A financial provision order or a property adjustment order in favour of a spouse cannot be made unless a decree nisi of divorce or of nullity or a decree of judicial separation, as the case may be, has been granted. Moreover, no such order made on or after the granting of a decree nisi of divorce or of nullity can take effect unless the decree has been made absolute (ss.23(5) and 24(3)). A spouse must rely on maintenance pending suit, or a matrimonial order made by a magistrates' court, up until the date of decree absolute in the case of divorce or nullity or until the date of a decree of judicial separation. If the proceedings for divorce, nullity or judicial separation are dismissed, no order can be made in favour of a spouse.

In contrast, a financial provision order for the benefit of a child of the family may be made and may become effective before or on granting a decree or at any time thereafter (s.23(2)). Moreover, where proceedings for divorce, nullity or judicial separation are dismissed after the beginning of the trial, the court may nevertheless make a financial provision order for the benefit of a child, either forthwith, or within a reasonable period after the dismissal (*ibid.* See further *P.(JM.)* v *P.(L.E.)* [1971] P 217). These provisions do not apply to property adjustment orders for the benefit of a child which can be made only on or after the granting of a decree, and which will only take effect in proceedings for divorce or nullity, on decree absolute. (See Chapter 17, Part 2.)

## 7. Duration of continuing financial provision orders

The term specified in an order for secured or unsecured periodical payments in favour of a party to a marriage may begin not earlier than the date of the making of the application for an order (MCA 1973, s.28(1)). The application will generally have been made in the petition or answer so that in appropriate cases the court may back-date payments, and if it thinks that payments pending suit have been inadequate, the deficiency may thus be remedied. (See Chapter 9.)

An order for periodical payments in favour of a party to a marriage cannot extend beyond the death of either of the parties to the marriage, but an order for secured periodical payments may extend for the life of the party in whose favour it is made. However, where either form of order is made in proceedings for divorce or nullity the term must come to an end on the remarriage of the party in whose favour the order is made (s.28(1)). Where either form of order is made in favour of a party to a marriage in proceedings for judicial separation or in proceedings under s.27 of the Matrimonial Causes Act 1973, and the marriage in question is subsequently dissolved or annulled but the order continues in force, the order will, notwithstanding anything in it, cease to have effect on the remarriage of that party, except in relation to arrears due under it on the date of the remarriage (s.28(2)). It is also provided for the avoidance of doubt that references to "remarriage" include a marriage which is by law void or voidable (s.52(3)).

It has already been noted above that the court may make an order for periodical payments for a limited term. At the end of that term the order will automatically cease to have effect unless the term is extended by the court exercising the power of variation conferred by s.31 (see below). No such extension can be made if the court on making the original order for periodical payments gave a direction under s.28(1A) directing that no application for such an extension could be made. (See Part 2(b) above.)

The limitations relating to financial provision orders and transfer of property orders in favour of children of the family are considered in Chapter 17.

## 8. Variation

### (a) The powers of the court

(i) Periodical payments

Where a court has made an order for periodical payments or secured periodical payments, it has power to vary or discharge the order or to suspend any provision thereof temporarily and to revive the operation of any provision so suspended (MCA 1973, s.31(1) and (2)). This applies also to orders for maintenance pending suit and interim orders for maintenance made under s.27 of the Matrimonial Causes Act 1973 (see Chapter 16 for s.27). These powers apply also in relation to any instrument executed in pursuance of an order for secured periodical payments (s.31(3)). Where the court makes an order in exercise of such powers it may also remit the payment of any arrears due under the order or any part thereof (s.31(2A). See Chapter 22).

Thus the court can clearly increase or decrease the amount of the periodical payments and in the latter case it may reduce the sum payable to a nominal amount. In the case of an existing order for a nominal amount it may increase the amount payable to such sum as it considers appropriate.

Where the existing order provides for payment to be made for a limited term only, then the court can, in general, vary the order by extending the term for which payments are to be made. Such an application must be made before the expiry of the limited term. This will not, of course, be possible where the court which made the order also exercised its power under s.28(1A) to direct that the recipient of the payments shall not be entitled to apply under s.31 for an extension of the term specified in the order.

Where the existing order is unlimited as to time, the court may discharge the order immediately or it may direct that the variation or discharge of the order shall not take effect until the expiration of such period as may be specified in the order of variation or discharge (s.31(10)). This enables the court to continue an order, or to continue an order at a certain level, for a limited term so as to provide an opportunity for the recipient to adjust and become financially independent or at least less dependent. *(Quaere:* where it provides for the discharge of an order at the end of the fixed term, can it also make a direction under s.28(1A)?) In other words, on an application under s.31 the court may impose an "immediate clean break" or a "deferred clean break".

The court may vary an order for periodical payments retrospectively to a date before the date of the application for variation (*McDonald* v *McDonald* [1964] P 1; *Morley-Clarke* v *Jones* [1986] Ch 311). Indeed the variation may extend back to the original order and may include the substitution of a new payee. However, such retrospective variation can have no effect on the tax consequences of payments made before the date of the variation in accordance with the terms of the order as it originally stood (*Morley-Clarke* v *Jones*. This is now less important in view of the changes made by the Finance Act 1988: see Chapter 18). A variation may be backdated even though the practical effect is to remit arrears outstanding under the previous order, i.e. by virtue of a reduction in the amount of the previous order (*McDonald* v *McDonald*). The back-dating of an increase in the rate of periodical payments, if necessary for a period of years, can be justified where the periodical payments have been at an unduly low rate for the period concerned. Normally, however, "the countervailing effects of a shortfall in proper financial support in the past and the effect of the increase in the size of the order eventually made as a result in the fall of the value of the pound will be compensated in a rough and ready way over a comparatively short period of retroactive effect by the exercise of his general discretion by the judge in determining both the size of the order and the length of the backdating" (*per* Purchas LJ in *S* v *S* [1987] 2 All ER 312 at p. 319). It will be an improper exercise of discretion where the object of back-dating is to provide the recipient with a capital sum which could not be ordered directly in view of the prohibition on the making of a lump sum order on an application to vary an order for periodical payments (see (v), below). Thus in *S* v *S* the judge at first instance had back-dated the variation of a periodical payments order for a period of seven years producing a lump sum of £80,000. It was conceded that it was not possible to justify periodical payments at the rate ordered throughout the seven year period. The Court of Appeal concluded that it was an attempt to give the wife by indirect means a lump sum to enable her to discharge her indebtedness and in particular to pay the sum of £61,000 due to the Inland Revenue. The Court of Appeal provided for backdating for a period of months only.

An attempt to analyse the present day value of the provision made in the original order, and to adjust the original order by reference to the changed value of the pound, may be of only limited assistance because of the differing incidence of tax prevailing at the two dates (*per* Purchas LJ in *S* v *S* [1987] 2 All ER 312 at p. 318). Thus in *S* v *S* the gross amount of the original order of £25,000 was adjusted by reference to the value of the pound as shown by the retail price index to produce a figure of £70,250 which was very close to the figure of £70,000 ordered at first instance. However, when the tax position of the parties was taken into account the net spendable income at the time of the original order was £6,786. Application of the same inflation factor to this figure produced a present day value of £19,069. In contrast the net figure available on the order of £70,000 made by the judge was £30,090.

## (ii) Lump sum payments

An order for the payment of a lump sum cannot be varied except that where the order provides for the lump sum to be paid by instalments the court may vary the instalments. It has been generally thought that even in such a case, the amount of the lump sum cannot be increased or reduced and there can be no order for the repayment of any instalment already paid, but the amount and timing of the remaining instalments can be varied. However, in *Tilley* v *Tilley* (1980) 10 Fam Law 89 the Court of Appeal directed that no further payment should be made in respect of the balance of a lump sum still outstanding. The original order, made by consent, had provided for the transfer of property from the husband to the wife and for the payment by the wife to the husband of £4,000 within three months and a further £3,500 within six years. The £4,000 was paid, but the wife subsequently found herself in financial difficulties and could only pay the £3,500 by selling the home in which she lived with the children. The court directed that there should be no further payment to the husband, but Donaldson LJ said that if there was any application thereafter for periodical payments or lump sum payments for the children, the court faced with such an application ought to take into consideration the £3,500 which in effect the husband had contributed to the maintenance of the children.

## (iii) Property adjustment orders

A property adjustment order is not in general variable. Thus where there had been an order transferring the husband's interest in the matrimonial home to the wife subject to a charge in favour of the husband, it was held that there is no power to vary that order in the light of changed circumstances by extinguishing the charge (*Nikoloff* v *Nikoloff* (1977) 7 Fam Law 129. Latey J also refused to extend time for an appeal against the original order as this would clearly defeat the intention of Parliament in s.31. However, an embargo on the house being sold before the youngest child reached 17 was deleted). On the other hand, an order authorising an earlier redemption of a charge than contemplated in the original order does not amount to a variation. Thus in *Popat* v *Popat* [1991] 2 FLR 163 the court had made an order in 1989 for the transfer of the former matrimonial home vested in the joint names of the parties into the sole name of the wife subject to the existing mortgage and to a charge in favour of the husband to secure one-third of the net value of the property. The charge was not to be enforced until the earlier of the following events - the death of the wife, the wife's remarriage or cohabitation with another man for more than a period of six months or the child of the marriage attaining the age of 17 years or on completion of full-time education by the child. In 1990 the wife wished to redeem the charge though none of the specified events had occurred. The Court of Appeal held that an order authorising her to redeem the charge upon payment of £19,085 was not a variation of the original order. The only purpose of the charge imposed by the original order was to provide security to the husband for the one-third share in the equity. The only function of the court was to satisfy itself that the amount being offered was the proper amount in accordance with the terms of the charge, and once that amount was tendered the wife was entitled to have the charge redeemed as the order contained no limitation upon the right to redeem.

Where, as in *Carson* v *Carson* [1983] 1 WLR 285, the court has made an order under s.24(1)(b) for a settlement in the form of a Mesher order providing for the postponement of sale of the former matrimonial home, there is no power to make an order under s.24(1)(a) for the transfer of the former husband's interest in that property to the wife who is in occupation. This was an attempt to make a second property adjustment order in relation to the same capital asset which was clearly contrary to the policy of s.31. It was also clear that the judge when making the original order had clearly intended to dispose of all outstanding claims for financial relief and to effect a comprehensive settlement of all financial and property issues between the parties. (Leave to appeal out of time against the order was again refused because it would have had the effect of outflanking s.31.) The court left open the position where some other capital asset was involved, though Sheldon J expressed the view (agreeing with Ewbank J at first instance) that the fact that an order has been made under one subsection of s.23 or 24 does not of itself preclude a later application for an order under another such subsection (*ibid.* at p. 293). This could be important if, for example, a party acquired further assets by inheritance or gift as in *Pearce* v *Pearce* (1981) 1 FLR 261.

It is customary for a Mesher order "to contain some provision for the court to make further orders in future unascertained events as to the administration or execution of the trusts established by the order" (see Oliver LJ in *Thompson* v *Thompson* [1985] 2 All ER 243 at p. 247). Thus in *Mesher* v *Mesher* [1980] 1 All ER 126 itself the property was not to be sold until the child of the marriage reached a specified age or "until further order". An application made under the liberty to apply so reserved must be an application for the working out of the original order rather than an application to vary the order. In *Thompson* v *Thompson* Oliver LJ said that the court must "consider the application for the purpose of ascertaining whether what is sought is to give effect to the original order in accordance with its spirit and construction or whether it is made with a view, in effect, to producing a different substantive result from that originally contemplated" (at p. 249). He acknowledged that there might be borderline cases where the question may not be easy to decide, but it is not right for the court to decline jurisdiction simply on the ground that any "further" order would necessarily be a variation. In that case the application was made by the wife who was in occupation of the property and wished to move to another area. It was held that she was seeking to give effect to the original order and not to vary it and the court had jurisdiction to hear the application, and the case was remitted to the county court for consideration on the merits. An application by the party not in occupation of the property made with a view to obtaining an early realisation of his share would, on the other hand, almost certainly be regarded as an application to vary. Oliver LJ made it clear that the insertion of the reference to a further order is not for the purpose of meeting contingencies which may occur after the specified period, thus enabling the period to be extended, but to cater for events which may occur before that specified period expires. The words "further order" are to be construed as "further order in the meantime", unless the context indicates the contrary.

(See, for example, *Chamberlain* v *Chamberlain* [1973] 1 WLR 1557 where the sale was suspended until every child of the family had ceased to receive full-time education "or thereafter without the consent of the parties or order of the court". The further order there envisaged could only be an order for the execution of the trust for sale of the property on the failure of the trustees to agree on a sale.) The Law Commission has recommended that the court be given power to vary property adjustment orders in certain circumstances (Law Com. No. 192, *The Ground for Divorce*, paras. 6.2 - 6.7).

(iv) Orders for the sale of property
The court's power of variation, discharge, suspension and revival extends to any order made under s.24A(1) for the sale of property (MCA 1973, s.31(2)(f)).

(v) Embargo on capital provision on an application to vary periodical payments
No property adjustment order can be made on an application for the variation of an order made under s.23 for periodical payments or secured periodical payments in favour of a party to a marriage or in favour of a child of the family (MCA 1973, s.31(5)). No order for the payment of a lump sum can be made on an application for the variation of an order for periodical payments or secured periodical payments made under s.23 (or s.27) in favour of a party to a marriage. However, where no application for a property adjustment order or for a lump sum payment has been previously made the court may make such orders on an original application, for the court has power to make such orders on granting a decree or at any time thereafter. Although this point has arisen principally in cases where no application has been made because no power existed to make such orders at the time the decree was granted (*Powys* v *Powys* [1971] P 340; *Jones* v *Jones* [1971] 3 All ER 1201; *Williams* v *Williams* [1971] P 271), the same applies where the power existed but for some reason no application was made (*Pearce* v *Pearce* (1981) 1 FLR 261). In such cases leave of the court would have to be obtained, and it has been said that such applications should not be allowed to undermine or outflank the general policy of the Acts of 1970 and 1973 in relation to variation (*Powys* v *Powys* [1971] P 340 at p. 355. But see Ormrod LJ in *Chaterjee* v *Chaterjee* [1976] Fam 199 at p. 207. See Part 5 above).

The inability of the court to order a lump sum payment (or in some instances to make a property adjustment order) on an application to vary or discharge an order for periodical payments is a potential obstacle to the achievement of a clean break. In *Peacock* v *Peacock* [1991] 1 FLR 324 at p. 330 Thorpe J said that cases "in which spouses move to the goal of clean break by two stages are commonplace. In such cases it is surely unfortunate if the court does not have the jurisdiction to set and enforce the fair level of capital commutation." (See the subsequent recommendations of the Law Commission in Law Com. No. 192, paras. 6.8 - 6.10.) However, although the court does not have power to order a husband to make a lump sum payment in commutation of the wife's periodical payments, it may terminate the husband's obligation to make periodical payments upon the voluntary payment by him of an appropriate sum. In *S* v *S* [1986] Fam 189 Waite J adopted a broad interpretation of the embargo on lump sum payments in s.31(5) as this would assist the application of the clean break principle. He said (at p. 200) that: "Parliament must be presumed to have intended ... that the courts should be allowed the maximum freedom to help former spouses to pursue independent lives, liberated from the running irritant of financial interdependence." The court must, of course, first be satisfied that "such a course would accord with the paramount requirements of the welfare of any child of the family under age and that the effect of the offer is such as to enable the wife to adjust within an appropriate period to the termination of her payments, without undue hardship" (*ibid*. at p. 201).

The ability of the court to achieve a clean break in this way depends upon a suitable offer being made by the husband. General guidance in relation to the appropriateness of an offer was given by Booth J in *Boylan* v *Boylan* [1988] 1 FLR 282 at p. 291. She said that:

"... it appears to me that any offer made for this purpose must take as its starting point the income to which the wife is agreed or held to be entitled. Regard must be had to the fact that the wife's entitlement to payments under an order would continue during the joint lives of the parties and that if her claims under the Inheritance (Provision for Family and Dependants) Act 1975 are to be dismissed she will need an income for the remainder of her life. As against those matters, it would be appropriate ... to take into consideration the advantage to the wife of having a capital sum which will provide her with a secure income, always bearing in mind that in a case such as this the court is not seeking to put free capital into the wife's hands: see *Preston* v *Preston* (1981) 2 FLR 331."

All these, and no doubt other factors must be considered and quantified and Booth J considered that when dealing with substantial figures it might well be wise for the parties to receive expert financial guidance as well as legal advice.

In *Boylan* v *Boylan* [1988] 1 FLR 282 Booth J found that the appropriate figure for periodical payments for the wife in the light of the changed circumstances was £16,000 per annum. Having regard to her age - 46 - and her limited earning capacity which was estimated at some £5,000 per annum gross, the offer of £40,000 made by the husband was clearly quite inadequate. It was based on a radically different premise, namely that the wife was entitled by way of periodical payments to a sum substantially less than £10,000 per annum less tax for a limited period of three to four years during which time she could be expected to qualify herself in some way to earn her own living. Booth J did not think it right for the court to suggest an alternative figure as there had not been full argument on all the relevant financial factors. It would, of course, be open to the husband to make a further application for termination of the periodical payments on the basis of a more appropriate lump sum payment. In *S* v *S* [1986] Fam 189 Waite J also found the husband's offer of a lump sum of £120,000 (coupled with a release of his charge on the wife's house) was inadequate to justify the termination of periodical payments which would otherwise be increased to £70,000 per annum. On general grounds of principle and having regard to the paramount interests of the daughter in having her parents' financial difficulties disposed of once and for all, he thought it appropriate to indicate that the amount of the lump sum should be £400,000 so that the husband was given the option within a limited time of obtaining a termination of the periodical payments on payment of that sum. (The Court of Appeal did not have before it this aspect of the case, but upheld the figure of £70,000 in respect of periodical payments though it deleted a provision back-dating the variation for a period of some seven years. It substituted a provision back-dating the variation for a period of months. See [1987] 2 All ER 312.)

Where the parties have arrived at an agreement for the commutation of periodical payments, one of the parties may seek to renege on the bargain. In *Peacock* v *Peacock* [1991] 1 FLR 324 Thorpe J held that a distinction had to be drawn between the position where the reneging party was the intended recipient of the capital sum and the position where it was the potential payer who sought to renege. In the former case the court has jurisdiction to make the only order essential to enforce the contract, namely the order dismissing the claim to periodical payments. In the latter case the court has no jurisdiction to order what he will no longer perform consensually, namely the provision of a capital sum or asset that represents a fair commutation of the future claims. This was unsatisfactory. In *Peacock* it was the husband who had indicated that he was not prepared to carry out his agreement to transfer his interest in the matrimonial home to the wife, so Thorpe J proceeded to vary the order for periodical payments on the basis that no capital transfer would be made by the husband while at the same time indicating the orders he would have made if the husband's consent had continued to be forthcoming - which included an order for payment by the wife of a small lump sum payment. This gave the husband the opportunity of giving the matter further consideration.

*(b) The basis on which the court is required to act*
In its original form s.31 of the Matrimonial Causes Act 1973 required the court, in exercising its powers of variation and discharge, to have regard to all the circumstances of the case, including any change in any of the matters to which the court was required to have regard when making the order to which the application related. The section was amended by s.6 of the Matrimonial and Family Proceedings Act 1984 so as to apply to applications for variation and discharge the same basic principles as were made applicable by that Act to original applications for orders for financial provision and property adjustment. Whereas the court must still have regard to all the circumstances of the case, first consideration is now required to be given to the welfare while a minor of any child of the family who has not attained the age of 18. Further, the court must now consider whether an order for periodical payments or secured periodical payments should be varied so as to require the payments to be made or secured only for such further period as will in the opinion of the court be sufficient to enable the party in whose favour the order was made to adjust without undue hardship to the termination of those payments (s.31(7)). In other words the court must consider whether an immediate or a deferred "clean break" has now become appropriate.

The new guidelines were intended to apply to orders made under the old law, for they were intended to encourage evolution rather than revolution. (See Law Com. No. 112, para. 45.) The Law Commission considered that it would be wholly artificial to require the court to exclude from consideration changes in legislative attitudes to such matters as a wife's earning potential. However, while the same guidelines apply to orders made before and after the 1984 amendments, it is appropriate to give weight to the circumstances in which the original order was made. The way in which the courts have exercised their powers to vary existing orders is considered in the next chapter together with the cases concerned with original applications for financial provision and property adjustment.

The requirement that the court must have regard to all the circumstances of the case means that the court, when dealing with an application to vary a periodical payments order, is not confined to considering the alterations in the actual means of the parties. In *Lewis* v *Lewis* [1977] 1 WLR 409 the Court of Appeal said that the judge had been right to look at all the circumstances as they were when the matter came before him - untrammelled by the existence of the previous order – and to make an order that was reasonable in those circumstances. (The court distinguished *Foster* v *Foster* [1969] 1 WLR 1155 where in relation to the previous legislation the court said that the correct approach was to start from the original order and see what changes had taken place since the order, and then to amend the order in rough proportion to those changes if that was possible.) However, it is important to ensure that an application for variation is not in reality an attempt to appeal. Thus in *Bromiley* v *Bromiley* [1987] FLR 71 where the divorce court order had been registered in a magistrates' court, it was held that an application by the husband for a variation within two months of the previous variation simply on the basis that he could not afford to pay the sum ordered was, in the absence of any change of circumstances, simply an attempt to appeal to a different bench of magistrates.

Where there has been a considerable lapse of time since the original order and no application to increase the amount of periodical payments in line with inflation, the fact that the husband may well have arranged his affairs in reliance upon the fact that no further claim has been made will be very relevant in considering the order that should be made (*McGrady* v *McGrady* (1978) 8 Fam Law 15). Similarly, although the court has power to back-date a variation, this should be exercised with caution for a husband who has arranged his affairs on the basis that his liability will not change until a new order is made may have to find the extra money from savings or by borrowing (*Moon* v *Moon* (1979) 1 FLR 115).

On an application to vary an order for periodical payments the court can take into account not only a party's conduct between the dissolution of the marriage and the original order, but also his or her conduct between the making of the original order and the hearing of the application to vary it. Any conduct during these periods which interfered with the other party's life or standard of living (whether or not it affected the other party's finances) and which was so gross and obvious that to order the other party to support the party whose conduct was in question would be repugnant to justice, is relevant in considering the application to vary an order (*per* Sheldon J in *J(HD)* v *J(AM)* [1980] 1 WLR 124 at p. 131). In that case the fact that the former wife had conducted a sustained campaign of malice and persecution against the former husband and his new wife could not be ignored in deciding the provision that should be made by the husband. However, taking a broad view, and bearing in mind that the former wife still had a contribution to make to bringing up the daughter of the marriage, it was not appropriate to deprive her of all provision. The periodical payments were allowed to remain at their existing level of £1,000 per annum and were not raised as requested by the former wife to a figure which, on financial considerations alone, would have been in the region of £2,500 per annum.

## 9. Appeals

### (a) Rights of appeal

There is a right of appeal from a district judge to a judge. This was formerly governed by r. 124 of the Matrimonial Causes Rules 1977 and was by way of a re-hearing (*G (formerly P)* v *P (Ancillary Relief: Appeal)* [1978] 1 All ER 1099). This right of appeal is now governed by r. 8.1(2) of the Family Proceedings Rules 1991 and is to some extent more limited in scope. In *Merritt* v *Merritt* [1992] 1 WLR 471 Bracewell J held that such appeals were now to be dealt with on the same basis as appeals from a judge to the Court of Appeal, so that fresh evidence could only be adduced in limited circumstances. In *Lauerman* v *Lauerman* [1992] 1 WLR 734 at p. 735 Thorpe J took the view that the intention underlying the new rule was that "the old practice of hearing these appeals *de novo* should be moderated to the extent that the judge of the division should ordinarily proceed upon the basis of the district judge's findings of fact without further evidence from appellant or respondent". However, he said there remains "a residual discretion to reinvestigate areas of fact or to admit further evidence if the justice of the case seems to demand it". Above all, it was intended that the judge of the division should not be bound by "the strict principles that inhibit the court of review from substituting its discretion for the discretion of the court below". The approach of Thorpe J has now been approved by the Court of Appeal in *Marsh* v *Marsh* [1993] 1 WLR 744.

An appeal lies to the Court of Appeal from a judge. The Court of Appeal is entitled to interfere with the judge's exercise of discretion only in limited circumstances. The classic statement is that of Asquith LJ in *Ballenden (formerly Satterthwaite)* v *Satterthwaite* [1948] 1 All ER 343 at p. 345:

"We are here concerned with a judicial discretion, and it is of the essence of such a discretion that on the same evidence two different minds might reach widely different decisions without either being appealable. It is only where the decision exceeds the generous ambit within which reasonable disagreement is possible, and is, in fact plainly wrong, that an appellate body is entitled to interfere."

### (b) Appeals out of time

(i) Basis on which leave to appeal will be granted

A court may, in certain circumstances, exercise its discretion to grant leave to appeal out of time from an order for financial provision or property adjustment on the basis of new events which have occurred after the date on which the order was made. Although on general principles changes in circumstances after the date of an order should be dealt with on an application to vary, there is no power to vary an order for the payment of a lump sum or for the transfer of property. Accordingly, the ability to challenge such orders by way of appeal has proved crucial in a number of cases, but leave to appeal may only be granted if certain strict conditions are satisfied. These were specified by Lord Brandon in *Barder* v *Caluori* [1988] AC 20 at p. 43, as follows:

(1) New events must have occurred since the making of the order which invalidate the basis, or fundamental assumption, upon which the order was made, so that if leave to appeal out of time were to be given, the appeal would be certain, or very likely to succeed.

(2) The new events must have occurred within a relatively short time of the order having been made. Although the length of time cannot be laid down precisely Lord Brandon regarded it as extremely unlikely that it could be as much as a year, and thought that in most cases it will be no more than a few months.

(3) The application for leave to appeal out of time should be made reasonably promptly in the circumstances of the case.

(4) The grant of leave to appeal out of time should not prejudice third parties who have acquired, in good faith and for valuable consideration, an interest in the property which is the subject matter of the relevant order.

In *Barder* v *Caluori* a consent order provided that within twenty-eight days the husband should transfer to the wife his legal and equitable interest in the jointly owned matrimonial home. Before the order was executed, but after the time for appeal had expired, the wife killed their children and committed suicide. The wife's mother opposed the husband's application for leave to appeal out of time. Lord Brandon said that the consent order had been made upon the fundamental, though tacit, assumption "that for an indefinite period, to be measured in years rather than months or weeks, the wife and the two children of the family would require a suitable home in which to reside. That assumption was totally invalidated by the death of the children and the wife within five weeks of the order being made." The judge had been entitled to exercise his discretion by granting leave to appeal out of time and there was no ground on which that exercise of discretion by him could properly be reversed by the Court of Appeal. The judge's order, setting aside the consent order on the ground that it had been vitiated by a fundamental mistake common to both parties, was restored. (See also *Passmore* v *Gill* [1987] 1 FLR 441.)

In the earlier case of *Wells* v *Wells*, decided in 1980 but not reported until [1992] 2 FLR 66, the Court of Appeal had set aside a consent order where after the date of that order the wife had begun to associate with another man (whom she had known before) and then began living with him and married him some six months later. Ormrod and Brandon LJJ held that the original order had been based on a state of affairs falsified by later events and that a new order, appropriate to the new circumstances should be substituted. (See the comments of Lord Brandon in *Barder* v *Caluori* [1988] AC 20 at p. 42.) This may be contrasted with the later case of *Cook* v *Cook* [1988] 1 FLR 521 where the husband alleged that he discovered after the consent order (which provided for him to transfer to the wife his interest in the former matrimonial home in satisfaction of her claims) had been made, that, contrary to what had been asserted in Form 11 by the wife, namely that she had no intention of cohabiting with another man, she had started to cohabit with another man and intended to cohabit with him permanently. However, Neill and Ralph Gibson LJJ accepted that this was not a case in which there was a complete change of circumstances, but only a development in an already existing relationship. There was a relationship which, as the husband knew perfectly well, was already a close one before the consent order was made. This had ripened further until actual cohabitation, as some would understand it, took place. Moreover, an examination of the figures relating to the resources of the parties showed that the judge was entitled to conclude that there would be no real difference if the matter were reopened and looked at all over again. The first condition in *Barder* v *Caluori* had not therefore been fulfilled. (See also *Chaudhuri* v *Chaudhuri* [1992] 2 FLR 73 and *Rundle* v *Rundle* [1992] 2 FLR 80.)

It may be possible to reopen an order for financial provision by way of an appeal out of time where there turns out to be a substantial discrepancy between the valuation of the matrimonial home or other property at the time the order was made and the price obtained on a sale of the property within a relatively short time thereafter. Thus in *Warren* v *Warren* (1983) 4 FLR 530 the judge had made an order for payment to the wife of a lump sum of £16,000 representing approximately one-third of the value of £52,000 attributed to the former matrimonial home. The husband did not comply with the order, though he did carry out some improvements, and some nine months later the house was sold for £92,500. The Court of Appeal held that events showed that the judge had computed the lump sum on a wholly erroneous basis through no one's fault. It was, therefore, proper to reopen the matter. The court regarded the increase in the value of the house as a windfall to be divided equally between the parties after giving full credit to the husband for his expenditure on the property. However, Griffiths LJ (at p. 537) said:

"The extraordinary discrepancy in this case must not be taken by the profession as any encouragement to bring appeals to this court wherever there is a difference between a valuation and the ultimate sale price."

The decision in *Warren* v *Warren* was distinguished in *Edmonds* v *Edmonds* [1990] 2 FLR 202. In *Warren* the valuation had been agreed by the parties on a basis that was recognised as erroneous, whereas in *Edmonds* the valuation had not been agreed but made on the basis of the only expert evidence available to the registrar. Secondly, in *Warren* the parties had not had the opportunity of correcting the false assumption whereas in *Edmonds* the husband had asserted throughout his belief that the valuation should be much higher, but had failed to adduce sufficient evidence to rebut the expert evidence called by the wife upon which the court was entitled to rely. The events leading up to a sale at £110,000, as compared with an earlier valuation of £70,000, were not, on the facts of the case, new events within condition (1) of *Barder* v *Caluori* for the fact that the value of the property would almost certainly increase was known to all and reflected in the terms of the original order.

In *Thompson* v *Thompson* [1991] 2 FLR 530 at p. 538 Mustill LJ said that, where the change relied on is the ascertainment of the true value of an asset or liability after an order has been made on the basis of a mere estimate, two situations must be distinguished. The first is where the change consists of a discovery that the estimate was unsound when made. In this situation he said that "usually ... the court must inquire whether the applicant was in some way responsible for the erroneous valuation". If he was then he may well not be entitled to the indulgence of being allowed to appeal out of time. He took this to be the ground of the distinction drawn in *Edmonds* v *Edmonds* above. The same applies if the applicant himself put forward a valuation which his opponent and the court were willing to adopt. However, "the mere fact that the valuation was agreed at the time when the order was made cannot be conclusive for or against an application to reopen it later, if the interests of justice so require." (*Ibid.*) The second situation is where a valuation, reasonable when made, has afterwards become unexpectedly out of date. In this case he said that "... it makes no difference how the valuation came into existence: if it was put forward by the applicant for leave to appeal or not; if it was challenged by him or not. The fact is that something new has happened." (*Ibid.*) In that case a clean break had been ordered by a division of the assets of the parties on the basis that the husband's business was worth £20,000. A week later, after the time for appealing had expired, the husband sold the business for £45,000. Although this represented an increase of 125 per cent, Mustill LJ (at p. 537) said that in considering whether new events have occurred which invalidate the basis upon which the clean break had been ordered percentages should be used with caution, "for it is easy to see that a modest-seeming percentage change in the figure for an asset or a liability may have a disproportionate practical effect on the order under appeal." He continued:

"We think it much better for the reviewing court, when considering questions of degree, to look in broad terms at the balance of the financial relationship created by the order under review, and then ask itself how that balance has been affected by the new state of affairs."

In *Thompson* v *Thompson* [1991] 2 FLR 530 at p. 538 Mustill LJ also gave further consideration to the nature of the change of circumstances which would be regarded as sufficient. He accepted that, broadly speaking "... it should make no difference whether something has happened to alter the evaluation of assets or liabilities, or other factors already taken into account in the order originally made, or whether an entirely new factor has come into play - such as the receipt of an unexpected legacy." This could not be an absolute rule in a field where possible permutations of fact are so diverse, and two qualifications were necessary. First, "the change should not have been brought about by the conscious fault of the person who seeks to take advantage of it". However, "merely to say that the applicant must not have brought the change on himself is not enough, for this would disqualify an applicant who had been ruined by an honest error of business judgment". Secondly, the cause must not have been foreseen and taken into account when the order was made, for if it was it cannot be "new".

(ii) Approach to be adopted by the court where leave to appeal is granted

In *Barder* v *Caluori* and *Passmore* v *Gill* [1987] 1 FLR 441 the Court of Appeal found it unnecessary to do more than set aside the order that the husband transfer his interest in the former matrimonial home to the wife. In both cases the wife had been joint owner of the home so that the effect was to leave her estate with the half share to which she had been entitled before the assessment under s.25 of the 1973 Act had been carried out. In *Smith* v *Smith* [1991] 2 All ER 306 the matrimonial home had been vested solely in the husband who had been ordered to pay the wife a lump sum of £54,000 (which was approximately equal to half the value of his assets) in full and final settlement of her claims. Leave to appeal was granted to the husband following the wife's suicide some six months after the original order. The Court of Appeal held that the correct approach in these circumstances was to start again from the beginning and to consider what order should be made on the facts before the judge, but on the basis that the wife is known to have only six months or so to live. The effect was to reduce drastically the appropriate provision for the needs of the wife, but needs are not the only matter which the court is required to consider. Butler-Sloss LJ said (at p. 311):

"A wife with few or no needs, who had none the less made a significant contribution to the marriage, has in my judgment a right to recognition of that contribution in money terms where there are assets available to meet it so long as the court does not act to the unjust detriment of the other spouse."

It was a long marriage of over 30 years with both spouses having made considerable and valuable contributions. The Court of Appeal ordered payment of a lump sum to the wife and considered the ultimate destination of the wife's estate an irrelevant consideration. In fact it passed under the wife's will to her daughter. (See also *Barber* v *Barber* [1993] 1 FCR 65.)

# Chapter 11

# The exercise of the court's power

## 1. The statutory criteria

Before the Matrimonial Proceedings and Property Act of 1970 there was only limited statutory guidance as to the factors to be taken into account by the court in exercising its powers to order maintenance and its limited powers to adjust property rights. Thus in proceedings for divorce or nullity the court was empowered, if it thought fit, to make such orders for the maintenance of the wife by the husband as it thought "reasonable having regard to her fortune (if any), his ability and the conduct of the parties" (Matrimonial Causes Act 1965, ss.16(1) and 19). In other cases there was even less guidance, the court being merely directed to make such orders as it thought fit or thought just (*ibid*. ss.20(1) and (2)). However, s.5 of the Act of 1970 - subsequently s.25 of the Matrimonial Causes Act 1973 - set out in some detail the matters to which the court was to have regard in exercising the much wider powers conferred by the 1970 Act and now found in the 1973 Act.

In its original form, s.25 required the court, in deciding whether to exercise its powers to order financial provision or adjustment of property rights in favour of a party to the marriage or to order a sale of property under s.25A and, if so, in what manner, to have regard to all the circumstances of the case including the specific matters set out in paragraphs (a) to (g) of subs.(1). It was then required to exercise its powers so as to place the parties, so far as it was practicable and, having regard to their conduct, just to do so, in the financial position in which they would have been if the marriage had not broken down and each had properly discharged his or her financial obligations and responsibilities towards the other. In deciding whether to exercise its powers to order financial provision or adjustment of property rights in relation to a child of the family and, if so, in what manner, the court was required to have regard to all the circumstances of the case including the specific matters set out in paragraphs (a) to (e) of subs.(2). It was then required to exercise its powers so as to place the child, so far as it was practicable and, having regard to the considerations mentioned in relation to the parties to the marriage in s.25(1)(a) and (b) (resources and needs), just to do so, in the financial position in which the child would have been if the marriage had not broken down and each of the parties to the marriage had properly discharged his or her financial obligations and responsibilities towards him. (*Ibid.* s.25(2). See also s.25(3) in relation to a child who was not a child of the family. As a result of the amendments made to the 1973 Act by the Matrimonial and Family Proceedings Act 1984, these provisions are now subss.(3) and (4) respectively of s.25, and are considered in Chapter 17.)

Some of the criteria appeared especially relevant to periodical payments, and others to lump sum awards or property adjustment orders, but it had been emphasised by the Law Commission that the two types of financial provision could not, and should not, be kept wholly distinct, and that all criteria were, or might be, relevant to both types of order (Law Com. No. 25, para 83). This seemed clear from the wording of the section and in *Trippas* v *Trippas* [1975] Fam 134 at p. 143, Scarman LJ stated that the powers to make financial provision orders and property adjustment orders were to be exercised in accordance with the one policy, namely that set out in s.5 of the Act of 1970 and subsequently embodied in s.25 of the Act of 1973. The modifications to this policy introduced by the Matrimonial and Family Proceedings Act 1984 are considered below.

## 2. Applying the statutory criteria – the "new approach"

The principles to be applied by the court in exercising its discretionary powers in the light of the statutory criteria were considered by the Court of Appeal for the first time after full argument in *Wachtel* v *Wachtel* [1975] Fam 72. At first instance Ormrod J had expressed the view that the court should give effect to the new approach to family problems which was explicit in the Divorce Reform Act 1969 and implicit in the Act of 1970. The Divorce Reform Act had changed the conceptual basis of divorce from matrimonial fault or offence to irretrievable breakdown of the relationship of marriage, retaining some elements of the old concept, but using them essentially as evidence of irretrievable breakdown. It was, therefore, no longer appropriate to talk about an "innocent" or a "guilty" wife in this context. The provisions of s.5 of the Act of 1970, together with the wide new powers to interfere with proprietary rights, suggested that Parliament had "intended to bring about a shift of emphasis from the old concept of 'maintenance' of the wife and children by the husband to one of the redistribution of assets and, what might be called, 'purchasing power'". This view was approved by the Court of Appeal where Lord Denning MR, delivering the judgment of the court, said (at p. 91):

"The Act of 1970 is not in any sense a codifying statute. It is a reforming statute designed to facilitate the granting of ancillary relief in cases where marriages have been dissolved under the Act of 1969, an even greater measure of reform. It is true that in certain of the lettered sub-paragraphs of section 5(1) of the Act of 1970 one can find reflections of certain earlier well known judicial decisions. But this was not to ensure that earlier decisions on conduct should be slavishly followed against a different jurisdictional background. Rather it was to secure that the common sense principles embodied in the lettered sub-paragraphs, which found their origin in long standing judicial decisions, should continue to be applied where appropriate in the new situation. We regard the provisions of sections 2, 3, 4 and 5 of the Act of 1970 as designed to accord to the courts the widest possible powers in readjusting the financial position of the parties and to afford the courts the necessary machinery to that end, as for example is provided in section 4."

The basis of this "new approach" was that when "the marriage comes to an end, the capital assets have to be divided; the earning power of each has to be allocated" (*per* Lord Denning MR in *Wachtel* v *Wachtel* [1973] Fam 72 at p. 91). In exercising its powers to effect such a division and such an allocation, the court was required, having regard to all the circumstances of the case including the matters specifically mentioned in s.25, to try to achieve the target set out at the end of s.25(1). In considering what the financial position of the parties would have been if the marriage had not broken down, it was made clear that it was no longer appropriate to regard the wife's expectations as limited to maintenance out of the husband's income supplemented by any income of her own, together with the right to live in a house in which she has no share or only a limited share. She must be treated as potentially entitled to benefit at some time from her husband's capital assets (*per* Bagnall J in *Harnett* v *Harnett* [1973] Fam 156 at p. 164).

Lord Denning also made it clear that there was to be a new approach to the "conduct" of the parties, a factor which had for so long exercised a dominating influence on divorce and financial arrangements. No longer was one spouse "guilty" and the other "innocent". "In most cases both parties are to blame or, as we would prefer to say - both parties have contributed to the breakdown." In such circumstances it was no longer appropriate to make a reduction or discount on account of a wife's misconduct. Lord Denning explained the position as follows (at p. 90):

"It has been suggested that there should be a 'discount' or 'reduction' in what the wife is to receive because of her supposed misconduct, guilt or blame (whatever word is used). We cannot accept this argument. In the vast majority of cases it is repugnant to the principles underlying the new legislation, and in particular the Act of 1969. There will be many cases in which a wife (though once considered guilty or blameworthy) will have cared for the home and looked after the family for very many years. Is she to be deprived of the benefit otherwise to be accorded to her by section 5(1)(f) because she may share responsibility for the breakdown with her husband? There will no doubt be a residue of cases where the conduct of one of the parties is in the judge's words ... 'both obvious and gross', so much so that to order one party to support another whose conduct falls into this category is repugnant to anyone's sense of justice. In such a case the court remains free to decline to afford financial support or to reduce the support which it would otherwise have ordered. But, short of cases falling into this category, the court should not reduce its order for financial provision merely because of what was formerly regarded as guilt or blame. To do so would be to impose a fine for supposed misbehaviour in the course of an unhappy married life ..."

The reduced importance of conduct had a profound effect on applications for financial provision and property adjustment. In the majority of cases it could be put on one side and this was generally welcomed. However, it has already been noted in Chapter 1 that the new law dealing with the financial and property consequences of divorce came under criticism both on account of the hardship that continued to be suffered by some divorced wives and on account of the hardship suffered by those on whom the burden of support fell - the divorced husband and particularly his new family.

The statutory target also came in for considerable criticism. First, in a very large number of cases - perhaps most cases - it proved to be an impracticable target. (See Ormrod J in *Wachtel* v *Wachtel* [1973] Fam 72 at p. 77.) The limited resources available in the majority of cases made it difficult to avoid at least some worsening in the position of both parties. Secondly, whether or not resources were limited, it was also criticised as embodying an outdated concept of lifelong support. (See Law Com. No. 103 para. 29.) Moreover, it was said that it implied that the court should "place a young woman who marries a millionaire and who is deserted by him three weeks later in the financial position in which she would have been if the marriage had not broken down, even if she is not pregnant and has not interrupted her career" (Law Com. No. 103, para. 59 quoting the Scottish Law Commission Memorandum No. 22, Vol 2, para. 3.4). In fact the target did not stand by itself, because the court was required to consider all the circumstances of the case including the seven specified factors. In some cases the courts did not even make an attempt to achieve the target where this was obviously inappropriate, e.g. in very short marriages where the husband was especially wealthy and the wife had suffered no adverse financial consequences (e.g. *Taylor* v *Taylor* (1975) 119 SJ 20; *H* v *H (Financial Provision: Short Marriage)* (1981) 2 FLR 392).

In the light of these and other criticisms, the Law Commission recommended that: "To seek to place the parties in the financial position in which they would have been had the marriage not broken down should no longer be the statutory objective" (Law Com. No. 112, para. 46). In the reformulation of s.25 effected by s.3 of the Matrimonial and Family Proceedings Act 1984 the statutory target was abolished. On the other hand, it was recommended that the direction to the court to "have regard to all the circumstances of the case" (including certain specified matters) should be retained, but with the addition of certain provisions designed to give a clear indication of how the discretion - which would remain the central feature of the law - should be applied to the facts of individual cases. It was recommended that the guidelines should be revised to emphasise, first, that the provision of adequate financial support for children should be an overriding priority. Secondly, "the importance of each party doing everything possible to become self-sufficient should be formulated in terms of a positive principle; and weight should be given to the view that, in appropriate cases, periodical financial provision should be primarily concerned to secure a smooth transition from the status of marriage to the status of independence" (Law Com. No. 112, para. 46).

Part II of the Matrimonial and Family Proceedings Act 1984 sought to give effect to those recommendations. In particular s.3 recast s.25 of the Matrimonial Causes Act 1973 and inserted a new s.25A.

## 3. The reformulated statutory criteria

*(a) The criteria on an original application*
It is now provided in s.25(1) of the Matrimonial Causes Act 1973 that it shall be the duty of the court in deciding whether to exercise its powers under s.23, 24 or 24A

and, if so, in what manner, to have regard to all the circumstances of the case, first consideration being given to the welfare while a minor of any child of the family who has not attained the age of eighteen. In exercising the powers to order financial provision, an adjustment of property rights or a sale under s.24A in relation to a party to the marriage, the court must in particular have regard to the matters set out in paragraphs (a) to (h) of s.25(2). These correspond to paragraphs (a) to (g) of the old s.25(1) subject to two amendments and with the addition of one new paragraph.

The new paragraph is paragraph (g) which deals with "conduct" which formerly appeared in the target at the end of the old s.25(1). The old paragraph (g) now becomes paragraph (h). The two amendments are to paragraphs (a) and (f) and consist of the italicised words in the paragraphs as set out below. The factors are now as follows:

(a) the income, earning capacity, property and other financial resources which each of the parties to the marriage has or is likely to have in the foreseeable future, *including in the case of earning capacity any increase in that capacity which it would in the opinion of the court be reasonable to expect a party to the marriage to take steps to acquire*;

(b) the financial needs, obligations and responsibilities which each of the parties to the marriage has or is likely to have in the foreseeable future;

(c) the standard of living enjoyed by the family before the breakdown of the marriage;

(d) the age of each party to the marriage and the duration of the marriage;

(e) any physical or mental disability of either of the parties to the marriage;

(f) the contributions which each of the parties has made *or is likely in the foreseeable future to make* to the welfare of the family, including any contribution by looking after the home or caring for the family;

(g) the conduct of each of the parties, if that conduct is such that it would in the opinion of the court be inequitable to disregard it;

(h) in the case of proceedings for divorce or nullity, the value to either of the parties to the marriage of any benefit (for example, a pension) which, by reason of the dissolution or annulment of the marriage, that party will lose the chance of acquiring.

In exercising the powers to order financial provision, property adjustment, or sale in relation to a child of the family, the court is required by subs.(3) of s.25 to have regard in particular to the following matters:

(a) the financial needs of the child;

(b) the income, earning capacity (if any), property and other financial resources of the child;

(c) any physical or mental disability of the child;

(d) the manner in which he was being and in which the parties to the marriage expected him to be educated or trained;

(e) the considerations mentioned in relation to the parties to the marriage in paragraphs (a), (b), (c) and (e) of subs.(2) set out above.

Crucial in furthering the policy of self-sufficiency and the clean break are the provisions of the new s.25A. Subsection (1) requires a court exercising its powers to order financial provision or property adjustment in favour of a party to a marriage to consider whether it would be appropriate so to exercise those powers that the financial obligations of each party towards the other will be terminated as soon after the grant of the decree as the court considers it just and reasonable. Subsection (2) requires a court ordering periodical payments, secured or unsecured, to consider whether it would be appropriate to require those payments to be made or secured only for such term as would in the opinion of the court be sufficient to enable the party in whose favour the order is made to adjust without undue hardship to the termination of his or her financial dependence on the other party. Finally, as noted in the previous chapter, subs.(3) enables a court to dismiss an application for periodical payments by a spouse if it considers that no continuing obligation should be imposed on either party to make such payment. This enables a "clean break" to be imposed and not merely to be achieved by agreement.

*(b) Criteria on applications to vary existing orders*
Before examining the new criteria in more detail it is important to note that similar provisions have been introduced in relation to applications to vary or discharge existing orders including those made before the amendments made by the Matrimonial and Family Proceedings Act 1984 came into force. The Law Commission believed that its new guidelines should also apply to such existing orders (Law Com. No. 112, para 44). The most important reason was that its proposals were intended to be merely evolutionary. It did not contemplate any abrupt change in the way in which the law was administered, and it did not therefore expect there to be any flood of successful variation applications. Moreover, it also had to bear in mind that in considering variation applications the courts looked at the matter afresh and sought to make whatever order was reasonable in the circumstances of the case as they are at the time, untrammelled by the existence of the previous order (*Lewis* v *Lewis* [1977] 1 WLR 409). It would have been wholly artificial to require the court to exclude from consideration changes in legislative attitudes to such matters as the wife's earning potential.

On the other hand, the Law Commission thought that the court should take into account the circumstances in which, and the basis on which, the order was originally made. In particular it should give weight to the circumstances in which the order was made, e.g. that the wife had been given a large maintenance award and a small lump sum. By virtue of s.31(7) the court, in exercising the powers of variation and discharge conferred by that section, is required to have regard to all the circumstances of the case, first consideration being given to the welfare while a minor of any child of the family who has not attained the age of eighteen, and the circumstances of the case are to include any change in any of the matters to which the court was required to have regard when making the original order to which the application relates. Moreover, in the case of a periodical payments or secured periodical payments order made on or after the grant of a decree of divorce or nullity, the court must consider whether in all the circumstances, and after having regard to any such change, it would be appropriate to vary the order so that the payments under the order are required to be made or secured only for such further period as will in the opinion of the court be sufficient to enable the party in whose favour the order was made to adjust without undue hardship to the termination of those payments.

It is submitted that the same basic principles apply whether the court is considering the appropriateness of an immediate or deferred clean break by virtue of s.25A on an original application for periodical payments or by virtue of s.31(7) on an application to vary or discharge an existing order for periodical payments. (See Chapter 10, Part 8 for further consideration of the power to vary or discharge.)

The position in relation to a deferred clean break seems clear. Before the court can make an order for periodical payments for a limited term only and before it can vary an existing order so that payments will continue only for a limited period, the court must be satisfied that the party in whose favour the order is made or continued will be able to adjust without undue hardship to the termination of those payments within that period. However, while the standard may be the same in both situations the burden to be discharged by the party seeking termination of the order may well differ. Thus the fact that an order for periodical payments has been in existence for some years may well be a highly relevant factor in assessing the hardship that termination would cause and the appropriate period of adjustment, especially if no capital provision was made for the recipient at the time of the original order. Moreover, while on an original application the court is likely to be able to exercise its powers to make capital as well as income provision this will frequently not be the case when it is considering an application to vary an existing order for periodical payments. Thus if an order for the payment of a lump sum has been made on an earlier occasion, then the achievement of a clean break may be dependent on the willingness of the other party to make a further payment. (See Chapter 10, Part 8 (a)(v).)

The position in relation to an immediate clean break is less clear. In *Morris* v *Morris* [1985] FLR 1176 at p. 1179 May LJ said:

"I think that it is essential to draw a distinction, however, as indeed did Parliament, when one is considering whether or not to make a clean break, between the occasion of any first order under the financial provisions of the relevant legislation after a decree on the one hand, and an occasion of an application to vary such an order - it may be many years after the original order was made - on the other".

There is certainly a difference between the structure of s.25A dealing with original applications and s.31 dealing with applications to vary or discharge existing orders. Thus s.31 contains no provision directly comparable with subs.(1) of s.25A which requires the court to consider whether its powers should be exercised so that the financial obligations of each party towards the other will be terminated as soon after the grant of the decree as the court considers just and reasonable. The only equivalent provision in s.31 is in subs.(7) which requires the court to consider whether payments should be made only for such further period as will in the opinion of the court be sufficient to enable the recipient to adjust without undue hardship to the termination of the payments. While this appears to lay down a stricter test - the avoidance of undue hardship as opposed to a just and reasonable test - it must be noted that subs.(2) of s.25A also lays down the test of avoiding undue hardship in relation to original applications for periodical payments. It can be argued that s.25A(2) applies only to a deferred clean break after a limited term order, but it seems unlikely that Parliament intended to provide a lower standard for an immediate clean break than for a deferred clean break on an original application under s.23. In other words, in performing its duty under s.25A(1) to consider whether a termination of financial obligations would be just and reasonable, the court must also consider subs.(2), and it would only be just and reasonable to impose an immediate or deferred clean break on an original application if an adjustment was possible without undue hardship. It is submitted that the same test should apply in relation to applications under s.31 though the burden on the party seeking the immediate or deferred clean break may well be different.

In *Morris* v *Morris*, on an application to vary an order made some seven years previously, the judge had added a provision that the payments should cease when the husband was no longer employed by the National Trust which provided him with tied accommodation, or reached the age of 65, whichever was the earlier. May LJ commented that the judge seemed "to have proceeded solely on the basis that it was time that ... both parties recognised the facts of their respective lives and that she should set a termination date for the persisting acrimony that there had been between them on financial matters". The judge had clearly failed to consider whether the recipient would be able to adjust without undue hardship to the termination of the payments as required by s.31(7)(a) (*ibid.* at p. 11).

## 4. The interests of the children

The Law Commission recommended that "the provision of adequate financial support for children should be an overriding priority" (Law Com. No. 112, para. 46). It was concerned that "the impression that the making of provision for the children" was "regarded as a matter of secondary importance to the making of provision for the former spouse" was widespread (*ibid.* para. 24). It saw two advantages in making the position of children avowedly a priority. First, it is often the case that the allocation of a larger proportion of the overall maintenance provision for the children's benefit makes the maintenance obligation more acceptable to the payer (usually the father). Secondly, adequate recognition would be given to the value of the custodial parent's role while discouraging the belief that such payments may be regarded as an automatic lifetime provision intended for the benefit of the custodial parent (usually the wife) perhaps for many years after the children have ceased to live with her.

In implementing the recommendations of the Law Commission the Matrimonial and Family Proceedings Act 1984 does not make the welfare of children paramount or overriding. The new s.25(1) requires the court in deciding whether to exercise its powers under s.23, 24 or 24A and if so, in what manner, to have regard to all the circumstances of the case, first consideration being given to the welfare while a minor of any child of the family who has not attained the age of eighteen. The effect of the wording was explained by Sir Roualeyn Cumming-Bruce in *Suter* v *Suter and Jones* [1987] Fam 111 at p. 123 as follows:

"Having regard to the prominence which the consideration of the welfare of the children is given in s.25(1), being selected as the first consideration among all the circumstances of the case, I collect an intention that this consideration is to be regarded as of first importance, to be borne in mind throughout consideration of all the circumstances including the particular circumstances specified in s.25(2). But if it had been intended to be paramount, overriding all the other considerations pointing to a just result, Parliament would have said so. It has not. So I construe the section as requiring the court to consider all the circumstances, including those set out in subsection (2) always bearing in mind the important consideration of the welfare of the children, and then to try to attain a financial result which is just as between husband and wife."

The Court of Appeal found that the judge in the lower court had erred in treating the welfare of the children as paramount and on that basis awarding the wife periodical payments of £100 per month. The payments were reduced to a nominal amount of £1 per annum. The court also expressed the view that the presence of children need not prevent a "clean break" in appropriate circumstances though on the facts of the case the uncertainties were such as to make a "clean break" inappropriate. (See further Part 5 below.)

The statutory wording accordingly provides more flexibility than a requirement that the interests of the children be first and paramount. The Law Commission recognised that the financial position of children is inextricably linked with that of the parent with whom the child is to reside, and that provision will necessarily be made for the wife to enable her properly to minister to the children's needs (Law Com. No. 112, para. 24). It is not practicable, at any rate in relation to families with limited means, first to calculate maintenance for the children and then to calculate maintenance for the spouse with their care. The practice is to calculate a package as a whole and then to look at its effect on the parties. (See the evidence of the Law Society to the Special Standing Committee, Fourth Sitting March 27, 1984, cols. 203 *et seq.*) However, the existence of a formula-based maintenance assessment in respect of a child seems bound to have an effect on the approach of the court in considering provision for the applicant spouse with whom the child resides.

While it has generally been considered inappropriate to provide for capital payments to children (see Chapter 17, Part 2), the disposition of the matrimonial home has commonly been postponed while they are still dependent (see Chapter 12). Indeed Sir John Arnold P in his evidence to the Special Standing Committee described the new s.25(1) as being "to a large extent a reflection of current practice although it was the first time that the matter has been given a structured expression in legislation" (*ibid.* col. 77). In other words, he said "the approach of the courts is already basically one in which, in considering matters of maintenance and periodical payments and the provision or preservation of residential accommodation, the needs of the children have a priority in the minds of the judges".

However, while the welfare of a child may require first consideration, regard must also be had to the position of the parent against whom an order for financial provision is sought. In *R* v *R* [1988] 1 FLR 89 the judge had made orders for periodical payments of £5.50 per week for two children and £1 per week for a third child. Eastham J in the Court of Appeal said that if the financial needs of the children were the only consideration which the court had to take into account it was quite clear that a total of £12 per week would not be sufficient to meet the needs of the three children. However, he pointed out at p. 93 that "the financial needs of the three children, albeit a most important factor and, since the Matrimonial and Family Proceedings Act 1984 an even more important factor than it had been under the Matrimonial Causes Act 1973, nevertheless it is not the only factor and the court is obliged under the new s.25 of the 1973 Act, while dealing with orders in relation to children of the family, to take into account all the matters set out in subs.(3) of the section; sub-para. (e) imposes a duty on the court to take into account (a), (b), (c) and (e) of subs.(2) of the new section, which includes the income, earning capacity, property, financial resources and the financial needs, obligations and responsibilities of each of the parties to the marriage; and in considering the exercise of the powers, it is all subject to the fact that the court has to have regard to all the circumstances of the case". Slade LJ at p. 97 was prepared to accept broadly the principle that a person having an obligation to maintain his children is under an obligation to order his financial affairs with due regard to his responsibility to pay reasonable mainte-nance for his children and to meet his reasonable financial obligations. On the facts it was found that the husband had not acted unreasonably or irresponsibly in purchasing a house for his new family. In the view of the court the judge had been perfectly justified and right in looking at the matter from a family point of view not only when he was considering "all the circumstances of the case", but also when considering the resources and obligations of both families. Nevertheless, the order of £1 per week for the third child was not justifiable not only because there was room for saving on certain items by the husband, but also because the husband had previously voluntarily paid £5.50 for the child at an earlier date so that he had him-self clearly regarded that sum as proper maintenance. That figure was substituted for the figure of £1 per week. (See also *Blower* v *Blower* [1986] 1 FLR 292 which was concerned with the corresponding provision in the Domestic Proceedings and Magistrates' Courts Act 1978. Heilbron J said that the court was also required to have regard to the financial needs, obligations and responsibilities of each of the parties and, moreover, there was nothing in the Act to restrict obligations and responsibilities to those which were legally enforceable.)

In *Delaney* v *Delaney* [1990] 2 FLR 457 the husband and his new partner had given up the tenancy of a one-bedroom flat and purchased a three-bedroom house with the assistance of a mortgage. The Court of Appeal rejected the judge's view that he did not need a home of that size for the purpose of access to his three chil-dren who lived with his former wife in the former matrimonial home. Ward J (at p. 462) said:

> "In my judgment, this father was reasonably entitled to say that for the welfare of his children, their welfare being the court's first consideration under s.25 ..., he should have accommodation sufficient for proper access and so suitable to be able to offer them staying access."

(See Chapter 17, Part 7, for an account of the Child Support Act 1991, and in parti-cular subpart (*h*) for a consideration of the limited extent to which the needs of the absent parent's new family unit are taken into account in the maintenance assess-ment.) It should be noted that first consideration is required to be given to the wel-fare of a child only while he or she is a minor. (See *Leadbeater* v *Leadbeater* [1985] FLR 789, where a child of the family did not attain the age of 18 for a further five months.) Moreover, the requirement applies only to a child of the family and does not, therefore, apply to the children of a spouse's "new family" though the spouse's obligations to the new family will certainly be relevant under s.25(2)(b). (For a consideration of the concept of "child of the family" see Chapter 17.)

## 5. Self-sufficiency and the clean break

### (a) What is a "clean break"?

The best known statement of the clean break principle is by Lord Scarman in *Minton* v *Minton* [1979] AC 593 at p. 608 when he said:

"The law now encourages spouses to avoid bitterness after family breakdown and to settle their money and property problems. An object of the modern law is to encourage each to put the past behind them and to begin in a new life which is not overshadowed by the relationship which has broken down."

More recently in *Tandy* v *Tandy*, October 24 1986 Lexis Enggen, Waite J in the Court of Appeal said:

"The legislative purpose ... is to enable the parties to a failed marriage, whenever fairness allows, to go their separate ways without the running irritant of financial interdependence or dispute."

The essence of a "clean break", therefore, is the final settlement of financial and property questions between the spouses so as to remove the opportunity for future conflict between the parties and the need for future litigation. The avoidance of bitterness is the advantage much stressed though even in cases where there is no bitterness a clean break will have the advantage of enabling the former spouses to plan their new lives without the possibility of the ghost of a former spouse appearing from the wainscot to disrupt the life of the new family (*per* Sir George Baker P in *D* v *D* [1974] The Times 3 October). Accordingly, the central feature of a clean break is the termination of the liability of a former spouse to make periodical payments for the maintenance of the other spouse - until a claim for periodical payments is dismissed there remains the possibility of future applications for variation of an existing nominal or substantive order or, indeed, the making of an original application where for some reason such an application has not previously been pursued. However, in its most extended form it means that as far as possible all capital claims should also be settled.

Lump sum orders can only be made once and cannot be varied, but conflict may arise where an application for a lump sum payment is not clearly disposed of either by dismissal or by a clearly identifiable order for a lump sum (see *Brown* v *Kirrage* (1981) 11 Fam Law 141). Regard must also be had to the case where no application for a lump sum payment has been made so that the possibility of an original application being made in the future remains. Similar considerations arise in relation to orders for the transfer of property (see Chapter 10). The potential for future conflict is also created by an order which involves postponement of the sale of the former matrimonial home even though the main features of such an order cannot be varied (see Chapter 12). Thus in *Harman* v *Glencross* [1986] Fam 81 at p. 96 Balcombe J said that "from the wife's point of view a Mesher-type of order, or one of its variants, has its disadvantages. It leaves her linked financially with her husband, even though the modern practice, now enshrined in s.25A(1) of the Matrimonial Causes Act 1973, is to favour the 'clean break' wherever possible ...". He went on to say that an outright transfer of the husband's interest in the matrimonial home may be the most appropriate way to protect fully the wife's right to have a roof over the heads of herself and the children. However, an outright transfer of the home into the name of one former spouse, subject to a charge to secure payment of a proportion of the ultimate proceeds of sale, involves the possibility of future litigation even though it may have the psychological advantage of giving the transferee spouse a greater sense of security (see Chapter 12). Indeed in *Schuller* v *Schuller* [1990] 2 FLR 193 at p. 199 Butler-Sloss LJ said that the deferred charge on the former matrimonial home sought by the wife "would fly in the face of the duty upon the court to try wherever possible to create a clean break". The Court of Appeal upheld the decision of the judge to award the wife, who was securely housed in her own inherited flat, a modest lump sum which the husband, who was occupying the home, could afford. The wife's other claims were dismissed.

On the other hand in *Clutton* v *Clutton* [1991] 1 All ER 340 at p. 344 Lloyd LJ took the view that a Martin order in favour of the wife, with a charge in favour of the husband, did not offend against the principle of the clean break (for the meaning of a Martin order see Chapter 12, page 324). He said: "A charge which does not take effect until death or remarriage could only be said to offend against the principle of the clean break in the most extended sense of that term". The wife feared that she would be spied on by the husband for the purpose of establishing whether or not she was cohabiting with another man so as to trigger enforcement of the charge. Lloyd LJ said that this was far outweighed by the bitterness which the husband would naturally feel if he subsequently found the former matrimonial home occupied not only by the wife but by her new husband or cohabitee. Ewbank J (at p. 346) said that the "clean break principle does not ... mean that the other spouse is to be deprived for all time of any share". Postponement until death, remarriage or cohabitation does not produce the same problem as a Mesher order and is not generally disadvantageous to the occupying spouse. It does ensure that the other spouse receives eventually an appropriate share in the "jointly acquired asset".

### (b) The duty of the court

It has already been noted that there is now a duty on the court, in exercising its powers to order financial provision or property adjustment in relation to a party to a marriage, to consider whether it would be appropriate so to exercise those powers as to achieve an immediate or a deferred clean break. (See Part 3 of this chapter and ss.25A and 31(7).)

The duty of the court is to consider whether a clean break is appropriate, and such consideration must be "a real consideration, and not just a payment of lip service" to the words of the legislation (*per* Balcombe LJ in *Whiting* v *Whiting* [1988] 1 WLR 565 at p. 575). However, while the obligation to consider is an unqualified one, provided that the court has duly considered the point, the court has a wide discretion as to whether or not to impose a clean break (see Slade LJ at p. 579). In *Whiting* v *Whiting*, where the court was considering an application to vary an existing order for periodical payments, Stocker LJ said that "... the statutory obligation to consider whether in all the circumstances of the case it would be appropriate to vary the order does not impose on a judge an obligation to vary the order and impose a 'clean break' unless there are reasons, which he considers compelling, for doing so". Thus s.25A does not require a termination of periodical payments unless a good reason can be shown to the contrary. In *Barrett* v *Barrett* [1988] 2 FLR 516 the Court of Appeal made it clear that there is no presumption that periodical payments were to be terminated as soon as possible unless the wife could show some good reason why they should not be. Butler-Sloss LJ said (at p. 519):

"It is obviously desirable that people should not remain locked into matrimonial financial situations if in justice to both sides that can be brought by an order to an end, either immediately on decree absolute or within as short a period thereafter as possible. But if there is to be determination unless there is good reason not to be, then ... it should have been set out in the Act. But it is not ..."

### (c) Achieving a clean break

### (i) An immediate clean break

An immediate clean break can be achieved by virtue of s.25A(3) without the agreement of the spouse whose application for periodical payments is dismissed. The court may dismiss such an application for periodical payments with a direction that the applicant shall not be entitled to make any further application in relation to that marriage for an order for periodical payments if the court considers that no continuing obligation should be imposed on *either* party to make or secure periodical payments in favour of the other. Despite this form of wording it was held in *Thompson* v *Thompson* [1988] 1 WLR 562 that the application of one party may be dismissed even though there is no application from the other party so that the latter's right remains, nominally at least, still in existence. This could be significant where fortunes are reversed. (See *Whiting* v *Whiting* [1988] 1 WLR 565.)

An immediate clean break can also be achieved on an application to vary an existing order for periodical payments under s.31.

### (ii) A deferred clean break

A deferred clean break may be achieved by an order for periodical payments for a limited term only, namely a term sufficient for the recipient of the payments to make the necessary adjustment to financial independence. Before the expiration of that term the recipient may apply under s.31 for a variation of the order by an extension of the term unless the court exercised its power under s.28(1A) to direct that the recipient shall not be entitled to make such an application. Whether or not it is realistic to expect the recipient to make the necessary adjustment to financial independence within the specified term will be a matter for the court to determine on the evidence of her financial resources and in particular her employment prospects, age and state of health. The test is whether the recipient would suffer undue hardship, and it would appear that the onus is on the spouse seeking a limitation to show that there would be no undue hardship. It is submitted that where the court does make an order for periodical payments for a fixed term then only in the clearest cases should the court add a direction under s.28(1A). Having regard to the uncertainties that usually exist, it will generally be preferable to leave the recipient with the possibility of applying for an extension of the term. Indeed, in many cases it will be inappropriate and unfair even to place such an onus on the recipient. If an order is unlimited as to time then it remains open to the payer to return to the court to seek a discharge of the order if it appears that the recipient has failed to make reasonable efforts to increase her income.

In *Morris* v *Morris* [1985] FLR 1176 the judge had varied an existing order for periodical payments by adding a provision that it should cease to have effect when the husband (then aged 60) no longer had tied employment or reached the age of 65, whichever was the earlier. The Court of Appeal removed this provision taking the view that it was far too early to decide that the order should terminate in five years' time at the latest. The position would have to be looked at and monitored as it developed, as the parties grew older, and as they retired or got fresh employment as the situation might be. While it was appropriate to take into account the desirability of the parties recognising the facts of their respective lives and setting a termination date for the persisting acrimony that there had been between them on financial matters, it was essential to consider whether the wife could adjust before the specified date without undue hardship. This the judge had failed to do. Moreover, while it would have been open to the wife to return for an extension of the order, May LJ said (at p. 1182) that if the order was left as it was he thought that "the petitioner/ appellant, if she were minded to come back to court, would in practice be in a worse position than she ought to be if there were no such termination in the order".

In *Barrett* v *Barrett* [1988] 2 FLR 516 the judge had made an order for periodical payments of £25 a week in favour of the wife for a period of four years or until she remarried, whichever was the earlier. The wife had part-time employment but had not been able to take full-time employment because she was caring for the youngest child of the family. The Court of Appeal removed the provision limiting the payments for four years, noting that it was not possible to know whether that period was insufficient for her to adjust to termination without undue hardship. The limited term order put an onus on her which was not justified by s.25A(2). Butler-Sloss LJ said (at p. 521):

"I ... do not think that a wife in these circumstances at this age, who has not had full-time employment for many years, looking for and willing to find work and indeed prepared to take a course to make her more fit to get employment, and still not finding a job, should be obliged to go back to the court some time shortly before the four years are up and say 'I cannot find work: I do not know what to do'. It would be far more suitable for the husband to first write to the wife's solicitors and say: 'Why are you not getting work; What efforts have you made?' and if he is not satisfied, to go back to court and say the time has come, as under the new s.31 he would have the right to do, to have this order brought to an end if she was not making genuine but unsuccessful efforts to get employment."

However, "in order to encourage her in that approach" to finding employment the court was minded to accept an undertaking that she would notify the husband if and when she did obtain employment. Butler-Sloss LJ said, at p. 522, that he "for his part has the right to require of her solicitors or herself why she has not obtained a job. There is nothing unusual in asking for that, and further to justify what jobs she has applied for, and what efforts she has genuinely made after the conclusion of her treatment. In those circumstances, if the court took the view in future that she has not tried hard enough to get employment, the court would have the power under s.31 to impose the termination of ... the order ...".

## (d) When is a clean break appropriate?

(i) The original views
Despite the increasing recognition of the attractions of a "clean break", its limitations were recognised. Thus the Law Commission in Report No. 112, para. 28, said:
"... Moreover, it must be accepted that the occasions on which it is possible for the parties to arrive at a final, once for all settlement, on the occasion of their divorce will be comparatively few, and almost non-existent where there are young children. To seek to attain a "clean break" in many - perhaps the majority of cases - would simply be to drive divorced wives on to supplementary benefit. That (it has been said) is not the policy of the present legislation; nor (in our view) should it become the policy of the reformed legislation which we now envisage. Nevertheless, the response to the Discussion Paper showed strong support for the view (with which we agree) that such finality should be achieved wherever possible, as for example where there is a childless marriage of comparatively short duration between a husband and a wife who has income, or an earning capacity, or in cases of a longer marriage, where there is an adequate measure of capital available for division."
In his evidence to the House of Commons Special Standing Committee on the 1984 Bill, the President of the Family Division commenting on the provision of s.25A(1) and (2) said that the imposition of financial obligations for limited periods was to a large extent a factor which already operated, "for instance in cases in which an early retirement on the part of the paying party can be foreseen or where the payee requires financial support during a training course". He said:
"I can discern no reason why the court should consider that the particular course would be appropriate in cases in which it is not appropriate. It might be appropriate enough in the case of a short childless marriage during the whole of the period of which both spouses have continued their pre-marriage employment. It would be entirely inappropriate in cases in which the wife had a continuing charge of young children or where the marriage has been long and the wife has not worked during it or during the larger part of it and is middle-aged at the time of the divorce. It would be equally inappropriate where the evidence suggests an impossibility or great difficulty in obtaining employment however well equipped for this purpose the spouse might be. The function of convincing the court by the evidence that it is appropriate to terminate financial support or to order it for a limited period will have to be discharged by the party advocating that course and it is upon consideration of that evidence that the court's decision would have to rest."

## (ii) Short childless marriages

A clean break is likely to be appropriate in the case of a short childless marriage when the court may have regard to the effects which the marriage has had on a party. Thus in *Attar* v *Attar (No.2)* [1985] FLR 653 it was appropriate to allow the wife support to the extent of £15,000 per annum for two years while she adjusted to the consequences of a very short marriage and found work. This was provided by means of a lump sum payment of £30,000 which the wealthy husband could afford and obviated the need for an order for periodical payments.

## (iii) Where the spouses are self-supporting

Where both parties are self-supporting, a clean break may be achieved at least in income terms by the dismissal of any claim for periodical payments. Continuing provision for children may be necessary and appropriate for a limited term and the accompanying capital adjustment may not immediately achieve a clean break in the most extended sense of the term. Where one of the parties is not yet self-supporting and periodical payments have to be continued for an appropriate period, a clean break in income terms may be achieved at the end of that period by the discharge of the order for periodical payments under s.31. In either case the view has been expressed that "... to make mutual orders for periodical payments in nominal amounts just in case something should happen to either party, or ... as a 'last backstop' is to negate entirely the principle of the 'clean break' ..." (*per* Balcombe LJ in *Whiting* v *Whiting* [1988] 1 WLR 565 at p. 576). The majority of the Court of Appeal in that case (Stocker and Slade LJJ, with Balcombe LJ dissenting) considered that on the facts the judge had not been obviously wrong in taking the view that the maintenance order in favour of the wife "should be kept alive in case unforeseen contingencies, such as redundancy or illness, should in the future deprive the wife (who has done everything she could to pull herself on her feet) of her ability to provide for herself and make it necessary for her again to look to the husband for her needs, so far as he might be able to meet them" (*per* Slade LJ at p. 580).

In *Whiting* v *Whiting*, while the wife had become financially independent after having the benefit of a substantive order for periodical payments while she qualified as a teacher, the husband had been made redundant and now earned considerably less than he had previously. Indeed it was difficult to see how, short of his winning the pools, he was ever likely to be in a position to support her in the future (*per* Balcombe LJ at pp. 576-577). It seems clear from the judgments of the majority that their own inclination would have been to terminate the periodical payments order. Thus Stocker LJ (at p. 578) said:

> "It may well be that judges faced with the situation such as prevailed in this case, in which it is unlikely that the financial position of one spouse will ever justify any order other than a nominal one, will come to the conclusion that, in the absence of special factors, a proper exercise of their discretion will require a 'clean break' to be imposed ..."

(see also Slade LJ at p. 581). Nevertheless, they were unable to find that the court was entitled to substitute its own conclusion for that reached by the judge in the exercise of his discretion. Importance was also attached to the wife's lack of capital resources. Slade LJ, after noting that if redundancy or bad health were to intervene,

the wife's present good earnings might cease prematurely, said (at p. 580):
"This might not matter if she had substantial capital resources. However, because of her commitments as wife and mother, she has had a less good opportunity than the husband to build up any capital resources. She has not been able to accumulate any savings and has not received any capital sum on the break up of the marriage beyond her half share in the net proceeds of the house ... pursuant to the order [of the court]. This house, we were told, had previously been held by the two parties as joint tenants. Apart from the equity of redemption in her fairly modest home, she has virtually no capital".

Balcombe LJ, dissenting, acknowledged that there was no capital sum paid by the husband to the wife at the time of separation to commute in advance her "right" to provide payments. However, Waite J in *Tandy* v *Tandy* October 24, 1986 Lexis Enggen had said that "... there will be circumstances in which fairness to one side demands and to the other side permits, a severance of the maintenance tie in cases where no capital resources are available". Moreover, in *Whiting* v *Whiting* the wife had a share of the capital resources in that she had a share of the proceeds of the house, and that is how she now had her own home.

Finally, it is important to note that Slade LJ (at p. 581) concluded that:
"Judges who are called on to exercise the relevant powers conferred by s.31(7) of the 1973 Act (or under the corresponding provisions of s.25A) may find that the task is not an easy one. I venture to hope that the decision of this court, albeit reflecting a difference of opinion among its members, will serve as a reminder that the 'consideration' made requisite by the newly introduced statute must be real and substantial and that the easier course of declining to order a clean break may not in all cases be the right one."

A wife may be in no immediate need of periodical payments due in part at least to cohabitation with another man. In such circumstances the courts have declined to equate cohabitation with remarriage and effect a clean break. If a substantive order is unnecessary, the courts have preferred to make a nominal order rather than a discharge of the order (see *Suter* v *Suter and Jones* [1987] Fam 111). In *Hepburn* v *Hepburn* [1989] 1 FLR 373 at p. 376 Butler-Sloss LJ said that she did not share the view that nominal orders were a hangover from the previous period and were undesirable.

(iv) Clean break where there are children
In a number of cases decided before the 1984 Act amendments came into force, the court had expressed the view that where there were children for whom the parties shared a continuing obligation there was likely to be little or no room for the father and mother to have a clean break from each other. See e.g. *Pearce* v *Pearce* (1979) 1 FLR 261 and *Moore* v *Moore* (1980) 11 Fam Law 109. In *Moore* Ormrod LJ said:
"It is one thing to talk about a 'clean break' when there are sufficient financial resources to make a comprehensive settlement. Where there are no capital resources as here, it is unrealistic to talk about a 'clean break' if there are children. It is not possible for the father and mother of dependent children to have a clean break from one another ... So, in my judgement the so-called principle of the 'clean break' has no application where there are young children".

However, in *Suter* v *Suter and Jones* [1987] Fam 111 at p. 121 Sir Roualeyn Cumming-Bruce agreed with the submission of counsel that the new s.25A imposes a mandatory duty on the court in every case to apply itself to the questions set out in s.25A(2) whenever a court decides to make a periodical payments order in favour of a party to a marriage. He said that the "judgments in the cases before 1984 have to be read with that in mind. Though the parties may have to co-operate with each other over children still dependent on them, it may be possible on the facts to recognise a date when the party in whose favour the order is made will have been able to adjust without undue hardship to the termination of financial dependence on the other party". The judge must, therefore, specifically address himself to the question whether "this" wife could and should find a way of adjusting her way of life so as to attain financial independence of her husband. On the facts it was not possible at that time to predict with confidence when the wife would have been able to make the adjustment which would lead to the inference that it would then be just and reasonable to terminate her right to claim periodical payments from her husband. The children were growing up and it was likely that it would become progressively easier for the wife to organise and increase her earning capacity. But there were too many uncertainties to predict the development of events over the next ten years. Likewise, it was too early to predict the financial advantages which on the judge's finding she could expect to derive, if she wished, from her association with the co-respondent.

In contrast, in *Mortimer-Griffin* v *Mortimer-Griffin* [1986] 2 FLR 315 a clean break was achieved even though the one child of the marriage was aged fourteen and might go on to higher education which indicated a need for support for some years to come. After the marriage had broken down the wife had retrained as a teacher and had assumed sole responsibility for the maintenance of herself and her daughter. The husband had subsequently been made redundant and was now unemployable as a result of a physical disability. It is not in fact clear from the report whether the wife's claim for periodical payments was made and, if made, dismissed, but Sir John Donaldson MR said (at p. 317):

"As a result of the various orders which have been made ... the husband is clear of all existing past and future liability to maintain his wife, although it is fair to point out ... that in view of the circumstances which exist between the husband and wife, it is not conceivable - unless there was some very substantial change in their respective circumstances - that any court would have made an order requiring the husband to maintain the wife."

In fact not only was he free of liability towards his former wife but he was effectively clear of liability to maintain his daughter.

Where there are children needing care, then in the absence of substantial capital assets a deferred clean break is a more likely outcome. Indeed in *C* v *C (Financial Provision)* [1989] 1 FLR 11, noted above, an immediate clean break was not achieved in view of the demands of child care on a wife with very substantial capital assets. Although the most likely outcome is an order for periodical payments in favour of the wife for a limited term while the child is of school age, the court may conclude that the wife's earning capacity may cease to be affected by child care responsibilities at an earlier date. In *Waterman* v *Waterman* [1989] 1 FLR 380 the judge had evidence of the wife's earning capacity from which he concluded that periodical payments for a wife caring for a five year old child should cease after five years when the child would be aged ten years. In the Court of Appeal Sir Stephen Brown P had some hesitation in accepting this assessment of the appropriate period but thought it was not plainly wrong. In view of the uncertainty the court did, however, delete the prohibition under s.28(1A) preventing the wife from applying for extension of the limited term.

(v) The "clean break" and state support

In *Moore* v *Moore* (1980) 11 Fam Law 109 Ormrod LJ said that it was not the policy of the law to impose a clean break when the effect would be to drive a wife on to supplementary benefit. The Law Commission said that this was not the policy of the existing legislation, and that it should not become the policy of the reformed legislation which it envisaged. This remains the case where one spouse clearly has the capacity to support or at least provide a meaningful contribution to the support of the other former spouse who is not in a position to adjust to complete financial independence. More difficult are the cases where the available resources are so limited that one party is dependent on state support and the other is unable to make a contribution sufficient to remove her from dependence on state support. The limited contribution which he can make passes by way of partial reimbursement to the state and confers no benefit on his former spouse. This situation has been governed by the principle in *Barnes* v *Barnes* [1972] 1 WLR 1381 whereby the supporting party is expected to make such contribution as is appropriate having regard to the relationship between the level of subsistence and what is left to him after meeting the terms of the order (see Chapter 19). Although this may produce fairness it can involve repeated litigation in the form of applications for variation. This principle must now be reconciled with the principle embodied in the 1984 amendments of seeking to achieve a clean break.

This was attempted by Waite J in the Court of Appeal in *Ashley* v *Blackman* [1988] Fam 85 at p. 92 when he said:

"... I do not think that there is necessarily any legislative inconsistency in introducing on the one hand the clean break objective for mandatory consideration in variation cases, and preserving on the other hand a formula for the exercise of the discretion which perpetuates in such cases the principle of *Barnes* v *Barnes* [1972] 1 WLR 1381. The implied Parliamentary intention ... is that the courts should for the future bear both those policy aspects in mind and strike whatever balance - or if need be make whatever choice - between them that the requirements of justice in the particular circumstances appear to dictate. The devious or the feckless husband will still be prevented from throwing his proper maintenance obligations on the state. The genuine struggler, on the other hand, will be spared the burden of having to pay to his former spouse indefinitely the last few pounds that separate him from total penury. Between the two extremes there will be ample opportunity for flexible orders which give proper weight to both heads of policy, including in suitable cases a use of the phased or tapered termination process over a period of time which the substituted s.31(7) ... appears to contemplate."

That case was in his view "a classic instance for applying the clean break objective" (*ibid.*). The parties had been divorced in 1971 after a marriage lasting thirteen years. A periodical payments order had been made in favour of the wife and there had been three previous applications for variation. The former wife, aged 48, suffered from schizophrenia and the periodical payments (at that time £14 per week) which she had been receiving from the husband represented only a small fraction of her income, the bulk of which was provided in one form or another by the State. The husband, aged 55, had remarried and having brought up the children of the marriage now had two further children. His very modest income was insufficient to attract income tax and every penny he paid simply reduced the amount of state benefit to which the wife would otherwise be entitled. The Court of Appeal made an order under s.31(7) terminating the periodical payments. Waite J said:

"No humane society could tolerate, even in the interests of saving its public purse, the prospect of a divorced couple of acutely limited means remaining manacled to each other indefinitely by the necessity to return at regular intervals to court for no other purpose than to thrash out at public expense the precise figure which the one shall pay to the other, not for any benefit to either of them, but solely for the relief of the tax-paying section of the community to which neither of them has sufficient means to belong."

(See also Ward J in *Delaney* v *Delaney* [1990] 2 FLR 457 at p. 461 and Chapter 19, Part 6.)

### (e) Undue hardship and financial independence

Where the court proposes to make an order for periodical payments it must consider whether it would be appropriate to require those payments to be made or secured only for such term as would in the opinion of the court be sufficient to enable the party in whose favour the order is made to adjust without undue hardship to the termination of his or her financial dependence on the other party (s.25A(2)). The implication must be that if the court is proposing to impose an immediate clean break then there has been, or at least will be, no financial dependency. In other words there will be no undue hardship from an immediate dismissal of the application for periodical payments for the applicant, on the basis of her own income, earning capacity and assets, or as a result of capital payments or transfers in her favour, or both. She will be financially independent or "self-sufficient". In *Ashley* v *Blackman* [1988] Fam 85 at p. 93 Waite J said that "... Parliament intended by the use of that formula to include situations where the period of adjustment would be nil because the hardship would be nil". The concepts of "undue hardship" and "financial independence" or "self-sufficiency" call for further consideration.

First it seems implicit in the statutory provisions that a party may have to accept some hardship as a result of a clean break. Where the available resources of the parties are limited, some diminution in their financial position may be inevitable as a result of the existence of two households rather than one. Where a clean break is desirable because of the bitterness following breakdown of the marriage, the fact that a party does not receive, or no longer receives, periodical payments from the other but has to rely on his or her own earning capacity and resources may cause some degree of hardship. This should not prevent a clean break.

Secondly, before determining whether there would be undue hardship resulting from the termination of periodical payments, the court must make some assessment of the applicant's expectation in the light of all the circumstances of the case. The expression "undue hardship" is not to be regarded as a reference solely to the needs of an applicant wife in a narrow sense. Similarly, the idea of moving to "financial independence" does not mean that the court is concerned only with whether the wife can support herself, and the mere fact that she can obtain employment does not necessarily justify termination of periodical payments. The question is whether she can support herself at the appropriate standard.

In the unreported decision of the Court of Appeal in *Ring* v *Ring* December 19, 1986 Lexis Enggen, Waite J said that the provisions of s.25A(2) were "clear indications that something more will normally be required than a mere parting of the ways on terms which enable each side to take what is theirs without regard to inequalities of financial strength or earning power". The judge had made an error of principle when he terminated the wife's future maintenance rights on the basis of a lump sum which left her with little or nothing more than her equitable entitlement from the spouses' joint assets. It had contained no element of commutation or compensation for the loss of the wife's *prima facie* right to maintenance from a husband with high earnings.

In *Boylan* v *Boylan* [1988] 1 FLR 282 at p. 289 Booth J, after pointing out that the court must have regard to all the circumstances of the case, said:

"It is, therefore, relevant to this issue that the wife is the former spouse of a man of substantial wealth and it is by that standard that her reasonable requirements should be judged and an assessment made as to whether or not she would suffer 'undue hardship' on the termination of the payments".

The court rejected the argument for the husband that the court's approach should be based on the wife's needs which then amounted to £10,000 per annum. Her needs constituted only one factor, and the fact that a wife is thrifty is not a reason for reducing the amount of payments to her any more than it would be a reason for increasing them if she were a spendthrift. The wife could reasonably expect to participate in the husband's wealth for she had contributed, albeit in a small way, by working in the business which was the source of that wealth and which was started at about the same time as the marriage. The only circumstances in which the wife's rights to periodical payments could be terminated in such a way as would not cause undue hardship to her would be upon payment by the husband of a sum sufficient to provide her with an income comparable with that which she would receive by way of periodical payments. The husband's offer had been based on the amount to cover her needs for a limited period and was wholly inadequate.

In *Gojkovic* v *Gojkovic* [1990] 1 FLR 140 at p. 144 Butler-Sloss LJ said that not only is an applicant's future earning capacity relevant but so also is the standard of living enjoyed by the family before the breakdown of the marriage. The proposed standard of living of both spouses must be a relevant consideration and, where finances permit, they should not be wholly out of proportion to each other. The judge had found that the wife had made an exceptional contribution to the wealth generated during their relationship and marriage, a contribution greater than that often made by wives after long marriages. The wife had earned her share, and that share was not to be calculated exclusively in relation to her needs which in a narrow sense could have been met by the offer of suitable accommodation and a lump sum producing an income of £30,000 a year net.

## 6. Discretion and the one-third rule

*(a) The discretion conferred on the courts*
The wide discretion conferred upon the courts by ss.23, 24 and 25 of the 1973 Act has been emphasised on a number of occasions. In *Trippas* v *Trippas* [1973] Fam 134 at p. 144 Scarman LJ said that it was "essential that the court should retain the complete flexibility of approach that the statute there emphasises - all the circumstances of the case, past, present, and in so far as one can make a reliable estimate - future".

There have also been a number of warnings about the way in which reported cases should be viewed. Thus in *Martin (BH)* v *Martin (D)* [1978] Fam 12 at p. 20 Ormrod LJ said:

"It is the essence of such a discretionary situation that the court should preserve, so far as it can, the utmost elasticity to deal with each case on its own facts. Therefore, it is a matter of trial and error and imagination on the part of those advising clients. It equally means that decisions of this court can never be better than guidelines. They are not precedents in the strict sense of the word. There is bound to be an element of uncertainty in the use of wide discretionary powers given to the court under the Act of 1973 and no doubt there always will be, because as social circumstances change so the court will have to adapt the ways in which it exercises discretion."

*(b) The so-called "one-third rule"*
In view of the width of the court's discretion it is not surprising that some element of certainty was sought. To some extent at least, this has been provided by the so-called "one-third rule". In *Wachtel* v *Wachtel* [1973] Fam 72 at p. 94 Lord Denning said that a good starting point was to regard the wife as entitled at some time to one-third of the combined resources of the parties. This figure was, however, only a starting point as he explained:

"But this so-called rule is not a rule and must never be so regarded. In any calculation the court has to have a starting point. If it is not to be one-third, should it be one-half or one-quarter? A starting point at one-third of the combined resources of the parties is as good and rational a starting point as any other, remembering that the essence of the legislation is to secure flexibility to meet the justice of particular cases, and not rigidity, forcing particular cases to be fitted into some so-called principle within which they do not easily lie. There may be cases where more than one-third is right. There are likely to be many others where less than one-third is the only practicable solution. But one-third as a flexible starting point is in general more likely to lead to the correct final result than a starting point of equality or a quarter."

He went on to say that if the court was only concerned with the division of capital assets it would be tempting to divide them in half, which was the course taken by

Ormrod J at first instance. However, he noted that most wives are not content with a share of the capital assets, and also want their former husbands to support them by making periodical payments. In addition, he will normally be making payments for the children, even if they are with her, and in view of these calls on his future earnings, it was not generally appropriate for her to have both half the capital assets and half the earnings, but she would usually get a share of each.

It became clear that there were a number of situations where the one-third rule was inappropriate. First, it is inappropriate where the parties are of small means when the dominating factor is the necessity of providing for the needs of the parties and any children (*Cann* v *Cann* [1977] 1 WLR 938; *Scott* v *Scott* [1978] 1 WLR 723 *per* Cumming-Bruce LJ at p. 728). Secondly, it is likely to be inappropriate where the available resources are very large and one party is substantially better off than the other (*Preston* v *Preston* [1982] Fam 17). In *Slater* v *Slater* (1982) 3 FLR 364 at p. 369 Sir John Arnold P said that "... in very big cases and in very small cases the one-third guideline is not particularly helpful, but in cases in between, in my view, it is a very useful guideline provided that it is clearly understood that, to the extent that the facts of individual cases so dictate, it is necessary to depart from the guideline in one direction or another." One cause for departure, which was relevant in that case, may be the requirement that the husband should be left with sufficient money to meet his proper commitments. The Court of Appeal must consider the net effect of the orders on the parties. This approach came into favour in cases such as *Stockford* v *Stockford* (1982) 3 FLR 58 and *Furniss* v *Furniss* (1982) 3 FLR 46 where resources were limited if not small. This was accompanied by criticisms of the one-third rule by Ormrod LJ in particular. Thus in *Furniss* v *Furniss* (at p. 51) he said that the fact that high interest rates had to be paid on mortgages even on the most modest of houses on the one hand and subsidies were available to people with little money on the other, made the one-third calculation on gross incomes wholly unsatisfactory. "Many times this court had said that in these days the one-third approach is not helpful. It may help sometimes, it may give a right idea of the position, but generally it misleads."

Criticism in another context came in *Potter* v *Potter* [1982] 1 WLR 1255 when the Court of Appeal said that in cases involving the redistribution of capital, the one-third approach was not appropriate. In straightforward cases of applications for periodical payments where the incomes of the parties are readily ascertainable, the one-third guideline was a useful rule of thumb adopted by the profession for many years as an approach to the kind of income liability under which a husband might expect to find himself. However, as that case showed, the practical disadvantage of the one-third approach in relation to capital assets was that it was first necessary to arrive at a global figure to which it could be applied. That raised problems of valuation which were acute where the husband was engaged in a one-man business. Dunn LJ suggested that the proper approach in a case of that kind was to take the wife's reasonable requirements and balance those against the husband's ability to pay. that would involve a general consideration of his sources of income and capital, and in particular his liquidity position. Criticisms of the one-third rule may also be found in *Smith* v *Smith* (1983) 4 FLR 154; *Hall* v *Hall* [1984] FLR 631 at p. 633 and *Sharp* v *Sharp* [1984] FLR 752 at p. 755.

However, in *Bullock* v *Bullock* [1986] 1 FLR 372 at p. 475 Sir John Arnold P referring to *Potter* v *Potter* and *Smith* v *Smith* said that he did not think that these decisions constituted a direction to the court to reject the learning of *O'D* v *O'D* [1976] Fam 83 where the award of the lump sum to be paid by the husband was based on a computation of one-third of the value of the husband's fortune and was upheld by the Court of Appeal. The adoption of the one-third convention by the judge in the case did not make her judgment one which should be overturned. Parker LJ (at p. 375) agreeing, said that "in the present case, there is no question of it being necessary to destroy the income-producing asset in order to comply with the award". In other cases where it is so necessary, other considerations might apply.

In *Dew* v *Dew* [1986] 2 FLR 341 at p. 344 Anthony Lincoln J said that he did not consider that any *dicta* in *Potter* v *Potter* were intended to fetter the wide discretion to be exercised in accordance with the guidance offered by s.25 of the 1973 Act as amended, or to exclude the one-third or any other approach which will assist the court in such an exercise. "The fraction may serve as a starting point from which one can take a bearing in one's journey through the provisions of s.25 of the Act of 1973. It may be left behind, perhaps far behind, in the search for an equitable distribution, or it may be returned to as the appropriate apportionment." Accordingly he did not regard *Bullock* as being in conflict with *Potter* or as "reinstating" the one-third approach, since the latter never became defunct as a helpful guide in some but not all cases. Moreover, he said *Potter* was a very different case. The objective of the Court of Appeal there was to make good a deficiency in a wife's income and this could best be done by an award of a capital sum against the husband to produce such income. The purpose was not to apportion and redistribute the capital assets as such. In *Bullock* the husband's capital assets were valued at over £1 million and the wife's assets at £60,000. One-third of the total gave £350,000 pointing to a lump sum of £290,000 for the wife. However, after taking into account the requirements of s.25 and the fact that the husband's assets were not readily realisable she was awarded a lump sum of £135,000 payable in three instalments. Anthony Lincoln J said (at p. 346): "I do not lose sight of the initial starting point of just under £300,000 which is left far behind but is not wholly invisible".

The one-third rule was not intended to be more than a starting point to be justified or departed from after a consideration of the factors referred to in s.25. It was intended to do justice in "what one might call the average run of cases" (*per* Ormrod LJ in *S* v *S* [1977] Fam 127 at p. 130). Lord Denning in *Wachtel* v *Wachtel* [1973] Fam 72 at p. 95 thought it would be suitable in cases where the marriage had lasted for many years and the wife had been in the home bringing up the children. He acknowledged that it might not be applicable when the marriage had lasted only a short time, or where there were no children and she could go out to work. In the former case her contributions will probably have been small and hence she will have "earned" a smaller share of available resources. In the latter case it is arguable that since the husband will not have to make income provision for children (and perhaps only limited provision for the wife), the starting point for capital provision should be one half rather than one-third. This would seem to apply with particular force if she has brought up children but they are no longer dependent. (But see *W* v *W* [1977] Fam 107.)

Where a clean break is to be imposed, so that no income provision is to be made for the wife, one of the underlying reasons for the rule as stated by Lord Denning is not present and it seems more difficult to justify one-third as the starting point. In earlier cases where the court considered that periodical payments would be inappropriate in view of likely recurring difficulties of enforcement, a wife was awarded larger capital provision than one-third (see e.g. *Weisz* v *Weisz* [1975] The Times 16 December; *Bryant* v *Bryant* (1976) 120 SJ 165; and *Griffiths* v *Griffiths* [1979] 1 WLR 1350). Again in *Eshak* v *Nowojewski* (1981) 11 Fam Law 115, where the wife had remarried, Sir John Arnold P said that the "general approach in a case in which there is no question of periodical payments for a spouse is to regard the spouse's claim as starting at any rate with the idea of an equal division. Of course that idea would yield to the circumstances of any particular case". (Contrast *Dennis* v *Dennis* (1976) 6 Fam Law 54 and *Kadylak* v *Kadylak* (1975) 5 Fam Law 19.)

A reduced role for the one-third rule was to be expected with the increased emphasis on achieving a clean break following the Matrimonial and Family Proceedings Act 1984, even though provision for the children might have to continue. When this is coupled with the earlier recognition that there are situations where it is clearly unhelpful and inappropriate and criticisms arising from a rigid application in some cases, it is understandable that the one-third rule appears no longer to have the influence it once had. Nevertheless, some reference to the one-third rule continues to be made in the reported cases. Thus in *Hope-Smith* v *Hope-Smith* [1989] 2 FLR 56 the judge, in calculating the lump sum to be paid to the wife out of the proceeds of sale of the former matrimonial home, had clearly assessed the sum as a portion of the anticipated available net proceeds of sale, starting at one-third which he then increased so as to provide a sum more nearly approximating to that which the wife would need to rehouse herself with the aid of a mortgage. This resulted in a figure of 37.9 per cent. Unfortunately the sum payable had not been expressed as a fraction but as a fixed sum, and on appeal an order for payment of a percentage of the proceeds of sale was substituted. Although this was fixed at 40 per cent there was no criticism of the judge's starting point of one-third even though it was not his finishing point.

In *Gojkovic* v *Gojkovic* [1990] 1 FLR 140 at p. 146, where the husband had very considerable assets, Butler-Sloss LJ noted that the judge had tested the lump sum order he proposed to make "in other ways" - half the value of the hotel she had been running and approximately one-third of the joint assets - though he was at pains to say that he was not making his decision in reliance upon either of these bases. In *Peacock* v *Peacock* [1991] 1 FLR 324 where a clean break could not be achieved on an application to vary an order for periodical payments in the absence of an agreed payment by the husband in commutation, Thorpe J granted the wife's application for an increase in the order to £1,500. He said (at p. 331):

"Whilst that figure is considerably below the one-third rule of thumb, it reflects the fact that the wife has the use of the husband's share of the property".

It might need to be reviewed after the husband had received his share of the property.

It seems that the one-third rule may still be a useful starting point or checking device but it is important to remember its limited objectives. It is important also to have regard to its rationale which in some respects is difficult to reconcile with the rationale of the clean break.

## 7. Matters affecting particular criteria

*(a) The income, earning capacity, property and other financial resources which each of the parties to the marriage has or is likely to have in the foreseeable future, including in the case of earning capacity any increase in that capacity which it would in the opinion of the court be reasonable to expect a party to the marriage to take steps to acquire*

(i) Income and earning capacity

In considering income the court must take into account not only basic pay, but also overtime pay or the ability to earn it (*Klucinski* v *Klucinski* [1953] 1 All ER 683). If the court is satisfied that a husband is earning less than he could if he wished, then it may take into account his earning capacity. The same applies where it is satisfied that a man who is unemployed is capable of working, though in both situations whether it is reasonable to take into account potential earning capacity will depend upon the facts of the particular case. Thus in *McEwan* v *McEwan* [1972] 1 WLR 1217, a decision in relation to the matrimonial jurisdiction of the magistrates' courts, the court took into account the potential earning capacity of a retired detective constable aged 59. In the light of evidence about the demand for labour in his home town the court inferred that he was voluntarily unemployed. In *Griffiths* v *Griffiths* [1974] 1 WLR 1350 the court concluded on the evidence that it was reasonable to attribute to a 51 year old husband who had been employed as a consulting engineer, but had been unemployed for three years, a potential earning capacity of £5,000 per annum. In *K* v *K (Conduct)* [1990] FLR 225 the husband had an earning capacity, although it might take him some time to find employment. He had not made reasonable efforts to find employment since he had lost his job several years previously, and no order for periodical payments was made in his favour against his wife who had a significant income. He was, however, awarded a lump sum larger than his half share of the home in view of his need for accommodation. On the other hand, in *Bennett* v *Bennett* (1978) 9 Fam Law 19 where the husband had resigned from a good job after 19 years because of a clash of personality with his managing director and was subsequently unable to find comparable employment, the Court of Appeal said that the judge had paid too little regard to the difficulties which the husband faced and to a natural unwillingness on his part to accept new employment at substantially reduced remuneration. (See also *Williams* v *Williams* [1974] Fam 55 discussed in Chapter 19.)

There will also be cases where the husband's income may be difficult to ascertain in view of the way in which he carries on his business affairs by making use of capital and the ability to borrow. In *Robinson* v *Robinson* (1981) 2 FLR 1 at p. 14 Scarman LJ said that a man was not to be criticised for that, but that the "courts must keep their common sense and they must look to the standard of life that the man nevertheless maintains - in fact, at his whole life-style - and one does not need any very great research into the authorities to observe that the courts have consistently refused to be blinded by arithmetical science in determining the ability of a rich man to make provision for his wife and children" (see also *J* v *J* [1955] P 215; *Schlesinger* v *Schlesinger* [1960] P 191; *Newton* v *Newton* [1990] 1 FLR 33 and *E* v *E* [1990] 2 FLR 233).

There are also cases where a husband receives allowances designed to cover expenses incurred in the course of his employment, but which nevertheless cover matters which he would, to some extent at least, otherwise have to discharge out of his income. These sums should be taken into account even though they cannot be dealt with as a matter of strict calculation on one side or other of the account (*Chichester* v *Chichester* [1936] P 129; *Sibley* v *Sibley* (1981) 2 FLR 121. For the distinction between matters which should be "brought into account" and matters "to be taken into account" or into "consideration" see Ormrod LJ in *Macey* v *Macey* (1982) 3 FLR 7 at p. 11).

(ii) Potential earning capacity

The wording of paragraph (a) was amended by the Matrimonial and Family Proceedings Act 1984, s.3, to require the court to have regard not only to the earning capacity which a party was likely to have in the foreseeable future, but also to *any increase in that capacity which it would in the opinion of the court be reasonable to expect a party to the marriage to take steps to acquire.* Potential earning capacity of an applicant spouse is likely to be a crucial part of the court's assessment of whether, and, if so, when, his or her financial dependence on the other party can be terminated so as to achieve a deferred clean break. This change was intended to emphasise the importance of a factor which the courts had already taken into account in a number of cases. In *Brady* v *Brady* (1973) 3 Fam Law 78 Sir George Baker P had said that there was "no reason why a wife whose marriage has not lasted long and who has no child, should have a 'bread ticket' for life". (See also *Graves* v *Graves* (1973) 117 SJ 679.) In *Soni* v *Soni* [1984] FLR 294 at p. 297 Sheldon J, agreeing with this view, went on to say:

"In all likelihood, moreover, the younger the wife may be and the shorter the marriage (particularly if there are no children) the more difficult it will be for her to persuade the court that she is unable to earn her own living and to order her husband to make any substantial continuing provision for her. But there can be no hard and fast rule, and the decision in each case must depend upon its particular facts."

The real issue in that case was whether the wife, over a period of some seven years, had made reasonable efforts to obtain employment. Sheldon J concluded that unavailing though most of her efforts had been, throughout the relevant period she had made reasonable efforts "to obtain not only 'teacher' and other training suitable to enable her to make the best use of her professional abilities, but also employment in factories, shops and offices". She had also been handicapped by a combination of factors for which her husband could not escape some responsibility. Sheldon J found her claim for basic periodical payments entirely reasonable but said that as soon as her course of training (or any subsequent more advanced course that she might be advised to take) was completed, she had to redouble her efforts to obtain employment and that it was likely to be more difficult for her to persuade the court that any failure by her thereafter to obtain work was due entirely to factors beyond her control. (See also *Khan* v *Khan* (1981) 2 FLR 131.)

Accordingly, if the applicant is fairly young, the marriage short, and there are no children, financial support is unlikely to be other than of a rehabilitative nature, i.e. only for such period as may be required to enable the dependent party to realise her potential earning capacity - and that period is likely to be short.

On the other hand, if the wife has young children to look after it has been recognised that it may be difficult or impossible for her to undertake employment or at least full-time employment in the short or medium term. In these circumstances the wife's future potential earning capacity may be difficult to predict, particularly over a period that may be as long as ten years, though as the children grow up it is likely to become progressively easier for the wife to organise and increase her earning capacity. (See Sir Roualeyn Cumming-Bruce in *Suter* v *Suter and Jones* [1987] Fam 111 at p. 122.) In *Fisher* v *Fisher* [1989] 1 FLR 423 it was recognised that the existence of an illegitimate child born to the wife after decree nisi was clearly a factor affecting her ability to provide a suitable income for herself. It was envisaged that it would be at least two years before the wife was free of her full-time obligations to the child, then aged 7 years, when he probably would be able to spend the bulk of the day at school rather than returning home for lunch. In addition there had to be a reasonable time for the wife to adjust, to receive appropriate training, and to take steps before it could be said whether employment was available or not. Purchas LJ (at p. 435) said that a court hearing a renewed application for discharge of the order for periodical payments in favour of the wife would not receive kindly a premature application by the husband any more than it would be tolerant to a case presented by the wife which demonstrated that, far from honouring her acceptance that she should get back to work, she had made no material efforts in this direction.

In certain circumstances the court's assessment of a wife's potential earning capacity may be such that it feels able to put a limit on the period for which periodical payments should be made to her. In *C* v *C* *(Financial Provision)* [1989] 1 FLR 11 the wife was aged 49, capable and talented, fluent in two languages and was going to end up with a substantial amount of capital. There was no doubt that a clean break would be appropriate in due course, but for the present the younger son was aged 13 and the fact that she would have to care for him for most of the school holidays meant that her capacity to earn was to some extent reduced. Ewbank J proposed that periodical payments should terminate shortly after the son attained the age of 18. It would, of course, be open for the wife to return to the court to seek an extension of the payments if predictions regarding earning capacity proved to be too optimistic. In view of the uncertainties involved, the court will be very reluctant to include a provision under s.28 (1A) of the 1973 Act prohibiting such an application. In *Waterman* v *Waterman* [1989] 1 FLR 380 the wife, aged 38, had custody of a child aged 5 following the breakdown of a short marriage and a period of cohabitation totalling some 33 months. The Court of Appeal held that an order for periodical payments in her favour to terminate after 5 years was appropriate. However, the judge had not been justified in including a provision under s.28 (1A) prohibiting an application for an extension of that term. There were too many uncertainties about the wife's future position. She had been a secretary until she had begun to live with the husband, and since the divorce she had taken a computer course as well as a course in book-keeping in order to enhance her earning capacity. Her employment opportunities were restricted by the need to care for the child, but the court accepted that a 10 year old child did not require the same degree or intensity of care as a 5 year old. As the child grew older the difficulty of part-time employment would be reduced. Nevertheless, Purchas LJ acknowledged that he would probably not have made even a fixed term order himself.

In *Mitchell* v *Mitchell* [1984] FLR 387 the Court of Appeal felt able to increase the share of the husband in the ultimate net proceeds of sale of the home which was to be sold when the younger child completed his full-time education. The crucial feature of the case, said Dunn LJ, was the wife's earning capacity. She was a qualified and experienced typist who had worked full-time for three years during the marriage. He concluded (at p. 391) that once both children, then aged 17 and 13, had left school and were at work there was "no reason why the wife should not work full-time" and once that happened he would not be surprised if her earnings as a secretary typist, if she chose to work in London, should be comparable to those of the husband if not as substantial. In any event she should be able to earn enough to raise a small mortgage to help her buy the sort of house that she needed.

The courts have also recognised the difficulties of middle-aged and older women who may have cared for children over a lengthy period of time and whose work experience and qualifications are consequently limited. In *Leadbeater* v *Leadbeater* [1985] FLR 789 the wife who had been a secretary at the time of the marriage said that she had not adapted to the new methods, such as word processing, now used in offices. Balcombe J (at p. 796) accepted that at the age of 47 it was "wholly unreasonable to expect her to do so" but she had shown initiative and found a part-time job earning £1,680 per annum. He thought the hours of work could be increased and he credited her with earning capacity of £2,500. In *Barrett* v *Barrett* [1988] 2 FLR 516 the wife was aged 44 and still caring for the youngest of three children of the marriage. Butler-Sloss LJ (at p. 521) acknowledged the difficulty of a wife of that age, "who has not had full-time employment for many years, looking for and willing to find work and indeed prepared to take a course to make her more fit to get employment and still not finding a job". Although she had part-time employment, her future was too uncertain to make an order for periodical payments only for a fixed term. (See also *B* v *B* [1989] 1 FLR 119 and *B* v *B* [1990] 1 FLR 20.)

However, despite acknowledging the difficulties of middle-aged women with little or no current experience and skills, the courts have credited them with limited, but by no means always nominal, earning capacity. Thus in *M* v *M (Financial Provision)* [1987] 2 FLR 1 Heilbron J found that the job prospects of a wife who had spent most of a 20-year marriage at home caring for the household and child, but who had done some part-time secretarial work, were not good, but credited her with earning capacity of approximately £6,000. In *Boylan* v *Boylan* [1988] 1 FLR 282 Booth J found that the wife aged 46 with no formal training or qualifications, but having undertaken occasional unskilled jobs during the marriage, could be credited with a small earning capacity of £5,000 per annum. (See also *Robinson* v *Robinson (No. 2)* [1986] 1 FLR 48.)

(iii) Support from third parties

Where a party has formed another association, this may - and in the case of the husband, very often will - increase his needs and responsibilities. It may, on the other hand, provide additional resources not only in the form of an additional source of income, but also in the form of a home for that party. Indeed the very fact that one party has a secure home with a new partner has been a very important factor in determining the form of order made in relation to the matrimonial home. (See Chapter 12.)

Actual remarriage will automatically terminate any order for periodical payments and no application for capital provision can be made thereafter (see s.28 and Chapter 10). Since the court may hear an application for provision after remarriage provided that it was initiated before remarriage, it may be in the position of having to take account of the fact of remarriage. An applicant's entitlement on the basis of his or her contributions should not be affected, but the remarriage is bound to have a bearing on the assessment of the applicant's financial resources and needs (see *H* v *H* [1975] Fam 9). In relation to the prospects of remarriage, Lord Denning MR in *Wachtel* v *Wachtel* [1973] Fam 72 said at p. 96 that this should not affect a wife's share for "she has earned it by her contribution in looking after the home and caring for the family". This should certainly be the case when the court is concerned with the division of the capital assets on the basis of contributions, but the position is not so clear when the court is considering provision for needs. If the court is "considering to what extent the husband should be called upon to take a smaller share of the assets and to concede a greater share to the wife on the basis of her need or their comparative financial position, prospects of remarriage are ... clearly relevant ..." (*per* Eveleigh LJ in *Tinsdale* v *Tinsdale* (1983) 4 FLR 641 at p. 648). Thus in *Tinsdale* v *Tinsdale* the Court of Appeal did not consider it right to transfer the whole of the husband's interest in the matrimonial home to the wife, and postponed the sale of the home until the wife remarried or cohabited. In *Duxbury* v *Duxbury* [1987] 1 FLR 7, where the husband had substantial assets, Ackner LJ (at p. 12), while acknowledging that in certain cases the wife's prospects of remarriage may not only be a relevant but also an operative factor, attached no weight to such prospects in deciding how much to award by way of a lump sum. The amount necessary to provide for the wife's reasonable needs having been determined, he said (at p. 13) "How she spent it was her affair". If a redistribution of the assets of the family as envisaged in *Wachtel* extends to income-earning capacity as well as to capital assets, then it can be argued that a dependent or quasi-dependent spouse may have earned at least some support while his or her own income-earning capacity is adjusted so far as this may be possible. Against this must be set the fact that s.25 is clearly not concerned simply with the division of assets on the basis of contributions. The possibility of remarriage may also highlight the importance of capital provision, which will be unaffected by remarriage, as against periodical payments. (See *O'D* v *O'D* [1976] Fam 83; *Cumbers* v *Cumbers* [1974] 1 WLR 1331.)

Even though a party has not remarried, the courts may take into account support provided by a cohabitee of that party. In *W* v *W* [1976] Fam 107 the fact that the wife had a joint interest in her new home, where she lived with the father of her illegitimate child, was held to be relevant even though she claimed her interest in the property was not hers beneficially. The interest gave her security and a roof over her head, and this resulted in a small reduction in the lump sum payment she received. (See also *Wynne* v *Wynne and Jeffers* [1981] 1 WLR 69; *Ibbetson* v *Ibbetson* [1984] FLR 545.) The extent of support being derived from a third party is a question of fact and must be established by evidence, though a cohabitee cannot be compelled to file an affidavit of means (*Wynne* v *Wynne and Jeffers*). Thus in *Campbell* v *Campbell* [1976] Fam 347, where the wife's proposed marriage had fallen through, Sir George Baker P declined to draw the inference that she was being supported by the third party. (See also *Tomlinson* v *Tomlinson* [1980] 1 All ER 593.)

The court is not limited to considering the actual amount of support, but can consider the amount which it would be reasonable for the cohabitee to provide. In *Suter* v *Suter and Jones* [1987] Fam 11 the court concluded that as the wife was for practical purposes living with the co-respondent in the former matrimonial home (vested in her alone as a result of the transfer by the husband of his interest), it was just and reasonable to make an order on the basis that she required the co-respondent to contribute not less than £600 per annum to the expenses of the house which she had invited him to enjoy. The Court of Appeal reduced the periodical payments to be made to the wife to a nominal amount. The court declined to dismiss her claim for periodical payments not only because of the uncertainty about her own future earning capacity, but also because of the uncertainty in relation to the financial advantages which on the judge's finding she could expect to derive, if she wished, from her association. There had already been one interruption in the continuity of their cohabitation. She might become increasingly and financially dependent on him. She might not.

On the other hand, in *Duxbury* v *Duxbury* [1987] 1 FLR 7 no account was taken of the fact of cohabitation of the former wife of a very wealthy man. The cohabitee was in comparison a man of insubstantial means so that there was little prospect of the wife receiving significant support from him. The lump sum calculated on the basis of what the wife had earned and on her needs was not reduced because of the cohabitation, and it was irrelevant that she might spend some of it on the cohabitee thus having less for her own benefit.

The possibility of cohabitation is now commonly incorporated into an order postponing sale of the former matrimonial home as an event triggering sale. Thus in *Tinsdale* v *Tinsdale* (1983) 4 FLR 641, where the court postponed sale during the wife's lifetime or until she remarried or became dependent upon another man, Dunn LJ (at p. 648) said that he had "in mind that if she cohabited with another man in the premises then obviously that man ought to take over the responsibility of providing accommodation for her".

On an application to vary or discharge an order for periodical payments it is now clear that while settled cohabitation by a recipient ex-wife with a man is not to be equated with remarriage, or to be given decisive weight, it does constitute a change of circumstances within s.31(7), and cohabitation and the decision not to remarry and the reasons for it are conduct which it would be inequitable for the courts to disregard within s.25(2)(g) considered below (*per* Waterhouse J in *Atkinson* v *Atkinson* [1988] Fam 93 at p. 108). In that case the Court of Appeal upheld the decision of the judge to continue a substantive order for periodical payments in favour of the former wife notwithstanding her cohabitation. However, the amount payable was to be reduced from £6,000 to £4,500 in a year's time on the basis that the cohabitee (who had been made redundant) ought by then to have been able to obtain more remunerative employment. Waterhouse J said that the judge had found that the wife had no means of generating income herself and there was no evidence that she would be able in the foreseeable future to adjust without undue hardship to termination of the periodical payments. A reduction beyond that ordered would reduce her to virtual poverty level. In *Hepburn* v *Hepburn* [1989] 1 FLR 373 the wife had cohabited for over six years with a man, and had become involved in his business interests. The Court of Appeal held that the judge had been entitled to conclude that the former wife ought not to be paid any money at that time, but that in view of the uncertainties, it would not be right to bring the order permanently to an end. A nominal order was upheld and Butler-Sloss LJ said (at p. 378) that "... it is not the job of a court to put pressure on parties to regularize their irregular unions". (See also *S* v *S* [1990] 1 FLR 20.)

Although the availability of the resources of a new partner of one former spouse may be taken into account in determining the provision that is necessary for that spouse, they cannot be taken into account as if they are direct resources of the spouse. The fact that a husband has the benefit of the income or capital of a new wife or a cohabitee may mean that a greater part of his own income is available to make provision for his former wife and children. However, where, for example, the husband is unemployed and has no income, an order for periodical payments cannot be made against him on the basis that payments will be made from the new partner's resources (*Brown* v *Brown* [1981] The Times 14 July; *Macey* v *Macey* (1982) 3 FLR 7; *Re L (Minor) (Financial Provision)* (1981) 1 FLR 39). In *Slater* v *Slater* (1982) 3 FLR 364 at p. 373 May LJ said "... one cannot use a second wife's assets directly to benefit the first wife. It would be wrong to consider her income and that of the husband as a joint fund from which to provide maintenance for the first wife ... but on the other hand, I think that one can take some account of the assets which the second wife may be fortunate enough to possess to provide what I can best describe as a 'cushion' against the net effect that any order in favour of the first wife will have upon the husband's finances". (Contrast earlier cases where a party was being supported through the generosity of friends or business associates when the court looked at his current personal expenditure: *W* v *W* (No. 3) [1962] P 124; *Ette* v *Ette* [1965] 1 All ER 341. It was clear in these cases that he had money at his disposal.)

The fact that other adult members of the family may be living in the home of one party is also relevant, but their contribution must be looked at more broadly. Thus in *Rodewald* v *Rodewald* [1977] Fam 192 at p. 201, where the husband had his 20 year old son and his 21 year old daughter living with him, Ormrod LJ said that "it is wholly unrealistic to try to quantify the contribution which members of a family make in a case like this". He thought that it "is far better to take it broadly that the father's overheads are less than they would be if he did not have these two children living with him in the house". Such considerations "should not come in at the stage when one is seeking to choose a starting point but when one is looking for a sum which will produce broad justice in a particular case". In *Macey* v *Macey* (1982) 3 FLR 7 at p. 11 Ormrod LJ said that "there are certain factors - usually figures capable of fairly accurate assessment - which should be 'brought into account', and which are to be contrasted with matters which are to be 'taken into account' ". He preferred the phrase "taken into consideration".

(iv) Future property

The court is required to take into account not only property and financial resources which a party has at the time the application is heard, but also property and financial resources which a party is likely to have in the foreseeable future. Such property or financial resources may arise as a result of investments made by a spouse, for example in life assurance or, by virtue of his or her employment, in the form of a gratuity or lump sum payment under an occupational pension scheme. (See *Priest* v *Priest* (1981) 1 FLR 189 and *Milne* v *Milne* (1981) 2 FLR 286 considered in Chapter 10.)

It may also be appropriate to take into account property which may come to a party under the terms of a settlement or will. The court must make an assessment of the worth (and likelihood) of this prospect. In *Calder* v *Calder* [1976] The Times 29 June, the court took into account a vested remainder which the husband had in one Canadian settlement and a contingent remainder which he had in another settlement. Ormrod LJ said that these interests could not be ignored because, on a balance of probabilities, the husband would become a wealthy man when they fell into possession. The husband already had assets of his own which enabled the court to provide for an immediate lump sum payment with a larger sum to be paid in the future. (See also *B* v *B* [1990] 1 FLR 20 at p. 27.) On the other hand, the possibility of a party inheriting property from a wealthy parent may be too uncertain and too far in the future to enable any order for capital provision to be made at present. (See *Hardy* v *Hardy* (1981) 2 FLR 321 considered in Chapter 10, and *Ring* v *Ring* Court of Appeal December 19, 1986 Lexis Enggen.) In *Michael* v *Michael* [1986] 2 FLR 389 at    p. 395 Nourse LJ said:

"... I am of the clear opinion that s.25(2)(a) of the Act of 1973 as amended, while it is primarily concerned with property and financial resources in which there is a vested or contingent interest, is not exclusively so concerned. Indeed, its broad and somewhat informal language demonstrates that it was intended to operate at large and not in some strait-jacket tailored to the sober uniforms of property law. Thus, there can be no doubt that it could in certain circumstances extend to something which in the language of the law is a mere expectancy or *spes successionis*, for example an interest which might be taken under the will of a living person."

He considered a case where there was clear evidence, first, that the respondent's father was suffering from a terminal illness, secondly, that his will left property of substantial but uncertain value to the respondent, and thirdly, that it was highly improbable that he would revoke it. In such a case it could, in his view, hardly be doubted either that the property was property which the respondent was likely to have in the foreseeable future or that the application should be adjourned until the death of the father. However, those facts he considered to be very special - and they demonstrated that rarely will such an interest fall within s.25(2)(a). In the normal case, uncertainty both as to the prospect of inheritance and as to the time at which it will occur and would make it impossible to hold that the property was property which the party was likely to have in the foreseeable future. In *Michael* v *Michael* there was considerable uncertainty as to whether the wife would take any interest under her mother's will, and the mother's high blood pressure was not such as to pose a serious threat to her life in the near future. (See also *Morgan* v *Morgan* [1977] Fam 122.)

This may be contrasted with *MT* v *MT (Financial Provision: Lump Sum)* [1992] 1 FLR 362 where there was no doubt that the husband would be entitled to a fixed share in the estate of his elderly father under German law and there was a possibility that he would inherit a larger share. Moreover, the prospect of such inheritance had dominated the financial decisions of the parties during the marriage. An adjournment of the wife's application until the death of the husband's father was therefore appropriate.

(v) After-acquired property

Where an application is made a considerable time after the separation of the parties, it is relevant to take into account the fact that the assets of the respondent have been acquired after the separation. In some cases, such as *Lombardi* v *Lombardi* [1973] 1 WLR 1276, the fact that the husband's position has greatly improved through the efforts of himself and his cohabitee or new wife, long after the original separation, will be a very important consideration. It is unlikely that any - or at least any substantial - order will be made which involves the use of assets acquired in this way. In *S* v *S (Financial Provision)* [1990] 2 FLR 252 the Court of Appeal held that Booth J had been entitled to take the view that when the court was considering the wife's claim for ancillary relief some nine years after the dissolution of the marriage it was not appropriate to look at the husband's financial position as if the marriage had just come to an end.

On the other hand, there are no "reserved funds, or reserved sources of money to which the court should not in proper cases have resort" (*per* Ormrod LJ in *Pearce* v *Pearce* (1981) 1 FLR 26 at p. 267). Thus where, as in *Pearce* v *Pearce*, a husband has acquired assets by gift or inheritance, it may be very reasonable to resort to such assets - particularly where he has hitherto failed to discharge his responsibility to his former wife or children. It may also be relevant to take into account assets acquired by an applicant wife by way of gift or inheritance. Thus, in *Schuller* v *Schuller* [1990] 2 FLR 193, after the parties had separated in 1977 the husband had remained in the matrimonial home while the wife went to work as a housekeeper for an elderly friend who bought a flat in their joint names. On the friend's death she inherited the whole interest in the flat in which she continued to live, and was residuary beneficiary of his estate which was worth something over £4,000. The Court of Appeal held that the judge had properly taken into account the wife's after-acquired assets in deciding the provision to which she was entitled. Nourse LJ (at pp. 200-201) said that "there can be nothing wrong at all in a judge taking the view that each party should be able to keep the house in which he or she lives, especially if it can be kept without further incumbrance. That is a form of equality which is so desirable as to outweigh any minute attention to questions such as how and when and whence the houses were acquired". He did, however, say that there is no special magic in an equal division of all the parties' assets according to their current values. In *Primavera* v *Primavera* [1992] 1 FLR 16 some nine years after the original dissolution of the marriage the wife inherited her mother's estate consisting primarily of a house. In compliance with her mother's wishes she divided the proceeds of sale between herself and her two daughters although, in contrast to her husband who was a man of substantial wealth, she was not in a strong financial position. Glidewell LJ concluded that the wife's actions had been justified, but he emphasised that in a different and perhaps more normal situation where the parties were of more modest means, it might well be that the effect of the wife's inheritance would be a material consideration which it would be quite wrong not to put into the balance to some extent when considering an application to vary the order for periodical payments.

(vi) Damages for personal injuries
There used to be a difference of judicial opinion as to whether damages for personal injuries should be taken into account as part of the resources of a party within paragraph (a). In *Armstrong* v *Armstrong* (1974) 4 Fam Law 156 the judge deducted, from the value of the husband's farm, the sum received by the husband by way of general damages for personal injuries and invested by him in the farm. In the Court of Appeal Buckley LJ upheld this decision on the basis that the husband had suffered and that the compensation was personal to him. Stephenson LJ expressed doubt, but agreed that it was not justifiable to interfere with the judge's decision. (See also *Jones* v *Jones* [1976] Fam 8.) In *Smith* v *Smith* November 28, 1974 unreported, Bar Library Transcript No. 380A Ormrod J expressed strongly the view that the sum of £2,500 damages which had been awarded to the husband for personal injuries must be taken into account as part of his resources, and this view was upheld by the Court of Appeal. This view prevailed in *Daubney* v *Daubney* [1976] Fam 267 where all the previous cases were considered by the Court of Appeal. However, even on this view, Scarman LJ accepted that it is relevant to note that such compensation is given for pain and suffering and loss of amenity. It would not be a correct exercise of the discretion under s.25 to make an order which in effect would deprive the spouse of all benefit from such compensation (*ibid.* at p. 967. See also *Cawkwell* v *Cawkwell* (1978) 9 Fam Law 25). In *Wagstaff* v *Wagstaff* [1992] 1 WLR 320 at p. 325 Butler-Sloss LJ said that that should not be taken as saying that no part of damages awarded under the head of pain and suffering should be charged by the other spouse. Lord Donaldson MR (at p. 327) said that such compensation was a financial asset which, like money earned by one spouse by working excessively long hours or in disagreeable circumstances, was, subject to human selfishness, available to the whole family before the breakdown of the marriage, and like any other asset was to be taken into account when the court came to exercise its powers under s.25.

Any alteration of a husband's financial position as a result of divorce or breakdown of marriage should be wholly disregarded when it comes to assessing the damages recoverable from a third party even though the divorce has resulted from injuries caused to the plaintiff husband by the negligence of that third party. (See *Pritchard* v *J H Cobden Ltd* [1988] Fam 22.)

(vii) Social security benefits
The relevance of social security benefits is considered in Chapter 19.

(viii) Gross or net income
In assessing the joint income of the parties, it was emphasised by Ormrod LJ in the Court of Appeal in *Rodewald* v *Rodewald* [1977] Fam 192 that it was the two *gross* incomes that should be combined. It was to that total that the one-third rule should be applied to produce a starting point, as was done in *Wachtel* v *Wachtel* [1973] Fam 72. "Gross income" means income before deduction of income tax, but certain other deductions are generally made at this stage such as essential expenses in connection with earning the income and national insurance contributions. More recently in *Furniss* v *Furniss* (1982) 3 FLR 46 at p. 51 Ormrod LJ described the gross calculation as old fashioned, and said that courts must apply s.25 which requires the court to have regard to the needs of both parties. The prevailing economic climate of very high interest rates on mortgages, and subsidies available to people with low incomes, made the one-third calculation on the gross income of the parties wholly unsatisfactory. He said that the only satisfactory approach was to examine the net effect on the joint income of the parties. However, it is clear from the later case of *Stockford* v *Stockford* (1982) 3 FLR 58 that he was not suggesting the application of the one-third rule to the net incomes of the parties. In that case Ormrod LJ took the gross incomes of the parties and assessed their respective needs in accordance with paragraphs (a) and (b). The next stage was to assess the actual impact of any order for periodical payments on the parties' respective financial means as far as possible, looking broadly at the overall position rather than entering upon a detailed investigation of household budgets. The "net effect" method outlined involved working out the husband's liability to tax on the basis of a hypothetical order and deducting from his gross income the aggregate national insurance contributions, "etc", the amount of the order and his tax liability, which gave a figure for his available resources. In the case of the wife it involved adding up her earnings, allowances, and the amount of the hypothetical order, which gave the resources available to her. The two figures could then be compared and related to their respective needs, and the hypothetical order adjusted accordingly.

A crucial feature in *Stockford* v *Stockford* was the husband's large mortgage interest liability which made it impossible for the periodical payments to the wife to be raised from their relatively low level. This approach is, therefore, likely to be advantageous to a husband who is forced to raise a substantial mortgage to purchase an alternative home for himself when his former wife is allowed to remain in the former matrimonial home. The court said that he was contributing indirectly to her standard of living by "allowing" her to remain in the former matrimonial home in which he had an interest. However, it is important to note that the court inferred that the judge had thought that the husband had not been extravagant in his purchase of accommodation. While the cost of the husband's accommodation is a factor under paragraph (b), the court must consider whether that cost is reasonable in all the circumstances, i.e. for a man of that income with his existing liabilities for his first family. Indeed the court may have to consider the reasonableness of other items of expenditure on the part of the husband. If the husband has been extravagant or unreasonable, then this can be reflected in arriving at the correct net result in so far as he is concerned. In *Slater* v *Slater* (1982) 3 FLR 364 it was found that on the basis of the order made by the judge the husband's actual expenditure exceeded his income by a considerable sum. The crucial fact was the decision of the husband and his new wife to live some distance from his place of employment with the result that substantial travelling expenses were incurred. Sir John Arnold P (at p. 372) concluded that although it was understandable that the husband should fall in with the wishes of his new wife as to the place of their residence, "for a man who had the burdens which the husband did have, of having to support according to the law, his former wife and the three children of his former marriage, it was an extravagant decision".

Although the assets and income of a husband's new wife cannot be used directly to benefit the first wife, it is quite proper to have regard to the income of the new wife in order to determine the net effect of a proposed order on the husband. (See the comments of May LJ in *Slater* v *Slater* (1982) 3 FLR 364 at p. 373 quoted in sub-paragraph (iii) above.) Where the wife is in receipt of social security benefits it may be possible to ignore the effect of the order upon her but, in such circumstances, it is important to consider the net effect of any proposed order on the income of the husband and to relate the amount available to him to social security rates of benefit. (See *Allen* v *Allen* [1986] 2 FLR 265 *per* Purchas LJ at p. 269, and Chapter 19.)

It is still necessary to have some starting point for the purposes of arriving at a suitable hypothetical order to which the net effect can be applied. In *Slater* v *Slater* both Sir John Arnold P and May LJ said that in considering the appropriate amount of financial provision it was useful to have some guideline to start with. This might be an existing order which it was sought to vary, it might be the level of maintenance currently being provided voluntarily, an offer made or, in an appellate court, the order made below. If there was no other such guideline, and it was not a case of great wealth or poverty, the one-third guideline might be taken. Sir John Arnold P (at p. 370) continued:

"Having reached a provisional conclusion as to what, if any, departure from the guideline is proper on the facts of the particular case, it is then right in a suitable case to test that provisional conclusion on an examination of what the net effect of such an order would be, and then to make any necessary adjustment to one's provisional conclusion. It is often relevant, as was suggested in *Preston* v *Preston* (1981) 2 FLR 331, to test one's provisional conclusion against the one-third guideline when that has not been initially adopted."

(ix) The value of capital assets

In considering capital provision the court must take into account the net value of a party's assets (*Dennis* v *Dennis* (1976) 6 Fam Law 54). Regard should be had not only to the mortgage on the matrimonial home, but also to the possible charge in favour of the Law Society for legal aid costs (*Hanlon* v *Hanlon* [1978] 1 WLR 592. See Chapter 13). A professional valuation is desirable even in small cases though it is sometimes possible for the parties between them, because of experience of similar houses in the neighbourhood, to arrive at an agreed valuation which is a reasonably reliable one (see Ormrod LJ in *Chand* v *Chand* (1978) 9 Fam Law 85). It is provided in *Practice Direction* [1981] 1 WLR 1010 that where a dispute arises as to the value of any property, a valuation should be made without order by an agreed valuer or, in default of agreement, by an independent valuer chosen by the President of the Royal Institution of Chartered Surveyors. (See also further guidance by Booth J in *Evans* v *Evans* [1990] 1 WLR 575.)

The difficulties and expense involved in the detailed valuation of a business have been emphasised on a number of occasions. Thus in *Potter* v *Potter* [1982] 1 WLR 1255 Dunn LJ gave a clear warning against attempting to reach a global figure as to the value of the husband's assets. In that case the husband was engaged in a one-man business, and Dunn LJ said (at p. 1257) that valuation of a business was "a necessarily hypothetical exercise because the only way it can be done is to assume that the business will be sold, and that, of course, is the one thing which in fact is not going to happen, and very rarely does happen". Some £12,000 had been spent in fees on a detailed valuation of the business which at the end of the day was an almost irrelevant consideration. He concluded (at p. 1258):

"In a case of this kind the proper approach of the court should be to take the wife's reasonable requirements and balance those against the husband's ability to pay. *That involves a general consideration of his sources of income and capital and, in particular, of his liquidity.*" (Author's italics.)

This view was followed by Anthony Lincoln J in *B* v *B* [1989] 1 FLR 119 where some £50,000 had been spent by the parties in a dispute as to the extent and value of the husband's assets. He considered it meaningless or irrelevant to state that the husband's architectural practice was worth nothing or worth £300,000. He continued (at p. 121):

"It is not to be sold. It produces the family's income. What is important is to establish the husband's ability to meet the wife's reasonable requirements. One useful guide in this regard is the pattern of the husband's actual expenditure over the years. I accept that the overall asset position should not be wholly disregarded but it should be given a broad and general consideration looked at against a backcloth of his broad and general standard of life."

In that case it was appropriate to sell the matrimonial home, thus enabling a substantial lump sum payment to be ordered in favour of the wife. (See also Booth J in *Evans* v *Evans* [1990] 1 WLR 575 at p. 576.)

In considering the feasibility of a lump sum payment being provided out of a husband's business it is essential to have regard to the question of liquidity. In *Potter* v *Potter* [1982] 1 WLR 1255 at p. 1259 Dunn LJ emphasised "that it is important, in a case where the capital sum is to be raised by a man engaged in a one-man business (as this man is) the sum should not be so large as to cripple the income-producing asset represented by the business". In the earlier case of *P* v *P* [1978] 1 WLR 483 at p. 487 Ormrod LJ had complained of "a very marked tendency ... to treat valuation figures as if they were the equivalent of cash ... where they are not". In that case the farm occupied and worked by the wife and vested in her name was valued at about £100,000. Ormrod LJ said that:

"It is wholly unrealistic ... to approach this case on the footing that this wife is equivalent to a person who has £100,000 invested in readily realisable securities or in cash or on deposit or whatever."

Roskill LJ described it as a "paper figure" and said at p. 492 that many deductions, including capital gains tax, would have to be made if the farm was sold. It was also the asset which enabled the wife to earn her living and provide for the children. In contrast, although the husband in *O'D* v *O'D* [1976] Fam 83 had substantial assets many of which were extremely difficult to realise, it became clear that by a very simple rearrangement between himself and his father he would have no difficulty in raising a large sum of money as one of the companies in the group in which he and his father were shareholders had a very large amount of liquid cash in a bank account. Ormrod LJ said that in making an assessment of a husband's current financial position and future prospects "the court is concerned with the reality of the husband's resources, using the word in a broad sense to include not only what he is shown to have, but also what could reasonably be made available to him if he so wished. Much will depend on the interpretation of accounts, balance sheets and so on, which will require in many cases the expert guidance of accountants. It will rarely be possible to arrive at arithmetically exact figures. The court must penetrate through the balance sheets and the profit and loss accounts to the underlying realities, bearing in mind that prudent financial management and skilled presentation of accounts are unlikely to overstate the husband's real resources and, on the other side, that there may be a great difference between wealth on paper and true wealth. Valuations may overstate or understate the results of realisation of assets, many of which may not be realisable within the immediate or foreseeable future" (at p. 90. See also *Smith* v *Smith* (1983) 4 FLR 154; *Newton* v *Newton* [1990] 1 FLR 33).

Where both spouses have interests in a family company their strict entitlements should not normally be given any greater weight than is usually given to entitlement to the beneficial interest in a matrimonial home when applying s.25. Thus in *P* v *P* [1989] 2 FLR 241 the husband had built up a successful haulage business in which the wife had also been allotted shares. Anthony Lincoln J rejected the husband's application for the transfer of the wife's shares to him and the wife's application for an order providing for a buy-out of her shares. The apportionment of shares between the couple had been made at a time when the marriage was functioning reasonably and had superseded an earlier apportionment in which the wife had received only one share and the husband the remaining ninety-nine shares. The apportionment did not reflect, and was not intended to reflect, the wife's contribution either to the company or to the marriage. The couple had not been thinking of individual entitlements but of the family as a whole on each occasion. No one had sought to suggest that the wife should not have the lion's share of the proceeds of sale of the matrimonial home without regard to her entitlement, and the company as a capital asset should be treated in the same way. That was not to say that the wife in conflict with a third party about her shares could not assert her title, but under s.25 that was not the position. In the circumstances, therefore, it was appropriate to give only general consideration to so-called entitlement to shares in the company. The retention of her shares would enable the wife to reap the benefits in the middle-term future arising out of a flotation, liquidation or possible buy-out, bearing in mind, of course, that the company was the source of the future income and support of the family - a successful enterprise which should not be changed. (For the position where third parties have an interest in a company see *Nicholas* v *Nicholas*

[1984] FLR 285, considered in Chapter 10. See also *Practice Direction* [1981] 1 WLR 1010 considered above.)

(x) Ascertaining a party's financial resources

Where a respondent or a petitioner is served with a notice in Form 11 or Form 13 in respect of an application for maintenance pending suit or financial provision, then unless the parties are agreed upon the terms of the proposed order, he must, within 14 days, file an affidavit in answer to the application containing full particulars of his property and income. If he does not do so, the court may order him to file an affidavit containing such particulars (Family Proceedings Rules 1991, r. 2.58). Within 14 days after the service of any such affidavit on the applicant or within such other time as the court may fix, the applicant must file an affidavit in reply containing full particulars of his property and income (*ibid.*). Where an application is made for a property adjustment order, the application must state briefly the nature of the adjustment proposed and the notice in Form 11 or Form 13, as the case may be, must, unless otherwise directed, be supported by an affidavit by the applicant stating the facts relied on in support of the application. Any person served with such a notice may serve an affidavit in answer within 14 days (Family Proceedings Rules 1991, r. 2.59). Affidavit evidence is made mandatory for the parties themselves in financial proceedings. There is no express requirement that the evidence of any other witnesses shall be by affidavit, but the practice is for the evidence of such witnesses also to be given in affidavit form. The parties may agree between themselves that the evidence of experts such as valuers and accountants can be submitted originally in the form of a proof or report, but otherwise the practice is to insist upon all evidence being first given by affidavit. This has the obvious advantage of enabling each side's case to be communicated to the other side in advance, so that the issues can be clarified in good time before the hearing and unnecessary adjournments can be avoided. However, the mere fact that the evidence of a particular witness other than a party to the suit has not been given by affidavit does not make his or her evidence inadmissible *per se.* The judge has a discretion whether to admit it or not, a discretion which he will normally exercise in the light of an inquiry as to whether the evidence in question can be admitted without taking the opposing party unfairly by surprise. (See further Waite J in *Krywald* v *Krywald* [1988] 2 FLR 401 at p. 409.)

After affidavits have been filed mutual discovery should take place without order, 14 days from the last affidavit, unless some other period is agreed, with inspection 7 days thereafter (Family Proceedings Rules 1991, r. 2.63; *Practice Direction* [1981] 1 WLR 1010). Any party to an application for ancillary relief may by letter require any other party (1) to give further information concerning any matter contained in any affidavit filed by or on behalf of that other party or any other relevant matter, or (2) to furnish a list of relevant documents, or (3) to allow inspection of any such document. In default of compliance by any such other party, application may be made to the district judge for directions (*ibid.*). In the unreported case of *Re M*, Butler-Sloss J appears to have taken the standard of what should be ordered under this rule as being anything which was reasonably necessary for the purpose of performing the balancing exercise which is required under s.25 of the

1973 Act. This was referred to as a very sensible sort of test by Sir John Arnold P in *Thyssen-Bornemisza* v *Thyssen-Bornemisza (No. 2)* [1985] FLR 1069 at p.1079.

If a dispute arises as to the extent of discovery or as to answers to a questionnaire, an appointment for directions should be taken out. Where the district judge considers that to answer any question would entail considerable expense and there is doubt whether the answer would provide any information of value, he may make the order for the question to be answered at the questioner's risk as to costs. The district judge may refuse to order an answer to a question if he considers that its value would be small in relation to the property or income of the party to whom the question is addressed (*Practice Direction* [1981] 1 WLR 1010. See *Hildebrand* v *Hildebrand* [1992] 1 FLR 244 where the court considered the extent to which a party should be compelled to answer a questionnaire and interrogatories). In the case of a wealthy party it may be oppressive to order him to incur the expenditure of time and money involved in giving discovery of the complex details of his holdings of wealth. Accordingly the courts have recognised the so-called "millionaire's defence", i.e. where the husband concedes that his wealth is large enough and liquid enough to fund any order that the court might make to satisfy the wife's reasonable needs (see Waite J in *S* v *S* [1986] 3 WLR 518 at p. 525). Thus in *Thyssen-Bornemisza* v *Thyssen Bornemisza (No.2)* [1985] FLR 1069 at p. 1080 Sir John Arnold P said that "... the largest amount which could legitimately be provided for whether by a lump sum order under s.23 or an adjustment of property order under s.24 or by a combination of the two mechanisms, is not so large that it could be increased over and above what would be justified by the possession by the husband of a fortune of £400 million by the proof of a larger fortune than that". Accordingly the discovery which had been made was such as to satisfy the requirement that was "reasonably necessary for the performance of the balancing exercise under s.25 and the proper implementation of the provisions of ss.23 and 24 in the circumstances of this case". The same approach was adopted in *Attar* v *Attar (No. 1)* [1985] FLR 649 when the husband accepted that he was worth more than £2 million which was ample to satisfy any claim for a lump sum the wife could have after a short marriage. Booth J said that the position might have been very different if the husband had pleaded in his affidavit that his wealth was tied up in assets which were not available to him and out of which he could not pay a lump sum. This he had not done. (*Ibid.* at p. 651.)

In *G* v *G (Financial Provision: Discovery)* [1992] 1 FLR 40 Bracewell J held that a wife was entitled to require from her husband information about the partnership of which he had recently become a member although no partnership deed had yet come into existence. However, there was no jurisdiction to order a responsible person in the partnership to provide such information, and the husband was instead ordered to use his best endeavours to produce a letter from such a person giving the required information.

At the hearing of an application for ancillary relief there is power to order the attendance of any person for the purpose of being examined or cross-examined, and at any stage of the proceedings to order the discovery and production of any document or to require further affidavits (Family Proceedings Rules 1991, r. 2.62).

In the absence of full and frank information by the husband as to his financial position the court is entitled to draw inferences adverse to the husband as to his capacity to make provision (*Ette* v *Ette* [1964] 1 WLR 1433; *Weisz* v *Weisz* [1975] The Times 15 December; and the discussion in Chapter 12). In *Desai* v *Desai* (1983) 13 Fam Law 46, Anthony Lincoln J said that in the light of the husband's lack of candour and an inadequate disclosure of his financial situation he was entitled to look behind the veil that had been drawn by the husband to hide his true situation. A party who failed to disclose all the facts to the court had only himself to blame if the court was forced to make robust inferences of his shortcomings. However, in *E* v *E* [1990] 2 FLR 233 at p. 242 Ewbank J said that while the failures of the husband in relation to disclosure would justify any inferences which were proper to draw against him, it would be wrong to draw inferences that the husband had assets which, on an assessment of the evidence, he was satisfied the husband did not have. He concluded that at the end of a very long case the investigation had not established any assets of substance which had not been disclosed, except for the technical ownership of some land in Israel and the use of a house there. It was, of course, a different matter when the question of costs was being considered. There is no power to order a person other than a party to the marriage to file an affidavit of means etc. (As to the extent of the provisions of the Bankers' Books Evidence Act 1879 as amended by the Banking Act 1979, see *Williams* v *Williams* [1988] 1 FLR 455.)

*(b) The financial needs, obligations and responsibilities which each of the parties to the marriage has or is likely to have in the foreseeable future*

(i) Basic requirements

The court will obviously be concerned with the basic requirements of the husband, the wife and the children for food, clothing and accommodation. In the case of parties of limited means it may be able to do little more than allocate the slender resources available to cover these basic needs, taking into account at the appropriate stage the availability of social security benefits (see Chapter 19). In *Browne* v *Pritchard* [1975] 1 WLR 1366 at p. 1370 Ormrod LJ said:
"Whenever a court is dealing with families of limited resources, 'needs' are likely to be much more important than resources when it comes to exercising discretion. In most individuals and most families the most urgent need is a home. It is therefore to the provision of homes for all concerned that the courts should direct their attention in the first place."
The "need" for a home, particularly on the part of dependent children of the family, has probably been the most important factor determining the amount of provision ordered and the form of that provision. Thus in *Browne* v *Pritchard* the wife had a secure home in a council flat, and a sale of the matrimonial home would have rendered the husband and the children who lived there homeless. The effect of the order was that the wife's interest in the home was not to be realised until the children's need for a home had been satisfied, i.e. when the younger boy was 18. In *P* v *P* [1978] 1 WLR 483 at p. 490 Ormrod LJ said that the court was concerned with

the bare, basic realities of life. "Who is going to provide the money to keep these children and then bring them up properly?". It was overwhelmingly clear that it was the wife who would have to do so out of the farm business she was then running. A larger capital sum than the judge had ordered her to pay could not be raised out of the farming business unless it was sold. "No court would or should in a case such as this make a lump sum order which has the effect of making it impossible for the earner parent to continue to earn a living and so maintain the family and the children and so on".

The court must, however, take into account the needs of each of the parties to the marriage. It must "balance the reasonable requirements of the former wife against the reasonable requirements of the former husband" (*per* Cumming-Bruce LJ in *Chadwick v Chadwick* [1985] FLR 606 at p. 608). The accommodation required by the party with whom any children of the family are living will obviously have to be sufficient for their needs as well as for the needs of the caring parent. The needs of the other parent, and the difficulty of satisfying them even as a single person, must not be underestimated (see Booth J in *Peacock v Peacock* [1984] 1 WLR 532 at p. 536). In *Allen v Allen* [1986] 2 FLR 265 the Court of Appeal found that the recorder had not been justified in regarding the modest house purchased by the husband after the breakdown of the marriage, with the aid of a mortgage, as anything more than necessary accommodation to which the husband was entitled. It was costing no more than the money he would pay to his mother, and certainly no more than he would have to pay if he became a tenant, whether in private or council accommodation.

It has also been recognised that the needs of the other parent may extend to a home sufficiently large to provide accommodation for the children for regular staying access. Thus in *Ibbetson v Ibbetson* [1984] FLR 545 at p. 553 the judge said that "... a three bedroom house for a man who has regular staying access amounting to twelve weeks a year for two girls aged 12 and 10 is in no way in excess of his needs. It may be a pleasant detached house, but comparison must be made to the wife's present and probable future home and the living standards to which the children are accustomed". In *Delaney v Delaney* [1990] 2 FLR 457 the husband had given up the tenancy of a one bedroom flat, which was unsuitable for access by the children, and, with the woman he hoped to marry, purchased a property on a basis which involved an increased financial commitment. The Court of Appeal did not find this unreasonable even though it left him with insufficient resources to maintain fully his former wife and children. Ward J (at p. 462) said that whether the man was judged by a standard of "extravagant expenditure" (the test applied in *Furniss v Furniss* (1982) 3 FLR 46) or of living to an improper standard (the approach applied in *Barnes v Barnes* [1972] 1 WLR 1381) or of behaving unreasonably (the approach in *Preston v Preston* (1981) 2 FLR 331), he did not find it possible to judge him to have gone beyond the limits of what was permissible. He thought that two bedrooms may have been sufficient, but three bedrooms did not far exceed his need having regard to the fact that the wife lived in a three bedroom house. Ward J continued:

"In my judgement, the approach of this court in this case must be first to have regard to the need of the wife and children for proper support. Having assessed that need, the court should then consider the ability of the husband to meet it. Whilst this court deprecates any notion that a former husband and extant father may slough off the tight skin of familial responsibility and may slither into and lose himself in the greener grass on the other side, none the less this court has proclaimed and will proclaim that it looks to the realities of the real world in which we live, and that among the realities of life is that there is life after divorce. The respondent husband is entitled to order his life in such a way as will hold in reasonable balance the responsibilities to his existing family which he carries into his new life, as well as his proper aspirations for that new future. In all life, for those who are divorced as well as for those who are not divorced, indulging one's whims or even one's reasonable desires must be held in check by the constraints imposed by limited resources and compelling obligations."

Accordingly, in assessing the needs of each party the court should compare the position of each party and should seek to avoid any significant discrepancy between their respective accommodation and standard of living generally. However, there may be exceptional cases such as *Hedges* v *Hedges* [1991] 1 FLR 196. In that case the husband was a boarding school teacher and, following the breakdown of a short marriage of some four and a half years, he had purchased a house with the assistance of a 90 per cent mortgage. He did not live there; it was acquired partly as an investment and partly to protect his position lest he should lose his tied accommodation at the school. In contrast the wife was living in rented accommodation and was in employment where the prospects of a large enough increase in salary to make a mortgage possible seemed remote. The prospect of her becoming the owner of a house or flat was at present unrealistic. This apparently striking contrast in their respective positions in relation to accommodation would be a factor of great weight in some situations, but Mustill LJ (at p. 203) acknowledged that the case was rather special. He said: "This is not a case where the husband continues to occupy the matrimonial home, or where the wife gave up her own home to join him. Nor, indeed has the husband bought a house and gone to live in it himself". The purchase was no different in principle from an investment in, for example, the purchase by instalments of a deferred annuity susceptible of being commuted to a lump sum. It was a prudent provision for later years of life. Certainly the size of the provision was something at which to look when deciding how much the husband could reasonably be expected to spare out of his net revenue. It did not require "a pitching of the figure of periodical payments on the assumption that the [wife] is entitled to have a mortgage and a house of her own" (*ibid.*). The wife was awarded a small lump sum and periodical payments for 18 months, a provision which would keep her afloat until she was able to move from temporary work into better-paid permanent employment. It is important to note that this was a short marriage, and it was not a case where the failed marriage had caused a setback in the wife's position in the employment market or in her other sources of income for which compensation was in justice due.

Where resources are limited the situation may be made even more difficult where the husband remarries, thereby incurring obligations towards his new wife and any children of the new family. Previously the view seems to have been that his obligations to his new family, though a relevant factor, were not of such weight as his obligations to his former wife and the children of the dissolved marriage (*Cockburn* v *Cockburn* [1957] 1 WLR 1020; *Roberts* v *Roberts* [1970] P 1 at p. 8). The same applied where a husband co-habited with a woman, thereby incurring "moral" obligations towards the new family (*Roberts* v *Roberts*). However, in *Barnes* v *Barnes* [1972] 1 WLR 1381 at pp. 1384-1385 Edmund Davies LJ considered paragraph (b) and said that "the fact that the husband has undertaken the legal responsibilities of maintaining a new wife must be fully borne in mind and be given the same degree and weight as his responsibilities in any other financial respect". In those cases where the availability of income support to the wife is crucial, the balancing of the man's obligations to the two families will be in accordance with the principle applied in *Barnes* v *Barnes* (see Chapter 19). In *Slater* v *Slater* (1982) 3 FLR 366 at p. 369 Sir John Arnold P said that a new wife's resources were relevant in relation to the question of how far it is necessary for the husband to support his new wife, how far she is really a burden upon him financially, how far she is able, from her own resources, to make a contribution to the household sufficient to enable him to use his own resources for his own support and his other burdens, including, of course, any children of the new marriage but including also his former wife and the children from his former marriage. In that case the husband's decision to live some distance from his place of work because of the wishes of his new wife was found to be unreasonable in view of the expense of travelling involved. On the other hand, in *R* v *R* [1988] 1 FLR 89 the Court of Appeal said that it would have been folly for the husband and his new wife to have disposed of a house they had purchased for the accommodation of the new family when they obtained accommodation as joint managers of a public house. Such accommodation was only available to them while they were managers, and events showed how reasonable this was because the new wife had, on medical grounds, been unable to continue with that employment and had also given birth to a child.

Where the court has assessed the amount necessary to provide for the wife's reasonable needs at the appropriate standard, then how the wife spends the provision made for her is her affair. Thus in *Duxbury* v *Duxbury* [1987] 1 FLR 1 at p. 13 Ackner LJ said that the fact that the wife might spend some of it on the man with whom she cohabited - who as a result would benefit from it - would merely reduce the satisfying of her reasonable needs which in that case was assessed to require the sum of £28,000 per annum. It was just as irrelevant that she should be spending part of her money upon him as if she had decided to have living with her an impecunious friend or an elderly relative who, again, would be an expense which she herself would be defraying out of the income which had been assessed as being appropriate solely for her needs.

Where substantial assets are available, it has been said that "needs" can be regarded as equivalent to "reasonable requirements" taking into account other factors such as age, health, length of marriage and standard of living (*per* Ormrod LJ in *Page* v *Page* (1981) 2 FLR 198 at p. 201). Thus in *Preston* v *Preston* [1982] Fam 17 Ormrod LJ considered that the wife was entitled to expect a very high standard of living which would include a home in a house or flat at the top end of the market, and probably a second home in the country or abroad, together with a very high spending power. This meant a very high after-tax income, but account had to be taken of her ability to spend or invest capital so as to reduce the impact of taxation. (See also *O'D* v *O'D* [1976] Fam 83.)

In *P* v *P* [1989] 2 FLR 241 the wife was awarded a lump sum of £240,000 out of the net proceeds of sale of the matrimonial home amounting to £260,000 to meet her capital requirements. This was to cover the provision of a suitable four bedroom house in the appropriate area within easy reach of the children's present schools (£190,000), a sum to enable her to move and to purchase new fittings and furniture (£12,000), the cost of a car (£10,000) and one half of her costs (£28,000). There was no reason to include a sum as a nest-egg or for contingencies, because her stake in the family company had considerable future value and she might be able to move to a smaller house when the children left home. (See also *B* v *B* [1989] 1 FLR 119 and *B* v *B* [1990] 1 FLR 20.)

Where sufficient assets exist, a wife's reasonable requirements may extend to a sum sufficient to enable her to get started in business. In *Nicholas* v *Nicholas* [1984] FLR 285 the Court of Appeal found that it was appropriate to provide the wife with a lump sum which not only provided her with reasonable housing accommodation for herself, but also gave her sufficient capital to buy a bigger home and equip it as a guest house so as to obtain some income. This presented the only opportunity she was likely to have of obtaining an independent income by using such experience as she had acquired. Even so, the lump sum of £80,000 was less than would have been required to purchase or provide the equivalent of the matrimonial home in which she lived, but the standard and extent of accommodation provided was not an appropriate measure of her needs after dissolution of the marriage. The husband had no present housing need because he was living with another woman in a house which he had enabled her to purchase or improve by a capital advance. In *Gojkovic* v *Gojkovic* [1990] 1 FLR 140 the Court of Appeal found that the judge had been entitled to take into account the wife's desire to buy a hotel. She had been a working wife with recognised expertise in the management of hotels, and her reasonable needs were not met simply by a sum which would make her self-sufficient. The court was not concerned only with her needs but with the very considerable contribution she had made to the building up of substantial business assets.

*(c) The standard of living enjoyed by the family before the breakdown of the marriage*

The standard of living previously enjoyed by the family has always been recognised as an important factor, and may now be an important factor in assessing the needs of the parties under paragraph (b) above. It is also now an important factor in determining whether a financially dependent spouse can adjust to the termination of financial support without undue hardship. In an ordinary case such a spouse should not be expected to adjust to a significantly lower standard of living if the other spouse has the means to provide support. (See *Boylan* v *Boylan* [1988] 1 FLR 282.)

Where resources are limited, the practical impact may be small for some reduction in the previous standard of living will generally be inevitable. In that event the court should ensure that as far as possible both parties enjoy thereafter a comparable standard of living (*Scott* v *Scott* [1978] 1 WLR 73; *Ibbetson* v *Ibbetson* [1984] FLR 545). However, since it may be necessary for the former matrimonial home to be appropriated for the benefit of one former spouse who has care of the children, some imbalance may be unavoidable (see Purchas J in *Martin* v *Martin* [1976] Fam 167 at p. 182 and, in different circumstances, *Hedges* v *Hedges* [1991] 1 FLR 196). Where resources are more substantial, it may be possible to take full account of the standard of living enjoyed by the parties during the marriage. It has been noted in relation to paragraph (b) that in this context "need" is to be construed as "reasonable requirements". In *Calderbank* v *Calderbank* [1976] Fam 93 the parties had lived in a large house with a good standard of living financed by the wife who was a woman of means. The wife was ordered to pay to the husband (who had no capital) a lump sum of £10,000 which would enable him to acquire a house "suitable to his way of life" and in which he could live and "in which he can see his children" when they came to stay with him. (See also *Ibbetson* v *Ibbetson* and *Delaney* v *Delaney* [1990] 2 FLR 457.) In *Vicary* v *Vicary* [1992] 2 FLR 271 it was held that payments made during the marriage to assist the children of the wife by a previous marriage could properly be taken into account under paragraph (c) so that financial provision for the wife might be such as to enable her to make similar gifts in the future. The husband had acquiesced in, or contributed to, such payments and there were ample resources available after providing for the needs of the parties.

Where, during the marriage, the wife accepted a modest standard of living in the hope that the family would benefit later, paragraph (c) should not be taken as justifying a lower standard of provision than is now possible by virtue of the husband's affluence which may be due, in part at least, to the earlier sacrifices. Accordingly, if earlier sacrifices enabled the husband to plough back into his business a large proportion of the profits so that it has developed into a considerable enterprise, this can properly be reflected in the provision made (*Preston* v *Preston* [1982] Fam 17; and *B* v *B* [1990] 1 FLR 20 at p. 30). On the other hand, where a marriage has been very short the fact that the parties, as a result of their wealth, enjoyed a very high standard of living will be of limited relevance. Indeed, in *Attar* v *Attar (No. 2)* (1984) 6 FLR 653 Booth J said that in the circumstances of the case the standard of living was a matter which had to be put on one side. The parties had cohabited for only about seven weeks over a period of six months, and a part of this was their honeymoon. The standard of living enjoyed by the parties during this period could not safely be taken as reflecting the standard of living they might have enjoyed in their cohabitation together. In *Leadbeater* v *Leadbeater* [1985] FLR 789 at p. 796 Balcombe J, in determining the income requirements of the wife, took into account the lifestyle enjoyed by her both before and after her marriage to the husband, because it was common ground that during the short marriage she had enjoyed a much enhanced lifestyle.

*(d) The age of each party to the marriage and the duration of the marriage*
It will not generally be appropriate for the same financial consequences to follow a marriage which has lasted only a few weeks as one which has lasted for twenty-five years.

In the first place there is likely to have been less contribution to the acquisition of property and to the care of the family. Thus in *Taylor* v *Taylor* (1975) 119 SJ 30 where a husband had purchased a matrimonial home in joint names but the marriage lasted only a few weeks, it was appropriate to transfer the wife's interest to the husband thereby restoring the property to him absolutely. In *Drinkwater* v *Drinkwater* [1984] FLR 627, where the marriage had lasted for only about three years, the Court of Appeal held that there was no reason for the home to remain unsold longer than was necessary to provide a home for the children, especially in view of the large contribution to its purchase made by the husband. In concluding that a *Mesher* order was appropriate, Stephen Brown LJ said (at p. 630) that the fact that there was such a short marriage rendered it quite inequitable that the husband should be kept out of any share of the capital savings of the family so as to provide for an indefinite period a home for the wife alone. (See also *Walsh* v *Corcoran* (1983) 4 FLR 59.) In *Leadbeater* v *Leadbeater* [1985] FLR 789 at p. 799 Balcombe J said that the major factors which he had to take into account were (a) the wife's reasonable needs, which he assessed at a lump sum of £50,000 to achieve a clean break, and (b) the length of the marriage, namely four years. It seemed to him proper to make a discount from that capital sum, primarily because of the short length of the marriage, though partly too on account of payments made by the husband to discharge some of her liabilities. Acknowledging that the application of a discount was somewhat arbitrary, he applied a discount of 25 per cent to produce a figure of £37,500 which was the sum ordered.

Secondly, in a short marriage there are less likely to be adverse financial consequences as was the case in *Taylor* v *Taylor* where the wife had not given up her employment or her flat in London. Even before the changes made by the Matrimonial and Family Proceedings Act 1984 emphasised the desirability of a clean break, it had been accepted that in the case of a very short marriage between two young persons, neither of whom has been adversely affected by the consequences of the marriage and each of whom is fully capable of earning his or her own living, the approach of the court should normally be to order periodical payments for a limited time to allow the party who is in the weaker financial position - usually the wife - to adjust herself to the situation. Thereafter it would be possible to achieve the wholly desirable result of a clean break, if necessary facilitated by a small lump sum payment (*per* Balcombe J in *H* v *H* (1981) 2 FLR 392 at p. 299. See also *Graves* v *Graves* (1973) 117 SJ 679; *Wagner* v *Wagner* (1981) 1 FLR 154; *Khan* v *Khan* (1981) 2 FLR 131). In *Fisher* v *Fisher* [1989] 1 FLR 423 at p. 429 Purchas LJ said that the purpose of ss.25A and 31(7) of the 1973 Act introduced by the 1984 Act:

"... was to discourage in cases of marriages of short duration, particularly where no children were involved, orders for periodical payments which were known colloquially as 'meal tickets for life'. The new provisions required the court in every case to consider in particular, but not to the exclusion of other relevant factors, whether 'it would be appropriate' to limit the term in such a way as to provide a positive stimulus to the spouse in whose favour an order for periodical payment is made to achieve either partial or total financial independence of the supportive spouse."

In *Attar* v *Attar (No. 2)* (1984) 6 FLR 653 where the wife who had been an air stewardess, and the husband, a very wealthy national of Saudi Arabia, had lived together for a very short period, Booth J said that the proper approach was to allow the wife a period of two years to readjust to her situation from that of living abroad to coming back to England and establishing herself in England. She was awarded a lump sum designed to give her for two years the net income she had enjoyed before marriage. In *Hedges* v *Hedges* [1991] 1 FLR 196 at p. 203, where the effective life of the marriage was four and a half years, Mustill LJ said: "This is not a case where the failed marriage has caused a setback in the appellant's position in the employment market, or in her other sources of income for which compensation is in justice due". The Court of Appeal upheld the award of a lump sum of £2,500 and periodical payments of £200 per month for eighteen months for the wife who was aged 37.

Where there are children, then even if the wife is young and the marriage has been short, the period of adjustment is likely to be longer - although a deferred clean break remains the objective. See *C* v *C (Financial Provision)* [1989] 1 FLR 11; *Waterman* v *Waterman* [1989] 1 FLR 380, and the discussion of potential earning capacity in relation to paragraph (*a*) above.

Even if a marriage has been short and childless, the adverse consequences may be serious if the parties are not young. Thus in *S* v *S* [1977] Fam 127 the parties entered into marriage when over the age of 50. The wife sold her own home and gave the proceeds to her son, but the marriage broke down some two years later. The court said that it was important in short marriages, particularly where the people concerned were not young, to look very closely to see what the effect of the marriage had been, mainly on the wife, but also on the husband. She was undoubtedly much worse off as a result of the marriage, and the primary consideration was to look at her needs. Her need for a home could be satisfied by a property settled on her until her death or remarriage but with no entitlement to capital beyond a small lump sum. This may be contrasted with *Robertson* v *Robertson* (1983) 4 FLR 387 where the marriage had lasted some three years and the wife was aged 44 and the husband aged 58 at the time of the marriage. The wife was currently unable to earn her own living due to her state of health, but she had been unable to earn her own living for the eleven years before the marriage. She was unlikely to be able to work while the stress of litigation with her landlords continued. Balcombe J (at p. 392) accepted that the proper order for periodical payments would be to cover a period until such time as it could be seen whether or not the wife's health recovered. He accepted the "primary submission that with a short marriage between mature people of this kind, the wife not having given up any job that she previously had and therefore not having lost her earning potential simply because of the marriage, it would be inappropriate to make an order in her favour for periodical payments for the rest of her life". In addition to an order for a lump sum payment of £15,000, he made an order for periodical payments at the rate of £5,000 per annum, approximately one-third of their joint incomes, for a period of some eighteen months and thereafter at the nominal rate of 50p a year.

In contrast it is obvious that on the breakdown of a lengthy marriage, a wife who has had no career of her own is likely not only to have made a considerable contribution to the welfare of the family within paragraph (f), especially if there are children, but also to have greater need of support. If she has also been employed in the husband's business activities, this will also be significant under paragraph (f) considered below.

Even if a marriage has lasted for many years a wife may have no claim at all where the parties have led separate lives for most of their marriage (*Lombardi* v *Lombardi* [1973] 1 WLR 1276; *Krystman* v *Krystman* [1973] 1 WLR 927; *Fraser* v *Fraser* (1982) 3 FLR 98).

After a certain lapse of time a party to a marriage is entitled to take the view that there will be no revival or initiation of financial claims against him or her. The longer the lapse of time the more secure should he or she feel in the rearrangement of financial affairs, and the less should any such claim be encouraged or entertained. Where a marriage has irretrievably broken down, the parties are to be encouraged to deal with all outstanding issues as reasonably expeditiously as possible (*per* Wood J in *Chambers* v *Chambers* (1981) 1 FLR 10. He said that by inference the principle of the clean break indicates that financial issues should be decided within a reasonably short time of breakdown). However, the position may be otherwise where the husband has made great efforts to conceal his financial position (*Re W (deceased)* (1975) 119 SJ 439). Moreover, a wife may have no choice but to delay applying or proceeding with her application where there is no prospect of obtaining provision at the time of the marriage breakdown in view of the husband's financial position, but application is made as soon as the husband's financial position justifies it (*Pearce* v *Pearce* (1981) 1 FLR 261; *Hardy* v *Hardy* (1981) 2 FLR 321). Nevertheless, even in that situation the longer the delay the more difficult will be the wife's task: it can be argued, for example, that the husband's assets have no relation to the former marriage; indeed, on the contrary, they may owe a good deal to a new marriage. (But see *Tandy* v *Tandy* CA October 24 1986 Lexis Enggen, discussed under paragraph (f) below, where after a brief period of cohabitation there had been a very long period of separation during which the wife brought up their child single-handed.)

A period of pre-marital cohabitation is not the same as a period of marriage (*per* Sir George Baker P in *Campbell* v *Campbell* [1976] Fam 347 at p. 352). However, the court may take such a period of cohabitation into account as one of the circumstances of the case, and the weight to be attached to it is a matter for the court's discretion. There will be some cases where the inability of the parties to legitimise their relationship calls for a measure of sympathy which will enable the court to take what has happened during the period of cohabitation into account as a very weighty factor (*per* Eveleigh LJ in *Foley* v *Foley* [1981] Fam 160). This was so in *Kokosinki* v *Kokosinki* [1980] Fam 72 where Wood J said that he could not do justice between the parties unless he took into account the wife's conduct during the twenty-five years that she and her husband had cohabited before the ceremony of marriage. She had been faithful, loving and hard working and had helped to build up the family business, whilst at the same time managing the home and helping to bring up their son. She had earned herself some part of the value of the family business even though the marriage had lasted nominally some five years and effectively only a much shorter period. She was awarded a lump sum payment of £8,000 out of the husband's assets of some £47,500. (See also *Chaterjee* v *Chaterjee* [1976] Fam 199 and *Day* v *Day* [1988] 1 FLR 278.)

This may be contrasted with *Campbell* v *Campbell* [1976] Fam 347 and *H* v *H* (1981) 2 FLR 392. In the latter case the marriage lasted only some seven weeks although the parties had lived together over a number of years. In holding that the period of cohabitation was not relevant in the circumstances of the case, Balcombe J (at p. 399) said:

"To consider it as equivalent to a true period of marriage would be cynical in the extreme. It lacked any semblance of permanence; there were no children, and on the several occasions when they separated both considered themselves free to take another partner."

*(e) Any physical or mental disability of either of the parties to the marriage*

To a large extent these factors will also be reflected in the income or earning capacity of the spouses on the one hand and their needs on the other. (See *Robertson* v *Robertson* (1983) 4 FLR 387; *Chadwick* v *Chadwick* [1985] FLR 606; *Sakkas* v *Sakkas* (1987) 17 Fam Law 414; *Newton* v *Newton* [1990] 1 FLR 33; *K* v *K (Conduct)* [1990] 2 FLR 225 at p. 231.) The availability of the National Health Service will also be taken into account. In *Seaton* v *Seaton* [1986] 2 FLR 398 the husband had suffered a severe stroke after the parties had separated and shortly before their marriage was dissolved. As a result he was severely incapacitated and was unable to look after himself. He had no earning capacity but received a disability pension. He was looked after by his parents. The Court of Appeal upheld the dismissal of his claim for an order for periodical payments against his wife who was earning sufficient to produce a surplus after paying for her necessities. The court took the view that, thanks to the fact that his parents had voluntarily assumed the burden of looking after him, he did not in fact have any significant needs. The judge had found it difficult to envisage how any contribution by way of periodical payments by the former wife would have any material effect in enhancing the life of the husband, because his limited opportunities for pleasure appeared to be reasonably satisfied already, given the dramatic quality of his continuing and prospective physical and mental disability. Sir Roualeyn Cumming-Bruce (at p. 403) said:

"There is no question of this applicant adjusting at all to the termination of his previous financial dependence upon his wife as it was at the time when they were still cohabiting. There is no question of any adjustment which would enable the husband in any way to modify his total dependence on others for his care and his support. That falls at the moment on his parents, thanks to their voluntary decision, and when it terminates his only prospect is total dependence upon the resources of the State."

In relation to persons suffering from mental disorder within the meaning of the Mental Health Act 1983, certain special considerations apply. Thus although orders may be made against a person in respect of whom a receiving order has been made under that Act, they will be subject to limitations under the Act (see *CL* v *CFW* [1928] P 223). Where the court makes an order requiring payments (including a lump sum) to be made, or property to be transferred, to a spouse and the court is satisfied that the person in whose favour the order is made is incapable, by reason of mental disorder with the meaning of the Act, of managing and administering his or her property and affairs, then subject to any order, direction or authority made or given in relation to that person under the Act, the court may order the payment to be made or, as the case may be, the property to be transferred, to such persons having charge of that person as the court may direct (Matrimonial Causes Act 1973, s.40).

*(f) The contributions which each of the parties has made or is likely in the foreseeable future to make to the welfare of the family, including any contribution made by looking after the home or caring for the family*

(i) Contributions by looking after the home and family
Although a wife may obtain a proprietary interest in the matrimonial home or other property by reason of financial contributions direct or indirect, she can obtain no such interest by virtue of any other general contribution to the family welfare (see Chapter 2). This injustice can be remedied on the grant of a decree of divorce, nullity or judicial separation by the making of an order for a lump sum payment or a transfer of property order in favour of the wife, for such contributions must be taken into account under paragraph (f). In *Wachtel* v *Wachtel* [1973] Fam 72 at pp. 93-94 Lord Denning MR considered the object of paragraph (f) and said:
"... we may take it that Parliament recognised that the wife who looks after the home and family contributes as much to the family assets as the wife who goes out to work. The one contributes in kind. The other in money or money's worth. If the court comes to the conclusion that the home has been acquired and maintained by the joint efforts of both, then, when the marriage breaks down, it should be regarded as the joint property of both of them, no matter in whose name it stands. Just as the wife who makes substantial money contributions usually gets a share, so should the wife who looks after the home and cares for the family for twenty years or more."
In that case the wife was regarded as having made a substantial contribution to the home over a period of some eighteen years and had been an excellent mother. In *Trippas* v *Trippas* [1973] Fam 134 at p. 144 Scarman LJ noted that the wife had made no specific contribution to the business life or business earnings of her husband but "for over twenty-five years of marriage she maintained his home; she brought up his children, and she provided ... the general and moral support to a man sometimes hard pressed by business worries that a good wife does". More recently in *Mortimer-Griffin* v *Mortimer-Griffin* [1986] 2 FLR 315 at p. 316 Sir John Donaldson MR said that "... it would be quite wrong to suggest that if a husband earns money and a wife looks after a child, that means that the two cannot be equated, one with the other, even if it is easier to put a figure on the husband's activities than on the wife's activities".
  Even when a marriage has been of short duration the court may conclude, as it did in *Cumbers* v *Cumbers* [1974] 1 WLR 1331, that a wife has "really played a part in the marriage which deserves compensation of a capital nature" (*per* Lord Denning MR at p. 1334). In that case the marriage had lasted only some eighteen months and the husband had paid the whole of the deposit on the purchase of the matrimonial home. However, there was a child of the marriage, and the wife had not only looked after the child but had worked and contributed to the household expenses. (See also *Tandy* v *Tandy* October 24, 1986 Lexis Enggen, where the effective length of the marriage was very short but the wife had brought up the child of the marriage as a single parent.) This may be contrasted with *H* v *H* [1975] Fam 9 at p. 16 where Sir George Baker P, while acknowledging that the wife had earned a share in the former matrimonial home, said:

"If the concept of earning is to be applied to a domestic situation, then it should be applied with all its normal consequences. One is that if the job is left unfinished you do not earn as much."

In some respects the facts were exceptional in that the wife had left to live with, and subsequently marry, another man while the four children of the marriage, then aged 8, 6, 5 and 4, had remained with the husband. In practical terms, therefore, it can be said that the wife's contribution to the welfare of the family had been limited and her capital provision was smaller than that which would have been appropriate if she had cared for the family over a longer period.

There will be some cases where one party will have made very little or no contribution to the welfare of the family. Thus in *West* v *West* [1978] Fam 1 the wife had unreasonably refused to join her husband in the home he had purchased and set up a family of their own as she had preferred to stay with her own parents. Although the case was mainly concerned with the question of whether the wife's conduct was "gross and obvious" (see paragraph (g) below), Ormrod LJ said that the very limited provision made for the wife could be justified under paragraphs (d) and (f). He said that she had cared for the children in her own "family" home. In *E* v *E* [1990] 2 FLR 233 Ewbank J concluded that from 1987 the wife's contribution to the welfare of the family was negative, and from 1980 onwards it had been minimal. She had been extravagant in her expenditure and had retreated from the children after 1980. She had ceased to be a full member of a household that was well provided for in material terms and with staff to take care of everything. (See also *Walsh* v *Corcoran* (1983) 4 FLR 59.)

The wording of paragraph (f) was amended by the Matrimonial and Family Proceedings Act 1984 to include a reference to contributions which a party is likely to make in the foreseeable future. This will require the court to have regard to the contribution which a wife may still have to make in the future in relation to the upbringing of minor children.

(ii) Contributions to expenditure
Although "... originally introduced in order to do justice to wives and mothers who stayed at home to look after the home and family" (*per* Ewbank J in *E* v *E* [1990] 2 FLR 233 at p. 247), it is not only contributions in the form of care of the home and family which can be taken into account under paragraph (f). It also covers financial contributions to household expenditure and to the acquisition of the matrimonial home and its contents. The court can thus take indirect financial contributions into account without the problems that arose in proceedings under s.17 of the Married Women's Property Act 1882 (see Chapter 2). In this respect it is important to look not only at the cash contributions, but also at the commitments accepted by each party. Thus in *Earley* v *Earley* [1975] The Times 25 June, where the home was vested in the wife subject to a lump sum payment to the husband, it was necessary to have regard to the fact that the wife would thereafter have the obligation of discharging the mortgage repayments and to the fact that the husband would be receiving an immediate cash payment without the house being sold.

Where improvements have been made by one spouse to a home vested in the name of the other, it is not appropriate to make a separate award under s.37 of the

Matrimonial Proceedings and Property Act 1970 when the matter can be considered as part of the overall position on divorce by taking into account under paragraph (f) the amount spent by the spouse on the improvements (*Griffiths* v *Griffiths* [1974] 1 WLR 1350 at pp. 1358-1359 and 1362. See Chapter 2 Part 6).

(iii) Contributions to the acquisition of other assets
Apart from those cases in which "a wife has faithfully carried out the duties and functions of a loving wife and mother" there are cases in which, in addition, "she had been practically involved and has participated in a family business project, whether in farming, industry, or otherwise, or possibly in the acquisition of an asset" (*per* Wood J in *Page* v *Page* (1981) 2 FLR 198 at p. 205). The extent of such participation will vary and is a matter of evidence, but the wife "may well be able to make out a case for a slice of that part of the family wealth which she had helped to create" (*ibid.*). In *Preston* v *Preston* [1982] Fam 17 at p. 25 Ormrod LJ said that "active participation by the wife either by working in the business or by providing finance, will greatly enhance her contributions to the welfare of the family under paragraph (f), and may lead to a substantial increase in the lump sum over and above her 'reasonable requirements'". This, in effect, recognises that she has "earned" a share in the total assets and should be able to realise it and use it as she chooses (*S* v *S* Unreported July 16, 1980 (CA) Transcript No. 664). In *Gojkovic* v *Gojkovic* [1990] 1 FLR 140 the judge found that the wife had made an exceptional contribution to the substantial wealth generated during their relationship and marriage, a contribution greater than that often made by wives after long marriages. The wife had earned her share as envisaged in *Page* v *Page* and was awarded a lump sum of £1 million to take account of this in addition to providing for her reasonable needs.

The fact that a wife has received remuneration for her efforts in the family business does not necessarily mean that recognition under paragraph (f) is inappropriate. Thus in *Dew* v *Dew* [1986] 2 FLR 341 at p. 346 Anthony Lincoln J concluded that the wife had made a substantial contribution both in the family company and in the home. She was not, as the husband certainly was, indispensable to the life and prospects of the company, but she helped as a back-up for the husband to exploit his own industrial talent. She was generously remunerated for her work in the company, but in his estimation there remained "a significant margin of gratuitous contribution as well as her housekeeping" which required that her contribution be taken into account "carrying her award well above the figure for her reasonable requirements".

(iv) Gifts and inheritances
Where one spouse has inherited or been given property, this too may be taken into account as part of his or her contribution under paragraph (f). Thus in *P* v *P* [1978] 1 WLR 483 at p. 489 Ormrod LJ said in relation to paragraph (f) that:
"It is at this point ... that effect should be given to the fact that the freehold in this farm is the property of the wife, having been given to her by her father, and it should be regarded for the purposes of section 25 as part of her contribution, together with the work she has put into it and presumably the profits that have been ploughed back into it."

It was also necessary to take into account the husband's efforts in improving the property by building up the stock and improving the fertility of the land, though it was clear that by comparison the wife's contributions were very large indeed. In *B* v *B* [1990] 1 FLR 20 the wife worked without remuneration and had put "a large part of her inheritance into the family kitty, relieving the husband of capital and income expenditure", though it was not a case where assets had been created by her efforts. Ward J (at p. 31) concluded that assets had been preserved to some extent; debts had been prevented by the use of the wife's money and by her efforts - "But no great capital assets had been create". It was a case, therefore, "where the wife should get the fullest of the conventional awards".

(v) Timing of contributions
In *Kokosinski* v *Kokosinski* [1980] Fam 72 Wood J said that paragraph (f) referred only to events which occur after the ceremony of marriage. On this basis care of the home and family during a period of premarital cohabitation could not be taken into account, but he thought that the court could take into account behaviour which has occurred outside the span of the marriage, at least where the conduct has affected the finances of the other spouse. In *Martin* v *Martin* [1976] Fam 335 Purchas J saw no reason to restrict the ambit of paragraph (f) to conduct before the breakdown of the marriage. If one or both of the parties have by their dealings with the assets enjoyed by the family either greatly enhanced or severely reduced or destroyed those assets, these are matters to which the court may properly have regard. In that case the wife - acting on her own after the marriage had broken down, and notwithstanding the husband's actions - had managed to save the farm that they had previously worked together. This was a decisive factor underlying the decision to vest the farm in the wife absolutely. (See also paragraph (g).)

(vi) Death of a spouse
The contribution of the wife during a marriage of over thirty years was taken into account in determining the appropriate amount to be paid to her estate when she died shortly after the original order had been made (*Smith* v *Smith* [1991] 2 All ER 306 at p. 311. See also *Barber* v *Barber* [1993] 1 FCR 65).

*(g) The conduct of each of the parties, if that conduct is such that it would in the opinion of the court be inequitable to disregard it*

(i) The scope of the paragraph
This paragraph was introduced by the Matrimonial and Family Proceedings Act 1984 to deal with conduct that was formerly referred to in the statutory target, and which had been abolished by that Act. It was noted above that in *Wachtel* v *Wachtel* [1973] Fam 72 Lord Denning MR made it clear that conduct was no longer to be regarded as relevant in the majority of cases. The conduct of both parties was to be considered, and if the conduct of one was substantially as bad as the other then they would weigh equally in the balance. The conduct of one party was to be relevant only if it was "obvious and gross" so that there was a substantial disparity between the parties.

In *Armstrong* v *Armstrong* (1974) 4 Fam Law 156 Stephenson LJ referred to conduct which it would be "inequitable or unjust to disregard", thereby foreshadowing the new statutory formulation. The intention underlying paragraph (g) was in fact to set out in statutory form the effects of the case law beginning with *Wachtel*, but concern was expressed in 1984 that the new formulation involved a change of emphasis which could result in an examination of conduct in every divorce case. Unfortunately, in *Kyte* v *Kyte* [1988] Fam 145 at p. 154 Purchas LJ raised further doubts on the point. He thought that it might well be that the use of the words "it would in the opinion of the court be inequitable to disregard it" gave a broader discretion to the court than that envisaged in the cases since *Wachtel*. However, he did not consider it necessary to decide the matter as the behaviour established against the wife would satisfy the test under either approach, and since the point had not been argued it would be wrong to express a concluded view. Accordingly those cases where conduct would have been found to be "gross and obvious" will undoubtedly fall within paragraph (g), but it remains possible that cases where the conduct falls short of that standard may also fall within the new wording of the paragraph.

It must also be borne in mind that even if conduct is found to be relevant within paragraph (g), its practical effect on the orders made may be very limited. It must be balanced against all the other relevant factors, and provision for the needs of the parties and children may leave little scope for giving effect to conduct. Thus in *K* v *K (Conduct)* [1990] 2 FLR 225 at p. 230 Scott-Baker J said that it would be inequitable to disregard the husband's conduct in relation to his failure to obtain employment and the consequences of his drink problem. He concluded that it would not be just to make an order against the wife for periodical payments to be made to the husband although she had a good income and he did not. However, the husband had a great need for accommodation and he was awarded a lump sum payment of £60,000 out of the proceeds of sale of the jointly owned matrimonial home valued at some £100,000. It was appropriate that he should have more than simply his half-share, but not very much more.

(ii) Conduct associated with the breakdown of the marriage
It is understandable that "gross and obvious" conduct should be sought and found in terms of misconduct associated with the breakdown of a marriage. Nevertheless, such conduct on the part of one spouse must be balanced against the conduct of the other spouse. In *Vasey* v *Vasey* [1985] FLR 596 at p. 603 Dunn LJ said in relation to the comparable provision in the Domestic Proceedings and Magistrates' Courts Act 1978 that conduct would be a relevant factor only in an exceptional case:
"because experience had shown that it was dangerous to make judgments about the cause of the breakdown of the marriage without full enquiry, since the conduct of the spouse could only be measured against the conduct of the other and marriages seldom broke down without faults on both sides."
This echoes the views expressed in *Wachtel* v *Wachtel* [1973] Fam 72 where the court found that the responsibility for the breakdown of the marriage rested equally on both parties, and *Trippas* v *Trippas* [1973] Fam 134 where there was nothing to choose between the parties each of whom had been living with another partner.

More recently in *Leadbeater* v *Leadbeater* [1985] FLR 789 Balcombe J concluded that it would not be inequitable to disregard conduct. If he had to take into account the husband's conduct in bringing a 16 year old girl to live in the home, then equally he had to take into account the wife's attitude over her son, her alcoholism, and her adultery.

In *Dixon v Dixon* (1974) 5 Fam Law 58 the conduct of the husband was regarded as gross and obvious when he committed adultery with his own daughter-in-law and went to live with her. In *Bailey v Tolliday* (1983) 4 FLR 543 the wife had carried on a sexual relationship with her father-in-law which had been concealed from the husband. As a result of that relationship a child was born. Waite J (at p. 550) said that it would be contrary to reason to disregard the effect which the wife's conduct had had upon the marriage because it would offend a reasonable person's sense of justice. It would be contrary to conscience to leave it out of account because of the effect which it had had upon the husband. In *Ibbetson v Ibbetson* [1984] FLR 545 the judge considered it would be repugnant to justice not to take the circumstances of the breakdown of the marriage and the consequences of it into account. He said (at p. 553): "The admitted facts are that after fifteen years of marriage Mrs Ibbetson leaves her husband in Saudi Arabia taking the children with her to go and live with his former best friend in a house in Leicester and she makes no complaint of any kind against Mr. Ibbetson. In my view this must be a relevant factor". (See also *Blezard v Blezard* (1980) 1 FLR 253; *Backhouse v Backhouse* [1978] 1 All ER 1158.)

In *Kyte v Kyte* [1988] Fam 145 at p. 156 Purchas LJ said that the conduct of the wife in actively assisting or, alternatively, taking no steps to prevent her husband's attempts at suicide knowing that she stood to gain by his death, together with her wholly deceitful conduct in relation to her association with her new partner, would amount to conduct of a gross and obvious kind which would have fallen within the concept under the old law. In his judgment it would be inequitable to ignore it even against the conduct of the husband whose manic depression contributed to the unhappy conditions which existed during the marriage and afterwards. The husband had been ordered to transfer his interest in the home to the wife and this was allowed to stand by the Court of Appeal which, however, reduced the lump sum of £14,000 ordered by the judge to £5,000 on account of the wife's conduct.

In *West v West* [1978] Fam 1 at p. 9 Sir John Pennycuick V-C said that the word "gross" did not carry any sort of moral judgement. It meant no more than "of the greatest importance", and the same seems true of the new formulation. In *West v West* the wife was so closely tied to her own family that she would not join her husband and set up a family of her own with her husband in a home of their own. The judge had found that this attitude stemmed from factors in her make-up which were not under her control. Since the wife was not fully to blame for her attitude, he had concluded that her conduct was not gross and obvious. However, the Court of Appeal took the view that a refusal or failure by a wife ever to join her husband in spite of his having bought a house for her must be described as "gross" unless it is found that the house is totally and absolutely unsuitable for her occupation. A more extreme case was *M v M* (1982) 3 FLR 83 where the wife had killed the two children of the marriage, but was found not guilty of murder by reason of insanity. Reeve J held that the conduct of the wife was undeniably of the greatest importance in causing the irretrievable breakdown of the marriage. Accordingly, although no moral blame could be attached to it in view of the medical evidence, it was conduct which it would be inequitable to leave out of account. Even so, the wife was not deprived of her share of the proceeds of sale of the matrimonial home and was awarded a small lump sum payment, though no provision was made for periodical payments. (Contrast *Evans* v *Evans* (1981) 2 FLR 33.)

(iii) Conduct relating to financial matters
Financial mismanagement or irresponsibility in relation to assets of the family may be relevant conduct. In *Martin* v *Martin* [1976] Fam 167 Purchas J said that he could not exclude from his consideration of all the circumstances under s.25(1), as it then was, the fact that the husband had charged the farm - the main family asset - and, through unsuccessful ventures in connection with another woman, wholly or nearly wholly dissipated about £33,000 of capital. On the other hand, the wife, acting on her own and notwithstanding the actions of the husband, had managed to save the farm as a viable concern and had reached a position where there was a reasonable profit. In *Primavera* v *Primavera* [1992] 1 FLR 16 at p.23 Glidewell LJ said that he was inclined to the view that the wife's disposition of the inheritance received from her mother did not properly fall within paragraph (g), but in the end that did not matter because it was clearly a circumstance of the case to which, under s.31(7), the court was required to have regard (see above). He was also of the view that the general financial mismanagement of which the wife had been guilty in the past was not a relevant consideration. While accepting that in an appropriate case financial mismanagement by a party might be a circumstance to which the court was required to have regard under s.31(7), he did not accept that it should go into the scales in a case where the husband was a man of the wealth of the husband in the case before him.

(iv) Conduct amounting to a positive contribution
While conduct may be thought of primarily as a factor reducing the amount of financial provision which the court might otherwise have awarded to a party, it may also increase that amount. Thus in *Kokosinski* v *Kokosinski* [1980] Fam 72 at p. 85 Wood J held that the court could not do justice between the parties unless it took into account the wife's conduct during the twenty-five years that she and her husband had been cohabiting before the ceremony of marriage.

Moreover, conduct in the sense of "misconduct" must be balanced against such positive conduct by the same person. In *Wachtel* v *Wachtel* [1973] Fam 72 at p. 90 Lord Denning MR said:

> "There will be many cases in which a wife (though once considered guilty or blameworthy) will have cared for the home and looked after the family for very many years. Is she to be deprived of the benefit otherwise to be awarded to her by [s.25(2)(f)] because she may share responsibility for the breakdown with her husband?"

Thus in *West* v *West* [1978] Fam 1, although the wife's conduct in failing to set up home with her husband was clearly to be taken into account, it had to be balanced against the fact that she had cared for the children in her own "family" home.

Income provision for her was reduced to one-eighth of their combined incomes. The decision in *Bateman* v *Bateman* [1979] Fam 25 provides another example of such a balance being struck. The wife resented the time spent by the husband on his career, and during many rows she was often the aggressor. She twice inflicted wounds of some gravity on the husband and on one occasion he had to enter hospital. Purchas J held that although the wife's conduct had substantially contributed to the breakdown of the marriage and was a relevant factor, the wife had over the years made a valuable contribution to the family by looking after the home and bringing up the children. Bearing in mind the husband's shortcomings, she should by no means be deprived of all financial provision, but would be granted reduced orders.

(v) Conduct after separation or divorce
It is apparent that conduct that affects the property and/or financial resources of the parties may be relevant even though it occurs after their separation or indeed after dissolution of the marriage. In *Jones* v *Jones* [1976] Fam 8 the husband, some two months after decree absolute, attacked the wife with a knife and inflicted a number of wounds one of which caused a severe disability of the wife's hand. The husband was convicted of causing grievous bodily harm and was sentenced to three years' imprisonment. Orr LJ (at p. 15) said that "conduct" was capable of applying to something that happened after the breakdown of the marriage, or indeed after the decree absolute. Megaw LJ (at p. 16) emphasised that the husband's attack made it most unlikely that the wife would thereafter be able to earn anything or, anyway, to earn anything substantial. (See also *Hall* v *Hall* [1984] FLR 631.)

Although the husband's conduct in *Jones* had occurred after the decree absolute, it had occurred before the wife's application for provision had been determined. The Court of Appeal was therefore able to take it into account by vesting the former matrimonial home in her absolutely and deleting an obligation on the part of the wife to pay one-fifth of the equity to the husband on certain future events, which had been imposed by the judge. Conduct occurring after an order has been made cannot affect orders for lump sum payments or transfers of property - these are not subject to variation or discharge under s.31 of the Matrimonial Causes Act 1973, though in certain limited circumstances leave to appeal out of time may be granted. (See *Barder* v *Caluori* [1988] AC 20 and Chapter 10, Part 9(b).) Such conduct may be relevant where the order is for periodical payments and thus subject to variation or discharge under s.31.

It will certainly be relevant to the extent that it effectively reduces the other party's means, income, or ability to earn his living. In *J(HD)* v *J(AM)* [1980] 1 WLR 124, on an application to vary an order for periodical payments, Sheldon J held that any conduct by a party may be relevant whether or not it directly affects the other's finances if it is such as to interfere with the other's life and standard of living and which is "gross and obvious" so as to "cause the ordinary mortal to throw up his hands and say 'Surely that woman is not going to be given any money' or 'is not going to get a full award' " (quoting Sir George Baker P in *W* v *W* [1976] Fam 107 at p. 110). In that case the former wife had conducted a sustained campaign of malice and persecution against the husband and his new wife, and Sheldon J held that this could not be ignored.

(vi) Cohabitation

A difficult question is the extent to which the cohabitation of the former wife with another man can and should be regarded as conduct which it would be inequitable to disregard in determining the financial provision appropriate for the former wife. In *MH* v *MH* (1982) 3 FLR 429 at p. 437 Wood J said that it was neither fair, just nor reasonable for a woman to be in a better position by virtue of cohabitation rather than remarriage, and reduced the amount of the periodical payments to take account of the support received by the former wife from her new partner. In *Atkinson* v *Atkinson* [1988] Fam 93 at p. 108 Waterhouse J accepted that the cohabitation of the wife, the decision not to remarry and the reasons for it are conduct which it would be inequitable for the court to disregard within the terms of s.25(2)(g). He said (at p. 108):

> "The variety of human folly is, of course, infinite and there may well be cases in which the ex-wife's conduct in the context of cohabitation, such as financial irresponsibility or sexual or other misconduct, may make it necessary and appropriate that a periodical payments order should be discharged or reduced to a nominal amount. Again, the overall circumstances of the cohabitation, particularly the financial consequences, may be such that it would be inappropriate for maintenance to continue ...".

That had been the case in *Suter* v *Suter and Jones* [1987] Fam 111 where the Court of Appeal held that the fact that the wife had "invited her lover to live for the foreseeable future in the former matrimonial home with herself and the children, without seeking or receiving any contribution to the expenses of maintaining that home" was conduct which it was inequitable to disregard. The order for periodical payments was reduced to a nominal order, the matrimonial home having already been transferred to her. In *Atkinson* v *Atkinson* the Court of Appeal upheld the reduction in the amount of the periodical payments from £8,000 to £4,500 on account of the cohabitation, but concluded that any further reduction would be inappropriate as it would reduce the wife virtually to poverty level.

On the other hand, in *Duxbury* v *Duxbury* [1987] 1 FLR 7 the Court of Appeal held that the judge was justified in not taking into account the fact of the wife's cohabitation with another man in determining the amount of the substantial lump sum intended to provide for her future needs. Ackner LJ (at p. 13) said that it was an irrelevant factor. He said that, having calculated the sum necessary to meet her reasonable needs: "How she spent her money was her affair". She has the freedom to lead her own life as she chooses following divorce.

It is clear from these cases that cohabitation is not to be equated with remarriage and given "decisive weight". It is "not the job of a court to put pressure on parties to regularise their unions" (*per* Butler-Sloss LJ in *Hepburn* v *Hepburn* [1989] 1 FLR 373 at p. 378). An order for periodical payments is unlikely to be discharged on account of the cohabitation of the recipient, but the amount of the payments may be reduced - or reduced to a nominal amount - to take account of the financial support she may be (or should be) deriving from the cohabitee.

*(h) In the case of proceedings for divorce or nullity of marriage, the value to either of the parties to the marriage of any benefit (for example, a pension) which, by reason of the dissolution or annulment of the marriage, that party will lose the chance of acquiring*

(i) Loss of pension rights

The effect of the dissolution or annulment of a marriage on the legal status of the parties makes it likely that a wife will lose the chance of acquiring some financial benefits. First, and perhaps most obviously, she will lose the chance of acquiring any benefit as his widow if she should survive him. The position in relation to the state pension is considered in Chapter 19. In relation to a private pension it is necessary to establish clearly the precise benefits involved. The principal benefits are the pension and any lump sum to which the husband will become entitled on retirement and any widow's pension which may be payable following the husband's death after retirement. It is also necessary to take into account any widow's pension payable should the husband die in service and any lump sum payable to his estate. (See the Memorandum *Maintenance and Capital Provision on Divorce* (1991) published by the Family Law Committee of the Law Society, para. 3. 3.)

At the present time the courts have no special power to deal with future pension rights, and they can only make use of their general powers to order financial provision or property adjustment in an attempt to provide some relief. In exercising their powers the courts are required under paragraph (a) to take into account resources which a party may have in the foreseeable future. The Family Law Committee, in its Memorandum, noted that the courts have seemed to limit the foreseeable future to about four or five years and that where a divorce occurs more than ten years before a pension is due, the wife is unlikely to benefit (*ibid*. para. 3. 4). The Memorandum recommends that the courts should be given power to make pension adjustment orders, but no legislation seems likely in the short term. (See also the Consultation Paper issued by the Lord Chancellor's Department in 1985: *Occupational Pension Rights on Divorce*.)

As the law stands at present the court may try to compensate a spouse for loss of pension rights in a number of ways. First, it can make an order for payment of a lump sum deferred until receipt by the former husband of a lump sum or gratuity. Thus in *Milne* v *Milne* (1981) 2 FLR 286 the husband was ordered to pay to the wife a sum equal to one-half of the amount to which he or his estate would become entitled under the pension scheme when such sum became payable under the scheme, provided that the wife was living at that date. (See also *Priest* v *Priest* (1981) 1 FLR 189 and the discussion in Chapter 10.) Alternatively, the application can be adjourned until the husband receives the lump sum on retirement. The difficulties and limitations are discussed in Chapter 10. If the husband dies, such an application could not be pursued and it would be necessary to consider a claim under the Inheritance (Provision for Family and Dependants) Act 1975 (see Chapter 21). The court has no power under that Act to interfere with the discretion exercised by pension fund trustees (see Chapter 23).

The court may take into account the loss of pension rights as one of the factors in determining the financial provision which is appropriate. It can then order a larger payment by way of compensation. Thus in *Richardson* v *Richardson* (1978) 9 Fam Law 86, where the husband was due to retire in some three years' time and receive a civil service pension and lump sum payment of £9,000, the judge had left out of account the impact of those rights. The Court of Appeal increased the lump sum payment ordered from £7,750 to £12,000. However, in many cases the husband will not have sufficient assets to provide adequate compensation (see *Julian* v *Julian* (1972) 116 SJ 763, and Chapter 9 where the power of the court to refuse a decree in certain circumstances is considered). The court may also decline to make a clean break which might otherwise have been thought appropriate, thereby preserving the wife's right to seek a variation of a periodical payments order on the basis of the husband's pension (see *M* v *M (Financial Provision)* [1987] 2 FLR 1). The court has no power to order the husband to take out and maintain a life insurance policy to make provision for the wife (*Milne* v *Milne*), or to order the assignment of pension rights. On the other hand, it may be possible to make these and other arrangements by consent (see *Parker* v *Parker* [1972] Fam 116 and Chapter 9).

(ii) Loss of succession rights

Once a marriage has been dissolved or annulled, one former spouse will not be entitled to succeed on the intestacy of the other. A former spouse is also unlikely to be given the benefits he or she would otherwise have received under the other's will in the event of survival, or by gift *inter vivos*. Following breakdown of a marriage one former spouse is unlikely to make a new will in favour of the other, and an existing will is likely to be altered. (The automatic revocation of provisions in existing wills on divorce is discussed in Chapter 20.) Strictly such prospective loss is not due to the change in status brought about by divorce or annulment, but to the breakdown of the marriage. This distinction does not appear to have been drawn in *Trippas* v *Trippas* [1973] Fam 134 where the Court of Appeal considered the significance of what was then paragraph (g) and is now paragraph (h). The principle question was the effect of the receipt by the husband, some nine months after the parties separated, of a capital sum exceeding £80,000 for the sale of a business. The receipt of such a sum had been discussed by the parties before their separation, and it seems that the husband had said that there would be something for the wife. When the payment was received the husband made a gift of £5,000 to each of his sons, but gave nothing to the wife. Scarman LJ, after referring to what is now paragraph (h), said that it was reasonable to infer that had they been living together at the time, the wife could have expected in cash or in kind some sort of benefit accruing to her from the sale of the business. Even if she had at that time received nothing in the form of cash, if they had gone on living with each other she would have benefited generally from the availability of the capital, and the sum could also be regarded as a substitute for a pension. Had they lived together until he died, some provision would have been made for the wife by gift or will or settlement from the capital sum. In the circumstances the court considered that an order for payment of a lump sum of £10,000 to the wife was appropriate.

In *O'Donnell* v *O'Donnell* [1976] Fam 83 it was argued that the court in *Trippas* v *Trippas* had misunderstood the true intention and effect of paragraph (g) in applying it, even to this limited extent, to the peculiar facts in that case. It was pointed out that the paragraph is not applicable to cases of judicial separation, and that it should therefore be confined to cases where the wife has lost the chance of a future benefit owing to loss of her status as a wife. (See *Talbot* v *Talbot* [1971] The Times 19 October in relation to the strict view taken on a similar expression in s.5: Chapter 9.) The Court of Appeal did not think it necessary to decide the point, even if it was open to them to do so, because in the case before them the matters which the judge had taken into account under paragraph (g) (as it then was) could equally well be taken into account under paragraph (a) as part of the present and future resources of the husband. The same could be said in relation to *Trippas*.

The wider view seems to have been taken in *Thyssen-Bornemisza* v *Thyssen-Bornemisza (No. 2)* [1985] FLR 1069. In that case both parties were domiciled in Switzerland and accordingly under Swiss law the wife, if she had continued to be married to the husband at the time of his death, would have been entitled as of right to one-quarter of his estate. Griffiths LJ said (at p. 1081):

"There can be no doubt that that is a factor that the judge is required to take into account, but of course it is not a factor peculiar to this case because of Swiss law. It is a factor that is almost certainly present in every case of dissolution of marriage because in the ordinary course of things if the parties are married at the date of the husband's death the overwhelming probability is that the wife will benefit significantly either under the will or on an intestacy, so there is nothing special about the fact in this case other then the magnitude of the figures."

He went on to say that in cases where the parties do not have much money it is a factor that is unlikely to be significant. In cases of great wealth, where it is possible for the court to make proper provision for the wife to enable her to go on enjoying the same standard of living to the end of her days, it was difficult to see what particular weight should be given to this factor, especially in a case where the wife had not contributed in any way by her efforts to the husband's fortune.

# Chapter 12

# Dealing with the matrimonial home

## 1. The courses of action open to the court

In many, perhaps most, cases the main, and often the only item of property with which the court is concerned is the matrimonial home of the parties and it therefore merits special attention as indeed it received in *Wachtel* v *Wachtel* [1973] Fam 72. Ormrod LJ described *Wachtel* as the prototype of a large class of cases with which the court deals every day. "It was," he said, "essentially a case of two people starting their married life with little or nothing but their earning capacities, and together founding a family and building up by their joint efforts such capital as they were able to save. Typically, their main capital asset was the matrimonial home, bought on a mortgage and paid for out of income". Such cases were "true examples of equal partnership," and such expressions as "family assets" and "the wife earning her share" were wholly apposite" (*O'D* v *O'D* [1976] Fam 83 at p. 88). Circumstances vary a good deal more than the statement would seem to suggest, but he was concerned to distinguish the *Wachtel* type of case from the situation where one spouse has brought into the marriage substantial capital assets or acquires such assets during the marriage by inheritance or gift. The approach of the courts in that situation was considered in Chapter 11.

Where the matrimonial home is the principal, perhaps the only, asset, there are four basic courses open to the court.

(1) It may order the home to be sold and the proceeds of sale divided between the parties in such proportions as it determines.

(2) It may order the sale of the home to be postponed so that one spouse and any children may continue to live there for a period to be determined by the court. When it is no longer appropriate for the home to be retained as such, the sale can take place and the proceeds divided as determined by the court.

(3) It may vest the matrimonial home (or allow it to remain vested) in one spouse absolutely and, where appropriate, provide compensation for the other spouse in the form of a capital sum payable immediately or alternatively at some future date.

(4) It may order the home to be settled on one spouse for life.

It is important to take into account the impact of costs and the effect of the statutory charge that may arise in favour of the Legal Aid Board (see Chapter 13). The tax implications of orders affecting the matrimonial home are considered in Chapter 18.

## 2. Sale of the matrimonial home

*(a) The need to provide homes*

An immediate sale of the former matrimonial home and a division of the proceeds between the former spouses is perhaps at first sight the most obvious course to take in winding up the marriage partnership. However, the sale of the home to provide one spouse with his or her share or a lump sum payment may cause considerable hardship to the other spouse who continues to live in the house. The spouse who left the home may have formed another attachment and perhaps remarried, or may be otherwise provided with accommodation, for example by the local authority. If the party who has secure accommodation elsewhere has made little contribution to the acquisition of the home during a short marriage, a sale will be inappropriate and the property may be vested in the sole name of the occupying spouse (see *Walsh* v *Corcoran* (1983) 4 FLR 59 and Part 4 below).

In *Browne* v *Pritchard* [1975] 1 WLR 1366 the former wife who had left the home had remarried, though her "new" husband had left her and she was living on social security. Nevertheless, she had obtained a council flat which, as Ormrod LJ pointed out, was "a valuable asset". The former husband, who had remained in the home with his two children by a former association, was unemployed and also living on social security. To order a sale would, in the opinion of Ormrod LJ, have been "socially disastrous". It was the provision of homes for all concerned which was the first priority. The former wife had argued that she should have her share of the house in money, whatever difficulties it might impose on the husband, but Ormrod LJ said (at p. 1371):

"If the marriage had not broken down ... she would never have touched a penny of the value of the house, because investment in a home is the least liquid investment that one can possibly make. It cannot be converted into cash while the children are at home and often not until one spouse dies unless it is possible to move into much smaller and cheaper accommodation."

In the earlier case of *Smith* v *Smith* (1974) 118 SJ 167 he had pointed out the basic limitations of this course when he said:

"The effect of forcing a sale of the home followed by a division of the balance of the proceeds of sale after paying off incumbrances would be to leave each party with a sum of money which was useless when it came to obtaining alternative accommodation."

In *Martin (BH)* v *Martin (D)* [1978] Fam 12, the crucial factor seems to have been that the registrar had found that the wife's half share in the equity of the matrimonial home would be insufficient to buy another house for her. Stamp LJ concluded that if the house was sold and the wife left without any secure accommodation she would suffer greater hardship than would be suffered by the husband in postponing the sale. The husband lived in a council house with the party cited whom he expected to marry. He therefore had a secure roof over his head and had no immediate need of capital. Ormrod LJ said that it was a case in which the needs of the parties outweighed their resources. There were no children to be taken into consideration. (See also *Dopson* v *Cherry* (1975) 5 Fam Law 52.)

*(b) Entitlement to enjoyment of capital*

The decision in *Martin (BH)* v *Martin (D)* may be contrasted with the earlier decision of the Court of Appeal in *Goodfield* v *Goodfield* (1975) 5 Fam Law 197 where the parties were of similar age and the only child of the family was over 17 though still living with her mother in the former matrimonial home. The husband had formed a stable association with another woman and it provided him with a home. The county court judge had upheld the agreement of the parties that the beneficial interest in the matrimonial home should be divided between them in equal shares, but ordered that the wife be permitted to remain in the house until her remarriage, her death, or the sale of the property, such sale not to take place without her express consent. In the Court of Appeal, Scarman LJ noted that the effect of the order was to deprive the husband of the benefit of his interest in the matrimonial home for a very prolonged period, whereas if the marriage had not broken down each party would have continued to enjoy the benefit of the capital asset. The judge had not had regard, or sufficient regard, to the plight of the husband. While the wife would be in a difficult accommodation market it was inconceivable that a single woman with £4,750 behind her and a steady job could not find accommodation if she was forced to. While that accommodation might not be the accommodation to which she had been accustomed for 20 years it was a sadness of matrimonial breakdown that neither side was able to maintain quite the standard of life they were able to maintain when they were united. The wife had to accept a measure of disadvantage if s.25 was to be applied and justice done to the husband as well as to her. He considered that:

"A matrimonial home for a family such as this was not only a place in which both could live; it was a security for old age, a capital resource to which they could turn in times of trouble or emergency. Postponing the sale indefinitely meant that the husband was deprived of the backing of that capital asset."

It was acknowledged that a postponement of the benefit of the capital asset for a period of time was often a reasonable burden to place upon a spouse, e.g. where there were young children living with the wife. Even where there were no children, to consider postponement might be justified if the husband had other capital or was earning a substantial income. However, the fact that he had acquired what appeared to be a stable home with the lady with whom he was living went only to his accommodation problem, whereas the hardship imposed by the order was the deprivation of immediate access to his capital asset. An order was made that the home should be sold, but not until one year had elapsed from the date of the order unless in the meanwhile the wife had died, or remarried, or consented to such a sale. Until such a sale the wife was to be entitled to remain in occupation, but with the duty to pay the rates and mortgage instalments. Upon sale the proceeds were to be divided equally.

*(c) Striking a balance*

While each case must depend upon its own particular circumstances, the facts of *Martin* and *Goodfield* are similar in many respects, though *Goodfield* appears to have received no more than a brief mention in *Martin*. They can be reconciled on the basis that in *Martin* the court considered that the wife would not be able to accommodate herself securely with her share of the proceeds and her other resources, whereas in *Goodfield* the court envisaged no such difficulty. This was the view taken by the Court of Appeal in *Blezard* v *Blezard* (1981) 1 FLR 253 where Orr LJ said that an order depriving the husband of his share of the value of the matrimonial home until the death of the wife was wrong in the circumstances of the case as the wife's share of the equity of the home would enable her to purchase alternative accommodation. The Court of Appeal did in fact provide for a postponement of the sale for some four years until the younger child attained 18, but thereafter it saw no reason why the husband should be deprived of his capital. The proceeds of sale were to be divided two-fifths to the husband and three-fifths to the wife. It was considered appropriate that the husband should receive less than a half share in view of the wife's undertaking to discharge mortgage repayments until sale. It does not seem that in arriving at this unequal division in the wife's favour, the court was seeking to provide the wife with a sum sufficient to purchase alternative accommodation as an equal division would probably have sufficed. However, the division of the proceeds of sale can be adjusted so as to ensure that the spouse who remains in occupation of the home will have sufficient to purchase alternative, but smaller, accommodation. This may have been a factor in *Bennett* v *Bennett* (1978) 9 Fam Law 19 where the Court of Appeal ordered a sale of the former matrimonial home occupied by the wife and children. The wife was to receive two-thirds of the net proceeds of sale after discharging the mortgage, or £17,000, whichever of those sums was the greater. It was not disputed that if the wife were to obtain a sum of the order of £17,000, she would be in a position to buy, in the same locality, a suitable home for herself and the children. (See also *Bambrough* v *Bambrough* (1983) 4 FLR 27 and *Compton* v *Compton* (1984) 5 FLR 706.)

In *Grimshaw* v *Grimshaw* (1981) 11 Fam 75 the Court of Appeal distinguished *Goodfield,* and Ormrod LJ said that it was crucial that the court in that case was satisfied that the money received by the wife was sufficient to enable her to find alternative accommodation. Whereas the judge in *Grimshaw* had ordered an immediate sale with an equal division of the proceeds, the Court of Appeal gave the wife the option of paying £4,000 within 12 months in return for the transfer of the husband's interest in the house to her subject to a 15 per cent charge on the ultimate proceeds of sale. The £4,000 would enable the husband to raise the balance for a mobile home and could be raised by the wife and son on mortgage. Neither party had alternative accommodation and in this respect the case differs from most reported cases. In *Mason* v *Mason* [1986] 2 FLR 212 the Court of Appeal agreed that the husband and his new family ought not to be entitled to remain in the former matrimonial home, thereby depriving the wife of her share of the family capital, even though it was acknowledged that he might experience difficulty in rehousing himself and his new family in the private sector. An order for a lump sum payment to the wife of an amount greater than her half share to compensate her for dismissal of her claim for periodical payments was upheld even though it would force a sale of the home, but more time was allowed for payment as it seemed that the increasing profitability of the husband's business might by then have given him greater capacity to raise a mortgage. The wife was securely housed in a council house and if the husband and his new family had to accept council accommodation they would be in no worse position than that in which the wife found herself and would in all probability be able to purchase that accommodation on favourable terms as the wife was now able to do. It was also pointed out that the husband's intractability had prevented a satisfactory settlement on the basis of a sale before crippling costs had been incurred and, but for the impact of costs, the home would have provided sufficient funds with which to have rehoused all the persons involved.

Accordingly, in considering whether to order an immediate sale of the former matrimonial home a crucial factor is the accommodation of the parties. If one spouse is securely accommodated elsewhere the court will be reluctant to order a sale of the home occupied by the other unless the proceeds of sale will be sufficient to provide alternative accommodation, or other accommodation can be obtained by the latter spouse. If, on the other hand, the non-occupying spouse is not satisfactorily housed the court will have to balance the hardship which would be suffered by the occupying spouse if a sale were ordered. The decision in *Goodfield* v *Goodfield* (1975) 5 Fam Law 197 serves as a reminder that in considering the actual or prospective accommodation of the spouses following divorce, some worsening in the position of both spouses may be inevitable. Moreover, although one spouse may be anxious to remain in the former matrimonial home, perhaps with the children, this may be neither provident nor sensible where more modest accommodation in size and/or value would be sufficient. Thus in *C* v *C (Financial Provision)* [1989] 1 FLR 11 Ewbank J concluded that it was not necessary for the wife to remain in a six bedroom house. In *Evans* v *Evans* [1990] 2 All ER 147 Booth J ordered the former matrimonial home, occupied by the wife and children, to be sold and the proceeds of sale, after discharge of the mortgage and costs of sale, to be paid to the wife for the purpose of providing herself and the children with alternative accommodation within her financial means. On the other hand, *Martin (BH)* v *Martin (D)* [1978] Fam 12 serves as a reminder that under s.25 the court is not only concerned with dividing the property between the parties according to their contributions. It is also concerned with the needs of the parties, and in particular with the fact that as a result of the marriage one of the parties, generally the wife, may well be in an economically weaker position to support herself and to provide for her needs. The assets of the other party may have to be utilised to help provide for those needs, and if the husband's assets are tied up to provide accommodation for the wife, then presumably he will be called upon to pay less by way of periodical payments than if the wife had to provide her own accommodation.

Where the husband has remained in occupation, a sale may be refused where it would cause him hardship and there is no evidence that he could rehouse himself. (See *Chinnock* v *Chinnock* (1981) 1 FLR 249 where the wife and children were securely housed in council accommodation.) The need to provide a home for children may, of course, be an overriding factor in the short term.

Where the value of the former matrimonial home is substantial, a sale may be the best way not only of providing funds for the purchase of more modest accommodation, but also for providing a lump sum payment for the other reasonable requirements of the occupying party. This may avoid having to resort to the husband's business which might be crippled or endangered by the need to provide a lump sum. (See *B* v *B* [1989] 1 FLR 119; *P* v *P* [1989] 2 FLR 241.)


## 3. The postponed trust for sale

### (a) Preserving the home for one spouse
Where it is important to preserve the former matrimonial home as a home for one former spouse, but inappropriate to deprive the other former spouse of all interest in it, the court may vest the home in the joint names of the spouses, or allow it to remain so vested, and provide that the sale shall be postponed for a period when it is required as a home. Both spouses retain an interest in the proceeds of sale and this is an alternative approach to vesting the property in the name of one former spouse alone subject to a charge in favour of the other (see Part 4 below, and for a comparison see Hayes and Battersby, *Property Adjustment Orders and the Matrimonial Home* [1981] Conv. 404 and *Property Adjustment: Order or Disorder in the former Matrimonial Home* [1985] Fam Law 213 and *Property Adjustments: Further thoughts on Charge Orders* [1900] Fam Law 142). It was the course adopted by the Court of Appeal in *Mesher* v *Mesher* [1980] 1 All ER 126 which was decided in 1973 and gave its name to one form of order. An alternative form of order was adopted in *Martin (BH)* v *Martin (D)* [1978] Fam 12 which provides for a different period of postponement.

### (b) The Mesher order

(i) The nature of the order
In *Mesher* v *Mesher* the matrimonial home was held by the parties jointly. The order provided that the parties should continue to hold the house on trust for sale and should hold the proceeds of sale and rents and profits until sale on trust for themselves in equal shares provided that as long as the daughter of the marriage was under 17 or until further order the house should not be sold. In *Allen* v *Allen* [1974] 1 WLR 1171 the former home vested in the husband alone was ordered to be transferred to the spouses, jointly to be held on trust for sale. The wife was to be given occupation with the children, and the property was not to be sold until the younger boy was 17 or he had finished his full-time education.

(ii) The advantages
The advantage of a Mesher order is that it not only preserves the home for one former spouse who will be able to bring up the children there, but it does so without depriving the other former spouse of all interest in the property. Moreover, bearing in mind the effect of inflation, the latter would enjoy the benefit of any increase in the value of the property which he or she would not receive if the property were wholly vested in the other subject to a charge for a fixed sum as in *Hector* v *Hector* [1973] 1 WLR 1122. (This problem can also be overcome by providing the other spouse with a charge for a proportion of the proceeds of sale. For the tax consequences of each form of order, see Chapter 18.)

(iii) The problems

If the home is to be retained then provision must be made for the outgoings on the property, though in some cases, such as *Alonso* v *Alonso* (1974) 4 Fam Law 164, the property may itself provide some income from lodgers. Where the wife remains in the home with the children her earnings are likely to be limited and, as *Chamberlain* v *Chamberlain* [1973] 1 WLR 1557 shows, she will generally need assistance by way of periodical payments. It is not, therefore, a course which permits a clean break in its widest sense to be made between the parties, and by its emphasis on an ultimate sale and division of the proceeds of sale may appear more threatening than an order vesting the property in the occupying spouse subject to a charge in favour of the other.

The principal disadvantage of a Mesher order is, however, the problem facing the wife when the children have completed their education or reached the specified age when the property has to be sold. This was described by Latey J in *S* v *S* [1976] Fam 18 at p. 23 as follows:

"This wife like so many wives when there are children has come off worse as a result of the breakdown of the marriage. It is a sad fact of life that, where there are children, both husband and wife suffer on marriage breakdown, but it is the wife who usually suffers more. The husband continues with his career, goes on establishing himself, increasing his experience and qualification for employment - in a word, his security. With the children to care for a wife usually cannot do this. She has not usually embarked on a continuous and progressing career while living with her husband caring for their child or children and running the home. If the marriage breaks down she can only start in any useful way after the children are off her hands and then she starts from scratch in middle life while the husband has started in youth."

In that case he observed that the wife would be 36 or more before she could begin to forge any real career with prospects of continuity and perhaps some pension rights. The only security for her future lay in the existing home which was ordered to be vested in her absolutely.

This then is the danger which in *Carson* v *Carson* [1983] 1 WLR 285 at p. 291 Ormrod LJ said was "staring us in the face". That case showed that the court will not generally have power to review the position at the end of the period of postponement (see Chapter 10, Part 8(a)(iii)). A Mesher order had been made in 1975, and in 1981 the wife who had remained in the home with the children sought to have the entire interest in the property transferred to her. The Court of Appeal held that there was no power under s.31 of the Matrimonial Causes Act 1973 to vary a property settlement order, while an application for a transfer of property order was an attempt to get a second settlement of the same asset and should be refused. The court also refused leave to appeal out of time against the original order. The Mesher order received a good deal of criticism in the late 1970s and especially in the judgment of Ormrod LJ in *Martin* v *Martin* [1978] Fam 12 at p. 21. The dangers of the Mesher order continued to be emphasised in cases during the 1980s including *Carson* v *Carson* (1981) 2 FLR 352 and *Harvey* v *Harvey* [1982] Fam 83. In *Mortimer-Griffin* v *Mortimer-Griffin* [1986] 2 FLR 315 at p. 319 Parker LJ, endorsing criticism by Sir John Donaldson MR in that case, said:

"It has been criticised since its birth; it is an order which is likely to produce harsh and unsatisfactory results. For my part, I hope that criticism, if it has not got rid of it, will at least ensure that it is no longer regarded as the 'bible'."

(iv) Situations where a Mesher order remains appropriate

Despite continuing criticisms it has been recognised that there remain situations where a Mesher order is appropriate, and this was recognised most recently by Lloyd LJ in *Clutton* v *Clutton* [1991] 1 All ER 340 at p. 346.

First, it has been accepted that it was an appropriate form of order in *Mesher* v *Mesher* itself. In that case the former wife was living in the house with the daughter, then aged 9, and a man she proposed to marry. She was to discharge all outgoings including the mortgage interest, but any capital repayments were to be discharged equally by the parties. The former husband was living with another woman, whom he intended to marry, in a house which had been purchased in their joint names. The woman had provided a substantial cash payment towards the purchase price, the balance coming from a mortgage advance. The crucial factor in *Mesher* v *Mesher* was that when the case came before the court both parties were intending to remarry and the primary concern in the case was to preserve a home for the children. It was not a case, therefore, where the wife would find herself alone and with insufficient money to provide herself with accommodation when the sale eventually occurred. Clearly if, on the other hand, there is no immediate prospect of remarriage and the wife has no independent career of her own and is unlikely to have sufficient capital to purchase alternative accommodation, the Mesher type of order is inappropriate (see *Hanlon* v *Hanlon* [1978] 1 WLR 592).

Secondly, a Mesher order may be appropriate where the family assets are amply sufficient to provide both parties with a roof over their heads if the matrimonial home were sold, but nevertheless the interests of the children require that they remain in the matrimonial home. In such a case it may be just and sensible to postpone the sale until the children have left home since, *ex hypothesi*, the proceeds of sale will then be sufficient to enable the wife to rehouse herself. This was the example given by Lloyd LJ in *Clutton* v *Clutton* [1991] 1 All ER 340 at p. 346. However, he emphasised that where there is doubt as to the wife's ability to rehouse herself, a Mesher order should not be made. That was the position in *Clutton* itself where even if the wife was given two-thirds of the equity valued at £50,000 as suggested by the husband, it was very uncertain whether in a few years' time when the daughter left home this would be sufficient to enable the wife to rehouse herself. (Contrast *Sharp* v *Sharp* [1984] FLR 752.)

Thirdly, where the marriage has been very short and the contribution of the occupying spouse to its acquisition has been small in comparison with the contribution of the other spouse, a Mesher order may be appropriate for the benefit of the children. This was the case in *Drinkwater* v *Drinkwater* [1984] FLR 627 where Fox LJ (at p. 629) said:

"... the marriage was a very short one, the husband made a substantial contribution to the purchase price (much larger than the wife's), it is his only asset and if there were no children it is difficult to see why the house should not be sold straight away. That might be inconvenient for the wife but the fact remains that it would be the only fair way of dealing with the financial interests of the parties in this property at that point of time. The only reason why it is necessary to continue the wife's occupation of the house during what is likely to be another fourteen years at least is to secure the interests of the children. But in a case of this sort where the marriage has been so short, once that has been achieved then it seems to me that, having regard to their respective financial positions and contributions, the fair course at that point of time is to enable the husband to be put in possession of his share of this house. That can only be done by giving him his share of the proceeds of sale by a sale at that point of time."

It should be noted that the husband was not in secure accommodation, had a low income and poor employment prospects and no capital.

Fourthly, where the net amount which would be produced by a sale of the property is relatively small and in financial terms equality would be equitable, the court may have no alternative but to make a Mesher order to preserve the home for the children. Thus in *Anthony* v *Anthony* [1986] 2 FLR 353, after allowing for payment of the substantial costs which had been incurred and which would give rise to the statutory legal aid charge, only about £10,000 would remain available to the parties out of the matrimonial home. It should be noted, however, that at first instance the judge had made an order vesting the property in the husband alone subject to payment of a lump sum and that the wife was seeking a Mesher order on the basis that she would be responsible for all the outgoings on the house but with the benefit of orders for periodical payments in respect of two children. The Court of Appeal concluded that the only feasible course of action to enable the wife to remain in the home with the two younger children was to make a Mesher order but noted that if the order was made without qualification there could be no sale for as long as twelve years as the youngest child was only six. Parker LJ (at p. 359) said that the court cannot look safely into the future with sufficient certainty to make that an unalterable provision. Accordingly, there should be liberty to apply for the trust for sale to be exercised earlier in the event of circumstances arising which either party might feel justified an earlier sale.

Fifthly, where a creditor is seeking to obtain and enforce a charging order against the husband's beneficial interest by seeking a sale of the matrimonial home, then the normal course should be to postpone the sale of the house for such period only as may be necessary to protect the right of occupation of the wife and children rather than transfer the husband's interest to the wife (*per* Balcombe LJ in *Harman* v *Glencross* [1986] Fam 81 at p. 99). Thus in *Austin-Fell* v *Austin-Fell* [1989] 2 FLR 497 the court made a Mesher type order under which enforcement of a charging order obtained by a bank against the husband's beneficial interest in the matrimonial home would be postponed for some ten years. (See further Chapter 8.)

(v) The terms of a Mesher order

If a Mesher order is considered appropriate a number of points must be considered. First, the court must consider the period of postponement which is appropriate to cover the children's dependency. The reported cases show that the ages 16, 17 or 18 have all commended themselves from time to time. However, an arbitrary date by reference to the age of the youngest child is frequently inconvenient. In *Harvey* v

*Harvey* [1982] Fam 83 at pp. 87-88 Purchas J said:

"In the circumstances prevailing today, it would be rash to presume that at the age of 16 each of these children will no longer be a responsibility of the wife. Experience shows that very often young people stay in their homes longer than that during the early stages of what one hopes will be their early careers, so that in any event I would have considered that 16 was far too early a point in time at which to allow a sale of the roof over the wife's head, without any kind of relief."

A more satisfactory form of order is probably that adopted in *Chamberlain* v *Chamberlain* [1973] 1 WLR 1557 where sale was postponed until the youngest child completed full-time education or thereafter with the consent of the parties or by order of the court.

It is desirable that a Mesher order should contain a provision for the court to make further orders in relation to the administration or execution of the trust established by the order (*per* Oliver LJ in *Thompson* v *Thompson* [1985] 2 All ER 243 at p. 247). The common form therefore postpones sale until certain specified events "or further order" thereby implying a liberty to apply. The reason for this was explained by Oliver LJ in *Thompson* v *Thompson* as follows:

"The court, on making a property adjustment order in a case where there are minor children still to be accommodated in the matrimonial home, is confronted with the difficulty that it is seeking to legislate for a future which is, of necessity, uncertain. One or other of the parties, or the child or children, may die or become incapacitated; the party having custody may go bankrupt, emigrate or merely wish to move house. The family circumstances may change entirely so that the suspension on the execution of the trust for sale may be no longer regarded as appropriate, and this may happen in all sorts of quite unpredictable ways. It is obviously not possible, even for a skilled equity draftsman, to cater for every conceivable circumstance. For this reason, although the order finally decides the rights of the parties so far as their beneficial interests are concerned it is necessary that the flexibility of administration of the trust be preserved. That can be achieved in practice only by enabling the parties to apply back to the court for directions if circumstances occur rendering an earlier sale desirable."

An application in pursuance of such a provision must, however, be a working out of the original order and must not be in effect an attempt to vary the original order (*ibid.* at p. 249. See also Chapter 10, Part 8). Thus the court may, in exercise of its power under s.24A of the Act, order a sale of the property at a date earlier than that contemplated by the events specified in the original order if the object is to give effect to the spirit of the original order, but not if it is sought to produce a different substantive result. In *Thompson* v *Thompson* an earlier sale was ordered for the benefit of the occupying party, but in *Norman* v *Norman* [1983] 1 WLR 295 Wood J refused to order a sale to enable the former husband who was in ill health and in need of accommodation to use part of the proceeds of sale to purchase a home. In *Thompson* v *Thompson* [1985] 2 All ER 243 at p. 249 Oliver LJ found it difficult "to conceive of a 'further order' extending the specified period (on the expiration of which the parties are given an immediate right to have the trust executed) which does not constitute a variation."

Secondly, the right of occupation should be expressly conferred upon the former spouse who is to care for the children, and the other spouse, generally the husband, should be excluded, as was done in *Allen* v *Allen* [1974] 1 WLR 385.

Thirdly, it may be desirable to include a provision for a change of home, i.e. that the existing home might be sold and the proceeds invested in a new property to be held on the same terms as the old property. The occupying spouse may need to move for employment or education reasons, but it would seem that he or she has no power to compel the other spouse to contribute his or her share of the proceeds to the purchase of a new house. There are problems in relation to the powers of trustees for sale of land to invest the proceeds of sale in the purchase of further land so that suitable provision should be included in the original order.

Where it becomes necessary to apply for a further mortgage advance and improvement grants to carry out substantial repairs necessary to the matrimonial home which is subject to a Mesher order, then if the husband refuses to join in such applications the court may appoint a receiver to take the husband's place for this purpose (*Harvey* v *Harvey* [1987] 1 FLR 67).

### (c) The Martin order

(i) The nature of the order

The major disadvantage of a Mesher order is the problem that faces the occupying spouse-seeking accommodation when the limited period of postponement comes to an end. An obvious way of dealing with this disadvantage is to provide for a longer period of postponement where this is compatible with the interests of the other spouse. In *Martin (BH)* v *Martin (D)* [1978] Fam 12 at p. 21 Ormrod LJ said:

"There is no magic in the fact that there are children to be considered. All it means is that the interests of the children take priority in most cases, so that often there can be no question of sale while the children are young. But the situation that will arise when the children reach the age of 18 requires to be carefully considered. Otherwise a great deal of hardship may be stored up in these cases by treating it as a rule of thumb that the matrimonial home should then be sold."

In that case the husband was living in a council house with a woman he intended to marry and had no immediate need for a capital sum to support his present way of life. The wife's share of the equity would not be enough to enable her to purchase alternative accommodation. The Court of Appeal upheld an order giving the wife the right to occupy the home during her life or until her remarriage or such earlier date as she should cease to live there. Thereafter, it was to be held on trust for the parties in equal shares. An earlier example of such an order can be found in *Flatt* v *Flatt* (1974) 4 Fam Law 20 where the wife had left the husband after some 34 years of marriage. The court ordered the home to be held by both parties on trust for sale and provided that the husband should continue to live there as long as he wished. The form of order in *Martin* v *Martin* has subsequently been adopted in a number of reported cases. (See e.g. *Harvey* v *Harvey* [1982] Fam 83; *Brown* v *Brown* [1981] The Times 11 December; *Tinsdale* v *Tinsdale* (1983) 4 FLR 641.)

(ii) The terms of the order

The first point that arises relates to the events other than the death of the occupying spouse which should be the occasion for a sale. It is clearly appropriate to provide for sale of the property in the event of remarriage of the occupying spouse in view of the general policy of the 1973 Act to terminate periodical payments on that event. It is now also usual to provide for sale if the occupying spouse cohabits with another person for a specified period. In *Tinsdale* v *Tinsdale* (1983) 4 FLR 641 the Court of Appeal ordered that the matrimonial home should continue to be held in joint names on trust for sale in equal shares, the sale to be postponed during the wife's lifetime or until she remarried or became dependent on another man, because (*per* Dunn LJ at p. 648) "I have in mind that if she cohabits with another man in the premises then obviously that man ought to take over the responsibility in providing accommodation for her". The more common approach now seems to be to provide that cohabitation must last for a specific period such as six months. (See *Grimshaw* v *Grimshaw* (1981) 11 Fam Law 75; *Scipio* v *Scipio* (1983) 4 FLR 654.)

Where a sale is postponed for what may be a very lengthy period in the case of a Martin order it may be appropriate that the occupying party pay an "occupation rent" in recognition that she is having the enjoyment of a property which is owned jointly with the other former spouse. This course was adopted by the Court of Appeal in *Flatt* v *Flatt* (1974) 4 Fam Law 20 where the husband was ordered to pay to the wife £247 a year so long as he was in the house having the whole benefit of it. This was considered more fully in *Harvey* v *Harvey* where the Court of Appeal provided that the wife should pay to the husband an occupation rent to commence only after the mortgage had been paid off or the youngest child had attained the age of 18, whichever was the later. The wife had responsibility for payment of the mortgage. This was followed in *Brown* v *Brown* where, on appeal, the court varied a Mesher order so as to allow the wife to occupy the house until her remarriage, death or voluntary decision to leave. If she occupied the house after the youngest child attained the age of 18 she was required to pay an occupation rent to the husband. The court said that that form of order offered some way out of the position in regard to a former matrimonial home at the bottom end of the market which, if it was sold, would not give either party enough capital to allow the purchase of a house in the private sector. It should be noted again that the husband in this case had a council flat and no need of an immediate capital sum. On the other hand in *Scipio* v *Scipio* (1983) 4 FLR 654 the Court of Appeal, while approving a Martin order, considered the requirement for the occupying wife to pay an occupation rent as from the date when the children completed their full-time education to be inappropriate having regard to the discrepancy between the husband's income and the wife's income.

## 4. Vesting the matrimonial home in one party

*(a) Vesting the property in the occupying spouse*
The vesting of the former matrimonial home in the sole name of the former spouse whose home it remains was the course favoured by Lord Denning in *Wachtel* v *Wachtel* [1973] Fam 72. In considering what should be done with a matrimonial home he said (at p. 96):

"Take a case like the present when the wife leaves the home and the husband stays in it. On the breakdown of the marriage arrangements should be made whereby it is vested in him absolutely; free of any share in the wife, and he alone is liable for the mortgage instalments. But the wife should be compensated for the loss of her share by being awarded a lump sum. It should be a sum sufficient to enable her to get settled in a place of her own, such as by putting down a deposit on a flat or house. It should not however be an excessive sum. It should be such as the husband can raise by a further mortgage on the house without crippling him.

Conversely, suppose the husband leaves the house and the wife stays on in it. If she is likely to be there indefinitely, arrangements should be made whereby it is vested in her absolutely free of any share in the husband: or if there are children, settled on her and the children. This may mean that he will have to transfer the legal title to her. If there is a mortgage, some provision should be made for the mortgage instalments to be paid by the husband, or guaranteed by him. If this is done, there may be no necessity for a lump sum as well. Furthermore, seeing that she has the house, the periodic payments will be much less than they otherwise would be."

In *Wachtel* itself no action was necessary in relation to the legal estate which was vested in the husband, for it was he who remained in the home with one of the children of the marriage. The appropriate course was to compensate the wife for her share in the property by the payment of a lump sum. If the home is vested in the joint names of the parties there will generally be an order requiring the non-occupying spouse to transfer his or her interest to the other.

Two qualifications to the statement of Lord Denning must be noted in the light of subsequent decisions. First, he contemplated the possibility that instead of vesting the property absolutely in the wife it might be settled on her and the children. This course was adopted at first instance by Latey J in *Chamberlain* v *Chamberlain* [1973] 1 WLR 1557 but the Court of Appeal held that such an order was inappropriate unless there were special considerations which required the children to make demands on their parents after the conclusion of their full-time education. This view has been followed in subsequent cases. (See Chapter 17, Part 2(b)(iii).) Secondly, Lord Denning's statement may be taken to imply that the expectations of husband and wife are to be viewed differently though there is nothing in the relevant sections of the 1973 Act to indicate this. However, in *Calderbank* v *Calderbank* [1976] Fam 93 it was made clear that husbands and wives are to be dealt with upon a basis of complete equality, though that complete equality may, and often will, have to give way to the particular circumstances of their married life. Thus equal treatment does not necessarily mean equal division of the assets for their circumstances may be different. It does mean that in appropriate circumstances, as in *Calderbank*, the wife may be ordered to pay a lump sum to the husband when she remains in the matrimonial home. Indeed, even when the circumstances are more modest than in that case the husband may be expected to obtain some compensation when the home is vested in the wife (see e.g. *Hector* v *Hector* [1973] 1 WLR 1122). There will be some cases, of course, as envisaged by Lord Denning, where the wife will not only have the matrimonial home vested in her, but will also receive a lump sum payment. This is likely to happen where a clean break is achieved by dismissal of the wife's application for periodical payments where the husband has sufficient means to do this.

*(b) Compensating the non-occupying spouse*

(i) An immediate lump sum payment
The most obvious way of compensating the non-occupying spouse for not having an interest in the former matrimonial home, and the method envisaged by Lord Denning in *Wachtel* v *Wachtel*, is by means of an order for a lump sum payment in favour of that spouse. An important factor influencing the size of the lump sum payment will, of course, be the interest which the recipient had in the home, even though vested in the name of the other spouse. However, it will also be affected by other matters including those set out in paragraphs (a) to (h) of s.25(2). Thus if the non-occupying spouse has a secure home elsewhere, and available resources are limited, there may be less justification for awarding him or her a substantial lump sum payment reflecting his or her full interest in the home. (See e.g. *Backhouse* v *Backhouse* [1978] 1 WLR 243.) A smaller lump sum may also be justified where the marriage has been short, and/or where the contribution of the non-occupying spouse to the acquisition of the home and to the welfare of the family within paragraph (f) has been limited. (See e.g. *H* v *H* [1975] Fam 9; *Kadylak* v *Kadylak* (1975) 5 Fam Law 195.)

There are cases, too, where the occupying party's resources are such as to make it difficult or impossible for the court to order a lump sum payment as large as might be appropriate on the basis of the other factors. (See e.g. *Mentel* v *Mentel* (1976) 6 Fam Law 53; *Porter* v *Porter* (1978) 8 Fam Law 143.) It has been said on a number of occasions that where resources are limited a lump sum order should not cripple the party against whom it is made. (See Lord Denning in *Wachtel* v *Wachtel* [1973] Fam 72 at p. 96.) In many cases the only way in which an occupying party can find a sufficient sum to make a lump sum payment is by obtaining a further mortgage advance on the home. Often not even this will be possible, especially where it is the wife who remains in occupation and it is the husband who has to be compensated. In these circumstances, no immediate lump sum is possible. There are then two ways in which the court may seek to compensate the non-occupying spouse.

(ii) Lump sum payable by instalments
First, it may be possible to make an order for payment of a lump sum by instalments, but as these would probably have to be financed out of income (with no tax relief) it will not often be a feasible course of action.

(iii) Deferred lump sum payment and charge
Secondly, the payment of the lump sum may be postponed and the non-occupying spouse given a deferred charge on the home by way of security. This means that the legal and beneficial interest in the home is vested in one spouse alone subject to a charge in favour of the other spouse to secure payment of (a) a fixed sum of money, or (b) a proportion of the proceeds of sale. A charge for a fixed sum is "open to con-

siderable objections in a period of rapid inflation which 'gives' the party subject to the benefit of the charge no share in any increase in value between the date of the order and the date when the amount secured becomes payable." It limits that party to a lump sum "which by the time it was paid was very much less valuable" (*per* Buckley LJ in *Alonso* v *Alonso* (1974) 4 Fam Law 164). Such an order was made in *Hector* v *Hector* [1973] 1 WLR 1122, but as a result of the criticism the standard form of order will now generally provide for a charge to secure payment of a lump sum equivalent to a proportion of the proceeds of sale. (See also *McDonnell* v *McDonnell* [1977] 1 WLR 34 and *Hope-Smith* v *Hope-Smith* [1989] 2 FLR 56.)

The charge is registrable as a general equitable charge (C(iii)) in the case of unregistered land (Land Charges Act 1972, s.2(4)). In the case of registered land it will be a minor interest and will be overridden on a transfer unless protected by a notice or caution (Land Registration Act 1925, ss.3(xv), 20, 22, 49, 54, 59). The tax consequences of this form of order also need consideration, and are discussed in Chapter 18.

As in the case of a postponed trust for sale, it is necessary for the court to determine the appropriate period of deferment. In *Browne* v *Pritchard* [1975] 1 WLR 1366, where the husband remained with two children in the matrimonial home vested in the joint names of the parties, the wife's interest was extinguished and she was given a charge to secure one-third of the net proceeds of sale. The charge was not to be realised until six months after the younger of the two children living with the husband became 18 with liberty to apply for the charge to be realised sooner if circumstances made that desirable. The wife and another child were securely housed in a council flat. The end result was very similar to that achieved by a Mesher order, and the major disadvantage is similar, namely that the occupying party may be in a difficult position in relation to accommodation when the home has to be sold. It may be possible to meet this difficulty by reducing the size of the payment to the non-occupying spouse so as to leave the occupying spouse with sufficient funds to purchase a smaller property when the children have left home. However, in more recent cases the court has come to the conclusion that the only effective protection for the occupying spouse may be to postpone realisation of the charge for his or her life. This is similar in effect to a Martin order. Such protection must of course be balanced against the hardship to the non-occupying party who may be deprived of capital for a very long time. Indeed he may obtain no personal enjoyment as his share may be paid to his estate after his death. In *Barrett* v *Barrett* (1981) 11 Fam Law 75, where the husband was 20 years older than the wife, Ormrod LJ said that a charge which continued for the benefit of the husband's estate was simply an emotive matter which was valueless to everybody and should not be imposed. Nevertheless, where the non-occupying party is securely housed elsewhere and has no immediate need of capital, a deferment which may last for the life of the occupying spouse may strike a fair balance.

Such a course was adopted in *Dunford* v *Dunford* [1980] 1 WLR 5 where the home was transferred to the wife subject to a charge in favour of the husband for 25 per cent of the proceeds of sale deferred until the death of the wife or the sale of the home. (See also *Draskovic* v *Draskovic* (1981) 11 Fam Law 87; *Ross* v *Ross* [1989] 2 FLR 257.) In *Chinnock* v *Chinnock* (1978) 1 FLR 249 it was the husband who remained alone in the former matrimonial home as the wife and child were living in a council house. There was no evidence that the husband could rehouse himself and he could not raise a lump sum to compensate the wife for her one-third interest without a sale of the home. A sale was not appropriate and the court ordered that the husband hold the property subject to a charge of one-third of the net proceeds of sale of the property, such charge to be free of interest and not enforceable until the husband either sold the property or died. The inclusion of sale as an event giving rise to payment of the lump sum has been criticised as unduly restrictive, and some provision allowing transfer of the charge to a new home may be appropriate as a move may be desirable for employment purposes or because of the education of the children.

The charge may also be made realisable on remarriage of the occupying party and, especially in the case of a wife, in the event of her cohabiting with a man. In *Grimshaw* v *Grimshaw* (1981) 11 Fam Law 75 the husband's charge was to be realisable on the occurrence of one of a number of events including the cohabitation of the wife with another man for a period of six months. Ormrod LJ said that the court was not enthusiastic about the cohabitation provision, but such a provision has now become common practice. In *Chadwick* v *Chadwick* [1985] FLR 606 it was argued that in the special circumstances of the case a sale on remarriage or cohabitation by the wife might cause her hardship and was inappropriate. She suffered from a disease which imposed upon her formidable disabilities limiting her mobility and capacity for work and there was a risk that she might "marry or decide to invite for cohabitation, a gentleman who could not afford to establish her in another bungalow, in spite of the fact that she would be able to put up 50 per cent of the value of the [existing] bungalow, after its sale, less costs of sale and the impact of the Law Society's charge" towards such a purchase (*per* Cumming-Bruce LJ at p. 608). This argument was rejected by the Court of Appeal which said that the court had to balance the reasonable requirements of the wife with those of the husband who was being deprived of his share of the capital for what might be a very long period.

On the other hand, in *Greenham* v *Greenham* [1989] 1 FLR 105 the Court of Appeal was concerned to avoid the need for the occupying spouse to move house at an advanced age. The judge had ordered the husband to pay to the wife a lump sum equal to 20 per cent of the proceeds of sale of the former matrimonial home, in which the husband, then aged 63, continued to live, upon the earliest of the following events: (1) the sale of the property by the husband, (2) the husband's seventieth birthday, or (3) the husband's death. The Court of Appeal deleted the provision relating to the attaining of the age of 70. Balcombe LJ (at p. 108), noting that the wife had been provided with a home, said that the wife had not demonstrated a sufficient need to justify requiring the husband to sell the home when he reached that age. Although it appeared that he would have sufficient money to buy himself alternative accommodation it would still involve him in having to move home at an age when he might not wish to do so.

*(c) Cases where no compensation is appropriate*

There are cases where it is appropriate to vest the matrimonial home in one spouse without any form of compensation being made to the other. This course has been taken in cases where a husband has shown himself unable or unwilling to make any financial provision. In *Bryant* v *Bryant* (1976) 6 Fam Law 108 the husband had shown that he was prepared to flout the orders of the court and there was no reasonable prospect of his keeping up any periodical payments on his release from prison. Transferring the husband's interest in the matrimonial home to the wife would not only give the wife and the children a roof over their heads, but would also provide an income for her because part of the house was let to tenants. In *Niblett* v *Niblett* (1973) 3 Fam Law 185 the wife, who continued to live in the former matrimonial home with the two daughters of the marriage, had no capital apart from her half share in the equity on the house. Her earning capacity was limited as one of the girls was a semi-invalid, and she was being assisted by social security to keep up the payments. The husband was no better off and only a nominal order for periodical payments in favour of the wife was possible. His income might improve, but it was very bad at the time, and in all the circumstances the Court of Appeal considered that the judge could have done nothing else except order the husband to transfer his half share in the former matrimonial home to the wife subject to the mortgage. Accordingly, quite apart from the question of blame, the only way in which adequate provision can be made for the wife's needs may be to vest the former home in her absolutely without any compensation to the husband. This was the case in *S* v *S* [1976] Fam 18 and in *Jones* v *Jones* [1976] Fam 8 where the wife's ability to support herself had been prejudiced by injuries inflicted on her by her former husband, and she would be quite unable to raise any money for future payment of a lump sum except through the sale of the home. It is probably preferable to consider *Jones* v *Jones* from the point of view of the wife's needs rather than the husband's conduct, though conduct may be a factor which results in a husband receiving no compensation (see Chapter 11, Part 7(g)). *Bryant* v *Bryant* should also be viewed as protecting the wife and children rather than punishing the husband (*per* Stephenson LJ).

Another aspect of conduct is the contribution made by a party to the acquisition of the home and to the welfare of the family. Where the contribution of one party has been very small, no compensation may be appropriate when the home is vested in the other party. Thus in *Poulter* v *Poulter* (1974) 4 Fam Law 86 the former matrimonial home vested in the joint names of the parties had been purchased with funds provided by the wife's father, and Reeve J considered that "the husband had put nothing into the house and could have nothing out of it". In that case the marriage had lasted for some nine years, but this fact appears to have been of little importance. In a very short marriage there will have been little opportunity to contribute to the welfare of the family within s.25(2)(f). In *Taylor* v *Taylor* (1975) 119 SJ 30 the marriage lasted for some four months though there was an even shorter period of cohabitation. The wife retained her job and had suffered no financial loss as a result of the marriage or its breakdown. She had contributed nothing to the purchase price of the house and next to nothing to the household expenses. She had never earned anything to entitle her to a share and in the circumstances an order extinguishing her interest in the former matrimonial home was appropriate. In *Walsh* v *Corcoran* (1983) 4 FLR 59 there had also been a very short marriage and the wife had made virtually no contribution to the welfare of the family or to the acquisition of the home and the Court of Appeal made an order that the wife transfer her interest in the home to the husband on payment by him of £3,000 which he had offered.

In *Schuller* v *Schuller* [1990] 2 FLR 193 the Court of Appeal rejected the suggestion that the wife should have the benefit of a deferred charge on the former matrimonial home to secure payment of the balance of a half share in the proceeds of sale. It was suggested that such a charge should take effect either on the death of the husband or on earlier sale of the property. Apart from ignoring the effect of the wife's after-acquired assets, this would deprive the husband of a number of possibilities. One was the right that any man has to leave his money to whom he wished. Moreover, if at some stage he was in need of money for medical attention or nursing home fees and had to sell the property he would have to pay out a major sum to the wife. Butler-Sloss LJ said (at p. 199) that: "... such an order would also fly in the face of the duty upon the court to try wherever possible to create a clean break".

## 5. Settlement for life

In certain circumstances the need, and indeed the expectation, of one party can be satisfied merely by the use of a home for life without any capital interest ultimately accruing to his or her estate. This is more likely to arise where the parties have married relatively late in life and the marriage has been short and childless. Thus in *S* v *S* [1977] Fam 127 both parties had been married previously, and married each other when they were both aged over 50. The marriage had broken down after a short time and the court concluded that the primary need of the wife was for a home. However, at her age it was not necessary that she should have a freehold house in her name. The court made an order for £11,000 to be settled on the wife to purchase a house on trust which would come to an end on her death or remarriage. The house would revert to the husband or his estate on the wife's death so that his family would not, in the long run, be deprived of the capital represented by the home. She was also awarded a small lump sum.

In *Johnston* v *Johnston* (1976) 6 Fam Law 17 a marriage between a widower of 68 and a widow of 61 ended within a year when the husband obtained a decree of nullity on the basis of his own incapacity to consummate the marriage. The court made an order for settlement of the husband's entire interest in the flat which had been their home on the wife for life and then to the husband absolutely. It was made clear that the wife only had a personal right of residence and if she ceased to live there, her interest would end. In *Curtis* v *Curtis* (1981) 11 Fam Law 55 the court made an order that money be provided by the wife through the medium of a trust for a house or flat to be bought for the husband to live in during the remainder of his life and on his death the wife was to have the property absolutely. This course was preferable to the award of a smaller lump sum which he could dispose of absolutely, but which would be quite inadequate for him to find alternative accommodation.

A settlement may be effected either by the machinery of a strict settlement or by the use of a trust for sale. If the former is used then the machinery and provisions of the Settled Land Act 1925 apply and the legal estate must be vested in the occupying party as tenant for life who will have the power to dispose of it. In *S* v *S* and *Curtis* v *Curtis* the reports give no indication of the machinery to be used, but in

*Johnston* v *Johnston* it was specifically provided that the settlement was to take effect through the medium of a trust for sale. (For the advantages and disadvantages of the strict settlement and the trust for sale in this context, see Hayes and Battersby, *Property Adjustment Orders and the Matrimonial Home* [1981] Conv. 404 at p. 417.)

# Chapter 13

# Costs and legal aid

## 1. General principles

*(a) The starting point*
The general approach to costs in applications for financial provision and property adjustment was recently considered by the Court of Appeal in *Gojkovic* v *Gojkovic (No. 2)* [1991] 2 FLR 233. The starting point is that costs *prima facie* follow the event (*per* Butler-Sloss LJ at p. 236 referring to Cumming-Bruce LJ in *Singer* v *Sharegin* [1984] FLR 114 at p. 119). The concept of "no order for costs" where both parties have been reasonable in their approach to the dispute was rejected (at p. 239) as not being of general application in the Family Division save in children cases. Nevertheless, the starting point may be displaced much more easily than, and in circumstances that would not apply, in other divisions of the High Court. Butler-Sloss LJ (at p. 236) explained the position as follows:

"In applications for financial relief, the applicant (usually the wife) has to make the application in order to obtain an order. If the financial dispute can be resolved, it is usual, and normally in the interests of both parties, that the applicant should obtain an order by consent; and if money is available, and in the absence of special circumstances, such an agreement would usually include the applicant's costs of the application. If the application is contested and the applicant succeeds, in practice in divorce registries around the country where most ancillary relief applications are tried, if there is money available and no special factors, the applicant spouse is *prima facie* entitled to, and likely to obtain, an order for costs against the respondent."

She went on to point out that there are a number of circumstances which may affect or even distort the order for costs that would otherwise have been expected to be made. Thus the behaviour of one party, such as in material non-disclosure, or excessive zeal in seeking disclosure, is likely to be an important factor to be taken into account by the court in exercising its discretion (*Robinson* v *Robinson (No.2)* [1986] 1 FLR 37; *E* v *E* [1990] 2 FLR 233). An order for costs may also be affected by the inadequacy of the assets to provide for the needs of the parties (see *Martin* v *Martin*

[1976] Fam 335; *Singer* v *Sharegin*). The incidence of legal aid will also affect the position. Accordingly "the ambit and extent of the discretion of the court is consequently, and rightly, far wider than in other civil proceedings" (*per* Butler-Sloss LJ at p. 237).

*(b) Estimates for costs*
In view of the impact of costs on the assets available to make appropriate provision, estimates of costs on each side are now required to be prepared for submission to the court at the commencement of the hearing and at any pre-trial review of the application (*Practice Direction (Ancillary Relief: Costs Estimates)* [1988] 1 WLR 561, superseding *Practice Direction (Estimate of Costs)* [1982] 1 WLR 1082). The estimates should be available by the time the case is fixed for hearing and should differentiate between costs already incurred and the expected costs of the hearing, so far as the latter can be ascertained. In *Leadbeater* v *Leadbeater* [1985] FLR 789 at p. 794 Balcombe J considered how costs should be treated in estimating the assets of the parties. He accepted that "there should be added back into the assets of each party what has already been paid by that party on account of costs, less only such part of that figure ... that would never in any event be recoverable, in particular ... the difference between the figure for solicitor own client costs and what might be recovered on taxation by way of an order for party and party costs, subject to the further gloss that there should be deducted any part of that element (i.e. the difference between solicitor and own client and party and party costs) that may have been incurred unreasonably. On the same basis, ... there should be omitted from the party's liabilities, any future liability for costs except, again, such part of that future liability as might properly never be recoverable." This might not apply in cases where the assets are very small, but otherwise this approach means that a party's schedule of assets should exclude reference to costs except those that are irrecoverable. This avoids anticipating the order for costs to be made at the end of the case.

*(c) The desirability of agreement*
The courts have on numerous occasions expressed concern about the situation that arises where the court is unable to make appropriate provision for the parties and their children because of their liability for costs. In *Evans* v *Evans* [1990] 2 All ER 147 Booth J, with the concurrence of the President of the Family Division, gave some general guidelines to be followed by the practitioner in the preparation of a substantial ancillary relief case. (See further Chapter 11, Part 7(a).) In *Singer* v *Sharegin* [1984] FLR 114 at p. 119 Cumming-Bruce LJ emphasised the immense importance of the obligation upon solicitors and counsel in all cases not only to form accurate estimates as to costs but to inform their lay client what the impact of costs is likely to be and the risk involved if "they insist on sticking to what they regard as their own sensible point of view and so refuse to make, or accept, an offer involving much compromise on both sides". In *Sharp* v *Sharp* [1984] FLR 752 the wife's solicitors had taken up the position that they were not prepared even to meet the husband's solicitors to negotiate because they required certain information about the husband's means. Dunn LJ (at p. 757) said "... it is dangerous for solicitors in this class of litigation to take up a position of that kind, namely that they insist on a

particular result (the absolute transfer of the matrimonial home) and it is unfortunate that they refused even to sit around the table and have any kind of discussions with the husband's solicitors". He drew attention to the possibility that if solicitors act in a way which may be regarded either as an abuse of the process of the court or oppressive, then the court has jurisdiction to order the solicitors personally to pay the costs thrown away. (See *Davy-Chiesman* v *Davy-Chiesman* [1984] Fam 48 though the facts there were very different.)

*(d) Open offers and Calderbank offers*
It is important to consider the desirability of making open offers or Calderbank offers with a view to achieving a settlement. In *E* v *E* [1990] 2 FLR 233 at p. 237 Ewbank J said that the making of open offers in a case such as that before him (where the assets were substantial) was a practice to be encouraged, particularly when the costs were going to be very substantial - in that case some £300,000.

As an alternative to an open offer a respondent may make a Calderbank offer which derives its name from *Calderbank* v *Calderbank* [1976] Fam 93. In that case Cairns LJ suggested a procedure whereby a letter makes an offer "without prejudice" to the issue of financial provision or property adjustment, but reserves the right to refer to it on the issue of costs. The offer is accordingly not revealed to the court until after the order is made. The court is required to take account of Calderbank offers (and indeed open offers) in exercising its discretion as to costs (RSC Ord 62, r. 9; CCR Ord 11, r. 10). Both parties must make full and frank disclosure of all relevant assets and the respondent must make a serious offer worthy of consideration. If these preconditions are satisfied then it is incumbent on the applicant to accept or reject the offer and, if the latter, to make his or her position clear and indicate in figures what she/he is seeking (a counter-offer). It is incumbent on both parties to negotiate if possible and at least to make an attempt to settle the case (*per* Butler-Sloss LJ at p. 238). If no agreement is reached and the order ultimately made does not exceed the sum offered, then *prima facie* the applicant will pay the costs after the date of the communication of the offer. In *McDonnell* v *McDonnell* [1977] 1 WLR 34 at p. 38 Ormrod LJ made it clear that the offer will influence, but not govern, the exercise of discretion in relation to costs. The question is whether the recipient of the offer, on the basis of the facts known to him and his advisers and without the advantage of hindsight, ought reasonably to have accepted the proposals in the letter, bearing in mind the difficulty of making accurate forecasts. If the order eventually made exceeds the offer, then *prima facie* costs should follow the event with the proviso that other factors may alter that *prima facie* position as noted above. Thus in *S* v *S (Financial Provision)* [1990] 2 FLR 252 the husband had made a Calderbank offer of £400,000, which the wife had summarily rejected. Booth J eventually ordered the husband to pay sums totalling £435,000, but made no order as to costs to reflect the court's disapprobation of the delay on the part of the wife in the conduct of her application. In the Court of Appeal Purchas LJ (at p. 260) said that the question of how Calderbank letters which nearly, but do not quite, cover the order should be dealt with was essentially a matter for the exercise of discretion by the trial judge in the circumstances of each particular case, and it could not be said that, merely because the Calderbank letter did not cover the full amount awarded, the judge was obliged as a matter of law to award costs against the unsuccessful offeror.

It is essential that the preconditions mentioned are fulfilled. A Calderbank offer or an open offer will not protect a respondent if he has not made a full disclosure of his assets at such time as to allow the applicant an appropriate time to consider what is in fact a reasonable offer. In *Gojkovic* v *Gojkovic (No. 2)* [1991] 2 FLR 233 it was not until less than one month before the date set for the hearing that the husband provided an accountant's report as to his assets and made an open offer which the wife rejected. She refused to make a counter-offer. On the eve of the hearing the husband made a Calderbank offer which fell dramatically short of the lump sum of £1 million eventually ordered which was the amount claimed by the wife in reply to that offer. The pressure of time was such that she and her advisers could not be seriously criticised for not formulating a counter-offer earlier. The husband had knowledge of the counter-offer on the first day of the hearing but did not settle during the nine days which followed. The judge had been wrong to make no reference to that offer and it was not appropriate to make no order for costs. The wife was awarded costs from the date she rejected the open offer until the end of the hearing before the judge. (See also *Robinson* v *Robinson (No. 2)* [1986] 1 FLR 37 at p. 50.)

In *Moorish* v *Moorish* (1984) 14 Fam Law 26 Cumming-Bruce LJ suggested that the respondent was under a duty to act reasonably to protect himself against costs by making an offer by way of a Calderbank letter which fairly reflected his potential liability in the proceedings. It is also possible for an applicant to make a reverse Calderbank offer to accept a specified amount (*B* v *B* (1981) 12 Fam Law 92).

## 2. Legal aid

*(a) The importance of understanding the implications of legal aid*
In *Anthony* v *Anthony* [1986] 2 FLR 353, where both parties had been granted legal aid, the divorce proceedings had been protracted, acrimonious and costly. Parker LJ (at p. 355) noted that nearly half the value of the equity in the matrimonial home, which was initially available to provide for the parties and their children, had already been eaten up by costs. He said:

"This is a sad but all too familiar situation and for my part I cannot stress too strongly that it is incumbent on solicitors to explain and constantly reiterate to legally aided clients that legal aid does not mean that they conduct litigation free of charge for ever."

*(b) The liability of an assisted person for the costs of the other party*
The fact that a spouse is in receipt of legal aid does not prevent an order for costs being made against him if he is unsuccessful at any stage of the proceedings. However, where a person receives legal aid in connection with any proceedings his liability by virtue of an order for costs is limited to "the amount (if any) which is a reasonable one for him to pay having regard to all the circumstances, including the means of the parties and their conduct in connection with the dispute" (Legal Aid Act 1988, s.12(1)). In many cases, of course, the means of the assisted party will be

insufficient to pay anything in the way of costs, but in *McDonnell* v *McDonnell* [1977] 1 WLR 34 the court took into account the fact that the wife had obtained a lump sum of £2,000 when it assessed her liability to pay her husband's costs to the extent of £500 following his successful appeal against the form of the order relating to the former matrimonial home.

In *Collins* v *Collins* [1987] 1 FLR 226, where both parties were in receipt of legal aid, the Court of Appeal held that the judge was not entitled to increase the amount of the lump sum to be paid by the husband so as to include a contribution by the husband to the wife's costs which had been increased by the misleading behaviour of the husband.

### (c) Recovery of costs by the Legal Aid Board

The Legal Aid Board has a duty to recover costs which it has incurred on behalf of an assisted person. It will look first to costs payable by the other party under an order for costs. In so far as the amount recovered under such an order does not cover the costs incurred on behalf of the assisted person, the Board will look to the contribution paid by the assisted person. In respect of any balance the Legal Aid Board has a first charge on any property which is recovered or preserved for the assisted person in the proceedings.

### (d) The statutory charge

(i) The nature of the charge
The Legal Aid Act 1988, s.16(6) provides that, except so far as regulations otherwise provide:
  (a)  any sums remaining unpaid on account of a person's contribution in respect of the sums payable by the Legal Aid Board in respect of any proceedings; and
  (b)  a sum equal to any deficiency by reason of his total contribution being less than the net liability of the Board on his account,
are to be a first charge for the benefit of the Board on any property which is recovered or preserved for him in the proceedings.

(ii) Exemptions from the charge
Exemptions from the charge are set out in the Civil Legal Aid (General) Regulations 1989, reg. 94. These include:
  (a)  any periodical payment of maintenance;
  (b)  the first £2,500 of any money, or of the value of any property, recovered or preserved by virtue of orders (or agreements having the same effect as orders) made under:
    (i)  s.23(1)(c) or (f); 23(2); 24; 27(6)(c) or (f), or 35 of the Matrimonial Causes Act 1973;
    (ii)  s.2 or 6 of the Inheritance (Provision for Family and Dependants) Act 1975;
    (iii)  s.17 of the Married Women's Property Act 1882;
    (iv)  s.2(1)(b) or (d), 6(1) or (5), or 20(2) of the Domestic Proceedings and Magistrates' Courts Act 1978;

(v) the provisions of Schedule 1 to the Children Act 1989.

### (iii) Property recovered or preserved

In *Hanlon* v *The Law Society* [1980] 2 All ER 199 at p. 209 Lord Simon of Glaisdale said that "... property has been recovered or preserved if it has been in issue in the proceedings: recovered by the claimant if it has been the subject of a successful claim, preserved to the respondent if the claim fails. In either case it is a question of fact, not of theoretical risk". He went on to say that in property adjustment proceedings "... it is only property the ownership or transfer of which has been in issue which has been 'recovered or preserved' so as to be the subject of a legal aid charge. What has been in issue is to be collected as a matter of fact from pleadings, evidence, judgment and/or order". He saw no reason "for extending the words to items of property the ownership or possession of which has never been questioned". In that case the court had made an order under s.24 requiring the husband to transfer the matrimonial home to the wife. It had been vested in the husband's name alone but the wife had contributed equally in money and work to the family and marriage. The House of Lords held that the whole interest in the matrimonial home, and not merely the husband's beneficial interest in it, had been in issue. Had there been a clear concession by the husband that, as a matter of prior entitlement - i.e. before the exercise of the court's discretion under ss.24 and 25 - the husband's beneficial interest in the house was limited to a half share then the wife would have "recovered" only her husband's share and would not have been engaged in "preserving" her share. However, no such concession or admission had been made by the husband. (See Lord Scarman at p. 214.)

Even though there was no issue in relation to the ownership of the matrimonial home or other property or other beneficial interest therein, a charge will arise if the possession of such an interest was realised. This was established in *Curling* v *The Law Society* [1985] 1 WLR 471 where the matrimonial home was jointly owned by the spouses. The husband, who was seeking custody of their two children, opposed the suggestion of the wife that the home should be sold and the proceeds divided equally. He sought, in effect, a Mesher order whereby the home would not be sold until the children ceased to be dependent. Eventually the parties reached a compromise whereby the husband abandoned his claim for custody and under a consent order the husband purchased the wife's interest in the home for £15,000. The wife unsuccessfully sought a declaration that the sum was not subject to the statutory charge. Oliver LJ (at p. 482) said:

"What clearly was in issue in this case was whether the house should be sold or retained by the petitioner as his residence, or, to put it another way, whether the respondent was going to receive her share of any money representing her share before the children attained full age. That, as the judge said, was the obstacle which she overcame as a result of the consent order made in the proceedings. What was potentially a distant prospect of receiving her share at some time in the future was translated into an immediate entitlement."

The mere fact that the petition contained a claim for a property adjustment order in relation to a specifically identified property is not by itself conclusive of the question whether the respondent's interest in the property is in issue in the proceedings, but it may be treated as raising a *prima facie* inference that the property was in issue. (See Oliver LJ in *Curling* v *The Law Society* [1985] 1 WLR 470 at p. 481 disapproving of *Jones* v *The Law Society* (1983) 4 FLR 733.) The mere claim for an order under s.24 does not necessarily impugn the respondent's title to the property as it may involve a Mesher order which merely postpones the immediate enjoyment of an ackowledged interest, or it may even involve the bare vesting of a legal estate to give effect to a subsisting equitable interest (*ibid.*). However, if the parties are agreed as to their respective interests in the matrimonial home, it is important that this should be made clear in the correspondence and other documents from the outset.

In *Stewart* v *The Law Society* [1987] 1 FLR 223 in proceedings for variation of a periodical payments order an agreement was reached, incorporated in a consent order, whereby the husband agreed to pay the wife £7,000 which was expressed to be in commutation of the wife's right to receive and claim periodical payments. Latey J held that this could not be regarded as a periodic payment of maintenance, but was a capital payment to which the statutory charge attached. This was approved in *Watkinson* v *The Legal Aid Board* [1991] 1 WLR 419 where the Court of Appeal refused to characterise a payment of £10,000, made as part of an agreement terminating the wife's right to periodical payments, as the final payment. It was a lump sum and subject to the statutory charge.

The charge imposed on property recovered or preserved is imposed in respect of the costs of the totality of the proceedings covered by the legal aid certificate and is not limited to the particular proceedings taken to recover the property. (See Lord Scarman in *Hanlon* v *The Law Society* [1980] 2 All ER 199 at p. 213.) Thus in *Hanlon* the charge covered the costs of the divorce proceedings as a whole, including proceedings for custody and access, and was not limited to costs incurred in relation to the proceedings for a property adjustment order under s.24. Moreover, if there are successive applications in relation, for example, to periodical payments made under the same legal aid certificate, then any capital sum received as part of a compromise to terminate the periodical payments will be subject to the statutory charge to cover the costs of all applications made under the certificate. This occurred in *Watkinson* v *The Legal Aid Board* [1991] 1 WLR 419 where Lord Donaldson MR (at p. 425) said that the moral was:

"First that solicitors should never apply for a certificate to be amended, if they could equally well apply for a fresh certificate ... Second, that in matrimonial proceedings, where there is likely to be what might almost be described as an 'annual pay round' in the form of successive applications for a revision of the amount of periodical maintenance payments, solicitors should use every endeavour to procure the discharge of a legal aid certificate once its purpose has been fulfilled ... and before any new step in the proceedings is taken for which legal aid will be required."

(iv) Enforcement and postponement of the charge

The Legal Aid Board may enforce a charge in any manner which would be available to a chargee in respect of a charge given *inter partes*. The Board must not agree to the release or postponement of the enforcement of any such charge except where regulation 96, 97 or 98 applies, and then only in accordance with the provisions of these regulations.

There used to be no power to postpone enforcement of the charge attached to lump sum payments. Such a power is now given by regulation 96 in respect of orders and agreements made after 1 December 1988. Regulation 96 applies where in proceedings under the Matrimonial Causes Act 1973 there is recovered or preserved for the assisted person a sum of money which by order of the court, or under the terms of any agreement reached, is to be used for purchasing a home for himself or his dependants. Where the assisted person

  (a) wishes to purchase a home in accordance with the order or agreement, and
  (b) agrees in writing on a form approved by the Board (complying with the conditions set out in subparagraph (3)),

the Board may, if the Area Director is satisfied that the property to be purchased will provide adequate security, agree to defer enforcing any charge over that sum. It is obviously advisable that the order or agreement makes it clear that the purpose of the lump sum payment is to enable the recipient to purchase a home. (See *Scallon* v *Scallon* [1990] 1 FLR 194 at p. 198.) The agreement will provide for payment of simple interest on the amount outstanding on the charge from the date of registration to the date of discharge. It will also provide for the execution of a charge on the property purchased with the lump sum in favour of the Legal Aid Board. This also applies to lump sum payments in proceedings under the Married Women's Property Act 1882, the Inheritance (Provision for Family and Dependants) Act 1975, and Schedule 1 to the Children Act 1989.

Even if the conditions for postponement are satisfied, the Legal Aid Board still has a residual discretion to refuse. However, in *Scallon* v *Scallon* [1990] 1 FLR 194 at p. 198 Parker LJ said:

"... in my view, the court is entitled to proceed on the basis that the Legal Aid Board would so exercise its discretion as to further and not to defeat an order of this court. In a case where the entire order of the court would be frustrated if the charge were enforced and the reality was that neither party could obtain a home, it appears to me to be unlikely in the extreme that the Board would exercise the charge and thus frustrate the order of the court."

Accordingly, in that case, when the court was considering the amount of the lump sum payment it was not appropriate to deduct from the sum payable to the wife (based on a proportion of the proceeds of sale of the home) any figure for legal aid costs. (See also Purchas LJ at p. 200. *Simmons* v *Simmons* (1983) 4 FLR 803 distinguished.)

Postponement of the enforcement of a charge over property recovered or preserved for an assisted person is provided for under regulation 97 where by order of the court or under the terms of any agreement reached, the property is to be used as a home for the assisted person or his or her dependants. The Area Director must be satisfied that the property provides adequate security for the sum charged and the assisted person must agree to pay interest on the sum outstanding in accordance with the form of agreement which he or she is required to sign. There is also provision dealing with postponement of the charge where the assisted person wishes to purchase a different property in substitution for the property which is the subject of the order or agreement (regs. 97(5) and 98).

# Chapter 14

# The effect of foreign decrees and proceedings

## 1. The scope of the court's powers

The powers of the court under ss.23 and 24 are exercisable only on or after the grant of a decree under the Act of 1973. Subject to one limited exception - the power to order periodical payments under s.23 in favour of a child of the family when a petition is dismissed - those powers cannot be exercised where a marriage has been dissolved or annulled by a decree of a foreign court which is recognised by English courts. The consequences for a party residing in England or Wales could be serious. (See *Torok* v *Torok* [1973] 1 WLR 1066 - where the wife succeeded in obtaining a decree in England shortly before the foreign proceedings were concluded - and *Quazi* v *Quazi* [1980] AC 744.) He or she could, of course, seek financial provision in the court which granted the decree, but the attitude of the foreign court might be very different from that of an English court applying the principles of the 1973 Act. Moreover, the foreign court might have no power, or be unable to exercise any power, to adjust property rights in a matrimonial home situated in England or Wales.

The problem is one which arises only if the foreign decree is one which will be recognised by an English court as effectively terminating the marriage. The first step is, therefore, to consider whether the foreign decree is one which will be recognised according to the general principles now contained in the Family Law Act 1986 Part II. Secondly, even if a foreign decree is one which would be recognised under those general principles, recognition may be refused on one or more of the grounds set out in s.51 of that Act. If recognition is refused under s.51 this would permit a decree together with ancillary relief to be sought under the Matrimonial Causes Act 1973. The circumstances in which a foreign decree will be recognised in an English court and when recognition may be refused are considered in Part 2 below.

If the foreign decree is one which will be recognised by an English court, application for financial relief may now be made under Part III of the Matrimonial and Family Proceedings Act 1984 which was intended to relieve the hardship that could arise. This is considered in Part 3 below.

## 2. The validity of a "foreign" decree

### (a) The general rules of recognition

The Family Law Act 1986 provides first that the validity of any divorce or annulment granted by a court of civil jurisdiction in any part of the British Islands will be recognised throughout the United Kingdom (s.44(2)). Secondly, the validity of a divorce or annulment obtained in a country outside the British Islands (an "overseas divorce") will be recognised in the United Kingdom if, and only if, it is entitled to recognition by virtue of ss.46 to 49 of the Act or by virtue of any other enactment (s.45). Section 46 draws a distinction between divorces, annulments and legal separations obtained by means of "proceedings" and those obtained otherwise than by means of proceedings. For this purpose "proceedings" means judicial or other proceedings (s.54(1)).

The validity of an overseas divorce, annulment or legal separation obtained by means of proceedings will be recognised if -

(a) the divorce, annulment or legal separation is effective under the law of the country in which it was obtained, and

(b) at the relevant date either party to the marriage -

   (i)  was habitually resident in the country in which the divorce, annulment or legal separation was obtained, or

   (ii)  was domiciled in that country, or

   (iii) was a national of that country.

(s.46(1)).

The relevant date means the date of the commencement of proceedings (s.46(3)).

The validity of an overseas divorce, annulment or legal separation obtained otherwise than by means of proceedings will be recognised if -

(a) the divorce, annulment or legal separation is effective under the law of the country in which it was obtained;

(b) at the relevant date -

   (i)  each party to the marriage was domiciled in that country, or

   (ii)  either party to the marriage was domiciled in that country and the other party was domiciled in a country under whose law the divorce, annulment or legal separation is recognised as valid, and

(c) neither party to the marriage was habitually resident in the United Kingdom throughout the period of one year immediately preceding that date.

(s.46(2)).

The relevant date means the date on which the divorce, annulment or legal separation was obtained (s.46(3)). For the purposes of s.46 a party to a marriage is to be treated as domiciled in a country if he was domiciled in that country either according to the law of that country in family matters or according to the law of the part of the United Kingdom in which the question of recognition arises (s.46(5)).

### (b) Refusal of recognition

Recognition of the validity of -

(a) a divorce, annulment or judicial separation granted by a court of civil jurisdiction in any part of the British Islands, or

(b) an overseas divorce, annulment or legal separation,

may be refused in any part of the United Kingdom if the divorce, annulment or separation was granted or obtained at a time when it was irreconcilable with a decision determining the question of the subsistence or validity of the marriage of the parties previously given (whether before or after the commencement of this part of the Act) by a court of civil jurisdiction in that part of the United Kingdom or by a court elsewhere and recognised or entitled to be recognised in that part of the United Kingdom (s.51(1)).

Recognition by virtue of s.45 of the validity of an overseas divorce, annulment or legal separation obtained by means of proceedings may be refused if it was obtained

(i) without such steps having been taken for giving notice of the proceedings to a party to the marriage as, having regard to the nature of the proceedings and in all the circumstances, should reasonably have been taken; or

(ii) without a party to the marriage having been given (for any reason other than lack of notice) such opportunity to take part in the proceedings as, having regard to those matters, he should reasonably have been given.

In relation to similar wording in s.8(2) of the Recognition of Divorces and Legal Separations Act 1971 it was said that this meant that the spouse against whom the decree had been obtained must have been offered an adequate and effective opportunity of being heard and putting his or her views to the foreign court. A mere ability to take part in the formalities did not constitute such an opportunity. In determining whether the facility offered was adequate the court might take into account the severity of the foreign law. If a foreign court took the view that only strict and precise approaches to it were required and accepted, it should not object if a court of another country with more liberal views found that the whole proceedings jarred its conscience. (See *Joyce* v *Joyce and O'Hare* [1979] Fam 93, where recognition was refused. Compare *Hack* v *Hack* (1976) 6 Fam Law 177.)

In the case of a divorce, annulment or legal separation obtained otherwise than by means of proceedings, recognition may be refused under s.45 if -

(i) there is no official document certifying that the divorce, annulment or legal separation is effective under the law of the country in which it was obtained; or

(ii) where either party to the marriage was domiciled in another country at the relevant date, there is no official document certifying that the divorce, annulment or legal separation is recognised as valid under the law of that other country.

Whether a divorce, annulment or legal separation was obtained by proceedings or otherwise, recognition may be refused if recognition would be manifestly contrary to public policy (s.51(3)). The courts have been reluctant to define or describe "public policy" in this context though in *Joyce* v *Joyce and O'Hare* [1979] Fam 93 Lane J appears to have regarded recognition as contrary to public policy if the decree would effectively prevent the wife from enforcing her claim for any financial provision and would leave her without an effective remedy with regard to the former matrimonial home vested in the joint names of the spouses. Recognition was refused on this ground to a Bolivian decree in *Kendall* v *Kendall* [1977] Fam 208 where the wife had been deceived by her husband's lawyers into applying for a divorce in a language she did not understand. Hollings J was also satisfied that if the

Bolivian court was apprised of the circumstances it would take steps to invalidate the decree. In this case there was a jointly owned home in England which could then be dealt with under the Matrimonial Causes Act 1973.

Even if one of the grounds in s.51 is established the court has a discretion whether or not to refuse recognition of a foreign decree. (See *Newmarch* v *Newmarch* [1978] Fam 79 and *Joyce* v *Joyce and O'Hare* [1979] Fam 93 in relation to the Recognition of Divorces and Legal Separations Act 1971.) It would, of course, be important to consider the advantages of applying for financial relief under Part III of the Matrimonial and Family Proceedings Act 1984 if the necessary conditions are satisfied (see *Tahir* v *Tahir* [1993] SLT 194).

## 3. Applications for financial relief under Part III of the Matrimonial and Family Proceedings Act 1984

*(a) The scope of Part III*
Applications for financial relief under Part III of the 1984 Act may be made by either party to a marriage where (a) the marriage has been dissolved or annulled, or the parties to the marriage have been legally separated, by means of judicial or other proceedings in an overseas country, and (b) the divorce, annulment or legal separation is entitled to be recognised as valid in England and Wales, provided the applicant has not remarried (s.12(1) and (2). "Remarriage" includes a marriage which is by law void or voidable: s.12(3)). The provisions are retrospective in effect, i.e. application can be made by a person whose marriage was dissolved before they came into force on 16 September 1985 (*Chebaro* v *Chebaro* [1987] Fam 127). In addition to showing that the jurisdictional requirements of the Act are satisfied, before the court can exercise its powers to order financial relief an applicant must surmount two hurdles set up to ensure that financial relief is confined to those cases in which it is appropriate for the court in England and Wales to intervene and to protect potential respondents from harassment by claims for the making of which there is no substantial ground.

*(b) The jurisdictional requirements*
The court has jurisdiction to entertain an application for financial relief if any one of the following three jurisdictional requirements is satisfied:
  (a) either of the parties to the marriage was domiciled in England and Wales throughout the period of one year ending with the date of the application for leave under s.13 or was so domiciled on the date on which the divorce, annulment or legal separation obtained in the overseas country took effect in that country; or
  (b) either of the parties to the marriage was habitually resident in England and Wales throughout the period of one year ending with the date of the application for leave or was so resident throughout the period of one year ending with the date on which the divorce, annulment or legal separation obtained in the overseas country took effect in that country; or
  (c) either or both of the parties to the marriage had at the date of the application for

leave a beneficial interest in possession in a dwelling-house situated in England and Wales which was at some time during the marriage a matrimonial home of the parties to the marriage.

(s.15(1). See Law Com. No. 117, paras. 2.7-2.8).

Under (a) and (b) the court's jurisdiction is based on the domicile of either party or on one year's habitual residence of either party in England and Wales at either of two alternative dates, namely (i) the date of the application for leave, or (ii) the date when the overseas divorce or annulment took effect in the overseas country. An alternative basis for jurisdiction is provided by (c) - the presence of a matrimonial home in England or Wales. This was recommended by the Law Commission to deal with the situation where both parties live abroad after the foreign divorce, but have in fact lived in England or Wales, perhaps for a substantial period during the marriage, and the only substantial asset is the matrimonial home within the jurisdiction (Law Com. No. 117, para. 2.9). The former matrimonial home may be owned by either or both of the parties to the marriage, but one of the parties must still have an interest in the home at the date of the application for leave. The existence of proceeds of sale of the property will be insufficient to confer jurisdiction. Where jurisdiction is exercisable only by virtue of (c), no interim order for maintenance may be made (s.14(2)), and the court's powers to make orders for financial provision and property adjustment are restricted to making orders dealing with the matrimonial home or with the proceeds of sale thereof (s.20).

Where the jurisdiction to entertain proceedings would fall to be determined by reference to the jurisdictional requirements imposed by Part I of the Civil Jurisdiction and Judgments Act 1982, then the fact that the applicant can show that the jurisdictional requirements of the 1984 Act are satisfied does not obviate the need to satisfy the requirements imposed by Part I of the 1982 Act. Accordingly, if the latter are not satisfied then the court must not entertain the proceedings (s.15(2)). Conversely, the court may entertain the proceedings if the requirements of the 1982 Act are satisfied even though the requirements of the 1984 Act are not satisfied. (This might be the case on the basis of habitual residence of the applicant spouse for less than one year (Article 5(3)), or the domicile of the spouse in the Convention sense (Articles 2 and 5(3)).)

Under the 1982 Act the jurisdiction of the court in England and Wales in respect of various proceedings is generally limited to cases where the respondent is domiciled in England and Wales, but this is subject to the existence of certain areas of "special jurisdiction". One area of "special jurisdiction" which may include relief within Part III of the 1984 Act comprises "matters relating to maintenance" (Article 5(2)). In relation to matters falling within this category a person domiciled in one contracting State may be sued in the courts of the place where the "maintenance creditor" is domiciled or habitually resident or (if the matter is ancillary to divorce or similar proceedings) in the courts of the country which by its own law has jurisdiction to entertain the divorce or similar proceedings. There is no definition of "maintenance" in the Convention and it is by no means clear whether relief within Part III of the 1984 Act would be regarded as "maintenance" by the European Court of Justice given that it is first granted after the marriage has been dissolved. It is also not clear whether property adjustment orders as well as lump sum orders can be classed as "maintenance" for this purpose. Another area of special jurisdiction which might include relief within Part III of the 1984 Act comprises rights *in rem* in, or tenancies of, immovable property in respect of which Article 16(1) gives exclusive jurisdiction to the courts of the country where the property is situated. It may also be the case that, under the 1982 Act, a court in England and Wales could take jurisdiction to make orders for relief under Part III of the 1984 Act on the basis of the agreement of the parties or submission to the jurisdiction (Articles 17 and 18). It may also be noted that the rules laid down in the Convention do not apply to "rights in property arising out of the matrimonial relationship", though the meaning of this expression is not entirely clear. (See *de Cavel* v *de Cavel* [1980] ECR 731 and the Report by P Jenard on the Convention - Official Journal 1979 No. C59/1, 10-11.)

*(c) Application for leave*
Under s.13 leave of the court must be obtained before an application can be made. The court must not grant leave unless it considers that there is a substantial ground for the making of the application for financial relief. An application for leave is made *ex parte* and, in considering whether a substantial ground exists, the court has to estimate, on the basis of the applicant's uncontroverted statements, his or her prospects of success in satisfying the court that it would be appropriate for an order for financial provision to be made. It is essential for the judge to have all the material facts as known to the applicant placed before him (see *W* v *W (Financial Provision)* [1989] 1 FLR 22). The court may, as in *W* v *W,* set aside an order made *ex parte* if it is shown that an applicant has failed to make a full and frank disclosure of material facts as a result of which the court has made an order substantially different from the order it would have made if such a disclosure had taken place. A further application for leave may be made accompanied by proper disclosure. In *W* v *W* the court, having become fully apprised of the facts, treated the matter as a further application by the wife with the husband being compensated as to costs. The wife was given leave to apply for financial relief limited to an application in respect of two properties in England. The existence of an order for financial provision or an order for transfer of property made in any country outside England and Wales is not, in itself, a bar to the granting of leave (s.13(2)). The court may impose conditions on the granting of leave, e.g. a condition that the applicant should seek to have a foreign order discharged or undertake not to enforce a foreign order (s.13(3)).

In *Holmes* v *Holmes* [1989] Fam 47 at p. 53 Purchas LJ said that looking at the phrase "substantial ground for the making of an application" in the immediate context of the Act he had formed the view "that what is required is that the applicant should demonstrate to the court that there are in all the circumstances surrounding the application for financial relief - the orders that may or may not have been made, the presence or absence of powers to grant financial relief in the foreign forum - reasons for saying that there is a substantial ground for making the application ...". In other words "a substantial ground upon which the court could be invited to exercise its powers under s.12 within the jurisdiction of s.15". He went on to say that in particular, "when the court comes to consider such an application, it will have to take into account under s.16(1) whether in all the circumstances of the case it will be appropriate for such an order to be made by a court in England and Wales. If it is not satisfied that it would be appropriate (and that is a positive onus), the court shall, as a matter of mandatory instruction, dismiss the application". He emphasised that if on the application for leave to apply it is clear that if leave were given the application must founder at the first hurdle of s.16(1), then it would clearly be wrong for the court to grant leave to apply in the first instance. Accordingly it is not possible to isolate the considerations which arise under this group of sections (see also Z v Z *(Financial Provision: Overseas Divorce)* [1992] 2 FLR 291).

*(d) Appropriateness of the venue*

If an applicant obtains leave an application can be made if one of the jurisdictional requirements is satisfied. However, before the court can make an order for financial relief it must consider whether in all the circumstances it would be appropriate for such an order to be made by the court in England and Wales. If the court is not so satisfied, it must dismiss the application (s.16(1)). The court will already have considered this question to some extent in giving leave under s.13. The intention was that it should be possible to raise the issue of "appropriateness" of the court in England and Wales separately from, or together with, the matters relevant to the exercise of the court's discretion in deciding whether to exercise its powers and if so in what way. (See Law Com. No. 117, para. 2.6.)

In considering the question of "appropriateness" the court must, under s.16(2), consider all the circumstances of the case and in particular have regard to the following matters:

(a) the connection which the parties to the marriage have with England and Wales;

(b) the connection which those parties have with the country in which the marriage was dissolved or annulled or in which they were legally separated;

(c) the connection which those parties have with any other country outside England and Wales;

(d) any financial benefit which the applicant or a child of the family has received, or is likely to receive, in consequence of the divorce, annulment or legal separation, or by virtue of any agreement or the operation of the law of a country outside England and Wales;

(e) in a case where an order has been made by a court in a country outside England and Wales requiring the other party to the marriage to make any payment or transfer any property for the benefit of the applicant or a child of the family, the financial relief given by the order and the extent to which the order has been complied with or is likely to be complied with;

(f) any right which the applicant has, or has had, to apply for financial relief from the other party to the marriage under the law of any country outside England and Wales and, if the applicant has omitted to exercise that right, the reason for the omission;

(g) the availability in England and Wales of any property in respect of which an order under Part III of the Act in favour of the applicant could be made;

(h) the extent to which any order made under Part III is likely to be enforceable;

(i) the length of time which has elapsed since the date of the divorce, annulment or legal separation.

In *Holmes* v *Holmes* [1989] Fam 47 at p. 53 Purchas LJ said that in paragraph (f) specific provision is made for the court to bear in mind whether or not the hardship which was recognised before the passing of the Act exists in the case in question. That hardship arose when the courts in this country had no power to grant financial relief where a marriage was terminated in foreign proceedings in which no financial order had been made. Part III now enables the court in England and Wales to step in and fill the gap by making an order for financial provision. On the other hand, it does not mean that merely because a foreign court has power to grant relief, no application will ever be entertained under Part III. However, it was not, in his view, the intention of Parliament to vest in the English courts any power to review or correct "orders made in a foreign forum by a competent court in which the whole matter has been examined in a way exactly equivalent to the examination which would have taken place if the application had been made in the first instance in the courts here" *(ibid.* at p. 311). In that case, following a divorce in New York the court in that State had made an order for maintenance and orders dealing with the property of the spouses. The judge was held to have properly refused leave under s.13. Russell LJ said (at p. 313):

> *"Prima facie* the order of the foreign court should prevail save in exceptional circumstances, and a good case for any interference with it or adjustment of it or any supplementation of it should be apparent before any leave is granted under section 13 where the foreign court is properly seized of the dispute ... So far as it is possible, duplicity of proceedings should be avoided in this as in all other fields in the interests of the parties and their children as well as in the interests of justice and the comity of nations." (See also *Z* v *Z (Financial Provision: Overseas Divorce)* [1992] 2 FLR 291.)

### *(e) Orders for financial provision and property adjustment*

#### (i) General powers of the court

If the court is satisfied that it is appropriate for it to order financial relief it is empowered to make any one or more of the orders which it could make under the Matrimonial Causes Act 1973 if a decree of divorce, nullity or judicial separation had been granted, i.e. any of the financial provision orders mentioned in s.23(1) of that Act or any of the property adjustment orders mentioned in s.24(1) of that Act (s.17(1)). Where the court makes a secured periodical payments order, an order for the payment of a lump sum or a property adjustment order, or at any time thereafter the court may make an order for the sale of property under s.24A(1) of the 1973 Act (s.17(2)).

#### (ii) Restricted powers where jurisdiction founded on a matrimonial home in England and Wales

Where the court has jurisdiction to entertain an application for an order for financial relief by reason only of the situation in England and Wales of a dwelling-house which was a matrimonial home of the parties (see s.15(1)(c)), the powers of the court are restricted to making one or more of the orders specified in s.20(1). These are as follows:

(a) an order that either party to the marriage shall pay to the other such lump sum as may be specified in the order;
(b) an order that a party to the marriage shall pay to such person as may be specified in the order for the benefit of a child of the family, or to such child, such lump sum as may be so specified;
(c) an order that a party to the marriage shall transfer to the other party, to any child of the family or to such person as may be specified in the order for the benefit of such child, the interest of the first-mentioned party in the dwelling-house, or such part of that interest as may be so specified;
(d) an order that a settlement of the interest of a party to the marriage in the dwelling-house, or such part of that interest as may be so specified, be made to the satisfaction of the court for the benefit of the other party to the marriage and of the children of the family or either of them;
(e) an order varying for the benefit of the parties to the marriage and of the children of the family or either or any of them any ante-nuptial or post-nuptial settlement (including such a settlement made by will or codicil) made on the parties to the marriage so far as that settlement relates to an interest in the dwelling-house;
(f) an order extinguishing or reducing the interest of either of the parties to the marriage under any settlement so far as that interest is an interest in the dwelling-house;
(g) an order for the sale of the interest of a party to the marriage in the dwelling-house.

Thus no order for periodical payments or secured periodical payments can be made. Property adjustment orders can only relate to the interest of a party to the marriage in the former matrimonial home or the proceeds of sale of such an interest. Where the court makes an order for the payment of a lump sum by a party to the marriage, the amount of the lump sum must not exceed (or where more than one such order is made, e.g. in favour of a party to the marriage and in favour of a child of the family, the total amount of the lump sums must not exceed in aggregate) the proceeds of sale of that party's interest in the dwelling-house after deducting any costs incurred in the sale, or, if that interest is not sold, the amount which in the opinion of the court represents the value of that interest (s.20(2)). Where the interest of a party to the marriage in the dwelling-house is held jointly or in common with any other person or persons, an order for sale may include the interest of any such third party (s.20(3). See s.24(6) of the Matrimonial Causes Act 1973 for the court's duty to receive representations from such third parties before making such an order). However, the maximum amount of any lump sum order is determined by reference only to the interest of the party to the marriage in the dwelling-house (*ibid.*).

(iii) Interim orders
Where leave for the making of an application is granted under s.13 and it appears to the court that the applicant or any child of the family is in immediate need of financial assistance, the court may make an interim order for maintenance. An interim order is one requiring the other party to the marriage to make to the applicant or to the child such periodical payments for such term as the court thinks reasonable. The

term may begin not earlier than the grant of leave and end on the date of the determination of the application for an order for financial relief (s.14(1)). An interim order may be made subject to such conditions as the court thinks fit (s.14(3)). There is no power to make an interim order if the court has jurisdiction to entertain the application by reason only of the fact that either or both of the parties had a beneficial interest in a former matrimonial home in England and Wales (s.14(2)) - i.e. under s.15(1)(c).

(iv) Supplemental provisions
Various provisions of Part II of the Matrimonial Causes Act 1973 are made applicable to interim orders under s.14 and to orders for financial provision and property adjustment under s.17 so that similar consequences apply as if the orders had been made in proceedings under that Act (s.21).

(v) Basis on which the powers are exercisable
In deciding whether to exercise its powers to order financial relief under s.17 and, if so, in what manner, the court is required to have regard to all the circumstances of the case, first consideration being given to the welfare while a minor of any child of the family who has not attained the age of eighteen (s.18(1) and (2)). In exercising the powers in relation to a party to a marriage the court is also required to have regard in particular to the matters mentioned in s.25(2)(a) to (h) of the Matrimonial Causes Act 1973. It is also under duties corresponding with those imposed by s.25A(1) and (2) of that Act where it decides to exercise under s.17 powers corresponding with the powers referred to in those subsections. In exercising the powers in relation to a child of the family the court is required to have regard in particular to the matters mentioned in s.25(3)(a) to (e) and (4)(a) to (c) of the 1973 Act (s.18(3). See Chapter 17). Where an order has been made by a court outside England and Wales for the making of payments or the transfer of property by a party to the marriage, the court in England and Wales in considering the financial resources of the other party to the marriage or a child of the family, must have regard to the extent to which that order has been complied with or is likely to be complied with (s.18(6)). On an application for a consent order for financial relief under s.17 the court may, unless it has reason to think that there are other circumstances into which it ought to inquire, make an order in the terms agreed on the basis only of the prescribed information furnished with the application (s.19(1). See also subs.(2) in relation to variation). This has the same objective as s.7 which applies to applications for consent orders under the Matrimonial Causes Act 1973. (See Chapter 15.)

(vi) Transfer of tenancies
Where an application is made by a party to a marriage for financial relief the court has the same power to make an order transferring to the applicant a protected, statutory or secure tenancy as it has under the Matrimonial Homes Act 1983 on or after a decree of divorce, nullity or judicial separation in England and Wales (s.22). As under the Matrimonial Homes Act 1983, s.1(10), the applicant must show that the dwelling-house has at some time during the marriage been a matrimonial home of the parties (see Chapter 4).

(vii) Anti-avoidance provisions
Provision is also made for orders restraining or setting aside dealings with property by a party to a marriage intended to prevent or reduce financial relief under s.14 or s.17 of the Act (ss.23 and 24).

## 4. Stay of proceedings in England and Wales

*(a) The court's powers*
The extension of the jurisdictional basis for divorce by the Domicile and Matrimonial Proceedings Act 1973 increased the possibility of proceedings for dissolution of marriage being commenced in England and Wales as well as in some other jurisdiction. At the same time the inherent jurisdiction of a court in England and Wales to grant a stay of proceedings in England and Wales was limited. An English court would only exercise its inherent jurisdiction to stay proceedings in England to enable an action to proceed in another forum if the English proceedings were regarded as oppressive (see *St. Pierre* v *South American Stores Ltd* [1936] 1 KB 382 at p. 398). Accordingly, the 1973 Act conferred upon the court specific powers to stay divorce proceedings in England and Wales where proceedings had also been commenced in another jurisdiction. The Act provided for "obligatory" stays and for "discretionary" stays.

*(b) "Obligatory" stays*
First, paragraph 8 of Schedule 1 provides that a party to divorce proceedings in England and Wales may obtain a stay of those proceedings when proceedings for divorce or nullity are also in being in a "related jurisdiction", i.e. Scotland, Northern Ireland, Jersey, Guernsey or the Isle of Man. If an application for a stay is made before the beginning of the trial or first trial of the divorce proceedings in England and Wales, the court must order them to be stayed if it appears that:
(a) the parties have resided together since the date of the marriage; and
(b) the place where they resided together when the proceedings in the court were begun, or, if they did not then reside together, where they last resided together before those proceedings were begun, was in the related jurisdiction; and
(c) either of the parties was habitually resident in that jurisdiction throughout the year ending with the date on which they last resided together before the date on which the proceedings in the court in England and Wales were begun.
The Law Commission in its Report No. 48, *Jurisdiction in Matrimonial Causes,* which preceded the 1973 Act, assumed that in cases of conflict between proceedings in England and Wales on the one hand, and proceedings in another part of the British Isles on the other, a basis of jurisdiction would exist in both countries. In other words, one or other spouse would be domiciled or have the necessary residential qualification in each country at the time each of the two sets of proceedings was commenced. The conditions set out in paragraph 8 accordingly lay down a further connecting factor to indicate that proceedings should be permitted to continue in one country rather than in the other. In general terms, the Law Commision considered that, as between two competing British jurisdictions, the country most closely

connected with the marriage should exercise jurisdiction, and in this respect the place where the spouses last resided together is very important. However, since the last residence together in a country may have been very short, the requirement was added that one of the parties must have been habitually resident in that country for a minimum period of one year prior to the separation.

If the party to divorce proceedings in England and Wales applying for a stay is able to show that the conditions laid down in paragraph 8(1) are satisfied, then the court must grant a stay. Where the proceedings in England and Wales include proceedings for divorce and proceedings for other relief, e.g. nullity, the court is to stay only the divorce proceedings. The Law Commission considered that usually nullity proceedings should take precedence over divorce proceedings, for if there is no marriage, there can be no dissolution. Accordingly, nullity proceedings in England and Wales are not subject to stay as of right in favour of divorce proceedings (or indeed nullity proceedings) in a related jurisdiction. Nullity proceedings are, however, subject to the court's discretionary power of stay.

*(c) Discretionary stays*

The Domicile and Matrimonial Proceedings Act 1973 also provides that in certain cases matrimonial proceedings in England and Wales may be stayed by the court where there are concurrent proceedings elsewhere in respect of the same marriage, i.e. either in a related jurisdiction or abroad. Paragraph 9 of Schedule 1 to the Act provides that where before the beginning of the trial or first trial in any matrimonial proceedings which are continuing in the court it appears to the court:

  (a) that any proceedings in respect of the marriage in question, or capable of affecting its validity or subsistence, are continuing in another jurisdiction, and
  (b) that the balance of fairness (including convenience) as between the parties to the marriage is such that it is appropriate for the proceedings in that jurisdiction to be disposed of before further steps are taken in the proceedings in the court or in those proceedings so far as they consist of a particular kind of matrimonial proceedings,

the court may then, if it thinks fit, order that the proceedings in the court be stayed or, as the case may be, that those proceedings be stayed so far as they consist of proceedings of that kind.

In the first place, therefore, there must be two sets of properly constituted proceedings at the time when the application for a stay is made to the court in England and Wales (s.5(6)). The proceedings in the English court may be any "matrimonial proceedings", i.e. proceedings for divorce, judicial separation, nullity of marriage, a declaration as to the validity of a marriage of the petitioner, or a declaration as to the subsistence of such a marriage. This is in contrast to the position in relation to obligatory stays under paragraph 8 which applies only to divorce proceedings in England and Wales.

Secondly, proceedings may generally only be stayed before the beginning of the trial or first trial though it is provided that this does not include the separate trial of an issue as to jurisdiction only. However, if the court is satisfied that a person has failed to perform the duty imposed upon him to disclose particulars of proceedings in another jurisdiction, a stay may be ordered after the trial has begun (para. 9(4)).

Thirdly, it is provided that in considering the balance of fairness and convenience, the court must have regard to all the factors appearing to be relevant, including the convenience of witnesses and any delay or expense which may result from the proceedings being stayed, or not being stayed (para. 9(2)).

The Domicile and Matrimonial Proceedings Act 1973 did not abolish the inherent power of the court to stay proceedings (s.5(6)(b)), but in the context of divorce proceedings, that power lay dormant and reliance was placed on the discretionary power of the court under the 1973 Act in a modest number of cases (e.g. *Gadd* v *Gadd* [1984] 1 WLR 1435; *K* v *K* [1986] 2 FLR 411). The real issue underlying applications for stays under the 1973 Act has generally been the availability of the wide powers of an English court to order financial provision and/or property adjustment under the Matrimonial Causes Act 1973 if the marriage was dissolved by decree of an English court rather than by the court in the competing jurisdiction. However, during the last decade the English courts have, in other contexts, developed the inherent power to stay proceedings so as to incorporate the principle of *forum non conveniens*. This development could not be said to be complete until the decision of the House of Lords in *Spiliada Maritime Corporation* v *Cansulex* [1987] AC 460.

The present position may be summarised as follows:

(1) A stay will only be granted on the ground of *forum non conveniens* "where the court is satisfied that there is some other available forum, having competent jurisdiction, which is the appropriate forum for the trial of the action, i.e. in which the case may be tried more suitably for the interests of all the parties and the ends of justice" (*per* Lord Goff in *Spiliada* [1987] AC 460 at p. 476). The court will look to see what factors there are which connect the case with another forum and if, on the basis of that inquiry, the court concludes that there is another available forum which, *prima facie*, is clearly more appropriate for the trial of the action, it will ordinarily grant a stay, unless there are circumstances by reason of which justice requires that a stay should nevertheless not be granted. (*Ibid. per* Lord Goff at pp. 477-478.)

(2) If the court is satisfied that there is another available forum which is *prima facie* the appropriate forum for the trial of the action, the burden of proof - which generally rests on the party seeking a stay - will shift to the other party to show that there are special circumstances by reason of which justice requires that the trial should nevertheless take place in England. The court will consider all the circumstances of the case including the fact, if established, that the petitioner will not obtain justice in the foreign jurisdiction (*ibid.* at p. 476). However, the court should not, as a general rule, be deterred from granting a stay of proceedings simply because the plaintiff in England will be deprived of "a legitimate personal or juridical advantage", provided that the court is satisfied that substantial justice will be done in the appropriate forum overseas (*de Dampierre* v *de Dampierre* [1988] AC 92 at p. 110).

In *de Dampierre* v *de Dampierre* [1988] AC 92 at p. 109 Lord Goff concluded that while he was anxious not to fetter in any way the broad discretion conferred by the 1973 Act, it was "inherently desirable that judges at first instance should approach their task in cases under the statute in the same way as they now did in cases of *forum non conveniens* where there is a *lis alibi pendens*". In that case both husband and wife were French nationals who had married in France though they had moved to London some two years later where the child had been born. The wife had subsequently moved to New York where she lived with the child. The husband instituted divorce proceedings in France and some two months later the wife petitioned for divorce in England whereupon the husband applied in England for a stay of the wife's petition. It was clear that *prima facie* the courts of France provided the appropriate jurisdiction for the resolution of the dispute so that a stay should be granted unless justice required otherwise. French matrimonial law contains provision for "compensation" which unlike the provisions of the English law of financial provision places emphasis upon the question whether the breakdown of the marriage was due to the exclusive fault of one of the parties and (subject to exceptions) a party so at fault is deprived of the right to an award of compensation. Lord Goff said that while such an approach is no longer acceptable in England, "it is evidently still acceptable in a highly civilised country with which this country has very close ties of friendship ..." (at p. 110). It was, therefore, "impossible to conclude that, objectively speaking, justice would not be done if the wife was compelled to pursue her remedy for financial provision under such a regime in the courts of the country which provide, most plainly, the natural forum for the resolution of "the matrimonial dispute".

Lord Templeman, agreeing, said that it was not unfair to the wife in the present circumstances to deprive her of the advantages of seeking from an English court maintenance which she might not obtain from a French court. However, he emphasised that the court must identify and evaluate the advantage claimed by the wife and acknowledged that there were many circumstances in which it would be unfair to the wife to deny her the advantage of claiming maintenance from an English court. Thus, for example, "... if the husband's assets were wholly or mainly in England, or if the wife remained in England, or if the English proceedings would render the French proceedings wholly unnecessary, it might well be unfair to tell the wife to litigate in France and unfair to stay the wife's English proceedings. The extent of the possible disadvantage to a wife if she is confined to her remedies in a foreign forum is another relevant circumstance. For example, if French law provided that on divorce a guilty wife shall be punished and an innocent wife returned to her parents without maintenance or compensation, the wife, at any rate if resident in England, could fairly claim from an English court maintenance out of the husband's assets in England; the husband would behave unfairly if he refused to support his wife and sought a stay of the English proceedings. Fairness depends on the facts of each case and there is no short cut" (*ibid.* at p. 102). The earlier cases concerning applications under the 1973 Act must now be read in the light of the decision of the House of Lords in de *Dampierre* v de *Dampierre*. (See Schuz, (1989) 38 ICLQ 946.)

## 5. Stays of proceedings in foreign courts

A court in England and Wales has jurisdiction to restrain a party from commencing or continuing proceedings in another country. Such jurisdiction will be exercised only in exceptional circumstances and if the court is satisfied that the commencement or continuation of the proceedings in the foreign court would be vexatious or oppressive. This presupposes that the court in England and Wales has considered whether it is the natural forum for the adjudication of the dispute. It must also take account not only of injustice to the defendant if the plaintiff is allowed to pursue the foreign proceedings, but also the injustice to the plaintiff if he is not allowed to do so and is deprived of advantages in the foreign forum. It will be less difficult to obtain a stay if the injunction is sought only for a limited period and for a limited purpose (*per* Lord Goff in *Société Nationale Industrielle Aerospatiale* v *Lee Kui Jak* [1987] AC 871 at p. 896).

In *Hemain* v *Hemain* [1988] 2 FLR 388 the wife had filed a petition for divorce in England in December 1987 and the husband filed a petition for divorce in France in January 1988. In the same month the husband applied for a stay of the English divorce proceedings and this was due to be heard in May. The Court of Appeal upheld the grant of an injunction restraining the husband from proceeding with the divorce proceedings in France until his application for a stay of the English proceedings was heard in May. The balance of convenience was wholly in favour of maintaining the status quo, at any rate until after the hearing in May of the application for a stay. May LJ (at p. 392) said that "... in effect what the husband has done is to obtain a temporary injunction in relation to the wife's English proceedings, which is just the relief in respect of the French proceedings which, by resisting the application before the judge below and prosecuting the appeal, he is seeking to deny her. That in the present case ... is an injustice. It is, without using the epithets in too opprobious a sense, vexatious and oppressive and an abuse of the proceedings of this court."

An alternative method of dealing with the problem was canvassed, namely to dismiss the husband's application for a stay of the English proceedings unless he gave an undertaking to halt his French proceedings pending the hearing in May. The husband in that case apparently refused to give the required undertaking. This was a method to which resort might be had in other cases. It would preserve the status quo effectively by agreement between the parties without the necessity of granting an injunction as an exception to a general principle and without interfering with the proceedings in the French court or appearing to do so (*per* May LJ at p. 393).

# Chapter 15

# Agreements

## 1. The increased importance of agreements

Spouses may make agreements relating to financial provision or ownership or enjoyment of property at various stages of their relationship. While a marriage is happy the financial arrangements are likely to be informal and are modified to meet changing conditions with little difficulty. Even in relation to substantial assets, such as the matrimonial home, "a normal married couple" is unlikely to spend "the long winter evenings hammering out agreements about their possessions" (*per* Lord Hodson in *Pettitt* v *Pettitt* [1970] AC 777 at p. 810).

However, once a marriage runs into difficulty and the parties separate, and certainly when a marriage is terminated by divorce, the disposition of the income and capital of the parties must be determined expressly. In many cases the relationship between the parties will be such that this will have to be done by the court. In other cases it will still be possible for the parties to reach an agreement on such matters, an outcome which can be seen, and is increasingly being seen, as preferable to a court-imposed solution.

It is arguable that the spouses are generally the best judges of what is right for themselves, and are more likely to accept and live up to an arrangement that is of their own making than to an order imposed by a court. Moreover, an agreement made by the parties themselves may enable greater flexibility to be achieved than would be possible in a court order. The risks and uncertainties of a contested application are avoided, and there is also likely to be a considerable saving in costs. The amount of costs likely to be incurred in contested applications for financial provision and property adjustment is an important factor even to a party in receipt of legal aid. (See Chapter 13.)

## 2. Establishing an agreement

*(a) Application of general principles of the law of contract*
Agreements between spouses must, of course, comply with the general principles of
the law of contract if they are to be valid and enforceable. In view of the nature of
the relationship between a husband and his wife two preliminary questions in particular may arise in relation to arrangements between them. First, were the arrangements made by the spouses intended to produce a legally binding agreement, or
were they simply family arrangements, depending for their fulfilment on good faith
and trust, and not enforceable by legal proceedings? Secondly, were the arrangements made so obscure and uncertain that, though intended to be legally binding, a
court cannot enforce them? These two questions are often related, for the "question
of the uncertainty of the words used must ... be a matter of significance in considering the question whether or not there was an intention to enter into legal relations in
a matter of this nature" (*per* Megaw LJ in *Gould* v *Gould* [1970] 1 QB 275 at
p. 282. See also Edmund Davies LJ at p. 281). However, in *Jones* v *Padavatton*
[1969] 1 WLR 328 at p. 336 Fenton Atkinson LJ warned that lack of formality and
precision in expressing an arrangement is not necessarily an indication that no contract was intended.

*(b) Intention to create legal relations*
Where the spouses are living together in amity at the time they enter into an agreement, there is a presumption that they did not intend the agreement to be legally
binding. In *Balfour* v *Balfour* [1919] 2 KB 571 the husband, shortly before returning abroad to work, orally agreed to pay his wife £30 a month in consideration of
her agreeing to support herself without calling upon him for further maintenance.
The Court of Appeal unanimously held there was no legal contract, and Atkin LJ
expressly stated that the onus was on the person seeking to enforce the agreement to
show that it was intended to be legally binding (*ibid.* at p. 580). This, too, was the
view taken by the majority of the Court of Appeal in *Gould* v *Gould* [1970] 1 QB
275 where, after the spouses had separated, the husband promised to pay his wife
£15 a week, but with the qualification "as long as I can manage it". The majority,
Edmund Davies and Megaw LJJ, held that it had not been within the contemplation
of the parties to make a legally binding agreement - taking into account, in particular, the uncertainty of the terms and the absence of any *quid pro quo* from the wife.
Edmund Davies LJ accepted that the facts differed from those in *Balfour* v *Balfour*
in that the agreement was made after the parties had separated, and agreed that in
the circumstances the probability that a legally binding agreement was intended
might be greater than in the earlier case. Apart from this, neither he nor Megaw LJ
appeared to envisage any change in the onus of proof where an agreement had been
entered into after separation.

On the other hand, Lord Denning MR, dissenting, took the view, which he later
repeated in *Merritt* v *Merritt* [1970] 1 WLR 1211, that the presumption of fact
against an intention to create a legally binding agreement which applied to arrangements made by a husband and wife living in amity, did not apply to arrangements
made when they were separated or about to separate. Indeed in *Merritt* v *Merritt* (at

p. 1213) he went so far as to say that in such circumstances "it might safely be presumed that they intended to create legal relations". Widgery LJ (at p. 1214) found it "unnecessary to go so far as to say that there is a presumption in favour of the creation of legal relationships when the marriage is breaking up, but certainly there is no presumption against the creation of legal relations as there is when the parties are living happily together". Karminski LJ was content to deal with the problem as a question of fact.

In *Pettitt* v *Pettitt* [1970] AC 777 the members of the House of Lords accepted the general principle in *Balfour* v *Balfour*, though Lord Hodson thought it an "extreme case" (*ibid.* at p. 806) and Lord Upjohn thought it "stretched the doctrine to its limits" (at p. 816). Lord Upjohn thought that it had little, if any, application to the question of title to the property of the spouses, at all events to property of the magnitude of the matrimonial home. Moreover, both Lord Reid (at p. 796) and Lord Diplock (at p. 822) distinguished between the position where an agreement was still executory, and the position when the parties had performed their mutual promises. If the spouses so perform their mutual promises, the fact that they could not have been compelled to do so while the promises were still executory cannot deprive the acts done by them of all legal consequences on proprietary rights.

Where arrangements are made between other close relatives, such as parent and child, or uncle and nephew, at least in relation to the payment of an allowance there is also a presumption of fact against an intention of creating legal relations (*Jones* v *Padavatton* [1969] 1 WLR 328 *per* Salmon LJ at p. 332).

## (c) Public policy

An agreement between spouses who are living together regulating their legal rights in case they should separate in the future is void as being contrary to public policy (*Hindley* v *Westmeath* (1827) 6 B & C 200; *Westmeath* v *Westmeath* (1830) 1 Dow & Cl. 519(HL)). On the other hand, an agreement for immediate separation is not illegal (*Wilson* v *Wilson* (1848) 1 HL Cas 538), and a reconciliation agreement between spouses living apart, which provides for their legal rights if their attempt to live together again is unsuccessful, is not void even though it envisages a separation in the future (*Re Meyrick's Settlement* [1921] 1 Ch 311).

## 3. Special problems on marriage breakdown

Agreements between spouses on the breakdown and termination of marriage raise some special problems. First, they will often be negotiated at a time when one or both of the parties will be suffering from emotional strain as a result of the breakdown of their relationship and when there may be bitterness rather than goodwill between the parties. Thus "the circumstances surrounding a marriage breakdown do not always enhance evenness of bargaining power, particularly where emotional stress impairs judgment" (*per* Watson SJ in *In the Marriage of Wright* (1977) 29 Fed. LR 10 at p. 44). Secondly, one spouse may have little accurate information as to the financial resources of the other and may find it difficult to assess the reasonableness of the terms proposed. One spouse may, therefore, need protection against unfair advantage being taken by the other, and adequate remedies where this has occurred.

The interests of the state may also need consideration where the parties seek to limit or even exclude altogether the obligation of one spouse to the other as the effect may be to cast the burden of support on to the public purse. The state is also concerned with the interests of minor children who may be affected by an agreement to which they are not parties. This raises the question of the relationship between an agreement and the court's powers to order financial provision and property adjustment. To the extent that these powers remain exercisable notwithstanding an agreement they provide a means of rectifying unjust or out of date provision made by the agreement, though to that extent the sanctity of the agreement is weakened. On the other hand, if the parties wish to incorporate the whole or part of their agreement in a court order it becomes necessary to consider the attitude of the court towards the terms of the agreement. Whether or not an agreement is incorporated into a court order, changing circumstances may make an alteration desirable at least as far as continuing provision is concerned.

Accordingly, the following questions arise for consideration:

(1) To what extent do the court's powers remain exercisable notwithstanding a prior agreement?

(2) What is the attitude of the court when asked to give effect to an agreement by means of a consent order?

(3) What remedies are available to a spouse who is dissatisfied with the terms of the agreement or consent order?

(4) To what extent are agreements and consent orders variable to take account of changed circumstances?

## 4. The effect of an agreement on the court's powers

The ability of the parties to make their own arrangements on financial and property matters is subject to the well established rule in *Hyman* v *Hyman* [1929] AC 601 which renders void a provision purporting to restrict the right of a spouse to apply to the court for financial provision. It was said that "the wife's right to future maintenance is a matter of public concern which she cannot barter away" and it was "against the public interest" to permit the jurisdiction of the court in relation to maintenance to be ousted (*per* Lord Atkin at p. 629). Although *Hyman* v *Hyman* was concerned with a provision in a separation agreement (entered into at a time when divorce was not in contemplation) the same principle has been applied to agreements reached as a preliminary to divorce proceedings or in the course of such proceedings. Such agreements are now likely to be more important than the traditional separation or maintenance agreement. A provision in a "maintenance agreement" purporting to restrict any right to apply to a court for an order containing financial arrangements is now void by statute (s.34 of the Matrimonial Causes Act 1973).

Although it is not possible to oust the jurisdiction of the court it is open to the spouses to make an agreement which merely seeks to impose some limit on their rights and obligations in relation to financial provision. Thus in *Wright* v *Wright* [1970] 1 WLR 1219, as part of an agreement whereby the wife was allowed to proceed with her petition for divorce in an undefended suit, her counsel stated on the hearing of the petition that it was agreed that no order for maintenance should then be made and that it was her intention not to apply for maintenance until there was an unforeseen circumstance making it impossible for her to work at all or otherwise to maintain herself. A subsequent application for maintenance was dismissed, for although the agreement did not deprive the court of its power to award maintenance even in the absence of the circumstances mentioned, the existence of the agreement made it necessary for the wife to offer *prima facie* proof of unforeseen circumstances which made it impossible for her to work or otherwise maintain herself, and this she had not done. The Court of Appeal applied the same reasoning to the power to award a lump sum payment in *Brockwell* v *Brockwell* (1976) 6 Fam Law 46 and *Edgar* v *Edgar* [1980] 1 WLR 1410.

In *Edgar* v *Edgar* the spouses had entered into a separation deed in 1976 whereby the husband agreed to purchase a home for the wife in her name, to pay for alterations, to provide accommodation for the wife's mother, to buy the wife a motor car and to make substantial periodical payments to the wife and to each of the four children of the marriage. The wife acknowledged that she did not intend to seek further capital provision from the very wealthy husband whether by way of ancillary relief in divorce proceedings or otherwise. However, in subsequent divorce proceedings the wife obtained an order for the payment of a lump sum of £670,000. The Court of Appeal held, first, that in such cases there is jurisdiction to hear an application for a lump sum payment notwithstanding the deed and the court is bound to take into account all the considerations set out in s.25. Secondly, the existence of an agreement is a very relevant circumstance under s.25 and in the case of an arm's length agreement, based on legal advice between parties of equal bargaining power, is a most important piece of conduct to be considered under s.25. Thirdly, providing that there is such equality, the mere fact that the wife would have done better by going to court would not generally be a ground for giving her more in view of the importance to be attached to upholding agreements which do not offend public policy. Fourthly, if the court, on the evidence, takes the view that one spouse has taken an unfair advantage of the other in the throes of marital breakdown, "a time when emotional pressures are high, and judgment apt to be clouded" so that it would be unjust not to exercise its powers under s.23, it should exercise such powers even if no fraud, misrepresentation or duress is established which, at common law, would entitle a wife to avoid the deed (*ibid. per* Ormrod LJ at p. 1418). The Court of Appeal concluded that although the husband had superior bargaining power he had not been shown to have exploited it unfairly so as to induce the wife to act to her disadvantage. Since there was no evidence reflecting adversely on the husband's conduct in the negotiations and no adequate explanation of the wife's conduct either in entering into the covenant or in asking the court to disregard it, the wife had failed to show sufficient grounds to justify the court in relieving her from the effect of the deed of separation. The court accordingly set aside the order for payment of the lump sum.

This may be contrasted with *Evans* v *Evans* (1981) 2 FLR 33 where the wife had signed a document by which she (1) undertook to transfer her half share in the matrimonial home to the husband free of consideration, (2) consented to periodical payments of £5 per week for each child, (3) indicated that she made no claim on the contents of the matrimonial home, and (4) sought no maintenance for herself. Wood J refused to give any weight to the document which he described as "merely a statement of intention made by a sick woman at a time of stress". Although advised to seek independent advice she had declined to do so, and she had a history of psychiatric disturbance which also made it inappropriate to take her adultery into account as "gross and obvious conduct". She was awarded a lump sum of £1,500 in return for her interest in the matrimonial home and a nominal order for periodical payments which was to be reviewed as soon as the financial position of the husband, who was unemployed, improved.

Even if a spouse has obtained independent legal advice it may be appropriate to consider the quality of that advice. In *Edgar* v *Edgar* Ormrod LJ had referred to the possibility of "bad legal advice" being relevant to the question of justice between the parties. In *Camm* v *Camm* (1983) 4 FLR 577 at p. 580 he said that he had not been thinking in terms of negligence by the solicitor. It was "... not necessarily negligent advice to take a course or permit a client to take a course which a more experienced, or a stronger minded legal adviser would have discouraged". However, the quality of such advice was relevant, and he contrasted the position in the case before him with that in *Edgar* v *Edgar*. In *Edgar* v *Edgar* the wife was fully and strongly advised not to enter into the agreement but none the less went ahead, whereas in *Camm* v *Camm* there was much less clear legal advice by the wife's solicitors and the whole matter was dealt with on quite a different level. In that case the wife had entered into an arrangement which was manifestly unsatisfactory from her point of view in the light of her earning capacity which was modest and speculative. She was obviously under extreme pressure, coming partly from herself and partly from the fact that the husband was refusing to concede anything about periodical payments. (See also *K* v *K (Financial Provision)* [1992] FCR 265.)

The time which has elapsed since the date of the agreement is also a relevant consideration. Thus the husband may have taken steps in reliance upon the agreement to incur heavy expenditure which he otherwise would not have done or may do other things, such as taking on a very large mortgage, relying on the fact that he is not liable for periodical payments. However, if there is no evidence that the husband has moved to his disadvantage in reliance upon the agreement, the wife should not be penalised because she has put up with a smaller income than she would have had if she had been a wiser woman (see Ormrod LJ in *Camm* v *Camm* (1983) 4 FLR 577 at p. 586).

## 5. Incorporation of an agreement in a court order – consent order

*(a) The advantages of incorporation*
Where the parties have reached an agreement they will often wish some or all of its terms, as appropriate, to be embodied in an order of the court made on or after the granting of a decree under the Matrimonial Causes Act 1973. (See Chapter 16 for orders in magistrates' courts based on agreement.) This has the advantage that,

unlike the terms of a mere agreement, it will be enforceable without the necessity for an action by and a judgment in favour of the person entitled to money or property under an agreement. The legal effect of those provisions is then derived from the court order itself and does not depend any longer on the agreement between the parties (*per* Lord Diplock in *de Lasala* v *de Lasala* [1980] AC 546 at p. 560).

### (b) The discretion of the court

The court has a discretion whether or not to make an order in the terms agreed by the parties. In *Livesey* v *Jenkins* [1985] AC 424 at p. 436 Lord Brandon emphasised that the discretion to make an order under s.23 or s.24 of the 1973 Act had to be exercised in the manner ordained by s.25(1). It was, therefore, essential that the court was provided with information about all the circumstances of the case, including, *inter alia*, the particular matters specified in s.25(1) as it then was. Unless the parties ensured that that information was provided and was correct, complete and up to date, the court was not equipped to exercise, and therefore could not lawfully and properly exercise, its discretion as laid down by s.25(1). In contested cases this requirement was met by rules 73 to 76 of the Matrimonial Causes Rules 1977 dealing with the affidavit evidence to be filed (see now the Family Proceedings Rules 1991, rr 2.62-2.63). Rule 77 (now rule 2.62) provided for investigation by a registrar of an application and further information could be obtained. However, the situation with regard to consent orders, especially where no affidavits were filed at all and reliance was placed entirely on the exchange of information between the solicitors of the parties, was less satisfactory. There were at the time of the proceedings out of which the appeal arose no statutory provisions or rules of court relating specifically to the making of consent orders. It was common practice for registrars to make such orders without making any inquiries themselves, but relying simply on the fact that both parties were represented by solicitors, and that they could be relied on to have inquired adequately into all the matters to which regard had to be had under s.25(1) before advising their respective clients to agree to the making of consent orders by the court.

This practice was criticised in the Court of Appeal in *Jenkins* v *Livesey* [1984] FLR 452 at p. 456 by Sir John Arnold P and he indicated that in ordinary circumstances attendance before the registrar was necessary to enable answers to be given to any queries that he might have in the course of the exercise of the jurisdiction. A Practice Direction was issued which contained a reminder that in all cases where an application is made for financial provision or a property adjustment order, the court is required to have before it an agreed statement of the general nature of the means of each party signed by the parties or their solicitors.

There was concern about the burden that would be imposed on parties and their solicitors, especially by the increased need for appearances before the registrar. The Matrimonial and Family Proceedings Act 1984 sought to achieve a compromise. Section 7 of the Act inserted s.33A into the Matrimonial Causes Act 1973. This provides:

"(1) Notwithstanding anything in the preceding provisions of this Part of this Act, on an application for a consent order for financial relief the court may, unless it has reason to think that there are other circumstances into which it ought to inquire, make an order in the terms agreed on the basis only of the prescribed information furnished with the application."

This also applies to an application for a consent order varying or discharging an order for financial relief, (subs.(2)). An "order for financial relief" means an order under any of s. 23, 24, 24A or 27 of the 1973 Act. A consent order for this purpose means an order in the terms applied for to which the respondent agrees (subs.(3)).

The intention of s.33A (and of s.19 of the 1984 Act which is in similar terms and applies where financial relief is sought after a foreign divorce) was to enable the court to deal with consent applications "on the papers" unless there was any doubt about the propriety of the settlement. The "prescribed information" was clearly intended to place the court in a better position to perform its duty and to identify those cases which required further consideration, while not requiring all the information that would be necessary on a contested application. The information required is now prescribed by r.2.61 of the Family Proceedings Rules 1991 which provides that there shall be lodged with every application for a consent order under any of ss.23, 24, or 24A of the 1973 Act, two copies of a draft order in the terms sought, one of which must be indorsed with a statement signed by the respondent to the application signifying his agreement, and a statement of information which may be made in more than one document. This statement must include:

(a) the duration of the marriage, the age of each party and of any minor or dependent child of the family;

(b) an estimate in summary form of the approximate amount or value of the capital resources and net income of each party and of any minor child of the family;

(c) what arrangements are intended for the accommodation of each of the parties and any child of the family;

(d) whether either party has remarried or has any present intention to marry or to cohabit with another person;

(e) where the terms of the order provide for the transfer of property, a statement confirming that any mortgagee of that property has been served with notice of the application and that no objection to such a transfer has been made by the mortgagee within 14 days from such service; and

(f) any other specially significant matters.

It is also provided that where an application is made for a consent order varying an order for periodical payments it will be sufficient if the statement includes only the information in respect of net income mentioned in paragraph (b) above (r.2.61(2)). An application for a consent order for interim periodical payments pending the determination of an application for ancillary relief may be made in like manner (*ibid.*). Where all or any of the parties attend the hearing of an application for financial relief the rule provides that the court may dispense with the lodging of a statement of information, and give directions for the information which would otherwise be required to be given in such a statement to be given in such manner as it sees fit (r.2.61(3)).

A Practice Direction issued in 1986 stated that the rule was properly complied with if the statement was signed by solicitors on record as acting for the respondent. A suggested form of accompanying statement of information was set out in the schedule to the Practice Direction. Although the rule did not require the statement of information to be signed by either party, the direction stated that practitioners might consider it appropriate for the form to be signed by or on behalf of both parties as a means of establishing the accuracy of the information relating to their respective clients (*Practice Direction (Financial Provision: Consent Order)* [1986] 1 WLR 381). A subsequent Practice Direction issued in 1990 stated that experience had shown that the statement of information was being inadequately completed. The statement was revised to make it clear that the details of capital and net income should be stated as they are at the date of the statement and not as they would be following implementation of the orders. Additionally the statement should give the net equity of any property concerned and the effect of its proposed distribution. A revised form was set out in the schedule (*Practice Direction (Financial Provision: Consent Order) (No.2)* [1990] 1 WLR 150).

*(c) Scope of consent orders*

In so far as the terms agreed by the parties provide for financial provision or transfer of property which the court has power to order under s.23, 24 or 24A, little difficulty will arise in relation to the incorporation of these terms in a consent order. However, the agreement may contain terms which are not within these powers. Thus in *Livesey* v *Jenkins* [1985] AC 424 the agreement provided that the wife should be solely responsible, after the transfer to her of the husband's half share in the matrimonial home, for the mortgage on it and all other outgoings relating to it. It also provided that the husband and wife were to be solely responsible respectively for certain specified bank overdrafts and loan accounts. Lord Brandon pointed out that there was nothing in ss.23 and 24 of the Act of 1973 which directly empowered the court to make orders of this kind. The proper procedure for incorporating the obligations concerned into a consent order is by formulating them as undertakings given to the court. Such undertakings create an obligation towards the court and in the view of Lord Brandon are enforceable as effectively as direct orders. (But see *Re Hudson* [1966] Ch. 209.)

In *Dinch* v *Dinch* [1987] 1 WLR 252 at p. 255 Lord Oliver drew attention to the need "to take sufficient care in the drafting of consent orders in matrimonial proceedings to define with precision exactly what the parties were intending to do in relation to the disposal of the petitioner's claims for ancillary relief so as to avoid any future misunderstanding as to whether those claims, or any of them, were or were not to be kept alive". He stressed that it is the imperative professional duty of those entrusted with the task of advising the parties to consider with due care the impact which any terms that they may agree on behalf of their clients have or are intended to have upon any outstanding application for ancillary relief and to ensure that such appropriate provision is inserted in any consent order made as will leave no room for any future doubt or misunderstanding or saddle the parties with the wasteful burden of wholly unnecessary costs. (See also *Atkinson* v *Atkinson* [1984] FLR 524.) In addition to potential claims under the Matrimonial Causes Act 1973, regard must also be had to any potential claim under the Inheritance (Provision for Family and Dependants) Act 1975. Under s.15 of that Act the court may make an order that one party to a marriage shall not be entitled to make a claim under that Act on the death of the other party to the marriage (see Chapter 21).

*(d) The effect of incorporating an agreement into a court order*

Once financial arrangements which have been agreed by the parties have been made the subject matter of a consent order, they no longer depend upon the agreement of the parties as the source from which their legal effect is derived. Thereafter, their legal effect is derived from the court order. This important statement of principle was made by Lord Diplock in *de Lasala* v *de Lasala* [1980] AC 546, which was an appeal from Hong Kong, and was approved by the Court of Appeal in *Thwaite* v *Thwaite* [1982] Fam 1. It follows that a consent order must be treated as any other order and dealt with so far as possible in the same way as a non-consensual order. Thus the court's power to vary or discharge an order for periodical payments or for secured periodical payments extends to such orders made by consent, but there is no power to vary an order for the payment of a lump sum or for the transfer of property even though made by consent.

The court's power to vary "maintenance agreements" under ss.35 and 36 of the 1973 Act is not applicable to an agreement which has been incorporated into a court order. (For the position in relation to a consent order before decree absolute see *Aspden* v *Hildesley* [1982] 1 WLR 264 and the comments thereon in *Tommey* v *Tommey* [1982] 3 All ER 385.)

## 6. Remedies available to a spouse dissatisfied with the terms of an agreement or consent order

*(a) The choice of remedies*

A spouse who is dissatisfied with the terms of an agreement or a consent order may be able to obtain relief under statutory powers to vary the agreement or the consent order in which it has been incorporated. The power to vary agreements under ss.35 and 36 of the Matrimonial Causes Act 1973 is considered in Part 8(c) of this chapter. The power to vary court orders under s.31 of that Act was considered in Part 8 of Chapter 10. The power to vary is usually concerned with changes of circumstances subsequent to the date of the agreement or order.

Where it is sought to challenge an agreement on the basis of circumstances at the time when it was made it will be necessary to bring an action to set aside the agreement. Where it is sought to challenge a consent order on this basis, it may be done by way of an appeal from the judgment or order to a higher court or by bringing a fresh action to set the order aside (see Lord Diplock in *de Lasala* v *de Lasala* [1979] 2 All ER 1146 at p. 1155). In addition to an appeal on the basis of fresh evidence, an appeal may be made in limited circumstances on the basis of circumstances occurring shortly after the date of the order (see *Barder* v *Caluori* [1988] AC 20 considered on pages 246–250).

In the High Court a judge or district judge has no power to review by way of rehearing or an order for a new trial any "final" order made by himself or a fellow judge or district judge. The whole question of procedure was reviewed in detail by Ward J in *B-T* v *B-T* [1990] 2 FLR 1. He said (at p.10) that "... a judge or registrar has no power to mediate mournfully upon his own errors or, more pleasantly, upon his brother's errors". Thus even where it is alleged that an order has been obtained by misrepresentation the court has no jurisdiction to rehear or alter the order after it has been passed and entered, provided that it accurately expressed the intention of the court. In other words, while the court may correct an order which does not express the intentions of the court, it may not alter an order where it is said that it ought not to have been made, e.g. because of misrepresentation.

The position may be different in relation to interlocutory as opposed to final orders (see *Allsop* v *Allsop* (1980) 11 Fam Law 18). For this purpose, an order is interlocutory rather than final if the court that made it has a continuing power to vary its terms, as distinct from making orders in aid of enforcing those terms under a liberty to apply (see Lord Diplock in *de Lasala* v *de Lasala* [1980] AC 546 at p. 561). Thus the court has no power to vary a lump sum or a property adjustment order, and therefore such an order is a "final" order for this purpose even though it is interlocutory for the purposes of appeal. In *Allsop* v *Allsop* the Court of Appeal held that the registrar was entitled to set aside an order for a lump sum payment when the husband subsequently admitted that his affidavit of means had been deliberately false. It was an unusual case and, in so far as the court considered it was dealing with a "final" order, there were, in the view of Ward J in *B-T* v *B-T* [1990] 2 FLR 1 at p. 15, special reasons for the departure from established practice and the procedural safeguards afforded by a fresh action. He "would confine the *ratio* of *Allsop* to the proposition that the court has power to set aside its own order when the parties consent to its doing so or where the facts are not in dispute and the misrepresentation is plain beyond all argument". A different view could be taken in a county court with regard to a rehearing, at least in relation to consent orders. (See the discussion by Ward J in *B-T* v *B-T* [1990] 2 FLR 1 at p. 23.)

*(b) An action to set aside an agreement or consent order*
An agreement for financial provision may be set aside on a number of grounds in the same way as any other contract in an action brought for that purpose. Where an agreement has been incorporated in a consent order the appropriate procedure is, as noted above, a separate action to set aside the order. The advantage of a separate action to set aside a consent order as compared with an appeal is that it enables serious issues, such as allegations of fraud, to be properly tried. It may also prevent the wasting of unnecessary costs involved in bringing the discovery of the parties' means up to date (see Ward J in *B-T* v *B-T* [1990] 2 FLR 1 at p. 25). In *Robinson* v *Robinson* (1983) 4 FLR 102 at 114B Ormrod LJ said:
" From the point of view of convenience, there is a lot to be said for proceedings of this kind taking place before a judge at first instance, because there will usually be serious and often difficult issues of fact to be determined before the power to set aside can be exercised. These can be determined more easily, as a rule, by a judge at first instance."
He also thought that the judge could go on to make the appropriate order, which an appeal court could not do. However, in *B-T* v *B-T* Ward J (at pp. 12-13), while agreeing with the view of Ormrod LJ as to the advantages of a separate action, saw difficulty in the fact that the only relief sought by the claim in the fresh action could in effect be for a declaration that the order be set aside. A new trial of the matters in dispute in the ancillary relief application would have to follow. He was not sure

how, short of transferring the action to the Family Division and listing the ancillary relief application to follow the action to set aside, the judge could proceed instantly to make the appropriate order. Indeed, even such a pragmatic course presented difficulty because, until the order was set aside, there would be no ancillary relief proceedings pending and consequently no jurisdiction for the registrar (or district judge) to give directions to enable the matter to be brought before the judge. (See *H* v *B* [1987] 1 FLR 405.)

The grounds on which an agreement or consent order may be set aside are considered in Part 7 below.

*(c) Appeals from consent orders*
As orders of the court, consent orders are subject to the provisions which apply generally to appeals from orders made at first instance. Where a consent order has been made by a district judge, an appeal lies to a judge. On such an appeal fresh evidence can be considered, though on a less generous basis than that which applied before the coming into force of the Family Proceedings Rules 1991 (see now r. 8.1(2). The position is considered further in Chapter 10, Part 9(a)). Where a consent order has been made by a judge, leave to appeal to the Court of Appeal is necessary.

Where the court of first instance has not adjudicated upon the evidence, its decision cannot be challenged on the ground that the court has reached a wrong conclusion on the evidence before it (*per* Ormrod LJ in *Thwaite* v *Thwaite* [1982] Fam 1 at p. 8). Subject to this, final orders of all kinds can be challenged on appeal and may be set aside on other grounds. In *de Lasala* v *de Lasala* [1980] AC 546 Lord Diplock referred to two such grounds - fraud and mistake - but in *Thwaite* v *Thwaite* Ormrod LJ said that there were others, e.g. fresh evidence properly admitted by the appellate court and material non-disclosure. These are considered in Part 7 below.

*(d) Non-enforcement of consent orders*
Where an order is still executory, as in *Thwaite* v *Thwaite,* and one of the parties applies to the court to enforce the order, the court may refuse if, in the circumstances prevailing at the time of the application, it would be inequitable to do so.

*(e) Proceeding with an application under the Matrimonial Causes Act 1973*
A party who is dissatisfied with the terms of an agreement which has not been incorporated into a court order may proceed with applications under ss.23 and 24 of the Matrimonial Causes Act 1973. The effect of an agreement in such circumstances was considered in *Edgar* v *Edgar* [1980] 1 WLR 1410 and was discussed earlier in Part 4 (page 359). It may be a preferable way of proceeding than an action to set aside the agreement. Moreover, although it is a party who is dissatisfied with the agreement will find it preferable to proceed in this way, it may also be a more appropriate way of proceeding for a party who wishes to enforce an agreement which is not being performed by the other party who is dissatisfied with it. In *Sutton* v *Sutton* [1984] Ch D 184 John Mowbray QC sitting as a High Court judge was concerned with an application by a former wife for specific performance of an agreement relating to the former matrimonial home. He considered that there were

two reasons why public policy required the wife in that case to proceed under s.24 instead of enforcing the agreement. First, the public at large has an interest in seeing that a husband makes proper provision for his wife on divorce. Secondly, the husband, who had remarried and could not himself apply under s.24, would be protected by the ability of the court to take into account such factors as the true extent of the wife's savings, her inheritance from her father of a house, his injury at work and his remarriage. The agreement had also not been negotiated by solicitors. (See also *Simester* v *Simester* [1986] 1 WLR 1463, considered in Chapter 10.)


## 7. Grounds for setting aside agreements and orders

### *(a) Misrepresentation*

An agreement or consent order may be set aside on the ground that one spouse was induced to agree by the fraudulent misrepresentation of the other (see *Allsop* v *Allsop* (1981) 11 Fam Law 18 where the husband admitted fraudulent misrepresentation regarding his assets). However, the burden of proof is a heavy one - as is shown by the decision in *Wales* v *Wadham* [1977] 1 WLR 198. In that case the wife remarried some two months after the date of a consent order giving effect to an agreement whereby she obtained a substantial lump sum in addition to the half share in the former matrimonial home which had already been transferred to her. The allegation of fraudulent misrepresentation was made on the basis that throughout all the years of marriage since 1945 the wife had consistently expressed a conscientious and religious objection to remarriage after divorce. Tudor Evans J found that the wife's views when expressed were honestly held and not calculated to mislead the husband. He also accepted that the wife's principal motive in concealing the existence of her future second husband was not to save the settlement but because she did not want him to be involved in the divorce proceedings. He said (at p. 211):

"In order to prove a fraudulent misrepresentation, the husband must show that the wife made a statement of fact which was false to her knowledge or that she was reckless as to its truth and that such misrepresentation was intended to, and did cause the husband to enter into the contract."

Moreover:

"A statement of intention is not a representation of existing fact, unless the person making it does not honestly hold the intention he is expressing, in which case there is a misrepresentation of fact in relation to the state of that person's mind."

He found, however, that the wife had made an honest statement of her intention which was neither a representation of fact nor a dishonest expression of intent. (See the criticisms at (1977) 40 MLR 599.)

### *(b) Non-disclosure*

Each party concerned in a claim for financial provision and property adjustment owes a duty to the court to make full and frank disclosure of all material facts to the other party and the court. This principle does not depend in any way on the concept that the parties must, in reaching an agreement for a consent order, show *uberrima fides* in the contractual connotation of that expression. It depends rather on the statutory requirement imposed by s.25 of the Matrimonial Causes Act 1973 that the court must exercise its discretion to make orders under ss.23 and 24 in accordance with the criteria prescribed by that section and that unless the parties make full and frank disclosure of all material matters the court cannot lawfully or properly exercise such discretion. It is not open to parties, whether represented by lawyers or not, to disregard or to contract out of such requirements (see Lord Brandon in *Livesey* v *Jenkins* [1985] AC 424 at pp. 441 and 443 *et seq.*, referring with approval to the decision of the Court of Appeal in *Robinson* v *Robinson* (Practice Note) [1982] 1 WLR 786).

Difficulty in relation to non-disclosure has arisen principally in relation to two matters. The first is where a party has failed to disclose an intention to remarry. This was the position in *Livesey* v *Jenkins* where Lord Brandon criticised the decision of Tudor Evans J in *Wales* v *Wadham* [1977] 2 All ER 125 to reject the husband's claim based on the need for full and frank disclosure. It is the intention at the time of the consent order of the party who has remarried which is relevant, and there will be no non-disclosure if that party can show that the intention to remarry (or to cohabit) was genuinely formed only after that date, albeit within a relatively short time. The statement of information which is now required by r. 2.61 is designed to ensure that the intentions of the parties in relation to remarriage and cohabitation are clearly set out for the court. If such statements are incorrect then the other party may seek to challenge the consent order on the basis of fraud or misrepresentation. In *Toleman* v *Toleman* [1985] FLR 62 some three months after a consent order had been made, the wife's solicitors informed the husband's solicitors of the intention of the wife to remarry, and counsel for the husband had endorsed his brief to the effect that it was made on the basis that the wife had no intention of remarrying or cohabiting. The husband was granted leave to appeal out of time so as to enable him to test at a rehearing the question whether he had been misled at the time the order was being negotiated and whether the basis of the consent order had disappeared. (See Chapter 10, Part 9 for the possibility of seeking leave to appeal out of time on the basis of a change of circumstances on satisfying the conditions laid down by the House of Lords in *Barder* v *Caluori* [1988] AC 20.)

It is also essential that a party makes a proper and accurate disclosure of his or her financial position. Thus in *Robinson* v *Robinson* (Practice Note) [1982] 1 WLR 786 a requirement of full and frank disclosure in relation to the financial position of the husband was forcefully upheld by the Court of Appeal in a manner approved by the House of Lords in *Livesey* v *Jenkins* [1985] AC 424 at p. 443. In *Robinson* v *Robinson* the parties had been divorced in 1973 at which time the husband was ordered to make periodical payments for the wife and children. The amount of those payments was increased by the Court of Appeal later in the same year. In 1976, on an application by the husband for the periodical payments to the wife herself to be suspended or reduced, the judge discharged the order for such payments in her favour and made an order, to which the wife consented, under which she accepted a lump sum in full and final settlement of all her claims against the husband. In 1981 the wife applied to a judge at first instance for the two previous orders of 1973 and 1976 to be set aside on the ground that the husband had on each occasion misrepresented or inadequately represented his financial position. The Court of Appeal made clear the duty on the parties to make full and frank disclosure of their property and financial resources and Ormrod LJ said that "although intensive research might have revealed to the wife the husband's financial position, it was clear that both in 1973, and in the proceedings leading up to his application in 1976, the husband had not provided the wife with a full and frank disclosure to which she was entitled". He rejected the argument that the capital value of the husband's assets ought to have been investigated by the wife's advisers. It was the husband's duty to make full disclosure, and the wife was entitled to take the husband's affidavit and the affidavit of his accountant at their face value. Ormrod LJ also criticised manoeuvring with accounts prepared for other purposes. He said (at p. 787) that "all too much time is wasted in these cases in exchanging uninformative accounts of private companies and more effort must be made to give a true picture of the husband's financial position. If the husband wants to avoid the risk of a consent order being set aside he should make a frank disclosure to the wife before she agrees to it and the court makes the order". (See also *Vicary* v *Vicary* [1992] 2 FLR 271.)

That case may be contrasted with *Hill* v *Hill* (1984) 14 Fam Law 183 where Cumming-Bruce LJ distinguished *Robinson* v *Robinson* where he noted that the discrepancy in the value of the assets with which the Court of Appeal was concerned amounted to many thousands of pounds. The husband in *Hill* v *Hill* was not in any sense hiding his assets behind a smokescreen of figures, difficult of analysis, relating to a number of interrelated companies with assets and liabilities difficult to ascertain. It was a case in which the husband had himself disclosed the existence of some endowment policies with relatively small surrender values at the date of separation, and the wife's solicitors decided to bring the matter before the judge on the evidence as known without attempting to obtain information about the accurate surrender value of the policies and, as the judge had found, it might be a matter of judgment or taste as to whether it was right to describe the surrender value as minimal - as the husband had done. (See also *Barber* v *Barber* (1987) 17 Fam Law 125.) In *Livesey* v *Jenkins* [1985] AC 424 at p. 445 Lord Brandon also emphasised that it is not every failure of frank and full disclosure which will justify a court in setting aside an order. It will only be in cases when the absence of full and frank disclosure has led to the court making, either in contested proceedings or by consent, an order which is substantially different from the order which it would have made if such disclosure had taken place that a case for setting aside can possibly be made good. He warned that parties who applied to set aside orders on the ground of failure to disclose some relatively minor matter or matters the disclosure of which would not have made any substantial difference to the order which the court would have made or approved are likely to find their applications being summarily dismissed with costs against them or, if they are legally aided, against the legal aid fund.

*(c) Mistake*
(i) Common mistake
Although the spouses have admittedly reached an agreement, their consent may be nullified where they have both been mistaken as to some fundamental assumption upon which it was based. An example of such a common mistake in this context is to be found in *Galloway* v *Galloway* (1914) 30 TLR 531 where a man and a woman

entered into a separation deed on the mistaken and common assumption that they were in fact married to each other. Their marriage was in fact void and the deed was treated as of no effect.

(ii) Mutual mistake

An agreement may also be affected by a mutual mistake, that is where the parties have misunderstood each other and they are at cross-purposes. Thus the spouses may have agreed that the matrimonial home should be transferred from the husband to the wife, but they may be at cross-purposes as to the extent of the property involved (see *Parkes* v *Parkes* [1971] 1 WLR 1481). In such circumstances an objective test will be applied to determine what agreement, if any, they have reached.

In *Amey* v *Amey* [1992] 1 FCR 289 at p. 295 Scott Baker J said that "the test for whether a court will intervene and set aside a contract for mutual mistake or frustration is essentially the same as applied by Lord Brandon in *Barder* v *Caluori* [1988] AC 20 as the first of his three conditions for giving leave to appeal out of time, namely that: '... Events have occurred since the making of the order which invalidate the basis or fundamental assumption, upon which the order was made'". In that case the husband had paid the wife £120,000 pursuant to an agreement which effected an equal division of the value of their hotel business. It had been made on the basis of the contribution that each had made both financially and otherwise to the business and there was no fundamental assumption that the wife would live for any particular period after the agreement. Scott Baker J refused to set aside the agreement following the wife's unexpected death before the agreement could be incorporated into a court order.

(iii) Unilateral mistake

A unilateral mistake, i.e. where only one of the spouses has been mistaken, can render an agreement ineffective only if the other spouse knew or must have known of the mistake. It is also essential that the mistake was material, i.e. the mistaken party must be able to show that he or she would not have made the contract if he or she had known the truth. Thus in *Wales* v *Wadham* [1977] 1 WLR 199 the husband had also sought to have the agreement rescinded on the ground of unilateral mistake, namely that he was ignorant of the wife's intention to marry, though this was not pressed by his counsel - and Tudor Evans J was not convinced that the husband's mind was affected by a fundamental mistake of fact. In *Taylor* v *Taylor* (1976) BLT No. 228A an attempt made by a husband to have an agreement set aside on the ground of mistake was unsuccessful because the mistake was unknown to the wife. The husband contemplated a surrender by the wife not only of her own but also of the children's right to maintenance in return for the home being transferred to her. (See also *O'Dougherty* v *O'Dougherty* (1983) 4 FLR 407.)

In *Cross* v *Cross* (1983) 4 FLR 235 at p. 240 Wood J said:

"In some circumstances a court may refuse an order [for specific performance] upon the grounds of mistake even where mistake is unilateral if the plaintiff had contributed to the defendant's mistake however unintentionally. Even if the mistake be that of the defendant and not in any way induced by the plaintiff, the court may, nevertheless, refuse to make an order if to do so would be highly unreasonable or cause an injustice. Moreover, he who comes to equity must come with clean hands and any conduct of the plaintiff which would make the grant of specific performance inequitable can prove to be a bar."

Thus in that case the husband had agreed in July 1979 to transfer his interest in the matrimonial home (which was in the joint names of the spouse) to the wife as full and final settlement of her claims for financial provision. At that time he thought his wife and son were still living in the matrimonial home and that the agreement would conclude the matter and following divorce would enable him to remarry. In January 1980 the husband discovered that the wife had moved out of the matrimonial home in June 1979 to go and live with her present husband. Wood J considered that whether or not there was a strict duty upon the wife to disclose her change of circumstances and her future plans, it would in all the circumstances have been inequitable to enforce the agreement against the husband. He proceeded to consider the wife's application under the 1973 Act and divided the proceeds of the house between the parties with the larger share being allocated to the wife.

### (iv) Consent orders

Where an agreement has been incorporated into a consent order the issue is whether the court was given the wrong material when making the consent order and not whether the district judge or judge was wrong. In *Harrison v Harrison* (1983) 13 Fam Law 20 a consent order provided that the husband should transfer to the wife all interest in a house which he had inherited and for the payment of £1,000 to the wife in full settlement of her claims. No reference was made to the former matrimonial home which was jointly owned by the parties, but the husband maintained that it had been part of the agreement that the wife would transfer her half share to the husband and that this term had been omitted due to a mistake on the part of the husband's solicitors. The husband sought leave to appeal, but Balcombe J said that the appropriate vehicle for deciding whether there had been a mistake was by way of a fresh action and not by way of appeal so that there could be full and proper discovery which was crucial in the case. The issue was whether the registrar had been given the wrong material whilst making the consent order and not whether he had been wrong. In addition, what the husband wanted was a positive provision that the wife should transfer her interest in the matrimonial home to the husband, and that meant a rectification of the consent order. Balcombe J was not convinced that the court exercising its appellate jurisdiction had power to rectify the consent order. It could set the order aside and make a fresh order, but in the particular circumstances he might not have power to make an order in favour of the husband since the husband had remarried and he had not applied for financial provision before doing so.

### (d) Duress

An agreement may be set aside for lack of consent due to duress the essence of which is coercion by the use of, or the threat of, physical force. Although there may be some ground for saying that it can extend beyond physical pressure, it remains a narrow concept which is likely to be of limited use in this context. In *Backhouse v Backhouse* [1978] 1 WLR 243 Balcombe J refused to accept that the husband had used duress in the sense of threats to secure the signature of his wife to a transfer of her share in the home to him.

*(e) Undue influence*

Applications to set aside agreements on the basis of undue influence fall into one of two categories. The first category comprises cases where the relationship between the parties at or shortly before the agreement was such as to raise a presumption of undue influence on the part of the defendant over the plaintiff. In such a case the onus is on the person seeking to uphold the agreement to satisfy the court that the other party acted in circumstances which enabled him or her to exercise an independent will. In the second category of cases no such relationship can be shown to exist and the onus will be on the plaintiff to show affirmatively that the contract was the result of influence exercised by the defendant over him or her. The relationships giving rise to a presumption of undue influence are still capable of some development, but there is long-standing authority to the effect that a husband is not presumed to have exercised undue influence over his wife (*Howes* v *Bishop* [1909] 2 KB 390; *MacKenzie* v *Royal Bank of Canada* [1934] AC 468). Accordingly, where a spouse seeks to have an agreement set aside on the basis of undue influence, it will fall into the second category, and the onus will be on that spouse to establish that the necessary influence existed and was exercised.

In *Tommey* v *Tommey* [1982] 3 All ER 385 Balcombe J held that where an agreement had been incorporated into a consent order, undue influence, even if established, is not a ground for setting aside the order. He stressed the importance of certainty and finality in litigation and thought that the involvement of the court provided a safety net which should be large enough to catch most cases of exploitation. However, in *Livesey* v *Jenkins* [1985] AC 424 at p. 440, Lord Brandon said:

"The question of the effect of undue influence in circumstances of this kind does not arise on this appeal, and, that being so, it would be undesirable to express even a provisional opinion upon it. I think it right to say, however, that I am not persuaded that Balcombe J's decision on the question was necessarily correct."

Even in relation to an agreement not incorporated into a court order the burden on a party alleging undue influence will be a heavy one, particularly as the agreement is likely to have been entered into at a time when the parties have separated or are about to separate and in one sense the capacity of one spouse to influence the other has declined or disappeared. Where a marriage has broken down it is less likely that one spouse will be willing to place trust and confidence in the other to such an extent as to destroy independent judgment. On the other hand, it is a situation where one spouse may be particularly vulnerable and susceptible to pressure from the spouse in the stronger financial position. In recent cases the courts have shown that they are prepared to apply another long-standing equitable doctrine to new circumstances.

*(f) Unconscionable bargains*

(i) The scope of the doctrine

In *Lyle* v *Lyle* (1973) 117 SJ 70 Brandon J emphasised the importance for both parties to have an opportunity for reflection to consider the implications of an agreement, particularly where a spouse had opposed a divorce and then come round to the idea of acceptance. In that case he was satisfied that the wife who sought to upset an agreement which gave her substantial benefits had been advised by a very experienced counsel and solicitors. Indeed the agreement had been explained to her by Bagnall J when she was in the witness box in support of her petition. However, the position may be different where a spouse receives little or no benefit from an agreement and has no opportunity for independent advice. This is made clear by the decision in *Backhouse* v *Backhouse* where Balcombe J referred to a decision of Megarry J in 1968 - *Cresswell* v *Potter* - which was only reported in 1978 (see [1978] 1 WLR 243 and 255).

In *Cresswell* v *Potter* the wife, some months before her relatively short marriage was dissolved, had executed a deed whereby in return for an indemnity against liabilities under a mortgage, but for no other consideration, released and conveyed to her husband all her interest in the former matrimonial home which had been vested in their joint names. In *Backhouse* v *Backhouse* the marriage had lasted a good deal longer and the matrimonial home had also been conveyed into the joint names of the spouses. The husband remained in the home with the children after the wife left, and four months later the wife executed a transfer of the home into the husband's sole name. She had not sought advice and she received no monetary consideration for the transfer. In *Cresswell* v *Potter* the wife succeeded in her action claiming that the release was ineffective as against the proceeds of sale of the home and that she was entitled to a half share of those proceeds. In *Backhouse* Balcombe J did not have before him the issue of whether the transfer should be set aside, but approached the wife's applications for financial provision and property adjustment on the basis that a transfer had not been made.

In *Cresswell* v *Potter* Megarry J relied on the words of Kay J in *Fry* v *Lane* (1888) 40 Ch D 312 at p. 322 where many of the authorities on setting aside transactions at an undervalue were considered. Kay J had said:

"The result of these decisions is that where a purchase is made from a poor and ignorant man at a considerable undervalue, the vendor having no independent advice, a Court of Equity will set aside the transaction. This will be done even in the case of property in possession, and *a fortiori* if the interest be reversionary. The circumstances of poverty and ignorance of the vendor, and the absence of independent advice, throw upon the purchaser, when the transaction is impeached, the onus of proving, in Lord Selborne's words, that the purchase was 'fair, just and reasonable'."

There were, therefore, three requirements to be satisfied if an agreement was to be set aside on this basis:

* A plaintiff who is "poor and ignorant";
* A sale at a considerable undervalue; and
* Absence of independent advice.

(ii) A "poor and ignorant" plaintiff

Although the principle has not changed since 1888, Megarry J acknowledged that there might have to be some change in phraseology. Thus he thought that "poor" could be replaced by "a member of the lower income group" and "ignorant" by "less highly educated". In *Cresswell* v *Potter* [1978] 1 WLR 255 the wife had been a van driver and was then a Post Office telephonist. Megarry J (at p. 257) thought that "although no doubt it requires considerable alertness and skill to be a good telephonist", such a person could "properly be described as 'ignorant' in the context of property transactions in general and the execution of conveyancing documents in particular". He also thought that "poverty" was not confined to "destitution" and, as the wife was in receipt of legal aid and obviously of slender means, these requirements were satisfied.

In *Backhouse* v *Backhouse* [1978] 1 WLR 243 the wife was certainly not wealthy, but she was not in the view of Balcombe J "ignorant" in a sense that she was not an intelligent woman. Indeed he thought that "the wife is clearly, both from her past behaviour in relation to the financial affairs of the marriage and indeed from the impression she gave in the witness box, a business woman of some ability". He was satisfied that the reason why the wife signed over the transfer of the home was that she felt a sense of guilt at what she had done and he accepted that although she did not "see" the document, she knew what it was. However, Balcombe J (at p. 251) appears to have been satisfied in relation to this requirement on the basis that:

"When a marriage has broken down both parties are liable to be in an emotional state. The party remaining in the matrimonial home as the husband did in this case has an advantage. The wife is no doubt in circumstances of *great emotional strain*." (Author's italics.)

(iii) A sale at a considerable undervalue
There was little doubt on the facts of both cases that this requirement was satisfied. They may be contrasted in this respect with *Lyle* v *Lyle* (1973) 117 SJ 70 where the wife was to receive a substantial capital sum. In other cases it may not be so easy to decide what is an undervalue. Must it always be related only to the value of the property transferred, or should account be taken of any potential adjustment which the court itself might order under the Matrimonial Causes Act 1973? Would the wife in *Taylor* v *Taylor* (1975) 119 SJ 30, for example, have been parting with her interest in the matrimonial home at an undervalue if she had agreed to transfer it on the same terms as the court in fact ordered her interest to be transferred to the husband? Surely not. The marriage had been very short and she had made little or no contribution to the marriage and none to the acquisition of the house. It is submitted that all aspects of the bargain must be taken into consideration.

(iv) Absence of independent legal advice
In both *Cresswell* v *Potter* and *Backhouse* the deed under attack had been prepared by the husband's solicitors and given to the wife to sign by an enquiry agent in the former case and by the husband in the latter case. In neither case did the wife have independent legal advice. Megarry J noted that the authorities put before him where the transfer had been set aside related to transactions where it was regarded as usual, indeed essential, for the parties to have a solicitor. The absence of a solicitor to act for the wife therefore had a special significance for the "more usual it is to have a solicitor, the more striking will be his absence, and the more closely will the courts scrutinise what was done" ([1978] 1 WLR 255 at p. 258).

In *Cresswell* v *Potter* it was argued that if the wife had wanted advice, then she knew how to get it. Shortly before she had executed the deed she had consulted solicitors when she was having difficulty in getting some furniture and effects from the former matrimonial home. They had written a letter which had produced the desired result. However, Megarry J (at p. 259) said:

"... what matters ... is not whether she could have obtained proper advice but whether in fact she had it: and she did not. Nobody, of course, can be compelled to obtain independent advice: but I do not think that someone who seeks to uphold what is, to him, an advantageous conveyancing transaction can do so merely by saying that the other party could have obtained independent advice, unless something has been done to bring to the notice of the other party the true nature of the transaction and the need for advice."

This was echoed by Balcombe J in *Backhouse* when he accepted that "no-one can make a person go to solicitors if they do not wish to do so, but this wife was never invited to do so before she signed away what was her only substantial capital asset". He also accepted that, by analogy with s.34 of the Matrimonial Causes Act 1973, which precludes parties from contracting out of the right to apply to the court for an order containing financial arrangements, the court should not look with favour on assignments of proprietary interests in the matrimonial home made without the benefit of legal advice (see [1978] 1 WLR 243 at pp. 251-252).

Accordingly, where a solicitor acting for one spouse is instructed to prepare a deed of this nature after the marriage has broken down, great care is necessary in order to obviate the possibility of its being set aside in subsequent proceedings. While it is not essential that the other spouse obtains legal advice, it is essential that she should be advised to do so and that the essential nature of the transaction be brought home to her. In *Cresswell* v *Potter* [1978] 1 WLR 255 at p. 260 Megarry J pointed out that it would not have been very difficult to send to the wife a short covering letter which explained that by signing the release she would be giving up her half share in the property to the husband in return for nothing except an agreement by him that she would never have to pay anything under the mortgage, adding that she ought to consider getting independent advice before signing the document. He concluded:

"If in the teeth of that information the plaintiff had executed the release without obtaining such advice, I think that the requirement that there should be independent advice may well have been discharged. In other words, I do not think that the requirement of independent advice should be regarded as absolute - here there was no attempt to comply with the requirement, whether absolute or qualified."

This was the position in *Butlin-Sanders* v *Butlin* [1985] FLR 204. In this case the wife had received no consideration for her transfer of her interest in the former matrimonial home to the husband and she was not released from her obligations to the building society, although the husband had agreed to indemnify her. She (and her husband) fell within the "lower income group" and were "less highly educated". However, in contrast to the position in *Backhouse* and in *Cresswell* v *Potter*, the wife had received advice from a solicitor who had emphasised the difficulties. For reasons of her own - a desire for a divorce, a desire to make some recompense to the husband for the wrong she felt she had done him and a feeling that she had taken out of the joint property all that she was really entitled to - she was prepared to go ahead with the transaction in the face of the advice from her solicitor. The husband satisfied Balcombe J that when the wife transferred her interest in the home to him, "she knew what she was doing, she wanted to do it and she did it" (*ibid.* at p. 213). (It should also be noted that it was not until nearly four years after the conveyance that any action was taken by the wife to challenge the transfer, and this delay and its effect on the husband was also a factor.)

*(g) Change of circumstances*
In certain limited circumstances a court may properly exercise its discretion to grant leave to appeal out of time from an order for financial provision or transfer of property on the basis of new events which have occurred after the date on which the order was made. (See Chapter 10, Part 9.)

## 8. Variation of agreements and consent orders

*(a) Variation of consent orders under section 31 Matrimonial Causes Act 1973*
Where financial arrangements agreed upon between parties are made the subject of a consent order by the court, they no longer depend upon the agreement of the parties as the source from which their legal effect is derived. Their legal effect is derived from the court order and it follows that they must be treated as orders of the court and dealt with, so far as possible, in the same way as non-consensual orders (*per* Lord Diplock in *de Lasala* v *de Lasala* [1980] AC 546 at p. 560, adopted by Ormrod LJ in *Thwaite* v *Thwaite* [1982] Fam 1 at p. 8). Accordingly, the court's power to vary or discharge orders for periodical payments or secured periodical payments under s.31 of the Matrimonial Causes Act 1973 extends to orders made by consent (see *Brister* v *Brister* [1968] 1 WLR 390). The powers to vary an agreement under ss.35 and 36 of the Act (considered below) cease to apply. On the other hand, there is no power to vary an order for payment of a lump sum or for the transfer of property even though made by consent. Where no application for a lump sum payment or for a transfer of property order has been made previously, the court does have power to make such orders on a subsequent original application under s.23 or s.24 respectively. In such cases leave of the court must be obtained and it has been said that such applications should not be allowed to undermine or outflank the general policy of the legislation in relation to variation (*Powys* v *Powys* [1971] P 340 at p. 355. See Chapter 10). In *Ladbrooke* v *Ladbrooke* (1977) 7 Fam Law 213 an attempt to use such original applications to achieve what was tantamount to a variation of a consent order dealing with the disposition of the matrimonial home was unsuccessful. A consent order in 1972 had provided for the matrimonial home to be sold and the wife to receive £9,000 from the proceeds. She remained in the home until 1975 when she sought variation and orders under ss.23 and 24 on the ground that the property was now worth considerably more. Dunn J held that having regard to the agreement, its approval by the court, and the fact that the wife had benefited by staying in the house, it would be unjust to make further capital provision even though applications under ss.23 and 24 were permissible.

## (b) Variation of agreements as post-nuptial settlements

A separation deed making financial provision for a spouse may be a post-nuptial settlement (*Worsley* v *Worsley and Wignall* (1869) LR 1 P & D 648; *Tomkins* v *Tomkins* [1948] 1 All ER 237; *Jeffrey* v *Jeffrey (No.2)* [1959] P 122). The court has power on granting a decree of divorce, nullity or judicial separation or at any time thereafter, to make an order varying for the benefit of the parties to the marriage and of the children of the family or either or any of them, any post-nuptial settlement made on the parties to the marriage, or to make an order extinguishing or reducing the interest of either of the parties to the marriage under any such settlement (Matrimonial Causes Act 1973, s.24(1). See further Chapter 10).

## (c) Variation of maintenance agreements

### (i) The scope of the statutory provisions

Where an agreement has not been made the subject of a consent order, it may in certain circumstances be varied by the court under the provisions of ss.35 and 36 of the Matrimonial Causes Act 1973 if it falls within the definition of a "maintenance agreement" in s.34. Section 35 gives the power to alter maintenance agreements during the lives of the parties and s.36 gives power to alter maintenance agreements after the death of one party.

A "maintenance agreement" for this purpose means any agreement in writing made, whether before or after the commencement of the Act, between the parties to a marriage, being

(a) an agreement containing financial arrangements, whether made during the continuance or after the dissolution or annulment of the marriage; or

(b) a separation agreement which contains no financial arrangements in a case where no other agreement in writing between the same parties contains such arrangements.

"Financial arrangements" means provisions governing the rights and liabilities towards one another when living separately of the parties to a marriage (including a marriage which has been dissolved or annulled) in respect of the making or securing of payments or the disposition or use of any property, including such rights and liabilities with respect to the maintenance or education of any child, whether or not a child of the family (s.34(2)).

The purpose for which the agreement was made no longer matters, but the agreement must be in writing, and it must be made between the parties to a marriage. In *Young* v *Young* [1973] The Times 10 February, it was held that a separation agreement made between a husband, a wife and a third party was not a "maintenance agreement" for this purpose. The deed, which was made between the husband, the wife, and the husband's brother, and which provided the wife with periodical payments and the use of a house belonging to the husband and his brother jointly, could not, therefore, be altered as a maintenance agreement, though if proceedings for divorce or judicial separation were subsequently commenced, it might be varied as a post-nuptial settlement.

(ii) Alteration of agreement during the lives of the parties

Application for the alteration of a maintenance agreement can be made by either party to the High Court or a divorce county court provided that each of the parties to the agreement is for the time being either domiciled or resident in England and Wales. A magistrates' court can entertain such an application only if both the parties to the agreement are resident in England and Wales, and at least one of the parties is resident in the petty sessions area for which the court acts (s.35 (1) and (3)).

An order can be made only if the court is satisfied, either:

(a) that by reason of a change in the circumstances in the light of which any financial arrangements contained in the agreement were made, or, as the case may be, financial arrangements were omitted from it (including a change foreseen by the parties when making the agreement), the agreement should be altered so as to make different, or, as the case may be, so as to contain, financial arrangements; or

(b) that the agreement does not contain proper financial arrangements with respect to any child of the family.

(s.35(2). For the meaning of "child of the family" see Chapter 17).

If an application is based on the first ground it must be shown, first, that there has been a change in the circumstances in the light of which the agreement was made and, secondly, that by reason of a change in those circumstances, an alteration ought to be made. These requirements do not apply to an application based on the second ground.

In considering the circumstances in the light of which financial arrangements were made or omitted, the weight of opinion appears to favour an objective approach (see *Ratcliffe* v *Ratcliffe* [1962] 1 WLR 1455 and *Gorman* v *Gorman* [1964] 1 WLR 1440; cf. *K* v *K* [1961] 1 WLR 802). In *Gorman* v *Gorman* (at pp. 1445-1446) Willmer LJ said:

"While it may be quite right in a proper case to have regard to circumstances which the evidence proves did in fact influence the parties, I certainly do not think that it is possible to exclude any circumstances which as reasonable people they must have had in mind; otherwise, as it seems to me, it would always be possible for the respondent to an application under the Act of 1957 to say that the circumstances relied on (said to be the subject of a change) were circumstances which he never had in contemplation at all, and thereby deny the court jurisdiction to make any order."

It is no longer necessary to show that the change in the circumstances was not foreseen by the parties (reversing *K* v *K* [1961] 1 WLR 802), and the fact that the change of circumstances was brought about by the voluntary act of one of the parties will not prevent it being a "change of circumstances" for this purpose. However, this would be an important consideration when the court considered whether the agreement ought to be altered by reason of the change. Thus in *Ratcliffe* v *Ratcliffe* [1962] 1 WLR 1455, where fourteen months after entering into a maintenance agreement the husband had voluntarily given up employment at £1,400 a year and commenced a two-year course of study to qualify as a teacher during which period he would receive only free board and lodging and a small personal allowance, the court thought that though there had been a change in circumstances, it would not be right to make any alteration in the agreement by reason of that change.

The court to which an application is made may by order make such alterations in the agreement:

(a) by varying or revoking any financial arrangements contained in it; or

(b) by inserting in it financial arrangements for the benefit of one of the parties to the agreement or of a child of the family, as may appear to that court to be just having regard to all the circumstances, including, if relevant, the matters mentioned in s.25(4) of the Act. (These are considered in Chapter 17.)

Thereafter the agreement has effect as if any alteration made by the order had been made by agreement between the parties and for valuable consideration (s.35(2)). This makes it clear that the agreement survives and continues and the legal obligations of the parties remain contractual subject to the change (see *Warden* v *Warden* [1982] Fam 10 *per* Ormrod LJ at p. 13 and Waterhouse J at p.16). The court has power to backdate the variation of a maintenance agreement to the point at which in justice the variation should be made (see *Warden* v *Warden* overruling *Carr* v *Carr* [1974] Fam 65. This brings the position into line with the variation of court orders: *MacDonald* v *MacDonald* [1964] P 1).

The powers of a magistrates' court on such an application are limited (s.35(3)). First, in a case where the agreement includes no provision for periodical payments by either of the parties, a magistrates' court only has power to make an order inserting provision for the making by one of the parties of periodical payments for the maintenance of the other party or for the maintenance of any child of the family. Secondly, in a case where the agreement includes provision for the making by one of the parties of periodical payments, a magistrates' court only has power to make an order increasing or reducing the rate of, or terminating, any of these payments.

Where the High Court or a county court alters an agreement by inserting provision for the making or securing by one of the parties to the agreement of periodical payments for the maintenance of the other party, or by increasing the rate of periodical payments which the agreement provides shall be made by one of the parties for the maintenance of the other, the term for which the payments, or as the case may be, so much of the payments as is attributable to the increase are, or is to be made under the agreement, will be such term as the court may specify in the order. However, that term must not exceed:

(a) where the payments will not be secured, the joint lives of the parties to the agreement, or a term ending with the remarriage of the party to whom the payments are to be made, whichever is the shorter;

(b) where the payments will be secured, the life of that party, or a term ending with the remarriage of that party, whichever is the shorter. (s.35(4)).

Where the High Court or a county court alters an agreement by inserting provision for the making or securing by one of the parties of periodical payments for the maintenance of a child of the family, or by increasing the rate of periodical payments which the agreement provides to be made or secured for the maintenance of such a child, the term for which the payments or so much of the payments as is attributable to the increase, are, or is to be made or secured for the benefit of the child, will be such as the court may specify in the order. In deciding such term the court must apply the provisions of s.29(2) and (3) as to age limits (s.35(5)). See Chapter 17. The effect of the Child Support Act 1991 is also considered in Part 6(k)(ii) of that chapter).

Whereas the power of a magistrates' court is limited to ordering periodical payments there is no apparent limit on the kind of financial arrangements which the High Court or a divorce county court may insert by way of alteration. The section clearly contemplates an order providing for secured periodical payments, and there seems to be nothing to prevent the High Court or a divorce county court from altering a maintenance agreement by inserting an order for a lump sum payment. (Contrast s.31(5) which provides that no order for the payment of a lump sum can be made on an application to vary a periodical payments order or a secured periodical payments order in favour of a spouse.) Indeed, the expression "financial arrangements" extends to provisions governing the rights and liabilities of the parties in respect of "the disposition or use of any property" (s.34(2)).

If this is so it would be in marked contrast to the prohibition on lump sum payments and transfer of property orders in favour of spouses on applications for the variation of orders for periodical payments. In *Pace* v *Doe* [1977] Fam 18 it was argued that the use of the word "property" in the definition of "financial arrangements" enables a lump sum to be included in a maintenance agreement for it is a "financial arrangement" and part of the financial arrangements, and therefore it can be added to a maintenance agreement under s.35 if it is not already there. However, Sir George Baker P found it unnecessary to decide "whether a wife who had not remarried and who, because of changed circumstances, wanted a provision for a lump sum included in an existing agreement, could succeed and whether the court had jurisdiction to add such a provision" (*ibid.* at p. 23). This was because the wife in that case had remarried and it could not possibly have been intended that a lump sum order might be added to an existing agreement after a wife had remarried. An original application to the court for a lump sum payment after remarriage is expressly prohibited by s.28(3) of the Matrimonial Causes Act 1973, and he said it would be contrary to the philosophy of the Act to permit a wife to obtain a lump sum or transfer of property order in any such manner. Even if there was jurisdiction, the fact of remarriage made it "quite wrong and unjust to exercise a discretionary power of amendment to enable her to do something by a side door which she could not otherwise do". He also emphasised that s.35 "which has always caused trouble, has a long history: it has remained side by side with the new legislation and it is equally likely that Parliament never thought that lump sum orders, or financial provision orders including transfer of property orders, could be added to an agreement after the wife had remarried" (*ibid.* at p. 24). In *Furneaux* v *Furneaux* (1973) 118 SJ 204, where the former wife had not remarried, Payne J seems to have had no hesitation in saying that there was no power to vary an agreement by ordering a lump sum.

It is also uncertain as to whether the court can vary any capital provision in an agreement on an application under s.34. In *D* v *D* [1974] The Times 3 October, Sir George Baker P refused an application to vary an agreement which provided for the wife to transfer her interest in the matrimonial home to her husband in consideration of the payment of £1,500 by instalments. His decision was based on the merits of the wife's application, and he held that the fact that the property had increased in value since the date of the agreement, due partly to inflation, did not justify variation on the application of a wife who had been competently advised at the date of the agreement. The ghost of a former wife should not appear from the wainscot to disrupt her husband who had settled to a new life with a new wife. Nevertheless he did say that it was necessary to look at the facts of each case and, from the brief report of the case, there seems to have been no suggestion that the court had no jurisdiction to entertain an application for the variation of an agreement relating to capital rather than income provision. However, the court's powers apply only where a maintenance agreement is "for the time being subsisting". Accordingly, unless some continuing provision exists there would seem to be no jurisdiction. In relation to a purely capital settlement, jurisdiction would seem to exist only where, for example, payment was to be by instalments which had not yet been completed, or possibly, where the payment or transfer had not for some other reason been made. If the agreement also provided for a continuing obligation such as periodical payments or provision in respect of mortgage instalments, then there would seem to be no problem of jurisdiction. The position where the only continuing obligation consists of periodical payments for children was left open in *Pace* v *Doe* [1977] Fam 18 at p. 22.

The Act does not expressly state that further applications can be made on subsequent occasions, but there is no express prohibition of such applications. The implication seems to be that such applications can be made, and this is confirmed by the statement of Davies J in *Orton* v *Orton* (1958) (unreported, but noted at (1959) 109 NLJ 50) in relation to the Maintenance Agreements Act 1957, that there should be some degree of permanency about any order that is made, and that the Act was not really intended to encourage constant applications to vary the amount under the agreement.

(iii) Alteration of agreements after the death of one party
Where a maintenance agreement provides for the continuation of payments under the agreement after the death of one of the parties, and that party dies domiciled in England and Wales, the surviving party, or the personal representatives of the deceased party, may apply to the High Court or a county court for an order altering the agreement in the manner considered above (s. 36(1)).

Such an application cannot be made, except with the permission of the High Court or a county court, after the end of the period of six months from the date on which representation in regard to the estate of the deceased is first taken out (s.36(2)). The personal representatives of the deceased will not be liable under this provision for having distributed any part of the estate of the deceased after the expiration of six months on the ground that they ought to have taken into account the possibility that a court might permit an application to be made by the surviving party after that period. This does not prejudice any power to recover any part of the estate so distributed arising by virtue of the making of an order altering the agreement (s.36(6)). There is no provision for an application under s.36 to be made to a magistrates' court.

If a maintenance agreement is altered by a court on an application under s.36, the same consequences ensue as if the alteration had been made immediately before the death by agreement between the parties and for valuable consideration (s.36(4)).

# Chapter 16

# Financial provision in matrimonial proceedings

## 1. The position at common law

The common law imposed on a husband a duty to maintain his wife in accordance with his means, but imposed no corresponding duty on a wife to maintain her husband. (See for example *National Provincial Bank Ltd* v *Ainsworth* [1965] AC 1175, *per* Lord Hodson at p. 1219 and *per* Lord Upjohn at p. 1229.) This followed from the doctrine of unity of personality, and the wife's inability to hold property and hence to enter into any contract in her own right (see Chapter 1. For comment on the current position in relation to the doctrine of unity of personality see *Midland Bank Trust Co Ltd* v *Green (No. 3)* [1981] 3 All ER 744 and *Routhan* v *Arun DC* [1982] 2 QB 502). A husband would normally perform his duty by providing, first, a suitable home where he and his wife would live together, and, secondly, necessaries such as food and clothing. It was likely that he would provide his wife with an appropriate allowance to meet expenses of their common household, but the common law has never given the wife a right to a separate allowance (*National Assistance Board* v *Parkes* [1955] 1 QB 486 at p. 496; *Lilley* v *Lilley* [1960] P 158 at p. 178). In the latter case Hodson LJ said: "The common law right was not a right to an allowance but to be supported by being given bed and board, and under the Summary Jurisdiction (Separation and Maintenance) Act 1895 a wife could not complain of wilful neglect to maintain because the husband was foolish enough to take the housekeeping out of her hands any more than she could have done at common law (see *Jackson* v *Jackson* (1932) 48 TLR 206)". However, a wife living with her husband has been presumed to have his implied authority to pledge his credit for necessary household expenses (*Jewsbury* v *Newbold* (1875) 26 LJ Ex 247; *Phillipson* v *Hayter* (1870) LR 6 CP 38. For an application of the principle to medical expenses incurred in respect of a wife, see *Gage* v *King* [1961] 1 QB 188).

This authority did not arise from the fact of marriage, but from the wife's usual position of housekeeper from which it could be inferred that the husband had held her out as his agent. (The same authority will be implied in the case of a woman living with a man as his mistress if there is a "household": *Blades* v *Free* (1829) 9 B &

C 167; *Ryan* v *Sams* (1848) 12 QB 460.) It has been open to a husband expressly to forbid his wife to pledge his credit and there is no need for communication of this to any tradesman (*Jolly* v *Rees* (1863) 15 CB (N.S.) 628; *Debenham* v *Mellon* (1880) 6 App Cas 24 (HL)). However, if he has in the past held out his wife to a particular tradesman as having apparent authority it is necessary to give an express warning to that tradesman (*Drew* v *Nunn* (1879) 4 QBD 661 (CA); *Debenham* v *Mellon* (1880) 6 App Cas 24 at pp. 34, 36-37. A disclaimer published in a newspaper will then only be effective if the husband can prove that it came to the tradesman's notice). A husband has also been unable to rebut the presumption of implied authority by showing that his wife already has a sufficient allowance with which to purchase necessaries (*Morel Bros & Co Ltd* v *Westmoreland* [1904] AC 11) or that she is already supplied with sufficient of the goods in respect of which a claim is made against him.

Generally, a wife has not been entitled to separate maintenance in a separate home unless she has had a good reason for living apart from her husband (*Lilley* v *Lilley* [1960] P 158; *Price* v *Price* [1951] P 413). The common law duty of the husband to maintain his wife is suspended while she is in desertion but it revives on termination of the desertion (*Jones* v *Newtown and Llanidloes Guardians* [1920] 3 KB 381). If she commits adultery which has not been connived at or condoned then her right to be maintained ceases altogether (*Wright and Webb* v *Annandale* [1930] 2 KB 8). Indeed, if the wife's conduct is such as to induce in the husband a reasonable (though of course mistaken) belief in her adultery, then he is not obliged to maintain her as long as he continues to have reasonable grounds for that belief (*Allen* v *Allen* [1951] 1 All E.R 724; *Chilton* v *Chilton* [1952] P 196; *Dyson* v *Dyson* [1954] P 198; *Naylor* v *Naylor* [1962] P 253).

A wife might, however, be living apart from her husband because he has deserted her or because she has been forced to do so by his misconduct. In such circumstances, in the absence of misconduct on her part, she is still entitled to be maintained (*Holborn* v *Holborn* [1947] 1 All ER 32). If a husband then failed to provide for his wife she was entitled to pledge his credit for necessaries suitable to their joint style of living before the separation. The basis of this right was the so-called "agency of necessity" (*Bazeley* v *Forder* (1868) LR 3 QB 559). This could not be terminated by the husband forbidding his wife to pledge his credit or even by expressly forbidding tradesmen to give her credit. However, its value was limited because tradesmen were naturally reluctant to give credit if they were likely to become involved in a matrimonial dispute.

The wife's agency of necessity was abolished by s.41 of the Matrimonial Proceedings and Property Act 1970, but this leaves untouched the authority which she is presumed to have while running the husband's household, or any authority which she may have been held out by the husband as having.

The practical utility to a wife of the husband's common law obligation to maintain her has been limited owing to the difficulty of enforcement, but its influence has been considerable. First, as noted in an earlier chapter, it has played an important part in protecting the wife's occupation of the matrimonial home after a marriage has broken down but before it has been terminated by divorce (see Chapter 5 Part 10). Secondly, although a wife obtained statutory remedies which were much more effective in enabling her to obtain maintenance, the courts have referred to the common law obligation in interpreting the scope of these remedies. Thus statute enabled a wife to seek maintenance in a magistrates' court, and later in the High Court and a county court, on the ground that her husband had wilfully neglected to provide reasonable maintenance for her (Matrimonial Proceedings (Magistrates' Courts) Act 1960, s.1(1)(h); Matrimonial Causes Act 1973, s.27). This was held to be a statutory method of enforcing the common law obligation of maintenance (see *Gray* v *Gray* [1976] Fam 324; *Newmarch* v *Newmarch* [1978] Fam 79; *Jones* v *Newtown and Llanidloes Guardians* [1920] 3 KB 381; *Price* v *Price* [1951] P 413). Statute subsequently gave a husband a more limited right to seek maintenance from his wife, and eventually the Domestic Proceedings and Magistrates' Courts Act 1978 made the principle, that "it is the duty of each spouse to support the other and that the nature of the duty is the same in the case of each spouse", the basis of the statutory remedies in the magistrates' court and in the High Court and county court (Law Com. No. 77, para. 9.24).

The common law obligation of a husband to maintain his wife is thus of little, if any, importance today having been superseded by the statutory remedies in the magistrates' court under the 1978 Act and in a county court under s.27 of the Matrimonial Causes Act 1973 which are considered in this chapter. Its importance in relation to occupation of the home has also decreased as a result of the increased statutory protection. (See Chapters 5 and 6.)

Once a marriage has been terminated by divorce then of course the husband's obligation is also terminated and financial provision thereafter is dependent entirely on statute. The comprehensive statutory system relating to financial provision and adjustment of property rights for the benefit of the husband as well as a wife and children on the granting of a decree of divorce or nullity is considered in Chapters 10 and 11. However, it should be noted that this system applies, with certain modifications, on the granting of a decree of judicial separation, for although the marriage continues to exist thereafter, the decree "ends the obligation to live together and almost invariably denotes the death of the marriage. In some cases, especially those involving members of certain religious denominations which do not countenance divorce, it may be the only severance of the legal tie which the parties contemplate" (Law Com. No. 25, para 65).

## 2. Financial provision in magistrates' courts

It has been noted in Chapter 5 that the matrimonial jurisdiction of magistrates' courts originated in the Matrimonial Causes Act 1878. That Act attempted to provide a remedy for the ill-treated wife, not by punishing the husband but by providing the wife with the financial means to live apart from her husband. The jurisdiction was gradually extended until the Summary Jurisdiction (Separation and Maintenance) Act 1895, which can be said to have conferred a general matrimonial jurisdiction on magistrates. This Act remained the basis of the jurisdiction until 1960 though further grounds were added in the intervening years, and in 1937 a husband was given the right to apply for an order in certain limited circumstances. The

Matrimonial Proceedings (Magistrates' Courts) Act 1960 attempted to rationalise and modernise the law, but the matrimonial offence remained the basis for obtaining an order for maintenance. The contrast between this much criticised approach and the reformed divorce law after the Divorce Reform Act 1969 led to the Law Commission being invited by the Home Secretary to set up a Working Party which produced a Working Paper in September 1973 (Law Com. Working Paper No. 53, *Matrimonial Proceedings in Magistrates' Courts*). In that Working Paper (para 24) it was suggested that the objective of the matrimonial jurisdiction of the magistrates should be to enable them to intervene on the application of either party to a marriage:

(i) to deal with family relations during a period of breakdown which is not necessarily permanent or irretrievable
  (a) by relieving the financial need which breakdown can bring to the parties,
  (b) by giving such protection to one or other of the parties as may be necessary, and
  (c) by providing for the welfare and support of the children, and
(ii) to preserve the marriage in existence, where possible.

The analogy of the "casualty clearing station" used in the Working Paper (para 24) was strongly criticised by the Finer Committee in its Report published in 1974 (*The Report of the Committee on One Parent Families* Cmnd. 5629, paras 4.380-4.385). The Finer Committee considered that the Working Party had allowed itself to be misled concerning the actual role of magistrates' courts in matrimonial breakdown by the attractions of the analogy. Thus, while the Working Party accepted that magistrates' courts were used only by a particular social class, it "immediately blurs the implications of this conclusion by creating a further distinction to the effect that the superior jurisdiction deals with irretrievable breakdown, whereas the summary jurisdiction handles breakdowns which are not irretrievable" (para 4.380). Moreover, evidence showed that very many of the casualties of marriage breakdown who sought the help of magistrates' courts become long-term patients (para 4.382). (Research conducted by the Law Research Unit at Bedford College suggested that the people who used the magistrates' courts came to a great extent from the lowest socio-economic classes, the lowest economic class predominating. The upper and middle classes have not to any great extent had recourse to the magistrates' courts to obtain relief for the breakdown of their marriage before the petition for divorce.)

The Finer Committee put in the forefront of its recommendations a proposal for the establishment of a unified institution, the family court, administering a single and unified system of family law in place of the three systems administered respectively by the divorce courts, the magistrates' courts and the supplementary benefit authorities. In the debate on the Report of the Finer Committee in the House of Commons, the Secretary of State for Social Services said that the Government could "... see no prospect of accepting the recommendation for family courts" (Hansard, October 20, 1975 Vol. 898, Cols. 57-60. See also the answer of the Lord Chancellor: Hansard (House of Lords) December 17, 1975 Vol. 366, Cols. 1560-61). The Law Commission concluded that whatever might be the future prospects of a family court, there could be no doubt that the reform of the substantive law was an immediate requirement (Law Com. No. 77 para 1.10). In October 1976 the Law

Commission published its *Report on Matrimonial Proceedings in Magistrates' Courts* (Law Com. No. 77).

In the Report it was accepted that there was evidence that very many of the casualties of marriage breakdown, once they had obtained a matrimonial order from the magistrates, did not seek any more permanent cure for their marital ills. It concluded (para 1.12):

"Where reconciliation takes place, no further cure is required. Where there is no reconciliation, it is important that the parties should be aware of the availability of divorce and of legal aid to help them in divorcing. Effective arrangements are required to ensure that advice on such mattters is readily available, but provided it is, we think it realistic to expect that the function of the magistrates' courts in a dual system will to an increasing extent be that envisaged in our working paper. The reforms which we recommend in our present report will, we hope, contribute to the efficiency with which that function is performed."

The draft Bill annexed to the Report formed the basis of the Domestic Proceedings and Magistrates' Courts Act 1978. That part of the Act dealing with financial provision was brought into force on 1 February 1981. Some amendments were made by the Matrimonial and Family Proceedings Act 1984 with effect from 12 October 1984. These were in line with the amendments made by that Act to the exercise of the powers to order financial provision and property adjustment on or after divorce under the Matrimonial Causes Act 1973.

Applications under Part 1 of the Domestic Proceedings and Magistrates' Courts Act 1978 were formerly known as "domestic proceedings" and a magistrates' court sitting for the purposes of hearing domestic proceedings was known as "the domestic court". The Children Act 1989, s.92(1), provided that the expression "domestic proceedings" should be replaced by the expression "family proceedings" and that the "domestic court" should be known as the "the family proceedings court". Special provisions apply to the composition of the family proceedings court and in relation to the arrangements for the sitting of that court. (See generally the Magistrates' Courts Act 1980, ss.65-74.)

### 3. Orders for financial provision under the Domestic Proceedings and Magistrates' Courts Act 1978

*(a) The bases for obtaining an order under the Act*
There are three basic ways in which an order for financial provision may be obtained in a magistrates' court under the Domestic Proceedings and Magistrates' Courts Act 1978:

(1) by an application for an order under s.2 on the basis of one of the grounds set out in s.1;

(2) by an application for an order under s.6 on the basis of an agreement reached by the spouses;

(3) by an application for an order under s.7 on the basis of existing voluntary financial arrangements where the parties are living apart.

In addition a magistrates' court is given power to make interim maintenance orders in certain circumstances during the pendency of any such application. It is also necessary to have regard to the powers of a court under the Maintenance Orders (Facilities for Enforcement) Act 1920 and the Maintenance Orders (Reciprocal Enforcement) Act 1972 to confirm provisional orders made by a court abroad and to make provisional orders for confirmation abroad.

*(b) Application for orders under section 2*
(i) Grounds
Either party to a marriage may apply to a magistrates' court for an order for financial provision under s.2 on the ground that the other party to the marriage:
  (a) has failed to provide reasonable maintenance for the applicant; or
  (b) has failed to provide, or to make a proper contribution towards, reasonable maintenance for any child of the family; or
  (c) has behaved in such a way that the applicant cannot reasonably be expected to live with the respondent; or
  (d) has deserted the applicant.
(s.1. For the meaning of "child of the family" see s.88(1) and Chapter 17).
These grounds replace the long list of matrimonial offences on which an application could be made under the 1960 Act. (The Law Commission has more recently recommended that grounds (c) and (d) should be abolished: Law Com. No. 192, *The Ground for Divorce* (1990) paras. 4.27-4.28.) Section 1 also gives effect to the general principle that it is the duty of each spouse to support the other on a basis of equality. There is no longer any requirement that the failure to provide maintenance should be "wilful".

In relation to "failure to provide reasonable maintenance" it is submitted that the court should first consider what provision it would order on the basis of the criteria set out in s.3 of the Act if a ground for an order was established. If the respondent is making lower provision then there will be a failure to provide reasonable maintenance. An applicant relying on ground (c) may be receiving reasonable maintenance, but can safeguard her position by obtaining an order before she leaves the respondent on account of his conduct. Similarly a deserted applicant may be receiving reasonable maintenance, but the Law Commission considered that she should not be required to wait until maintenance has ceased before making her application (Law Com. No. 77, para 2.11).

An application must be made in the appropriate form in Schedule 1 to the Family Proceedings Courts (Matrimonial Proceedings etc.) Rules 1991 (SI 1991 No. 1991).

Where an application is made for an order under s.2, the court, before deciding whether to exercise its powers under that section, must consider whether there is any possibility of reconciliation between the parties to the marriage. Moreover, if at any stage of the proceedings on that application it appears to the court that there is a reasonable possibility of such a reconciliation, the court may adjourn the proceedings for such period as it thinks fit to enable attempts to be made to effect a reconciliation (s.26(1). Where the court adjourns any proceedings under this provision, it may request a probation officer or any other person to attempt to effect a reconciliation between the parties: s.26(2)).

(ii)  Orders the court can make

Where the applicant satisfies the court of any of the grounds in s.1 of the Act, the court may make any one or more of the following orders:

(a) an order that the respondent shall pay to the applicant such periodical payments, and for such term, as may be specified in the order;

(b) an order that the respondent shall pay to the applicant such lump sum as may be so specified;

(c) an order that the respondent shall make to the applicant for the benefit of a child of the family to whom the application relates, or to such child, such periodical payments, and for such term, as may be so specified;

(d) an order that the respondent shall pay to the applicant for the benefit of a child of the family to whom the application relates, or to such a child, such lump sum as may be so specified.

(s.2(1)).

The position in relation to financial provision for a child of the family is considered in Chapter 17. Particular regard must now be had to the effect of the Child Support Act 1991.

It will be seen that magistrates are no longer restricted to ordering weekly periodical payments, but may order maintenance to be paid for such term and at such intervals as may be specified. They may also make an order for a limited period of time (confirming *Chesworth* v *Chesworth* (1973) 4 Fam  Law 22. See also *Khan* v *Khan* (1981) 2 FLR 131). The term specified in an order for periodical payments in favour of a party to a marriage must not begin earlier than the date of the making of the application for the order and must not extend beyond the death of either of the parties to the marriage (s.4(1)). Thus periodical payments may be backdated to the date when the application was made. There is also power to make an order operating from a future date which may be useful where a man is unemployed at the time of the hearing, but has arranged to start work in the near future. There is, however, no power to order periodical payments to be secured.

Where an order for periodical payments in favour of a party to a marriage remains in force after that marriage is subsequently dissolved or annulled, the order will cease to have effect on the remarriage of the party in whose favour it was made except in relation to any arrears due under the order at the date of the remarriage (s.4(2). "Remarriage" includes a marriage which is by law void or voidable: s.88(3)). The remarriage of the party liable to pay does not automatically affect the order, but its effect on his resources may be relevant if he applies for a variation under s.20.

Magistrates now have power to order payment of a lump sum, but the amount of any lump sum must not exceed £1,000 or such larger amount as the Secretary of State may from time to time by order fix for this purpose (s.2(3). The figure was raised from £500 by SI 1988 No. 1069). However, it is provided that the court may make an order for the payment of a lump sum notwithstanding that the person required to pay the lump sum was required to pay a lump sum by previous order under the Act (s.2(3)). Thus while there is a limit on the amount that can be ordered on any one occasion, a lump sum may be ordered on more than one occasion. (Contrast the position under s.23 of the Matrimonial Causes Act 1973. See Chapter

10.) Moreover it seems that on the same occasion the court may order £1,000 for a party to the marriage and £1,000 per child (see *Burridge* v *Burridge* (1982) 126 SJ 276 - lump sum of £500 for wife and £125 for each of the two children payable by instalments). It is also provided that an order for payment of a lump sum may be made for the purpose of enabling any liability or expenses, reasonably incurred before the making of the order in maintaining the applicant or any child of the family to whom the application relates, to be met (s.2(2). See *Burridge* v *Burridge*). An order may also provide for the lump sum to be paid by instalments (s.63 Magistrates' Courts Act 1980, s.75).

(iii) A means of payment order
Where a magistrates' court orders money to be paid periodically by one person to another, the court must at the same time exercise one of the powers, to determine the means of payment, conferred by s.59 of the Magistrates' Courts Act 1980 as substituted by the Maintenance Enforcement Act 1991 (see Chapter 22).

(iv) Matters to which the court is to have regard in exercising its powers
The matters to which the court is required to have regard in exercising its powers to order financial provision under s.2 are set out in s.3. This section was recast by s.9 of the Matrimonial and Family Proceedings Act 1984 with a view to ensuring that applications for financial provision in magistrates' courts under the 1978 Act would be governed as far as possible by the same rules and the same substantive law as governs proceedings in the divorce court.

Where an application is made for an order under s.2 of the Act, it is the duty of the court, in deciding whether to exercise its powers under that section and, if so, in what manner, to have regard to all the circumstances of the case, first consideration being given to the welfare while a minor of any child of the family who has not attained the age of eighteen (s.3(1)). In relation to the exercise of its powers under s.2(1)(a) or (b) to order the respondent to make periodical payments or a lump sum payment to the applicant, the court is required in particular to have regard to the following matters set out in subs.(2):

(a) the income, earning capacity, property and other financial resources which each of the parties to the marriage has or is likely to have in the foreseeable future, including in the case of earning capacity any increase in that capacity which it would in the opinion of the court be reasonable to expect a party to the marriage to take steps to acquire;

(b) the financial needs, obligations and responsibilities which each of the parties to the marriage has or is likely to have in the foreseeable future;

(c) the standard of living enjoyed by the parties to the marriage before the occurrence of the conduct which is alleged as the ground of the application;

(d) the age of each party to the marriage and the duration of the marriage;

(e) any physical or mental disability of either of the parties to the marriage;

(f) the contributions which each of the parties has made or is likely in the foreseeable future to make to the welfare of the family, including any contribution by looking after the home or caring for the family;

(g) the conduct of each of the parties, if that conduct is such that it would in the opinion of the court be inequitable to disregard it.

The matters to be taken into account by the court in exercising its powers to make financial provision for children under s.2(1)(c) or (d) are set out in s.3(3). These are considered in Chapter 17 (page 420).

The original s.3 was modelled on s.25 of the Matrimonial Causes Act 1973 with modifications necessary to reflect the different circumstances of applications in magistrates' courts. The new s.3 is similarly modelled on the new s.25 of the 1973 Act. The changes are thus along similar lines. Thus paragraph (a) is amended to include in the case of earning capacity any increase in that capacity which it would in the opinion of the court be reasonable to expect a party to the marriage to take steps to acquire. Paragraph (f) is amended to include contributions which a party to the marriage is likely in the foreseeable future to make to the welfare of the family, and paragraph (g) now refers only to conduct.

In *Macey* v *Macey* (1982) 3 FLR 7 at pp. 10-11, Wood J rejected an attempt to distinguish between the operation of s.3 of the 1978 Act and s.25 of the Matrimonial Causes Act 1973 and said:

"In my judgment it would be most unfortunate if different principles were to obtain in magistrates' courts and the higher courts for making of financial orders. The wording of s.3 of the 1978 Act has clearly been modelled upon that of s.25 of the 1973 Act and there are indications which show an intention to bring the powers of the magistrates more into line with those of the higher courts - for instance, the new power to award a lump sum: section 2(1)(b) of the 1978 Act. It had been held in *Roberts* v *Roberts* [1970] P 1, 6 that: '... the justices' discretion as to quantum of maintenance should be exercised on the same principles as those adopted in the High Court.' I can find nothing in the wording of s.3 of the 1978 Act to indicate that any alteration should be made to this well-established principle. Thus, the approach of the magistrates under s.3 of the 1978 Act should follow the same principles as those followed by the higher courts under s.25 of the 1973 Act."

It is submitted that the same applies to the relationship between the reformulated sections, but it must be borne in mind that the 1978 Act contains no "clean break provision" such as is found in s.25A of the 1973 Act, since the marriage continues to subsist. It is also possible that the assessment of periodical payments may be affected by the fact that a magistrates' court has only a restricted power to order payment of a lump sum and no power to order a transfer or settlement of property.

The principal reported cases dealing with financial provision in a magistrates' court under the 1978 Act are as follows: *Brown* v *Brown* [1981] The Times 14 July; *Coleman* v *Wheeler* (1981) 2 FLR 99; *Khan* v *Khan* (1981) 2 FLR 131; *Re L (Minors) (Financial Provision)* (1981) 1 FLR 34; *Macey* v *Macey* (1982) 3 FLR 7; *Wills* v *Wills* [1984] FLR 672. (See Chapter 11 for a consideration of s.25 of the Matrimonial Causes Act 1973 where the relevant decisions in relation to the 1978 Act are also considered in relation to the various statutory factors.)

Adultery is no longer an absolute bar to financial relief, but conduct which has relevance to the marriage is relevant to liability and quantum. The Law Commission believed that the decision in *Wachtel* v *Wachtel* [1973] Fam 72 had demonstrated that on the basis of such a provison as in paragraph (g), which followed the wording of s.25(1) of the 1973 Act, the courts would have no difficulty "in identifying the limited class of cases in which the conduct of the parties should properly influence their decision" (Law Com. No. 77 para. 2.23).

In *Gengler* v *Gengler* [1976] 1 WLR 275 the Divisional Court expressed the view that a fair and useful starting point for justices assessing maintenance for a wife was to treat her as entitled to a sum equal to one-third of the parties' joint earnings less her own earnings. However, objections have been voiced to the application of the one-third rule in the magistrates' court on the ground that it is based on the supposition that the wife will also receive one-third of their capital assets and that it is unjust to limit the amount she can claim by way of periodical payments when the husband cannot be compelled to transfer any capital assets to her (Cretney 127 New LJ 555; Ellis, 92 LQR 487. For a consideration of the "one-third rule" see Chapter 11). However, in very many cases the limited means of the parties will restrict the scope of what the court can achieve. It will face the difficult task of trying to provide for the needs of two households, and the availability of income support may be crucial (see Chapter 19, Part 6).

*(c) Applications for orders under section 6 - payments agreed by the parties*
Either party to a marriage may apply to a magistrates' court for an order under s.6 on the ground that either the applicant or the other party to the marriage has agreed to make such financial provision as may be specified in the application. This is designed to provide an effective means by which, where a marriage has temporarily broken down, the parties to the marriage can obtain the assistance of the courts in regulating the financial arrangements between themselves without having to parade before the court their marital difficulties (Law Com. No. 77, para 4.4). On such an application the court may order that the applicant or the respondent shall make the financial provision specified in the application if:
  (a) it is satisfied that the applicant or the respondent as the case may be has agreed to make that provision, and
  (b) it has no reason to think that it would be contrary to the interests of justice to exercise its powers under s.6.
Where the respondent is not present or represented by counsel or solicitor at the hearing of the application, the court must not make an order unless there is produced to the court such evidence as may be prescribed by rules of (a) the consent of the respondent to the making of the order, and (b) the financial resources of the respondent (s.6(9). See Family Proceedings Courts (Matrimonial Proceedings etc.) Rules 1991, r.17). In a case where the financial provision specified in the application includes or consists of provision in respect of a child of the family to be made by the applicant to the respondent for the benefit of the child, or to the child, such evidence of the financial resources of the child must be produced to the court as may be prescribed by the rules. As from 5 April 1993, the operation of this section is subject to the limitations imposed by the Child Support Act 1991 (see Chapter 17 Part 6).

"Financial provision" for this purpose is basically the same as that which may be ordered under s.2, except that there appears to be no limit on the amount of any lump sum payment (s.6(2), (6), (7)). Where the financial provision specified in an application includes or consists of provision in respect of a child of the family, the court must not make an order unless it considers that the provison which the respondent has agreed to make in respect of that child provides for, or makes a proper contribution towards, the financial needs of the child (s.6(3)). If the court decides that it would be contrary to the interests of justice to make an order on the terms specified in the application, or that any financial provision for a child of the family does not provide for or make a proper contribution towards the financial needs of that child, it may in certain circumstances make an order for some other financial provision, if the parties agree. It may do so if it is of the opinion that (i) it would not be contrary to the interests of justice to make an order for the making of some other financial provision specified by the court, and that (ii) in so far as that other financial provision contains any provision for a child of the family, it provides for, or makes a proper contribution towards, the financial needs of that child (s.6(5)). The position in relation to provision for a child of the family is considered further in Chapter 17 (page 428).

*(d) Applications for orders under section 7 - powers of the court where parties are living apart*

A provision which was not in the original Bill, and is not derived from the recommendations of the Law Commission, was introduced at the Report stage in the House of Commons with a view to enabling a spouse to have existing voluntary financial arrangements placed on a formal legal basis even though there is no ground for an application under s.1 or any agreement to seek an order. Where the parties to a marriage have been living apart for a continuous period exceeding three months, neither party having deserted the other, and one of the parties has been making periodical payments for the benefit of the other party or of a child of the family, the latter party may apply to the court for an order under s.7. Such an application must specify the aggregate amount of the payments so made during the period of three months immediately preceding the date of the making of the application. If the court is satisfied that the respondent has made the payments specified in the application, the court may make one or both of the following orders:

(a) an order that the respondent shall make to the applicant such periodical payments, and for such term, as may be specified in the order;

(b) an order that the respondent shall make to the applicant for the benefit of a child of the family to whom the application relates, or to such a child such periodical payments, and for such term, as may be so specified.

(s.7(2)).

The provisions of s.4 relating to the duration of orders for financial provision apply to an order under (a) as they apply to a similar order under s.2 (s.7(6)). The provisions of s.5 relating to the age limit and the duration of orders for financial provision apply to an order under (b) as they apply to a similar order under s.2 (s.7(7)). As from 5 April 1993 the operation of this power is subject to the limitations imposed by the Child Support Act 1991 (see Chapter 17 Part 6).

Thus this provision applies only where the parties are living apart by agreement and will not apply if either party is in desertion. The court must be satisfied that the respondent made "periodical payments", i.e. more than one payment, and that he made the periodical payments specified in the application. The payments must have been made for the benefit of the applicant or a child of the family, but not necessarily in the form of direct payments to the applicant. It would seem that, for example, the payment of rent in respect of accommodation occupied by the applicant would satisfy this requirement. If the conditions are satisfied, the court may only make orders for periodical payments and cannot order payment of a lump sum.

Moreover, in exercising its powers under s.7, the court is subject to certain specific limitations. In the first place it must not require the respondent to make payments which exceed in aggregate, during any period of three months, the aggregate amount paid by him for the benefit of the applicant or a child of the family during the period of three months immediately preceding the date of the making of the application. Secondly, the court must not require the respondent to make payments to or for the benefit of any person which exceed in amount the payments which the court considers that it would have required the respondent to make to or for the benefit of that person on an application under s.2 of the Act. Thirdly, the court must not require payments to be made to or for the benefit of a child of the family who is not a child of the respondent unless the court considers that it would have made an order in favour of that child under s.2 of the Act (s.7(3)). Finally, where the court considers that the orders which it has power to make under s.7, (a) would not provide reasonable maintenance for the applicant, or (b) if the application relates to a child of the family, would not provide, or make a proper contribution towards reasonable maintenance for that child, it must refuse to make an order under s.7, but it may then treat the application as if it were an application for an order under s.2 of the Act (s.7(4). See Family Proceedings Courts (Matrimonial Proceedings etc.) Rules 1991, r.18).

In exercising its powers under s.7, the court is required to have regard to the same considerations as on an application for an order under s.2, i.e. the matters set out in s.3. However, for this purpose the reference in subs.(2)(c) to "conduct which is alleged as the ground for the application" is to be replaced by a reference to "the living apart of the parties to the marriage" (s.7(5)).

The position in relation to financial provision for a child of the family is considered further in Chapter 17.

*(e) Interim orders*

Where an application is made for an order under s.2, 6 or 7 the magistrates' court has power to make an "interim maintenance order" at any time before making a final order on, or dismissing, the application, or on refusing by virtue of s.27 to make an order on an application which it considers would be more conveniently dealt with by the High Court. The High Court has the same power on ordering an application to be reheard by a magistrates' court, either after the refusal of an order under s.27 or on an appeal under s.29 (s.19(1). For s.27 and for s.29 see pages 398 and 399 respectively).

An "interim maintenance order" is one which requires the respondent to make to the applicant or to any child of the family who is under the age of eighteen, or to the applicant for the benefit of such a child, such periodical payments as the court thinks reasonable (s.19(1). For the meaning of "child of the family" see s.88(1) and

Chapter 17 Part 5. For the effect of the Child Support Act 1991 see Chapter 17 Part 6). Where an application is made for an order under s.6 by the party to the marriage who has agreed to make the financial provision specified in the application, an interim maintenance order may require the applicant to make payments to the respondent or to or for the benefit of any child of the family under the age of eighteen (s.19(3A)). If the person with whom the child has his home is a parent of the child but not a party to the marriage, the court has the power to make an interim maintenance order requiring the respondent to make periodical payments to that parent for the benefit of the child (s.19(2)). It will be noted that an interim maintenance order may provide only for periodical payments and there is no power to order a lump sum payment. It may provide for payments to be made from such date as the court may specify, not being earlier than the date of the making of the application for an order under s.2, 6 or 7 (s.19(3)). Where an interim maintenance order made by the High Court on an appeal under s.29 provides for payments to be made from a date earlier than the date of the making of the order, the interim order may provide that payments made by the respondent under an order made by a magistrates' court shall, to such extent and in such manner as may be provided by the interim order, be treated as having been paid on account of any payment provided for by the interim order (s.19(3)).

An interim order made on an application for an order under s.2, 6 or 7 ceases to have effect on whichever of the following dates occurs first:
(a) the date, if any, specified for the purpose in the interim order;
(b) the date of the expiration of the period of three months beginning with the date of the making of the interim order;
(c) the date on which a magistrates' court either makes a final order on, or dismisses, the application.
(s.19(5)).
However, unless a final order has been made or the application dismissed, the magistrates' court has power by order to provide that the interim order shall continue in force for a further period. In this event it will cease to have effect on whichever of the following dates occurs first:
(a) the date, if any, specified for the purpose in the further order;
(b) the date of the expiration of the period of three months beginning with the date of the making of the further order, or if there is more than one extension, beginning with the date of the making of the order granting the first extension;
(c) the date on which the court either makes a final order on, or dismisses, the application.
(s.19(6)).
In the case of an interim order made by the High Court, an extension order may be made by the magistrates' court by which the application for an order under s.2, 6 or 7 is to be reheard.

The court may not make more than one interim maintenance order with respect to any application for an order under s.2, 6 or 7 (s.19(7). This is without prejudice to the powers of a court to make an interim order on any further such application). Accordingly, the total possible life of an interim maintenance order is six months. In the first instance it cannot extend beyond three months, but it can be continued (on more than one occasion) up to the end of a further three months. No appeal lies from the making of or refusal to make, the variation of or refusal to vary, or the revocation of or refusal to revoke, an interim maintenance order (s.19(8). For the power to vary or revoke - see s.20, below).

*(f) The effect of cohabitation*
An order which requires periodical payments to be made to one of the parties to a marriage (whether for his own benefit or for the benefit of a child of the family) is enforceable notwithstanding that the parties to the marriage are living with each other at the date of the making of the order or that, although they are not living with each other at that date, they subsequently resume living with each other. However, the order will cease to have effect if, after that date, the parties continue to live with each other, or resume living with each other for a continuous period exceeding six months (s.25(1). This applies to orders under s.2, 6 or 11(2) and interim orders under s.19). This provision is intended to make it easier for a spouse to seek a reconciliation without losing the benefit of an order. It is provided that the expression "living with each other" is to be construed as "living with each other in the same household" (s.88(2)). This is taken from s.2(6) of the Matrimonial Causes Act 1973 and adopts the approach in *Hopes* v *Hopes* [1949] P 227. (See Law Com. No. 77, para. 2.54.) The six-month period of cohabitation must be continuous for its function is to provide an indication that the parties have resumed living together permanently.

Unless the court otherwise directs, an order which requires periodical payments to be made to a child of the family continues to have effect and to be enforceable notwithstanding that the parties to the marriage in question are living with each other at the date of the making of the order or, although they are not living with each other at that date, they subsequently resume living with each other (s.25(2)). An order under s.7 can, of course, only be made when the parties are living apart. Such an order will cease to have effect immediately if the parties resume living with each other.

On an application by either party to a marriage a magistrates' court may make an order declaring that an order for periodical payments has ceased to have effect by virtue of the fact that the parties have resumed living with each other, and specifying the date on which it ceased to have effect (s.25(4)).

*(g) Variation and revocation of orders*
Where a magistrates' court has made an order for periodical payments under s.2 it has power to vary or revoke that order and to make an order for payment of a lump sum whether or not a lump sum payment has been ordered on a previous occasion (s.20(1) and (7)). The power to vary an order includes the power to suspend any provision thereof temporarily and to revive any provison so suspended. The amount of any lump sum must not exceed the amount specified by s.2(3), i.e. at present £1,000.

The same power is given to vary or revoke an order for periodical payments under s.6, and a lump sum payment can now be ordered to be made by a party to the marriage even if the original order did not provide for the payment of a lump sum by that party (s.20(2) as amended by the Matrimonial and Family Proceedings Act 1984, s.11). The amount of the lump sum payment may exceed the statutory maximum if the person who is to pay the lump sum (whether applicant or respondent) agrees (s.20(8)). An order for periodical payments under s.7 can also be varied or revoked, but no lump sum can be ordered (s.20(3). No lump sum can be made on an original application under s.7). An interim maintenance order can also be varied or revoked, but the court must not, in exercising its power of variation, extend the period for which the order is in force (s.20(5)).

Where the court varies an order for the making of periodical payments it may provide that the payments as so varied shall be made from such date as it specifies, not being earlier than the date of the making of the application to vary (s.20(9)). In exercising its powers of variation and revocation the court must, so far as it appears just to do so, give effect to any agreement which has been reached between the parties in relation to the application. If there is no such agreement, or if the court decides not to give effect to the agreement, the court must have regard to all the circumstances of the case, first consideration being given to the welfare while a minor of any child of the family who has not attained the age of 18, and the circumstances of the case include any of the matters to which the court was required to have regard when making the existing order (s.20(11)). If the original order was made under s.6 or on appeal, then regard must be had to the matters relevant on an application under s.2.

Generally an application for the variation or revocation of an order for periodical payments may be made by either party to the marriage (s.20(12), i.e. orders under s.2, 6, 7, 11(2) or 19. For the position in relation to orders for payment to or for the benefit of a child, see Chapter 17 page 419).

There is no express power to vary a lump sum payment. However, where a court has made an order for payment of a lump sum by instalments, then on an application made by either the person liable to pay or the person entitled to receive the lump sum, it has power to vary that order by varying the number of instalments payable, the amount of any instalment payable, and the date on which any instalment becomes payable (s.22). It may also be noted that in proceedings for enforcement the court has power to remit arrears and this may enable the court to reduce or extinguish a lump sum (s.32(1) and s.95 Magistrates' Courts Act 1980. See Chapter 22 Part 2(g)). There is no way in which a lump sum can be increased or recovered once it has been paid.

## (h) Relationship with the High Court

(i) Cases more suitable for the High Court

Where, on hearing an application for an order under s.2, a magistrates' court is of the opinion that any of the matters in question between the parties would be more conveniently dealt with by the High Court, it must refuse to make any order on the application. No appeal lies from that refusal. However, if in any proceedings in the High Court relating to or comprising the same subject-matter as that application the High Court so orders, the application must be reheard and determined by a magistrates' court acting for the same petty sessions area as the court which refused to make any order (s.27 Domestic Proceedings and Magistrates' Courts Act 1978). Thus an order for financial provision on the ground of failure to provide reasonable maintenance may also be sought in the High Court under s.27 of the Matrimonial Causes Act 1973 (see page 404). The powers of that court under that section are wider than the powers of a magistrates' court and enable an unlimited lump sum to be ordered as well as secured provision. In a case where the respondent has substantial assets it may be reasonable for a magistrates' court to decline to proceed with the case (see Law Com. No. 77 para. 4.96). This course may also be appropriate where it is felt that the High Court is better equipped to carry out a full investigation into a party's means (see *Brown* v *Brown* (1972) 117 SJ 87).

### (ii) Concurrent proceedings

There is no statutory limitation on the powers of a magistrates' court where there are concurrent proceedings in the divorce court. The magistrates should "look at the whole thing and as a matter of public policy and general convenience decide what is the right thing for them to do" (*per* Ormrod J in *Lanitis* v *Lanitis* [1970] 1 WLR 503 at p. 509. See Law Com. No. 77, paras. 4.97 - 4.98).

### (iii) Power of divorce court to discharge orders

Where after a magistrates' court has made an order for financial provision, proceedings between and relating to the marriage of the parties are commenced in the High Court or a county court then the court in which the proceedings or any application made therein are or is pending may, if it thinks fit, direct that the order made by the magistrates' court shall cease to have effect on such date as may be specified in the direction (s.28(1)). This does not apply to an order for payment of a lump sum by a magistrates' court.

### (iv) Appeals

Generally, where a magistrates' court makes or refuses to make, varies or refuses to vary, revokes or refuses to revoke an order for financial provision, an appeal lies to the High Court (s.29(1)). However, there is no right of appeal in respect of an interim maintenance order or against a refusal by a magistrates' court under s.27 to hear an application on the ground that it would be more conveniently dealt with by the High Court. On an appeal the High Court has power to make such orders as may be necessary to give effect to its determination of the appeal, including such incidental or consequential orders as appear to the court to be just. In the case of an appeal from a decision of a magistrates' court made on an application for or in respect of an order for the making of periodical payments, the High Court has power to order that its determination of the appeal shall have effect from such date as it thinks fit, not being earlier than the date of the making of the application to the magistrates' court (s.29(2)). Where the High Court reduces the periodical payments required to be made, or discharges the order, it may order the person entitled to the payments under the order of the magistrates' court to pay to the person liable to make payments under that order, such sum in respect of payments already made in compliance with the order as the court thinks fit. If any arrears are due under the order of the magistrates' court, the High Court has power to remit the payment of those arrears or any part thereof (s.29(3)). Any order of the High Court made on appeal (other than an order directing that an application shall be reheard by a magistrates' court) is for the purposes of the enforcement and variation of the order to be treated as if it were an order of the magistrates' court from which the appeal was brought, and not of the High Court (s.29(5)).

*(i) Jurisdiction*

(i) General principles
A magistrates' court has jurisdiction to hear an application for an order for financial provision under the 1978 Act if at the date of the making of the application either the applicant or the respondent ordinarily resides within the commission area for which the court is appointed (s.30(1)). However, there will be no jurisdiction if the respondent resides outside the United Kingdom, even, it seems, if the respondent consents or submits to the jurisdiction (see *Forsyth* v *Forsyth* [1948] P 125. But see the suggestion to the contrary in Cheshire and North, *Private International Law* 12th ed. p. 703). The domicile of the parties is not relevant (s.30(5)).

Where the respondent resides outside the United Kingdom a magistrates' court may have jurisdiction to make a maintenance order against him under the Maintenance Orders (Facilities for Enforcement) Act 1920 or the Maintenance Orders (Reciprocal Enforcement) Act 1972.

Part I of the 1972 Act provides a means whereby an order can be made against a respondent in a "reciprocating country", i.e. one so designated by Order in Council under the Act on the basis that an agreement for reciprocal facilities has been made between the United Kingdom and that country (see Reciprocal Enforcement of Maintenance Orders (Designation of Reciprocating Countries) Orders 1974 (SI 1974 No. 556); 1975 (SI 1975 No. 2187; 1979 (SI 1979 No. 115); 1983 (SI 1983 No. 1125)). The Act provides for the repeal of the 1920 Act (s.22(2)), but this provision is not yet in force because all the countries to which the 1920 Act applied have not yet been designated as "reciprocating countries" under the 1972 Act. When a country has been designated as a "reciprocating country" an order has also been made revoking the application of the 1920 Act to that country. The scheme of the 1920 Act, which accordingly still applies to some countries, is similar to that of Part I of the 1972 Act which is considered below. It is, however, narrower in some respects. Thus Part I of the 1972 Act has a wider definition of the type of orders covered and the principle of a provisional order made in one country followed by confirmation of the order in the other country - the "shuttlecock procedure" - applies also to variation or revocation of orders (1972 Act, ss.5 and 9 as amended by the Domestic Proceedings and Magistrates' Courts Act 1978, s.54).

Part II of the 1972 Act provides for the reciprocal enforcement of claims for the recovery of maintenance between the United Kingdom and countries to which the United Nations Convention on the Recovery Abroad of Maintenance dated 20 June 1956 at New York extends. These countries, known as "convention countries", are also specified by Order in Council (Recovery Abroad of Maintenance (Convention Countries) Order 1975 (SI 1975 No. 423, SI 1982 No. 1530).

In Part III of the 1972 Act s.40 authorises the application by Order in Council of the provisions of the Act, with such exceptions, adaptations and modifications as may be specified in the Order, to other arrangements relating to applications made by or against persons resident in the United Kingdom. Orders have been made under s.40 in respect of arrangements with the Republic of Ireland (SI 1974 No. 2140), certain states in the United States of America (SI 1979, No. 1314) and the Hague Convention countries (SI 1979 No. 1317; SI 1983 No. 885; SI 1983 No. 1523; SI 1987 No.1282. The countries are Czechoslovakia, France, Italy, Netherlands, Portugal, Sweden, Switzerland, Germany).

(ii) Orders under Part I of the Maintenance Orders (Reciprocal Enforcement) Act 1972

Under Part I of the Act a magistrates' court has jurisdiction to hear an application for a maintenance order against a person residing in a reciprocating country if the application is one which the court would have jurisdiction to determine under the Domestic Proceedings and Magistrates' Courts Act 1978 or the Children Act 1989 if that person (a) were residing in England and Wales, and (b) received reasonable notice of the date of the hearing of the application (s.3(1) as amended by the Maintenance Orders (Reciprocal Enforcement) Act 1992, s.1 and Sched.1). Any maintenance order made will, however, be a provisional order only, and will have no effect until it has been confirmed by a competent court in the reciprocating country in which the respondent is residing (ss.3(2) and 21(1) as amended). Once the order has been so confirmed it is to be treated for all purposes as if the magistrates' court which made the order had made it in the form in which it is confirmed and as if the order had never been a provisional order (s.3(6)). A "maintenance order" for this purpose means an order which provides for the periodical payment of sums of money towards the maintenance of any person, being a person whom the person liable to make payments under the order is, according to the law applied in the place where the order was made, liable to maintain (s.21(1). In the case of a maintenance order which has been varied, it means that order as varied).

A magistrates' court has no power to refuse to hear such an application on the ground that the matter in question is one which would be more conveniently dealt with by the High Court (i.e. under Domestic Proceedings and Magistrates' Courts Act 1978, s.27. See s.3(4) as amended by the Maintenance Orders (Reciprocal Enforcement) Act 1992).

When a magistrates' court makes a provisional maintenance order then a certified copy of the order, together with other specified documents, must be sent to the Secretary of State with a view to their being transmitted to the responsible authority in the reciprocating country in which the payer is resident if he is satisfied that the statement relating to the whereabouts of the payer gives sufficient information to justify that being done (s.3(5). See also the Magistrates' Courts (Reciprocal Enforcement of Maintenance Orders) Rules 1974 (SI 1974 No. 668) and SI 1980 No. 108). No appeal lies from a provisional maintenance order made by a court in the United Kingdom (s.12).

A similar procedure provides for the confirmation by a court in England and Wales of a provisional order made in a reciprocating country (s.7).

(iii) Orders under Part II of the Maintenance Orders (Reciprocal Enforcement) Act 1972

Where a person in England and Wales claims to be entitled to recover in a convention country maintenance from another person and that other person is for the time being subject to the jurisdiction of that country, the applicant may apply to the Secretary of State to have his claim for the recovery of maintenance transmitted to that country (s.26(1)). An application to the Secretary of State must be made through the appropriate officer, who is the clerk of a magistrates' court acting for the petty sessions area in which the applicant is residing (s.26(3) and (6)). On receiving an application from the appropriate officer the Secretary of State must transmit it, together with any accompanying documents, to the appropriate authority in the convention country, unless he is satisfied that the application is not made in good faith, or that it does not comply with the requirements of the law applied by that country (s.26(4)). Accordingly, there is no provision for transmitting a provisional order to a convention country, but a claim may be transmitted to be determined in the convention country where the proposed respondent is living and in accordance with the law of that country.

Where the Lord Chancellor receives from the appropriate authority in a convention country an application by a person in that country for the recovery of maintenance from another person who is for the time being residing in England and Wales, he must send the application, together with any accompanying documents, to the clerk of a magistrates' court acting for the petty sessions area in which that person is residing (ss.27A and 27B as inserted by the Maintenance Orders (Reciprocal Enforcement) Act 1992). See the Magistrates' Courts (Recovery Abroad of Maintenance) Rules 1975 (SI 1975 No. 488) as amended by SI 1980 No. 1584). The application must be treated for the purposes of any enactment as if it were an application for a maintenance order under the Domestic Proceedings and Magistrates' Courts Act 1978, and the court hearing the application may make any order which it has power to make under s.2 of that Act (*ibid.* s.28 as amended by the Maintenance Orders (Reciprocal Enforcement) Act 1992). Also interim orders under s.19(1). Part 1 of the 1978 Act, except ss.6 to 8, 16 to 18, 20ZA, 25 to 27, and 28(2) apply in relation to the application and to any order made on the application). Where an application is made for the recovery of maintenance from a person residing in England and Wales who is the former spouse of the applicant it must be treated as an application for an order under s.2 of the 1978 Act notwithstanding that their marriage has been validly dissolved by a divorce granted in a convention country which is recognised as valid by the law of England and Wales. On hearing the application the magistrates' court may, subject to certain limitations, make any order which it has power to make under s.2 of the 1978 Act if it is satisfied that the defendant has failed to comply with the provisions of an order for the payment of maintenance for the benefit of the applicant or a child of the family made by reason of the divorce proceedings in the convention country by the court which granted the divorce or by any other court in that country (s.28A(1), (2) and (3) as amended by the 1992 Act). The limitations are, first, that an order for the making of periodical payments for the benefit of the applicant or any child of the family must not be made unless the order made in the convention country provides for the making of periodical payments for the benefit of the applicant, or, as the case may be, that child. Secondly, an order for the payment of a lump sum for the benefit of the applicant or any child of the family must not be made unless the order made in the convention country provides for the payment of a lump sum to the applicant or, as the case may be, to that child. If a magistrates' court makes an order on an application, the clerk of the court must register the order in the prescribed manner in that court (*ibid.* s.27C(7). An order may be transferred to another court if the payer is no longer resident within the jurisdiction of the original court. See s.32). Again, therefore, it is a claim rather than an existing order which is transmitted from the convention country through the Lord Chancellor to a court in England and Wales.

(iv) Orders under Part III of the Maintenance Orders (Reciprocal Enforcement) Act 1972

The arrangements which are given effect by Orders in Council made under s.40 vary. Thus the arrangements with the Republic of Ireland authorise a magistrates' court in England and Wales not only to make a provisional order against a person resident in the Republic, but also to confirm that order itself (see Reciprocal Enforcement of Maintenance Orders (Republic of Ireland) Order 1974 (SI 1974 No. 2140), r.3). The arrangements with the Hague Convention countries authorise a magistrates' court to make an order against a person residing in one of those countries which is not provisional (see Reciprocal Enforcement of Maintenance Orders (Hague Convention Countries) Order 1979 (SI 1979 No. 1317), r.3). However, the arrangements with certain states in the United States of America merely provide for claims to be forwarded through the justices' clerk of the local magistrates' court to the American state so that a maintenance order can be made under the law of that state against a person in that state (see Recovery of Maintenance (USA) Orders 1979 (SI 1979 No. 1314); 1981 (SI 1981 No. 606); 1984 (SI 1984 No. 1824); Home Office circular 172/1979).

*(j) Jurisdiction to vary or revoke*

A magistrates' court which has made an order for periodical payments under Part I of the Domestic Proceedings and Magistrates' Courts Act 1978 may hear applications for variation or revocation of that order (s.20ZA as inserted by the Maintenance Enforcement Act 1991). A magistrates' court may proceed with an application under s.20 notwithstanding that the respondent has not received written notice of the application.

An order made by virtue of Part I of the 1972 Act may be varied or revoked either by the court which made the original provisional order or the court which confirmed it. Thus a provisional order made by a magistrates' court in England and Wales and confirmed in a reciprocating country may be varied or revoked by that magistrates court (s.5(1)), and a magistrates' court in England and Wales has power to confirm a provisional order made by a court in a reciprocating country varying or revoking such an order (s.5(5)). Similarly, a provisional order made in a reciprocating country which is confirmed by and registered in a court in England and Wales may be varied or revoked by the court in England and Wales in which it is registered (s.9(1)). The powers do not extend to so much of the order as provides for payment of a lump sum (Civil Jurisdiction and Judgments Act 1982, Sched. 10 para. 4). The court also has power to confirm a provisional order made by the court in the reciprocating country which made the original registered order varying or revoking it (s.4(6)). However, certain variations made by a magistrates' court in England and Wales can only be made by provisional orders, and until they are confirmed by the court in the reciprocating country, such orders will have no effect. Thus, if the order was made by a magistrates' court in England and Wales, that court can vary it by increasing the rate of payments only by a provisional order unless either (a) both parties appear in the proceedings, or (b) the applicant appears and the other party is duly served (s.5(3)). An order made in a reciprocating country which has been confirmed by and registered in a magistrates' court in England and Wales, can only be varied by that court by a provisional order, if (a) both parties are residing in the United Kingdom, or (b) the application is made by the person entitled to the payments, or (c) the variation consists of a reduction in the rate of payments and is made solely on the ground that there has been a change in the financial circumstances of the person liable to make the payments since the order was made or confirmed, and the court in the reciprocating country has no power under its law to confirm provisional orders varying maintenance orders (s.9(2)). A magistrates' court in England and Wales may not revoke a registered order otherwise than by a provisional order unless both parties are residing in the United Kingdom (s.9(3)). Where a registering court makes a provisional order varying or revoking a registered order there is provision for forwarding that provisional order for confirmation in the reciprocating country (s.9(5)).

An order made by virtue of Part II of the 1972 Act must be varied in the country in which it was made. Thus where an applicant in England and Wales seeks to vary an order made in a convention country, he or she may apply to the Secretary of State to have his application for variation of that order transmitted to the convention country (s.26(2)). Similarly where an order has been made by a court in England and Wales there is provision for an application for variation by an applicant resident in a convention country to be transmitted through the Secretary of State to the court in England and Wales (s.34(3)).

## 4. Orders under s.27 Matrimonial Causes Act 1973

*(a) The background*
In 1949 a wife was given the right to apply to the High Court for maintenance on the basis of the wilful neglect of her husband to maintain her and without seeking any other form of relief (Law Reform (Miscellaneous Provisions) Act 1949). This was seen by the courts as a statutory method of enforcing the husband's common law duty to maintain her. The result was that if a husband was no longer under any obligation to maintain her because, e.g. she had committed adultery, then she could not establish wilful neglect and no order could be made. This did not change when, in 1970, a husband was given a limited right to seek an order against his wife although there was no common law obligation on a wife to maintain her husband (Matrimonial Proceedings and Property Act 1970, s.6(1)(b). See *Gray* v *Gray*

[1976] Fam 324). A wife could be ordered to make payments to her husband only if his earning capacity was impaired through age, illness or disability. The Law Commission acknowledged that in accordance with the policy adopted in proceedings for divorce, nullity and judicial separation, a husband should be entitled to apply in all circumstances. However, it considered that "without a complete re-casting of the section and a complete reformulation of mutual obligations to maintain, this would hardly be workable" (Law Com. No. 25 *Report on Financial Provision in Matrimonial Proceedings*, para. 19). This was done by the Domestic Proceedings and Magistrates' Courts Act 1978 (s.63, following the recommendations of the Law Commission in Law Com. No. 77 para. 9.24) which, as has already been noted, recast the grounds on which financial provision could be obtained in a magistrates' court.

The reformulated section removes the requirement that the failure to maintain must have been "wilful" and embodies the principle that "it is the duty of each spouse to support the other and that the nature of the duty is the same in the case of each spouse" (Law Com. No. 77 para. 9.24). Adultery ceases to be an absolute bar to an order, though conduct is relevant when the court is determining whether to make an order in favour of a spouse. The grounds are identical with the first two grounds on which a spouse may apply to a magistrates' court for an order under s.1 of the 1978 Act.

*(b) The grounds for making an order*
On the application of either party to a marriage a county court may make orders for financial provision of the applicant spouse and any child of the family on the ground that the other party to the marriage (the respondent):
  (a) has failed to provide reasonable maintenance for the applicant, or
  (b) has failed to provide, or to make a proper contribution towards, reasonable maintenance for any child of the family.
(s.27(1) as substituted by s.63 Domestic Proceedings and Magistrates' Courts Act 1978). If the application is defended the case will be transferred to the High Court.

Generally there must be a valid subsisting marriage. However, in *Newmarch* v *Newmarch* [1978] Fam 79 it was held that it was open to the wife, despite the validity of a foreign decree of divorce, to seek confirmation of an interim maintenance order made under s.27 and to obtain a substantive maintenance order, for under s.27 a discretion remained to make an order in proceedings which had been commenced before the parties had been divorced by the foreign decree (contrast *Turczak* v *Turczak* [1970] P 198).

In deciding whether the respondent has failed to provide reasonable maintenance for the applicant, and what order, if any, to make in favour of the applicant, the court is required to have regard to all the circumstances of the case including the matters mentioned in s.25(2) of the Act, and where an application is also made in respect of a child of the family who has not attained the age of eighteen, first consideration must be given to the welfare of the child while a minor (s.27(3) as amended by s.4 of the Matrimonial and Family Proceedings Act 1984). It is also provided that for this purpose s.25(2)(c) of the Act is to have effect as if the reference therein to the "breakdown of the marriage" was replaced by a reference to "the failure to provide reasonable maintenance for the applicant" (s.27(3B)).

In deciding whether the respondent has failed to provide, or to make a proper contribution towards, reasonable maintenance for the child of the family to whom the application relates, and what order, if any, to make in favour of the child, the court is required to have regard to all the circumstances of the case including the matters mentioned in s.25(3)(a) to (e) of the Act. Where the child of the family to whom the application relates is not the child of the respondent the court must also have regard to the matters mentioned in s.25(4) (s.27(3A)). It is also provided that for this purpose s.25(2)(c) shall have effect as if the reference therein to "breakdown of the marriage" was replaced by a reference to "the failure to provide, or to make a proper contribution towards, reasonable maintenance for the child of the family to whom the application relates" (s.27(3B)). A "child of the family" is defined in s.52 of the Act. As from 5 April 1993 orders for periodical payments can be made only to the extent permitted by the Child Support Act 1991 (see Chapter 17 Part 6).

*(c) Orders the court can make*

Where the applicant satisfies the court of one of the grounds mentioned above, the court may make any one or more of the following orders:

(a) an order that the respondent shall make to the applicant such periodical payments, and for such term, as may be specified in the order;

(b) an order that the respondent shall secure to the applicant, to the satisfaction of the court, such periodical payments, and for such term as may be specified in the order;

(c) an order that the respondent shall pay to the applicant such lump sum as may be specified in the order;

(d) an order that the respondent shall make to such person as may be specified in the order for the benefit of the child to whom the application relates, or to that child, such periodical payments, and for such term, as may be specified in the order;

(e) an order that the respondent shall secure to such person as may be specified in the order for the benefit of the child to whom the application relates, or to that child, to the satisfaction of the court, such periodical payments, for such term as may be specified in the order;

(f) an order that the respondent shall pay to such person as may be specified in the order for the benefit of the child to whom the application relates, or to that child, such lump sum as may be specified in the order.

(s.27(6)).

Where an order for periodical payments or secured periodical payments has been made for a limited term, then on general principles the court can, on an application under s.31 to vary the order, extend the term of the order. However, where such an order in favour of a party to a marriage is made on or after the grant of a decree of divorce or nullity, the court may now direct that that party shall not be entitled to apply under s.31 for an extension of the term (s.28(1A) inserted by s.5(2) of the Matrimonial and Family Proceedings Act 1984). This provision now ensures that, if the court considers it appropriate, finality can be achieved and is complementary to s.25A(2) (considered in Chapter 10).

An order for the payment of a lump sum under (c) and (f) may be made for the purpose of meeting any liabilities or expenses incurred in maintaining the applicant, or any child of the family to whom the application relates, before the application was made (s.27(7)(a)). An order for the payment of a lump sum may provide for the payment of that sum by instalments of such amount as may be specified in the order, and may require the payment of the instalments to be secured to the satisfaction of the court (s.27(7)(b)). An order for payment may only be made against a respondent spouse and there is no power to order the applicant spouse to make payments in favour of a child of the family.

### (d) Duration of continuing provision for a spouse

An order for periodical payments or secured periodical payments in favour of a spouse may be for such term as the court thinks fit subject to certain limits. The term specified in an order for periodical payments may begin not earlier than the date of the application, and cannot last longer than the joint lives of the spouses, that is, beyond the death of either spouse. If the court orders periodical payments to be secured, then the term may begin not earlier than the date of the application, and may extend for the life of the applicant spouse (s.28(1)). There is no automatic cessation of an order on subsequent dissolution or annulment of the marriage. (For power of revocation or variation, see below.) However, if the marriage is subsequently dissolved or annulled, but the order continues in force, then it will cease to have effect on the remarriage of the party in whose favour it was made except in relation to any arrears due under it on the date of such remarriage (s.28(2)). When the court is considering within these limits the appropriate term to be specified in an order made on or after the granting of a decree of divorce or nullity, it is now under a duty by virtue of s.25A(2) of the Act to consider whether it would be appropriate to specify a limited term (s.28(1) as amended by s.5(1) Matrimonial and Family Proceedings Act 1984).

Cohabitation by the parties, whether continued or resumed, does not affect the operation of an order (see Law Com. No. 77 paras. 9.12 to 9.16).

### (e) Duration of continuing provision for children

The provisions of the Matrimonial Causes Act 1973 relating to the duration of orders for periodical payments or secured periodical payments in favour of children in proceedings for divorce, nullity and judicial separation apply also to such orders made under s.27 of the Act. (See Chapter 17, Part 2.)

### (f) Interim orders

Where it appears to the court that the applicant or any child of the family to whom the application relates is in immediate need of financial assistance, but it is not yet possible to determine what order, if any, should be made on the application, the court may make an interim order for maintenance. This will be an order requiring the respondent to make to the applicant until the determination of the application such periodical payments as the court thinks reasonable (s.27(5)). On the making of a final order, a lump sum payment may be ordered to cover expenses incurred before the application was made. See above.

## (g) Variation, discharge and suspension of orders

Where a court has made an order for periodical payments or secured periodical payments, or an interim order, the court has power to vary or discharge the order or to suspend any provision thereof temporarily and to revive the operation of any provision so suspended (s.31(1) and (2)). These powers do not apply to an order for the payment of a lump sum, but they do apply to a provision in such an order for the payment of the lump sum by instalments. No order for the payment of a lump sum can be made on an application for the variation of an order for periodical payments or secured periodical payments in favour of a spouse (s.31(5)).

Where the person liable to make payments under a secured periodical payments order has died, an application to vary or discharge that order, or to suspend or revive any provision in it, may be made by the person entitled to payments under the order or by the personal representative of the deceased person. However, except with the permission of the court, no such application can be made after the end of the period of six months from the date on which representation in regard to the estate of that person is first taken out (s.31(6)).

An application for the variation of a periodical payments order or a secured periodical payments order in favour of a child may be made by the child himself if he has attained the age of 16 (s.27(6A)). Where a periodical payments order made in favour of a child ceases to have effect when the child attains the age of 16 or at any time after that date but before he attains the age of 18, then if, on an application to the court, it appears to the court that:

(a) the child is, will be or (or if the order were made) would be receiving instruction at an educational establishment or undergoing training for a trade, profession or vocation, whether or not he also is, will be or would be in gainful employment; or

(b) there are special circumstances which justify the making of an order,

the court may, by order, revive the periodical payments order from such date as the court may specify, not being earlier than the date when the application was made (s.27(6B)).

In exercising the powers of variation, discharge, suspension and revival the court must have regard to all the circumstances of the case, first consideration being given to the welfare while a minor of any child of the family who has not attained the age of eighteen. The circumstances of the case include any change in any of the matters to which the court was required to have regard when making the order to which the application relates. In the case of an order made on or after the grant of a decree of divorce or nullity, the court must consider whether in all the circumstances and after having regard to any such change it would be appropriate to vary the order so that payments under the order are required to be made or secured only for such further period as will in the opinion of the court be sufficient to enable the party in whose favour the order was made to adjust without undue hardship to the termination of those payments. Where the party against whom the order was made has died, the circumstances of the case also include the changed circumstances resulting from his death (s.31(7) as amended by s.6(3) Matrimonial and Family Proceedings Act 1984).

Where the court decides to vary or discharge a periodical payments or secured periodical payments order, then it has power to direct that the variation or discharge shall not take effect until the expiration of a period specified in the variation or discharge (s.31(10)). This enables the court to continue the order, or to continue an order, at a certain level, for a fixed term to provide an opportunity for the recipient to adjust and become financially independent or less dependent.

*(h) Enforcement*
The enforcement of orders under s.27 and their registration for enforcement in other parts of the United Kingdom is considered in Chapter 22.

*(i) Jurisdiction*
The court must not entertain an application under s.27 unless:
(a) the applicant or the respondent is domiciled in England and Wales on the date of the application; or
(b) the applicant has been habitually resident in England and Wales throughout the period of one year ending with that date; or
(c) the respondent is resident in England and Wales on that date. (s.27(2) as substituted by Domicile and Matrimonial Proceedings Act 1973 s.6(1).)

# Chapter 17

# Financial provision for children

## 1. The basis of financial provision for children

*(a) The position at common law*
It seems that the common law never imposed any civil liability on a husband or wife to maintain their children (*per* Lord Goddard CJ in *National Assistance Board* v *Wilkinson* [1952] 2 QB 648 at p. 657. See also *Thomasset* v *Thomasset* [1894] P 295). The absence of clear authority may be due to the fact that even if such a duty existed in theory there was no means whereby it could be enforced. A child had no implied authority to pledge his parents' credit either by virtue of an agency of necessity or otherwise. Such authority would be implied only if a parent had in some way constituted a child an agent in accordance with the ordinary principles of the law of agency (*Law* v *Wilkin* (1837) 6 A & E 718; *Mortimore* v *Wright* (1840) 6 M & W 487). Similarly, in the case of an illegitimate child neither the father nor the mother was liable for its maintenance at common law (*Ruttinger* v *Temple* (1863) 4 B & S 491), though as in the case of a legitimate child, a parent may give the child authority to incur a debt on his or her behalf.

*(b) Financial provision by statute*
The power to order financial provision for children has been conferred on the courts by a number of statutes. These statutes fall into two categories. First, there are statutes dealing principally with the affairs of adults, but which also confer power to order financial provision for children. These are the Matrimonial Causes Act 1973 and the Domestic Proceedings and Magistrates' Courts Act 1978. Secondly, there are statutes concerned only with children. These formerly included the Guardianship of Minors Act 1971, the Guardianship Act 1973 and the Children Act 1975. It had been the objective of the Law Commission to bring together in a single, coherent and modernised code the law relating to the care, upbringing and mainte-nance of children. However, it reluctantly concluded that it was only practicable to assimilate and incorporate into its scheme the powers then contained in the Acts of 1971, 1973 and 1975. Where the court also had power to make orders for the benefit

of an adult, as under the Matrimonial Causes Act 1973 and the Domestic Proceedings and Magistrates' Courts Act 1978, it was considered to be more convenient for all the orders to be made under the same Act (Law Com. No. 172, *Review of Child Law: Guardianship and Custody* (1988) paras. 1.5 *et seq.*). Accordingly, orders for financial provision and property adjustment for the benefit of a child continue to be possible under the statutes in the first category but, as from 5 April 1993, only to the extent permitted by the Child Support Act 1991 so far as orders for periodical payments are concerned (see (*c*) and Part 6 below). The powers to order financial provision contained in the statutes referred to in the second category have been assimilated and merged in the Children Act 1989 with little change in the substance of the existing law, but with the benefit of considerable simplification. This assimilation now extends to the powers of the court to order financial provision for wards of court previously governed by s.6 of the Family Law Reform Act 1969. In this category, too, the power to order periodical payments is limited by the Child Support Act 1991 (see below).

In addition to these statutory powers to order financial provision for children there are statutory provisions which are designed to enable certain public authorities to recover from parents a contribution, at least, towards sums expended on the maintenance of their children. The most important of these provisions are considered in Chapter 19. Again, the effect of the Child Support Act 1991 must be taken into account.

*(c) The machinery of the Child Support Act 1991*
The fact that a high percentage of absent parents do not make regular payments for the maintenance of their children has meant that more and more children, and the lone parents who care for many of them, have become dependent on public funds principally in the form of income support (see Chapter 19). This was one of the unsatisfactory features of the existing system of child maintenance noted in the White Paper "Children Come First" (1990) Cm.1264. Among the other problems noted in the White Paper was the inconsistency which resulted from the system of decisions on maintenance being based largely on discretion and made in numerous courts and hundreds of social security offices. It concluded that "in the interests of the children, a single system is needed and that system needs a structure of consistent and rational principles and clearly established priorities..." (para.1.6). The White Paper went on to propose, first, the introduction of a non-discretionary formula for the calculation of child maintenance applicable to all families where maintenance is an issue, thereby eliminating scope for inconsistency. Secondly, it proposed the establishment of a child support agency with the responsibility for tracing absent parents and for the assessment, collection and enforcement of maintenance payments. These proposals were, with modifications, carried into effect by the Child Support Act 1991 which restricts the jurisdiction of the courts to make or vary orders for periodical payments for children. This significant change in the handling of child maintenance is considered in the last Part of this chapter.

The new system began to come into operation on 4 April 1993 (The Child Support Act 1991 (Commencement No. 3 and Transitional Provisions) Order 1992, SI 1992 No. 2644). Although the existing powers of the courts to order periodical payments for children within the scope of the Act are now largely superseded, the courts retain a power to make "top-up" orders in certain circumstances and the powers of the courts to make orders for lump sum payments and property adjustment orders in favour of such children continue in effect. Moreover, there are children, such as stepchildren, who do not fall within the scope of the Act and therefore all the existing powers of the courts remain important in relation to such children. The existing statutory powers will be considered first.

## 2. Orders under the Matrimonial Causes Act 1973

*(a) The court's powers*
On granting a decree of divorce, a decree of nullity of marriage, or a decree of judicial separation, or at any time thereafter (whether, in the case of a decree of divorce or nullity of marriage before or after the decree is made absolute), the court may make orders for financial provision and orders adjusting property rights in favour of children of the family.

Under s.23 the court may make one or more of the following financial provision orders:

(a) that a party to the marriage shall make to such person as may be specified in the order for the benefit of a child of the family, or to such child, such periodical payments, for such term, as may be specified in the order;

(b) that a party to the marriage shall secure to such person as may be specified in the order for the benefit of a child of the family, or to such child, to the satisfaction of the court, such periodical payments, for such term, as may be so specified;

(c) that a party to the marriage shall pay to such person as may be specified in the order for the benefit of a child of the family, or to such child, such lump sum as may be so specified.

An order for the payment of a lump sum to or for the benefit of a child of the family may be made for the purpose of meeting any liabilities or expenses reasonably incurred by or for the benefit of that child before an application for a financial provision order in his favour was made (s.23(3)).

Under s.24 the court may make one or more of the following property adjustment orders:

(a) an order that a party to the marriage shall transfer to any child of the family or to such person as may be specified in the order for the benefit of such a child such property as may be specified in the order to which the party first mentioned is entitled either in possession or reversion;

(b) an order that a settlement of such property as may be so specified being property to which a party to the marriage is so entitled, be made to the satisfaction of the court for the benefit of the other party to the marriage and of the children of the family or either or any of them;

(c) an order varying for the benefit of the parties to the marriage and of the children of the family or either or any of them any ante- or post-nuptial settlement (including such a settlement made by will or codicil) made on the parties to the marriage. (For the meaning of "ante- or post-nuptial settlement" see Chapter 10.)

A financial provision order for the benefit of a child of the family may be made and may become effective before or on granting a decree or at any time thereafter (s.23(2). An order for maintenance pending suit cannot be made in favour of a child of the family). Moreover, where proceedings for divorce, nullity or judicial separation are dismissed after the beginning of the trial, the court may nevertheless make a financial provision order for the benefit of a child, either forthwith, or within a reasonable period after dismissal (s.23(2). For a consideration of the expression "after the beginning of the trial", see *P(JM)* v *P(LE)* [1971] P 217). These provisions do not apply to property adjustment orders for the benefit of a child which can be made only on or after the granting of a decree, and which will take effect in proceedings for divorce or nullity, only on decree absolute.

Generally no financial provision order or a transfer of property order can be made in favour of a child who has attained the age of 18 (s.29(1)). The term specified in an order for periodical payments or secured periodical payments in favour of a child may begin with the making of an application for the order in question and must not extend beyond the date when the child will attain the age of 18 (s.29(2)). In the first instance the term specified must not extend beyond the date of the birthday of the child next following his attaining the upper limit of the compulsory school age unless the court making the order thinks it right in the circumstances of the case to specify a later date (s.29(2)). However, the court may make an order for periodical payments or secured periodical payments or an order for a lump sum payment or a transfer of property in favour of a child who has attained the age of 18, and may include in an order for periodical payments or secured periodical payments in favour of a child who has not attained that age, a provision extending the term beyond the date when the child will attain that age, if it appears to the court that:

(a) the child is, or will be, or if such an order or provision were made would be, receiving instruction at an educational establishment or undergoing training for a trade, profession or vocation, whether or not he is also, or will also be in gainful employment; or

(b) there are special circumstances which justify the making of an order or provision.

(s.29(3)).

There is no objection to the term extending beyond the date when the child attains 21.

A periodical payments order in favour of a child will, notwithstanding anything in the order, cease to have effect on the death of the person liable to make payments under the order except in relation to any arrears due under the order on the date of death (s.29(4)).

*(b) The exercise of the powers*

(i) Factors to be taken into account

It has already been noted in Chapter 11 that the basis on which the powers to order financial provision and property adjustment conferred by the 1973 Act are to be exercised was re-cast by the Matrimonial and Family Proceedings Act 1984. Section 25(1) of the 1973 Act now provides that it is the duty of the court in deciding whether to exercise those powers and, if so, in what manner, to have regard to all the circumstances of the case, first consideration being given to the welfare while a minor of any child of the family who has not attained the age of 18. Section 25(3) now provides that as regards the exercise of the powers of the court to order financial provision or property adjustment or sale in relation to a child of the family, the court shall in particular have regard to the following matters:

(a) the financial needs of the child;
(b) the income, earning capacity (if any), property and other financial resources of the child;
(c) any physical or mental disability of the child;
(d) the manner in which he was being, and in which the parties to the marriage expected him to be, educated or trained;
(e) the considerations mentioned in relation to the marriage in paragraphs (a), (b), (c) and (e) of s.25(2), i.e. (a) the income, earning capacity, property and other financial resources which each of the parties has or is likely to have in the foreseeable future, (b) the financial needs, obligations and responsibilities which each of the parties to the marriage has or is likely to have in the foreseeable future, (c) the standard of living enjoyed by the family before the breakdown of the marriage, and (e) any physical or mental disability of either of the parties to the marriage.

In *S* v *X and X (Interveners)* [1990] 2 FLR 187 Ward J held that the court was directed by s.25(2)(a) only to inquire into the means of the father and not into the means of the interveners who had been appointed testamentary guardians of the child on the death of the mother. The child had been committed to the joint custody of the interveners and the father with care and control to the interveners and access to the father. It would not be right to compel discovery against the interveners as part of an inquiry into their means though there was in any event ample evidence which indicated that they were capable of providing for the child. Ward J said (at p. 190):

"I cannot see that financial resources of the child would include any moral promise made by the interveners to maintain him. In my judgment, the scheme of the Act requires the balancing exercise to be essentially between the needs, which in this case everybody agreed would include educational needs, of the boy and the ability of the father to meet those needs, he being duty-bound to maintain his legitimate child."

(ii) Financial resources

The "financial resources" of a child include the interest of a child under a trust. The extent to which such an interest can be taken into account will depend upon the nature of the interest of the child and, in the case of an interest under a discretionary trust, upon the assessment made by the court as to what the child could reasonably expect to receive in reality. Thus in *Jones* v *Jones and Croall* [1989] 1 All ER 1121 the Court of Appeal held that while the judge had been correct to regard a trust fund as a financial resource of the children the financial provision for whom was the subject matter of the application, he had misdirected himself in simply assuming that the whole income should be available for the children. The court had "to perform a careful balancing exercise to ensure that the children's needs are met without requiring the father to pay more than he can properly afford while at the same time not placing improper pressure on the trustees to exercise their discretion in such a way that they would not otherwise have thought it right to exercise it." In performing this balancing exercise Booth J considered it helpful for the court to consider a number of matters.

First, the court must evaluate any statement made by a trustee as to the future exercise by him of his discretion under the trusts. In *Jones* v *Jones* this was made difficult by the fact that the solicitors who were the trustees for the children's fund also acted for the grandmother on her application for financial provision for the children. The discretionary trust had been established by the will of the children's mother who had died in 1987 leaving an estate worth some £17,500 which constituted the trust fund. The trustees were empowered in their discretion to pay the whole or any part of the income or capital from the trust for the benefit of either of the children until they reached the age of 18 when they became entitled to the trust fund absolutely. The trustees' stated aim was to preserve the fund until the children reached the age of 18 and not to advance funds for their maintenance unless they were compelled to do so. They had until then only advanced one modest sum of £140 to buy gifts for the children as a small consolation for the death of their mother. It was conceded, however, that despite their stated intention to preserve the trust fund, the trustees might, nevertheless, be willing to advance monies to provide things for the children which could not otherwise be afforded.

Secondly, it is necessary for the court to have regard to the nature of the trust under which the child is a beneficiary. In *Jones* v *Jones* the trust fund represented an inheritance which in the normal course of events the children would not have received until a much later stage in their lives. The family was from a modest financial background and the fund was likely to be the children's only major capital asset which, had the mother lived, would have continued to be invested in the bricks and mortar of her home yielding no income but appreciating in value with the rise in property prices. Had it not been for the mother's untimely death, there would have been no question of the children deriving any benefit from the property other than the fact that it provided a roof over their heads. The fund had not been established for the purpose of providing for the children's maintenance and education as was the case in *Lilford* v *Glynn* [1979] 1 WLR 78. In that case the father had settled £30,000 in 1969 to be used for the payment of school fees for his two daughters with the remainder to be used for the children's benefit. In 1971 it was agreed that the trustees would pay the school fees directly to the school with the husband making periodical payments for the children. In 1976, on the wife's application to vary, Payne J ordered that the husband should pay the entire school fees for the daughters then aged 13 and 15 thus leaving the trustees free to use the trust income in other ways for the benefit of the children, or, if the trustees thought fit, to accumulate it with the capital so as to benefit the children when they were older. This would avoid the complication of extracting income from the trustees towards the payment of the fees. In the Court of Appeal Orr LJ said that the court was not concerned only with the mechanism of payment of the school fees. The husband had clearly created the trust with the main object of meeting the cost of the girls' education and had provided for that purpose a sum, the income of which, together with the expenditure of a modest part of the capital in the purchase of educational annuities, may well have appeared likely to be sufficient for that purpose and probably would have been but for subsequent inflation. In these circumstances it would be unjust to the husband to place on him a primary liability to pay the fees leaving the trustees free, if they should think fit, to accumulate the income of the trust for the prospective benefit of the children after their education had been completed. To do so would defeat the object for which the trust had been created. Accordingly, in lieu of the order made by the judge the Court of Appeal accepted an undertaking from the husband that he would pay, term by term, any balance of the school fees which the trustees did not pay and would provide security for such payments and for periodical payments.

Thirdly, when the court is considering an application for financial provision by a beneficiary under a trust, it must have regard to the obligation of the person against whom an order is sought to maintain the applicant. Thus in *Jones* v *Jones* Booth J said that the court should not lose sight of the fact that the mother's death in no way altered the duty of the father to maintain the children in accordance with his means. It would be wrong to treat the trust fund which had come about as a result of the mother's death as representing something of a windfall for the father, absolving him to a great extent from the burden he would otherwise have had to bear in maintaining his children.

(iii) The appropriate standard of provision

In considering the provision appropriate for a child under the 1973 Act, the courts have proceeded on the basis that in "the vast majority of cases the financial position of a child of a subsisting marriage is simply to be afforded shelter, food and education according to the means of his parents" (*per* Bagnall J in *Harnett* v *Harnett* [1973] Fam 156 at p. 161, cited by Orr LJ in *Lilford* v *Glynn* [1979] 1 WLR 78 at p. 86). The provision called for on breakdown of marriage is therefore related to dependency and is likely to be of an income nature so that cases where capital provision will be appropriate will be rare. Section 29 of the 1973 Act also contains restrictions on the powers of the court to order provision for a child beyond the age of 18. Although provision may be made for a child who has attained the age of 18, it will again be related to dependency. Thus provision may be ordered while full-time education or training is continuing beyond the age of 18, as in *Downing* v *Downing* [1976] Fam 228 where a university student was given leave to intervene in her parents' divorce proceedings. Provision may also be made for a child who has attained the age of 18, and who is not in full-time education or training, if there are "special circumstances" which justify the making of the order. This would seem to cover the position of a child suffering from a mental or physical disability. (See the statements in *Chamberlain* v *Chamberlain* [1973] 1 WLR 1557 at p. 1564 and *Lilford* v *Glynn* [1979] 1 WLR 78 at p. 84.)

The reformulation of s.25 of the 1973 Act by the Family and Matrimonial Proceedings Act 1984 requires the court to have regard to all the circumstances of the case, first consideration being given to the welfare while a minor of any child of the family who has not attained the age of 18. It has already been noted that this provision, which refers only to a "child of the family", requires first consideration to be given to the welfare of a child only while he or she is a minor. It does not appear to have made any change in the general attitude of the courts to financial provision for children. In the subsequent case of *Kiely* v *Kiely* [1988] 1 FLR 248 at p. 252 Booth J agreed that "the statutory scheme is to enable the court to make proper financial provision for children as children or dependants".

In any event, in exercising its powers to order financial provision and property adjustment as between the parties to a marriage, a dominating factor for the court from the beginning has been the need to secure housing for the children while they are dependent. This has frequently affected the allocation of capital between the parents and even more frequently involved some restriction on the enjoyment of their capital. However, the general view has been that there is no further obligation on a parent to make capital provision for a child who is capable of self-support. Thus in *Chamberlain* v *Chamberlain* [1973] 1 WLR 1557 the judge had ordered that the husband's interest in the matrimonial home should be extinguished and the house settled on the wife for life with remainder to the children absolutely. In the Court of Appeal Scarman LJ said (at p. 1564):

"... I think that the judge erred in settling the house so that the beneficial interest at the end of the day became that of the children in equal shares ... There are no circumstances here to suggest that any of the children had special circumstances which required them to make demands on their parents after the conclusion of their full time education. The capital asset, the house, was acquired by the work and by the resources of their parents, and provided that the parents meet their responsibilities to their children as long as the children are dependent on them, this seems to me an asset which should then revert to the parents."

The court made a Mesher order providing that the house should not be sold until the three children had finished their education. (See Chapter 12 for the form of a Mesher order.) The same appproach was adopted in *Lilford* v *Glynn* [1979] 1 WLR 78 at p. 86 where the father, who was a millionaire, had, as noted above, already created a settlement for the children's education. The Court of Appeal held that although the court had power under s.24(1)(b) to order a settlement which by its nature would continue to endure for the benefit of a child after the child had attained the age of 18, the court, having regard to s.25(2) (as it then was) should not regard any father, however rich he might be, as having financial responsibilities and obligations to provide a settlement for a child who was under no disability and whose maintenance and education were secure.

In *Kiely* v *Kiely* [1988] 1 FLR 248 the Court of Appeal set aside an order that the husband pay a lump sum of £4,000 to each of his two children when the younger child reached 18 (in about 6 years' time) or on the sale of the matrimonial home, whichever was the sooner. There was no evidence of need on the part of the children, or special circumstances which called for capital provision to be made for their benefit. Moreover, the husband did not have the means to provide the lump sums other than by the sale of the property which was the children's home. The objective of the order had in reality been to recompense the wife for the husband's failure to comply with the periodical payments order, she being unable to seek further capital for herself. In *Draskovic* v *Draskovic* (1981) 11 Fam Law 87 the husband proposed that his interest in the former matrimonial home should be given to his children. If this had been done the charge of the Law Society for costs would have been defeated and Balcombe J held that not only was there no special reason for making provision for the children, but that in the circumstances it would be against the public interest to accede to the proposal. (For the operation of the charge see Chapter 13.)

Modest capital provision for children was upheld by the Court of Appeal in *Griffiths* v *Griffiths* [1984] Fam 70. The judge had ordered the husband to pay to his former wife £2,750 as a lump sum for the benefit of the two children of the family. Dismissing the husband's appeal, Dunn LJ noted that in *Chamberlain* v *Chamberlain* Scarman LJ had added the important proviso that the parents meet their responsibilities to their children. In *Griffiths* the husband had not met his responsibilities towards the children in that he had neither paid nor offered to pay any sum at all to the children or for their benefit since he left the matrimonial home. The amount ordered represented part of the husband's half share of the proceeds of sale of the former matrimonial home. The husband had already spent a good deal of the remainder of his share on a car and on various items for his new home with another woman in her council house. He was receiving unemployment and supplementary benefit. It was very unlikely that the order would have been upheld if the husband had intended to use the money for the purpose of providing accommodation for himself and his partner, but this was not the case. Watkins LJ said (at p. 78) that, generally speaking, the moneys which are available as a result of the breakdown are used as far as possible satisfactorily to create decent living conditions in both new homes, for the benefit not only of the parties who have joined together, but for all the children affected by the upheaval. It was clear that in the absence of a lump sum payment the children would have been unlikely to derive any financial benefit from their father. The position was similar in this respect to the position in *Kiely* v *Kiely*. However, in that case payment could only have been made by a sale of the former matrimonial home in which the children lived. In *Griffiths* the former home had been sold and the children were living elsewhere with their mother. Where there is capital which is not needed for the provision of accommodation there would seem to be a strong argument for considering a modest lump sum payment to make up for a parent's failure to provide periodic maintenance, but it should be related to some specific need or be capable of producing a significant income by way of supplement.

In *Griffiths* the court questioned the advisability of an order for payment of the lump sum to the mother in the hope that she would faithfully discharge the kind of trust thereby imposed upon her to use the whole of it sensibly for the purpose of maintaining the children of the broken marriage. Watkins LJ said that he would prefer that any lump sum which is ordered to be paid by a father to a mother for this purpose should be secured in some way so that the income from it will be used for the maintenance of the children and the capital preserved so that it may eventually revert to the father's use or be given to the children when they reach majority or thereabouts. However, the sum involved in that case was so small that the income it would produce would be wholly inadequate properly to maintain two children, and therefore the order was allowed to stand.

In *Bateman* v *Bateman* [1979] Fam 25, Purchas J made an order that the former matrimonial home should be held on trust for sale but the sale postponed until the wife ceased to use the home as her main place of residence, or remarried or died, whichever was the earliest event, and thereafter the house was to be sold and the proceeds distributed as to 25 per cent to the wife and 75 per cent equally amongst the surviving children or their issue. The husband had a home elsewhere and laid no claim to the matrimonial home though he had actually agreed that the home should be settled on the wife for life or until remarriage with the property passing to the children absolutely thereafter.

In determining the provision appropriate for a spouse it was stated by the Court of Appeal in *Page* v *Page* (1981) 2 FLR 198 that it was not relevant to take into account his or her wish to be put in a position to make provision by will for adult children who are in no way dependent on their parents. (See also *S* v *S* unreported, 16 July 1980.) However, a different view may be taken where payments have been made to children during the marriage with the approval of the other spouse. Moreover, it is a matter for the applicant spouse to decide how she should dispose of property awarded to her on the basis either of her needs or her contribution to the marriage (see *Vicary* v *Vicary* [1992] 2 FLR 271; *Smith* v *Smith* [1991] 2 All ER 306; *Barber* v *Barber* [1993] FCR 65).

### 3. Orders under the Domestic Proceedings and Magistrates' Courts Act 1978

*(a) Orders under s. 2*

(i) The court's powers
Where one party to a marriage applies to a magistrates' court and satisfies the court of any of the grounds in s.1 of the 1978 Act the court may, under s.2, make an order for periodical payments and/or an order for a lump sum payment to the applicant for the benefit of a child of the family to whom the application relates, or to such child. (See Part 6 below for the effect of the Child Support Act 1991 in relation to periodical payments, and Chapter 16 for a consideration of the position where the respondent is resident outside England and Wales.)

Generally, no order for periodical payments or for payment of a lump sum can be made in favour of a child who has attained the age of 18 (s.5(1)). The term specified in an order for periodical payments in favour of a child may begin with the date of the making of an application for the order in question or any later date, and must not generally extend beyond the date when the child will attain the age of 18 (s.5(2)). Indeed in the first instance the term specified must not extend beyond the date of the birthday of the child next following his attaining the upper limit of the compulsory school age unless the court thinks it right in the circumstances of the case to specify a later date. However, the court may make an order for periodical payments or an order for a lump sum payment in favour of a child who has attained the age of 18, and may include in an order for periodical payments in favour of a child who has not attained that age, a provision extending the term for which the payments are to be made beyond the date when the child will attain that age, if it appears to the court:

(a) that the child is, or will be, or if such an order or provision were made would be, receiving instruction at an educational establishment or undergoing training for a trade, profession or vocation, whether or not he is also, or will also be, in gainful employment; or

(b) that there are special circumstances which justify the making of the order or provision.

(s.5(3)).

There is thus no objection to the term extending beyond the date when the child attains 21. A periodical payments order in favour of a child will, notwithstanding anything in the order, cease to have effect on the death of the person liable to make payments under the order (s.5(4)).

Where an order for periodical payments to or in respect of a child ceases to have effect on the date on which the child attains the age of 16 or at any time after that date but before or on the date on which he attains the age of 18, then the court has power to revive that order if application is made by the child before he attains the age of 21. The order may be revived from such date as the court may specify, not being earlier than the date of the making of the application (s.20(1)).

(ii) Matters to which the court is required to have regard

Where an application is made for an order under s.2, the court in deciding whether to exercise its powers to order financial provision under that section and, if so, in what manner, is required to have regard to all the circumstances of the case, first consideration being given to the welfare while a minor of any child of the family who has not attained the age of 18 (DPMCA 1978, s.3(1) as amended by s.9 of the Matrimonial and Family Proceedings Act 1984). In relation to the exercise of its powers to order periodical payments or a lump sum payment to or for the benefit of a child of the family the court is required in particular to have regard to the following matters:

(a) the financial needs of the child;

(b) the income, earning capacity (if any), property and other financial resources of the child;

(c) any physical or mental disability of the child;

(d) the standard of living enjoyed by the family before the occurrence of the conduct which is alleged as the ground of the application;

(e) the manner in which the child was being and in which the parties to the marriage expected him to be educated or trained;

(f) the matters mentioned in relation to the parties to the marriage in paragraphs (a) and (b) of s.3(2), i.e. the income, earning capacity, property and other financial resources of each of the parties to the marriage and the financial needs, obligations and responsibilities of such parties: see further Chapters 11 and 16.

(s.3(3)).

In deciding whether to exercise its powers in favour of a child of the family who is not the child of the respondent and if so, in what manner, the court is required to have regard to the matters set out in s.3(4). (See Part 5 of this chapter.)

*(b) Orders under s.6*
Under s.6 of the Act a magistrates' court may on the application of one party to a marriage, and subject to certain conditions, order the other party to make such periodical payments or lump sum payment as he or she has agreed to make to the applicant for the benefit of a child of the family, or to that child. (See Chapter 16 and Part 7 of this chapter for the effect of the Child Support Act 1991.)

Where an application is made by a party to a marriage for an order under s.6 then, if there is a child of the family who is under the age of 18, the court must not dismiss or make a final order on the application until it has decided whether to exercise any of its powers under the Children Act 1989 with respect to the child (s.8 as amended by the Children Act 1989, Schedule 13, para 36. For the powers of the court to order financial provision under the Children Act 1989, see Part 4 below).

*(c) Orders under s.7*
Under s.7 of the Act, where the parties to a marriage have been living apart for a continuous period exceeding three months, a magistrates' court may, on the application of one party, and subject to certain limitations, order the other party to make periodical payments to the applicant for the benefit of a child of the family or to that child on the basis of payments made by the respondent party during the period of separation. (See Chapter 16 and Part 6 of this chapter for the effect of the Child Support Act 1991.)

Where an application is made by a party to a marriage for an order under s.7 then, if there is a child of the family who is under the age of 18, the court must not dismiss or make a final order on the application until it has decided whether to exercise any of its powers under the Children Act with respect to the child (s.8 as amended by the Children Act 1989, Schedule 13, para. 36. For the powers of the court to order financial provision under the Children Act 1989, see below).

## 4. Orders under the Children Act 1989

*(a) The scope of the court's powers*
The powers of the court to order financial relief with respect to children are set out in Schedule 1 of the Act (s.15(1)). The Schedule distinguishes between two categories of application. First, it provides for an application to be made by a parent or guardian of a child, or by any person in whose favour a residence order is in force with respect to a child. Such an application may result in an order or orders being made against a parent or against both parents of the child. Secondly, the Schedule provides for an application to be made by a person who has attained the age of 18 for an order for financial relief against either or both of his parents. (Reference should be made to Part 6 for the effect of the Child Support Act 1991.)

*(b) Applications by parents, guardians etc*

(i) Orders the court may make

On an application to the High Court or to a county court by a parent or guardian of a child, or by a person in whose favour a residence order is in force with respect to a child, the court may make one or more of the following orders (para. 1(1) and (2)):

(a) an order requiring either or both parents of a child -
   (i)  to make to the applicant for the benefit of the child; or
   (ii) to make to the child himself,
   such periodical payments, for such term, as may be specified in the order;
(b) an order requiring either or both parents of a child -
   (i)  to secure to the applicant for the benefit of the child; or
   (ii) to secure to the child himself,
   such periodical payments, for such term, as may be specified in the order;
(c) an order requiring either or both parents of a child -
   (i)  to pay to the applicant for the benefit of the child; or
   (ii) to pay to the child himself,
   such lump sum as may be specified in the order;
(d) an order requiring a settlement to be made for the benefit of the child, and to the satisfaction of the court, of property -
   (i)  to which either parent is entitled (either in possession or in reversion); and
   (ii) which is specified in the order;
(e) an order requiring either or both parents of a child -
   (i)  to transfer to the applicant, for the benefit of the child; or
   (ii) to transfer to the child himself,
   such property to which the parent is, or the parents are, entitled (either in possession or in reversion) as may be specified in the order.

The words seem wide enough to enable orders to be made in respect of children born before the Act came into force as well as in respect of children born later. This view was taken by Ward J in *H* v *O* [1992] 1 FLR 282 in respect of s.11B of the Guardianship of Minors Act 1971 (inserted by the Family Law Reform Act 1987) which has now been superseded by the provisions under consideration. In *K* v *K* *(Minors: Property Transfer)* [1992] 1 WLR 530, the Court of Appeal considered the scope of the power to make an order requiring either parent to transfer property to the other parent for the benefit of the child, or to the child, then contained in s.11B of the Guardianship of Minors Act 1971. Nourse LJ rejected the argument that "benefit" meant only financial benefit and was not intended to provide merely a welfare benefit. In that case the parents of four young children were unmarried and were the joint tenants of a four-bedroomed council house. Custody, care and control had been given to the mother but the father remained in the home, an ouster injunction having been refused. The Court of Appeal held that the power to order a transfer of property could, in appropriate circumstances, be used to oust one parent from the family home by transferring his rights as tenant to the other parent. However, a retrial was ordered as the judge had based his order solely on what was best for the children and had failed to carry out the balancing exercise required by s.12A of the 1971 Act. (Paragraph 4 of Schedule 1 of the Children Act 1989 is in similar terms.)

On an application to a magistrates' court the powers are more limited. A magistrates' court may only make one or both of the orders in (a) and (b) above.

The above powers may be exercised at any time (para. 1(3)). An order for periodical payments may be varied or discharged by a subsequent order made on the application of any person by or to whom payments were required to be made under the previous order (para. 1(4)). Where the court has made an order under the above powers, it may at any time make a further order for periodical payments, secured periodical payments, or for a lump sum payment with respect to the child concerned. It may not make more than one order for a settlement of property or for a transfer of property against the same person in respect of the same child (para. 1(5)).

The court may also exercise any of the powers on making, varying or discharging a residence order even though no application has been made to it under Schedule 1 (para. 1(6)).

(ii) The applicants
An application for a financial provision order or for a property adjustment order can be made by a parent or guardian of a child or by a person in whose favour a residence order is in force. A "residence order" is an order settling the arrangements to be made as to the person with whom a child is to live (s.8(1)). Under s.10 of the Act the court may make a residence order in any family proceedings in which a question arises with respect to the welfare of any child either on an application for such an order or if it considers that such an order should be made even though no such application has been made.

Application for a residence order may be made without leave not only by a parent or guardian of a child but also by:
(a)  any party to a marriage (whether or not subsisting) in relation to whom the child is a child of the family;
(b)  any person with whom the child has lived for a period of three years;
(c)  any person who -
    (i)  in any case where a residence order is in force with respect to the child, has the consent of each of the persons in whose favour the order was made;
    (ii)  in any case where the child is in the care of a local authority, has the consent of that authority, or
    (iii) in any other case, has the consent of each of those (if any) who have parental responsibility for the child.
Application can be made by any other person with leave of the court (s.10(1)).

"Family proceedings" for this purpose means any proceedings under (a) the inherent jurisdiction of the High Court in relation to children and (b) the Matrimonial Causes Act 1973, the Domestic Violence and Matrimonial Proceedings Act 1976, the Adoption Act 1976, the Domestic Proceedings and Magistrates' Courts Act 1978, ss.1 and 9 of the Matrimonial Homes Act 1983, Part III of the Matrimonial and Family Proceedings Act 1984 and Parts I, II and IV of the Children Act 1989.

(iii) Child resident outside England and Wales
Where one parent of a child under the age of 18 lives in England and Wales an order for periodical payments or secured periodical payments may be made against that parent in respect of that child even though the child lives outside England and Wales with (a) another parent, or (b) a guardian, or (c) a person in whose favour a residence order is in force with respect to the child (para. 14).

*(c) Applications by children over 18*
An application can be made by a person who has attained the age of 18 for an order for financial provision against either or both of his parents (para.19). On such an application the court may make one or both of the following orders:
  (a) an order requiring either or both of the applicant's parents to pay to the applicant such periodical payments, for such term, as may be specified in the order;
  (b) an order requiring either or both of the applicant's parents to pay to the applicant such lump sum as may be specified in the order.
An order can be made only if it appears to the court:
  (a) that the applicant is, or will be or (if an order were made) would be receiving instruction at an educational establishment or undergoing training for a trade, profession or vocation, whether or not while in gainful employment; or
  (b) that there are special circumstances which justify the making of an order.
An application cannot be made by a person under this provision if, immediately before he reached the age of 16, a periodical payments order under the Act (or certain other specified provisions) was in force with respect to him. The specified provisions are s.6(3) of the Family Law Reform Act 1969, s.23 or 27 of the Matrimonial Causes Act 1973, or Part I of the Domestic Proceedings and Magistrates' Courts Act 1978.

The powers of the court to order financial provision on the application of a person over the age of 18 are exercisable at any time, but no order can be made at a time when the parents of the applicant are living with each other in the same household. An order for periodical payments may be varied or discharged by a subsequent order made on the application of any person by or to whom payments were required to be made under the previous order. Where the court makes an order in favour of a person over the age of 18 under this provision, it may from time to time - while that order remains in force - make a further such order.

*(d) Matters to which the court is to have regard in making orders*
In deciding whether to exercise its powers to order financial provision and property adjustment under the Act, and if so in what manner, the court must have regard to all the circumstances including -
  (a) the income, earning capacity, property and other financial resources which the person against whom the order may be made, the applicant for the order and any other person in whose favour the court proposes to make the order, has or is likely to have in the foreseeable future;
  (b) the financial needs, obligations and responsibilities which each such person has or is likely to have in the foreseeable future;
  (c) the financial needs of the child;

(d) the income, earning capacity (if any), property and other financial resources of the child;
(e) any physical or mental disability of the child;
(f) the manner in which the child was being, or was expected to be, educated or trained.

(para. 4).

The balancing exercise which this requires means that an order must not be based solely on what is best for the children and without regard to the position of the parent against whom it is made. (See *K* v *K (Minors: Property Transfer)* [1992] 1 WLR 530 in relation to the provision formerly in s.21A of the Guardianship of Minors Act 1971.)

In deciding whether to exercise its powers to order financial provision or property adjustment against a person who is not the mother or father of the child, and if so in what manner, the court must in addition have regard to:

(a) whether that person had assumed responsibility for the maintenance of the child and, if so, the extent to which and the basis on which he assumed that responsibility and the length of the period during which he met that responsibility;
(b) whether he did so knowing that the child was not his child;
(c) the liability of any other person to maintain the child.

Where the court makes an order against a person who is not the father of the child, it must record in the order that the order is made on the basis that the person against whom the order is made is not the child's father (para. 4). The position is now consistent with that under the Matrimonial Causes Act 1973 and the Domestic Proceedings and Magistrates' Courts Act 1978.

*(e) Duration of orders for periodical payments*
The term specified in an order for periodical payments or secured periodical payments made under para 1, i.e. on an application by a parent or guardian or person in whose favour a residence order is in force with respect to the child, may begin with the date of the making of the application for the order in question or any later date. It must not in the first instance extend beyond the child's seventeenth birthday unless the court thinks it right in the circumstances of the case to specify a later date. It must not in any event extend beyond the child's eighteenth birthday unless it appears to the court that:

(a) the child is, or will be or (if an order were made extending beyond that age) would be receiving instruction at an educational establishment or undergoing training for a trade, profession or vocation, whether or not while in gainful employment; or
(b) there are special circumstances which justify the making of an order extending beyond the age of 18. (para. 3).

A periodical payments order in favour of a child will, notwithstanding anything in the order, cease to have effect on the death of the person liable to make payments under the order. Where an order is made requiring periodical payments to be made or secured to the parent of a child, the order will cease to have effect if (a) any parent making or securing the payments, and (b) any parent to whom the payments are made or secured, live together for a period of more than six months (para. 3(4)).

## (f) Provisions relating to lump sum payments

An order for payment of a lump sum made under para. 1, i.e. on the application of a parent or guardian or person in whose favour a residence order is in force with respect to the child, may be made for the purpose of enabling any liabilities or expenses (a) incurred in connection with the birth of the child or in maintaining the child, and (b) reasonably incurred before the making of the order, to be met (para. 5).

The amount of any lump sum required to be paid by an order made by a magistrates' court cannot exceed £1,000 or such larger amount as the Secretary of State may from time to time by order fix for this purpose.

An order for the payment of a lump sum may provide for the payment of that sum by instalments. Where the court provides for the payment of a lump sum by instalments the court, on an application made either by the person liable to pay or the person entitled to receive that sum, has power to vary that order in some respects. The court may vary (a) the number of instalments payable; (b) the amount of any instalment payable; or (c) the date on which any instalment becomes payable. It cannot vary the total amount of the lump sum. It has already been noted that a court cannot make more than one lump sum order under para. 1 against the same person in respect of the same child.

## (g) Variation of orders for periodical payments

An order for periodical payments may be varied or discharged by a subsequent order made on the application of any person by or to whom payments were required to be made under the previous order (paras. 1(4) and 2(5)). In exercising its powers to vary or discharge an order for periodical payments or secured periodical payments the court must have regard to all the circumstances of the case, including any change in any of the matters to which the court was required to have regard when making the order (para. 6). The power of variation includes the power to suspend any provision of the order temporarily and to revive any provision so suspended. Where the court varies the payments required to be made under the order, it may provide that the payments as so varied shall be made from such date as the court may specify, not being earlier than the date of the making of the application.

An application for the variation of an order for the making or securing of periodical payments to or for the benefit of a child under the age of 18 may be made by the child himself if the child has reached the age of 16. Where an order ceases to have effect on the date on which the child reaches the age of 16, or at any time after that date but before or on the date on which he reaches the age of 18, the child may apply to the court which made the order for an order for its revival. On such an application the court may revive the order from such date as it may specify (not being earlier than the date of the making of the application) if it appears to the court that -

(a) the child is, will be or, if an order were made, would be receiving instruction at an educational establishment or undergoing training for a trade, profession or vocation, whether or not while in gainful employment; or

(b) there are special circumstances which justify the making of an order for revival.

Any order which is revived may be varied or discharged on the application of any person by or to whom payments are required to be made under the revived order.

An order for the making or securing of periodical payments in favour of a child under the age of 18 may be varied or discharged, after the death of either parent, on the application of a guardian of the child concerned (para. 6). Where the parent liable to make payments under a secured periodical payments order has died, an application for the variation or discharge of the order may also be made by the personal representatives of the deceased parent (para. 7). No application for the variation of such an order can be made after the end of the period of six months from the date on which representation in regard to the estate of that parent is first taken out, except with the permission of the court. Where an application to vary an order for secured periodical payments is made after the death of the parent liable to make payments under the order, the circumstances to which the court is required to have regard as mentioned above also include the changed circumstances resulting from the death of the parent.

*(h) Interim orders*

The court may, at any time before it disposes of an application for financial relief, make an interim order -
(a) requiring either or both parents to make such periodical payments, at such times and for such term as the court thinks fit; and
(b) giving any direction which the court thinks fit.

An interim order may provide for payments to be made from such date as the court may specify, not being earlier than the date of the making of the application for financial relief. An interim order ceases to have effect when the application is disposed of or, if earlier, on the date specified in the order. If a date has been specified in the order then this may be varied by substituting a later date (para. 9).

*(i) Revocation of orders under other Acts*

Where a residence order is made with respect to a child at any time when there is in force a financial relief order under any Act other than the Children Act 1989 and requiring a person to contribute to the child's maintenance, the court may make an order revoking the financial relief order, or varying it by altering the amount of any sum payable under that order or by substituting the applicant for the person to whom any such sum is otherwise payable under that order (para. 8). Such an order may be made on the application of -
(a) any person required by the financial relief order to contribute to the child's maintenance; or
(b) any person in whose favour a residence order with respect to the child is in force.

## 5. The definition of a "child of the family"

*(a) The statutory provisions*

Under the Matrimonial Causes Act 1973 and the Domestic Proceedings and Magistrates' Courts Act 1978 the relevant court has power to order provision for "any child of the family". The concept of a "child of the family" is also relevant under the Children Act 1989. This expression includes not only the children of both spouses, i.e. the children of the marriage, but also certain other children who are part of the family unit, and for whom provision may therefore be necessary when that family unit breaks down. This means that there may be some person other than the spouses who is also liable to maintain a particular child who is a child of the family. Thus, for example, where the former marriage of a spouse has been dissolved his or her former spouse may be liable to maintain a child of the former marriage, while his or her present spouse is also liable to maintain the child as a child of the family which came into existence on the second marriage (see *Newman* v *Newman* [1971] P 43). Similarly, not only will the father of a child born outside marriage generally be liable to maintain the child, but so may a person who subsequently marries the mother of the child if the child becomes a child of the family which comes into existence on that marriage (see *Snow* v *Snow* [1972] Fam 74). In these circumstances it will be necessary for a court to balance the responsibilities of the various people liable to maintain a particular child, having regard now to the effect of the Child Support Act 1991. That Act, being concerned with the obligation of a parent to maintain his or her child, is narrower in its application than the Acts which apply to "children of the family".

Until the relevant parts of the Domestic Proceedings and Magistrates' Courts Act 1978 came into force on 1 February 1981, the expression "child of the family" had a different meaning for the purposes of the matrimonial jurisdiction of the magistrates' court from that which applied to all proceedings under the 1973 Act. The 1978 Act brought the meaning of the expression in the magistrates'jurisdiction into line with that in the 1973 Act and it has the same meaning in the Children Act 1989 (MCA 1973, s.52(1); DP & MCA 1978, s.88(1); CA 1989, s.105(1)).

The expression "child of the family" in relation to the parties to a marriage, now means:

(i) a child of both those parties; and

(ii) any other child ... who has been treated by both those parties as a child of their family.

The first limb of this definition will include all children of both parties to a marriage, whether or not born during the marriage, and including adopted children (Adoption Act 1976, s.39(1)). A child may be a "child of the family" under the second limb even though he or she is not the natural or adopted child of either spouse. In that event the crucial question to be determined by the court is whether the child has been treated by both spouses as a child of the family. The "treatment" test was intended to avoid the difficulties arising from the test of acceptance which applied in the divorce courts until 1971 and in the magistrates' courts until 1981. The statutory provisions, however, differ slightly in wording in relation to an exclusion from the second limb. The 1973 Act excludes "a child who has been boarded-out with [the] parties by a local authority or voluntary organisation". The 1978 Act refers to a child who is being so boarded-out with the parties. The latter definition was preferred by the Law Commission in its Review of Child Law (Law Com. No. 172, para. 4.46) as it saw no reason to exclude children for whom the local authority or voluntary organisation is no longer responsible. The Children Act 1989 excludes a child who is placed with those parties as foster parents by a local authority or voluntary organisation.

Before a child can be held to have been treated as "a child of the family" in relation to the parties to a marriage, there are two requirements that must be satisfied. First, there must be a "family". Secondly, there must be behaviour towards the child which amounts to treating the child as part of that family.

*(b) The statutory requirements*

(i) A "family"
There is no family for this purpose until marriage takes place. It will be very unusual for no family to come into existence on marriage, but this might be so where the wife was pregnant at the time of the marriage and the parties then separated immediately without ever living together. Sometimes the family may have existed only briefly. Thus in *W* v *W (Child of the Family)* [1984] FLR 796 the husband married the wife when she was pregnant by another man. The husband was aware that he was not the father of the expected child but decided to accept it. He was a serving soldier who obtained leave to visit his wife in hospital when the child was born some six weeks after the marriage, but then returned to his unit. A month or so later he spent two weeks' leave with his wife and the baby in her parents' home when he treated the child as his own. The marriage effectively ended when he returned to his unit. The Court of Appeal found there was evidence that a family, "although not much of one", came into existence at the date of the marriage.

Although a family may have come into existence on marriage this does not mean that the "family" subsists until the marriage is dissolved. Thus in *M* v *M* (1981) 2 FLR 39 it was accepted that the husband was not the father of a child born to the wife in 1972 after the parties had separated in April 1971. Between 1971 and the divorce proceedings in 1977 they had led entirely separate lives and though the husband had visited his wife from time to time there had been no resumption of cohabitation. The Court of Appeal held that there could not be said to have been at any time during the child's life a family, comprising the husband and wife, of which he could be treated as a part.

(ii) "Treated" as a child of the family
Whether or not a party has "treated" a child as a "child of the family" is a question of fact. This is to be judged objectively by looking at and carefully considering what the party did and how he behaved towards the child (*Teeling* v *Teeling* [1984] FLR 808). In *M* v *M* (1981) 2 FLR 39 at p. 45 Ormrod LJ said that "the court should look at this question ... broadly and answer it broadly as far as possible, trying to reach the sort of conclusion that any ordinary sensible citizen would reach if he asked the question." In that case the husband had, while living apart from his wife, taken part in a pretence for her benefit by behaving in the presence of the family as if the child was his own natural child rather than a "child of the family". Moreover, Walton J said that, while it may be difficult to give a precise meaning to "treated" for this purpose, it did suggest that "it is more than what happens on a few isolated occasions" (*ibid.* at p. 46. See also Ormrod LJ in *D* v *D* (1981) 2 FLR 93 at p. 96).

The need for caution, particularly in relation to a step-parent who has married a non-custodial parent, was emphasised by Orr LJ in *D* v *D* (1981) 2 FLR 93 at p. 96. He said that it would "be very unfortunate if by the application of some principle akin to estoppel a situation was reached in which a mother's second husband by consenting to generous visits of the child to the mother, would be held to have accepted (*sic*) the position of the child being a child of the family. That would ... give rise to an unhappy situation in which a husband who has married a wife with a child by a previous marriage might be tempted to restrict access to the mother in order to avoid any possibility of the child being held to be a child of the family". In that case the child had lived with her maternal grandparents for many years, but made fairly frequent visits to the home of her mother and stepfather some six miles away. The Court of Appeal found that it was the grandparents' home which was essentially the child's home at all times. She was essentially a visitor to the mother's home and it was not analogous to the case of a child at boarding school who is unquestionably based with his or her mother, coming home for all the holidays and regarding that as his or her home. There was plainly in existence another household in which a relationship with the child of a parental character existed.

Where a child has lived in the same household as a spouse who is not his or her natural parent it will now be very difficult for that spouse to show that he or she has not treated the child as a "child of the family". In *Carron* v *Carron* [1984] FLR 805 when the parties married, the wife brought two children aged 8 and 2, of whom the husband was not the father, to live with them in the matrimonial home. Ormrod LJ said (at p. 805): "You cannot live with children of this age for four years without treating them as children of the family". In *Teeling* v *Teeling* [1984] FLR 808 a child, of whom the husband was not the father, was born to the wife during a period of separation. Soon after the birth the wife returned with the baby to the matrimonial home where she lived with the husband and two daughters of the marriage for some six months. Ormrod LJ said that *de facto* the baby had been treated as a child of the family and it did not matter that the wife had said that the husband was not to regard the child as his.

In *W (RJ)* v *W (SJ)* [1972] Fam 152 it was not disputed that the two children concerned had been treated by the husband as his own up until the time when he discovered his wife's adultery. Park J distinguished his own decision in *R* v *R* [1968] P 414 where he had held that under the previous legislation there could be no "acceptance" of a child without the knowledge of the material facts relating to paternity. Under the present legislation the husband's lack of knowledge relating to the paternity of the children was immaterial in deciding whether he had "treated" them as children of the family. However, before a party can be said to have "treated" a child as a child of the family there must be some behaviour on his part towards the child. In *A* v *A* [1974] Fam 6 it was held that it is only possible to behave towards a child after the child has been born and is capable of being perceived by one or more of the senses. In that case the husband, a soldier, believed that he was the father of a child that his wife was expecting when he married her. A week after the marriage he returned to his unit in Germany and when the child was subsequently born it was clear from the pigmentation of its skin that the husband was not the father. The husband never resumed cohabitation with the wife and took no interest in the child. It was held that he had not treated the child as a child of the family.

This interpretation has been criticised as being extremely narrow and capable of causing hardship in a case where the husband had been aware all along that he was not the father of the child that his wife was expecting (Bromley & Lowe, *Family Law* 8th ed. p. 369). This was the position in *Caller* v *Caller* [1968] P 39 where the husband, who had married the wife when she was pregnant and deserted her three weeks before the child was born, was held, under the previous legislation, to have "accepted" that child as a child of the family. This was distinguished in *A* v *A* [1974] Fam 6 at p. 15 by Bagnall J who considered that his decision went a long way to eliminate the hardship that could arise from the decision in *W (RJ)* v *W (SJ)* [1972] Fam 152. His decision would mean that before deciding whether to treat any particular child as a child of the family the man will be able to ascertain two facts which he may regard as crucial in making his decision. He will be able to see the child, and in particular the pigmentation of its skin, and he will know the precise date on which the child was born.

*(c) The consequences of a child being a child of the family*
The fact that a child is held to be a "child of the family" does not necessarily mean that a non-parent spouse will be ordered to make financial provision for the child. It is provided that the High Court or a county court in deciding whether to exercise its powers to order financial provision or an adjustment of property rights under the 1973 Act, and a magistrates' court in deciding whether to exercise its powers to order financial provision under the 1978 Act, against a party to a marriage in favour of a child of the family who is not the child of that party and, if so, in what manner, must have regard (among the circumstances of the case) to:
  (a) whether that party had assumed responsibility for the child's maintenance and, if so, the extent to which, and the basis upon which, that party assumed such responsibility and the length of time for which that party discharged such responsibility;
  (b) whether in assuming and discharging such responsibility that party did so knowing that the child was not his or her own;
  (c) the liability of any other person to maintain the child.
(MCA 1973, s.25(4); DP & MCA 1978, s.3(3)). The Children Act 1989 (Schedule 1, para. 4(2)) also provides that a court in deciding whether to exercise its powers to order financial relief against a person who is not the father or mother of the child concerned, and if so in what manner, must have regard to the same factors.

In *Teeling* v *Teeling* [1984] FLR 808 at p. 810 Ormrod LJ said that if ever a case was *de minimis* so far as the assumption of any responsibility by a husband for the child was concerned, it was that case. It was clear that no court applying its mind to paragraph (a) could come to any other conclusion than that the husband had assumed minimal responsibility in respect of the child. In the circumstances, he emphasised that there was no point in fighting the issue as to whether the child had been treated as a child of the family.

The liability of another person to maintain a child is not confined to liability under a judgment or order, but extends to any liability enforceable at law. If an order has been made, then the liability is *prima facie* the amount of the order subject, if the order has been made some time previously, to the liability of the order to be varied. If no order has been made, the liability is that amount of maintenance which would be ordered if proceedings in a proper form were taken to enforce the liability (*per* Bagnall J in *Snow* v *Snow* [1972] Fam 74 at p. 91). It is not enough that there is someone else liable to maintain the child, and regard must be had to the capacity of that person to maintain the child (*Snow* v *Snow* [1972] Fam 74 *per* Lord Simon of Glaisdale at p. 101 and *per* Edmund Davies LJ at p. 118). In *Carron* v *Carron* [1984] FLR 805 at p. 806 Ormrod LJ emphasised that there was no reason why two maintenance orders against different persons should not be in existence simultaneously in respect of the same child.

## 6. The Child Support Act 1991

### (a) The operation of the Act

The background to the Act has been considered in Part 1(*c*) of this chapter and in Chapter 1. The system introduced by the Act will not be fully in place for several years. While the majority of child maintenance cases will eventually be dealt with by the Child Support Agency provided for by the Act, it would not have been possible for it to take on all the potential cases - estimated at around two million - all at once.

The assessment of maintenance under the Act commenced on 5 April 1993. However, during a transitional period beginning with 5 April 1993 and ending with 6 April 1997 no application under s.4 of the Act for child support maintenance in relation to a qualifying child may be made where:

(a) there is in force a maintenance order or a maintenance agreement in respect of a qualifying child and the absent parent, or there is pending before any court an application for such a maintenance order; or

(b) benefit is being paid to a parent of that child.

This restriction is gradually removed on a phased basis during that part of the transitional period beginning with 8 April 1996. (For further details see the Child Support Act 1991 (Commencement No. 3 and Transitional Provisions) Order 1992, SI 1992 No. 2644.)

The Act provides for the appointment of child support officers who are entrusted with the task of making maintenance assessments under the Act (s.13).

The relationship between the new machinery when it is fully operational and the courts is considered in (*k*) below.

It is also important to note that, as was acknowledged by the Lord Chancellor, the Act contains "a rather larger than usual number of regulation - making powers" (HL Debates, Vol. 526, col. 778). Thus while the principles and the intention of the scheme are set out in the Act, detailed provisions are left to be dealt with by regulations to be made by the Secretary of State.

### (b) The duty to maintain

The Act imposes on each parent of a qualifying child a responsibility for maintaining him (s.1(1)).

A child is a "qualifying child" for this purpose if (a) one of his parents is, in relation to him, an absent parent, or (b) both of his parents are, in relation to him, absent parents (s.3(1)). The parent of a child is an absent parent in relation to him if (a) that parent is not living in the same household with the child, and (b) the child has his home with a person who is, in relation to him, a person with care (s.3(2)). A person is a "person with care" in relation to any child if he is a person (a) with whom the child has his home; (b) who usually provides day to day care for the child (whether exclusively or in conjunction with any other person); and (c) who does not fall within a prescribed category of person (s.3(3)). It is provided that (a) parents, (b) guardians, and (c) persons in whose favour residence orders under s.8 of the Children Act 1989 are in force must not be prescribed categories for this purpose (s.3(4)). There may be more than one person with care in relation to the same qualifying child (s.3(5)).

A parent means any person who is in law the mother or father of the child (s.54). A person is a child for the purposes of the Act if:

(a) he is under the age of 16; or

(b) he is under the age of 19 and receiving full-time education (which is not advanced education)

    (i) by attendance at a recognised educational establishment; or

    (ii) elsewhere, if the education is recognised by the Secretary of State; or

(c) he does not fall within (a) or (b) but -

    (i) he is under the age of 18, and

    (ii) prescribed conditions are satisfied with respect to him.

(s.55(1)).

A person is not a child for the purposes of the Act if he (a) is or has been married; (b) has celebrated a marriage which is void; or (c) has celebrated a marriage in respect of which a decree of nullity has been granted (s.55(2)).

*(c) Discharging the duty to maintain*

An absent parent is to be taken to have met his responsibility to maintain any qualifying child for the purposes of the Act by making periodical payments of maintenance with respect to the child of such amount, and at such intervals, as may be determined in accordance with the provisions of the Act (s.1(2)). Where a maintenance assessment made under the Act requires the making of periodical payments, it is the duty of the absent parent with respect to whom the assessment was made to make those payments (s.1(3)). Periodical payments which are required to be paid in accordance with a maintenance assessment are referred to in the Act as "child support maintenance" (s.3(6)).

*(d) Application for a maintenance assessment*

(i) Application by a parent on his or her own initiative

An application may be made to the Secretary of State for a maintenance assessment to be made under the Act with respect to a qualifying child by a person who is in relation to that child (a) the person with care, or (b) the absent parent (s.4(1)). Where a maintenance assessment has been made in response to such an application, the Secretary of State may, on the application of the person with care or the absent parent with respect to whom the assessment was made, arrange for (a) the collection of the child support maintenance payable in accordance with the assessment, and (b) the enforcement of the obligation to pay child support maintenance in accordance with the assessment (s.4(2) and (3)). No application may be made under s.4 if there is in force with respect to the person with care and absent parent in question a maintenance assessment made in response to an application under s.6 considered in (ii) below. A person who has applied to the Secretary of State may at any time request him to cease acting under s.4 and the Secretary of State must comply with any such request subject to any regulations (s.4(2), (3), (6) and (8)).

A person who applies to the Secretary of State under s.4 for a maintenance assessment must, so far as that person reasonably can, comply with such regulations as may be made by the Secretary of State with a view to providing the Secretary of State or a child support officer (appointed under s.13 of the Act) with the information which is required to enable (a) the absent parent to be traced (where that is necessary), (b) the amount of child support maintenance payable by the absent parent to be assessed, and (c) that amount to be recovered from the absent parent (s.4(4)). This obligation will not apply in circumstances to be prescribed and it may also be waived by the Secretary of State in circumstances to be prescribed (s.4(7)). See now the Child Support (Maintenance Assessment Procedure) Regulations 1992, SI 1992 No. 1813, Part II.

(ii) Application by a person receiving benefit
Where income support, family credit or any other benefit of a prescribed kind is claimed by or in respect of, or paid to or in respect of, the parent of a qualifying child, he or she must authorise the Secretary of State to take action under the Act to recover child support maintenance from the absent parent if (a) he or she is a person with care of the child, and (b) he or she is required to do so by the Secretary of State (s.6(1)). This has effect regardless of whether any of the benefits mentioned are payable with respect to any qualifying child (s.6(8)). The authorisation extends to all children of the absent parent in relation to whom the parent giving authorisation is a person with care (s.6(4)). The authorisation must be given, without unreasonable delay, by completing and returning to the Secretary of State an application (a) for the making of a maintenance assessment with respect to the qualifying child or children, and (b) for the Secretary of State to take action under the Act to recover on her behalf, the amount of child support maintenance so assessed (s.6(5)).

The Secretary of State must not require the parent to give him such authorisation if he considers that there are reasonable grounds for believing that (a) if the parent were to be required to give that authorisation, or (b) if she were to give it, there would be a risk of her, or of any child living with her, suffering harm or undue distress as a result (s.6(2)). This was intended to meet the concern that a caring parent might have about the disturbing effect which renewed contact with the absent parent might have on the household. If the Secretary of State decides that it is appropriate to seek authorisation from the caring parent, then s.46 provides for a sanction on the caring parent who fails to provide that authorisation or to comply with any regulation made under s.6(9) requiring her to provide information to enable a maintenance assessment to be made or maintenance to be recovered. In those circumstances the child support officer may give a reduced benefit direction, that is a direction, binding on the adjudication officer, that the amount payable by way of any relevant benefit to, or in respect of, the parent concerned be reduced by such amount, and for such period, as may be prescribed (s.46(11)).

Before making such a direction a child support officer must serve written notice on the parent requiring her, before the end of the period specified in the notice in accordance with the regulations, either to comply or to give him reasons for having failed to do so (s.46(2)). When the specified period has expired, the child support officer must consider whether, having regard to any reasons given by the parent (either in writing or orally), there are reasonable grounds for believing that, if she were to be required to comply, there would be a risk of her or of any children living with her suffering harm or undue distress as a result of complying (s.46(3)). If the child support officer considers that there are such reasonable grounds, he must (a) take no further action under s.46 in relation to the failure in question, and (b) notify the parent in writing accordingly (s.46(4)). If the child support officer considers that there are no such grounds, he may give a reduced benefit direction and he must then send a copy of it to the parent (s.46(5) and (6)). Any person who is aggrieved by a decision of a child support officer to give a reduced benefit direction may appeal to a child support appeal tribunal against the direction (s.46(7). See further s.46(8), s.20(2) to (4) and s.21).

The Lord Chancellor indicated that it was intended to give a parent with care, who is required to give authorisation to the Secretary of State, a "cooling off" period - probably of six weeks - before the case is referred to a child support officer to consider action under s.46. This would give her an opportunity of thinking over the whole question and would be in addition to the period of notice to which she is entitled under s.46 (Hansard HL, Vol. 531, col. 543). He also emphasised that the child support officer will be required to make the same sort of judgement about the risk to the caring parent as the Secretary of State has to make at the outset under s.6(2). This means that two different people will be looking at the reasons for a caring parent's refusal to comply (*ibid*. col. 544).

The rate and period of reduction of benefit will be set out in regulations and "will need to be pitched at the minimum level to make caring parents think seriously about non-cooperation without good grounds" (*per* the Lord Chancellor). It was indicated that the benefit reduction should last for eighteen months. For the first six months the reduction would be set at 20 per cent of income support adult personal allowance - just under £8 a week at the then current benefit levels. For the final twelve months the reduction rate will be lowered to 10 per cent. It will, of course, be open to the caring parent to comply with the request for authorisation or information at any time and if she does so then the reduced benefit direction will be withdrawn. (See further the Child Support (Maintenance Assessment Procedure) Regulations 1992, SI 1992 No. 1813, Part IX "Reduced Benefit Directions".)

*(e) Making the maintenance assessment*

(i) Referral to child support officers
Any application for a maintenance assessment made to the Secretary of State is to be referred by him to one of the child support officers (appointed by the Secretary

of State under s.13) whose duty it is to deal with the application in accordance with the provisions made by or under the Act (s.11(1)). The amount of child support maintenance to be fixed by any maintenance assessment is to be determined in accordance with the provisions of Part I of Schedule 1 of the Act. Part II of the Schedule makes further provision with respect to maintenance assessments (s.11(2) and (3)).

### (ii) Periodical review

Maintenance assessments will be regularly reviewed to take account of changes in the cost of living and in the circumstances of the parties. The Secretary of State is required to make arrangements to secure that, where any maintenance assessment has been in force for a prescribed period, the amount of child support maintenance fixed by that assessment ("the original assessment") is reviewed by a child support officer as soon as is reasonably practicable after the end of that prescribed period (s.16(1)). A review is to be conducted as if a fresh application for a maintenance assessment had been made by the person in whose favour the original assessment was made (s.16(3)). On completing a review, the child support officer concerned must make a fresh maintenance assessment, unless he is satisfied that the original assessment has ceased to have effect or should be brought to an end (s.16(4)).

### (iii) Reviews on change of circumstances

Where a maintenance assessment is in force the absent parent or person with care may apply to the Secretary of State for the amount of child support maintenance fixed by that assessment ("the original assessment") to be reviewed on the ground that by reason of a change of circumstances since the original assessment was made, the amount of child support maintenance payable by the absent parent would be significantly different if it were to be fixed by a maintenance assessment made by reference to the circumstances of the case as at the date of the application (s.17(1) and (2)). Such a review must be conducted as if a fresh application for a maintenance assessment had been made by the person in whose favour the original assessment was made (s.17(5)). On completing a review under this provision the child support officer concerned must make a fresh maintenance assessment unless:

(a) he is satisfied that the original assessment has ceased to have effect or should be brought to an end; or

(b) the difference between the amount of child support maintenance fixed by the original assessment and the amount that would be fixed if a fresh assessment were to be made as a result of the review is less than such amount as may be prescribed.

(s.17(6)).

### (iv) Reviews of decisions of child support officers

Provision is made for the decision of a child support officer to be reviewed by another child support officer who played no part in taking the decision which is to be reviewed where either of the parties involved thinks that it is wrong (s.18). Thus where an application for a maintenance assessment is refused, or an application for a review of a maintenance assessment which is in force on the basis of a change of circumstances is refused, the person who made the application may apply for the refusal to be reviewed. Where a maintenance assessment is in force, the absent parent or the person with care may apply for the assessment to be reviewed on the basis that there is an error in the assessment. Where a maintenance assessment is cancelled, the absent parent or the parent with care may apply to the Secretary of State for the cancellation to be reviewed. Where an application for the cancellation of a maintenance assessment is refused, either parent may apply for that refusal to be reviewed.

(v) Duty of child support officer to conduct review
A child support officer to whom an application is referred must conduct the review applied for unless in his opinion there are no reasonable grounds for supposing that the refusal, assessment or cancellation in question:
  (a) was made in ignorance of a material fact;
  (b) was based on a mistake as to a material fact;
  (c) was wrong in law.
  (s.18(6)).
If the child support officer conducting a review is satisfied that a maintenance assessment or a fresh maintenance assessment should be made, he must proceed to make an assessment or a fresh maintenance assessment, taking account of any material change of circumstance since the decision being reviewed was taken (s.18(9) and (10)).

(vi) Reviews at the instigation of child support officers
Where a child support officer is not conducting a review, but is nevertheless satisfied that a maintenance assessment which is in force is defective by reason of:
  (a) having been made in ignorance of a material fact;
  (b) having been based on a mistake of a material fact;
  (c) being wrong in law,
he may make a fresh maintenance assessment on the assumption that the person in whose favour the original assessment was made has made a fresh application for a maintenance assessment (s.19(1)). Where a child support officer is not conducting such a review but is nevertheless satisfied that if an application were to be made under s.17 or s.18 it would be appropriate to make a fresh maintenance assessment, he may do so (s.19(2)). Before making a fresh maintenance assessment under these provisions a child support officer must give such notice of his proposal to make a fresh maintenance assessment as may be prescribed (s.19(3)). See further the Child Support (Maintenance Assessment Procedure) Regulations 1992, SI 1992 No. 1813, particularly Parts IV to VII.

(vii) Appeals
A person who is aggrieved by the decision of a child support officer (a) on a review under s.18, or (b) to refuse an application for such a review, may appeal against that decision to a child support appeal tribunal established under s.21 of the Act (s.20(1)). No appeal under this provision can be brought after the end of the period of 28 days beginning with the date on which notification was given of the decision

in question, except with leave of the chairman of a child support appeal tribunal (s.20(2)). Where an appeal is allowed, the tribunal must remit the case (with directions if considered appropriate) to the Secretary of State who must arrange for it to be dealt with by a child support officer (s.20(3) and (4)). Any person who is aggrieved by a decision of a child support appeal tribunal, and any child support officer, may appeal to a Child Support Commissioner on a question of law (s.24(1)). An appeal on a question of law lies to the Court of Appeal from any decision of a Child Support Commissioner (see s.25).

*(f) Jurisdiction*
A child support officer has jurisdiction to make a maintenance assessment with respect to a person who is (a) a person with care, (b) an absent parent, or (c) a qualifying child, only if that person is habitually resident in the United Kingdom (s.44(1)). This means that a maintenance assessment can be made only if all the parties concerned in an application are habitually resident in the United Kingdom. Where one of the parties is regarded as habitually resident outside the United Kingdom, there is no jurisdiction to make an assessment under the Act and application will have to be made through the courts whose discretionary powers make them better placed to deal with the varying circumstances. (See the Lord Chancellor, HL Debates, Vol. 531, col. 540 and Chapters 13 and 16.) The requirement of habitual residence does not apply to a person with care who is not an individual (s.44(2)). Regulations may provide for the cancellation of a maintenance assessment where the person with care, absent parent or qualifying child with respect to whom it was made ceases to be habitually resident in the United Kingdom (s.44(3)). See further the Child Support (Maintenance Arrangements and Jurisdiction) Regulations 1992, SI 1992 No. 2645.

*(g) Welfare of children*
Where, in any case which falls to be dealt with under the Act, the Secretary of State or any child support officer is considering the exercise of any discretionary power conferred by the Act, he must have regard to the welfare of any child likely to be affected by his decision (s.2). This would not appear to be limited to a qualifying child but might extend to children living with the absent parent.

*(h) The formula for maintenance assessments*

(i) General principles
The amount of child support maintenance to be fixed by any maintenance assessment is to be determined in accordance with the provisions and formulae set out in Schedule 1 of the Act. (s.11(2) and (3)). There are four basic elements involved in the calculation of child support maintenance. These are:
* the maintenance requirement;
* the assessable income;
* the deduction rate; and
* the protected income.

(See further the Child Support (Maintenance Assessments and Special Cases) Regulations 1992, SI 1992 No. 1815, hereinafter "CS (MA & SC) Regs 1992".)

(ii) The maintenance requirement

This is the amount, calculated in accordance with the formula set out in paragraph 2 of Schedule 1, which is to be taken as the minimum amount necessary for the maintenance of the qualifying child or, where there is more than one qualifying child, all of them. The formula is:

$$MR = AG - CB$$

"MR" is the amount of the maintenance requirement. "AG" is the aggregate of the following amounts: (a) such amount or amounts (if any), with respect to each qualifying child as may be prescribed; (b) such amount or amounts (if any), with respect to the person with care of the qualifying child as may be prescribed; and (c) such further amount or amounts (if any) as may be prescribed. In the White Paper, *Children Come First* vol.1, para. 3.4, it is stated that the maintenance requirement will consist of those income support allowances which would be paid for the children and for the parent who is responsible for their care, if that family had no other income. (See now reg 3 CS (MA & SC) Regs 1992.) These are (a) the personal allowances for the children, which will vary with the age of the child; (b) the family premium; (c) the lone parent premium where the child is living with a lone parent; and (d) the adult personal allowance which represents the care needed by the child. (See Chapter 19.) "CB" is the amount payable by way of child benefit or, where there is more than one qualifying child, the aggregate of the amounts so payable with respect to each of them. For the purpose of calculating child benefit it is to be assumed that child benefit is payable with respect to any qualifying child at the basic rate. "Basic rate" has the meaning for the time being prescribed. (See now reg 4 CS (MA & SC) Regs 1992.)

Thus at present rates the maintenance requirement in relation to a qualifying child under the age of 11 would be as follows:

| | |
|---|---|
| Allowance for dependent child under the age of 11 | £15.05 per week |
| The lone parent premium | 4.90 |
| The family premium | 9.65 |
| Adult personal allowance | 44.00 |
| | £73.60 per week |
| Less child benefit | 10.00 |
| Total | £63.60 per week |

(iii) The assessable income

The general principle is that assessable income is calculated by deducting a parent's exempt income from a parent's net income. A parent's net income will be calculated or estimated in accordance with regulations made by the Secretary of State, and will be income after payment of tax and national insurance contributions. (See now regs 7 and 8 CS (MA & SC) Regs 1992.) Exempt income will also be calculated or estimated in accordance with regulations to be made by the Secretary of State and represents the weekly amount which it is considered a parent needs for his or her own essential day to day expenses. It will be based on income support allowances, and will include reasonable housing costs and the costs of any children for whom he or she is liable. (See now regs 9 and 10 CS (MA & SC Regs 1992.) The calculation of exempt income is not affected by the fact that a liable person has a new partner. Thus the new partner's income will not be taken into account in calculating how much maintenance is to be paid and no account is taken of the new partner's expenses or expenses in relation to the new partner. (See White Paper, para. 3.16.) However, when a liable person has other natural children of his own then he is liable to maintain both the children of his first relationship and the children of any subsequent relationship. Accordingly, the exempt income will be revised to include an allowance for the further natural children of the liable parent and the proportion of housing costs attributable to the liable person himself and those children (*ibid.* para. 3.17). No allowance is made for his stepchildren, i.e. the children of any new partner by another relationship, though consideration is being given to limited circumstances in which it might be appropriate for a liable person to include the care of stepchildren in his exempt income, for example where the other natural parent is dead (*ibid.* para. 3.19). The income remaining after deduction of exempt income is the assessable income - the assessable income of both parents will be taken into account though, of course, there will be no payment to be made by the caring parent.

Where the deduction of a parent's exempt income from his or her net income results in that parent's assessable income being a negative amount, his or her assessable income is taken as nil. Where income support or any other benefit of a prescribed kind is paid to or in respect of a parent who is an absent parent or a person with care, that parent is for this purpose taken to have no assessable income. However, even if the absent parent is on benefit, it was felt that he should at least make a small contribution to meeting his maintenance liability by a deduction from his benefit at the same level as those which could currently be made, e.g. to meet arrears on various bills, and within existing limits for such deductions (HC Debates, Vol. 192, col. 186). Thus by virtue of s.43 the power of the Secretary of State to make regulations under s.51(1)(r) of the Social Security Act 1986 providing for deduction from benefits, may be exercised in relation to cases where an absent parent is taken to have no assessable income because he or she is in receipt of benefit, with a view to securing that (a) payments of prescribed amounts are made with respect to qualifying children in place of payments of child support maintenance, and (b) arrears of child support maintenance are recovered. (See the CS (MA & SC) Regs 1992, reg 28 which prescribes for (a) 5 per cent of the income support personal allowance for a single claimant aged not less than 25, i.e. £2.20 in 1993-94.)

(iv) The deduction rate

A percentage of the assessable income of each parent will be taken into account in order to meet the maintenance requirement, where possible. It is intended that, until the maintenance requirement is met, assessable income should be shared equally between the absent parent and his children who qualify under the Act. (See the CS (MA & SC) Regs 1992, reg 5 which specifies 0.5.) A smaller percentage will apply in individual cases after the maintenance requirement has been met. The White Paper takes a rate of deduction of 15 per cent for illustrative purposes (para. 3.22).

(See the CS (MA & SC) Regs 1992, reg 6 which specifies 0.25.) There will be an upper limit to the operation of the formula, and in high income cases above that limit the caring parent will be able to seek additional maintenance from the courts.

(v) The protected income

The protected income represents the level below which no family of a person liable to maintain a child will be allowed to fall as a result of his meeting his maintenance obligations and his essential living expenses. This is intended to provide an employed father (and his new family) with a safety net so that although this will be set by reference to income support rates (including housing costs), there will be a margin above them in order not to discourage absent parents from working or provide stimulus to default (HC Debates Vol. 192, col. 188). The White Paper indicated that £5 per week should be the amount which can be earned in addition to income support - the earnings disregard (para. 3.23). (See the CS (MA & SC) Regs 1992, reg 11 which specifies £8.00. Where the income of the absent parent, any partner of his and any child of his family exceeds the sum of the amounts taken into account under reg 11, then in calculating the protected income 10 per cent of the excess is also to be taken into account.) It is accordingly provided that where a maintenance assessment has been made with respect to an absent parent, and payment by him of the amount so assessed would reduce his disposable income below his protected income level, then the amount of the assessment is to be adjusted in accordance with such provisions as may be prescribed with a view to securing, so far as is reasonably practicable, that payment of the amount so assessed will not reduce his disposable income below his protected income level (Sched. 1, para. 6).

The amount of an absent parent's disposable income is to be calculated, or estimated, in accordance with regulations made by the Secretary of State. Such regulations may, in particular, provide that, in such circumstances and to such extent as may be prescribed (a) the income of any child who is living in the same household with the absent parent, and (b) where the absent parent is living together in the same household with another adult of the opposite sex (regardless of whether or not they are married), the income of that other adult is to be treated as the absent parent's income for the purposes of calculating his disposable income (Sched. 1, para. 6). (See CS (MA & SC) Regs 1992, reg 12.) Since the income which is to be protected is the income for the family for which the liable person is, in fact, financially responsible, the incomes and appropriate expenses of all the people in that family - including the new partner and stepchildren - will be taken into account (*ibid.* para. 3.24). It will be seen that where payment of the amount of maintenance calculated in accordance with general principles would leave the absent parent with less than his protected level of income, the amount of maintenance payable will be adjusted so as to leave him with that level of income.

The Secretary of State may prescribe a minimum amount of child support maintenance. Where the amount of child support maintenance which would otherwise be fixed by a maintenance assessment is nil, or less than the prescribed minimum amount, the amount to be fixed by the assessment must be the prescribed minimum amount (Sched.1, para. 7). See the CS (MA & SC) Regs 1992, reg 13 which specifies 5 per cent of the income support personal allowance for a single claimant aged not less than 25, i.e. £2.20 in 1993-94.

*(i) Making the maintenance assessment*

In order to determine the amount of any maintenance assessment, the first step is to calculate:

$$(A + C) \times P$$

where "A" is the assessable income of the absent parent, "C" is the assessable income of the other parent where that parent is the person with care (and otherwise has such value as may be prescribed), and "P" is such number greater than zero but less than 1 as may be prescribed. Where the result of this calculation is an amount equal to, or less than the amount of the maintenance requirement for the qualifying child or qualifying children, the amount of maintenance payable by the absent parent for that child or those children is to be an amount equal to: $A \times P$, that is the assessable income of the absent parent multiplied by the prescribed number.

Thus where the absent parent is liable to maintain a child under the age of 11 years the maintenance requirement will be £63.60 calculated as shown in (ii) above on the basis of rates in force in 1993-94. The exempt income of the absent parent will be as follows:

| | |
|---|---|
| Personal allowance | £44.00 |
| Housing costs - say | 32.00 |
| Exempt income | £76.00 |

(For further items that may be included see the CS (MA & SC) Regs 1992, reg 9.) The assessable income of the absent parent will be calculated as follows:

| | |
|---|---|
| If he has net income of, say | £180 per week |
| Deduct exempt income | 76 |
| Assessable income | £104 per week |

If this is multiplied by the prescribed rate of 0.5 this will result in a maintenance payment due from the absent parent of £52 per week and will leave him with a net income of £128 per week. This is in excess of his protected income of £84 which is calculated as follows:

| | |
|---|---|
| Single person's allowance | £44.00 per week |
| Housing costs - say | 32.00 |
| Margin | 8.00 |
| Protected income | £84.00 |

Accordingly no adjustment is necessary. For further items that may be included see the CS (MA & SC) Regs 1992, reg 11.

However, if the absent parent has remarried and has a further natural child and a stepchild, the protected level of income would be £156.75 calculated as follows:

| | |
|---|---|
| Children's allowances | £30.10 per week |
| Couple's allowance | 69.00 |
| Family premium | 9.65 |
| Housing costs - say | 40.00 |
| Margin | 8.00 |
| Protected level of income | £156.75 |

The absent parent's income after meeting the *prima facie* maintenance assessment of £52 is £128 per week together with child benefit for two children of £18.10, making a total income per week of £146.10. This is below the level of his protected income of £156.75 per week, so the maintenance payment must be reduced by

£10.65 per week so that he will be liable to pay £41.35 per week and will be left with his protected level of income.

Where the result of the calculation is an amount which exceeds the amount of the maintenance requirement for the qualifying child or children, then the amount of maintenance payable by the absent parent for that child or those children is to consist of (a) a basic element and (b) an additional element. The basic element is calculated by applying the formula -

$$BE = A \times G \times P$$

where A and P are as above. The value of G is to be determined by applying the formula -

$$G = \frac{MR}{(A + C) \times P}$$

The additional element is to be calculated by applying the formula -

$$AE = (1 - G) \times A \times R$$

where G is as calculated by applying the previous formula and A is as above, i.e. the absent parent's income. R is such number greater than zero but less than 1 as may be prescribed. The prescribed figure is 0.25: see CS (MA & SC) Regs 1992, reg 6.

Thus assume a maintenance requirement of £64 as above in respect of a child under the age of 11 years. If the absent parent has a net income of £300 per week and makes mortgage payments of £54 per week his assessable income will be calculated as follows:

| | |
|---|---|
| Net income | £300 per week |
| Deduct exempt income: | |
| personal allowance | £44.00 |
| housing costs | 54.00 |
| | £98.00 per week |
| Assessable income | £202 per week |

The maintenance requirement of £64 is met when he has paid 0.5 of the first £128 of his assessable income. In addition he will pay 0.15 of the remaining £74 of his assessable income which is £18.50. His total payment is accordingly £82.50 per week.

The application of the formulae is as follows:

(i) $BE = A \times G \times P$

$BE = 202 \times 0.63 \times 0.50 = 63.60$ rounded to £64

(ii) $G = \dfrac{MR}{(A + C) \times P}$

$G = \dfrac{64}{(202 + 0) \times 0.5} = \dfrac{64}{101} = 0.63$

(iii) $AE = (1 - G) \times A \times R$

$AE = (1 - 0.63) \times 202 \times 0.25 = 18.68$ rounded to £18.50

*(j) Interim maintenance assessments*

Where it appears to a child support officer who is required to make a maintenance assessment that he does not have sufficient information to enable him to make an assessment in accordance with the provision made by or under the Act, he may make an interim maintenance assessment (s.12(1)). Before making an interim maintenance assessment a child support officer must, if it is reasonably practicable to do so, give written notice of his intention to make such an assessment to the absent parent concerned and the person with care concerned (s.12(4)). The proposed interim assessment must then not be made before the end of such period of notice as may be prescribed (s.12(5)). See further the Child Support (Maintenance Assessment Procedure) Regulations 1992, SI 1992 No. 1813, Part III.

*(k) Relationship between maintenance assessments and the powers of the courts*

(i) The powers of a court to make maintenance orders
In any case where a child support officer would have jurisdiction to make a maintenance assessment with respect to a qualifying child and an absent parent of his on an application made by a person entitled to apply for such an assessment, no court may exercise any power which it would otherwise have to make, vary or revive any maintenance order in relation to the child and absent parent concerned (s.8(1) and (3)). This prohibition applies even though the circumstances of the case are such that a child support officer would not make an assessment if it were applied for (s.8(2)). A court is not prohibited from revoking a maintenance order (s.8(4)).

A court is not prevented from exercising any power it has to make a maintenance order in relation to a child if a maintenance assessment is in force with respect to the child and:
(a) the amount of child support maintenance payable in accordance with the assessment was determined by reference to the formula including the additional element, and
(b) the court is satisfied that the circumstances of the case make it appropriate for the absent parent to make or secure the making of periodical payments under a maintenance order in addition to the child support maintenance payable by him in accordance with the maintenance assessment.
(s.8(6)).

Thus courts are permitted to exercise their powers to order periodical payments to top up awards based on the formula in high income cases which are above the upper limit of the formula's operation. There are similar provisions enabling a court to make maintenance orders for the sole purpose of meeting some or all of the expenses incurred in connection with the provision of instruction or training for a child (s.8(7)), or for the sole purpose of meeting some or all of any expenses attributable to a child's disability (s.8(8)). A court is also not prevented from exercising any power which it has to make a maintenance order in relation to a child if the order is made against a person with care of the child (s.8(10)).

Courts will continue to be able to make maintenance orders in relation to stepchildren and other children who are not within the scope of the Act, and existing powers to make orders for lump sum payments and property adjustment orders for the benefit of children will remain exercisable even in relation to children within the Act. The courts' powers to make orders in respect of financial and property arrangements between spouses, including the power to order periodical payments for a spouse who is a parent, are not restricted by the Act, though it should be borne in mind that the maintenance requirement for a qualifying child contains a carer's allowance. However, concern has been expressed about the effect of the power to make maintenance assessments under the Act on the arrangements for the disposition of property between the spouses, and in particular that the principle of the clean break might be undermined. (See the Second Report of the Social Security Committee, Changes in Maintenance Arrangements (1991). For the position in relation to maintenance agreements see *(l)* below.) The Lord Chancellor emphasised the view that where one party has the care of children and is therefore often restricted in the work he or she can take on, it would not be right to apply the clean break principle. In any event, he said, while one has children who are under age there can be no question of a clean break between the parents and the children (HL Debates, Vol. 526, col. 836). Nevertheless, it is not unusual for a husband of limited means to be persuaded to transfer his interest in the matrimonial home to his wife, who will provide a home there for the children, in the expectation that no further claim for maintenance will or is likely to be made. The decision in *Hulley* v *Thompson* [1981] 1 WLR 159 has already shown that a father's obligation to his children is not necessarily discharged by such a transfer (see Chapter 19). In the light of such concerns the Lord Chancellor and the Secretary of State have pointed out that the formula takes account of such circumstances because of the inclusion of housing costs. Thus if an absent parent transfers his share in the home to the caring parent his housing costs are likely to be greater than they would have been if he had kept the family home for himself. The formula allows him to use those costs by way of deduction against the amount of maintenance he is required to pay. The housing costs of the caring parent are likely to be lower than they might otherwise have been, so the result will be that the absent parent will pay less maintenance (HL Debates, Vol. 526, col. 835; HC Debates, Vol. 192, col. 194. See also the White Paper, paras. 4.9-4.11, and the CS (MA & SC) Regs 1992, regs 15-18).

The Act also envisages the possibility of child maintenance agreements being incorporated into consent orders. The Lord Chancellor may by order provide that, in such circumstances as may be prescribed, s.8 shall not prevent a court from exercising any power which it has to make a maintenance order in relation to a child, if (a) a written agreement (whether or not enforceable) provides for the making or securing, by an absent parent of the child, of periodical payments to or for the benefit of the child, and (b) the maintenance order which the court makes is, in all material respects, in the same terms as that agreement (s.8(5)).

(ii) Existing orders and maintenance assessments

Where an order of a kind prescribed by regulations to be made by the Secretary of State is in force with respect to any qualifying child with respect to whom a maintenance assessment is made, the order will either (a) cease to have effect so far as it relates to the making or securing of periodical payments, to such extent as may be determined in accordance with the regulations, or (b) have effect where the regulations so provide subject to such modifications as may be so determined (s.10(1)). See the Child Support (Maintenance Arrangements and Jurisdiction) Regulations 1992, SI 1992 No. 2645, reg 3.

## (l) Maintenance agreements

The Act does not prevent any person from entering into any maintenance agreement for the making or securing of periodical payments to or for the benefit of any child (s.9(1) and (2)). On the other hand, the existence of a maintenance agreement does not prevent any party to the agreement, or any other person, from applying for a maintenance assessment with respect to any child to or for whose benefit periodical payments are to be made or secured under the agreement (s.9(3)). Any provision in such an agreement which purports to restrict the right of any person to apply for a maintenance assessment is void (s.9(4)). Where the Act (s.8) would prevent any court from making a maintenance order in relation to a child and an absent parent of his, no court may exercise any power that it has to vary an agreement so as (a) to insert a provision requiring that the absent parent make or secure the making of periodical payments by way of maintenance to or for the benefit of that child, or (b) to increase the amount payable under such a provision (s.9(5)).

Where an agreement of a kind prescribed by the regulations to be made by the Secretary of State is in force with respect to any qualifying child with respect to whom a maintenance assessment is made, then, so far as it relates to the making or securing of periodical payments, it will either (a) be unenforceable to such extent as may be determined in accordance with the regulations, or (b) where the regulations so provide, will have effect subject to such modifications as may be so determined (s.10(2)). See the Child Support (Maintenance Arrangements and Jurisdiction) Regulations 1992, SI 1992 No. 2645, reg 4.

## (m) Collection and enforcement

### (i) Collection

The Secretary of State may arrange for the collection of any child support maintenance payable in accordance with a maintenance assessment where (a) the assessment is made by virtue of s.6, i.e. as a result of an application by a person receiving benefit, or (b) an application has been made by the parent with care or by the absent parent under s.4(2) for him to arrange for its collection (s.29(1)). Where a maintenance assessment is made, payments of child support maintenance under the assessment must be made in accordance with regulations made by the Secretary of State (s.29(2)). The regulations may, in particular, make provision (a) for payments of child support maintenance to be made - (i) to the person caring for the child or children in question; or (ii) to, or through, the Secretary of State; or (iii) to, or through, such other person as the Secretary of State may, from time to time, specify; (b) as to the method by which payments of child support are to be made; (c) as to the intervals at which such payments are to be made. They may also empower the Secretary of State to direct any person liable to make payments in accordance with the assessment - (i) to make them by standing order or similar means, and (ii) to open a bank account from which payments under the assessment may be made in accordance with the method of payment which that person is obliged to adopt (s.29(3)). See further the Child Support (Collection and Enforcement) Regulations 1992, SI 1992 No. 1989, Part II.

The Secretary of State may also arrange for the collection of any periodical payments or secured periodical payments of a prescribed kind which are payable for the benefit of a child even though he is not arranging for the collection of child support maintenance with respect to that child (s.30(2)).

Where the Secretary of State is arranging for the collection of any payments under the preceding paragraphs, he may also arrange for the collection of any periodical payments, or secured periodical payments, of a prescribed kind which are payable to or for the benefit of any person who falls within a prescribed category (s.30(1)). Thus, although the determination of spouses' maintenance remains a matter for the courts the White Paper (para. 5.25) indicated that as "a matter of convenience to the parents, it might be helpful if the Child Support Agency were able to collect spouses' maintenance as well as child maintenance where one parent has to pay both sums of maintenance to the other." Provision for this is made by s.30. (See the Child Support (Collection and Enforcement of other Forms of Maintenance) Regulations 1992, SI 1992 No. 2643.)

(ii) Deduction from earnings orders
Where any person is liable to make payments of child support maintenance, the Secretary of State may make a deduction from earnings order against the liable person to secure payment of any amount due under the maintenance assessment in question (s.31(1) and (2)). Such an order may be made so as to secure the payment of arrears or future amounts of child support maintenance, or both (s.31(3)). A deduction from earnings order must be expressed to be directed at a person (the employer) who has the liable person in his employment and has effect from such date as may be specified in the order. It operates as an instruction to the employer to make the deduction from the liable person's earnings and pay the amount deducted to the Secretary of State (s.31(4) and (5). See further subs.(6), (7) and (8)). The Secretary of State is given power to make provision with respect to deduction from earnings orders by regulations (s.32(1)). The regulations may include a provision that a liable person may appeal to a magistrates' court if he is aggrieved by the making of a deduction from earnings order against him, or by the terms of any such order, or there is a dispute as to whether payments constitute earnings or as to any other prescribed matter relating to the order (s.32(5)). On such an appeal the court must not question the maintenance assessment by reference to which the deduction from earnings order was made (s.32(6)). See further the Child Support (Collection and Enforcement) Regulations 1992, SI 1992 No. 1989, Part III.

(iii) Liability orders
It was not thought reasonable that the Child Support Agency should be able to take further enforcement action purely on its own authority. Provision is therefore made for the agency to apply to a magistrates' court for a liability order and, if that order is granted, to use various enforcement methods available for enforcing civil debt. (See HL Debates, Vol. 526, col. 778.) Thus where a person who is liable to make payments of child support maintenance (the liable person) fails to make one or more of those payments and it appears to the Secretary of State that:
   (a) it is inappropriate to make a deduction from earnings order against him (because, for example, he is unemployed), or

(b) although such an order has been made against him, it has proved ineffective as a means of securing that payments are made in accordance with the maintenance assessment in question,

then the Secretary of State may apply to a magistrates' court for a liability order against the liable person (s.33(1) and (2)). On such an application the magistrates' court must make the order if satisfied that the payments in question have become payable by the liable person and have not been paid (s.33(3)). The court must not question the maintenance assessment under which the payments of child support maintenance fell to be made (s.33(4)).

Where a liability order has been made against a liable person, the Secretary of State may levy the appropriate amount by distress and sale of the liable person's goods in accordance with s.35 and regulations made thereunder. Such regulations may provide for an appeal to a magistrates' court by any person aggrieved by the levying of, or an attempt to levy, a distress (s.35(7)). See further the Child Support (Collection and Enforcement) Regulations 1992, SI 1992 No. 1989, Part IV. Where a liability order has been made against a person, the amount in respect of which the order was made, to the extent that it remains unpaid, is, if a county court so orders, recoverable by means of garnishee proceedings or a charging order, as if it were payable under a county court order (s.36(1)).

Where the Secretary of State has sought to levy an amount by distress under s.35 or to recover an amount by virtue of s.36 and that amount, or any part of it, remains unpaid, he may apply to a magistrates' court for the issue of a warrant committing the liable person to prison (s.40(1)). On any such application the court must (in the presence of the liable person) inquire as to (a) the liable person's means, and (b) whether there has been wilful refusal or culpable neglect on his part. If, but only if, the court is of the opinion that there has been wilful refusal or culpable neglect on the part of the liable person, it may:

(a) issue a warrant of commitment against him; or

(b) fix a term of imprisonment and postpone the issue of the warrant until such time and on such conditions (if any) as it thinks just.

(s.40(2) and (3)).

A warrant issued under this section must order the liable person to be imprisoned for a specified period, but to be released on payment of the amount stated in the warrant (s.40(6)). The maximum period of imprisonment which may be imposed is to be calculated in accordance with Schedule 4 of the Magistrates' Courts Act 1980 but must not exceed six weeks (s.40(7)).

Where the Secretary of State is authorised under s.4 or s.6 to recover child support maintenance payable by an absent parent in accordance with a maintenance assessment following the failure by the absent parent to make one or more of the payments due, and he recovers any such arrears, he may, in such circumstances and to such extent as may be prescribed, retain them if he is satisfied that the amount of any benefit paid to the person with care of the child or children in question would have been less had the absent parent not been in arrears with his payments of child support maintenance (s.41(1) and (2)). An absent parent may also be liable to interest with respect to arrears of child support maintenance (s.41(3)).

## (n) Termination of assessments

A maintenance assessment will cease to have effect on the death of the absent parent or of the person with care or on there no longer being any qualifying child with respect to whom it would have effect. It will also cease to have effect where a new assessment is made with respect to the qualifying child (Sched. 1, para. 16. Provision is also made for cancellation of an assessment).

# Chapter 18

# Financial provision and taxation

## 1. Introduction

Taxation is an important influence on the finances of most families, but families that break up also have special problems. The importance of considering the tax implications of financial provision and property adjustment has been stressed by the courts on a number of occasions. Thus in *S* v *S* [1977] Fam 127 at p. 136 Ormrod LJ said:

"To my mind, in a case of this kind it is impossible for a court to arrive at a sensible or satisfactory solution unless the parties do put before the court tax calculations. They are not, in this type of case, very complicated, and they immediately show the real position of each party on whatever is the assumption that the calculation is based upon. Without it, it is pure guesswork and I would urge that counsel make it part of their argument in this type of case always to work out the tax effects of the proposals which each individual counsel is urging on the court, so that the actual results on the client can be seen clearly, and the court can then choose between one argument and the other, or modify one submission in favour of one party or the other, being fully aware of the effect of what the court is doing."

The Finance Act 1988 not only introduced a new system of taxation of the income of married couples with effect from 6 April 1990, but it also made an important change of principle in relation to the treatment of maintenance payments for income tax purposes. The essence of the "old system" was the transfer of income from the person making the payments to the person receiving the payments so that the income ceased to be that of the payer and become that of the payee for income tax purposes. Where the tax liability of the payee on that slice of transferred income was lower than the tax liability of the payer would have been, a significant saving of tax might result. This subsidy for marriage breakdown was greater for better-off families where the payer had a high marginal rate of tax and was able to make substantial maintenance payments. The subsidy was of particular significance where the recipient was the child of the person making the payments. (In *Sherdley* v *Sherdley* [1988] AC 213 it was held that a father could apply for an order against himself for the benefit of a child with the object of saving tax amounting in that case to over £4,000 per annum.) Under the "new system" introduced by the Finance Act 1988 maintenance payments do not operate as transfers of income for income tax purposes but are treated as applications of the income of the person making the payments. Only limited relief is available, and to this extent the tax calculations referred to by Ormrod LJ will be less significant. However, although the subsidy may have been largely removed, it will still be important to know the tax burden on the parties. Moreover, the "old system" continues to apply, with modifications, to "existing obligations" as defined in s.36(4) of the Finance Act 1988. This means that two systems of taxation of maintenance payments will exist side by side for some time to come and while the Finance Act 1988 introduced a simple system for the taxation of maintenance payments, the transitional arrangements mean that considerable complexity will continue to exist during this period.

## 2. Income tax

*(a) The basic principles*
The present system of income tax imposes, first, a lower rate of tax (20 per cent in 1993-94) on the first £2,500 of an individual's taxable income. Secondly, the basic rate of income tax (currently 25 per cent) is imposed on an individual's taxable income exceeding £2,500 up to a specified amount (£23,700 in 1993-94). Thirdly, higher rate of tax (currently 40 per cent) is payable on so much of an individual's taxable income as exceeds that specified amount (ICTA 1988, s.1; FA 1991, s.21; FA 1992, s.9; FA 1993, s.51).

In order to ascertain an individual's taxable income it is first necessary to ascertain the amount of income according to the rules of each Schedule under which tax is levied. Where tax has been deducted before receipt, e.g. under the PAYE system, it is the gross amount which is included in calculating the individual's "statutory income". This is essential in order to determine liability to the higher rate of tax, but credit will, of course, be given in respect of the tax already suffered by deduction at source so that such income is then subjected only to excess liability if appropriate.

From the statutory income so calculated, there should be deducted "charges on income" in order to ascertain the individual's total income (ICTA 1988, s.385). Charges on income have included two items of particular relevance to taxation of the family, namely certain interest payments and "annual payments". Mortgage interest relief remains important though its scope was restricted to some extent by the Finance Act 1988 and the total amount of relief now seems to be "frozen" at the figure of £30,000 which is becoming increasingly inadequate with the rise in house prices and in the loans needed to finance the purchase of a matrimonial home. The Finance Act 1991, s.7 restricts relief to basic rate tax, so that relief is now given by deduction of tax on payment under the MIRAS scheme and no deduction is now necessary as a "charge on income" (see (c)(vii) below). In relation to annual payments the Finance Act 1988 has had a major impact on the taxation of financial provision following breakdown of a marriage (see s.36). The significance of annual payments as transfers of income from payer to recipient remains in relation to agreements and orders made before 15 March 1988, but payments under arrangements first made after that date are not annual payments and do not constitute a charge on the income of the person making the payments.

An individual's taxable income is ascertained by deducting from total income the personal reliefs to which he or she is entitled (ICTA 1988, s.256). Personal reliefs have been the traditional method of seeking to achieve "horizontal equity" by adjusting the burden of income tax according to the personal and family circumstances of an individual taxpayer. Although the number of reliefs has been reduced by the Finance Act 1988, those reliefs that remain have a significant effect on the tax burden of families. It should be noted that where allowances are unused in any particular tax year because they exceed the total income of the taxpayer, they cannot be carried forward to subsequent years and their benefit is to that extent lost.

### (b) Marriage and income taxation

The long-established rule was that a woman's income for a year of assessment during which she was a married woman living with her husband was deemed for income tax purposes to be his income and not hers, and was to be assessed on him (ICTA 1988, s.279). A husband was responsible for payment of tax on the joint income of the spouses, though the wife's income did not become the income of the husband except for the purposes of collection. It meant that the husband had to make the return in relation to his wife's income as well as his own though repayment to wives was allowed in some cases (s.281). The most important practical effect was that the aggregation of their incomes resulted in tax being levied at the rates appropriate to their combined income so that higher rates of tax may have been applicable than if their incomes had not been aggregated.

This system was the subject of considerable criticism, and various proposals for reform were discussed in recent years. The Finance Act 1988 effected a major reform of the taxation of married couples and provided for the introduction as from April 1990 of a completely new system of independent taxation. Under the new system a husband and wife are taxed independently on income of all kinds (Finance Act 1988, s.32). There were two objectives underlying the reform: (i) to give married women the same privacy and independence in their tax affairs as everyone else; and (ii) to bring to an end the ways in which the tax system could penalise marriage.

### (c) Marriage and taxation from 6 April 1990

#### (i) Independent taxation

The incomes of husband and wife are not aggregated for income tax purposes in the tax year 1990-91 and subsequent years of assessment (Finance Act 1988, s.32 repealing ICTA 1988, s.279). Accordingly, from 6 April 1990 spouses are taxed as independent persons on all income, regardless of whether it is earned or investment income.

All taxpayers, male or female, married or single, are entitled to the same basic deduction from total income. This "personal allowance", which for the year 1993-94 is £3,445, is available against all income, whether from earnings, pensions or savings (ICTA 1988, s.257 as amended by FA 1988, s.33). In addition, where a married man has his wife living with him there is an entitlement to a deduction from total income of £1,720. In the years 1990-91 and 1991-92 this "married couple's allowance" had to be set against the husband's income in the first instance, but if it exceeded his total income after all other deductions had been made from it, his wife was entitled to a deduction from her income of an amount equal to the excess. As from 6 April 1993 a married couple may allocate the married couple's allowance between them and a wife has the right to claim half the allowance (ICTA 1988, s.257B(1) as amended). No part of the basic personal allowance of either spouse is transferable to the other. This means that where a husband has no income or his income is less than that allowance, a couple may be worse off than under the old system under which the whole of the married man's allowance could be set against the wife's income. Transitional relief was available in 1990-91 and 1991-92 for couples in this situation whereby the excess of deductions to which the husband was entitled in 1989-90 over his income in the transitional years could be set against the wife's income after making the deductions to which she was entitled (ICTA 1988, s.257D).

(ii) Age allowances
A taxpayer who is aged 65 or more in a year of assessment is entitled to a higher personal allowance (£4,200 in 1993-94) and if he or she is aged 75 or more the personal allowance is further increased (£4,370 in 1993-94). In either case if the taxpayer's total income for the year of assessment exceeds a specified figure (£14,200 in 1993-94) then the increased personal allowance is reduced by two-thirds of the excess until the allowance is reduced to the basic personal allowance (ICTA 1988, s.257). The married couple's allowance is also increased (to £2,465 in 1993-94) if either spouse is aged 65 or more in a year of assessment and there is a further increase (to £2,505 in 1993-94) if either spouse is aged 75 or more in a year of assessment. Again, if the taxpayer's income exceeds a specified figure (£14,200 in 1993-94) then the increased allowance is reduced by two-thirds of the excess until the allowance is reduced to the basic married couple's allowance (ICTA 1988, s.257A).

(iii) Widow's bereavement allowance
Where a man dies in a year of assessment for which he is entitled to the married couple's allowance then his widow is entitled for that year of assessment to an allowance from her total income of an amount equal to the married couple's allowance, i.e. £1,720 in 1993-94. She is also entitled to the allowance in the next following year of assessment unless she married again before the beginning of the new tax year (ICTA 1988, s.262).

(iv) Additional personal allowance
This relief may be claimed by widows, widowers or other persons not entitled for the year of assessment to the married couple's allowance if a "qualifying child" is resident with him or her for the whole or part of a year (ICTA 1988, s.259). The amount of the allowance is the same as the married couple's allowance, i.e. £1,720 in 1993-94.
A "qualifying child" is a child who:

(a) is born or under the age of 16 years at the commencement of the year of assessment, or, if over that age is receiving full-time instruction at any university, college, school or other educational establishment, and

(b) is a child of the claimant or, not being such a child, is born in, or under the age of 16 years at the commencement of the year and maintained for the whole or part of that year by the claimant at his own expense.

(s.259(5)).

Only one allowance can be claimed on the basis of any particular "qualifying child". Thus where for any year of assessment two or more individuals are entitled to relief in connection with the same child, the amount of the allowance is to be apportioned between them. The apportionment will be as agreed between them or, in default of agreement, in proportion to the length of the periods for which the child in question is resident with them respectively in the year of assessment (ICTA 1988, s.260). Moreover, a claimant is entitled to only one deduction for any year of assessment irrespective of the number of qualifying children resident with him or her (ICTA 1988, ss.259(3) and 260(6)). However, where parents who have two (or more) children separate, it may be possible for each of them to claim the additional relief on the basis of a different qualifying child residing with them during at least part of the year of assessment.

Thus, even though the mother has residence orders in respect of both children and obtains relief on the basis of one of those children, the father may be able to claim relief on the basis that the other child spends part of the year with him, e.g. during school holidays. A parent who remarried would, of course, cease to be entitled to claim the relief, but this does not prevent the other parent being entitled if he or she has not remarried.

Where a man and a woman who are not married to each other live together as husband and wife for the whole or any part of a year of assessment then even though they may in the past each have been entitled to an allowance in respect of a different child, as from 6 April 1989 they are entitled to only one additional personal allowance (ICTA 1988, s.259(4A) inserted by Finance Act 1988, s.30). This will be in respect of the youngest of the children in respect of whom either would otherwise be entitled to the allowance.

(v) The effect of the new system

The new system had no practical effect on the position of the majority of married couples though couples where the wife was the only earner became worse off with the abolition of the wife's earned income allowance. Some couples are better off under the new system, most notably where the husband and wife are both earning and where income has been sufficiently high to attract the higher rate tax and to make it advantageous for the couple to elect for separate taxation of the wife's earnings. Whereas an election resulted in a loss of the married man's allowance and left the couple with two single allowances, under the new system not only will all income be separately taxed (so that less income may be taxed at the higher rate) but the husband and wife will be entitled to the married couple's allowance as well as to two single personal allowances.

Secondly, elderly couples may be better off. Both husband and wife will be entitled to a single person's age allowance, and the higher married couple's allowance is available. Elderly wives are more likely to have investment income to take advantage of the single person's age allowance, but in addition to this the allowance of each spouse will be tapered away where the individual income of each spouse exceeds a specified figure as compared with the past where the married age allowance was tapered away when their joint income exceeded the specified figure.

Thirdly, the new system benefits those couples where only the husband is the earner, but the wife has investment income. The wife is now independently taxed on that investment income thereby enabling her to utilise her own personal allowance and lower rate tax and basic rate tax bands, whereas in the past her investment income would have borne tax at the husband's marginal rate. If the non-earner has little or no capital, a tax saving may be achieved by a transfer of capital from the earner spouse to the non-earner spouse (a transfer of income by covenant will not be effective). This can be effected without incurring liability to capital gains tax (see page 459.) or inheritance tax (see page 462) and an outright transfer of legal and beneficial ownership seems unlikely to be regarded as affected by the settlement provisions in Part XV of the Taxes Act 1988 (see [1988] BTR 230). In view of the general reduction in tax rates the maximum saving to be achieved by such a transfer is around £5,000 per annum.

(vi) Independent taxation and property ownership

The aggregation of the income of a married woman with that of her husband dates from the period before the establishment of separate property by the Married Women's Property Act 1882. A little over a century later it can be said that the position in relation to income tax has been brought into line with the separation of the property of husband and wife. The importance of ascertaining their respective property rights on breakdown of the marriage and the difficulty of doing so has been evident for some time (see Chapter 2). Independent taxation of husband and wife makes it important for their respective income-producing property interests to be clearly identifiable during a marriage. Yet this will often not be the case where savings and investments may have been acquired in the name of one spouse alone or without any express consideration of the beneficial interests.

In an attempt to deal with the problem, s.282A of the Taxes Act 1988 (inserted by s.34 of the Finance Act 1988) provides that with effect from April 1990, income arising from property held in the names of a husband and wife is for the purposes of income tax to be regarded as income to which they are beneficially entitled in equal shares. (This does not apply to certain items of income: s.282A.) It is recognised that the vesting of legal title in joint names may not reflect beneficial entitlement in the property, and the spouses are provided with a means of clarifying the position where one spouse is entitled to the exclusion of the other or where they are beneficially entitled in unequal shares (ICTA 1988, s.282A(3)). This is a declaration by both spouses of their beneficial interests in (a) the income to which the declaration relates and (b) the property from which that income arises (ICTA 1988, s.282B). However, a declaration does not have effect in relation to income from property if the beneficial interests of the husband and wife in the property itself do not correspond to their beneficial interests in the income. It is, therefore, not open to one spouse to seek in this way to transfer income to the other spouse for income tax purposes by means of such a declaration without a transfer of the underlying property interest. This is a necessary complement to the rule which makes transfers of income from one spouse to another by covenant ineffective for tax purposes.

A declaration continues to have effect unless and until the beneficial interests of the husband and wife in either the income to which it relates, or the property from which the income arises, cease to accord with the declaration. A declaration does not have effect unless notice of it is given to the inspector in such form and manner as may be prescribed within sixty days beginning with the date of the declaration. It has effect in relation to income arising on or after the date of the declaration unless made before 6 June 1990 when it also has effect in relation to income arising before that date. (See generally s.282B.)

It remains to be seen what effect such a declaration will have in subsequent disputes between spouses following breakdown of the marriage. Unless there has been a mistake or fraud, it would seem difficult for a spouse to show that beneficial entitlement to the property concerned is other than that stated in the declaration. If the beneficial entitlement set out in the declaration is inconsistent with the contributions to the acquisition of the property then the declaration may be regarded as satisfying the requirements of s.53(1)(c) of the Law of Property Act 1925.

Section 282A does not apply where property is vested in the name of one spouse alone, though it is well established that the vesting of legal title is not conclusive as to the beneficial interest in the property (see Chapter 2). Where spouses are living together, difficulties of proof may well arise where it is claimed that one spouse holds the legal title upon trust for the other wholly or in part. Unless there is very clear proof that the spouse without legal title contributed to the purchase of an asset, the Revenue may understandably be reluctant to treat that spouse as having a beneficial interest. There will be a strong incentive, therefore, to transfer title into joint names or at least make an express declaration of the beneficial interests in the property concerned.

(vii) Mortgage interest relief

The situations in which an individual can obtain relief for interest paid, by a deduction in computing income for tax purposes, are limited. The most important instance in the family context is the relief which is available in respect of interest payable on a loan used to acquire a family home if certain conditions are satisfied. In relation to mortgage payments made on or after 6 April 1991, relief is limited to the basic rate of income tax (FA 1991, s.27).

The first condition is that the interest must be paid by a person for the time being owning an estate or interest in land in the United Kingdom or the Republic of Ireland on a loan applied in purchasing the estate or interest, or one absorbed into, or given up to obtain that estate or interest, or in developing the land or buildings on the land or to pay off a loan used for that purpose. Interest on a loan used to improve a house is eligible for relief only if the loan was made before 6 April 1988 (ICTA 1988, s.354).

Secondly, the land, caravan or houseboat must be used as the only or main residence of the person paying the interest (the borrower) (ICTA 1988, s.355). Whether a property is a borrower's "main" residence is a question of fact (*Frost* v *Feltham* [1981] 1 WLR 452. In contrast to the position in relation to capital gains tax it is not open to the taxpayer to choose which of two or more residences is to be regarded as his or her main residence for this purpose). A borrower may obtain relief for interest paid on a loan secured on a property which is not his main residence but which he uses as his residence or which he intends to use in due course as his only or main residence, if at the time he resides in living accommodation which for him is "job-related" (ICTA 1988, s.356). Relief is also now available in certain circumstances to a self-employed borrower who is required to live on other premises provided by another person under a contract entered into at arm's length. Where a borrower, entitled to relief in respect of a loan on his only or main residence, raises another loan for the purpose of acquiring another property for use as his only or main residence then, for a period of twelve months, relief will continue to apply in respect of interest on the first loan and will also apply to interest on the new loan as if no interest was payable in respect of the first loan. In other words the first loan will not be taken into account in calculating the £30,000 limit for the purposes of the new loan (see condition 3 below). In order to obtain the benefit of this provision the new property must actually be used by the borrower as his residence: *Hughes* v *Viner* (1985) 58 TC 437. The Revenue may extend the period of twelve months if it appears to be reasonable to do so. In respect of interest on a loan used to acquire property used as a main residence of a dependent relative (a former or separated spouse) of the borrower, relief is available only if the loan was taken out before 6 April 1988.

Where a husband and wife are not separated, only one residence may be treated as their only or main residence. Thus if the husband pays interest in respect of a loan on one residence as his only or main residence and the wife pays interest in respect of a loan on another residence as her only or main residence, then the residence which was purchased first will be treated as their only or main residence for the purpose of mortgage interest relief (ICTA 1988, s.356B(8) and FA 1988, Sched. 3, para. 14. This is in contrast to the position of unmarried couples who may still try to show that each has a different main residence, though the amount of relief available in respect of one residence is now restricted).

Thirdly, interest is eligible for relief only to the extent that the loan in respect of which it is payable does not exceed the "qualifying maximum" which is at present £30,000 (ICTA 1988, ss.356A and 367(5), FA 1988, s.41).

In the case of loans obtained before 1 August 1988 each borrower became (and now remains) entitled to a qualifying maximum of £30,000 reduced by the amount of earlier loans eligible for relief. Accordingly where a house was jointly purchased before that date by an unmarried couple, each was entitled (and remains) to relief on a loan up to the qualifying maximum of £30,000, giving a total relief of £60,000. In contrast, a husband and wife were treated as one person and thus were together eligible for relief only up to the qualifying maximum of £30,000. This difference was one of "the penalties of marriage", and was removed for the future by the Finance Act 1988 (s.42). The limit of relief in respect of loans taken out on or after 1 August 1988 will be related to a particular residence irrespective of the number of borrowers (ICTA 1988, s.356C(3)).

Accordingly, the position in relation to loans taken out on or after 1 August 1988 is as follows:

(a) Where the qualifying interest in relation to a residence is payable by one person, it is eligible for relief to the extent that the loan in respect of which it is payable does not exceed the qualifying maximum for the year of assessment (at present £30,000) reduced by the amount of earlier loans in respect of which the borrower is eligible for relief (ICTA 1988, s.356A(1)).

(b) Where the qualifying interest in relation to a residence is payable by more than one person, the interest paid by each of them is eligible for relief only to the extent that the amount on which it is payable by an individual borrower does not exceed his or her limit (the "sharer's limit"). The sharer's limit is arrived at by dividing the amount of the qualifying maximum during the period (£30,000) by the number of persons by whom qualifying interest is payable for the period in relation to the residence. Where one sharer's limit exceeds the amount of the loan on which interest is payable by him or her and the other sharer's limit is less than the amount of the loan on which interest is payable by the other sharer, the latter's limit is increased by the amount of the excess. (Where there are more than two sharers, provision is made for the division of the excess of one sharer to be shared amongst the other sharers with a short-fall.) Thus where there are two sharers, each is entitled to a share of relief of £15,000. If one has borrowed £35,000 and the other has borrowed £10,000, the excess of relief to which the latter is entitled (£5,000) is transferred to the former.

(c) As from 6 April 1990 each spouse is entitled to relief in his or her own right, but a husband and wife who are not separated may jointly elect that qualifying interest payable or paid by one of them shall be treated as payable or paid by the other. Where a third person is involved the spouses may still elect and the sharer's limit of one of them will be reduced and the sharer's limit of the other will be correspondingly increased (FA 1988, Sched. 3, para. 14).

Mortgage interest relief used to be given by way of a charge on income, thereby reducing the borrower's statutory income - and payments being made gross. Tax relief is now given by allowing the borrower to deduct tax at the basic rate on the interest paid under the Mortgage Interest Relief at Source Scheme - MIRAS.

## 3. Capital gains tax

### (a) General principles

Capital gains tax is levied on chargeable gains which accrue to a person on the disposal of assets in a year of assessment after deducting allowable losses (Taxation of Chargeable Gains Act 1992 (TCGA 1992) ss.1 and 2). In general a gain (or a loss) is the difference between the actual or deemed acquisition cost of an asset together with allowable expenditure thereon and the consideration received or deemed to be received on the disposal (TCGA 1992, Pt.II, Chapter I). In relation to an asset held on 31 March 1982, for the purpose of calculating any gain or loss on the disposal of the asset on or after 6 April 1988 it is assumed that on 31 March 1982 it was sold by the person making the disposal and immediately re-acquired by him at its market value on that date (TCGA 1992, s.35). Accordingly, any part of a gain which arose before April 1982 will be exempt from tax altogether. An indexation allowance may be claimed in relation to gains accruing since 31 March 1982 so that in theory at least the taxing of purely inflationary gains is ended (TCGA 1992, ss.53 and 54).

The amount of tax that would otherwise be chargeable may be reduced by a number of exemptions, the most important of which in the family context is that applicable on the disposal of the taxpayer's private residence or of an interest therein (TCGA 1992, s.222). Moreover, an individual is not chargeable to capital gains tax in respect of so much of his "taxable amount" (i.e. his chargeable gains less allowable losses for the year and losses brought forward) for any year of assessment as does not exceed the "exempt amount" for the year (TCGA 1992, s.3). In 1993-94 this is £5,800. Capital gains tax is now levied on the taxable amount at rates which are the same as the rates of income tax, ie. 1993-94 at 20%, 25% and 40% (TCGA 1992, s.4). The taxable amount of the capital gains, (after deducting the amount of the annual exemption) will be taxed as if it constituted the highest part of the taxpayer's income. Thus, if the taxpayer's taxable income exceeds his basic rate tax band (£23,700) then the whole of the gains will be subject to tax at the higher rate.

*(b) Marriage and capital gains tax*

The gains and losses of a husband and wife are calculated separately, and losses incurred by one of them are set against that spouse's gains. Up until 6 April 1990 the amount of capital gains tax on chargeable gains accruing to a married woman in a year of assessment, or part of a year of assessment, during which she was living with her husband, was assessed and charged on her husband and they were together entitled to only one annual exemption. In 1990-91 and subsequent years, a husband and wife living together are taxed independently in relation to capital gains and each is entitled to an annual exemption. The rate of capital gains tax applicable to the gains of a spouse will, therefore, depend only on the taxable income of that spouse to which his or her own gains will be added.

*(c) Transfers between spouses*

Where in any year of assessment a husband and wife are living together, the disposal of an asset by one to the other is to be treated as if the consideration were of such amount as would secure that on the disposal neither gain nor loss would accrue to the spouse making the disposal (TCGA 1992, s.58). No capital gains tax is, therefore, payable, but the spouse acquiring the asset is treated as having acquired it for whatever is the base value of the asset in the hands of the disposing spouse. There is, accordingly, no uplift in base value so that the effect is to postpone a charge on any gain, or an allowance for any loss, until the property is further disposed of outside the marital unit, when the gain or loss will be calculated by reference to the whole period of ownership of both spouses, or since 31 March 1982. Where an asset was held by a transferor on 31 March 1982, the general rule is that on a disposal after 5 April 1988 it will be deemed to have been sold and immediately re-acquired at its market value on that date. This rebasing rule will not apply to a disposal between husband and wife unless the transferor spouse makes an election that all gains and losses of all assets held on 31 March 1982 be calculated by reference to their market value on that date (TCGA 1992, s.35(3)(d), (5) and (9)). However, where there has been a transfer between spouses after 31 March 1982 then the transferee spouse will be treated as having held the asset on that date when making a further disposal which is not a no gain/no loss disposal (TCGA 1992, Sched. 3, para. 1).

*(d) Principal private residence exemption*

An exemption from capital gains tax which is of great importance in the family context is that which applies to a gain accruing to an individual on the disposal of a dwelling-house or part of a dwelling-house that has been his or her only or main residence throughout his or her period of ownership (TCGA 1992, s.222). The exemption also extends to land that is occupied and enjoyed with the residence as its garden or grounds up to 0.5 of a hectare, or such larger area as the Commissioners are satisfied is required for the reasonable enjoyment of it as a residence.

Where a person has more than one residence at the same time he or she may elect, by notice in writing to the inspector, which residence is to be treated as the main residence for this purpose. If no election is made, the question will be determined by the inspector, subject to a right of appeal (TCGA 1992, s.222(5). Notice of election must be given not more than two years from the beginning of the period for which it is to be effective and continues in effect until varied by a further notice). A man and his wife living with him can have only one residence or main residence so long as they are living together (TCGA 1992, s.222(6). Notice of election affecting both spouses must be given by both). A gain will be wholly exempt only if the dwelling-house has been an individual's only or main residence throughout the period of ownership (since 31 March 1982) or throughout that period except for all or any part of the last thirty-six months of that period (TCGA 1992, s.223(1). Certain periods of absence are permitted by s.223(3). See also Inland Revenue extra-statutory concessions D3 and D4). Where the dwelling house has not been so occupied the exemption will apply only to a fraction of the gain proportionate to the period when it was the only or main residence of the individual, and including the last thirty-six months of the ownership (TCGA 1992, s.223(2)).

Where the former matrimonial home, or an interest in it, is transferred by one spouse to the other following breakdown of the marriage, the transferor spouse will normally be able to take advantage of the principal private residence exemption (but see *M* v *M (Sale of Property)* [1988] FLR 389). If not, he or she may be able to take advantage of Inland Revenue extra-statutory concession D6 whereby the home may be regarded as continuing to be a residence of the transferring spouse from the date his or her occupation ceases until the date of transfer provided that:

(a) the home remains the only or main residence of the transferee spouse or ex-spouse; and

(b) during the period of absence the transferor has not elected that some other house should be treated for capital gains tax purposes as his or her main residence for this period.

Where property or an interest in property which has never been the only or main residence of either spouse is transferred following breakdown of a marriage the exemption will not be available and it is important that the impact of capital gains tax is taken into account in determining the orders to be made.

## 4. Inheritance tax

*(a) General principles*

Inheritance tax is charged on the value transferred by a chargeable transfer (Inheritance Tax Act 1984 (IHTA 1984), s.1). A chargeable transfer is a transfer of value (other than an exempt transfer) made by an individual (IHTA 1984, s.2). A transfer of value is any disposition made by a person ("the transferor") as a result of which the value of his estate immediately after the disposition is less than it would be but for the disposition, and the amount by which it is less is the value transferred by the transfer (IHTA 1984, s.3(1). For the meaning of "estate" see s.5. No account is to be taken of "excluded property" as defined in s.6). On the death of any person tax is charged as if, immediately before his death, he had made a transfer of value and the value transferred by it had been equal to the value of his estate immediately before death (IHTA 1984, s.4(1)). An *inter vivos* transfer of value by an individual which is not an exempt transfer will be a potentially exempt transfer to the extent that it constitutes either a gift to another individual or a gift into an accumulation and maintenance trust, a "disabled" trust or a trust with an interest in possession, e.g. a life interest (IHTA 1984, s.3A). This means that it will be assumed that the transfer will prove to be an exempt transfer until either seven years have elapsed since the date of the transfer or, if it is earlier, the death of the transferor (IHTA 1984, s.3A(5)). If the transferor survives the seven year period the transfer will be an exempt transfer. If he or she fails to survive the seven year period the transfer will be a chargeable transfer (IHTA 1984, s.3A(4)). Accordingly, no inheritance tax is payable when a potentially exempt transfer is made, and if the transferor survives the seven year period it will escape inheritance tax altogether. If the transferor dies within three years of the date of the transfer, then inheritance tax is charged on the value transferred at the full rate applicable on death. If the transferor dies more than three years after the date of the transfer, but within seven years thereof, inheritance tax is charged at a percentage of the death rate as follows:

(a) where the transfer is made more than three but not more than four years before the death, 80%

(b) where the transfer is made more than four but not more than five years before the death, 60%

(c) where the transfer is made more than five but not more than six years before the death, 40%; and

(d) where the transfer is made more than six but not more than seven years before the death, 20%.

(IHTA 1984, s.7(4)).

Inheritance tax is charged on the value transferred by a chargeable transfer on death or within seven years preceding death at the full death rate or rates subject to a deduction as outlined in the previous paragraph (IHTA 1984, s.7 and Sched. 1). In the tax year 1993-94 these are as follows:

| Portion of Value | | Rate of Tax |
|---|---|---|
| Lower Limit | Upper Limit | Per Cent |
| 0 | 150,000 | nil |
| 150,000 | - | 40 |

Inheritance tax is charged on the value transferred by a chargeable transfer made before death at one half of the rate or rates applicable on death (IHTA 1984, s.7(2)). This means that if the transferor dies within seven years of the transfer the tax chargeable has to be recalculated at the full rate so that additional tax may be payable. Moreover, the principle of cumulation means that the calculation of tax on a transfer must take into account chargeable transfers already made by the transferor in the period of seven years ending with the date of the transfer (IHTA 1984, s.7(1)). Thus if the transferor has within the preceding seven years made chargeable transfers amounting to £150,000 or more, inheritance tax will then be charged at 20 per cent or 40 per cent as the case may be. So long as a transfer of value is a potentially exempt transfer it is not taken into account in calculating the transferor's cumulative total. However, if the transferor fails to survive the seven year period and it becomes a chargeable transfer it is then brought into the transferor's cumulative total with effect from the date it was actually made.

*(b) Transfers between spouses*

Transfers between spouses, whether *inter vivos* or on death, are generally exempt transfers irrespective of the nature or amount of the property concerned (IHTA 1984, s.18(1)). If immediately before the transfer, the transferor, but not the transferor's spouse, is domiciled in the United Kingdom, the exemption is restricted to £55,000, less any amount previously taken into account for the purposes of this exemption (IHTA 1984, s.18(2)). For the exemption to apply it is not necessary for the spouses to be living together and accordingly the crucial date for the continued application of the exemption is the date of the decree absolute of divorce or nullity. A transfer of property, whether or not in pursuance of a court order, will be exempt up until that date but not thereafter. It has been noted in Chapter 10 that orders for the transfer of property, while they can be made on or after granting a decree nisi, only become effective on decree absolute. This does not prevent a transfer being made before decree absolute, but in many cases it will not be feasible to make a transfer before this date. (In *G* v *G* [1975] The Times 12 November the court refused to grant a decree absolute until the husband had undertaken to pay any capital transfer tax which might arise in respect of transfers made by him after the decree.) At this stage it may still be possible to rely on s.10(1) of the Inheritance Tax Act 1984. This provides that a disposition is not a transfer of value if it is shown that it was not intended, and was not made in a transaction intended to confer gratuitous benefit on any person and either (a) that it was made in a transaction at arm's length between persons not connected with each other, or (b) that it was such as might be expected to be made in a transaction at arm's length between persons not connected with each other. (On decree absolute husband and wife will cease to be "connected persons" for this purpose: IHTA 1984, s.270.) The Senior Registrar of the Family Division, with the agreement of the Inland Revenue, has issued a statement as follows:

"Transfers of money or property pursuant to an order of the court in consequence of a decree of divorce or nullity of marriage will in general be regarded
as exempt from capital transfer tax as transactions at arm's length which are not
intended to confer any gratuitous benefit.

If, exceptionally, such a benefit is intended it is the duty of the transferor to
deliver a capital transfer account ..." ((1975) 125 NLJ 841; 119 SJ 596).

It should be noted that the statement applies only to transfers in pursuance of court
orders.

By virtue of s.11 of the Inheritance Tax Act 1984 certain dispositions for the
maintenance of members of the family are not to be treated as transfers of value.
First, a disposition is not a transfer of value if it is made by one party to a marriage
in favour of the other party or of a child of either party, and is:

 (a) for the maintenance of the other party, or
 (b) for the maintenance, education or training of the child for a period ending not
    later than the year in which he attains the age of 18 or, after attaining that age,
    ceases to undergo full-time education or training.

 (s.11(1)).

In view of the general exemption for transfers between spouses it will not generally
be necessary to seek to rely on this provision during a marriage though it may be
necessary to do so where the transferee spouse is domiciled outside the United
Kingdom thereby restricting the amount of the general exemption. It may, however,
be possible to rely on this provision even after decree absolute for it is provided that
"marriage" in relation to a disposition made on the occasion of the dissolution or
annulment of a marriage, and in relation to a disposition varying a disposition so
made, includes a former marriage (IHTA 1984, s.11(6)). The provision therefore
covers a disposition to a former spouse if made on the occasion of the divorce, but it
is limited to "maintenance". While transfers in the form of periodical payments
would clearly be covered, the position in relation to lump sum payments or transfers
of property is less clear. The courts have rejected the idea that a lump sum payment
is merely another form of maintenance though in some cases, e.g. where difficulties
over enforcement are envisaged, a lump sum may be fulfilling the role of periodical
payments in part. In some cases, too, the transfer of property in the form of an interest in the matrimonial home may be seen as a way of providing maintenance.

Secondly, it is provided that a disposition is not a transfer of value if it is made in
favour of a child who is not in the care of a parent of his and is for his maintenance,
education or training for a period ending not later than the year in which (a) he
attains the age of 18, or (b) after attaining that age he ceases to undergo full-time
education or training. However, (b) applies only if before attaining that age the child
has for substantial periods been in the care of the person making the disposition
(IHTA 1984, s.11(2)).

Thirdly, a disposition is not a transfer of value if it is made in favour of an illegitimate child of the person making the disposition and is for the maintenance, education or training of the child for a period ending not later than the year in which
attains the age of 18, or after attaining that age, ceases to undergo full-time education or training (IHTA 1984, s.11(4)).

Where a disposition satisfies the conditions of the provisions of s.11 to a limited extent only, so much of it as satisfies them and so much of it as does not satisfy them are to be treated as separate dispositions (s.11(5)).

Finally, it may of course be possible to rely on other exemptions generally applicable. Thus the first £3,000 of transfers of value made by a transferor in a tax year are exempt. To the extent that transfers of value in the preceding year did not exceed £3,000, the balance may be brought forward (IHTA 1984, s.19).

## 5. Taxation of maintenance on the breakdown of marriage

### (a) The background

The Finance Act 1988 made sweeping changes in the taxation of periodical payments by way of maintenance. Under the new system such payments take effect outside the tax system subject only to limited relief. The generous tax relief that could be obtained under the old system by a person liable to make maintenance payments is no longer available. Such relief could be regarded as a subsidy which helped the family cope with the increased financial burdens generally resulting from marriage breakdown, but it was open to criticism as being poorly targeted. As noted earlier, it provided the biggest subsidy for those with incomes able to support large maintenance payments and with a high marginal rate of tax. (See Schuz, *Taxation of Maintenance Payments* [1985] BTR 306 and [1988] BTR 233.) However, the Finance Act 1988 sought to preserve relief enjoyed in relation to payments under existing obligations. Such payments are accordingly not subjected to the new system (unless the payer so elects) but are subject to a modified version of the old system.

### (b) Maintenance arrangements under the "old system"

#### (i) Payments to a spouse or former spouse

Until the tax year 1989/90 periodical payments made by a husband to his wife under an order of a court or a separation or maintenance agreement were "annual payments" for the purposes of the Taxes Act, even though paid weekly or monthly. The classification of payments as "annual payments" had important consequences for both husband and wife, for it meant that for income tax purposes the payments were treated as the income of the wife as recipient and not the income of the husband as payer. In other words, "annual payments" effected the transfer of income from husband to wife, while mere "voluntary payments" were simply an application of income by the husband and had no tax consequences. Annual payments were charged to tax as the income of the wife as recipient under Schedule D, Case III (ICTA 1988, s.18), but in many cases direct assessment on the wife was unnecessary because payments made by the husband were subject to deduction of tax under s.348 or 349 of the Taxes Act 1988. The gross amount of the annual payment was taken into account in computing the total income of the wife as recipient. If she was liable to higher rate tax a direct assessment was made under Schedule D, Case III in respect of her excess liability. If she was not liable to tax at the basic rate because, for example, her total income was insufficient to exhaust her personal reliefs, then she could make a repayment claim. On the other hand, in computing the total income of the husband the gross amount of the "annual payments" had to be deducted, for that was in effect no longer regarded as his income, but that of the wife. The husband was thus able to obtain relief against higher rate tax as well as basic rate tax, but having obtained relief from basic rate tax by deduction from the payments, allowance for the sum so deducted had to be made in calculating the amount payable to the Inland Revenue.

When payments were "small maintenance payments" as defined in the Taxes Act 1988, s.351, they were required to be made gross. Such payments were chargeable to tax in the hands of the recipient under Schedule D, Case III, though the basis of the provision was that in the majority of cases the recipient's total income was likely to be such that, after taking into account personal reliefs, no income tax was in fact payable. The provisions relating to small maintenance payments were repealed in relation to payments made on or after 6 April 1989 (FA 1988, s.148 and Sched. 14, Pt. IV).

(ii) Payments to or for children

Payments to or for a child had no effect for income tax purposes unless made under a binding agreement or a court order. An agreement or court order could provide for payments for a child in three ways.

First, an agreement or court order might provide for payments to be made by a husband to his wife or former wife for the maintenance of the child (*Stevens* v *Tirard* [1940] 1 KB 204). In this event the payments were treated as the income of the recipient spouse or former spouse and not of the child. The effect was to transfer income to the recipient spouse in the same way as provision for the recipient spouse herself.

Secondly, payments might be required to be made to a spouse or former spouse on trust for a child. However, this was held to be a settlement within s.663 of the Taxes Act 1988 so that if the child was under the age of 18 and unmarried, the payments would be deemed to remain the income of the parent making the payment (*Yates* v *Starkey* [1951] Ch 465). This form of order was, therefore, generally avoided.

Thirdly, an agreement or order might provide for payments to be made by a parent to a child. If the child was unmarried and under the age of 18 then the agreement constituted a "settlement" within s.663 of the Taxes Act 1988 so that income remained the income of the paying parent and did not become the income of the child (*Harvey* v *Sivyer* [1986] Ch 119). Where payment was provided for under a court order there was no settlement. The payments then became income of the child for tax purposes. The child could take advantage of his or her personal allowances (and basic rate tax band) and make a repayment claim in respect of basic rate tax deducted if this was appropriate. The paying parent could deduct the amount of the payments in calculating his total income and obtain relief in respect of higher rate tax as well as basic rate tax. It was, therefore, highly desirable that provision for a child should take the form of a court order for payment direct to a child. Such an order could be made by consent and the paying parent could apply for an order against himself (see *Sherdley* v *Sherdley* [1988] AC 213).

## (c) Existing obligations

### (i) Meaning
The old system applies with modifications to maintenance payments made under "existing obligations" which under the Finance Act 1988, s.36(4) comprise the following:

(a) an order made by a court (whether in the United Kingdom or elsewhere) before 15 March 1988, or before the end of June 1988 on an application made on or before 15 March 1988;

(b) a deed executed or a written agreement made before 15 March 1988 and received by an Inspector of Taxes before the end of June 1988;

(c) an oral agreement made before 15 March 1988, written particulars of which were received by an Inspector before the end of June 1988;

(d) an order made by a court (whether in the United Kingdom or elsewhere) on or after 15 March 1988, or under a written agreement made on or after that date, where the order or agreement replaces, varies or supplements an order or agreement within the old system. In this case it must be an obligation to make periodical payments as one of the parties to a marriage or former marriage to or for the benefit, and for the maintenance, of the other party or to any person under 21 for his own benefit, maintenance or education, or to any person for the benefit, maintenance or education of a person under 21 and the order or agreement replaced, varied or supplemented provided for such payments to be made for the benefit, maintenance or, as the case may be, education of the same person (s.36(5)).

### (ii) The position in 1988-1989
For the tax year 1988-89 the payments made under an existing obligation remained the taxable income of the recipient. However, a divorced or separated spouse who had not remarried who received payments for his or her maintenance or any child of the family was entitled in computing his or her total income to deduct an amount equal to the aggregate amount of the payments, or £1,490, whichever was the less (FA 1988, s.37). Where payments were made direct to a child under a court order and so became his or her income, these did not qualify for the deduction. The person making the payments under an agreement or an order continued to be entitled to relief on the same basis as in previous years. Payments would have been made subject to deduction of basic rate tax unless they were small maintenance payments.

### (iii) The position from 1989-90 onwards
From 1989-90 onwards payments under existing obligations do not amount to a charge on the income of the person making them whether made to a spouse for his or her own benefit, or for the benefit of a child of the family or made direct to a child of the family. Payments are to be made gross without deduction of basic rate income tax, but the payer is entitled to claim a deduction equal to the aggregate amount of the payments made in a tax year provided this does not exceed the aggregate amount of the payments due in the years 1988-89 (FA 1988, s.38). In other words, notwithstanding subsequent increases in the amounts payable under an

agreement or order, the amount of relief cannot exceed that available in the tax year 1988-89. All payments qualifying for relief in 1988-89 are aggregated for the purposes of calculating this limit.

Payments will continue to form part of the income of the recipient up to the aggregate amount of any payments made by the payer which formed part of the recipient's income for the year 1988-89 (FA 1988, s.38(1), (3) and (4)). In the case of payments made to a spouse for the maintenance of the recipient or a child of the family, the recipient, if he or she has not remarried, will be entitled to a deduction equal to the difference between the married person's relief and the single person's relief for 1989-90 and equal to the married couple's allowance from 1990-91 onwards (FA 1988, s.38(5) and (6)). Payments will be charged to tax under Case III of Schedule D or, if it arises outside the United Kingdom, under Schedule D, Case V (FA 1988, s.38(8)).

*(d) Maintenance arrangements under the "new system"*

(i) General principles
Under the "new system" introduced by the Finance Act 1988 periodical payments made by a husband to his wife under an order of a court or a separation or maintenance agreement, whether for the maintenance of the recipient spouse or of a child of the family, do not become the income of the recipient. Similarly payments made direct to a child under a court order no longer become the income of the child (ICTA 1988, s.347A(1)(b)). This also applies to maintenance payments arising outside the United Kingdom, i.e. under foreign orders and agreements which generally fall within Case V of Schedule D (see s.347A(4)). Accordingly, such payments are not assessable to tax as income of the recipient. This means that there is no advantage in a court order providing for payments to be made direct to a child and it will no longer be possible to utilise the personal allowance and basic rate tax band of the child.

Payments must be made gross, without deduction of tax at the basic rate. The person making a maintenance payment is not entitled to deduct the amount of the payments as a charge on his income in computing his income for tax purposes (ICTA 1988, s.347A(1)(a)). However, the payer, in computing his total income, will be entitled to deduct an amount equal to the aggregate amount of any "qualifying maintenance payment" made by him and falling due in a year but not exceeding the amount of the married couple's allowance for that year (ICTA 1988, s.347(2) and (3) and s.257A(1), and FA 1988, s.35). Only one such deduction may be claimed irrespective of the number of persons (former spouses or children) being maintained.

A "qualifying maintenance payment" is a periodical payment made under an order made by a court in a member state of the European Community, or under a written agreement, the proper law of which is the law of a member state or of part of a member state of the European Community, by a party to a marriage or former marriage to or for the benefit of the other party for the maintenance of the other party or to the other party for the maintenance of any child of the family (TA 1988, s.347B(1) as amended by Finance (No. 2) Act 1992, s.61). Thus payments qualify when made to the other spouse for the maintenance of a child of the family, but not when made direct to a child under a court order to that effect. If the marriage has been terminated, then payments cease to be qualifying maintenance payments when the recipient remarries. This means that payments to a custodial parent for the benefit of a child of the family will also cease to be qualifying maintenance payments for this purpose when that parent remarries. On the other hand, the remarriage of the party liable to make the payments will not affect the availability of the relief. Moreover the payer will then also be entitled to the married couple's allowance by virtue of the new marriage.

Where a party making qualifying maintenance payments also makes other maintenance payments attracting relief under the "old system" then the relief in respect of the "qualifying maintenance payments" is reduced by an amount equal to the aggregate amount of those other payments (s.347B(4)).

It is apparent that the new system has a dramatic effect on the availability of tax relief following separation and divorce. The maximum saving obtainable by the payer is (at current rates) 25% of the married couple's allowance if he is a basic rate taxpayer (£430) or 40% of that allowance if he pays tax at the higher rate (£688). The recipient spouse may in one way be better off if she has other income of her own. Since the maintenance payments are no longer her taxable income, the personal allowance (and basic rate tax band) to which she is entitled may now be set entirely against that other income (thereby producing a saving as compared with the old system). However, this must be balanced against the likely effect of the reduction in the relief available to the payer. The increased burden on the payer may reduce his capacity to pay maintenance, and lead to a reduction in the amount payable under a court order. The court will be concerned to consider the "net effect" of an order on the payer as well as the "net effect" on the recipient so that a downward variation of periodical payments may be justified. In so far as the "new system" benefits the recipient who is able to earn income of her own it can be said to encourage the policy in ss.25 and 25A of the Matrimonial Causes Act 1973 (see Chapter 11).

### (ii) Taxpayer's election

A person liable to make payments under an existing agreement or court order may elect to change from the old system to the new system. Such an election must affect all payments made by that person under existing agreements or orders (FA 1988, s.39(1)). The election must be made not later than twelve months after the end of the year of assessment for which it is to have effect. It has effect for any subsequent year of assessment and is irrevocable (s.39(2)). The payer must, within 30 days of the election, give notice of it to every recipient of a payment affected by the election (s.39(3)). The election must be made in such form and manner as the Board of Inland Revenue may prescribe.

Such an election will become advantageous when the married couple's allowance exceeds the maintenance in respect of which the payer was entitled to tax relief in 1988-89. It is also essential that payments are being made to a separated or former spouse, for a deduction equivalent to that difference is allowed only in respect of such payments and not in respect of payments direct to a child. If a recipient would prefer to receive payments tax free, it may be appropriate for the payments to be reduced either by agreement or by court order.

## (iii) School fees

A parent could obtain tax relief in respect of payments made for school fees on the same basis that relief could be obtained for general maintenance payments, i.e. that there was a transfer of income to the child concerned. Tax relief might also be obtained by a transfer of income to the mother for the benefit of the child, but the mother's personal reliefs might already be fully utilised. A court order was necessary to avoid the effect of s.663 of the Taxes Act 1988 which applied to agreements and meant that the income would remain that of the paying parent. It was also essential that the parent making the payments was not contractually liable to the school for the fees though there was no objection to the other parent, usually the mother, taking over the liability. In this way the relevant sums constituted periodical payments to the child though they would be received by the mother and used by her to discharge her liability for the school fees. The sum specified in the order would either be a gross amount (from which tax would be deducted) or, perhaps more commonly, an amount equivalent to such sum as after deduction of income tax at the basic rate would equal the school fees. The latter form avoided the need to apply for variation when school fees increased. The arrangements could be carried a stage further by a provision that the sum on account of fees should be paid direct to the school by the parent against whom the order was made. A precedent of an appropriate order is contained in Practice Direction [1987] 2 All ER 1084 amending an earlier Practice Direction [1983] 2 All ER 679 which does, however, contain an appropriate form of contract with the school.

No relief can be obtained in this way by virtue of an order for which application is first made after 15 March 1988. Relief may still be obtained where the payment of sums on account of school fees was provided for in an "existing obligation" (see FA 1988, s.36(4) and (*c*) above). Moreover, even if an "existing obligation" in favour of a child did not provide as such for school fees, it can be varied to include such provision, but the maximum relief available to the parent making the payments cannot exceed the total payments he was liable to make to his former or separated spouse and children in the year 1988-89. All payments must be made gross and without deduction of income tax since 5 April 1989.

## (iv) "Tax-free" provision for a spouse

All agreements and orders subject to the new system of taxation of maintenance payment should provide for the payment of gross sums, and such sums will be paid without deduction of tax. Agreements and orders made under the old system usually provided for payment of gross sums "less tax" or at least provided for payment of gross sums on the basis that tax at the basic rate would be deducted when they were paid. Since 5 April 1989, such payments must be made gross (FA 1988, s.38(7)). However, some agreements and orders sought to provide the recipient with a fixed amount so that whatever tax was payable and deducted he or she received that amount, no more, no less. An order for payment "free of tax" was construed as an order to pay such sum as after deduction of basic rate income tax equalled the sum specified in the order (*Jefferson* v *Jefferson* [1956] P 136). Since 5 April 1989 such an order requires the payment of the specified sum to be grossed up at the basic rate of income tax. Tax free orders were not often made and were much criticised (*Jefferson* v *Jefferson*; *J* v *J* [1955] 2 All ER 617). They are no longer necessary as the recipient will now always receive the gross amount.

An agreement for payment of "such sum as after deduction of income tax at the basic rate will leave £x" required only basic rate income tax to be taken into account so that it was in effect a covenant to pay £x grossed up at the current basic rate. If the recipient made a repayment claim in respect of his or her reliefs and allowances, he or she was under no obligation to hand over any repayment to the party making the payments. Since 5 April 1989 this will take effect as an agreement to pay the grossed up sum. Where the agreement provided for payment of "£x free of tax" the recipient was probably under an obligation to make a repayment claim where appropriate and to account to the payer for any repayment received. (See *Re Pettit* [1922] 2 Ch 765. It was also not clear whether the payer was liable for higher rate tax thereon.) The present position in relation to such a formula in an agreement is uncertain and it is arguable that it should be construed as requiring payment of £x rather than £x grossed up at the basic rate of income tax.

*(e) The foreign element*

(i) United Kingdom orders and agreements
As from 5 April 1989 a person liable to make payments under an order made by a court in the United Kingdom or an agreement governed by the law of a part of the United Kingdom will no longer be entitled to deduct income tax at the basic rate when making the payments. Thus, even where the order or agreement was made before 15 March 1988 payments must be made gross and this applies where the person liable to make payments is resident abroad (FA 1988, s.38. This applies to United Kingdom income tax. Where the payer is required under a foreign tax system to withhold foreign tax the recipient of the payments net of foreign tax may claim a foreign tax credit. See extra-statutory concession A-12).

Where the recipient of payments under a United Kingdom order or agreement is resident abroad then he or she nevertheless remains liable to United Kingdom income tax on income from a United Kingdom source. Thus if the order or agreement was made before 15 March 1988, the payments will continue to form part of the income of the recipient up to the aggregate amount of any payments made by the payer which formed part of the recipient's income for the year 1988-89 (s.38(1), (3) and (4)). As from 5 April 1990, the recipient will be entitled to his or her personal allowances in full if he or she is a Commonwealth citizen or otherwise falls within the provisions of s.278 of the Taxes Act 1988 (FA 1988, s.31. For the year 1989-90 he or she remained entitled only to a proportion of the allowances).

Where the payments are made under a court order or agreement made on or after 15 March 1988, they do not become assessable to tax as income of the recipient.

(ii) Foreign orders and agreements
Payments made under a foreign court order made before 15 March 1988, or under an agreement governed by foreign law made before that date, are assessed as

income of a recipient who is resident in the United Kingdom under Schedule D Case V (*IRC* v *Anderstrom* (1927) 13 TC 482; *Chamney* v *Lewis* (1932) 17 TC 318. Where an agreement is made abroad, *prima facie* the parties are taken to have intended the law of the place where it was made to govern their rights under it, but this presumption can be rebutted by evidence of some contrary intention on their part.) From 1989-90 onwards, such payments will continue to be assessed as the income of the recipient only up to the aggregate amount of any payments so assessed for the year 1988-89 (FA 1988, s.38(4)). The payments may be for his or her own benefit, or may be made to her for the benefit, maintenance or education of a child of the family under 21 years (s.38(1)).

The party making the payments under such an order or agreement must make the payments gross and is not entitled to deduct United Kingdom basic rate tax whether he is resident in the United Kingdom or not (*Keiner* v *Keiner* (1952) 34 TC 346). Moreover, he is not generally entitled to deduct the amount of the payments in calculating his total income for United Kingdom income tax purposes (*Bingham* v *IRC* (1955) 36 TC 254). However, if it appears to the Inland Revenue that payments have been made out of "foreign emoluments" in circumstances corresponding to those in which the payments would have reduced his liability to income tax, the payments may be allowed as a deduction in computing the amount of the emoluments (ICTA 1988, s.192(3). Foreign emoluments are the emoluments of a person not domiciled in the United Kingdom from an office or employment under or with any person, body of persons or partnership resident outside, and not resident in, the United Kingdom: TA 1988, s.192(1)). It is a condition of such a deduction that the payments are made out of the foreign emoluments and the Inland Revenue "... in the exercise of their discretion to allow such claims, will in practice require the claimant to show that he has not sufficient overseas income (on which United Kingdom tax is not chargeable) to enable him to make the payment without having recourse to the foreign emoluments." (IR 25 "The Taxation of Foreign Earnings and Foreign Pensions": Finance Act 1977, para 3.14).

Payments made under a foreign court order made after 14 March 1988 or under an agreement governed by foreign law made after that date are no longer assessed under Schedule D Case V and are exempt from United Kingdom income tax in the hands of the recipient. Generally the person liable to make such payments is not entitled to make any deduction in respect of such payments in computing his total income, i.e. he is not entitled to deduct an amount not exceeding the amount of the married couple's allowance as would be the case if the payments were made under an order made by a court in the United Kingdom or under an agreement governed by the law of part of the United Kingdom.

However, as from 1992-93 payments under an order made by a court in any member state of the European Community or under a written agreement the proper law of which is the law of a member state or part of a member state, will be "qualifying maintenance payments" for the purpose of s.347B of the 1988 Act. Accordingly, if the person making the payments is resident in the United Kingdom, he is entitled to deduct the amount of the payments up to £1,720 (ICTA 1988, s.347B as amended by Finance (No. 2) Act 1992, s.61).

## 6. The matrimonial home

*(a) Declaration of existing rights*
An order under s.17 of the Married Women's Property Act 1882 merely declares existing rights (see Chapter 2). This means that there is no disposal for capital gains tax purposes or transfer of value for inheritance tax purposes. An order under s.24 of the Matrimonial Causes Act 1973 may sometimes do no more than this, but "property adjustment orders" under that section can be made "without investigating too clearly or even at all proprietary titles" (*per* Anthony Lincoln J in *B v B (Real Property: Assessment of Interests)* [1988] 2 FLR 490). In that case the spouses had never occupied as their matrimonial home the property in dispute and a transfer of interest from one to the other would not escape capital gains tax by virtue of the principal private residence exemption. It was, therefore, necessary to evaluate the spouses' respective interests.

*(b) Mesher and Martin Orders*
Where the court makes a Mesher order or a Martin order, the transfer of any interest by either spouse to vest the beneficial ownership in joint names will result in the normal capital gains tax and inheritance tax consequences applying to that transfer. (It may be a "part disposal". See TCGA 1992, s.42. For the terms of a Mesher order and a Martin order, see Chapter 12.) In relation to capital gains tax it will usually be possible to take advantage of the private residence exemption. If not, relief may still be available by virtue of Inland Revenue extra-statutory concession D6 (see Part 3 (d) above). If any such transfer is made after decree absolute it will not be possible to rely on the exemption from inheritance tax for transfers between spouses. In that event it should be possible to rely on the provision of s.10(1) of the IHTA 1984 that a disposition not intended to confer gratuitous benefit is not a transfer of value (see Part 4 (b) above). However, in many cases no transfer of any beneficial interest will be involved though this may not be easy to establish.

The effect of a Mesher or Martin order is that both parties are jointly absolutely entitled to the home and there is no element of succession so that there is no settlement for capital gains tax purposes (*Booth v Ellard* [1978] STC 487). When the home is eventually sold, the former wife having been in occupation throughout the period of ownership will be exempt from capital gains tax in respect of her share of any gain by virtue of the private residence exemption. The former husband, on the other hand, will be liable to capital gains tax except to the extent that he can rely on a proportional exemption based on his period of occupation of the home and the last thirty-six months of ownership. The proportion which will be exempt will be calculated as follows:

$$\text{Husband's indexed gain} \times \frac{\text{husband's period of actual occupation} + \text{the last 36 months of ownership}}{\text{husband's total period of ownership}}$$

If the home was purchased before 31 March 1982, the total period of ownership and the period of actual occupation will be calculated from 31 March 1982 (FA 1988, Sched. 8 para. 8). If the husband left the home before that date then it may be that he is unable to take advantage of the exemption on the basis that at no time during the relevant period of ownership was the property his principal private residence. In this event it may be advantageous to calculate the gain on the basis of the actual pre-1982 acquisition date. (The rule providing for re-basing to 1982 does not apply where a smaller gain would accrue if the rule did not apply: FA 1988 s.96(3)(a).) Although this increases the period of ownership and may result in a higher gain, it will make it possible for the husband to take advantage of the principal private residence exemption by virtue of his pre-1982 occupation. The effect of that period of occupation (together with the last thirty-six months of ownership) may be to reduce the actual chargeable gain.

However, it now appears that the Inland Revenue takes the view that a Mesher order does create a settlement for capital gains tax purposes. (See the account of the correspondence between the Inland Revenue and the College of Law in the Solicitors' Family Law Association Newsletter, February 1993.) This would mean that when the postponement of sale comes to an end and the settlement terminates, the former spouses, as trustees, could rely on the principal private residence exemption on the basis that the house has been the only or main residence of a person, namely the wife, entitled to occupy it under the terms of the settlement (TCGA 1992, s.225). This is likely to be more favourable to the husband than if the order dos not create a settlement. (See Wylie, *Mesher Orders vs. Variable Deferred Charges* [1993] Private Client Business, p.179.)

It is submitted that neither a Mesher order nor a Martin order amounts to a settlement for inheritance tax purposes (IHTA 1984, s.43). Accordingly, on the death of either party his or her share will form part of his or her estate for inheritance tax purposes. If the husband dies first it may be argued that a settlement is created as a result of the former wife's right to occupy the home.

*(c) Transfer of property subject to a charge*
Where the court makes an order vesting the former matrimonial home in one spouse alone, it may order that spouse to pay a lump sum to the other or it may give the other a charge on the property to secure future payment of a specified sum or, more probably, a specified proportion of the proceeds of sale (see Chapter 12).

The transfer of an interest in the home to give effect to the order will frequently take place after decree absolute of divorce. It may give rise to a liability to capital gains tax, but it will usually be possible to take advantage of the private residence exemption (TCGA 1992, s.222), or of extra-statutory concession D6 (see above). If this is not possible because the property has never been the residence of the spouses (as in *Aspden* v *Hildesley* [1982] 1 WLR 264), the transferor may use the annual exemption - but "hold-over" relief under s.79 of the Finance Act 1980 is no longer available.

If the transfer is made after decree absolute of divorce it will not be possible to rely on the exemption from inheritance tax for transfers between spouses. However, s.10(1) of the IHTA 1984 provides that a disposition not intended to confer a gratuitous benefit is not a transfer of value. The Senior Registrar of the Family Division of the High Court, with the agreement of the Inland Revenue, has issued a statement which is quoted in Part 4 (b) above (see (1975) 125 NLJ 841; 119 SJ 596). The statement applies only to transfers in pursuance of a court order. If no exemption is applicable then the transfer will be a potentially exempt transfer so that no tax will be payable unless the transferor dies within seven years.

The immediate payment of a lump sum by way of compensation will not itself give rise to liability to capital gains tax, though the sale of property to raise the necessary funds may obviously do so. Liability for inheritance tax is again likely to be avoided by virtue of IHTA 1984, s.10(1). Where a lump sum payment is to be made in the future the position is more complicated. A specified sum payable in the future constitutes a debt and no capital gains tax will be payable when it is eventually paid (TCGA 1992, s.251). See also *Marren* v *Ingles* [1980] STC 500. Where the sum payable in the future and charged on the property is a specified proportion of the proceeds of sale, it is arguable that it still constitutes a debt so that no capital gains tax will be payable when it is eventually paid. On the other hand, it is arguable that the creation of the charge is the acquisition of an asset - the future right to money - by the person entitled to the charge, rather than the creation of a debt. On this basis capital gains tax would be payable, when the charge is eventually satisfied, on the difference between the value of the share of the proceeds at the date of the order and the value at the date of payment (see *Marson* v *Marriage* [1980] STC 177 and *Marren* v *Ingles*). It would also seem that since the person entitled to the charge has no beneficial interest in the property, he will be unable to take advantage of the principal private residence exemption by virtue of which he would be deemed to have been in occupation for thirty-six months immediately preceding the transfer (TCGA 1992, s.223(2)). (See Wylie *op. cit.*)

It is submitted that no settlement is created for inheritance tax purposes by an order in this form.

### (d) A settlement for life

In some cases the court may order one spouse to provide property to be used as a home for the other spouse for life or until remarriage so that it will revert to the spouse providing the property on termination of the other spouse's life interest. (See Chapter 12, *S* v *S* [1977] Fam 127; *Curtis* v *Curtis* (1981) 11 Fam Law 55.) This clearly involves an element of succession and a settlement is created for the purposes of capital gains tax and inheritance tax.

The creation of the settlement is a disposal for capital gains tax purposes and in many cases it will not be possible to rely on the private residence exemption or on Inland Revenue extra-statutory concession D6 (e.g. *S* v *S*. Some other exemption may, of course, be available; funds may be provided in cash). The creation of the settlement is unlikely to give rise to a potential charge to inheritance tax even if made after decree absolute because it will be regarded as made without any intention of conferring a gratuitous benefit (IHTA 1984, s.10).

If the settlement is created behind a trust for sale then on any disposal of the property by the trustees during the existence of the settlement it will be possible to rely on the private residence exemption for capital gains tax purposes (TCGA 1992, s. 225).

If the settlement terminates on the remarriage of the life tenant or on any other specified event other than her death, the settlor spouse becomes absolutely entitled and for the purposes of capital gains tax the trustees are deemed to dispose of the property at market value and to immediately re-acquire it as nominees for the settlor beneficiary (TCGA 1992, s.71). Any gain made will be exempt from capital gains tax under the private residence exemption (TCGA 1992, s.225). For the purposes of inheritance tax the life tenant is deemed to make a transfer of value of the property (IHTA 1984, s.52), but if the settlor husband is still alive, the reverter to settlor exemption should apply (IHTA 1984, s.53(3)). If the settlor is dead then inheritance tax will be payable as if the former wife had made a gift of the property (IHTA 1984, s.49(1)). It will generally be a potentially exempt transfer.

If the settlement terminates on the death of the life tenant there is again a disposal and a re-acquisition of the trust property by the trustees (TCGA 1992, s.71). Since the property reverts to the settlor, the disposal and re-acquisition by the trustees is at such consideration as to secure that neither gain nor loss accrues to them. This means that the settlor husband re-acquires the property at its market value at the date of the creation of the settlement. For the purposes of inheritance tax the property will form part of the estate of the life tenant (IHTA 1984, s.49(1)), and therefore part of the transfer of value which she is deemed to make on death (IHTA 1984, s.4(1)). If the settlor husband is still alive the reverter to settlor exemption will apply (IHTA 1984, s.53(3)). If the settlor husband dies during the settlement, i.e. before the life tenant dies, then the value of his reversionary interest in the property will be included in his estate for inheritance tax purposes (IHTA 1984, s.48(1)).

*(e) Mortgage interest relief*

Before 6 April 1988 a spouse or former spouse could obtain mortgage interest relief in respect of a loan which had been used to purchase property which was the residence of his or her spouse or former spouse. This was, of course, subject to the condition that the spouse claiming relief had an estate or interest in the property concerned. Thus a former spouse's right to relief was lost if the property was transferred into the sole ownership of the other former spouse. In such circumstances periodical payments (for which tax relief was then available) could be increased to cover mortgage interest payments by the owning and occupying former spouse who would claim mortgage interest relief. This also enabled the other spouse to obtain relief in respect of a loan up to the £30,000 maximum used to purchase a new home.

As from 6 April 1988 mortgage interest relief is only available in respect of a loan used to purchase property used as the residence of the person making the interest payments (FA 1988, s.44(1)). Relief is not available in respect of interest on a loan used to acquire a property used as the residence of a separated or former spouse. Indeed a spouse who leaves the matrimonial home after 6 April 1988 will cease to be entitled to relief on interest paid in respect of the mortgage on that home as it will no longer be his or her only or main residence. However, where interest is paid by a spouse or former spouse on a loan made before 6 April 1988, then if the last time interest was paid on it before that date it was eligible for relief only because the property concerned was used as the only or main residence of a separated or former spouse, relief will continue to be available where the property continues to be used as the only or main residence of the same separated or former spouse (FA 1988, s.44(2) and (3)). Where a husband continues to be entitled to relief in respect of a loan taken out before 6 April 1988 the amount of the loan does not have to be aggregated with the amount of any subsequent loan obtained by the husband to purchase a new home as his only or main residence for the purpose of the £30,000 loan limit.

Relief on mortgage interest payments made on or after 6 April 1991 is restricted to the basic rate of income tax (FA 1991, s.27 and Part 2 above).

# Chapter 19

# Financial provision and the state

## 1. The relevance of state provision for members of a family

There is now a considerable body of law concerned with the provision by various public authorities of services and benefits which have a profound impact on the financial position of many families. Thus in the first place, there is a comprehensive scheme of national insurance which provides for certain specific needs, such as those arising out of old age, unemployment, accidents, sickness and death. Secondly, there is a system of child benefit designed to assist parents in the cost of bringing up children. Thirdly, there is a system of income-related benefits (income support, family credit and housing benefit) together with a social fund designed to meet the needs of those whose resources are still inadequate to meet their needs despite any benefits received from the systems of national insurance or child benefit.

A full consideration of the operation of these and other benefits and services is beyond the scope of this book, for many of them are not specifically designed to meet the needs of a member of a family as such. Nevertheless, even in such cases account is generally taken of the fact that the recipient may be the member of a family with consequent responsibilities towards other members of the family. In any event it will be apparent that their impact on the financial problems of the family cannot be ignored. In *Reiterbund* v *Reiterbund* [1974] 1 WLR 788 at p. 795, where the court was concerned with the relevance of State benefits in determining whether a wife would suffer grave financial hardship as a result of dissolution of her marriage (see Chapter 9), Finer J said that two general points of practical application seemed to emerge:

"First, in the Family Division at any rate, we should recognise that much of the law of national insurance and supplementary benefits is of the greatest possible importance in the daily work of the Division. None of us can afford, in this respect, to make the always suspect separation between lawyer's law that we have to know, and the other law which we have to look up when necessary. The law of pensions and supplementary benefits requires as much expertise and demands as much study from practitioners as any other branch of the family law, of which it is, essentially, a part.

Secondly, it seems to me that when questions of the kind that I am considering arise in proceedings, the proper and convenient course is for the parties to obtain as much relevant information as possible from the records kept by the Department of Health and Social Security and then, so far as possible, to agree the information thus obtained. It would also be desirable for the parties to agree what the consequences might be, in terms of pension and benefit entitlement, of the contingencies which seem to be the most relevant ones to consider. Procedures of this kind are common form for the purpose of assisting the court to fix damages, and it seems to me that it would be most helpful if they were adopted in the field I now have under consideration."

The availability of such services and benefits means that as between members of a family the resources are increased. This will be important in deciding the extent of the financial responsibility of a spouse, and it is necessary to decide to what extent the various benefits, such as income support, should be taken into account by a court in deciding what order for financial provision, if any, is appropriate in any given case. This involves striking a balance between the interests of the members of a family on the one hand and the interests of the general tax paying public on the other. Accordingly, where no orders for financial provision are in force provision is made for recovery from liable relatives of at least part of the cost of providing support for members of a family. These questions are considered in the later Parts of this chapter. However, consideration will first be given to the position of a married woman in the national insurance scheme and to the main features of the child benefit scheme and to the three forms of income-related benefits - income support, family credit, and housing benefit.

## 2. The married woman and National Insurance

### (a) Contributions

The general principle is that insurance under the national insurance scheme is compulsory for all persons between school leaving age and retirement age. Entitlement to benefit has traditionally depended upon a person satisfying the relevant contribution requirements, either on the basis of his or her contributions or, in certain circumstances, on the basis of another person's contributions. However, a number of non-contributory benefits have now been introduced, such as invalidity pension, invalid care allowance, attendance allowance and mobility allowance.

Contributions from insured persons and employers are divided into five categories by s.1(1) of the Social Security Contributions and Benefits Act 1992 ("SSCBA 1992"). These are:

Class 1: a graduated contribution payable by employed earners who are earning in excess of a lower earnings limit and employers of such persons (SSCBA 1992, s.6).

Class 1A:payable in respect of cars made available for private use and in respect of car fuel (SSCBA 1992, s.10).

Class 2: a flat rate contribution payable by self-employed earners (SSCBA, s.11).

Class 3: a flat rate contribution payable voluntarily by earners and others with a view to enabling them to satisfy contribution conditions of entitlement to benefit (SSCBA, s.13).

Class 4: a graduated contribution payable in respect of profits or gains in excess of a prescribed limit derived from trades, professions or vocations which are chargeable to income tax under Schedule D (SSCBA, s.15).

Before the Social Security and Pensions Act 1975, s.3, came into force on 6 April 1977, a married woman could elect to pay a reduced Class 1 contribution or no Class 2 contribution at all in return for a diminished entitlement to benefits on the basis of her own contributions. Since the 1975 Act the general rule is that married women do not have this choice and must pay full contributions in return for entitlement to the full range of benefits on their own contributions. However, a considerable number of women remain for the present entitled to contribute at a reduced level, for example women married before 6 April 1977 who had chosen reduced liability (Social Security (Contributions) Regulations 1979 (SI 1979 No. 591) reg.100. The right to pay at a reduced level is lost in a number of circumstances including divorce: reg.101). A woman in this position will be unable to claim any contributory benefits in her own right, but will be able to claim a retirement pension on the basis of her husband's contributions. A married woman who is not employed or self-employed but remains at home to care for the family is not obliged to contribute. Alternatively, she may choose to make Class 3 contributions which will entitle her to certain benefits in her own right. If she does not contribute, her entitlement to benefits will depend on her husband's contributions.

*(b) Retirement pensions*

Provision is made by the Social Security Contributions and Benefits Act 1992 for a two-part State pension: (1) a basic pension; and (2) an additional or "earnings related pension". Where an employee is a member of a private pension scheme it is possible for the employer to contract out of the additional earnings related pension under the State scheme on the basis that it is replaced by the private pension. The basic pension remains payable and the employee pays a lower national insurance contribution. In considering the position of a married woman, two categories of State pension must be noted. First, she may be entitled to claim a Category A pension on the basis of her own contributions (s.44). Secondly, she may be able to claim a Category B pension on the basis of her husband's or her former husband's contributions (s.49). She cannot, of course, receive both pensions, but may secure the one more favourable to her. (She may supplement a Category A pension which, owing to deficient contributions, is less than the full amount with that part of the Category B pension to which she is also entitled, so as to bring the former up to the prescribed sum.)

Where a marriage has been ended by a decree of divorce or nullity it is possible for a former wife under the age of 60 to use some of her former spouse's contributions in qualifying for a Category A pension. Thus it is possible to substitute a former spouse's contribution for either:

(i) all the contribution years in the claimant's "working life" up to the end of the contribution year in which the marriage ended or the end of the last contribution year ending before the claimant reached pensionable age; or

(ii) all the contribution years from the beginning of the one in which the claimant married her former spouse up to the end of the one in which the marriage ended, or the end of the last contribution year ending before reaching pensionable age.

If she remarries before she attains the age of 60 then she will have to rely on her own or her new husband's contributions.

If a woman is over 60 at the time of the divorce then for the purpose of the basic retirement pension she can use her former husband's contribution record if it is better than her own. It can be used for all the contribution years in her working life up to the end of the year in which she reached the age of 59 or for all contribution years of the marriage up to the end of the year in which she attained the age of 59. Basic pension on the former husband's contributions will be paid when she retires or reaches the age of 65, together with any additional or graduated pension she may have earned from her own contributions.

## (c) Widow's benefits

A widow may be entitled on the basis of her husband's contributions to the following benefits:

(a) a "widow's allowance" which is a weekly benefit paid for 26 weeks from her husband's death if (i) on the death of her husband either (a) she was under pensionable age *or* (b) he was not at that time entitled to a Category A retirement pension AND (ii) he had satisfied the contribution conditions (SSCBA 1992, s.36);

(b) a "widowed mother's allowance" which is a weekly benefit commencing 26 weeks after her husband's death if she is entitled to child benefit or is pregnant by her husband and the husband had satisfied the contribution condition (SSCBA 1992, s.37 and Sched. 3, para. 5);

(c) a "widow's pension" payable if she is not in receipt of the widowed mother's allowance and was aged between 40 and 65 at the death of her husband or when her entitlement to widowed mother's allowance ceases (SSCBA 1992, s.38);

(d) a "Category B retirement pension" will be payable if she has attained the age of 60 or, if not, when she attains that age.

A "widow's allowance", a "widowed mother's allowance" and a "widow's pension" are not payable after a widow remarries or for any period during which she and a man to whom she is not marrried are living together as husband and wife (SSCBA 1975, ss.36, 37 and 38).

## (d) The effect of divorce or nullity

A decree of divorce or a decree of nullity in respect of a voidable marriage has two principal consequences for a woman under the age of 60.

First, she reverts to the status of a single woman for national insurance purposes. If she is employed or self-employed she becomes liable to pay the contributions appropriate to Class 1 or Class 2 as the case may be as from decree absolute. (If she had elected, as a married woman, to pay a reduced contribution by virtue of her married status then on divorce she loses her entitlement to pay at the reduced rate.) If she is not employed she will have to pay Class 3 contributions in order to maintain her eventual right to a retirement pension though she can use her former husband's contribution record as described above.

The second effect is that if her former husband predeceases her she will not be his widow and so cannot qualify for any widow's benefits. However, she will become entitled to a basic retirement pension in the circumstances described above.

A woman who is over the age of 60 at the date of a divorce or a decree of nullity is not liable to pay contributions if she is not working. She can qualify for the basic retirement pension on her former husband's contributions as described above.

### 3. Child benefit

Child benefit is a non-taxable weekly payment in respect of each child introduced by the Child Benefit Act 1975 to replace the system of family allowances and the child relief tax allowances. The rate of benefit is at present £10.00 in respect of the only, elder or eldest child, and £8.10 in respect of each other child. An additional £6.05 is payable in respect of the first or only child of certain single parents (SI 1976, No. 1267 as amended).

The general principle is that a person who is responsible for one or more children in any week is entitled to child benefit for that week in respect of the child or each of the children for whom he or she is responsible (SSCBA 1992, s.141).

A person is to be treated as a child for this purpose for any week in which (a) he or she is under the age of 16, or (b) he or she is under the age of 19 and receiving full time education (either by attendance at a recognised educational establishment or, if the education is recognised by the Secretary of State, elsewhere), or (c) he or she is under the age of 18 and not receiving full-time education and satisfies certain prescribed conditions relating to registration for work or for youth training (SSCBA 1992, s.142(1)). Generally, no person is entitled to child benefit in respect of a child who is married, unless the married child is not residing with his or her spouse, or, if he or she is so residing, where the spouse is receiving full-time education (SSCBA 1992, Sched 9. para. 3).

A person is to be treated as responsible for a child in any week if (a) he or she has the child living with him or her in that week, or (b) he or she is contributing to the cost of providing for the child at a weekly rate which is not less than the weekly rate of child benefit payable in respect of that child for that week (SSCBA 1992, s.143(1)). Where a person has had a child living with him or her at some time before a particular week he or she is to be treated as having the child living with him or her in that week notwithstanding their absence from one another unless, in the 16 weeks preceding that week, they were absent from one another for more than 56 days (equivalent to one half of that period) (SSCBA 1992, s.143(2)). A day of absence is to be disregarded for this purpose if it is due solely to the child receiving full-time education, or undergoing medical or other treatment or the fact that the child is in residential accommodation (SSCBA 1992, s.143(3). See further s.143(4) and Child Benefit (General Regulations) 1976 (SI 1976 No. 965) reg. 4).

Where two persons claim entitlement to child benefit in respect of the same child, priority will be determined in accordance with Schedule 10 of the Act (SSCBA 1992, s.144(2)). First, as between a person claiming child benefit in respect of a child for any week and a person to whom child benefit in respect of that child has already been awarded when the claim is made, the latter is entitled. This does not confer any priority where the week to which the claim relates is later than the third week following that in which the claim is made. Secondly, subject to this, a person entitled for any week by virtue of having the *child living with him* in that week has priority over a person entitled by virtue of *contributing* to the cost of providing for the child. Thirdly, as between a husband and wife residing together, the wife is entitled. Fourthly, subject to the above, as between a person who is and one who is not a parent of the child, the parent is entitled. Fifthly, subject to the above, as between two persons residing together who are parents of the child but not husband and wife, the mother is entitled. Finally, in cases not falling within any of the preceding categories, the parties may jointly elect that one of them shall be entitled. In default of such an election the person entitled will be such one of the parties as the Secretary of State may in his discretion determine.

## 4. Income-related benefits

### (a) General structure
The Social Security Contributions and Benefits Act 1992, s.123 provides for four "income-related benefits". These are:
(1)  Income support;
(2)  Family credit;
(3)  Housing benefit; and
(4)  Community charge benefit.
The general principle is that these benefits take the form of fixed payments comprising a basic allowance supplemented by standard additions for persons within specific groups. There is no discretionary element to meet special or emergency needs these are a matter for the "Social Fund" provided for in Part III of the Act. The remainder of this Part is concerned with income support, family credit and housing benefit.

### (b) Income support

#### (i) General principles
Income support was introduced by the Social Security Act 1986 to replace the system of supplementary benefit which had replaced national assistance. It provides means-tested support for individuals or families with no income from employment.

A person in Great Britain is entitled to income support only if a number of conditions are satisfied. These relate to age, capital and income requirements, remunerative work and availability for employment.

#### (ii) Age
The claimant must generally have attained the age of 18. A person who has attained

the age of 16 but not the age of 18 may obtain income support only in certain pre-scribed circumstances, e.g. if he is following an approved training course, is a lone parent or a member of a couple with children (SSCBA 1992, s.124).

### (iii) Capital and income requirements

No person is entitled to income support if his capital exceeds a prescribed amount which is at present £8,000 (SSCBA 1992, s.134(1) and reg.45). Where a claimant's capital exceeds £3,000 it is to be treated as equivalent to a weekly income of £1 per week for each complete £250 in excess of £3,000 but not exceeding £8,000. Where any part of the excess is not a complete £250 that part is to be treated as equivalent to a weekly income of £1. This is known as the claimant's "tariff income" (reg. 53).

Schedule 10 of the Income Support (General) Regulations (SI 1987 No. 1967) specifies various items of capital that are to be disregarded in calculating a claimant's capital (reg. 46(2)). These include the dwelling occupied as the home and any sum directly attributable to the proceeds of sale of any premises formerly occu-pied by the claimant as his home which is to be used for the purchase of other premises intended for such occupation within 26 weeks of the date of the sale or such longer period as is reasonable in the circumstances to enable the claimant to complete the purchase. Any personal possessions except those which had or have been acquired by the claimant with the intention of reducing his capital in order to secure entitlement to income support or to increase the amount of that benefit are also excluded. Capital is generally to be valued at its current market or surrender value, less 10 per cent where there would be expenses attributable to sale, and the amount of any incumbrance secured on it (reg. 49).

The claimant must show that he has no income or that his income does not exceed the applicable amount (SSCBA 1992, s.124(1)). The income of a claimant is calculated in accordance with Part V of the Regulations by determining the weekly amount of his income and adding to that amount the weekly amount of tariff income (reg. 28). Generally, earnings derived from employment as an employed earner and income which does not consist of earnings are to be taken into account over a period determined in accordance with regulations 29-31 and at a weekly amount deter-mined in accordance with regulation 32. A claimant is to be treated as possessing income of which he has deprived himself for the purpose of securing entitlement to income support or increasing the amount of that benefit (reg. 42). Any capital payable by instalments which are outstanding on the first day in respect of which income support is payable or the date of the determination of the claim, whichever is the earlier, is to be treated as income if the aggregate of the instalments outstand-ing and the amount of the claimant's other capital exceeds £8,000 (reg. 41). The claimant's capital is thus kept below the threshold of entitlement to income support.

Where a person claiming income support is a member of a family, the income and capital of any member of that family will generally be treated as the income and capital of that person (SSCBA 1992, s.136(1)). A "family" for this purpose may take one of three forms (s.137(1)):

(a) a married or unmarried couple;
(b) a married or unmarried couple and a member of the same household for whom one or both are responsible and who is a child or a person of a prescribed description;

(c) except in prescribed circumstances, a person who is not a member of a married or unmarried couple and a member of the same household for whom that person is responsible and who is a child (i.e. someone under 16) or a young person (i.e. someone aged 16-19) and in receipt of full-time education.

A "married couple" means a man and a woman who are married to each other and are members of the same household. An "unmarried couple" means a man and a woman who are not married to each other but are living together as husband and wife otherwise than in prescribed circumstances (SSCBA 1992, s.137(1)). A person is to be treated as responsible for a child or young person for whom he has primary responsibility (reg. 15(1)). Where a child or young person spends equal amounts of time in different households, or where there is a question as to who has primary responsibility for him, the child or young person is to be treated as being the primary responsibility of the person who is receiving child benefit in respect of him. If there is no such person then it will be the person who has made a claim for child benefit. In any other case it will be determined by the adjudication officer (reg. 15(2)). This does not apply to a child or young person who is entitled to income support (reg. 16).

Although the general principle is that the income of a child or young person is aggregated with that of a claimant, any earnings of a child or young person while still at school are to be disregarded. Where the income of a child or young person who is a member of the claimant's family exceeds the amount of the personal allowance and disabled child premium, if any, applicable in respect of that child or young person, the excess is not to be treated as income of the claimant (reg. 44(4)).

The capital of a child or young person who is a member of the claimant's family is not to be treated as capital of the claimant (reg. 47). However, where the capital of a child or young person exceeds £3,000, no allowance will be paid in respect of that child as part of the claimant's applicable amount and any income of that child or young person is not to be treated as income of the claimant (regs. 17 and 44(5)). Any capital of a child or young person payable by instalments which are outstanding on the first day in respect of which income support is payable or at the date of the determination of the claim, whichever is the earlier, is to be treated as income if the aggregate of the instalments outstanding and the amount of other capital of the child or young person exceeds £3,000 (reg. 44(1)). The capital is thus kept below the threshold for income support.

(iv) Not engaged in remunerative work

The claimant must show that he is not engaged in remunerative work and, if he is a member of a married or unmarried couple, that the other member is not so engaged (SSCBA 1992, s.124(1)). "Remunerative work" is work in which a person is engaged or, where his hours of work fluctuate, he is engaged on average, for not less than 16 hours a week being work for which payment is made or which is done in expectation of payment (reg. 5(1)). The number of hours was reduced from 24 to 16 with effect from 7 April 1992 and there is transitional protection for claimants working between 16 and 24 hours per week before that date (Income Support (General) Amendment (No. 4) Regulations 1991, SI 1991 No. 1559). This parallels the reduction in prescribed hours for the purposes of family credit (see (c)(iii) below).

(v) Availability for employment

The claimant must show that, except in prescribed circumstances, he is available and actively seeking employment and is not receiving relevant education (SSCBA 1992, s.124(1)). "Employment" for this purpose is defined in regulation 7. A child or young person is to be treated as receiving "relevant education" if, and only if, (a) he is receiving full-time education not being advanced education for the purposes of child benefit, or (b) although he is not receiving such full-time education he is treated as a child for the purposes of child benefit (reg. 12). A person "receiving relevant education" is not entitled to income support except in certain prescribed circumstances (SSCBA 1992, s.124(1)). This is intended to ensure that income support interlocks with child benefit so that generally if a parent is able to claim child benefit in respect of a young person and also include him in the family for the purposes of income support then the young person will not himself be separately entitled to income support. The prescribed circumstances in which a young person receiving relevant education may receive income support include cases where the young person is the parent of a child for whom he is treated as responsible under regulation 15 and is treated as a member of his household under regulation 16 or is living away from and is estranged from his parents (reg. 13).

(vi) The amount of income support

Where a person is entitled to income support, then if he has no income he will receive the "applicable amount". If he has income, he will receive the difference between his income and the applicable amount (SSCBA 1992, s.124(4)). The "applicable amount" is such amount or the aggregate of such amounts as are prescribed in the regulations (SSCBA 1992, s.135(1)). The prescribed amounts which are aggregated to make up a claimant's weekly applicable amount fall into three categories - personal allowances, premiums, and housing costs. The allowances and premiums are uprated in April each year.

The rates of personal allowance depend upon the age of the claimant and on whether he or she is living with a partner. The rates for the period commencing April 1993 are as follows:

| | |
|---|---|
| single person aged 18-24 | £34.80 per week |
| aged 25 or over | £44.00 per week |
| lone parent aged 18 or over | £44.00 per week |
| couple - one or both aged over 18 | £69.00 per week |
| dependent child aged under 11 | £15.05 per week |
| aged 11 to 15 | £22.15 per week |
| aged 16 to 17 | £26.45 per week |
| aged 18 | £34.80 per week |

(reg. 17 and Sched. 2 as amended).

Premiums are payable for certain groups, namely: families, lone parents, pensioners (ordinary and higher), the disabled, the severely disabled and disabled children. The "family premium" (currently £9.65) is payable where at least one member of the family is a child or young person, but only one such premium is payable irrespective of the number of children in the family (reg. 17(c)). The "lone parent premium" (currently £4.90) is payable where the claimant is a member of a family but has no partner (Sched. 2, para. 8).

Eligible housing costs include mortgage interest payments, interest on loans for repairs and improvements to the dwelling occupied as a home, payments by way of rent and service charges. They will be met where the claimant or, if he is one of a family, any member of his family is treated as responsible for the expenditure which relates to housing costs in respect of the dwelling occupied as the home which he or any member of his family is treated as occupying. A person is to be treated as responsible for the expenditure which relates to housing costs where:

(a) he or his partner is liable to meet those costs other than to a member of the same household;

(b) because the person liable to meet those costs is not doing so, he has to meet those costs in order to continue to live in the dwelling occupied as the home and either he was formerly the partner of the person liable, or he is some other person whom it is reasonable to treat as liable to meet the cost;

(c) he in practice shares those costs with other members of his household, other than close relatives of him or his partner, at least one of whom either is responsible under (a) or (b) or has an equivalent responsibility for housing benefit expenditure and for which it is reasonable in the circumstances to treat him as sharing responsibility.

Generally, a person is to be treated as occupying as his home the dwelling normally occupied as his home by himself or, if he is a member of a family, by himself and his family and he is not to be treated as occupying any other dwelling as his home. (See further Sched. 3, para. 4.) No amount may be met in respect of housing benefit expenditure (Sched. 3, para. 5).

If the claimant or, if he is a member of a couple or of a polygamous marriage, any partner of his is aged 60 or over, the whole of the eligible interest on a loan to acquire an interest in the dwelling occupied as the home will be met as a housing cost. If the claimant and any partner of his are aged under 60, then the whole of the eligible interest will be met as a housing cost only where the claimant has been in receipt of income support in respect of a continuous period of not less than 16 weeks. In any other case, i.e. during the first 16 weeks, only 50 per cent of the eligible interest will be met as a housing cost. However, where interest is payable on accumulated arrears of interest, the amount of such interest will be met as if it were eligible interest in so far as it represents interest on arrears incurred during the 16 week period to the extent that arrears do not exceed 50 per cent of the eligible interest that otherwise would have been payable during that period. "Eligible interest" means the amount of interest on a loan, whether or not secured by way of a mortgage, taken out to defray money applied for the purpose of (a) acquiring an interest in the dwelling occupied as a home; or (b) paying off another loan but only to the extent that interest on that other loan would have been eligible interest had the loan not been paid off (reg. 7(3)). Where a person who was formerly one of a couple or a polygamous marriage (i) has taken out, either solely or jointly with his former partner, a loan secured on the dwelling occupied as the home for some purpose other than (a) or (b), and (ii) has left the dwelling occupied as the home and either cannot or will not pay the interest on the loan, then, if that person's former partner has to pay the interest on the loan in order to continue to live in the dwelling, the interest paid by the former partner will be met as a housing cost as if the loan had been taken out for an authorised purpose (Sched. 3, para. 7(7)). Interest on loans for repairs and improvements to the dwelling occupied as the home will be met in certain circumstances (para. 8).

*(c) Family credit*

(i) General principles
Family credit was introduced by the Social Security Act 1986 to replace the system of Family income supplement. Its objective is similar - to provide assistance for persons who have responsibility for children and are working but are low paid.

A person in Great Britain is entitled to family credit if, when the claim for it is made or is treated as made, three conditions are satisfied. First, the claimant must satisfy certain income and capital requirements. Secondly, the claimant must show that he or his partner is engaged in remunerative work. Thirdly, the claimant must show that he or his partner is responsible for a child or young person (SSCBA 1992, s.128(1)).

(ii) Income and capital requirements
The claimant must establish that his or her income either:
  (1)  does not exceed the applicable amount which is prescribed annually by regulation and as from April 1993 is £69.00; or
  (2)  exceeds the applicable amount only by such an amount that after deducting from the appropriate maximum family credit a prescribed percentage of the excess of his income over the applicable amount some entitlement to family credit remains.
The prescribed percentage for the tapering marginal relief in (2) is at present 70 per cent (SSCBA 1992, ss.128(2) and Family Credit (General) Regulations 1987 (SI 1987 No. 1973), reg. 48).

No person is entitled to family credit if his capital exceeds a prescribed amount which at present is £8,000 (SSCBA 1992, s.134(1) and SI 1987 No. 1973, reg. 28 as amended). Where the claimant's capital exceeds £3,000 it is to be treated as equivalent to a weekly income of £1 for each complete £250 in excess of £3,000 but not exceeding £8,000. Where any part of the excess is not a complete £250, that part is to be treated as equivalent to a weekly income of £1 (reg. 36). This is referred to as the claimant's "tariff income". Schedule 3 of the Family Credit (General) Regulations specifies various items of capital that are to be disregarded as provided by regulation 29(2). The most important is the dwelling, together with any garage, garden and outbuildings, normally occupied by the claimant as his home. Personal possessions, except those acquired by the claimant with the intention of reducing his capital in order to secure entitlement to family credit or to increase the amount of that benefit, are also to be disregarded as are the assets of any business owned in whole or in part by the claimant and for the purpose of which he is engaged as a self-employed earner.

For the purpose of entitlement to family credit the income of a claimant is to be calculated on a weekly basis (a) by ascertaining the amount of his normal weekly income, and (b) by adding to that amount his "tariff income" (reg. 13). There are detailed rules for calculating the "normal weekly earnings" of employed earners and self-employed earners. In the case of an employed earner the relevant earnings to be taken into account are his net earnings, i.e. his gross earnings after deduction of income tax, national insurance contributions and one-half of any sum paid by way of a contribution to an occupational pension scheme (reg. 20). In the case of a self-employed earner the relevant earnings to be taken into account are his net profits, i.e. his gross receipts from his "self-employment" less (a) any expenses wholly and exclusively defrayed for the purposes thereof, and (b) one half of any qualifying premium payable for the provision of a pension (reg. 22). The income of a claimant which does not consist of earnings to be taken into account is his gross income together with capital treated as income (reg. 24). Maintenance payments received by the claimant are included (calculated in accordance with reg.16(2)) save that as from April 1992 there is a £15 per week maintenance disregard for single parents (see the Income-related Benefits Schemes (Miscellaneous Provisions) Amendment Regulations 1991, SI 1991 No. 2695). Under reg. 25 any capital payable by instalments which are outstanding at the date of the claim is to be treated as income if the aggregate of the instalments outstanding and the amount of the claimant's other capital calculated in accordance with Chapter VI of the Regulations exceeds £8,000. This preserves entitlement to family credit by keeping the claimant's capital below the threshold of disentitlement. Schedule 3 of the Regulations specifies sums to be disregarded in the calculation of income other than earnings. These include child benefit, income support, any housing benefit and generally any payment made to the claimant by a member of his household as a contribution towards his living accommodation costs.

A claimant's normal weekly earnings as an employed earner will generally be determined by reference to his weekly earnings for his employment over a period immediately preceding the week in which the claim is received, being a period of (i) 5 weeks if he is paid weekly, or (ii) 2 months, if he is paid monthly (reg. 14). A claimant's normal weekly earnings as a self-employed earner will generally be determined by reference to his weekly earnings over a period of 26 weeks immediately preceding the week in which the claim is received (see further reg. 15). A claimant's normal weekly income which does not consist of earnings is to be determined by reference to his weekly income over a period of 26 weeks immediately preceding the date of the claim or over such period immediately preceding that date as may, in a particular case, enable his normal weekly income to be determined more accurately (reg. 16).

Generally, the income and capital of any member of the claimant's "family" are to be treated as the income and capital of the claimant (SSCBA 1992, s.136(1)). "Family" for this purpose is defined in the same way as for income support (s.137(1). See above). However, this general principle is modified in the case of a child or young person. Any earnings of a child or young person are to be disregarded in the calculation of a claimant's earnings (Sched. 1, para. 2), but generally other income of the child or young person is to be treated as income of the claimant (reg. 10(1)). Where the income of a child or young person, other than income consisting of payments of maintenance (whether under a court order or not), exceeds the amount of family credit specified for that child or young person, that income is not to be treated as income of the claimant, and the amount of family credit for that child is to be nil (regs. 27(2) and 46(5)).

The capital of a child or young person who is a member of a claimant's family is not to be treated as capital of the claimant (reg. 30). However, where the capital of a child or young person exceeds £3,000 the credit in respect of that child or young person is to be nil and any income of that child is not to be treated as income of the claimant (regs. 46(4) and 27(3)). Any capital of a child or young person payable by instalments which are outstanding at the date of the claim is to be treated as income if the aggregate of the instalments outstanding and the amount of other capital of the child or young person would exceed £3,000. The capital of the child or young person is thus kept below the entitlement threshold for family credit (reg. 27(2)).

### (iii) Engaged in remunerative work

The claimant must show that he or, if he is a member of a married or unmarried couple, he or the other member of the couple, is engaged in remunerative work (SSCBA 1992, s.128(1)(b)). "Remunerative work" is work in which a person is engaged, or, where his hours of work fluctuate, is engaged, on average, for not less than 16 hours a week, being work for which payment is made or which is done in expectation of payment (see further reg. 4). Generally, a person is to be treated as engaged in remunerative work for the purpose of entitlement to family credit only if he carried out activities in the course of his work for not less than 16 hours in (a) the week of the claim, or (b) either of the two weeks immediately preceding the week of a claim and he has not become unemployed before the date of the claim (reg. 5). The prescribed number of hours was reduced from 24 to 16 with effect from 7 April 1992 in parallel with the change in the number of prescribed hours for income support purposes (Family Credit (General) Amendment Regs. 1991, SI 1991 No. 1520. See (*b*)(iv) above).

### (iv) Responsibility for a child or young person

The claimant must show that he or, if he is a member of a married or unmarried couple, he or the other member, is responsible for a member of the same household who is a child or a young person (SSCBA 1992, s.128(1)(d)). A person is to be treated as responsible for a child or young person who is normally living with him (see further reg. 7). Where a claimant or any partner is treated as responsible for a child or young person for this purpose, that child or young person and any child of that child or young person is to be treated as a member of the claimant's household (reg. 8).

### (v) Amount of family credit

Where a person is entitled to family credit because his income does not exceed the "applicable amount" he is entitled to the appropriate maximum credit in his case (s.128(2)). The applicable amount for this purpose is prescribed by regulation 47 and is usually uprated as from April each year. As from April 1993 the applicable amount is £69.00. The appropriate maximum family credit is the aggregate of the following credits:

(a) an adult credit in respect of a claimant or, if he is a member of a married or unmarried couple, in respect of the couple..................................................£42.50
(b) a child credit in respect of any child or young person for whom the claimant or his partner is treated as responsible, the amount depending on the age of the child:
   (i)   child aged less than 11 years............................................................. £10.75
   (ii)  child aged not less than 11 but less than 16 years.............................£17.85
   (iii) young person aged not less than 16 but less than 18 years.............. £22.20
   (iv) young person aged not less than 18 but less than 19 years ..............£31.00
(The figures given are those for the period from April 1993. See Schedule 2 of the regulations as amended.)

Where a person's income exceeds the applicable amount then he may still be entitled to family credit. However. the maximum family credit in his case is reduced by the prescribed percentage (70 per cent) of the excess of his income over the applicable amount. His entitlement will be the amount of the maximum family credit (if any) that remains after that deduction (s.128(2) and reg. 48).

Thus if a married couple have three children living with them, one aged 9 and two aged 15 and the net relevant income is £60.00, then the family credit entitlement is:

    1 adult credit.................................................. £42.50
    2 child credits (age 11 - 16)........................... £35.70
    1 child credit (under 11) ............................... £10.75
    Total payable.................................................£88.95
If the net relevant income is £99.00, the family credit entitlement is:

$$£88.95 - 0.7 \times (£99.00 - £69.00) =$$
$$£88.95 - £21 = £67.95.$$

(vi) Duration of family credit
Family credit is payable for a period of 26 weeks or such other period as may be prescribed, beginning with the week in which a claim for it is made or is treated as made. An award of family credit is then generally not affected by any change of circumstances during that period (SSCBA 1992, s.128(3)).

*(d) Housing benefit*

(i) General principles
Housing benefit is payable in the form of a rent allowance or a rent rebate in respect of rent or similar periodical payments which a person is liable to make in respect of the dwelling which he occupies as his home (SSCBA 1992, s.130(1) and the Housing Benefit (General) Regulations 1987 SI 1987 No. 1971). The claimant must also satisfy the specified income and capital requirements.

(ii) Payments in respect of a dwelling-house occupied as a home
The payments in respect of which housing benefit is payable are rent and similar

payments, such as service charges, but not mortgage payments (see reg. 10 and SSCBA 1992, s.130(2)). The claimant will usually be the person liable to make the payments but certain persons are treated as if they were liable to make payments in respect of a dwelling (reg. 6). These include (i) a person who is a married or unmarried partner of the person liable to make the payments, and (ii) a person who has to make the payments if he is to continue to live in the home because the person liable to make them is not doing so and either (a) he was formerly a partner of the person who is so liable, or (b) he is some other person whom it is reasonable to treat as liable to make the payments.

A "dwelling" for this purpose means any residential accommodation, whether or not consisting of the whole or part of a building and whether or not comprising separate and self-contained premises (SSCBA 1992, s.137(1)). A person is to be treated as occupying as his "home" the dwelling normally occupied as his home by himself or, if he is a member of a family, by himself and his family, and is not to be treated as occupying any other dwelling as his home (reg. 5(1)). "Family" is given the same meaning as in relation to income support (see SSCBA 1992, s.137(1) and (b)(iii) above).

### (iii) Income and capital requirements

The claimant must show that he has no income or that his income does not exceed the "applicable amount" subject to tapering marginal relief where his income does exceed that amount (SSCBA 1992, s.130(1)). The "applicable amount" is such amount, or the aggregate of such amounts as are prescribed (SSCBA 1992, s.135(1)). The amounts prescribed by the regulations which are aggregated to make up a claimant's weekly applicable amount are basically the same as the personal allowances and premiums prescribed under the income support system and noted above (see reg. 16 and Sched. 2 as amended). However, housing costs included in the income support system, such as mortgage interest payments, are excluded. In addition there is a higher single personal allowance for persons aged 16-24, and a higher lone parent allowance for persons under 18 and a higher lone parent premium.

A person is not entitled to housing benefit if his capital exceeds the prescribed amount which is at present £16,000 (SSCBA 1992, s.134(1) and reg. 37 as amended). Where the claimant's capital exceeds £3,000 it is to be treated as equivalent to a weekly income of £1 for each complete £250, in excess of £3,000 but not exceeding £16,000. Where any part of the excess is not a complete £250, that part is to be treated as equivalent to a weekly income of £1. This is referred to as the claimant's "tariff income" (reg. 45 and SSCBA 1992, s.134(2)). Schedule 5 of the regulations specifies various items of capital that are to be disregarded as provided by reg. 38(2).

For the purpose of entitlement to housing benefit the income of a claimant must be calculated on a weekly basis (a) by estimating the amount which is likely to be his average weekly income over the benefit period, and (b) by adding on to that amount his tariff income (reg. 21). There are detailed rules for calculating the "average weekly income" of employed and self-employed earners (regs. 28-32) and other income (reg. 33). A number of items are to be disregarded including an amount equal to any maintenance paid by the claimant to his former partner or in respect of his children other than children who are members of his household (Sched. 4, para. 27). Payments received by a claimant by way of maintenance are to be included save that as from April 1992 there is a £15 per week disregard for single parents (the Income-related Benefit Schemes (Miscellaneous Provisions) Amendment Regulations 1991, SI 1991 No. 2695).

Generally, the income and capital of any member of the claimant's "family" are to be treated as the income and capital of the claimant (SSCBA 1992, s.136(1)). "Family" for this purpose is defined in the same way as for income support (s.137(1)). However, this general principle is modified in the case of a child or young person. Any earnings of a child or young person are (with very minor exceptions) to be disregarded in the calculation of a claimant's earnings (Sched. 3, paras. 13 and 14), but generally other income of the child or young person is to be treated as income of the claimant (reg. 19(1)). Where the income of a child or young person exceeds the amount included in the calculation of the claimant's applicable amount for that child or young person by way of personal allowance and disabled child premium, if any, the excess is not to be treated as income of the claimant (reg. 36(1)).

(iv) Amount of benefit

Where a person is entitled to housing benefit because he has no income or his income does not exceed the applicable amount, he is entitled to the maximum housing benefit in his case (SSCBA 1992, s.130(3)). The amount of a person's maximum housing benefit in any benefit week is 100 per cent of his eligible rent (calculated on a weekly basis in accordance with regs. 69 and 70) less any deductions in respect of non-dependants (reg. 61). A non-dependant is a person who normally resides with the claimant and who is not a member of the claimant's family or within certain other categories. In essence non-dependants comprise persons who contribute or are deemed to contribute to the housing costs such as boarders (see reg. 3). The deductions in respect of non-dependants are not related to actual contributions or costs but are standard amounts specified in reg. 63 as amended. Thus in respect of a non-dependant aged eighteen or over who is in remunerative work earning at least £70.00 but less than £105 gross per week, a deduction of £8.00 per week will be made from the maximum housing benefit in calculating the amount of a rent rebate or allowance. If the gross income is £105 or more but less than £135, the deduction will be £12.00. If the gross income is £135 or more, the deduction will be £21.00. These figures are uprated in April each year.

Where a person's income exceeds the applicable amount, he may still be entitled to housing benefit. However, the appropriate maximum housing benefit in his case is reduced by a prescribed percentage (at present 65 per cent) of the excess of his income over the applicable amount (SSCBA 1992, s.130(3) and reg. 62). His entitlement to housing benefit will be the amount of the maximum housing benefit (if any) that remains after the appropriate reduction. If the amount of benefit involved is less than 50p per week then it will not be payable (reg. 64).

Where a person is entitled to housing benefit the benefit period will commence with the first week in respect of which he is so entitled or, if later, the benefit week in which the claim is received, and will be for such number of weeks as the appropriate authority shall determine having regard in particular to any relevant circumstances which the authority reasonably expects may affect entitlement in the future, but must not exceed sixty benefit weeks (reg. 66). The authority may determine that some other change of circumstances has occurred which should result in the benefit period ending with an earlier week (reg. 67).

## 5. Recovery of income support from members of a family – the so-called "liable relative" procedure

*(a) Orders obtained by the Secretary of State for Social Security under s.106 of the Social Security Administration Act 1992*

(i) The right of recovery
If income support is claimed by or in respect of a person whom another person is liable to maintain, or paid to or in respect of such a person, the Secretary of State for Social Security may, under s.106 of the Social Security Administration Act 1992 ("SSAA 1992"), make a complaint against the liable person for an order against him or her. On the hearing of the complaint the court is required to have regard to "all the circumstances" and, in particular, to the income of the liable person, and may order him or her to pay such sum, weekly or otherwise, as it may consider appropriate. In determining whether to order any payments to be made in respect of income support for any period before the complaint was made, or the amount of any such payments, the court must disregard any amount by which the liable person's income exceeds the income which was his during that period (s.106(3)). Any payments ordered are to be made (a) to the Secretary of State in so far as they are attributable to any income support (whether paid before or after the making of the order); (b) to the person claiming income support or (if different) the dependant; or (c) to such other person as appears to the court expedient in the interests of the dependant (s.106(4)). An order under s.106 is enforceable as a magistrates' court maintenance order (s.106(5)). As from 5 April 1993, it is necessary to consider the application of the Child Support Act 1991 in appropriate cases (see Chapter 17 Part 6).

(ii) Liability to maintain
For the purposes of an order under s.106 a man is liable to maintain his wife and any children of whom he is the father, and a woman is liable to maintain her husband and any children of whom she is the mother (SSAA 1992, ss.78(6) and 105(3)). A "child" means a person under the age of sixteen, but also includes a person who has attained the age of sixteen but not the age of nineteen and in respect of whom either parent, or some person acting in the place of either parent, is receiving income support.

The liability imposed by s.106 is absolute in the sense that it is not terminated by misconduct, such as adultery or desertion, on the part of the party receiving income support, but such misconduct may be regarded merely as one of the circumstances of the case to which the court is required to have regard (*National Assistance Board* v *Parkes* [1955] 2 QB 506). In any event, the right of recovery in respect of support provided for children cannot be affected by the conduct of the claimant. The right of recovery is not affected by a consensual separation irrespective of whether there is any agreement as to maintenance (*Stopher* v *National Assistance Board* [1955] 1 QB 486). Moreover, an order can be obtained against a husband under s.106 even though he has paid in full the amounts due under a separation agreement where his wife has been forced to seek income support when such payments become inadequate (*National Assistance Board* v *Prisk* [1954] 1 All ER 400), and the right of recovery is not affected by an agreement by a wife not to seek maintenance (*National Assistance Board* v *Parkes*). In *Hulley* v *Thompson* [1981] 1 WLR 159 a consent order in divorce proceedings provided that the husband pay no maintenance for the wife or the two children of the family, but that he transfer all his interest in the former matrimonial home to the wife. The husband, as father, was held to have a continuing obligation by virtue of s.17(1) of the Supplementary Benefits Act 1976 (now replaced by ss.78(6) and 105(3) of the Social Security Administration Act 1992) to maintain his children which could not be avoided by a consent arrangement. The fact that he had transferred the home to the mother of the children did not necessarily discharge his obligation, but it was a matter to be taken into account in assessing his contribution to their maintenance. *Prima facie* the father ought to pay the balance of what the mother was unable to pay for their maintenance and the matter was remitted to the justices to consider all the circumstances of the father and the mother.

Where a former wife is unable to support herself because, for example, she has to care for young or invalid children (see *S* v *S* [1976] Fam 18), her entitlement to income support is not affected if the former matrimonial home is vested in her absolutely. (Indeed her housing requirements will include the interest portion of any mortgage instalments.) Where it was vested in her as part of an arrangement whereby her claim to periodical payments was dismissed or she agreed to accept a small or nominal order, it may seem that her husband has been able to transfer his responsibility to the taxpayer, particularly where there is only a small or nominal payment for the children. However, this is not necessarily so as there are cases where an arrangement of this kind is the best that can be made where the husband's income is small. Indeed, by parting with his interest in the home, he may have made a very real contribution to the maintenance not only of the wife but of the children in excess of what he could realistically make out of his income. It is important that such considerations should be borne in mind in proceedings under s.106 of the 1992 Act in the same way as they are in proceedings under the Matrimonial Causes Act 1973.

(iii) Inclusion of sums paid to caring parent

Under these provisions as originally contained in s.24 of the Social Security Act 1986, where a parent claimed income support in respect of himself or herself as well as for his or her children an order could not extend to amounts paid in respect of the claimant parent as distinct from amounts paid in respect of his or her children if the other parent was not liable to maintain the parent receiving income support. This would be the position where the parents were no longer married or never had been married to each other. This was changed by s.8 of the Social Security Act 1990 inserting s.24A into the Social Security Act 1986. This has been replaced by s.107 of the Social Security Administration Act 1992 which enables the court to include in the order made under s.106 an amount, determined in accordance with regulations, in respect of any income support paid to or for the claimant parent. The Income Support (Liable Relatives) Regulations 1990 (SI 1990 No. 1777) reg. 2 provides that the amount which may be included in the sum which the court may order the parent to pay under s.106 is to be the whole of the following amounts which are payable to or for the claimant:

(a) any personal allowance for each of the children whom the other parent is liable to maintain;
(b) any family premium;
(c) any lone parent premium;
(d) any disabled child premium;
(e) any carer premium if, but only if, that premium is payable because the claimant is in receipt of, or is treated as being in receipt of, invalid care allowance by reason of the fact that he or she is caring for a severely disabled child or young person whom the other parent is liable to maintain.

(These sums are specified in Schedule 1 of the Income Support (General) Regulations 1987 (SI 1987, No. 1967)).

If the court is satisfied that in addition to these amounts the liable parent has the means to pay, the sum which the court may order him to pay under s.106 may also include all or some of the amount of any personal allowance payable to or for the claimant. In other words, once having looked at the allowances and premiums that are paid because there are children, the court may now also consider the cost to the mother in caring for the absent parent's children (see Hansard HC Vol. 170 col. 567). Where the sum which the court orders a person to pay under s.106 includes an amount in respect of income support in the form of a personal allowance for a lone parent, the order must separately identify the amount of the "personal allowance element" (s.107(2)). It should be noted that for this purpose a "child" means a person under the age of sixteen and does not include a young person aged sixteen to eighteen even though such a person is within the definition of a child for the purposes of s.106, and an order under that section may extend to income support paid in respect of that young person.

### (b) Voluntary agreements

Before seeking an order under s.106, the Department of Social Security will seek to recover payment from the liable relative by a voluntary agreement with him. The "liable relative officer" in the Department will contact the liable relative and seek an offer from him to discharge his liability. An offer will be accepted if it equals the amount of the income support provided. In deciding whether to accept a lesser amount the Department applies a formula to determine how much a liable person can afford to pay. This offsets the ordinary scale rate appropriate to him and any partner or children living with him, plus an allowance for his full rent (or mortgage) and an addition of one-quarter of his net earnings, against their net income. The excess is used as a basis for discussion, but the Department's officers have a discretion to reach agreement with him to pay a lesser amount if, for example, he has inescapable special expenses which exceed one-quarter of his net earnings.

*(c) Application for maintenance order and "diversion procedure"*
Proceedings under s.106 have been unnecessary where a lone parent has obtained an order against the liable relative in matrimonial proceedings. Indeed it has been regarded as preferable for the claimant parent to obtain such an order rather than for s.106 to be used. In many cases an order for maintenance will be of no direct financial benefit to a wife since the amount of the order will be less than the amount of income support she receives. It will, however, be advantageous where the court is likely to order the husband to pay an amount larger than that which the wife receives in the form of income support. Moreover, if she does obtain an order and subsequently goes out to work so that income support is withdrawn she will still have the advantage of the court order to supplement what she earns. Where the amount of an order is less than the full rate of her income support entitlement, she may authorise the clerk of the magistrates' court to divert payments received under the order to the Department of Social Security. When this so-called "diversion procedure" is operated, she receives an order book entitling her to income support (calculated on the basis that there is no maintenance order) which she can cash regularly in the ordinary way irrespective of the irregularity of payments under the order.

*(d) Transfer of s.106 order to parent*
Where an order is in force under s.106 against a liable parent in respect of the other parent or the children whereby payments are to be made to the Secretary of State, then if the dependent parent ceases to claim income support the Secretary of State may transfer to the dependent parent the right to receive the payments under the order, exclusive of any personal allowance element, and to exercise the relevant rights in relation to the order except so far as relating to that element. The Secretary of State may do this by giving notice in writing to the court which made the order and to the liable parent and to the dependent parent (s.107(3)).

A notice of transfer must not be given when there is in force a maintenance order made against the liable parent (a) in favour of the dependent parent or one or more of the children; or (b) in favour of some other person for the benefit of the dependent parent or one of more of the children. If a maintenance order is made at any time after such notice has been given by the Secretary of State, the order under s.106 will cease to have effect (s.107(4)). A "maintenance order" for this purpose means any order for the making of periodical payments or for the payment of a lump sum which is, or has at any time been, a maintenance order within the meaning of the Attachment of Earnings Act 1971. It also includes an order for the making of periodical payments or for the payment of a lump sum under Part III of the Matrimonial and Family Proceedings Act 1984 following an overseas divorce. A "child" for this purpose is again limited to a person below the age of sixteen (see s.107(15)).

Where payments under the order transferred are required to be made by standing order or similar means under s.59(6) of the Magistrates' Courts Act 1980, then if the clerk to the magistrates decides that payment by that method is no longer possible he must amend the order to provide that payments under the order are to be made by the liable parent to the clerk (SSAA 1992, s.107(5)).

The object of the provision is to make it easier for the lone parent who has not previously obtained a maintenance order to make the transition from income support to work by obviating the need for such a parent to commence new proceedings to obtain a maintenance order and thereby removing what was thought to be a significant disincentive to taking the step of going back to work (see Hansard Vol. 170, col. 569). However, it is important to note that the dependent parent will not become entitled to receive any personal allowance element in the order. It is provided that the Secretary of State ceases to be entitled (a) to receive any payment under the order in respect of any personal allowance element, or (b) to exercise the relevant rights so far as relating to any such element, notwithstanding that the dependent parent does not become entitled to receive any payment in respect of that element (s.107(6)). It may be possible for that parent to apply for an order in respect of his or her own maintenance under the Matrimonial Causes Act 1973 but any such order will terminate the order under s.106 in so far as it relates to the parent's personal allowance. Moreover, even in respect of the children, the transferred order will, it seems, be restricted to the amount of income support in respect of which the order was made.

If after a notice of transfer has been given by the Secretary of State the dependent parent makes a further claim for income support, then the Secretary of State may by giving a further notice in writing to the court which made the order and to the liable and dependent parents, transfer back from the dependent parent to himself the right to receive the payments and to exercise the relevant rights. Such a transfer revives the right of the Secretary of State to receive payment under the order in respect of any personal allowance element and to exercise the relevant rights to enforce or apply for variation so far as relating to any such element (s.107(8)).

A transfer from the Secretary of State takes effect on the day on which the dependent parent ceases to be in receipt of income support, and a transfer back to the Secretary of State takes effect on the first day in respect of which the dependent parent receives income support after the transfer from the Secretary of State took effect or such later day as may be specified for the purpose of the notice of transfer back from the Secretary of State irrespective of the day on which the notice of transfer is given (s.107(13)). A transfer does not transfer or otherwise affect the right of any person (a) to receive a payment which fell due to him or her at a time before the transfer took effect, or (b) to exercise any relevant rights in relation to any such payment. Where the Secretary of State gives notice of transfer to the dependent relative this does not deprive the Secretary of State of his right to receive such a payment in respect of any personal allowance element or to exercise the relevant rights in relation to such a payment. (For the effect of a re-transfer on the method of payment see s.107(9).)

*(e) Enforcement of maintenance orders by the Department of Social Security*
When payments are not being made by an absent parent under an existing maintenance order a recipient parent might be reluctant to seek enforcement of the order

by the court, particularly where income support is being paid to make up the short-fall. Section 108 of the Social Security Administration Act 1986 (re-enacting provisions introduced by s.8 of the Social Security Act 1990) now enables the Secretary of State for Social Security to enforce a claimant's own maintenance order for her when payments are not being made in full if the lone parent is claiming income support for herself and her family. This applies where a claimant who is a parent of one or more children is in receipt of income support either in respect of those children or in respect of both himself or herself and those children, and there is in force a maintenance order made against the other parent (i) in favour of the claimant or one or more of the children; or (ii) in favour of some other person for the benefit of one or more of the children. If in such a case the liable parent fails to comply with the terms of the maintenance order the Secretary of State may bring any proceedings or take any other steps to enforce the order that could have been brought or taken by or on behalf of the person in whose favour that maintenance order was made - "the primary recipient" (s.108(1) and (2)). The powers of the Secretary of State under s.108 are exercisable at his discretion and whether or not the primary recipient or any other person consents to their exercise, but any sums recovered are payable to or for the primary recipient as if the proceedings or steps in question had been brought or taken by him or on his behalf (s.108(3)). The powers conferred on the Secretary of State include:

(a)  the power to apply for registration of the maintenance order under
    (i)   s.17 of the Maintenance Orders Act 1950;
    (ii)  s.2 of the Maintenance Orders Act 1958; or
    (iii) Civil Jurisdiction and Judgment Act 1982; and
(b)  to make an application under s.2 of the Maintenance Orders (Reciprocal Enforcement) Act 1972.
    (s.108(4).)

Any court before which proceedings are brought by the Secretary of State under s.108 has the same powers in connection with those proceedings as it would have had if they had been brought by the primary recipient (s.108(2)). Moreover, in relation to those proceedings the Secretary of State must be treated for the purposes of any enactment or instrument relating to maintenance orders as if he were a person entitled to payment under the maintenance order in question though he does not thereby become entitled to any such payment (s.108(6)). The Secretary of State must be given notice by the court of any application (a) to alter, vary, suspend, discharge, revoke, revive, or enforce the maintenance order in question, or (b) to remit arrears under that maintenance order, and he is entitled to appear and be heard on the application though he is not given power to make any such application (s.108(5) and Income Support (Liable Relatives) Regulations 1990 (SI 1990 No. 1777, reg. 3). Where under s.108 the court makes an order for the whole or any part of the arrears due under the maintenance order in question to be paid as a lump sum the Secretary of State must inform the Legal Aid Board of the lump sum if a contribution required of the primary recipient might be recovered out of the lump sum (s.108(7)).

## 6. Social security benefit and financial provision

Where an application for financial provision is made under the Matrimonial Causes Act 1973 or the Domestic Proceedings and Magistrates' Courts Act 1978, the court is entitled to take into account the fact that income support is being paid to the applicant or that it is available to the applicant. On the one hand this may mean, as noted above, that the applicant receives little or no benefit from an award because income support will be withdrawn by a corresponding amount, but it is well established that the other spouse should not be allowed to shift his responsibilities on to the community more than is necessary. On the other hand, if the applicant wife is awarded a sum that will provide her (and any children in her care) with realistic support, the effect may be that the husband's income will itself fall below subsistence level. In that event income support would not be available to the husband to supplement his earnings.

The proper approach in the magistrates' court was indicated by the Divisional Court in *Ashley* v *Ashley* [1968] P 482. The court should first consider what would be an appropriate amount to order the husband to pay to the wife ignoring the fact that social security benefits would be available to her to make up any deficiency. However, if an order for such an amount would have the effect of reducing the husband to below subsistence level, a court should limit the amount of the order so that the husband will be left with an income at subsistence level. Sir Jocelyn Simon P pointed out (at p. 590) that the result would be that:

"Both parties and the children will then unhappily be at no better than subsistence level, but the result will be just as between the husband and his wife and children on the one hand, and between the husband and the general community as symbolised by the National Assistance Board on the other."

A similar approach was indicated by the Court of Appeal in *Barnes* v *Barnes* [1973] 1 WLR 1381 in relation to applications under the Matrimonial Causes Act 1973. In *Peacock* v *Peacock* [1984] 1 WLR 532 Booth J took the view that the same principles applied in applications for maintenance pending suit and interim periodical payments as in applications for final orders.

In deciding on what is subsistence level the courts have referred to the published figures for normal requirements for what was supplementary benefit and is now income support - the so-called scale rates. (See *Ashley* v *Ashley*; *Billington* v *Billington* [1974] Fam 24; *Winter* v *Winter* [1972] The Times 14 November.) In *Smethurst* v *Smethurst* [1978] Fam 52 Sir George Baker P applied the more generous formula used by the Supplementary Benefits Commission when negotiating with a liable relative. This would allow the husband to retain a margin over supplementary benefit scale rates - either £5 or one-quarter of his net earnings, whichever is the higher. This formula had first been revealed in the Report of the Finer Committee on One Parent Families (1974) Cmnd. 5629, paras. 4.184 *et seq.* However, this was rejected by the Court of Appeal in *Shallow* v *Shallow* [1979] Fam 1 where Ormrod LJ (at p. 5) said that "the formula has nothing to do with subsistence levels. It produces, in fact, nothing more than a negotiating figure for the use of the Commission's officers when seeking contributions from 'liable relatives'..." (see also *Fitzpatrick* v *Fitzpatrick* (1968) 9 Fam Law 16). The courts have sometimes departed from the subsistence level in the opposite direction, thereby leaving a man to support his new family with an income below subsistence level (see the remarks of Payne J in *Winter* v *Winter*). In *Billington* v *Billington* [1974] Fam 24 the Divisional Court held that although it would not normally be reasonable for a court to make a maintenance order or fix a protected earnings rate which would have the effect of bringing the husband's resources below the scale rate of supplementary benefit the court had a discretion under s.6(5) of the Attachment of Earnings Act 1971 in fixing the protected earnings rate and there was no principle of law which prohibited the justices fixing the rate below that level. In *Tovey* v *Tovey* (1978) 8 Fam Law 80 Ormrod LJ was prepared to reduce the husband's income to below subsistence level in order to impress on him that his primary duty was owed to the children of his marriage and not to those of his cohabitee. The court made this order even though the children would not actually benefit from it and its only effect would be to reduce the wife's entitlement to supplementary benefit by the same sum.

In *Ashley* v *Blackman* [1988] Fam 85 Waite J had to consider the effect on the principle in *Barnes* v *Barnes* of the imposition of a specific duty on the court in dealing with an application to vary or discharge an order for periodical payments under s.31 of the Matrimonial Causes Act 1973, to consider whether those payments could be terminated altogether thereby achieving a clean break. He said (at p. 92):

"... I do not think that there is necessarily any legislative inconsistency in introducing on the one hand the clean break objective for mandatory consideration in variation cases, and preserving on the other hand a formula for the exercise of the discretion which perpetuates in such cases the principle of *Barnes* v *Barnes* ...

The implied Parliamentary intention ... is that the courts should for the future bear both those policy aspects in mind and strike whatever balance - or if need be make whatever choice - between them that the requirements of justice in the particular circumstances appear to dictate. The devious or the feckless husband will still be prevented from throwing his proper maintenance obligations on the state. The genuine struggler, on the other hand, will be spared the burden of having to pay to his former spouse the last few pounds that separate him from total penury. Between those two extremes there will be ample opportunity for flexible orders which give proper weight to both heads of policy, including in suitable cases a use of the phased or tapered termination process over a period of time which the substituted section 31(7) of the Act of 1973 appears to contemplate."

The case before him was a classic instance for applying the clean break. (See Chapter 11.)

In *Delaney* v *Delaney* [1990] 2 FLR 457 the Court of Appeal had to consider the position of a husband who had given up the tenancy of a one-bedroom flat which was unsuitable for access by the children and, with the woman he hoped to marry, had purchased a property on a basis which involved an increased financial commitment. The court did not find this action unreasonable though the effect was that he had insufficient resources left properly and fully to maintain his former wife and children. The wife's earnings were such that she was entitled to family credits of £45.35 per week on the basis that there was no order for periodical payments. If an order was made in respect of either her or her children, that benefit would be reduced by 70p for every pound which she received up to that limit of £45.35. Ward J said (at p. 462):

"This court is entitled, as the authority of *Stockford* v *Stockford* (1982) 3 FLR makes clear, to approach the case on the basis that if, having regard to the reasonable financial commitments undertaken by the husband with due regard to the contribution properly made by the lady with whom he lives, there is insufficient left properly and fully to maintain the former wife and children, then the court may have regard to the fact that in proper cases social security benefits are available to the wife and the children of the marriage; that having such regard, the court is enabled to avoid making orders which would be financially crippling to the husband. Benefits are available to this family of which the judge was not made aware, and I have come to the conclusion that the husband cannot reasonably be expected to contribute to the maintenance of his previous family without financially crippling himself. In my judgment, it is far better that the spirit of effecting a clean break and starting with a fresh slate be implemented in this case, not by dismissing the claims of the wife and children, but by acknowledging that now and, it is likely, in the foreseeable future he will not be able to honour the obligations he has recognised towards his children."

The court made nominal orders in respect of each child. (See also *Allen* v *Allen* [1986] 2 FLR 265.)

If the husband is himself in receipt of income support it will rarely be appropriate to make other than a nominal order against him. In *Williams* v *Williams* [1974] Fam 55 the Divisional Court took the view that any attempt to award maintenance on the basis that there was some margin over and above the husband's expenditure, up to the amount of what was then supplementary benefit, was a futile exercise which should be avoided. In that case the husband was unemployed and in receipt of a full supplementary allowance, but the justices had refused to vary an order for periodical payments against him on the ground that they were not satisfied in regard to his efforts to find employment. The Divisional Court held that in continuing to pay the husband the full supplementary allowance, the Commission must have accepted that the husband was genuinely unable to find employment. This ought to have been taken into account and the case was remitted for a rehearing. This view was approved by Heilbron J in *Chase* v *Chase* (1983) 13 Fam Law 21.

However, there may be cases where an order may be appropriate. In *Freeman* v *Swatridge* [1984] FLR 762 at p. 767 Dunn LJ said:

"In many, perhaps the majority of, cases the amount of supplementary benefit received or receivable by the husband will be the appropriate amount to satisfy his financial needs and enable him to be at or just above subsistence level. But those rates are not to be blindly applied. They are no more than a guide. And in this case there was evidence ... which justified the judge in making the very modest order which he did make, namely 50p a week in respect of each child - perhaps no more than a token of his obligation to maintain his own children."

The evidence which the court took as justifying such an order was the fact that the husband had apparently been able to cope with making payments in respect of certain debts and yet his new family had apparently managed even though this must have reduced the amount available for food and other incidental outgoings. Wood J (at p. 766) also referred to the factor emphasised by Ormrod LJ in *Tovey* v *Tovey* (1978) 8 Fam Law 80 when he had said that "as a pure matter of public policy it was very undesirable that a man should not, even in a purely formal sense, continue to contribute to the children who were his primary liability. It was unfortunate that the liability was blurred by considerations such as the supplementary benefit regulations; they blurred that responsibility, which was very unfortunate."

In contrast, in *Fletcher* v *Fletcher* [1985] FLR 851 at p. 857 the court found there was no such margin and nominal orders in favour of the wife and children were appropriate. Sir John Arnold P said (at p. 857):

"... one has to asssume that there is at least a serious probability that there will be no margin between the level of subsistence and the amount of the supplementary benefit to justify the making of a substantial order, unless there are some circumstances in the case which suggest that is so; and in the absence of such circumstances the proper conclusion is that there is no such margin."

Apart from income support and family credit the availability of rent and rate rebates have been taken into account (*Walker* v *Walker* (1978) 122 SJ 193) and the same would now apply to community charge benefit. (See also *Viner* v *Viner (deceased)* [1978] CLY 3091; Chapter 21.)

Child benefit must also be taken into account, including the additional allowance for single parents (*Stockford* v *Stockford* (1982) 3 FLR 58). In *Moon* v *Moon* (1981) 1 FLR 115 at p. 118 Waterhouse J had said that the special allowance was for the special purpose of compensating a parent for the special difficulty of bringing up a family without the aid of a spouse, and should not be taken into account. (See also *Coleman* v *Wheeler* (1981) 2 FLR 99.) However, in *Stockford* v *Stockford* (1982) 3 FLR 58 at p. 62 Ormrod LJ said that this is wrong and the special allowance should be regarded as a resource of the wife, though it did not follow that the husband would benefit from it. (Contrast *Claxton* v *Claxton* (1982) 12 Fam Law 62 where attendance and mobility allowances for a second wife were not to be taken into account.)

# Chapter 20

# The family and the law of succession

## 1. Introduction

*(a) Devolution of property on death*
On the death of a person all property in which he or she had a beneficial interest not ceasing on death devolves on his or her personal representatives who, after payment of debts and other liabilities, will apply the residue in accordance with the provisions of the deceased's will or, if there is no will, or to the extent that the will is ineffective to dispose of the deceased's property, in accordance with the law relating to intestacy.

*(b) Intestate succession*
The law of intestate succession recognises the claims of certain members of a deceased person's family, notably a surviving spouse and the deceased's children, and is considered in the next section of this chapter. It will be seen that it consists of a system of fixed rules and, as it has to be applied to a variety of family circumstances, the resulting distribution may sometimes be unsatisfactory. Thus while it may provide entirely adequately for the family of a deceased who had entered into only one marriage which lasted for many years, it may operate unfairly where the surviving spouse had been married to the deceased for only a short period of time and there are children of the deceased by a previous marriage who may have been still dependent on him or her. The system also takes no account of unmarried cohabitation or of the claims of stepchildren (see e.g. *Re Callaghan (deceased)* [1985] Fam 1; *Re Leach (deceased)* [1986] Ch 226). In these and other circumstances it may be necessary for a family member to make an application under the Inheritance (Provision for Family and Dependants) Act 1975 for provision out of the estate of the deceased. The 1975 Act is considered in Chapter 21.

In 1989 the Law Commission published a report on *Distribution on Intestacy* recommending substantial changes in the law of intestate succession (Law Com. No. 187. See further Chapter 1).

## (c) Testate succession

The law of testate succession recognises the claims of the family only to a limited extent. There is only a limited obligation on a testator to take into account the claims of his or her family when making a will. Indeed, in the period up to 1938 their claims could be entirely ignored by a testator who could dispose of his or her property as he or she wished. A spouse had, and still has, no right to a fixed proportion of the estate of the deceased spouse except in cases of intestacy, but the Inheritance (Family Provision) Act 1938 introduced a limited restriction on the testator's freedom. It provided that where a will did not make reasonable provision for the maintenance of certain dependants of the deceased they could apply to the court for such reasonable provision to be made out of the deceased's estate. This jurisdiction was extended to cases of partial and total intestacy by the Intestates' Estates Act 1952, and a similar jurisdiction in relation to former spouses was introduced by the Matrimonial Causes (Property and Maintenance) Act 1958. This jurisdiction was further extended, particularly in relation to the surviving spouse, by the Inheritance (Provision for Family and Dependants) Act 1975 which is considered in Chapter 21.

The interests of the family are also protected against the possible adverse effect of a will made before marriage (and perhaps forgotten by the testator) by the long-established rule that a will is revoked by the testator's marriage. This rule was given statutory form by s.18 of the Wills Act 1837 which was reformulated by the Administration of Justice Act 1982, s.18. This rule protects the family only in so far as it benefits under the rules of intestate succession. Moreover, it is not designed to protect the family from a deliberate exercise of testamentary power which is intended to survive marriage, when recourse to the Inheritance (Provision for Family and Dependants) Act 1975 will be necessary. Thus it is now provided that where it appears from a will that at the time it was made the testator was expecting to be married to a particular person and that he intended that the will should not be revoked by the marriage, the will is not revoked by his marriage to that person. Further, where it appears from a will that at the time it was made the testator was expecting to be married to a particular person and that he intended that a disposition in the will should not be revoked by his marriage to that person, then (a) that disposition takes effect notwithstanding the marriage, and (b) any other disposition in the will also takes effect, unless it appears from the will that the testator intended the disposition to be revoked by the marriage (s.18(3) and (4) replacing s.177 of the Law of Property Act 1925). Another statutory exception to the general rule of revocation provides that a disposition in a will in exercise of a power of appointment takes effect notwithstanding the testator's subsequent marriage unless the property so appointed would in default of appointment pass to his personal representatives (s.18(2)).

Before 1983, divorce had no effect on the validity of any part of a will. However, s.18A of the Wills Act 1837, inserted by the Administration of Justice Act 1982 s.18 with effect from 1 January 1983, now provides that where, after a testator has made a will, a decree of a court dissolves or annuls his marriage or declares it void, (a) the will takes effect as if any appointment of the former spouse as an executor or as the executor and trustee of the will were omitted, and (b) any devise or bequest to the former spouse shall lapse and without prejudice to any right of the former spouse to apply for provision under the Inheritance (Provision for Family and Dependants) Act 1975. This applies only in so far as a contrary intention does not appear in the will. It will be noted that the whole will is not revoked by a decree of dissolution or annulment of the marriage and the dispositions to the other beneficiaries can thus take effect, though if the former spouse is the sole beneficiary then it will be ineffective to dispose of any property. However, the use of the word "lapse" has proved unfortunate. In *Re Sinclair deceased* [1985] Ch 446 the Court of Appeal held that it was to be construed as "failed" and not as directing that the other provisions in the will should take effect as if the former spouse had died in the testator's lifetime. This overruled the contrary view taken by Butler-Sloss J in *Re Cherrington deceased* [1984] 1 WLR 772. Thus in *Re Sinclair deceased* the testator had by his will left the whole of his estate to his wife absolutely with a proviso that if she predeceased him or failed to survive him by one month the estate was to pass to the Imperial Cancer Research Fund. The testator was subsequently divorced and died without having revoked his will. The Fund was not entitled to take the estate since neither contingency upon which it was to take had occurred and accordingly the estate devolved as on an intestacy.

### (d) Other forms of succession

Apart from the general principles of the law of succession, account must also be taken of (a) the statutory provisions which provide for the transmission of a tenancy to a member of a deceased tenant's family (see Chapter 7) and (b) the operation of the right of survivorship on the death of a beneficial joint tenant. Thus whereas the interest of a beneficial tenant in common will pass in accordance with the provisions of his or her will or under the rules of intestate succession, the interest of a beneficial joint tenant will pass unaffected by the will or those rules to the surviving joint tenant. (See Chapter 3.)

## 2. The system of intestate succession

### (a) General principles

The basic principles of the present system of intestate succession were introduced by the Administration of Estates Act 1925, though amendments have been made, in particular by the Intestates' Estates Act 1952 in relation to deaths after 31 December 1952, and by the Family Provision Act 1966 in relation to deaths after 31 December 1966. Under this system, on the death of a person intestate, as to any real or personal estate such estate is to be held by his personal representatives upon trust to sell the same and convert into money so much as does not already consist of money, with power to postpone such sale and conversion for such period as they may think proper (Administration of Estates Act 1925, s.33). After paying the funeral, testamentary and administration expenses and the debts and other liabilities of the deceased the residue of the estate is to be distributed in accordance with the provisions of Part IV of the Act of 1925 as amended. The position in relation to deaths after 31 May 1987 is considered in the following paragraphs of this section.

(i) Where the intestate leaves a surviving spouse

The interest taken by the surviving spouse of the intestate depends on whether or not certain other relatives of the intestate also survive.

First, if the intestate leaves no issue and no parent or brother or sister of the whole blood, or issue of a brother or sister of the whole blood, the residuary estate is held in trust for the surviving spouse absolutely.

Secondly, if the intestate also leaves issue, then the surviving spouse takes the personal chattels absolutely and a fixed net sum of £75,000 with interest thereon from the date of death to the date of payment and, subject thereto, the residuary estate is held (i) as to one-half upon trust for the surviving spouse during his or her life, and subject to such life interest on the statutory trusts for the issue of the intestate and (ii) as to the other half, on the statutory trusts for the issue of the intestate.

Thirdly, if the intestate leaves no issue, but leaves one or more of the following, that is to say, a parent, a brother or sister of the whole blood or issue of such a brother or sister, then the surviving spouse takes the personal chattels absolutely and a fixed net sum of £125,000 with interest thereon from the date of death to the date of payment and, subject thereto, the residuary estate is held (i) as to one-half in trust for the surviving spouse absolutely and (ii) as to the other half, in trust for the intestate's parents in equal shares or the survivor of them absolutely, or, if neither parent survives, on the statutory trusts for the brothers and sisters of the whole blood of the intestate. (See Administration of Estates Act 1925, s.46 as amended by the Intestates' Estates Act 1952 and the Family Provision Act 1966, s.1. The "fixed net sum" in each case may be increased by statutory instrument: see Family Provision (Intestate Succession) Order 1987 (SI 1987 No. 799). "Personal chattels" are defined in the Administration of Estates Act 1925, s. 55(1)(x).)

(ii) Where the intestate leaves issue but no surviving spouse

In this event the residuary estate is held on the statutory trusts for the issue.

(iii) Where the intestate leaves no surviving spouse or issue

If the intestate leaves no spouse or issue, but one or both parents, then the residuary estate is held in trust for the sole surviving parent absolutely or, where both parents survive, for them in equal shares absolutely.

(iv) Where the intestate leaves no spouse, issue or parent

If the intestate leaves no spouse, no issue and no parent, then the residuary estate is held in trust for the following persons living at the death of the intestate and in the following order, namely:

(1) on the statutory trusts for the brothers and sisters of the whole blood of the intestate; but if no person takes an absolutely vested interest under such trusts, then

(2) on the statutory trusts for the brothers and sisters of the half blood of the intestate; but if no person takes an absolutely vested interest under such trusts, then

(3) for the grandparents of the intestate and, if more than one survive the intestate, in equal shares; but if there is no member of this class, then

(4) on the statutory trusts for the uncles and aunts of the intestate (being brothers or

sisters of the whole blood of a parent of the intestate); but if no person takes an absolutely vested interest under such trusts, then

(5) on the statutory trusts for the uncles and aunts of the intestate (being brothers or sisters of the half blood of a parent of the intestate).

("Statutory trusts" are considered at page 509.)

In default of any person taking an absolute interest under the above provisions, the residuary estate passes to the Crown as *bona vacantia*.

## (b) The rights of a surviving spouse

### (i) The rights are given only if a spouse survives the intestate

The rights of succession given to a surviving spouse under the provisions outlined above will take effect only if it is established that the intestate was in fact survived by his or her spouse. Where the intestate and his or her spouse have died in circumstances rendering it uncertain which of them survived the other the provisions take effect as if the spouse had not survived the intestate (Administration of Estates Act 1925, s.46(3) added by the Intestates' Estates Act 1952, s.1(4)). This displaces the general presumption that where two or more persons have died in circumstances rendering it uncertain which of them survived the other or others, such deaths shall be presumed to have occurred in order of seniority, so that the younger is deemed to have survived the elder (Law of Property Act 1925, s.184).

### (ii) The effect of a decree of divorce, nullity or judicial separation

A person will not be entitled to an interest as a surviving spouse if his or her marriage to the intestate has been terminated by a decree absolute of divorce, but the grant of a decree nisi of divorce which has not been made absolute will not prevent that person succeeding as a surviving spouse (*Re Seaford* [1968] P 53). A person will not be entitled to an interest as a surviving spouse if his or her marriage to the intestate was void whether or not a decree of nullity has been pronounced (*Shaw* v *Shaw* [1954] 2 QB 429). In certain circumstances such a person may be able to apply for reasonable provision under the Inheritance (Provision for Family and Dependants) Act 1975. However, where a marriage was merely voidable, the surviving party will be entitled as a surviving spouse unless a decree of nullity has been granted and made absolute before the date of the intestate's death (*Elliott* v *Gurr* (1812) 2 Phillim 16; *A* v *B* (1868) LR 1 P & D 559. See also Matrimonial Causes Act 1973, s.16).

A decree of judicial separation does not terminate a marriage, and a surviving party will accordingly be a surviving spouse. However, it is now provided that, if while a decree of judicial separation is in force and the separation is continuing, either of the parties to the marriage dies after 1 January 1971 intestate as respects all or any of his or her real or personal property, the property as respects which he or she died intestate devolves as if the other party to the marriage had then been dead (Matrimonial Causes Act 1973, s.18(2)). This replaces the narrower provision in the Matrimonial Causes Act 1965 which still applies in relation to deaths occurring before 1 January 1971 (s.20(3)).

## (iii) Other rights of a surviving spouse

### • Redemption of life interest

Where a surviving spouse is entitled to a life interest in part of the residuary estate, he or she may elect to take the capital value of that interest calculated in accordance with the rules set out in the Act. Such an election must generally be made within 12 months from the grant of representation in respect of the estate (Administration of Estates Act 1925, s.47A as amended by the Administration of Justice Act 1977, s.28(2) and (3) and by SI 1977 No. 1491).

### • Rights in relation to the survivor's residence

Where the residuary estate of the intestate comprises an interest in a dwelling-house in which the surviving spouse was resident at the time of the intestate's death, the surviving spouse may require the personal representatives to appropriate that interest in the dwelling-house in or towards satisfaction of an absolute interest of the surviving spouse in the real and personal estate of the intestate (Intestates' Estates Act 1952, s.5 and Sched. 2). This includes the capital value of a life interest which the surviving spouse has elected to have redeemed. This provision does not refer to the matrimonial home of the intestate and the surviving spouse, but to the dwelling-house in which the latter was resident at the time of the former's death. This will, generally, also be the matrimonial home, but it need not be, and there is no requirement that the spouses shall have been residing together at the date of the intestate's death.

This right is not exercisable where the interest in the dwelling-house is (i) a tenancy, which at the date of the death of the intestate would determine within two years from that date; or (ii) a tenancy which the landlord, by notice given after that date, could determine within the remainder of that period. In certain cases the right is not exercisable unless the court so orders on being satisfied that the exercise of the right is not likely to diminish the value of other assets in the residuary estate or make them more difficult to dispose of (*ibid.* But see the provisions for transmission of tenancies: Chapter 7).

The right must be exercised by notice in writing to the personal representatives within 12 months of the grant of representation to the intestate's estate though the period may be extended by the court. The surviving spouse can require the dwelling-house to be valued before deciding whether to exercise the right and will be well advised to do so, for generally once the notice is given it cannot be revoked without the consent of the personal representatives. The value at which the dwelling-house is to be appropriated is its value at the date of appropriation and not at the date of the intestate's death (*Re Collins* [1975] 1 WLR 309). If the value of the house exceeds the value of the surviving spouse's interest, he or she may exercise the right subject to paying the excess value to the personal representatives (*Re Phelps* [1979] 3 All ER 373). In order to safeguard the right it is provided that the personal representatives must not sell or otherwise dispose of the interest in the dwelling-house within 12 months from the date of the grant of representation without the written consent of the surviving spouse except in the course of administration owing to want of other assets. This does not apply where the surviving spouse is the sole personal representative or one of the personal representatives (Intestates' Estates Act 1952, s.5, Sched. 2 para 4).

In those cases where the right is not exercisable, or in respect of other property, the personal representatives have a discretion to appropriate to the surviving spouse (Administration of Estates Act 1925, s.41).

*(c) The rights of the intestate's issue*

(i) The statutory trusts

Where the residuary estate of the intestate, or any part thereof, is directed to be held on the statutory trusts for the issue of the intestate, this means in trust for such of the children of the intestate, who are alive at the death of the intestate, who either attain the age of 18 or marry under that age, and if more than one, in equal shares. Where a child predeceases the intestate, but leaves issue living at the death of the intestate who either attain the age of 18 or marry under that age, then such issue take through all degrees, according to their stocks, in equal shares if more than one, the share which their parent would have taken if living at the death of the intestate (Administration of Estates Act 1925, s.47). The statutory power of advancement and the statutory provisions relating to maintenance and accumulation of surplus income apply.

(ii) Advancements

Any money or property which has been advanced to a child of the intestate must, subject to any contrary intention, expressed or appearing from the circumstances of the case, be taken as being paid or made in or towards satisfaction of the share or shares of his issue. It must, therefore, be brought into account, or "hotchpot", at a valuation calculated as at the date of the death of the intestate (see *Hardy* v *Shaw* [1967] Ch 82).

*(d) The rights of other relatives*

Where the residuary estate of an intestate or any part thereof is directed to be held on the statutory trusts for any class of relatives of the intestate, other than issue of the intestate, it is to be held on trusts corresponding to the statutory trusts for the issue of the intestate. In this case, however, there is no obligation to bring any money or property into account (Administration of Estates Act 1925, s.47(3)).

*(e) Legitimacy, legitimation, illegitimacy and adoption*

(i) General principles

Rights of succession on intestacy formerly depended entirely on legitimate relationships. However, the scope of legitimacy was extended by statute to deal with certain special cases and provision was made by statute for the legitimation of illegitimate children. The rights of illegitimate children and their parents were gradually extended and this process culminated in the Family Law Reform Act 1987 which carried into effect the recommendation of the Law Commission that "... a non-marital child should have the same rights of inheritance on the intestacy of his relatives as a marital child - and his relatives should likewise be able to inherit on his intestacy (Law

Com. No. 118, Illegitimacy (1982) para. 8.14). Special provision also now governs the effect of adoption on intestate succession.

## (ii) Illegitimacy

Section 18 of the Family Law Reform Act 1987 applies to the rules of intestate succession contained in Administration of Estates Act 1925 the general rule of construction contained in s.1 of the 1987 Act. This provides that:

"... references (however expressed) to any relationship between two persons shall, unless the contrary intention appears, be construed without regard to whether or not the father and mother of either of them, or the father and mother of any person through whom the relationship is deduced, have or had been married to each other."

The result is that illegitimacy "becomes in general irrelevant for the purposes of entitlement on intestacy" (the Solicitor General, Hansard H.C. Vol. 114, col. 256). This does not affect any rights under the intestacy of a person dying before 4 April 1988 when s.18 came into force (s.18(4)). Thus, e.g. a grandchild may now take on intestacy of his or her grandparent even though his or her parents were not married. Again, siblings now have rights of succession in each other's estates even though their parents were not married. However, as the Law Commission pointed out, in practice non-marital siblings may well take less frequently than marital siblings (Law Com. No. 118, para. 8.14). This is not because they are non-marital, but because they are related to the deceased only by the half-blood. The Act makes no change in the rules of distribution in the Administration of Estates Act 1925 whereby, for example, a half-brother of a deceased intestate does not take if the intestate left a surviving brother of the whole blood (s.46(1)).

In view of the difficulties that may arise in relation to establishing the identity of the father of an illegitimate child, s.18(2) provides that for the purposes of intestate succession a person whose father and mother were not married to each other at the time of his birth shall be presumed not to have been survived by his father, or by any person related to him only through his father, unless the contrary is shown (extending the provisions of the Family Law Reform Act 1969). This is essentially a rule of convenience and has the advantage of putting the burden of proof very clearly on a claimant (Law Com. No. 118, para. 8.32).

## (iii) Adoption

An adopted child is to be treated in law (a) where the adopters are a married couple, as if he had been born as a child of the marriage (whether or not he was in fact born after the marriage was solemnised), and (b) in any other case, as if he had been born to the adopter in wedlock (but not as a child of any actual marriage of the adopter) and as if he were not the child of any person other than the adopters or adopter (Adoption Act 1976, s.39). This means that an adopted child of a married couple is treated as the brother or sister of the whole blood of any other child or adopted child of his adoptive parents. In other cases the adopted child is treated as the brother or sister of the half-blood of any other child or adopted child of the adopter. It is also provided that the law of intestate succession is to be applied as if an adopted child had been born on the date of the adoption (Adoption Act 1976, s.42(2)). Since the

Administration of Estates Act 1925 provides that only persons "living at the death of the intestate" can take under the statutory trusts it seems that an adopted person and persons claiming through him cannot take on the intestacy of a person dying before the date of the adoption, i.e. the deemed date of birth of the adopted person (ss. 47(1)(i) and 55(2)). Thus although the provisions may have changed the position in relation to some testamentary gifts, the position in relation to intestate succession remains the same.

*(f) Partial intestacy*
Where a person dies leaving a will which effectively disposes of only part of his property, the remainder of his property is, subject to the provisions of the will, to be distributed in accordance with the provisions of the law of intestate succession outlined above. However, in certain cases benefits obtained under the will must be brought into account.

First, a surviving spouse must bring into account against the fixed net sum of £75,000 or £125,000, as the case may be, to which he or she is entitled, the value as at the date of death, of any beneficial interests received by him or her under the will other than personal chattels specifically bequeathed (Administration of Estates Act 1925, s.49(1)(a)).

Secondly, any beneficial interest acquired under the will by any issue of the deceased must be brought into account (*ibid.* s.39(1)(b)).

# Chapter 21

# Family provision

## 1. The scope of the family provision legislation

The aim of the system of family provision introduced by the Inheritance (Family Provision) Act 1938 was to ensure that reasonable provision was made for the maintenance of certain dependants of the deceased. It was not designed to enable members of the deceased's family to acquire a share in his estate without reference to their need for support, or, in other words, their dependency (see Chapter 1). This remains the position under the Inheritance (Provision for Family and Dependants) Act 1975 so far as persons other than the surviving spouse are concerned, but that Act has raised the standard of provision which can be made for a surviving spouse and equates it more closely to that which can be made for a divorced spouse in proceedings for divorce. The Law Commission stated in its *Second Report on Family Property: Family Provision on Death* (Law Com. No. 61 (1974) paras. 16 and 19):

"The first principle is that maintenance should no longer be retained as the objective in determining family provision for a surviving spouse (other than one who was judicially separated from the deceased) and that the court's powers should, as far as practicable, be as wide as its powers to award financial provision on divorce."

"The second principle ... is that for other dependants (including former spouses and judicially separated spouses) the function of family provision legislation should be confined, as it is at present, to securing reasonable provision for maintenance."

The Act also enlarged the class of persons who may apply for maintenance from the estate and gave the court wider powers to make whatever order might be appropriate in the circumstances, whether in the form of periodical payments, a lump sum (as before) or by a transfer or settlement of property, or a variation of a previous settlement. In order to make these wider powers effective the Act seeks to make additional property available to meet orders for family provision by a number of anti-avoidance provisions.

Application can be made under the Act of 1975 for provision out of the estate of a person dying on or after 1 April 1976 when the Act came into force (ss.1 and 27). Existing legislation continues to apply to the estate of persons dying before that date so that the higher standard of provision laid down for applications by surviving spouses will not apply in such cases. Orders made under existing legislation in such cases and orders already in existence at that date (other than interim orders) continue in force as if made under the 1975 Act. This means, for example, that the new provisions as to variation and discharge will be applicable (s.26(3) and (4)). The existing legislation has become less important with the passing of time since the general principle - which is retained in relation to applications under the 1975 Act - is that applications for orders cannot be made, except with the permission of the court, after the end of the period of six months from the date on which representation with respect to the estate of the deceased was first taken out (s.4. See page 551).

An application under the Act of 1975 cannot be made unless the deceased died domiciled in England and Wales (s.1(1)). The burden of proof that the deceased died so domiciled lies on the applicant (*Mastaka* v *Midland Bank Executor and Trustee Co Ltd* [1941] Ch 192. For the difficulties that can arise see Miller, *Family Provision: The International Dimension* (1990) 39 ICLQ 261).

## 2. The courts

Applications may be made to the High Court or to a county court (s.25(1)). In the High Court applications are assigned to the Chancery Division or the Family Division and a code of procedure common to both divisions is prescribed (R.S.C. Ord. 99). A county court now has jurisdiction to hear and determine any application for an order under s.2 of the Act irrespective of the value of the deceased's estate (County Courts Act 1984, s.25 as amended by the High Court and County Courts Jurisdiction Order 1991, SI 1991 No.724, art 2). Where a county court makes an order under s.2 the court then has all the jurisdiction of the High Court for the purpose of any further proceedings in relation thereto under s.6 which confers certain powers of variation (s.22(2). See page 549 for s.6. Applications in county courts are regulated by Ord 45A of the County Court Rules).

## 3. Who may apply?

The Act specifies five categories of applicant (s.1(1)).

### (a) The wife or husband of the deceased
This presupposes that there was a valid marriage between the applicant and the deceased which was still subsisting at the date of the latter's death. It is specifically provided that the category includes a person who in good faith entered into a void marriage with the deceased unless that marriage was dissolved or annulled during the lifetime of the deceased or that person has entered into a later marriage during the lifetime of the deceased (s.25(4)). The fact that such a person remarries after the

death of the deceased, but before an order is made, no longer affects the right to apply. In *Re Sehota* [1978] 3 All ER 385 it was held that a wife was entitled to apply under the Act even though the marriage was polygamous. In that case an application was permitted by the deceased's first wife, to whom he was still married, when he left a will disposing of his property to his second wife. Foster J saw no reason why applications should not be made by two wives where the deceased husband had left his property to a third party, e.g. a charity.

In *Whytte* v *Ticehurst* [1986] Fam 64 Booth J held that the claim of a surviving spouse under the 1975 Act ceased to exist on his or her death unless an order had been made. Only when an order has been made is there an enforceable cause of action which would continue to subsist for the benefit of the estate of the surviving spouse. This was followed by Sheldon J in *Re Bramwell* [1988] 2 FLR 263.

### (b) A former wife or husband of the deceased

This category was originally confined to a former spouse whose marriage with the deceased had been dissolved or annulled by a decree of a court in England and Wales under the Matrimonial Causes Act 1973 or earlier Acts replaced by that Act. However, it now extends to a person whose marriage with the deceased was dissolved or annulled under the law of any country outside England and Wales by a divorce or annulment which is entitled to be recognised as valid under English law (s.25(1) as amended by the Matrimonial and Family Proceedings Act 1984, s.25(2)). Remarriage removes a former spouse from this category even though the marriage is void or voidable (s.25(5)). Such a person will acquire rights to apply for financial provision against the other party to that marriage.

### (c) A child of the deceased

The Act of 1975 removed the various restrictions on applications by children of the deceased. However, it should be borne in mind that the fact that a child is given a right to apply does not mean that an award will be made. Maintenance is still the objective in relation to children, and an award will not be made without reference to the need for support. Nevertheless, although the best way of showing the need for support may be to show that the applicant child has been dependent on the deceased, this is not necessary so far as the right to apply is concerned. The Law Commission rejected the idea of an express requirement that the child was dependent on the deceased at the time of death, for this would rule out a claim against the estate of a parent who had unreasonably refused to support an adult child during his lifetime. (See *Re Debenham* [1986] 1 FLR 404 where the mother never seemed to have recognised any obligation to the child.) Moreover, an adult child who is fully self-supporting at the time of the parent's death may quite suddenly thereafter cease to be so (Law Com. No. 61, para. 75).

A "child" includes a child of the deceased even though the deceased was not married to the other parent, and a child *en ventre sa mère* at the death of the deceased (s.25(1)). A "child" also includes a person who had been adopted by the deceased. A person who was the natural child of the deceased but who has been adopted by another is not included even though adoption took place after the death of the deceased (*Re Collins* [1990] Fam 56).

*(d) A person (not being a child of the deceased) who, in the case of any marriage to which the deceased was at any time a party, was treated by the deceased as a child of the family in relation to that marriage*

Under the Act of 1938 a person could not apply on the basis of being a child of the deceased unless he or she was the deceased's own child or adopted child. Thus no application could be made by a person who was a child of the deceased's spouse by another person, or was the child of neither party, but who had nevertheless been treated as part of the deceased's family. The 1975 Act now permits an application to be made by any such person who has been treated by the deceased as a child of the family in relation to any marriage to which the deceased was at any time a party. This is similar to the provision made in the Matrimonial Causes Act 1973 (s.52(1). See Chapter 17, Part 5). Special considerations apply to children relying on paragraph (d) rather than on paragraph (c) (see s.3(3) of the 1975 Act).

It is not necessary for an applicant under paragraph (d) to have been "treated by the deceased as a child of the family" while he or she was a minor dependent child. A stepchild may be capable of qualifying even though he or she has not been treated by the deceased step-parent as an "unfledged person", i.e. by the assumption of parental responsibility and control. Thus in *Re Callaghan* [1985] Fam 1 by the time the deceased married the applicant's mother the applicant was 35 years of age, was himself married and no longer living in their home. Nevertheless, Booth J regarded the acknowledgement by the deceased of his own role of grandfather to the applicant's children, the confidences as to his property and financial affairs which he had placed in the applicant, and his dependence upon the applicant to care for him in his last illness, as examples of the deceased's treatment of the applicant as a child, albeit an adult child of the family. She said (at p. 6): "All these things are part of the privileges and duties of two persons who, in regard to each other, stand in the relationship of parent and child ...".

In *Re Leach* [1986] Ch 226 the applicant had been aged 32 and was living away from home when her father married her stepmother. She had never lived in the same household as her stepmother and had never been maintained by her. The close relationship which developed between them continued after her father's death some fourteen years later up until the stepmother died intestate when the applicant was over 50 years of age. Slade LJ said that the various matters taken into account by the judge viewed in isolation would not necessarily have enabled the applicant to qualify under paragraph (d). However, when they were looked at cumulatively, alongside the continuous nature of the relationship of mutual affection and trust between the applicant and the stepmother, it was impossible to say that there was no evidence on which the judge could properly hold that the applicant was eligible to apply. He said (at p. 237):

"I can see no reason why even an adult person may not be capable of qualifying under [paragraph (d)] provided that the deceased has, *as wife or husband* (or widow or widower) under the relevant marriage, expressly or implicitly, assumed the position of a parent towards the applicant, with the attendant *responsibilities and privileges* of that relationship. If things take their natural course, the privileges of the quasi-parent may well increase and the responsibilities may well diminish as the years go by." (Author's italics.)

He noted that in *Re Callaghan* the factors which had influenced Booth J in reaching her decision were clearly the privileges more than the responsibilities of quasi-parenthood which the deceased had assumed in relation to the applicant, during the period of his marriage to the applicant's mother. Slade LJ did however emphasise that the mere display of affection, kindness or hospitality by a step-parent towards a stepchild would not by itself be sufficient to amount to treatment by the step-parent of the stepchild as a child of the family.

On the other hand, it is clear from *Re Leach* that the treatment of an applicant by a surviving spouse after the death of the other spouse may be a relevant factor in deciding whether the applicant qualifies under paragraph (d), provided such treatment is referable to or "stems from" the marriage. In a case where the marriage has been terminated by the death of one of the spouses it would not be correct, for the purposes of paragraph (d), to regard the family unit created by that marriage as necessarily having come to an end on such death (*per* Slade LJ at p. 234). In *Re Callaghan* [1985] Fam 1 at p. 6 Booth J did not find it necessary to consider the argument that treatment by the deceased of the applicant as a child of the family before the marriage ceremony took place would of itself be sufficient to bring the applicant within paragraph (d), though she acknowledged that it was a powerful argument which found support from the judge at first instance in *Re Leach* [1984] FLR 590 at p. 597.

*(e) Any person (not being a person included in the foregoing paragraphs) who immediately before the death of the deceased was being maintained, either wholly or partly, by the deceased*

(i) The relationship with s.1(3)
It is provided in s.1(3) that for the purposes of s.1(1)(e) "a person shall be treated as being maintained by the deceased, either wholly or partly, as the case may be, if the deceased, otherwise than for valuable consideration, was making a substantial contribution in money or money's worth towards the reasonable needs of that person".

On the literal wording of the provisions it is arguable that s.1(1)(e) includes not merely a person "being maintained" by the deceased, but also someone who was to be "treated as being maintained" by him by virtue of the deeming provision in s.1(3). Moreover, as Sir Robert Megarry V-C pointed out in *Re Beaumont* [1980] Ch 444 at p. 450, there "is nothing in section 1(3) to state that someone who falls within section 1(1)(e) is also to be driven out of it unless he also satisfies section 1(3)". This would, however, produce the absurd result that if the proprietor of an old persons' home, a boarding house or hotel were to die, many of the residents who are paying for full board could say that they were being at least partly maintained by the proprietor before his death so that they satisfy s.1(1)(e) even though they did not satisfy s.1(3) since the proprietor was partly maintaining them for full valuable consideration. This, Sir Robert Megarry V-C thought, could not have been the intention of Parliament and he held that a claim could not be made by virtue of s.1(1)(e) unless the requirements of s.1(3) were satisfied. This interpretation was confirmed by the Court of Appeal in *Jelley* v *Iliffe* [1981] Fam 128. Stephenson LJ said (at p. 136):
"The deeming provision in section 1(3) exhaustively or exclusively defines what

section 1(1)(e) means by 'being maintained', and does not include in those words a state of affairs which is not within section 1(1)(e) and would extend its ambit. To qualify within section 1(1)(e) an applicant must satisfy section 1(3), as if before the words 'if the deceased' the draftsman of section 1(3) had inserted the word 'only'."

(See also Butler-Sloss LJ in *Bishop* v *Plumley* [1991] 1 WLR 582 at p. 587.)

(ii) "Immediately before the death of the deceased"
It is necessary for the applicant to show that he or she was being maintained by the deceased "immediately before the death of the deceased". If these words were construed literally as applying to the *de facto* situation at death, then a claim could be defeated because, e.g. during a terminal illness, the deceased was too ill to continue what had been regular payments to the applicant. In *Jelley* v *Iliffe* [1981] Fam 128, the Court of Appeal confirmed the rejection by Megarry V-C in *Re Beaumont* [1980] Ch 444 of this possibility. In considering whether a person was being maintained "immediately before the death of the deceased", Stephenson LJ said that "it is the settled basis or general arrangement between the parties as regards maintenance during the lifetime of the deceased which has to be looked at, not the actual, perhaps fluctuating, variation of it which exists immediately before his or her death". ([1981] Fam 128 at p. 136. See also *Re Kirby (deceased)* [1982] 3 FLR 249.) Accordingly, he said "a relationship of dependence which has persisted for years will not be defeated by its termination during a few weeks of mortal sickness".

On the other hand, the subsequent case of *Kourgky* v *Lusher* [1983] 4 FLR 65 shows that an applicant will not satisfy this requirement if there is clear evidence that the deceased had abandoned responsibility for maintenance of the applicant before his death. In that case the deceased had lived with the applicant from 1969, though with some interruptions when he had returned to his wife. In July 1979 he went on holiday with his wife and thereafter did not return to live with the applicant before his death intestate in August 1979.

If, as seems desirable, the court is required to go beyond a mere examination of the *de facto* state of affairs existing in the instant before death, it becomes necessary to consider the nature or quality of the basis or arrangement for which it should look. In *Re Beaumont* Sir Robert Megarry V-C had noted that under all other heads of s.1(1) the qualification is of an enduring nature. There must be a past or present marriage, paternity or maternity, or the treatment of the claimant as a child of the family in relation to a marriage of the deceased. If paragraph (e) made no more than a transient and fluctuating requirement, it would be strikingly out of line with the other paragraphs. While this is true it should be borne in mind that the Law Commission rejected the idea that the dependence that was required to exist at the date of death should also be required to have existed for some minimum period before death. It was pointed out that the length of the period of dependence would in any case be a factor that the court would have to take into account in deciding whether or not to award provision. If it was made a factor going to jurisdiction this would fetter unduly the court's discretion (Law Com. No. 61, para. 93).

In *Re Beaumont* [1980] Ch 444 at p. 455, Sir Robert Megarry V-C concluded that the arrangement which had to be looked for was an assumption of responsibility by the deceased for the applicant's maintenance. This was supported by the wording of s.3(4) of the Act which requires a court considering an application under paragraph (e) to "have regard to the extent to which and the basis upon which the deceased assumed responsibility for the maintenance of the applicant and to the length of time for which the deceased discharged that responsibility". Although this is not concerned with jurisdiction it does nevertheless assume that in any case within paragraph (e) there has in fact been an assumption of responsibility. In contrast to this, s.3(3) requires the court in considering applications by children of the deceased or persons so treated by the deceased to have regard "to whether the deceased had assumed any responsibility for the applicant's maintenance and, if so, to the extent to which and the basis upon which the deceased assumed that responsibility and to the length of time for which the deceased discharged that responsibility".

(iii) The assumption of responsibility
It was accepted by the Court of Appeal in *Jelley* v *Iliffe* [1981] Fam 128 that an applicant's right to apply under s.1(1)(e) depends on his proving that the deceased did *assume responsibility* for his maintenance. However, the Court of Appeal took a very different view from that taken by Sir Robert Megarry VC, as to the circumstances in which such an assumption of responsibility might be found to exist.

In *Re Beaumont* [1980] Ch 444 at p. 458 Sir Robert Megarry VC considered that the word "assumes" indicated that there must be some act or acts which demonstrated an undertaking of responsibility, or the taking of responsibility on one's self. The Act distinguished between "assuming" and "discharging" responsibility. It was for the applicant to establish that there had been an assumption of responsibility and not for the defendants to have to rebut any presumption of assumption of responsibility which was to be drawn from the bare fact of maintenance. In *Jelley* v *Iliffe* the Court of Appeal could not agree that the bare fact of maintenance raises no presumption that responsibility for it has been assumed. Stephenson LJ asked "... How better or more clearly can one take on or discharge responsibility for maintenance than by actually maintaining?" ([1981] Fam 128 at p. 137). In his view, s.1(1)(e) appears to have been aimed at giving relief to persons where the relationship to the deceased was such as to make it highly unlikely that any formal arrangements would have been made between them. Griffiths LJ read the phrase "assumed responsibility for" as being equivalent to "has undertaken" and as not adding much to the fact of maintenance. Accordingly, in his view, if the evidence shows "an arrangement subsisting at the time of death under which the deceased was making a substantial contribution in money or money's worth to the reasonable needs of the applicant, it will, as a general rule, be proper to draw the inference that the deceased has undertaken to maintain the applicant and thus 'assumed responsibility for the maintenance' within the meaning of s.3(4). It should not be necessary to search for any other overt act to demonstrate the 'assumption of responsibility'." (*Ibid.* at p. 142).

Generally, therefore, the fact that the deceased did provide maintenance for the applicant will give rise to the inference that the deceased had assumed responsibility for the maintenance of the applicant. However Stephenson LJ thought that the presumption arising from the fact of maintenance might "be rebutted by the circumstances including a disclaimer of any intention to maintain" (*ibid.* at p.137).

Griffiths LJ also envisaged a situation in which a deceased had been making regular payments to some person's support while at the same time making it clear that the recipient could not count on their continuing. Nevertheless he regarded such a situation as likely to be the exception rather than the rule (*ibid.* at p. 142).

Stephenson LJ made it clear that a distinction must be drawn between an intention to maintain during the lifetime of the giver who had something to offer and an intention to provide continuing support after death. If the deceased during his lifetime had disclaimed any intention to assume responsibility for the maintenance of the applicant then the latter would not be qualified to apply. On the other hand, the absence of an intention on the part of the deceased to provide continuing support after his death for a dependant will not disqualify the latter from applying for provision though it may well affect the decision of the court as to what provision, if any, is appropriate. Stephenson LJ pointed out that if it was necessary, or relevant, to prove an intention on the part of the deceased to maintain a dependant qualified to apply under s.1(1)(e) after the deceased's death, the only cases in which there would be the required qualification would be those where the deceased's intention had been defeated by accident, e.g. by his dying intestate leaving children or having made an invalid will in the dependant's favour. The scope of the Act was not so limited. He said (at pp. 137-138):

> "Its object is surely to remedy, wherever reasonably possible, the injustice of one, who has been put by a deceased person in a position of dependency on him, being deprived of any financial support, either by accident or by design of the deceased, after his death. To leave a dependant, to whom no legal or moral obligation is owed, unprovided for after death may not entitle the dependant to much or indeed any, financial provision in all the circumstances, but he is not disentitled from applying for such provision if he can prove that the deceased by his conduct made him dependent upon the deceased for maintenance, whether intentionally or not."

Accordingly a dependant of the deceased, i.e. a person for whose maintenance the deceased had assumed responsibility during his, the deceased's, lifetime, is not disqualified from applying merely because the lack of any provision on the deceased's death was intentional and not merely accidental. This is clearly right for applicants within the other categories of s.1(1) are not disqualified from applying merely because the lack of provision in a deceased's will or as a result of his intestacy was intentional.


(iv) Balancing the benefits

The final qualifying hurdle to be overcome by a potential applicant under s.1(1)(e) is to show that the maintenance he or she received from the deceased was "otherwise than for full valuable consideration". The effect of s.1(3) is to require the court to balance the benefits received by the applicant from the deceased against those provided by the applicant for the deceased. Unless the latter fall short of the former, the applicant will be disqualified from proceeding with his or her application because the "maintenance" received from the deceased will have been given for "full valuable consideration". Moreover, in *Jelley* v *Iliffe* [1981] Fam 128 at pp. 136 and 191, the Court of Appeal confirmed the view taken by Arnold J in *Re Wilkinson (deceased)* [1978] Fam 22, and by Sir Robert Megarry VC in *Re Beaumont* [1980] Ch 444 that the phrase "for full valuable consideration" is not to be construed as limited to benefits provided under a contract. This means that the court will often have the difficult task of trying to balance imponderables like companionship and other services against contributions by the deceased of money or accommodation.

In *Re Wilkinson* Arnold J found "with considerable uncertainty" that the services of the applicant who went to live in her sister's house were just outweighed by what the sister gave to her in board and lodging so that she was entitled to proceed with her application for provision out of her sister's estate. It has been pointed out that there is at least some "market" for housekeepers, but that the difficulties may be even greater in relation to claims by cohabitees ((1980) 96 LQR 534). In *Re Beaumont*, Sir Robert Megarry VC found it unnecessary to weigh the contributions of the male applicant against that of the woman with whom he had cohabited for many years because he held that there had been no assumption of responsibility by the latter for the maintenance of the applicant through the provision of accommodation and money. There was no difficulty in *Malone v Harrison* [1979] 1 WLR 1353 where the benefits provided by the deceased during the 12 years preceding his death for the applicant clearly outweighed benefits provided by her as his "part-time mistress". In *CA v CC* (1979) 123 SJ 35 the applicant had lived with the deceased for the four years preceding his death. She had met him when he had advertised for a housekeeper and had been employed on the understanding that she would share the deceased's bed and would receive money for the housekeeping but no wages. She subsequently had a child of whom he was the father. It was argued that she had not been maintained by the deceased, but had simply got an unusually good bargain in selling her services as a housekeeper. This was rejected by Sir George Baker P who said that she and the deceased had a stable affectionate relationship and that everything pointed to a family unit. She was a "*de facto* wife" who came within s.1(1)(e) and for whom provision had to be made. It appears, therefore, that there was no express balancing of benefits.

In *Jelley v Iliffe* [1981] Fam 128 the Court of Appeal advocated a broader approach to the problem. Griffiths LJ said (at p. 141):

"In striking this balance the court must use common sense and remember that the object of Parliament in creating this extra class of persons who may claim benefit from an estate was to provide relief for persons of whom it could truly be said that they were wholly or partially dependent on the deceased. It cannot be an exact exercise of evaluating services in pounds and pence."

He took the example of a man living with a woman as his wife and providing the house and all the money for their living expenses. She would, in his view, clearly be dependent on him and it would not be right to deprive her of her claim by arguing that she was in fact performing the services that a housekeeper would perform and it would cost more to employ a housekeeper than was spent on her and indeed, perhaps, more than the deceased had available to spend on her. He said (*ibid.* at p. 141):

"Each case will have to be looked at carefully on its own facts to see whether common sense leads to the conclusion that the applicant can fairly be regarded as a dependant."

Stephenson LJ expressed a similar view when he said (at p. 139):

"In my judgement the statute, whether literally or purposively construed, requires the court to take a broad commonsense view of the question whether the applicant for the statutory relief was a dependant of the deceased before death, and the ordinary man's answer to what, on this approach, is the right question, "Was this man dependent on this woman during her lifetime for maintenance, or did he give as good as he got?"

In that case the application had been struck out on the ground that the evidence in support of it did not disclose a reasonable cause of action. It was accepted in the Court of Appeal that while strictly the balancing operation is one that arises only at a later stage there would be a saving of costs if it can be done at a preliminary stage. However, if there is any doubt about the balance tipping in favour of the deceased's being the greater contribution, the matter must go to trial. If the balance is bound to come down in favour of the applicant's being the greater contribution, or if the contributions are clearly equal, there is no dependency of the applicant on the deceased, either because the latter depended on the former or there was mutual dependency between them, and the application should be struck out at the preliminary stage as bound to fail. In that case it was not clear beyond doubt on the applicant's affidavits that his contribution equalled or outweighed the benefit of rent-free accommodation he had received from the deceased. There was an arguable case that he was being maintained by the deceased and the matter was allowed to proceed to trial.

In *Bishop* v *Plumley* [1991] 1 WLR 582 at p. 587, Butler-Sloss LJ interpreted the statement of Griffiths LJ in *Jelley* v *Iliffe* to mean that the problem must be looked at in the round, "avoiding fine balancing computations involving the value of normal exchanges of support in the domestic scene". Thus in the ordinary case where the parties had lived together as husband and wife the provision of a secure home for the applicant would have been a substantial contribution creating a dependency in the applicant which will not be affected by such "normal exchanges of support in the domestic scene". In that case the Court of Appeal did not consider that the exceptional care which the applicant had provided for the deceased over a period of time immediately preceding his death went beyond such "normal exchanges of support". Butler-Sloss LJ said (at p. 587):

"I do not consider that her evidence that she did everything for him over a period of years can be assessed in isolation from the mutuality of the relationship. If a man or woman living as man and wife with a partner gives the other extra devoted care and attention, particularly when the partner is in poor health, is he or she to be in a less advantageous position on an application under the Act than one who may be less loving and give less attention to the partner? I do not accept that this could have been the intention of Parliament in passing this legislation."

## 4. The ground for an application – reasonable financial provision

*(a) The two-stage process*

An application for an order under s.2 of the Act can be made on the ground that "the disposition of the deceased's estate effected by his will or the law relating to intestacy, or the combination of his will and that law is not such as to make reasonable financial provision for the applicant" (s.1(1)). Thus, assuming the applicant is "qualified" to apply, the first of two possible stages in an application under the Act is for the court to determine whether or not reasonable financial provision has been made for the applicant. In some cases the provision which is reasonable will be nil, in which case the court will not interfere even if no provision has been made. The application will then fail as it will when the court determines that the provision made for the applicant is reasonable financial provision. The second stage is for the court to determine the extent to which it should exercise its powers under the Act to make reasonable financial provision for the applicant, but this only arises if it is satisfied that such provision has not been made. The second stage of the "composite problem" is clearly a question of discretion, but the first is not. "It is a question of fact, but it is a value judgment, or a qualitative decision," which ought not to be interfered with by the Court of Appeal unless it is satisfied that it was "plainly wrong" (*per* Goff LJ in *Re Coventry* [1980] Ch 461 at p. 487).

The wording of s.1(1) makes it clear that the test of reasonable financial provision to be applied in all cases is objective (see *Re Goodwin* [1969] 1 Ch 283 at p. 288 for a formulation of the objective test). Moreover, in relation to the first stage Goff LJ said in *Re Coventry deceased* [1980] Ch 461 at p. 488, that the "problem must be exactly the same whether one is dealing with a will or an intestacy, or with a combination of both. The question is whether the operative dispositions make, or fail to make, reasonable provision in all the circumstances."

### (b) The test of reasonable financial provision

Section 3 sets out in detail the matters to which the court is to have regard in determining (a) whether the deceased's will or the law of intestacy, or both, as the case may be, does make reasonable provision for the applicant, and (b) if such provision has not been made, what order should be made. It is provided that in considering the specified matters the court must take into account facts as known to the court at the date of the hearing (s.3(5)). This is in line with the objective approach to reasonable provision and removes the doubts which existed under the previous legislation as to whether the court could take into account any change of circumstances occurring after the date of the deceased's death. However, while the court must have regard to the state of the facts known at the date of the hearing, e.g. in relation to the earning capacity of an applicant or beneficiary or the value of the estate, it is not permissible to reach a conclusion that a will makes reasonable provision by having regard to legally unenforceable assurances given at the date of the hearing by beneficiaries under the will that they will not insist on their full legal rights. The court is concerned to establish what legal rights have been given to the applicant by the will and mere assurances that the testamentary provisions will not be adhered to are not sufficient (*per* Sir Nicholas Browne-Wilkinson VC in *Rajabally* v *Rajabally* [1987] 2 FLR 390 at p. 394).

### (c) Reasonable financial provision for a surviving spouse

In the case of an application by a surviving spouse, reasonable financial provision means "such provision as it would be reasonable in all the circumstances of the case for a husband or wife to receive, whether or not that provision is required for his or her maintenance" (s.1(2)). In the case of any other applicant it means "such financial provision as it would be reasonable in all the circumstances of the case for the applicant to receive for his maintenance" (*ibid.*). In this way the Act seeks to give effect to the recommendation of the Law Commission that the standard of provision for a surviving spouse should be higher than that for any other applicant. More information about these standards is to be found in s.3 of the Act, but the present formulation of the concept of reasonable financial provision for a surviving spouse is unsatisfactory. While it was intended - and has been recognised - that it is no longer limited to the function of providing maintenance, there is no clear identification in the Act or in the cases of the additional component. The new standard was inspired by, and partly formulated by reference to, the standard of provision applicable on divorce under the Matrimonial Causes Act 1973. Thus s.3(2) requires the court to have regard to the provision which the applicant might reasonably have expected to receive if on the day on which the deceased died the marriage, instead of being terminated by death, had been terminated by a decree of divorce. Further consideration will be given in due course to that requirement, but in the meantime consideration must be given to some general aspects of the concept.

It is submitted that provision for a surviving spouse has two objectives. The first objective may be to provide for the survivor's need for support - the "maintenance objective". The second objective should be to give recognition to the surviving spouse's contribution towards the accumulation of wealth which may happen to be vested in the name of the deceased spouse. It is, of course, possible for a surviving spouse to seek to establish a beneficial interest in part of the "deceased's estate in the same way as he or she might have done before the death" (see *Re Cummins* [1972] Ch 62). However, apart from other difficulties, contributions in the form of care for the home and family will not be enough to secure a share in this way (see Chapter 2). An order under the 1975 Act may therefore be designed to secure for the surviving spouse a share of the deceased's estate on the basis of both kinds of contribution - contributions in money or money's worth and contributions by caring for the family and the home. It is clear that the 1975 Act was intended to do this. Thus the Law Commission (Law Com. No. 61, para. 33) said:

"... we now propose criteria which would enable ... the court to adopt an approach similar to that ... adopted in divorce proceedings and *to recognise that a surviving spouse may be entitled to a share of the family assets by virtue of contributions to the welfare of the family* (see *Wachtel*)". (Author's italics.)

If the proposal for co-ownership of the matrimonial home had been implemented this would have reduced the importance of this aspect of family provision. Indeed in many modest estates it would probably have eliminated it. This has not occurred, though the spread of voluntary co-ownership will eventually have the same effect. Where the matrimonial home was held by the spouses as beneficial joint tenants then the deceased's share will automatically accrue to the survivor irrespective of the provisions of the will or the rules of intestate succession.

However, there remain a significant number of cases where the bulk of the estate including the matrimonial home will have been vested in the deceased. Even where the home has passed to the surviving spouse this will not necessarily be reasonable provision where the deceased has failed to provide out of the remainder of the estate the means of running and maintaining the home.

It is acknowledged that where the estate is of only modest size the need to provide support may call for some modification of the division of property that might otherwise be made. Nevertheless, a fairer balance is likely to be struck if there is a clearer recognition of the real beneficial interests as opposed to the mere vesting of title. Unfortunately the distinction has not always been clearly drawn in the cases.

In *Re Besterman deceased* [1984] Ch 458 there was a clear recognition by the Court of Appeal of the change effected by the 1975 Act in relation to reasonable financial provision for a surviving spouse. The deceased's estate was valued at £1.37 million and his will made relatively small provision for the widow with the bulk of the estate being left to the University of Oxford. The lump sum of £259,250 awarded to the widow at first instance was increased by the Court of Appeal to £378,000 on the basis that the judge's approach had been dominated by the "obligation of maintenance". It was described by Oliver LJ (at p. 479) as a very "pure" case in the sense that it was virtually free from any complicating factors such as conflicting obligations, legal or moral, relevant conduct or substantial means of the applicant or other extraneous considerations. It was also not a case in which the widow had contributed directly to the acquisition of the deceased's substantial wealth which he had largely acquired before he married the plaintiff at the age of fifty-four as his third wife. On the other hand, the marriage had lasted some eighteen years and Oliver LJ said (at p. 462) "there is no reason for assuming anything other than that the marriage was a contented one and that the plaintiff was a faithful and dutiful wife to whom the deceased owed all the duties ordinarily arising from the married state". Contribution to the welfare of the family unit of husband and wife must, therefore, have been an important factor in assessing the increased lump sum awarded.

In *Re Bunning deceased* [1984] Ch 480 the estate was more modest, but still relatively large - some £220,000 - and the widow had assets of some £98,000 largely derived from the deceased. The plaintiff was the deceased's second wife and had married him when he was over fifty. During their marriage she contributed not only to the welfare of the family unit but gave considerable help in his business. They had been separated for the last four years of the marriage and the deceased made no provision for the plaintiff in his will. Vinelott J concluded that the right figure for a lump sum payment was £60,000 and this was confirmed as appropriate in a number of ways. First, while he had not calculated the figure as a proportion of the spouses' aggregate resources, the figure of £60,000 would in fact achieve rough *equality*. Secondly, a lump sum of £60,000 was comparable with the life interest in the residue which in 1979 the testator himself had thought a reasonable provision to make for his wife. Thirdly, a sum of £60,000 would enable the plaintiff to buy the cottage she hoped to be able to buy and to provide the income she needed and provide a reserve adequate to allow for exceptional demands and unforeseen contingencies. It was also rather more than might have been awarded on divorce. Thus there was a proper recognition of the wife's contributions to the marriage in different ways. Her contribution to the business activities justified a share not only in the matrimonial home, but also in his other assets, though this had to be balanced against the fact that the assets had been largely accumulated before marriage. This latter factor might be thought to point to something less than half of the total assets, but this would not have produced a figure which would have enabled the widow to maintain herself at a level considered to be appropriate in the circumstances. Thus although Vinelott J makes no express distinction between the maintenance factor and the property factor in his calculation, both elements would seem to have played their part in producing the final result.

In *Stephens* v *Stephens* 1 July 1985, CA Lexis Enggen, the plaintiff widow had been given a right to live in the matrimonial home which had been vested in the deceased, and a life interest in the very small residue. The Court of Appeal did not distinguish expressly between the two aspects of provision, but concluded that the estate should be divided as to 60 per cent for the widow and 40 per cent for the residuary beneficiaries. The plaintiff, who was in her eightieth year, had used the proceeds of sale of her home in supplementing their living expenses during a twenty-year marriage. In terms of property division a half share might seem appropriate, and this she can be said to have obtained together with a further sum on account of maintenance. (In view of her advanced age a capitalisation of a life interest in the "deceased's half" of the estate would presumably have been relatively small.)

In *Rajbally* v *Rajbally* [1987] 2 FLR 390 the estate consisted of the former matrimonial home which the Court of Appeal held should be vested in the widow absolutely "to provide her with real security", subject to a lump sum of £7,000 being raised by mortgage for the deceased's son by a previous marriage whose ability to support himself was impaired by illness. The quarter share which the widow had been given by the will was not reasonable provision for it gave her no security in the home being a home to the maintenance of which she had contributed not only by her labour but also by substantial financial contributions from her earnings.

Although these cases do not provide clear positive guidance about the nature of the new standard of provision for a surviving spouse, there is a clear recognition that such provision is no longer limited to maintenance. The absence of a clear identification in the Act of the additional component has in other cases worked to the detriment of the surviving spouse. Foremost amongst these appears to be *Stead* v *Stead* [1985] FLR 16. In that case the plaintiff had been married to the deceased for twenty-four years though it was the second marriage for both of them. During the early part of the marriage they had little money and the plaintiff worked, and helped a great deal with the family finances. They had a farm which they worked, and when it was sold in 1966 they purchased their last matrimonial home for £3,000 and the plaintiff took in paying guests until 1970. Throughout the marriage they lived a frugal life with a modest income. When the deceased died in 1982 aged eighty-eight, he left an estate of £66,000 comprising the matrimonial home, valued at about £30,000, and liquid assets of about £34,000. By his will the deceased left "his" estate on trust with a life interest in the home to the plaintiff on condition that she paid all the outgoings: £6,000 to be invested to produce an income for her life and the residue to his two adult children. The Court of Appeal dismissed an appeal from an order for payment of a lump sum of £2,500 and periodical payments of £1,500. The plaintiff retained the right to live in the home, but with a reduced liability for outgoings. Purchas LJ accepted that at first sight it looked as if the plaintiff's claim to a share in the estate must be represented by a substantial capital amount. However he concluded that (p. 26):

"... the proper approach is to have in mind that the widow may well need some *capital provision to cover a limited number of eventualities*. As the President found in his judgment, *her requirements were so limited*. As [Counsel] submitted, in my judgment with some force, *if the widow were given more she would merely save it*. In the circumstances of this case .... the size of the lump sum should be appropriately restricted". (Author's italics.)

The Court of Appeal appears to have taken a very limited view of reasonable financial provision, having been concerned almost entirely with providing for the widow's requirements or needs, i.e. the maintenance aspect. It is submitted that insufficient regard was had to her contributions during the marriage by which she had earned a share in the assets which happened to be vested in her husband's name. Purchas LJ did acknowledge that "on an approach based upon her contribution to the family welfare by continuing to use [the home] it could be said that the widow is occupying her half of the estate, but of course she needs further financial provisions ....." (p. 27). In effect the widow was deprived of "her half of the estate" which happened to be vested in the deceased's name (except for a life interest in the home) because she needed the use of at least part of her husband's half of the estate. It is suggested that it would not be unreasonable for her to expect some support from the "husband's half" of the estate. The court appears to have been influenced by two factors, namely the ultimate destination of the assets of the estate and the importance of the power of testation. These are considered further below.

*(d) Reasonable financial provision for other applicants*

In the case of an applicant other than a surviving spouse "reasonable financial provision" means such financial provision as it would be reasonable in all the circumstances of the case for the applicant to receive for his or her maintenance (s.1(2) (b)). In *Re Coventry deceased* [1980] Ch 461 at pp. 484-485 Goff LJ said that whatever the precise meaning of the word "maintenance" (and he did not think it necessary to attempt any precise definition) it was clear that it is a word of somewhat limited meaning in its application to any person qualified to apply, other than a husband or wife. He referred to *Re E* [1966] 1 WLR 709 and *Millward* v *Shenton* [1972] 1 WLR 711. In the former case Stamp J, on an application under the 1938 Act, said that the purpose was not to keep a person above the breadline, but to provide reasonable maintenance in all the circumstances. In the latter case Lord Denning MR thought that maintenance could include a television and a car, depending on all the circumstances. In *Re Coventry deceased* Goff LJ thought that "breadline" would be more accurately described as "subsistence level". He concluded (at p. 485):

"What is proper maintenance must in all cases depend on all the facts and circumstances of the particular case being considered at the time, but I think it is clear on the one hand that one must not put too limited a meaning on it; it does not mean just enough to enable a person to get by, on the other hand, it does not mean anything which may be regarded as reasonably desirable for his general benefit or welfare."

In the same case Buckley LJ suggested (at p. 494) that s.1(2)(b) might be paraphrased as follows:

"In the case of any other application made by virtue of subsection (1) above, 'reasonable financial provision' means such financial provision as would be reasonable in all the circumstances of the case to enable the applicant to maintain himself in a manner suitable to those circumstances."

In *Re Coventry* both Oliver J at first instance and Goff LJ in the Court of Appeal disapproved of the decision in *Re Christie* [1979] Ch 168 in which the judge had treated maintenance as being equivalent to providing for the well-being or benefit of the applicant. In that case the deceased had by her will made in 1963 devised her interest in a London house to her daughter and her interest in a house in Essex to her son with the residue to be divided equally between the two children. She subsequently made a gift of her interest in the London house to her daughter and later sold the house in Essex and purchased a smaller house in which she lived. Although it seems that she had intended to change her will, she died without having done so. Thus the gift of the former house in Essex to the son failed whereas the daughter had already received her intended benefit. On an application by the son for reasonable financial provision the court ordered the new Essex house to be transferred to him. In *Re Coventry* [1980] Ch 461 at p. 490 Goff LJ said that this "may well have gone too far, though it was a strong case and one fully appreciates and sympathises with the deputy judge's desire to give effect to what appeared to be the clear wishes of the testator".

In *Re Dennis* [1980] 2 All ER 140 Browne-Wilkinson J thought that "the word 'maintenance' connotes only payments which, directly or indirectly, enable the applicant in the future to discharge the cost of his daily living at whatever standard of living is appropriate to him. The provision that is to be made is to meet recurring expenses, being expenses of living of an income nature. This does not mean that the provision need be by way of income payments. The provision can be by way of a lump sum, e.g. to buy a house in which the applicant can be housed, thereby relieving him *pro tanto* of income expenditure". Such a situation arose in *Re Callaghan deceased* [1985] Fam 1 where a stepson of the deceased intestate was awarded a lump sum of £15,000 out of an estate of £31,000 to enable him to purchase on advantageous terms the council house in which he lived. Booth J found that the applicant's wish to buy the house without the burden of a mortgage weighing upon him for the remainder of his working years was "a reasonable requirement for his maintenance" (at p. 7). In *Re Dennis* on the other hand the applicant son was in effect seeking a lump sum to pay capital transfer tax on *inter vivos* dispositions made to him by his deceased father. Browne-Wilkinson J said that there might be cases in which payment of existing debts might be appropriate as a maintenance payment, e.g. to pay the debts of an applicant in order to enable him to continue to carry on a profit-making business or profession.

## 5. Matters to which the court is to have regard in exercising its powers under s.2

*(a) Matters relevant to all applicants*
Section 3(1) of the Act sets out the matters relevant to claims by all applicants

though they will not necessarily be applied in the same way for all categories of applicants. In succeeding subsections of s.3 matters relevant to particular categories of applicants are set out without prejudice to the generality of subs.(1). The matters relevant to all applicants are:

(a) the financial resources and financial needs which the applicant has or is likely to have in the foreseeable future.
(b) the financial resources and financial needs which any other applicant for an order under s.2 of the Act has or is likely to have in the foreseeable future;
(c) the financial resources and financial needs which any beneficiary of the estate of the deceased has or is likely to have in the foreseeable future.

It is made clear by subs.(6) that the financial resources of a person include his earning capacity, and the financial needs of any person include his financial obligations and responsibilities. (In relation to potential earning capacity see *Re Ducksbury* [1966] 1 WLR 1226 and the cases in relation to divorce discussed in Chapter 11.) In *Re Crawford* [1983] 4 FLR 273 at p. 283 Eastham J dealing with the claim of a former wife of the deceased noted that she had only worked during the war for a couple of years as a shorthand-typist and in his judgment her earning capacity was nil at the age of 59. "She was not expected to work by the deceased" and he saw "no reason why at her age she should go out and seek paid employment". In *Re Collins deceased* [1990] Fam 56 Hollings J held that the fact that a daughter, aged 19 at the time of the hearing, was in receipt of social security benefits did not preclude consideration of whether the rules of intestate succession made reasonable financial provision for her on the death of her mother. She was awarded a lump sum payment of £5,000 out of a net estate of £27,000 for her maintenance "in times of unemployment". (See also *Re E* [1966] 1 WLR 709 and *Re Watkins* [1949] 1 All ER 695.) In *Harrington* v *Gill* (1983) 4 FLR 265 at p. 271 Dunn LJ said that the words "needs" or "need" in s.1(3) of the Act and also in s.3(1)(a), mean "reasonable requirements" which was the meaning given to the word "need" in the Matrimonial Causes Act 1973 by Ormrod LJ in *O'D* v *O'D* [1976] Fam 83.

In relation to paragraph (c) it is important to note that a "beneficiary" means not only a beneficiary under the will of the deceased or under the law of intestacy, but also a person in whose favour the deceased has nominated money or property or in whose favour the deceased has made a *donatio mortis causa* (ss.8 and 25(1)). The extent to which and the way in which financial benefits accruing to beneficiaries or to the applicant outside the will or the rules of intestate succession are taken into account are considered in Chapter 23.

(i) Any obligations and responsibilities which the deceased had towards any applicant for an order under s.2 or towards any beneficiary of the estate of the deceased.
The intention of the Law Commission was that even in relation to beneficiaries the emphasis should be on the extent of the deceased's obligations and responsibilities to them rather than on preserving their interests in the estate (Law Com. No. 61 para. 34).

(ii) The size and nature of the net estate of the deceased
In general terms it is clear that the larger an estate the more reasonable it is to

expect the deceased to have made some provision for a person to whom he had an obligation, while the smaller the estate, the more difficult it becomes to make provision for those who have a claim on him. In relation to the previous legislation Ungoed Thomas J said in *Re Clayton* [1966] 1 WLR 969 at p. 971 that the smallness of an estate was significant in three respects, and except in relation to surviving spouses where the court is no longer concerned merely with maintenance, the position is probably the same in relation to applications under the 1975 Act.

In the first place the smallness of the estate is relevant when considering the availability of State aid. Where an estate is so small and the means of the applicant "so exiguous that the only effect of making provision for the claimant will be *pro tanto* to relieve the National Assistance fund it would not be unreasonable for the deceased to take the view that there was no point in making provision for the claimant ..." (*per* Stamp LJ in *Re E* [1966] 1 WLR 709 at p. 715). On the other hand, where the estate is large the fact that those in need can resort to income support will not by itself justify failure to make any provision. In *Re Debenham* [1986] 1 FLR 404 a daughter was awarded periodical payments of £4,500 per annum from her mother's estate of £172,000 though the effect was to reduce the supplementary benefit which she and her husband received from £52 per week to nil.

Secondly, the smallness of the estate is relevant in considering the extent to which the estate can effectively contribute to the applicant's maintenance. In *Re Collins deceased* [1990] Fam 56 the comparatively small amount of the net estate was one of the factors which led to Hollings J awarding a small lump sum rather than periodical payments.

Thirdly, the smallness of the estate may be relevant in relation to the costs of an application which, if they are to be paid out of the estate, as is common, may leave very little for the applicant or the beneficiaries (see also Goff LJ in *Re Coventry deceased* [1980] Ch 461 at p. 486. See however the comments of Ormrod LJ in the Court of Appeal in *Re Fullard deceased* [1981] 2 All ER 796 at p. 799 in relation to costs. In unsuccessful applications by former spouses judges should look closely at the merits of the application before ordering that the estate pay the applicant's costs). This difficulty was to some extent alleviated when jurisdiction was given to county courts in cases where the net estate did not exceed a certain value at the date of death. This limit has been removed, and an application may now be made in a county court irrespective of the value of the deceased's estate (County Courts Act 1984, s.25 as amended by the High Court and County Courts Jurisdiction Order 1991, SI 1991 No. 724).

In relation to an application by a surviving spouse, the same considerations would not necessarily apply, for the court is no longer concerned merely with maintenance. As will be seen below, the court may be concerned with the extent to which the surviving spouse has earned a share in the "family property" on the basis of her contributions to the welfare of the family.

Where a large part of the deceased's estate was derived from or acquired with the assistance of the applicant or beneficiary, then this will clearly give that person a strong claim. A similar view has been taken where the bulk of the deceased's estate was derived from a parent of an applicant or beneficiary or acquired with the assistance of such a parent (see *Thornley* v *Palmer* [1969] 1 WLR 1037; *Sivyer* v *Sivyer*

[1967] 1 WLR 1482; *Re Brownbridge* (1942) 193 LTJ 185; *Re Styler* [1942] Ch 387). In *Re Leach (deceased)* [1985] 2 All ER 754 the applicant was awarded a lump sum equivalent to approximately one half of the net estate of her stepmother who had died intestate having succeeded to the bulk of the estate left by the applicant's father some years before. The fact that the bulk of the estate consists of what may be termed "family property" - in particular the matrimonial home - is likely to be of outstanding importance in relation to an application by a surviving spouse. The fact that a particular property was the matrimonial home or that the former matrimonial home forms the bulk of the estate is likely to be an important factor. Apart from the question whether, for example, a surviving wife has earned a share on the basis of her contributions to the family welfare or otherwise, the provision of suitable living accommodation has been an important factor in deciding the financial provision and property adjustment on divorce. (See Chapter 12.)

(iii) Any physical or mental disability of any applicant for an order under s.2 or any beneficiary of the estate of the deceased

These factors are likely to be reflected in the financial resources and needs of the interested parties. The availability of National Health Service facilities and other social security benefits may fall for consideration. In *Re Watkins* [1949] 1 All ER 695 Roxburgh J held that the testator was entitled to distribute his estate on the basis that his daughter, who was a patient in a private mental hospital, would be cared for in a State hospital after his death. (Contrast *Re Pringle* [1956] The Times 2 February. See also *Re Perry* [1956] The Times 19 April.)

(iv) Any other matter, including the conduct of the applicant or any other person, which in the circumstances of the case the court may consider relevant

The intention of the Law Commission (Law Com. No. 61 paras. 35 and 36) was that the courts should accept the same approach to conduct under the 1975 Act as the divorce courts have adopted since the decision of the Court of Appeal in *Wachtel* v *Wachtel* [1973] Fam 72 (see Chapter 11). This is borne out by the approach of Wood J in *Re Snoek (deceased)* (1983) 13 Fam Law 18 when he regarded the applicant widow's atrocious behaviour to her sick husband in the last years of his life as not quite cancelling out her earlier contribution in managing the family home and bringing up four children. She was awarded a modest lump sum of £5,000 out of an estate of £40,000 in which she had no interest under the deceased's will. In *Williams* v *Johns* [1988] 2 FLR 475 the applicant's behaviour had clearly caused her adoptive mother considerable shame and distress over the years and that was a matter which the court was entitled to take into account. However, it appears to have been no more than one factor in the decision that the applicant had failed to show any obligation to maintain her on the part of the deceased.

The deceased's reasons for making or not making provision for a particular person were specifically mentioned as a factor to be taken into account under the 1938 Act. Although no longer specifically mentioned they could be taken into account under this paragraph, though their importance has declined in view of the objective test of financial provision which now clearly applies. In *Re Coventry (deceased)* [1980] Ch 461 at pp. 488-489 Goff LJ said:

"... I think any view expressed by a deceased person that he wishes a particular person to benefit will generally be of little significance, because the question is not subjective but objective. An express reason for rejecting the applicant is a different matter and may be very relevant to the problem."

It is not unusual for the deceased to have left a signed statement giving the reasons why no provision or only limited provision has been made for a particular person. In *Williams* v *Johns* [1988] 2 FLR 475 there had been placed with the will a statement by the deceased that she had during her lifetime made provision for her adopted daughter beyond any reasonable expectation, that she had never received the response or affection from the daughter for which she had hoped, that their relationship had ended and she therefore felt no moral obligation towards her. It is not clear what weight was attached to this statement as the applicant daughter (aged 42) had been married and divorced and was unable to show any obligation on her mother to support her.

When the deceased made no will and so died intestate, the fact that there was evidence that the deceased intended to make a will in favour of the applicant has been taken into account (*Re Leach* [1986] Ch 226). Moreover, where the deceased has made a will it is apparent that the deceased's wishes as expressed in the will carry great weight. The desire of the court to give effect as far as possible to the wishes of the deceased as to the disposition of his property has been frequently mentioned. Thus in *Stead* v *Stead* [1985] FLR 16 at p. 22 Purchas LJ did not dissent from the submission that where there are alternative means of providing for an applicant, that course which least disturbs the testator's wishes ought to be taken. (See also Judge Mervyn Davies in *Re Besterman* [1982] 3 FLR 255 at p. 266; Vinelott J in *Re Bunning* [1984] Ch 480 at p. 499 and Balcombe LJ in *Stephens* v *Stephens*, CA July 1 1985 Lexis Enggen.)

It is provided by s.21 that in any proceedings under the Act of 1975 a statement made by the deceased, whether orally or in a document or otherwise, is admissible under s.2 of the Civil Evidence Act 1968 as evidence of any fact stated therein in like manner as if the statement were a statement falling within s.2(1) of that Act. Under s.2(1) oral or written statements made by a person can be admitted as evidence of any fact of which direct oral evidence by him would be admissible. Some doubts existed as to whether this covers statements by a deceased person who could never have given direct oral evidence since the proceedings in question are brought against his estate. Section 21 removes this doubt so far as proceedings under the 1975 Act are concerned.

Where the deceased had encouraged the applicant to think that he or she would receive benefits under the deceased's will this is a relevant matter which the court may take into account under paragraph (g), particularly if the applicant has entered into commitments on that basis (see *Re Leach* [1986] Ch 226).

*(b) Matters relevant to applications by spouses and former spouses*

(i) The statutory provision
In considering applications by surviving spouses and former spouses the court is required by s.3(2) to have regard to:

(a) the age of the applicant and the duration of the marriage;
(b) the contribution made by the applicant to the welfare of the family of the deceased, including any contribution made by looking after the home and caring for the family.

In the case of an application by a surviving spouse not judicially separated from the deceased at the date of death, the court is also required to have regard to the provision which the applicant might reasonably have expected to receive if on the day on which the deceased died the marriage, instead of being terminated by death, had been terminated by a decree of divorce.

## (ii) Age and duration of the marriage

The age of the applicant and the duration of the marriage are factors relevant to applications for financial provision in proceedings for divorce, nullity and judicial separation under the Matrimonial Causes Act 1973 (s.25(2)(d)). The approach adopted in that jurisdiction would seem generally appropriate under the Act of 1975. (See Chapter 11, Part 5.) In *Re Bunning* [1984] Ch 480 at p. 497 Vinelott J took into account, in particular, the fact that the wife was comparatively young and, in the circumstances of the case, entitled to a reasonable degree of financial security during what was likely to be a lengthy widowhood. The applicant was aged 56 at the time of the hearing with some earning capacity. Surviving spouses applying under the 1975 Act are often older. While advanced age may be a very relevant factor in deciding the form of provision by way of maintenance - so that periodical payments or a life interest in property may be more appropriate than an outright capital payment or transfer - the same considerations do not apply to the non-maintenance element in provision for a surviving spouse. In *Stead* v *Stead* [1985] FLR 16 the Court of Appeal appears to have been influenced by the advanced age of the plaintiff coupled with the argument that it is not the purpose of lump sum provision to enable the plaintiff to leave money to her children and others on her death. However, in *Re Besterman* [1984] Ch 458 at p.466 Oliver LJ had rejected, quite rightly it is submitted, the suggestion that the court ought to start with some sort of bias against making a provision which may ultimately have the effect of enabling the plaintiff to make provision for somebody else. First, he said: "That ... is something which is inherent in a lump sum order". Secondly, while such an argument might be appropriate in relation to applicants other than the surviving spouse where maintenance is a limiting factor, he said (at p. 470):

"In the case of a surviving spouse, however, the argument appears to me to amount simply to an indirect way of nullifying the express provisions of s.1(2) of the Act of 1975. It amounts to saying that, although by that section the reasonable provision is one which is, by definition, not restricted to maintenance, nevertheless, because it is a provision for the applicant and for nobody else, it is effectively limited to what is required for maintenance for the applicant".

More recently, in *Kusminow* v *Barclays Bank Trust Co Ltd* (1989) 19 Fam Law 66 Sir Stephen Brown P was urged to have regard to the fact that the applicant widow was aged 78 and that any capital sum awarded to her would be likely to go out of the deceased husband's family rather than to his two nephews. However, he took the view that notwithstanding her age it was not a case where money should be placed on trust, bearing in mind amongst other factors, the cost of administration and the fact that the beneficiaries were resident in Russia. It was a case where a final disposition should be made and he awarded a lump sum payment of £45,000 out of an estate of some £100,000.

Where a marriage has lasted for many years, the fact that they may have lived apart during the latter years does not necessarily mean that no provision should be made for the surviving spouse, though it is a relevant factor. In *Re Bunning* [1984] Ch 480 the parties had been separated for the last few years or so of their marriage which had lasted some 19 years. This factor had little effect on the provision made for the widow having regard not only to the fact that during the fifteen or sixteen years they had lived together she had been a "loyal, dutiful and hardworking wife" (*per* Vinelott J at p. 489) for her contributions had gone further. Although she had intended to continue working after her marriage to preserve her pension entitlement, she had found it impossible to do so while at the same time giving the testator the help and assistance he needed in his business, as both secretary and chauffeuse, as well as running the matrimonial home single-handed. An extreme situation arose in *Re Rowland deceased* [1984] FLR 813 where the applicant widow was aged 90 and had been married to the deceased for 62 years. Although they had been separated for the last 43 years, nevertheless in the early part of the marriage she had played her part appropriately as a mother and wife and Anthony Lincoln J was "satisfied that some small moral obligation was owed by the testator to his wife ... Despite the length of their separation, she had been his wife for eighteen years - by modern standards not a short marriage" (p. 818). On the other hand, he considered that "the duration of the separation and the estrangement must diminish the figure which would otherwise be awarded and must diminish it ... substantially (p. 819). (Contrast *Re Gregory* [1970] 1 WLR 1455.)

Substantial provision may be appropriate even after a marriage of short duration. Thus in *Re Dawkins (deceased)* [1986] 2 FLR 360 the widow was awarded a lump sum of £10,000 out of an estate of some £27,000 even though the marriage - the second marriage for both applicant and deceased - was of short duration, namely four years. While they had lived in a home belonging to the deceased, the applicant had spent most of her capital on day-to-day living and holidays and on paying off the deceased's bank overdraft.

In *Davis* v *Davis* [1993] 1 FLR 54 a life interest in the bulk of the estate was held to be reasonable financial provision for a widow who had been the deceased's second wife and married to him for some seven years. The trustees were able to purchase a house as her residence. See also *Re Clarke (deceased)* [1991] Fam Law 364.

(iii) Contribution to the welfare of the family
This factor is also similar to one of the factors which a court is required to take into account under s.25(2) of the Matrimonial Causes Act 1973 (para. (f) - see Chapter 11 Part 5). It would appear to have been an important factor in *Re Besterman (deceased)* [1984] Ch 458 where the Court of Appeal ordered a substantial lump sum payment. It was not a case in which the plaintiff widow had contributed directly to the acquisition of the deceased's substantial wealth which he had largely acquired before he married the plaintiff at the age of fifty-four as his third wife.

There were no children, but the marriage had lasted some eighteen years and Oliver LJ said (at p. 462) "... there is no reason for assuming anything other than that the marriage was a contented one and that the plaintiff was a faithful and dutiful wife to whom the deceased owed all the duties ordinarily arising from the married state". (See also the views expressed by Vinelott J in *Re Bunning (deceased)* [1984] Ch 480 at p. 489 referred to above.) In *Stephens* v *Stephens* CA July 1 1985 Lexis Enggen, both the plaintiff widow and the deceased had been married before and on their marriage the plaintiff had sold her own property and moved into the deceased's house. The bulk of the proceeds of sale had been spent over the years supplementing the money of the deceased which was available for living expenses. In view of the use by the widow of her own assets for living expenses, while the deceased had retained title to the home (in addition to more general contributions to the family welfare), it was considered only fair that she should be regarded as entitled to a share in at least the home. (See also *Re Dawkins (deceased)* [1986] 2 FLR 360 referred to above.)

It is important to emphasise that the contribution made by the applicant is only one factor to be taken into account. Experience of operation of the similar factor on divorce indicates that a share that might seem appropriate if this factor were viewed in isolation might be reduced having regard e.g. to the needs and resources, obligations and responsibilities of beneficiaries or other applicants as well as of the applicant himself.

(iv) Provision that would have been made on divorce

In the case of an application by a surviving spouse not judicially separated from the deceased at the date of death, the court is also required to have regard to the provision which the applicant might reasonably have expected to receive if on the day on which the deceased died the marriage, instead of being terminated by death, had been terminated by a decree of divorce (s.3(2). This provision is designed to give effect expressly to the recommendation of the Law Commission that the claim of the surviving spouse should be *at least equal* to that of a spouse on divorce and should be higher than the provision of maintenance appropriate for other applicants (Law Com. No. 61 para. 2(b)).

It is clear that the object of the requirement is not to equate financial provision for a surviving spouse with provision for a divorced spouse. Some statements, if read out of context, suggest the contrary. Thus in *Whytte* v *Ticehurst* [1986] Fam 64 at pp. 87-88, Booth J said that "... the purpose of this legislation was to enable the court to place the surviving spouse in the financial position he or she would have been in had a matrimonial decree been granted during the lifetime of the other". (See also Sheldon J in *Re Bramwell deceased* [1988] 2 FLR 263 at p. 267.) However, in *Re Besterman* [1984] Ch 458 at p. 469 Oliver LJ emphasised that in an application under the 1975 Act "the figure resulting from the section 25 exercise is merely one of the factors to which the court is to 'have regard' and the overriding consideration is what is 'reasonable' in all the circumstances. It is, however, obviously a very important consideration and one which the statute goes out of its way to bring to the attention of the court". In that case the judge had never in fact expressed any conclusion about what he thought would be the hypothetical provision on divorce. Oliver LJ noted that the award at first instance amounted to a little over one-sixth of the estate "which appeared to bear little relation to the provision that had been awarded to spouses of wealthy persons on divorce". In arriving at the increased figure of £375,000 (as compared with £259,250) he said that he had not taken the *Wachtel* proportion of one-third as a starting point but noted that it had been suggested as a useful cross-check. The effect of the award by the Court of Appeal was to give provision constituting approximately one-quarter of the available total and confirmed him "in the belief that it is not excessive" (at p. 479).

The mere fact that the applicant's marriage to the deceased was not in fact terminated by divorce does not mean that therefore, and *a fortiori*, she must be entitled to more generous provision than if the marriage had been so terminated (see Oliver LJ in *Re Besterman* [1984] Ch 458 at p. 478). This would obviously not be right where the applicant had been separated from the deceased, perhaps for a very long time, as in *Re Rowlands* [1987] FLR 813 for, apart from other considerations, the contribution of the applicant to the welfare of the family will be affected very much by the length of the actual as opposed to the nominal marriage. On the other hand, in *Re Bunning* [1984] Ch 480 the widow was awarded more than she would probably have obtained on divorce even though she was separated from the deceased for the last four or so years of a nineteen-year marriage to the deceased. Vinelott J (at p. 498) in arriving at the conclusion that the right figure for a lump sum payment was £60,000 thought that a divorce court "might well have regarded £36,000 as the appropriate as well as the maximum figure" for a lump sum payment under the 1973 Act. However, he said:

"The figure of £36,000 cannot be taken as limiting the provision which it is reasonable for the wife to receive out of the estate ... Not only is there now no longer need to provide for the husband, but he has no other dependants for whom to provide. In assessing what is reasonable provision I must bear in mind, on the one hand the matters specifically mentioned in section 3(2) of the Act of 1975 and, in particular, the fact that the wife is comparatively young and, having regard to the history which I have outlined, entitled to a reasonable degree of financial security during what is likely to be a lengthy widowhood. I must bear in mind, on the other hand, that the husband's assets were built up by his own efforts in large measure before he married. The court should not interfere with his right to dispose of those assets by his will except to the extent necessary to make reasonable provision for the wife."

More generous provision for a surviving spouse may thus be appropriate because the court may not be subject to the same practical restraints as those which frequently apply on divorce. This will obviously be so where there are no competing family claims on the assets, as in *Re Bunning*. There will also be cases where the deceased has made inadequate provision for the surviving spouse because of misapprehension or carelessness. The deceased may have believed himself to be wealthier than he was, or his property may have decreased in value or been depleted after the will was made. In *Re Besterman* the husband's solicitors had, on his instructions, written to assure the applicant that he had made ample provision for her, but Oliver J (at p. 465) thought that "... he had so far lost touch with the real value of money as not to appreciate the reality of her needs". In such circumstances more generous provision than that which would have been awarded on divorce seems appropriate.

On the other hand, there will be cases where reasonable provision may be less than that which would have been ordered on divorce. The earnings of the spouse who has died will no longer be available for the support of the family, and the members of his or her family will have to depend upon the capital of the estate in so far as their own earnings are insufficient. In *Moody* v *Stevenson* [1992] 2 WLR 640 Waite J said that the objective of the requirement in s.3(2) "is that the acceptable minimum posthumous provision for a surviving spouse should correspond as closely as possible to the inchoate rights enjoyed by that spouse in the deceased's lifetime by virtue of his or her prospective entitlement under the matrimonial law. There will, of course, be occasions when that objective turns out to be unattainable. One such occasion may arise when the death itself has triggered some event which eliminates an asset (such as an annuity) which would have been available to support a maintenance order on an application for *inter vivos* matrimonial relief". There may also be competing family claims, as where there are children by a previous marriage of the deceased. This may not only increase the claims for support but also bring the claims of the surviving spouse into conflict with the deceased's testamentary wishes. In *Dixit* v *Dixit* CA June 23 1988 Lexis Enggen, Sir Nicolas Browne-Wilkinson V-C said that s.3(2) did not mean that under the 1975 Act the court has to make the same provision as if there had been a divorce. He said:

"In my judgement the choice of words is not accidental; the two jurisdictions are materially different. The provision made under divorce is not a final disposition of the property by one parent for the benefit of himself and his spouse and children; the ultimate destination is not regulated by the divorce order. Whereas under the 1975 Act the court has the extremely delicate function of weighing the obligations by one spouse to another against the deceased's ordinary right to regulate the ultimate destination of his property by his will and in particular the obvious desire of the deceased in this case to provide for the children of both marriages equally by giving each of them a half share in one house or another."

In the recent case of *Moody* v *Stevenson* [1992] 2 WLR 640 the Court of Appeal considered the approach to be adopted to applications by surviving spouses. Waite J noted that the Act, in laying down the lengthy catalogue of matters to which the judge is bound by s.3 to have regard, did not specify in which order he should tackle them. He said (at pp. 650-651):

"Nevertheless, in cases where the applicant is a surviving spouse, the logical starting point, as it seems to us, would be an appraisal of the claimant's notional entitlement under the amended ss. 25 and 25A of the Matrimonial Causes Act 1973 ... assuming there has been a decree of divorce at the date of death (s.3(2)) and treating the assets in the deceased's estate as if they had been matrimonial assets valued as at the date of the hearing (s.3(5)). The result of that appraisal will then provide the judge with a yardstick by which, after taking into account any other s.3 matters to which he is required to have regard which have not already been considered by him in the appraising process, he will first determine, at stage one, whether the dispositions of the deceased's estate were such as to make reasonable financial provision for the applicant, and (if he finds that they were not) secondly determine, at stage two, what orders should be made in his discretion under s.2 of the Act."

In that case the deceased had made no provision for her husband as she considered he had adequate resources of his own. The court concluded that a family judge would have been most unlikely to regard the case as one for refusing financial relief to the husband altogether. In practical terms the disposition of the estate meant forcing him out of the matrimonial home at the age of 81 to seek local authority housing. The court directed a settlement of the matrimonial home on terms that would enable the applicant to go on living there as sole occupant so long as he was able to do so. Thereafter it would pass under the will to the deceased's stepdaughter.

(v) The position of surviving former spouses

The new higher standard of provision is not applicable in the case of a surviving former spouse whose claim will be limited to maintenance. Generally, such a person will have had the opportunity of applying for financial provision and property adjustment under the Matrimonial Causes Act 1973 on or after the grant of the decree of judicial separation or of divorce or nullity as the case may be. In *Re Fullard (deceased)* [1981] 2 All ER 796 the Court of Appeal held that in view of the wide powers of the court on applications under the 1973 Act, the number of cases in which it would be possible for a former spouse of the deceased to bring himself or herself within the terms of s.2 of the 1975 Act would be comparatively small. Moreover, in unsuccessful applications by former spouses judges should look closely at the merits of the application before ordering that the estate pay the applicant's costs (*per* Ormrod LJ at p. 799). Two exceptional cases were mentioned. The first is where a long period of time has elapsed since the dissolution of the marriage and periodical payments have continued to be paid up to the date of death when the deceased is found to have a reasonable amount of capital in his estate. The second is where a substantial capital fund was unlocked by the death of the deceased such as by insurance or pension policies, though Purchas J doubted whether the mere fact of accretion of wealth after the dissolution of the marriage would of itself justify an application (*ibid.* at p. 804). It is also arguable that account should be taken of the fact that there will be some cases where a marriage was dissolved before the court acquired wide powers to order financial provision and property adjustment on divorce on 1 January 1971. On this basis it may still be relevant to refer to *Re W (deceased)* (1975) 119 SJ 489 where a former wife aged 75 sought provision under the 1938 Act. She had divorced her husband 29 years previously and had never received any financial provision from him. The wife had not sought an order for financial provision for, at the time of the divorce, she had been earning more than the deceased. The deceased had subsequently taken care that his former wife never learnt about what his financial situation was. His stubbornness in resisting any efforts made by her to obtain money from him overcame her gentle and pliant nature so that she did not exert the pressure other wives might have done. The deceased had been able to amass capital partly because he had not been compelled to support his former wife.

In contrast, in *Re Fullard (deceased)* there had been a settlement of the parties' financial arrangements on divorce. Periodical payments were not appropriate, but the husband had transferred his share in the matrimonial home to the wife in return for £4,500. On his death the greater part of the husband's estate comprised that sum so that the former wife was in effect asking for her money back. The financial position of the former wife was much the same as that of the beneficiary under the will and the court held that it was reasonable for the deceased to have made no provision for his former wife. (See also *Brill* v *Proud* (1984) 14 Fam Law 59 where the court made an order for costs against the unsuccessful applicant to the extent of her legal aid contribution.)

On the other hand, in *Re Farrow (deceased)* [1987] 1 FLR 205 at pp. 212 and 213 Hollings J regarded *Re Fullard* as depending very much on the fact that a clean break had been achieved on the divorce and was thus very different from the situation before him. In *Re Farrow* the former wife had been awarded a lump sum of £50,000 in the divorce proceedings, part of which was to enable her to buy, repair and furnish the house in which she then lived and partly to produce income. Periodical payments of £5,000 had also been ordered but the husband died within a short time and she received very little support from the estate over the seven years up to the hearing of her application under the 1975 Act. The very large estate had passed to her two sons on the husband's intestacy, and she had lived off capital though she had also been extravagant. Hollings J held that provision for her support after the husband's death should have been made by him, and provision should be by way of providing continuing periodical payments on the basis that she had received all the capital to which she was entitled. She was also awarded a small lump sum of £15,000 to take account of the fact that she had been without periodical payments for a very long period after her former husband's death.

In the earlier case of *Re Crawford* (1983) 4 FLR 273 Eastham J declined to accept a general proposition that reasonable financial provision under the 1975 Act should be the same as periodical payments made to a former wife during the deceased's lifetime if those payments were either agreed or fixed by the court. He made an order for the payment of a lump sum sufficient to purchase an annuity of £4,000 per annum which appears to have been a little less than she had been entitled to under the consent order made in the divorce proceedings. However, in *Re Farrow* [1987] 1 FLR 205 at p. 212 Hollings J did not find the decision in *Re Crawford* helpful as laying down any general principles since its facts were so very special.

There may be some cases where the death of the deceased prevented his spouse or former spouse from making, or more probably, from proceeding with, an application under the Matrimonial Causes Act 1973, following a decree of judicial separation or a decree of divorce or nullity. In such a situation the court is empowered to treat the spouse or former spouse as if the decree of judicial separation had not been granted or the decree of divorce or nullity had not been made absolute, and thus to apply the higher standard applicable to surviving spouses not judicially separated from the deceased (s.14). This power is discretionary and it might not be appropriate to exercise it where, for example, the applicant has been guilty of unjustifiable delay in making or pursuing an application under the Act of 1973. The power is designed to deal with an exceptional situation and is exercisable only where the deceased dies within twelve months from the date on which the decree of divorce or nullity was made absolute or the decree of judicial separation was granted.

### (c) Matters relevant to applications by children

Where an application is made by a child of the deceased or by any other person treated by the deceased as a child of the family in relation to any marriage of the deceased, the court is also required to have regard to the manner in which the applicant was being, or in which he might expect to be, educated or trained (s.3(3)). In the case of an application by a child of the family under s.1(1)(d) the court is also required to have regard:

(a) to whether the deceased had assumed any responsibility for the applicant's maintenance and, if so, to the extent to which and the basis upon which the deceased discharged that responsibility and to the length of time for which the deceased discharged that responsibility;

(b) to whether in assuming and discharging that responsibility the deceased did so knowing that the applicant was not his own child;

(c) to the liability of any other person to maintain the applicant.

Where an applicant under paras. 1(1)(c) or (d) is a minor, then it will generally be reasonable for the deceased to have made some provision for him or her by will unless the deceased had already made adequate provision or such provision is made by another or the applicant is already fully self-supporting. The extent of the provision called for will vary, and what is reasonable will depend on a number of factors. Thus it would seem relevant to consider how close the actual, as distinct from the legal, relationship was between the applicant and the deceased. The fact that during his lifetime the deceased was providing for the applicant will strengthen the claim, but the reverse is not necessarily true. The fact that, during his lifetime, the deceased had failed to maintain the applicant may not have been reasonable and should not prevent proper provision if there are available assets. Even where there has been no contact between the applicant and the deceased provision may be appropriate. Thus in *Re Chatterton* [1980] Conv. 150 the deceased had made a will omitting his wife completely, and leaving one-quarter of his estate to his daughter, who had been born shortly after he had separated from his wife. The remainder of the estate was given to charities. Reeve J awarded the wife a lump sum of £1,000 on the basis of a very short marriage, and varied the terms of the will so that one half of the balance passed to the daughter at the age of 18 and the other half passed to the charities. The amount available for distribution was approximately £18,000 so that the amount to be held in trust for the daughter (then aged 8 or 9) was approximately £9,000. The Court of Appeal, noting that the deceased had never seen his daughter, nor even known her name, held that the award was sufficient provision for the daughter. In *CA* v *CC* (1979) 123 SJ 35 the deceased's entire estate passed to his legitimate son under a will made before he began to cohabit with the mother of his illegitimate son. Sir George Baker P held that, subject to the payment of a lump sum of £5,000 to the mother, the illegitimate son should share the estate (worth between £25,000 and £35,000) equally with the legitimate son who was living with the deceased's former wife.

Where an applicant is an adult who is in employment and so capable of earning his own living, some special circumstance is required to make a failure on the part of the deceased to make some financial provision for the applicant unreasonable (*per* Oliver J in *Re Coventry (deceased)* [1980] Ch 461 at p. 465, approved by

Buckley LJ at p. 495). Such an applicant faces a difficult task in getting provision made for him because the court is inclined to ask: "Why should anybody else make provision for you if you are capable of maintaining yourself?" The mere fact that the applicant finds himself in necessitous circumstances will not by itself render it unreasonable that no provision has been made for his maintenance out of the deceased's estate. Thus in *Re Dennis* the applicant was 38 years old and there was no evidence that he was in any way unfit. Although at the time he was out of work, he appeared to have as much chance as anybody else of obtaining employment and maintaining himself. He had already dissipated large sums of money given to him and in fact was seeking a large lump sum out of his father's estate to pay the capital transfer tax on an earlier gift (see also *Williams* v *Johns* [1988] 2 FLR 475).

It is not necessary for the applicant to show that there was a moral obligation on the part of the deceased to make such provision, but the existence of such a moral obligation would be one way of establishing a special circumstance which would justify provision. This is the correct interpretation of the decision of Oliver J in *Re Coventry deceased* [1980] Ch 461 which was approved by the Court of Appeal. In that case the applicant was the deceased's only son, aged 46 and in employment. The deceased died intestate and the main asset of his estate was the dwelling-house in which he had lived with his son. The house passed to the deceased's widow who had been separated from the deceased for many years. Oliver J said that to succeed, the applicant had to establish some sort of moral claim to be maintained by the deceased or at the expense of his estate beyond the mere fact of blood relationship. On appeal Goff LJ said (at p. 487): "Oliver J nowhere said that a moral obligation was a prerequisite of an application under section 1(1)(c); nor did he mean any such thing. It is true that he said that a moral obligation was required, but in my view that was on the facts of this particular case, because he found nothing else sufficient to produce unreasonableness."

A sufficient moral obligation has been found in a number of cases. Thus in *Re Callaghan* [1985] Fam 1 at p. 7, where the applicant stepson was aged 47 and married, Booth J said that the "obligations and responsibilities which the deceased had to the plaintiff were very considerable indeed; in effect they were the obligations of a widowed parent to a dutiful and responsible only child". Apart from the close relationship between the applicant and the deceased, the assets comprised in the estate were clearly derived from the applicant's mother who had married the deceased. The applicant was awarded a lump sum of £15,000 out of an estate of some £31,000 to enable him to buy the council house in which he lived without the burden of a mortgage weighing on him for the remainder of his working life. In *Re Leach* [1986] Ch 226 at p. 243, Slade LJ said that the judge could fairly and properly have regarded the deceased's statement of her testamentary intention to leave the applicant a half share in her house "as placing the deceased under some moral obligation to the plaintiff in relation to the disposition of her estate on death". This had encouraged the applicant stepdaughter, who was unmarried and aged 55 at the time of the application, to join with a friend in the purchase of a house. She was awarded a lump sum equal to about one half of the net estate, and emphasis was placed upon her need for financial assistance in discharging her share of the heavy running expenses (including mortgage repayments) of the house.

In *Re Leach* the relationship between the applicant and the deceased had been close but the deceased had never during her lifetime assumed responsibility for the applicant's maintenance; but this did not disqualify her from seeking relief. In *Re Debenham* [1986] 1 FLR 404 the deceased had refused to accept any responsibility for her daughter during childhood and had rejected all the daughter's approaches and left most of her substantial estate to charity. Ewbank J held the deceased had a moral obligation to provide for the daughter who was now aged 58 and married. The daughter and her husband had both been made redundant and were dependent on supplementary benefit. The most important factor, however, was that the daughter had developed epilepsy and was obviously a sick woman who was not capable of working.

The closeness or otherwise of the relationship between the applicant and the deceased may nevertheless be a relevant factor. In *Re Coventry* the deceased appears to have had no particular affection for his son who lived with him, though this was no more than one factor taken into account in assessing the deceased's obligation. In *Foskett* v *Smith* [1979] The Daily Telegraph 3 March, where a natural daughter and an adopted daughter were both in reasonable financial circumstances, Purchas J saw no reason to interfere with the father's will leaving his estate to his adopted daughter. The natural daughter had resented the adoption of her sister and for several years had ignored her father or treated him in an offhand manner up to his terminal illness. On the other hand, in *Re Ducksbury* [1966] 1 WLR 1226, an application under the 1938 Act, Buckley J held that the testator had not been justified in allowing his bitterness against his first wife to come between him and the applicant who was the elder of his two daughters by his first marriage. He also said that if a young woman who is able to earn her own living chooses to follow a course which results in her earning only a meagre living, that will not increase her moral claim on her parents. Nevertheless, in the circumstances the father had a moral obligation to make *some* provision for her.

In *Re Coventry* [1980] Ch 461 at p. 469, Oliver J had also said that s.3(3) pointed the way to the sort of circumstances in which it would be appropriate for an adult capable of earning his own living to seek provision under the Act. One such case was where the deceased had died whilst his adult son was being supported in the process of acquiring an occupational qualification and where no provision was made by the deceased for its completion. A claim would also seem appropriate where the applicant had given up work and precluded himself from earning an adequate living in order to devote himself to his father or mother. This was not the case in *Re Coventry* where there was "no more than a perfectly sensible arrangement which does not appear always to have worked entirely harmoniously - under which the deceased allowed his son and his family to have the benefit of the house in return for keeping him and paying a proportion of the outgoings" (*ibid.* at p. 476). In *Re Collins* [1990] Fam 56 the applicant daughter was aged 19 and living away from home with her boyfriend but was not yet established in employment. She was awarded a lump sum of £5,000 for her maintenance in times of unemployment and needs "and not paid to her on the basis merely of her being the daughter of the deceased" (*per* Hollings J at p. 62).

## (d) Matters relevant to applications by other "dependants"

Where an application is made under s.1(1)(e) on the basis of dependency on the deceased, the court is also required to have regard to the extent to which and the basis upon which the deceased assumed responsibility for the maintenance of the applicant, and to the length of time for which the deceased discharged that responsibility (s.3(4)). The amount of an award is likely to be based upon the degree of maintenance provided by the deceased during his lifetime though it may not be possible to continue provision at the same level where assets are insufficient and maintenance had been heavily dependent on the deceased's earning capacity. The court will also be able to consider whether or not it was the deceased's intention that maintenance should continue after his death. However, the weight to be attached to it may depend, among other things, on the manner in which, and the person to whom, the intention of the deceased was made evident.

In *Re Viner deceased* [1978] CLY 3091 the applicant aged 71 had received £5 per week from her brother for six months before his death. This provision had been made reluctantly and at the request of another sister of the deceased when the applicant had found herself in hard financial circumstances following the death of her husband. The sister had agreed to take a reduction in her own provision from the brother from £10 to £5 per week. Under the brother's will made some time earlier the applicant's sister received an annuity of £520, and the bulk of the estate of some £40,000 passed to a long-standing business associate of the brother. Master Chamberlain held that the provision which the court would make must take into account the fact that the maintenance paid to the applicant by the brother during his lifetime had been made grudgingly, and accordingly reasonable financial provision from his estate would be restricted to that made by the brother during his life. However, because a weekly sum of £5 would adversely affect the applicant's rent and rate rebates, a capital sum of £2,000 was awarded.

In *Malone v Harrison* [1979] 1 WLR 1353 the deceased had, in effect, monopolised the applicant for 12 years of her life from the age of 23. She was described by Hollings J as his "part-time mistress". The deceased had discouraged her from seeking gainful employment and encouraged her to rely on him for all her financial needs. Her earning capacity was plainly not good. Hollings J thought that as the deceased had been generous to the applicant in his lifetime so, within the limits set by the statute, should the court be in deciding what order to make. During the deceased's lifetime the applicant must have received at least £4,000 per annum from the deceased in one way or another, not including furs and jewellery and not including the annual value of two flats he had purchased for her. He assumed that she would spend or have to spend over the years capital as well as income, and that it was not the court's duty to provide for the beneficiaries under her will. On the other hand, it would not be right to include the value of her home, one of the flats, as expendable capital. He sought to enable the applicant to have, through income and capital, about £4,000 a year. During her potential earning period the annual sum required was £2,000. The applicant was 38 and, assuming earning capacity to 60, Hollings J applied a multiple of 11 producing £22,000. Her actuarial expectation of life was 76 and the additional period of 16 years should be covered. This was discounted by applying a multiple of 5 to the multiplicand of £4,000 producing

£20,000. The result of these necessarily broad estimated figures was the proper award, namely a sum approximate to the difference between the totals of the two sums - £42,000 and her present capital resources of £23,000. He ordered a lump sum of £19,000 to be paid out of the estate to the applicant.

Hollings J did consider whether, if he had power so to order, the applicant's home should be put in trust so that on her death it could revert to one or more of the other beneficiaries. However, the estate was large - some £480,000 - and having regard to the considerable sums already inherited by the beneficiaries such an adjustment was not necessary. It would not have benefited the one beneficiary whose interest might be concerned, the deceased's common law wife, and in any event he considered he had no power to make such an order.

In other circumstances a court may well feel that a life interest in a home may be more appropriate than an outright transfer of property. This was the course taken by Browne-Wilkinson J in *Re Haig* [1979] The Daily Telegraph 23 February where he considered that the failure of the deceased to provide a home for life for the woman, aged over 60, who had lived with him for about a year and a half prior to his death was unreasonable. In view of the gifts made to the applicant by the deceased during his lifetime there was no need to supplement her income out of the estate. In fact the court directed the sale of the house in which she lived and the purchase of another for her use during her life or until she remarried.

In *Harrington* v *Gill* (1983) 4 FLR 265 the applicant had moved into the deceased's house and lived with him there as man and wife until his death some eight years later. Dunn LJ said (at p. 271):

"The relevance of subs.(4) of s.3 is that, in considering reasonable requirements or reasonable financial provision under s.1(1), the court will, amongst other things, consider the extent to which the deceased has undertaken responsibility for the maintenance of the plaintiff, that is to say, the court will consider as a relevant factor the standard of living enjoyed by the plaintiff during the deceased's lifetime and the extent to which the deceased contributed to that standard of living."

He concluded that a reasonable man in the deceased's circumstances would have wanted the applicant, after the time they had spent together, to remain in the house and to have the use of the furniture. The applicant (now aged 74) was given a life interest in the house before it passed to the deceased's married daughter, and the furniture absolutely. The Court of Appeal upheld the judge's order for a lump sum payment of £5,000 and an order that a further sum of £5,000 be set aside to provide income for the applicant on top of her State pension.

In *Williams* v *Roberts* [1986] 1 FLR 349 the applicant had a home of her own into which the deceased had moved. During the last eight or nine years of the deceased's life it had been the applicant who had really cared for and, to the extent needed, provided the day-to-day nursing of the deceased. However, Wood J had no doubt that in so far as the future was concerned the applicant would have continued to be dependent upon a regular payment from the deceased and also have looked forward to some capital payment from time to time. In his view the 1975 Act did not require an approach involving a mathematical calculation, and he did not find the calculations in *Malone* v *Harrison* of assistance in the case before him.

Adopting a broad approach he awarded a lump sum of £20,000 out of an estate of over £100,000. In *CA v CC* (1979) 125 SJ 35 a female cohabitee was awarded a lump sum of £5,000 out of an estate of some £25,000 after some four years of cohabitation during which a child had been born. The applicant was aged only 25 and would probably be able to obtain employment when the child became of school age.

## 6. Orders which the court can make

### (a) The choice of orders
If the court is satisfied that reasonable financial provision has not been made for an applicant, it is empowered by s.2 to make one or more of the following orders:
  (a) an order for the making to the applicant out of the net estate of the deceased of such periodical payments and for such term as may be specified in the order;
  (b) an order for the payment to the applicant out of that estate of a lump sum of such amount as may be so specified;
  (c) an order for the transfer to the applicant of such property comprised in that estate as may be so specified;
  (d) an order for the settlement for the benefit of the applicant of such property comprised in that estate as may be so specified;
  (e) an order for the acquisition out of property comprised in that estate of such property as may be so specified and for the transfer of the property so acquired to the applicant or for the settlement thereof for his benefit;
  (f) an order varying any ante-nuptial or post-nuptial settlement (including such a settlement made by will) made on the parties to a marriage to which the deceased was one of the parties.

The court's powers are now therefore similar to those which it has in proceedings for divorce, nullity or judicial separation save that it is also given an express power to order the acquisition of property. (There is also no distinction between unsecured and secured periodical payments, for periodical payments must be derived out of the property of the deceased.) They are considerably wider than those which it possessed under the previous legislation when it could only order periodical payments or a lump sum payment. This extension of powers is clearly appropriate in view of the wider meaning given to "reasonable financial provision" in applications by surviving spouses, but they are available in applications by other persons so that maintenance can be provided in a more convenient manner. The only exception is that the power to vary an ante- or post-nuptial settlement made on the parties to a marriage to which the deceased was one of the parties, can only be exercised for the benefit of the surviving party to that marriage, or any child of that marriage, or any person who was treated by the deceased as a child of the family in relation to that marriage.

### (b) Periodical payments
The court is given a wide discretion as to the form in which an order for periodical payments may be expressed. Thus it may provide for:
  (a)  payments of such amount as may be specified in the order;

(b) payments equal to the whole of the income of the net estate or of such portion thereof as may be so specified;

(c) payments equal to the whole of the income of such part of the net estate as the court may direct to be set aside or appropriated for the making out of the income thereof of periodical payments under s.2;

or may provide for the amount of the payments or any of them to be determined in any other way the court thinks fit. Generally provision by way of periodical payments has been ordered as from the date of the deceased's death, but the court has a discretion, and may order provision as from the date of the judgment (see e.g. *Lusternik* v *Lusternik* [1972] Fam 125).

An order for periodical payments in favour of a surviving spouse not judicially separated from the deceased may continue in force after her remarriage. It does not terminate automatically on her remarriage as was the case under the 1938 Act (s.19(2)). It may be varied or discharged under the court's general power to vary or discharge (s.6). If the financial position of such a surviving spouse is materially improved by remarriage the periodical payments can be reduced or terminated, if appropriate, on an application under s.6. The court may include in an order for periodical payments in favour of a surviving spouse a proviso that payments should end on remarriage, but when such a proviso is included it may itself be varied or discharged (s.6(3)). Similarly, the remarriage of a party to a void marriage after the death of the other party will not automatically terminate an order for periodical payments in favour of the survivor. (But remarriage before the death of the other party will prevent an application being made under the Act.) On the other hand, an order for periodical payments in favour of a former spouse of the deceased or a surviving spouse where the marriage with the deceased was the subject of a decree of judicial separation continuing at the date of death, will terminate on the remarriage of the recipient except in relation to any arrears due under the order at the date of remarriage (s.19(2). This automatic termination on remarriage cannot be varied. (s.6(3)). "Remarriage" for this purpose includes a marriage which is by law void or voidable (s.25(5)).

An order for periodical payments in favour of a son of the deceased (not under a disability) need no longer terminate automatically on his attaining the age of 21 and an order in favour of a daughter (not under a disability) need no longer terminate automatically on her marriage.

The court is empowered to set aside part of the net estate to provide for periodical payments, thus enabling the remainder of the estate to be distributed (s.2(3)). One problem which remains under the Act of 1975 is that of making some allowance for a need which it is anticipated may arise in the future, but which does not exist at the present time. In an effort to balance the interests of applicants and beneficiaries the Act provides that no larger part of the net estate can be set aside than is necessary to provide for the periodical payments at the date of the order. Although such future needs might be dealt with on an application for the variation or discharge of an existing order under s.6, it will be seen that any provision ordered can only be made out of property already set aside to meet the existing order. Unless that property has increased substantially in value, any new order can only be made at the expense of the recipient. (See the course adopted in *Re Franks* [1948] Ch 62.)

*(c) Lump sum payments*

The power to order a lump sum payment was already possessed by the court under the previous legislation. At first it seems to have been regarded as more appropriate for use in small estates and indeed its use was so restricted until 1966. Decisions under the previous legislation had, however, already shown a greater readiness to use this power (e.g. *Re W (deceased)* (1975) 119 SJ 439) and, especially since the court is no longer concerned only with "maintenance" in the case of applications by surviving spouses, the power now has a more important role than in the past. An important characteristic of a lump sum payment is that it is not subject to variation, though where it has been ordered to be paid by instalments, as is now possible under the 1975 Act, the instalments may be varied (s.7. For the power of the court to order a lump sum payment on an application to vary a periodical payments order see s.6 (page 550)).

In *Re Besterman* [1984] Ch 458 at p. 476, Oliver LJ drew attention to the disadvantages of adopting the purchase price of an annuity as a method of calculating a lump sum. Apart from the danger of leading to a concentration on the maintenance aspect of provision for a surviving spouse, it is open to the criticism that the income which it is intended to provide is provided only if an annuity is actually purchased. This is not in general a prudent course in a time of inflation and postulates that there can be no resort to capital in the event of emergency. The "provision by way of a lump sum payment necessarily involves the plaintiff forgoing any right to come back to the court for further provision" as might be done in relation to periodical payments though only out of sums set aside for this purpose. This must be taken into account in assessing the amount of the lump sum, particularly where the size of the estate was such that there was no practical impediment to making a provision of an amount sufficient to cover possible future contingencies. The order made was based on the hypothesis that the capital producing the income would not remain intact, for a very much larger sum would have to be set aside if the income required was to be provided otherwise than by purchasing an annuity. The absence, which is inherent in a lump sum order, of an opportunity to return to the court means that in assessing the lump sum, the court must take rather greater account than might otherwise be the case of contingencies and inflation. He said (at p. 478):

"... I take the view that reasonable provision in this case would dictate that, in addition to a secure roof over her head, the widow should have available to her a capital sum of sufficient size not simply to enable her to purchase an adequate annuity according to present day needs, but to provide her with the income which she needs and a cushion in the form of available capital which will enable her to meet all reasonably foreseeable contingencies."

He pointed out that it is also inherent in a lump sum order that it enables the applicant to make provision for someone else who is not an applicant and to dispose of property by will. In the case of a small or relatively modest estate the periodical payments would be unlikely to make any significant contribution to the maintenance of an applicant, especially if there are competing obligations to take into account. A capital sum may, on the other hand, enable a specific purpose to be achieved, e.g. the purchase of a home as in *Re Callaghan* [1985] Fam 1 (£15,000), or may provide a cushion against the vicissitudes of life as in *Re Dawkins* [1986] 2

FLR 360 (£10,000) and *Re Collins* [1990] Fam 56 (£5,000). (See also *CA* v *CC* (1979) 123 SJ 35 (£5,000).)

*(d) Transfer or settlement of property*
These powers were introduced into the field of family provision on death by the Act of 1975 following the pattern of the court's powers in proceedings for divorce, nullity and judicial separation under the Matrimonial Causes Act 1973 (see Chapter 10. Property includes any chose in action: s.25(1)). An order for the transfer of property cannot be varied and no express power to vary or discharge an order for the settlement of property is given by the Act (see s.6. For the power to order a transfer of property on an application to vary a periodical payments order, see s.6(2). This does not apply to an order for settlement of property). However, the settlement itself may provide for foreseeable events. In *Moody* v *Stevenson* [1992] 2 WLR 640 the court directed a settlement of the former matrimonial home on terms which would allow the applicant widower to live there so long as he was able.

*(e) Acquisition of property*
This is a new power which does not appear in the Matrimonial Causes Act 1973. The Law Commission envisaged that this power could be used in cases where a home did not form part of the estate or where the applicant wished to move to a smaller home (Law Com. No. 61, para. 116. See *Powers* v *Haig* [1979] The Daily Telegraph 23 February).

*(f) Variation of marriage settlements*
The meaning of the expression "ante- or post-nuptial settlement" and the scope of the court's powers to vary such a settlement under the Matrimonial Causes Act 1973 have already been considered (see Chapter 10). The 1975 Act expressly states that the settlement must be one made on the parties to a marriage to which the deceased was one of the parties. The variation may consist of extinguishing a person's rights under a settlement, but only for the benefit of a surviving spouse or a child (s.2(1)(f)). If a settlement is not an ante- or post-nuptial settlement within the terms of this power, then if made by the deceased and it has the effect of defeating an applicant's claim for financial provision under s.2, it may be reviewed under the provisions of s.10 (see Chapter 23). It may also be a maintenance agreement within s.34(2) of the Matrimonial Causes Act 1973 and may then be varied under s.36 of that Act (see Chapter 15).

## 7. Consequential directions

It will commonly be necessary for the court to consider not merely whether a particular order should be made in favour of an applicant, but also how the burden should be borne as between the beneficiaries under the will or the rules of intestate succession. Thus it may not always be appropriate for a lump sum to be paid from the residue, as where, for example, substantial legacies are given to persons whose claims are much weaker than those to whom the comparatively small residue is given (see *Re Simson* [1950] Ch 38). Moreover, under the previous law it was held that the court could apportion the burden of any provision ordered unequally, not only between respective classes of beneficiaries, but between beneficiaries of the same class (*Re Preston* [1969] 1 WLR 317. See also *Malone* v *Harrison* [1979] 1 WLR 1353). The court can single out a needy beneficiary for special treatment in the sense that he or she may be relieved wholly or in part from the burden of contributing to the provision ordered for the applicant or applicants, but the court does not have power to increase the rights which a non-applicant beneficiary has under the intestacy law or the relevant will (*Re Campbell* [1983] NI 10).

Where the transfer of a specific item of property to an applicant seems appropriate, it may not be appropriate for the beneficiary to whom the property is specifically given by the deceased's will to bear the whole burden. The court is accordingly given power to include in any order such consequential and supplemental provisions as it thinks necessary or expedient, not only for the purpose of giving effect to the order, but also for the purpose of securing that the order operates fairly as between one beneficiary of the estate and another (s.2(3)).

In addition to this general power the court is given three specific powers. First, the court may order any person who holds any property which forms part of the net estate of the deceased to make such payment or transfer such property as may be specified in the order. This power is made necessary by the extended definition of the "net estate" in s.25(1) (see Chapter 23). That definition includes property which may be in the hands of persons other than the personal representatives. Secondly, the court may vary the disposition of the deceased's estate effected by the will, or the law relating to intestacy, in such manner as the court thinks fair and reasonable having regard to the provisions of the order and all the circumstances of the case. This makes it clear that the court has power to make some other provision out of the estate for a beneficiary of specific property which is transferred to or settled on an applicant by an order under s.2. Thirdly, the court may confer on the trustees of any property which is the subject of an order under s.2 such powers as appear to the court to be necessary or expedient. This implements the recommendation of the Law Commission that when the court orders property to be settled it should have power to confer wide powers on the trustees including all the discretionary powers commonly found in family trusts. (See Law Com. No. 61, para. 119.)

## 8. The effect of an order

Where an order is made under s.2 then the will or the law relating to intestacy, or both, as the case may be, have effect and shall be deemed to have had effect subject to the provisions of the order as from the deceased's death for all purposes (s.19(1). See also Inheritance Tax Act 1984, s.146). This specifically includes the purposes of the enactments relating to inheritance tax. Thus if an order under s.2 provides for the transfer to the surviving spouse of property specifically given to a stranger, advantage can be taken of the exemption from inheritance tax in respect of transfers to spouses.

## 9. Interim orders

Where on an application for an order under s.2 it appears to the court (a) that the applicant is in immediate need of financial assistance, but it is not yet possible to determine what order (if any) should be made under that section; and (b) that property forming part of the net estate of the deceased is or can be made available to meet the need of the applicant, the court may make an interim order (s.5(1)). An interim order may provide that, subject to such conditions or restrictions, if any, as the court may impose and to any further order of the court, there shall be paid to the applicant out of the net estate of the deceased such sum or sums and (if more than one) at such intervals as the court thinks reasonable. The order may provide for such payments to continue until an order is made under s.2 or the court declines to make an order under that section (s.5(1). Subsections (2), (3) and (4) of s.2 relating to the form and contents of final orders apply to interim orders: s.5(2)). It seems that the court's power under s.5 is not limited to making an order for periodical payments, but extends to making an order for payment of a lump sum. However, bearing in mind the scope and object of the section, periodical payments will generally be more appropriate.

In determining what order, if any, should be made the court must, so far as the urgency of the case admits, have regard to the same matters as those to which the court is required to have regard under s.3 of the Act in relation to a final order (s.5(3)). An order subsequently made under s.2 of the Act may provide that any sum paid to the applicant by virtue of an interim order shall be treated to such an extent and in such manner as may be provided by the subsequent order as having been paid on account of any payment provided for by that order (s.5(4)). This substantially re-enacts the previous legislation which was considered in *Re Ralphs* [1968] 1 WLR 1522. In that case an interim order was made in favour of an applicant widow which provided for weekly payments more or less corresponding with the income given to her by the provisions of the will, and provided that such payments were to be brought into account against such income. Cross J, having consulted the other Chancery judges, provided guidance for executors pending the hearing of an application. He stated that in the majority of cases where the applicant was given a benefit by the deceased's will, there would be no good reason for withholding it pending the hearing of the summons. He also expressed the view that executors, faced with an application for provision for maintenance, should form their own view as to what interim payments should properly be made from the deceased's estate. If they are not prepared to make such payments on their own responsibility, they should ask the parties who might be affected thereby for their consent. If consent is not forthcoming, the executors can apply to the court for leave to make the payment in question.

## 10. Variation and discharge

Where the court has made an order for periodical payments under s.2(1)(a) of the Act, it has power, by order, to vary or discharge the original order or to suspend any provision of it temporarily and to revive the operation of any provision so suspended (s.6(1)). This clearly enables the court, on an application for variation, to alter the periodical payments to be made to the recipient under the original order. The court's power on such an application is, however, specifically made wider in three respects (s.6(2)). In the first place, it may order periodical payments to be made to any other person who applied for an order under s.2, whether or not he was successful, or who would be entitled to apply for an order under s.2 were it not for the time limit on applications imposed by s.4 (see Part 11 below). Secondly, it may order the payment of a lump sum to any such person or to the recipient of the periodical payments under the original order. Thirdly, it can order the transfer of property to any such person or to the original recipient. It cannot make an order for the settlement or acquisition of property or for the variation of a marriage settlement.

However, any order can only affect what is called "relevant property", that is, property the income of which is at the date of the order applicable wholly or in part for the making of periodical payments to any person who has applied for an order under the Act (s.6(6)). It has been noted above that periodical payments under the Act can only come out of the property comprised in the estate and that the court on making an order generally sets aside part of the estate to meet such payments (s.2(3)). This enables the remainder of the estate to be distributed to the beneficiaries, but means that unless that distribution is to be undone, any powers which the court is given to alter the provision originally made must be limited to property retained to provide for the periodical payments. This means that while it is always possible to reduce periodical payments they can only be increased at the expense of periodical payments payable to another person unless the income from the property has increased. Similarly, an order for periodical payments in favour of a person not hitherto in receipt of such payments can only be made at the expense of the recipient under an original order. The powers to order the payment of a lump sum or the transfer of property can likewise only operate at the expense of an existing periodical payments order, though they may be exercised for the benefit of the person who has hitherto been receiving periodical payments where it is now considered more appropriate that capital provision should be made. Moreover, in such a case it does not matter that a similar order has been made in favour of such a person in the past, that is, there is no objection to a person receiving a second lump sum. (Contrast the position under the Matrimonial Causes Act 1973; see Chapter 10.)

The court's powers are further widened to deal with a provision in an order for periodical payments that they shall cease on the occurrence of a particular event or on the expiration of a particular period (s.6(3)). Provided an application is made within six months from the date of cessation, the court has power to make any order which it would have had power to make if the application had been made before the date of cessation. Thus while periodical payments under an order in favour of a surviving spouse do not automatically cease on remarriage, the order may itself provide for cessation of the payments on that event. Such a provision could be deleted on an application for variation made before remarriage, but where this has not been done, application can be made within six months of the remarriage by virtue of s.6(3) for the payments to be extended or revived as appropriate. (This is confirmed by s.6(10)). The court may instead order the payment of a lump sum or a transfer of property either to the former recipient of the periodical payments or to any other person entitled to apply for financial provision under the Act. Any order can, of course, only affect "relevant property", that is, for this purpose property the income of which was applicable for the making of the periodical payments immediately before they ceased on the occurrence of the specified event or the expiration of the specified period (s.6(6)). It should be noted that an order for periodical payments in favour of a surviving former spouse or a spouse judicially separated from the deceased terminates automatically on remarriage (s.19(2)). No variation of this automatic termination is possible (s.6(1)).

An application for variation or discharge under s.6 can be made by any of the following (s.6(5)):

(a) any person who has applied for an order under s.2 or would be entitled to apply were it not for the time limit imposed on applications by s.4;

(b) the personal representatives of the deceased;

(c) the trustees of any relevant property; and

(d) any beneficiary of the estate of the deceased.

In exercising its powers under s.6 the court is required to have regard to all the circumstances of the case, including any change in any of the matters to which the court was required to have regard when making the original order (s.6(7)).

Orders for lump sum payments and orders for the transfer of property are final and not subject to variation. Once made there is no question of ordering a re-payment or a re-transfer in the light of changed circumstances. The position is in this respect the same as that which prevails under the Matrimonial Causes Act 1973. Where a lump sum has been ordered to be paid by instalments the instalments may be varied (s.7).

## 11. Time limit for applications

An application for an order under s.2 cannot be made without the permission of the court after the end of the period of six months from the date on which representation with respect to the estate of the deceased is first taken out (s.4). An application is "made" when the originating summons is issued (*Re Chittenden* [1970] 1 WLR 1618). In considering for this purpose when representation with respect to the estate of a deceased person was first taken out, a grant limited to settled land or to trust property is to be left out of account, and a grant limited to real estate or to personal estate is to be left out of account unless a grant limited to the remainder of the estate has previously been made or is made at the same time (s.23).

The Act gives the court no guidance whatever as to any principles on which the jurisdiction to extend the time is to be exercised. The same was true before 1976 though until the Intestates' Estates Act 1952 there was no power at all to extend time. The 1952 Act permitted an extension on certain specified grounds only, and it was not until the Family Provision Act 1966 that these restrictions were removed. Earlier cases must therefore be viewed with caution. In *Re Ruttie* [1970] 1 WLR 89 Ungoed Thomas J thought it dangerous to establish prematurely any guiding principles without a wide experience which was not available in the early days of unfettered discretion. In *Re Salmon (deceased)* [1981] Ch 167 Sir Robert Megarry V-C, while disclaiming any intention to lay down principles, thought that after 14 years some progress could be made towards identifying some guidelines. He laid down six guidelines as to the basis on which the court should exercise its discretion in granting or withholding its permission for proceedings to be brought out of time. He was not purporting to lay down a comprehensive list, and in the later case of *Re Dennis (deceased)* [1981] 2 All ER 140 Browne-Wilkinson J added a seventh matter to be taken into account.

The first principle is that the discretion of the court is unfettered and is to be exercised judicially and in accordance with what is just and proper.

Secondly, the onus lies on the applicant to establish sufficient grounds for taking the case out of the general rule, and depriving those who are protected by it of its benefits. The burden is no triviality for the time limit is a substantive provision laid down in the Act itself. The applicant must make out a substantial case for it being just and proper for the court to exercise its statutory discretion to extend the time.

Thirdly, it is material to consider how promptly and in what circumstances the applicant has sought the permission of the court after the time limit has expired. This is not a crude matter of simply looking at the length of time that has been allowed to elapse, e.g. six weeks in *Re Ruttie* [1970] 1 WLR 89 as compared with two and a half years in *Re Gonin* [1977] 2 All ER 720. The whole of the circumstances must be looked at, and not least the reasons for the delay, and also the promptitude with which, by letter before action or otherwise, the applicant gave warning to the defendants of the proposed application. Thus if the warning was given within time, but for some good reason the proceedings were not commenced until a short while after time had run, the applicant's task would probably be relatively simple. Where there has been some error or oversight, it is important to consider whether the applicant has done all that was reasonably possible to put matters right promptly.

Fourthly, it is material to consider whether or not negotiations have been commenced within the time limit. If they have, and time has run out while they are proceeding, this is likely to encourage the court to extend the time. This was the case in *Re Ruttie* [1970] 1 WLR 89. Negotiations commenced after the time limit might also aid the applicant, at any rate if the defendants have not taken the point that time has expired.

Fifthly, it is relevant to consider whether or not the estate has been distributed before a claim under the Act has been made or notified. One of the prime reasons for insisting on a time limit is to enable an estate to be distributed within a reasonable time (*per* Browne-Wilkinson J in *Re Dennis (deceased)* [1981] 2 All ER 140 at p. 144). Section 20(1) provides that the Act is not to make the personal representative of a deceased person liable for having distributed any part of the estate of the deceased, after the end of the period of six months from the date on which representation with respect to the estate of the deceased is first taken out, on the ground that he ought to have taken into account the possibility that the court might permit the making of an application after the end of that period. This does not, however, prejudice any power to recover, by reason of the making of an order under this Act, any part of the estate from the beneficiary to whom it has been distributed. Sir Robert Megarry V-C in *Re Salmon* [1981] Ch 167 at p. 176 said:

"If it is always prejudicial to claimants not to receive money that they are entitled to receive at the earliest possible moment, it is likely to be even more prejudicial to have taken away from them money that they have actually received and have begun to enjoy. The point is strengthened if they have changed their position in reliance on what they have received, as by making purchases or gifts that they otherwise would not have made".

In *Re Ruttie* [1969] 3 All ER 1633 at p. 1637, where the estate had not been distributed, Ungoed Thomas J pointed out that an extension would cause no prejudice whatsoever to the defendant except the loss of the advantage of a rigid time limit, a loss the Act itself contemplates.

Sixthly, it is relevant to consider whether a refusal to extend the time would leave the claimant without redress against anybody. In *Re Gonin* [1977] 2 All ER 720 at p. 736 Walton J had considered the possibility that the plaintiff might sue her solicitors in negligence if in fact it was due to their faulty advice that her claim was not made in time. Sir Robert Megarry acknowledged that it could be said that the liability of the defendants ought not to depend upon the distribution of fault between the plaintiff and his or her solicitors. Nevertheless, however logic may affect the defendant's position, there is a real and plain difference to a plaintiff between having a claim against his or her solicitors instead of against the defendants, and having no claim at all. Even if the plaintiff is personally blameless the delays of his solicitors must be treated as the delays of the plaintiff, though injustice will often be avoided by the existence of the plaintiff's right to sue his solicitors for negligence.

In *Re Dennis deceased* [1981] 2 All ER 140 Browne-Wilkinson J said that a further seventh requirement which an applicant has to satisfy is to show that he has an arguable case, i.e. a case fit to go for trial. In this respect the court's approach is rather the same as it adopts when considering whether a defendant ought to have leave to defend in proceedings for summary judgment (see *Re Stone (deceased)* (1969) 114 SJ 36 where Lord Denning referred to there being "an arguable case" or a "triable issue"). In *Re Dennis* the applicant failed to show an arguable case in that he was merely seeking a capital sum to pay capital transfer tax due on an *inter vivos* gift made to him by his deceased father. This would not have contributed to the cost of his future living and so went beyond a claim for maintenance which was all he was entitled to seek.

It will generally be necessary for the court to balance the various factors. Thus in *Re Dennis (deceased)* Browne-Wilkinson J refused his consent, first because there had been a long delay, of which a part was unexplained and so far as could be seen, inexcusable, and secondly because the applicant had no arguable chance of success if the matter were to go forward. These factors outweighed the fact that the estate concerned was large and complicated and that the delay which had occurred had not, and would not, hold up the distribution of the estate. (See also *Re Bramwell (deceased)* [1988] 2 FLR 263.)

Where the court grants permission for an application to be made after the end of the six-month period, its powers are the same as if the application had been made within that period except under s.9. An order under that section in relation to the deceased's severable share of property of which, immediately before his death, the deceased was a beneficial joint tenant, can only be made in proceedings on an application under s.2 made within the six month period. The provisions of s.4 do not prevent applications being made under s.6 for the variation or discharge of an order for periodical payments. An application under s.6 can be made, *inter alia*, by a person entitled to make an application by virtue of s.1(1) but for whom no provision is made by an existing order. This may be because his original application was refused, or because he made no application or was unable to make an application because of the provisions of s.4. Although in a sense this permits an exception to the general time limit under s.4, it is essential that there is in existence an order providing for some other person. Moreover, an order under s.6 can only affect "relevant property", i.e. property the income of which is or was being applied wholly or in part in the payment of periodical payments specified in the order which is the subject of the application under s.6.

## 12. Excluding the Act

It is well established that a spouse cannot by agreement give up the right to apply for financial provision in matrimonial proceedings as it is against the public interest to permit the jurisdiction of the court to be ousted (see *Hyman* v *Hyman* [1929] AC 601; Matrimonial Causes Act 1973, s.34 and Chapter 15). Whether the same principle applied to the right to apply for provision under the Inheritance (Family Provision) Act 1938 was left open in *Zamet* v *Hyman* [1961] 1 WLR 1442. The Act of 1975 expressly provides a means whereby during the lifetime of a spouse the right of the other spouse to apply for provision out of his or her estate can be barred. In its original form s.15 required the agreement of both parties as well as the sanction of the court, but the Matrimonial and Family Proceedings Act 1984 removed the need for agreement and thereby enabled the court to impose a clean break (s.8). Section 15 now provides that on granting a decree of divorce, nullity or judicial separation, or at any time thereafter, the court if it considers it just to do so, may on the application of either party to the marriage, order that the other party to the marriage shall not on the death of the applicant be entitled to apply under s.2 of the Act. If such an order is made before a decree nisi of divorce or nullity has been made absolute, it will not be effective unless it is made absolute.

Before the court can make an order under s.15 it must consider it "just to do so". In *Whiting* v *Whiting* [1988] 1 WLR 565 at p. 577 Balcombe LJ said that in his view "before the court can consider it just to make an order depriving a divorced spouse of any opportunity to claim financial provision from the estate of the other spouse, it should be given some indication of what the estate is likely to consist of and some details of the persons whom the applicant considers to have a prior claim on his estate in the event of his decease". In that case he was prepared to accept that the husband's only capital asset was his interest in his existing house and that this was likely to be the only asset of substance in his estate. It was a reasonable inference that the husband considered his new wife and, presumably, his children, to have a prior claim on his estate in the event of his death, but nowhere in his evidence did he say so. The whole of his evidence was directed towards supporting his application for a discharge of the existing order for periodical payments and it appeared to have been assumed that his application under s.15 would stand or fall with that other application. The case to support an order under s.15 had not been made out though it was of course open to the husband to make a further application supported by the appropriate evidence as indicated by Balcombe LJ.

An order under s.15 was made in *Kokosinski* v *Kokosinski* [1980] Fam 72 where on divorce Wood J made an order under the Matrimonial Causes Act 1973 for the payment of a lump sum of £8,000 by the husband to the wife and dismissed her claim for periodical payments. He said (at p. 87) "There is no need for him to make capital provision for his dependants, who will have been adequately provided for". In *Re Fullard deceased* [1981] 2 All ER 796 where the Court of Appeal upheld the dismissal of an application under the 1975 Act by the former wife of the deceased, Ormrod LJ stressed the importance of s.15 and the advisability of obtaining agreement which was at that time necessary, and said (at p. 802):

"I regard s.15 as the form of insuring against applications under the 1975 Act which some people may very reasonably wish to do having made financial provision of a capital nature for the former spouse".

The policy of the 1984 Act in encouraging the clean break has obviously increased the desirability of obtaining an order under s.15.

## 13. Prevention of avoidance

Provision can only be ordered out of the "net estate" of the deceased. The definition of "net estate" has been considerably widened by the 1975 Act to prevent avoidance which was possible under the previous legislation. This aspect is considered in Chapter 23.

# Chapter 22

# Enforcement of orders

## 1. Introduction

The problem of enforcement arises principally in relation to orders for periodical payments which are not secured. Such orders involve a continuing obligation on the part of the persons against whom they are made with the consequent ever-present risk of default. In contrast, the obligations imposed by other forms of financial provision are normally discharged within a short time of the making of the order by the provision of security, the payment of a lump sum or the transfer or settlement of property as the case may be. Accordingly, the enforcement of such orders will generally arise, if at all, at the outset. If a person refuses or neglects to execute a deed securing periodical payments or transferring or settling property as ordered, the court may order that the deed shall be executed by a person nominated by the court for that purpose. When so executed the deed operates as if it had been executed by the person originally directed to execute it (Supreme Court Act 1981, s.39; County Courts Act 1984, s.38. See *Danchevsky* v *Danchevsky* [1975] Fam 17 where the wife attempted to enforce an order for sale by seeking committal of the husband. The Court of Appeal pointed out that an order for possession could have been enforced by a warrant for possession and the court could then have directed that the conveyance of the property be executed by some third person in place of the husband. This was preferable to committal). An order for the payment of a lump sum may be enforced in the same way as an ordinary judgment debt but not in bankruptcy proceedings (*Woodley* v *Woodley (No. 2)* [1993] 2 FLR 477).

However, an order for periodical payments not only involves a continuing risk of default, but gives rise to a different situation when default actually occurs. Such an order is not a final judgment, and arrears due under such an order are not enforceable as of right (*Robins* v *Robins* [1907] 2 KB 13). The court has a discretion and may allow time to pay or allow payment by instalments, and may even remit arrears in whole or in part. The arrears cannot, therefore, be recovered as an ordinary debt (*Kerr* v *Kerr* [1897] 2 QB 349) and are not provable in bankruptcy

(*Linton* v *Linton* (1885) 15 QBD 239; *Re Henderson* (1888) 20 QBD 508. See Insolvency Rules 1986, r. 12.3). On the other hand, such orders can be enforced in the ways provided notwithstanding the bankruptcy of the person against whom they are made (contrast the position in relation to payments under a maintenance agreement). A husband's obligation to make payments under a maintenance agreement comes to an end on his bankruptcy. A wife may prove in the bankruptcy of her husband for the value of the payments due to her under a covenant by him in a separation deed, but she cannot take proceedings against him for arrears whether they accrued before or after the bankruptcy, even though she has elected not to prove (*Victor* v *Victor* [1912] 1 KB 247 CA).

An undertaking given to the court and embodied in a written order has the same effect as a judgment or order in terms of the undertaking. Thus in *Gandolfo* v *Gandolfo* [1981] QB 359 the court held it was appropriate to treat the husband's undertaking to pay school fees as equivalent to an order for their payment, because it was an integral part of the order, and if it had not been given the periodical payments for the child would probably have been increased. It was also enforceable by the wife.

## 2. Enforcement of orders in the High Court or a county court

### (a) *Methods of payment*

Underlying the Maintenance Enforcement Act 1991 is the principle that it is much better to avoid default occurring than to take action once it has occurred (see HL Debates 29 November 1990, Vol. 523, No. 1073). The Act accordingly directs attention to the methods by which maintenance is to be paid. When making an order for maintenance, the High Court and a county court will not be limited to ordering payment to be made directly by one party to the other. By widening the courts' powers in relation to the method of payment the Act seeks to reduce the likelihood of arrears arising.

First, the Act gives the High Court or a county court power, when making a qualifying periodical maintenance order, to order that the payments required to be made by the debtor to the creditor under the maintenance order must be made (a) by standing order, or (b) by any other method which requires the debtor to give his authority for payments of a specific amount to be made from an account of his to an account of the creditor's on specific dates during the period for which the authority is in force and without the need for any further authority from the debtor (s.1(1), (4) and (5)). It may exercise this power either of its own motion or on an application made by an interested party. Where the High Court or a county court has made a qualifying periodical maintenance order, whether before or after the coming into force of the Act, it may exercise this power at any later time either on an application by an interested party or of its own motion, in the course of any proceedings concerning the order (s.1(3)). Where the court proposes to exercise this power it may order that the debtor open an account from which payments under the order may be made if, having given the debtor an opportunity of opening such an account, the court is satisfied that the debtor has failed, without reasonable excuse, to open such an account (s.1(6)).

Secondly, where the High Court or a county court makes a qualifying maintenance order it may now also make an attachment of earnings order under the Attachment of Earnings Act 1971 to secure payments under that maintenance order (s.1(1) and (4)). Prior to the Maintenance Enforcement Act 1991 an attachment of earnings order could only be made if the debtor applied or at least fifteen days had elapsed since the making of the maintenance order and the debtor had failed to make one or more of the payments required by the order and such failure was due to his wilful refusal or culpable neglect. These limitations having been removed the court may make an attachment of earnings order at the same time as it makes the qualifying maintenance order, either of its own motion or on an application by an interested party (s.1(1) and (3) and Sched. 2).

Where the High Court or a county court has made a qualifying periodical maintenance order, whether before or after the coming into force of the Act, it may at any later time exercise the powers to make an order for payment by standing order or similar means or an attachment of earnings order, either on an application made by an interested party or of its own motion, in the course of any proceedings concerning the order (s.1(3), (4) and (10)).

In deciding whether to exercise its powers to make either of such means of payment order the court, having (if practicable) given every interested party an opportunity to make representations, must have regard to any representations made by any such party (s.1(8)). "Interested party" for this purpose means (a) the debtor, (b) the creditors, and (c) in a case where the person who applied for the qualifying maintenance order in question is a person other than the creditor, that other person (s.1(10)). Where the court has made a "means of payment order" it may at any later time revoke, suspend, revive or vary that order either (a) on an application by an interested party or (b) of its own motion, in the course of any proceedings concerning the qualifying periodical maintenance order (s.1(7)).

A maintenance order means any order specified in Schedule 8 to the Administration of Justice Act 1970 and includes any such order which has been discharged, if any arrears are recoverable under it (s.1(10)). A periodical maintenance order for this purpose is an order (a) which requires money to be paid periodically by one person (the debtor) to another (the creditor) and (b) which is a maintenance order. Such an order is a qualifying periodical maintenance order if, at the time it is made, the debtor is ordinarily resident in England and Wales (s.1(2)). The reference to an order requiring money to be paid periodically by one person to another includes a reference to an order requiring a lump sum to be paid by instalments by one person to another (s.1(10)).

*(b) Methods of enforcement*

An order for periodical payments made in the High Court or in a county court may be enforced by the usual methods open to judgment creditors in those courts other than bankruptcy proceedings (*Re a Debtor* [1929] 2 Ch 146). An order made by a divorce county court can be transferred to the High Court if it cannot be conveniently enforced in the county court, and it then becomes enforceable as though it had been made by the High Court. In addition an order of the High Court or a county court may generally be registered in a magistrates' court for enforcement (see **Part 4**, below).

An order for payment of a lump sum made in the High Court or in a county court may be enforced by the usual methods open to judgment creditors in those courts with some exceptions noted below. As already mentioned, it may not be enforced in bankruptcy proceedings. (Where there is a strong *prima facie* case that relevant documents which have not been produced in the past are not likely to be produced in the future and might be removed or destroyed, an Anton Piller order may be obtained against a husband - particularly if he has shown that he was ready to flout the court's authority and mislead it so as to render the normal process of the law nugatory (*Emanuel* v *Emanuel* [1982] 1 WLR 669).)

The methods of enforcement fall into three categories:

(i)  those which are directed against the property of the person liable to make the payments;

(ii) proceedings which are directed against his person and which may lead to his committal; and

(iii) proceedings directed against his earnings by means of an attachment of earnings order.

*(c) Enforcement directed against property*

Execution may be levied against the property of the person liable to make periodical payments or a lump sum payment by the issue of a writ of *fieri facias* in the High Court (RSC Ord. 46 and Ord. 47; Family Proceedings Rules 1991, r. 7.1) or a warrant of execution in a county court (CCR Ord. 26; Family Proceedings Rules 1991, r. 7.1; County Courts Act 1984, s.85). No writ of *fieri facias* or warrant of execution can be issued to enforce payment of any sum due under an order for ancillary relief, or under an order under s.27 of the Matrimonial Causes Act 1973, where an application for a variation of the order is pending, except with leave of the registrar (Family Proceedings Rules 1991, r. 7.1). In the High Court application can also be made for a writ of sequestration (RSC Ord. 46, r. 5. But see the difficulties in *Clark* v *Clark* [1989] 1 FLR 174). A garnishee order may be sought in the High Court or in a county court as appropriate (RSC Ord. 49; CCR Ord. 30. See *Gandolfo* v *Gandolfo* [1981] 1 WLR 67 and *Cohen* v *Cohen* (1983) 4 FLR 451 - garnishee order against bank account in name of solicitors into which the proceeds of sale of the former matrimonial home had been paid).

An application can be made in the High Court and in a county court for a charging order on the property of the person liable to pay (Charging Orders Act 1979; RSC Ord. 50; CCR Ord. 30). Moreover, the effect of s.2(1) of the Charging Orders Act 1979 is to extend the availability of charging orders to cover cases where the interest sought to be charged is a beneficial interest in the proceeds of sale of land held under a trust for sale (*National Westminster Bank Ltd* v *Stockman* [1981] 1 WLR 67. See further Chapter 8). The High Court and a county court may also appoint a receiver by way of equitable execution (Supreme Court Act 1981, s.37(4); RSC Ord. 30, CCR Ord. 32), and may authorise the receiver to bring any necessary proceedings in the name of the estate owner of the property of which he has been appointed receiver (*Levermore* v *Levermore* [1979] 1 WLR 1277 - receiver authorised to take such proceedings in the husband's name as might be necessary to enforce a sale of the house vested in the joint names of the husband and his brother).

*(d) A judgment summons*

A judgment summons under the Debtors' Act 1869 can be issued in respect of periodical payments in the High Court and in a county court (s.5). A judgment summons requires the debtor to appear and be examined on oath as to his means, and on the hearing of the summons the judge may adopt one of the following courses:

(i) He may make an order committing the debtor to prison, but only if it is proved to his satisfaction that the debtor has, or has had since the date of the order, the means to pay the sum in respect of which he is in default, and has refused or neglected, or refuses or neglects to pay it (s.5(2). The burden of proof is on the creditor. Contrast the position in a magistrates' court in relation to a warrant of committal).

(ii) He may make a new order for payment of the amount due under the original order, together with the costs of the summons, either at a specified time or by instalments, in addition to any sums accruing due under the original order. (See Family Proceedings Rules 1991 r. 7.4.)

(iii) He may make an order for commitment, but may direct its execution to be suspended on terms that the debtor pays to the judgment creditor the amount due and costs, either at a specified time or by instalments, in addition to any sums accruing due under the original order (*ibid.* r. 7.4).

It had been thought that an order for payment of a lump sum could not be enforced in this way. However, in *Graham* v *Graham* [1992] 2 FLR 406 the Court of Appeal pointed out that the definition of a maintenance order for this purpose in Schedule 8 of the Administration of Justice Act 1970 now includes: "2A, An order for periodical or other payments made, or having effect as if made, under Part II of the Matrimonial Causes Act 1973". In appropriate cases payment of a lump sum can accordingly be enforced by judgment summons. Indeed, in *Graham* v *Graham* it was held that an order to bring a sum of money into court as security pending determination of an application for a lump sum payment was a maintenance order for this purpose. (See also *Woodley* v *Woodley* [1992] 2 FLR 417 and *Woodley* v *Woodley (No. 2)* [1993] 2 FLR 477.)

*(e) Attachment of earnings order*

It has been noted in (*a*) that under the Maintenance Enforcement Act 1991 the High Court and a county court, when making a qualifying maintenance order, may at the same time make an attachment of earnings order under the Attachment of Earnings Act 1971 to secure payments under that maintenance order (s.1(1) and (4)). The general principles are the same as those applicable in magistrates' courts (see 3(d) below). An order for payment of a lump sum cannot be enforced by an attachment of earnings order except where it is payable by instalments (see Attachment of Earnings Act 1971, s.2 and Sched. 1 para.3; Maintenance Enforcement Act 1991, s.1(10)).

*(f) Restrictions on the recovery of arrears*

The High Court and county courts have a discretion as to the amount of arrears which may be recovered, though they may not always have the opportunity of exercising that discretion. There is a general requirement that before any process is issued for the enforcement of an order made in matrimonial proceedings, an affidavit must be filed verifying the amount due under the order and showing how the amount is arrived at (Family Proceedings Rules 1991 r.7.1). However, a writ of *fieri facias* or sequestration may be issued on an affidavit of service of the original order and of non-payment and no notice need be given to the debtor who will thus have no opportunity of opposing the issue of the writ or asking the court to exercise its discretion.

This is subject to a provision that a person is not entitled to enforce through the High Court or any county court the payment of arrears due under an order for maintenance pending suit, an interim order for maintenance, or any order for unsecured or secured periodical payments under the Matrimonial Causes Act 1973, without the leave of the court if those arrears became due more than 12 months before the proceedings to enforce the payment of them are begun (Matrimonial Causes Act 1973, s.32). The court hearing an application for the grant of leave under this provision may refuse leave, or may grant leave subject to such restrictions and conditions as it thinks proper, including conditions as to the allowing of time for payment or the making of payment by instalments. The court may also, if it thinks fit, remit the payment of such arrears or any part thereof.

Before the Matrimonial Proceedings and Property Act 1970, the High Court and county courts had no express power to remit arrears, although since they had a discretion as to the extent to which arrears might be recovered, they could refuse to allow enforcement, and thus in effect remit the arrears. Moreover, on the variation or discharge of an order for periodical payments the new order could be backdated which would have the effect of remitting payments already due. It may still have been necessary to resort to these methods, for the power to remit arrears given by the Act of 1970, and contained in the Matrimonial Causes Act 1973, is exercisable only on an application for leave to enforce payment of arrears which became due more than 12 months previously, and in any event would seem to apply only to such arrears and not to arrears which have accrued within that period even where application for leave is made. However, it is now provided that where the court has made an order for maintenance pending suit, an interim order for maintenance, or an order for unsecured or secured periodical payments under the Act of 1973, then subject to s.31 of the Act, the court has the power to remit the payment of arrears due under such an order or any part thereof (Matrimonial Causes Act 1973, s.31(2A), introduced by s.51 of the Administration of Justice Act 1982).

There is uncertainty as to whether arrears due under an order of the High Court or a county court at the date of death of the person liable to pay are recoverable. The earlier cases support the view that arrears of maintenance could not be recovered (*Re Hedderwick* [1933] Ch 669; *Re Woolgar* [1942] Ch 318) though a contrary view was taken in relation to alimony (*Re Stillwell* [1916] 1 Ch 365). The more recent cases, however, suggest that arrears of maintenance can be recovered (*Sugden* v *Sugden* [1957] P 120; *W* v *W* [1916] P 113; *Re Hudson* [1966] Ch 209); and it would be unfortunate if a distinction was made between maintenance pending suit and financial provision orders.

## (g) Recovery of payments

Although the High Court and county courts have been able, in effect, to remit arrears, before the Act of 1970 they had no power to order the reimbursement of payments actually made. This meant that if, for example, a wife concealed from her husband a change in her circumstances that would have justified a reduction in the order so that her husband continued to pay the original amount, the court could reduce or discharge the order, but could not order her to repay what she had received. The Act of 1970 introduced two provisions, now contained in the Matrimonial Causes Act 1973, which enable the court to order reimbursement on the application of the person liable to make payments under an order, or his personal representatives, against the person entitled to the payments under the order, or her personal representatives. (Contrast the more limited provision in relation to orders in magistrates' courts - see Part 3 below.)

The first provision is concerned with the situation in which a person liable to make payments under an order, or his personal representatives, continues to make payments under the order after it has ceased to have effect by reason of the remarriage of the person entitled to receive payments, in the mistaken belief that the order was still subsisting (Matrimonial Causes Act 1973, s.38). The court may now order the recipient of the payments to pay to the applicant a sum equal to the amount of the payments made after the cessation of the order, or if it appears to the court that it would be unjust to make that order, it may order payment of such lesser sum as it thinks fit, or may dismiss the application.

It is also provided that no action may be brought against the recipient of the payments for recovery thereof as being money paid under a mistake of fact so that the discretion of the court cannot be avoided. An application under this provision may be made in proceedings for leave to enforce, or for the enforcement of payment of arrears under the order in question, but when not made in such proceedings must be made to a county court.

The second provision is concerned with the situation in which the payments made under the order have been in excess of what should have been paid having regard to a change in circumstances, though liability under the order has not ceased altogether as will be the case where the recipient has remarried (Matrimonial Causes Act 1973, s.33). If it appears to the court that by reason of (a) a change in the circumstances of the person entitled to, or liable to make, payment under the order since it was made, or (b) the changed circumstances resulting from the death of the person liable to make the payment, the amount received by the person entitled to the payments in respect of a period after those circumstances changed or after the death of the person liable, as the case may be, exceeds the amount which the person liable or his personal representatives should have been required to pay, the court may order payment to the applicant of such sum, not exceeding the amount of the excess, as it thinks just.

Applications for payments under this provision may be made in proceedings in the High Court or a county court for (a) the variation or discharge of the order, or (b) leave to enforce, or the enforcement of, the payment of arrears under that order. If an application is not made in such proceedings, it must be made to a county court.

Both provisions apply to orders for periodical payments or secured periodical payments for a spouse or any child of the family made on or after granting a decree of divorce, nullity or judicial separation, and to any such orders made under s.27 of the Matrimonial Causes Act 1973. Only the second provision applies to orders for maintenance pending suit and interim orders in proceedings under s.27, for the cessation of orders on remarriage of the recipient will not arise in relation to such orders.

## 3. Enforcement of orders in magistrates' courts

### (a) Methods of payment

An important feature of the machinery of a magistrates' court has been the role of the clerk as collecting officer. A magistrates' court has had a general power to order periodical payments to be made to the clerk of the court or to the clerk of any other magistrates' court (Magistrates' Courts Act 1980, s.59(1)). In the case of an order under Part 1 of the Domestic Proceedings and Magistrates' Courts Act 1978 or an order having effect as if made under Schedule 1 to the Children Act 1989 the court was required to make an order in this form unless, upon express representations by the applicant, it was satisfied that it was undesirable to do so (Magistrates' Courts Act 1980, s.59(2)). This has been modified by the Maintenance Enforcement Act 1991 which has substituted a new s.59 (s.2).

The new s.59(1) provides that in any case where a magistrates' court orders money to be paid periodically by one person (the debtor) to another (the creditor), the court must at the same time exercise one of the powers to determine the means of payment conferred by these sections. If the order is a qualifying maintenance order there are four possible means of payment orders from which the court must choose. (If the order is not a qualifying maintenance order, only the first two are available.) The possible orders under subs. (3) are:

(a) an order that payments under the order be made directly by the debtor to the creditor;

(b) an order that payments under the order be made to the clerk of the court or to the clerk of any other magistrates' court;

(c) an order that payments under the order be made by the debtor to the creditor by standing order or similar means;

(d) an attachment of earnings order under the Attachment of Earnings Order 1971 to secure payments under the order.

Where the court proposes to order payment by standing order or similar means, the court may also order that the debtor open a bank account from which payments under the order may be made if, having given the debtor an opportunity of opening such an account, the court is satisfied that the debtor has failed, without reasonable excuse, to open such an account (s.59(4)).

In deciding which means of payment order to make the court must have regard to any representations made (a) by the debtor, (b) by the creditor, and (c) if the person who applied for the maintenance order is a person other than a creditor, by that person, having (if practicable) given them an opportunity to make such representations (s.59(5)). Where the maintenance order is an order:

(a) under the Guardianship of Minors Acts 1971 and 1973,

(b) under Part 1 of the Domestic Proceedings and Magistrates' Courts Act 1978, or

(c) under, or having effect as if made under, Schedule 1 to the Children Act 1989, and the court does not propose to exercise its power to order payment by standing order or to make an attachment of earnings order, it must order payment to be made to the clerk of the court or to the clerk of any other magistrates' court unless upon representations expressly made in that behalf by the person who applied for the maintenance order it is satisfied that it is undesirable to do so (s.59(7)).

A maintenance order is a "qualifying maintenance order" if, at the time it is made, the debtor is ordinarily resident in England and Wales (s.59(2)). The reference to money paid periodically by one person to another includes, in the case of a maintenance order, a reference to a lump sum paid by instalments by one person to another (s.59(12)).

### (b) Enforcement by a magistrates' clerk

Where payments under a relevant United Kingdom order are required to be made periodically to or through the clerk of a magistrates' court or by standing order or similar means, and any sums payable under the order are in arrears, the clerk of the relevant court must, if the person for whose benefit the payments are required to be made so requests in writing, and unless it appears to the clerk that it is unreasonable in the circumstances to do so, proceed in his own name for the recovery of those sums (s.59A(1)). Where payments under a relevant United Kingdom order are required to be made periodically to or through the clerk of a magistrates' court, the person for whose benefit the payments are required to be made may, at any time during the period in which the payments are required to be so made, give authority in writing to the clerk of the relevant court to proceed in his own name for the recovery of any sums payable to or through him under the order in question which fall into arrears on or after the date of the giving of the authority. Where such authority has been given the clerk must proceed in his own name for the recovery of such arrears unless it appears to him that it is unreasonable in the circumstances to do so (s.59A(2) and (3)). Such authority may be cancelled by the person giving it and any proceedings commenced by virtue of the authority must not be continued (s.59A(4)). These provisions do not affect any right of a person to proceed in his own name for the recovery of sums payable on his behalf under an order of any court (s.59A(6)). See *Smith* v *Smith* (1976) 6 Fam Law 245.

A "relevant UK order" for this purpose means -

(a) an order made by a magistrates' court other than an order made by virtue of Part II of the Maintenance Orders (Reciprocal Enforcement) Act 1972;

(b) an order made by the High Court or a county court (including an order deemed to be made by the High Court by virtue of s.1(2) of the Maintenance Orders Act 1958) and registered under Part I of that Act in a magistrates' court; or

(c) an order made by a court in Scotland or Northern Ireland and registered under Part II of the Maintenance Orders Act 1950 in a magistrates' court.

Any reference to payments required to be made periodically includes, in the case of a maintenance order, a reference to instalments required to be paid in respect of a lump sum payable by instalments (s.59A(7)).

*(c) Penalty for failure to comply with maintenance order*
Where payments under a relevant English maintenance order are required to be made periodically to or through the clerk of a magistrates' court or by standing order or similar means, and the debtor fails to comply with the order in so far as the order relates to the manner of payment concerned, the relevant magistrates' court may order the debtor to pay a sum not exceeding £1,000 by way of a penalty (Magistrates' Courts Act 1980, s.59B).

*(d) Methods of enforcement*
The Magistrates' Courts Act 1980 provides that where default is made in paying sums due under an order of a magistrates' court, the court may issue either (a) a warrant of distress, which directs the police to levy the relevant sum by distress and sale of goods belonging to the defaulter, or (b) a warrant committing the defaulter to prison for a period varying from five days to six weeks according to the sum owed (s.76, s.93(7) and Sched. 4. For the power to postpone issue of a warrant see s.77). Payment of sums due under a magistrates' court maintenance order can be enforced by warrants of distress or committal only by an order made on a complaint (s.93(1)). The warrant of distress is little used in practice, but the warrant of committal remains important and is considered below. Orders may also be enforceable by an attachment of earnings order under the provisions of the Attachment of Earnings Act 1971 if such an order has not already been made at the same time as the maintenance order.

Where proceedings are brought for the enforcement of a magistrates' court maintenance order, the court may vary the order by exercising its powers to make one of the means of payment orders conferred by s.59(3)(a) to (d) (Magistrates' Courts Act 1980, s.76 as amended by the Maintenance Enforcement Act 1991, s.7). This does not apply where the maintenance order is not a qualifying maintenance order for the purposes of s.59. Where the court orders the whole or any part of any sum due to be paid by instalments the court may provide for the manner in which the instalments are to be paid (Magistrates' Courts Act 1980, s.95 as amended by Maintenance Enforcement Act 1991, Sched. 2 para. 8).

*(e) Committal*
No order for committal may be made in the absence of the defendant or in a case in which the court has power to make an attachment of earnings order unless the court is of opinion that it is inappropriate to make such an order. Moreover, the court must be satisfied that the default was due to the defendant's wilful refusal or culpable neglect (Magistrates' Courts Act 1980, s.93(6). See *James* v *James* [1963] 2 All ER 465 and *R* v *Luton Magistrates' Court, ex p. Sullivan* [1992] 2 FLR 196. A magistrates' court also has a general power to allow time for payment, or to order payment by instalments: s.75).

The imprisonment of a defendant under a warrant of committal does not operate to discharge him from his liability to pay the sum in respect of which the warrant was issued (s.93(8)), but he may not be imprisoned more than once in respect of the same arrears (Maintenance Orders Act 1958, s.17). On payment of the sum in respect of which an order for committal was made, the order ceases forthwith. On payment of part of that sum, the period of imprisonment is proportionately reduced (Magistrates' Courts Act 1980, s.79). While he is in custody no arrears accrue under the order being enforced unless the court that commits him otherwise directs *(ibid.* s.94. See *Starkey* v *Starkey* [1954] P 449).

Where a court has power to issue a warrant of committal it may, if it thinks it expedient to do so, fix a term of imprisonment and postpone the issue of the warrant until such time and on such conditions, if any, as it thinks just *(ibid.* s.77(2). See *Crossland* v *Crossland* [1993] 1 FLR 175). If the issue of the warrant is postponed on condition that the defendant maintains current payments becoming due under the order being enforced together with further payments on account of arrears, all amounts paid by him thereafter must first be appropriated to the arrears in respect of which the committal order was made (*R* v *Miskin Lower Justices, ex p. Young* [1953] 1 QB 533). It is not appropriate to commit to prison only in respect of the additional amount ordered to be paid periodically off the arrears without reference to the current order. The proper practice is for the committal to be in respect of the periodical amount of the order plus the amount to be paid in respect of arrears (see *Fowler* v *Fowler* (1981) 2 FLR 141). If the defendant fails to observe the conditions imposed, then the warrant may be issued subject to the power of the court, on the application of the defendant, to review the position in the light of what has happened since they made their original order (Maintenance Orders Act 1958, s.18; *James* v *James* [1963] 2 All ER 465 at p. 469).

### (f) Attachment of earnings orders

It has been noted that under s.59 of the Magistrates' Courts Act 1980 as amended by the Maintenance Enforcement Act 1991 an attachment of earnings order may be made at the same time as the court makes a maintenance order. Before the 1991 Act came into force an attachment of earnings order could only be made if the debtor applied or at least fifteen days had elapsed since the making of the maintenance order and the debtor had failed to make one or more of the payments required by the order and such failure was due to his wilful refusal or culpable neglect. These limitations have been removed (Maintenance Enforcement Act 1991, s.11 and Sched. 2, para. 1).

An application for an order can be made by complaint by:

(a) the person entitled to the payments; or

(b) the clerk of the court if there is in force an order requiring payments to be made to him, and if he is requested in writing to apply by the person entitled to the payments (i.e. where there is in force an order under s.59 of the Magistrates' Courts Act 1980, or s.19(2) of the Maintenance Orders Act 1950. The clerk must not generally take action unless requested to do so: Attachment of Earnings Act 1971 s.18(1)); or

(c) the debtor, i.e. the person liable to make the payments.

(Attachment of Earnings Act 1971, s.3(1) and s.19(1)). An order can also be made in proceedings brought to enforce a maintenance order by distress or committal (s.3(4)).

An attachment of earnings order is directed to the debtor's employer, and instructs him to make periodical deductions from the debtor's earnings and to pay the amounts deducted to the clerk of the court as collecting officer (s.6(1)). The order must specify the normal deduction rate and the protected earnings rate. The normal deduction rate is the rate, expressed as a periodical sum, at which the court thinks it reasonable for the debtor's earnings to be applied to meeting his liability under the maintenance order. The protected earnings rate is the rate, expressed as a periodical sum, below which, having regard to the debtor's resources and needs, the court thinks it reasonable that the earnings actually paid to him should not be reduced (s.6(5)). The normal deduction rate must be determined after taking into account any right or liability of the debtor to deduct income tax when making the payments, and must not exceed the rate which appears to the court to be necessary for the purpose of (a) securing payment of the sums falling due from time to time under the maintenance order, and (b) securing payment within a reasonable period of any sums already due and unpaid under the maintenance order (s.6(6)). Once an attachment of earnings order has been made no order or warrant of commitment may be issued in proceedings already begun for enforcement of the maintenance order (s.8(1)).

An attachment of earnings order may be varied or discharged on application or, in certain circumstances, by the court of its own motion (*ibid.* s.9(1) and (3) and Magistrates' Courts (Attachment of Earnings) Rules 1971 (SI 1971 No. 809) rr.12 and 13). If the debtor leaves the employment of the person to whom the order is directed, the order lapses and is of no effect until the court again directs it to an employer (s.9(4)). An order ceases to have effect in the following circumstances:

(a) if an order of commitment is made or a warrant is issued subsequently, or if the court subsequently exercises its power to suspend the issue of a warrant of commitment on conditions (*ibid.* s.8(3) as amended by the Magistrates' Courts Act 1980, Sched. 7);

(b) if an application is granted for registration of the maintenance order in the High Court (*ibid.* s.11) (see Part 4 below);

(c) in the case of a maintenance order which is an order of the High Court or county court and is registered in a magistrates' court, upon notice with a view to cancellation of the registration being given (see Part 4 below);

(d) if the maintenance order ceases to be registered in a court in England or becomes registered in Scotland or Northern Ireland (see Part 5 below);

(e) if the maintenance order is discharged, unless the court considers it should remain in force where arrears remain to be recovered.

### (g) Power to remit arrears

A magistrates' court hearing an application for the enforcement, revocation, revival, variation or discharge of a magistrates' court's maintenance order, may remit the whole or any part of the sum due under the order (Magistrates' Courts Act 1980, s.95). This power extends to an order of the High Court or a county court registered in a magistrates' court (Maintenance Orders Act 1958, s.3(2)). There is no statutory provision enabling an application to be made by itself asking for remission of arrears *simpliciter*. The power to remit arises only where an application of the nature referred to in s.95 is before the court.

Before remitting the whole or any part of a sum due, the court must, except where it appears to be unnecessary or impracticable to do so, cause the person in whose favour the order is made or, if that person is a child, the child or the person with whom the child has his home, to be notified of its intention and must afford to such person a reasonable opportunity to make representations to the court, either orally at an adjourned hearing or in writing, and such representations must be considered by the court (Magistrates' Courts Rules 1981, r. 44). In *R* v *Dover Magistrates' Court ex p. Kidner* [1983] 1 All ER 475, where there had been a failure to give notice to the wife, the Divisional Court made an order of *certiorari* quashing the order of the magistrates' court and remitting the matter to the magistrates so that they could reconsider the husband's application for remission after giving notice to the wife. In considering an application for remission of arrears the court has a wide discretion. In *R* v *Halifax Justices ex p. Woolverton* (1981) 2 FLR 369 at p. 371 Lord Widgery CJ said: "It is not easy to define exactly what the circumstances are in which a remission may be made because ... the terms of [the section] are very, very vague and general." However, the court held that it was wrong to order a remission of arrears as a penalty for not allowing access. In *Parry* v *Meugens* [1986] 1 FLR 125 Reeve J said that though the discretion was wide it must be exercised judicially. In that case the husband had deducted from payments of maintenance to his children sums equivalent to sums paid on behalf of his former wife. There was nothing to suggest that the justices had applied their minds to the fact that the maintenance payments were the children's money and were not payments due to the wife. Their failure to take any account of that vital consideration wholly vitiated the way they had exercised their discretion.

No statutory provision is made in the Magistrates' Courts Act 1980 for any appeal to the High Court against an order granting or refusing remission. Therefore, under s.111 of the Magistrates' Courts Act 1980 a decision on remission can be challenged by case stated on the ground of error of law or excess of jurisdiction and not otherwise *(per* Sir David Cairns in *Berry* v *Berry* [1987] Fam 1 at p. 23 where the earlier cases are discussed. *Fletcher* v *Fletcher* [1985] FLR 851 was confirmed and *Allen* v *Allen* [1985] Fam 8 was disapproved). This is in contrast to the position in relation to applications for variation or revocation where provision is made for an appeal by way of rehearing. Accordingly, an aggrieved party may have to use two different routes when seeking to "appeal" against a refusal of a magistrates' court to vary or discharge an order on the one hand and to remit arrears on the other hand. The High Court cannot deal with the merits of the decision of a magistrates' court in relation to remission (see the criticisms in *Berry* v *Berry*). However, in *S* v *S (Children: Periodical Payments)* [1993] 2 WLR 401 Thorpe J held that where magistrates have considered not only the appropriate level of continuing periodical payments for children, but also the enforcement or remission of past arrears already accumulated, the High Court had power to review their discretionary determination in relation to both matters on an appeal under s.94 of the Children Act 1989.

## (h) Limitation on the recovery of arrears

There is no statutory limit to the amount of arrears that may be recovered by enforcement proceedings but the normal practice is not to allow more than one year's arrears to be recovered and to remit earlier arrears. The earlier cases were reviewed by the Court of Appeal in *Russell* v *Russell* [1986] 1 FLR 465. In that case Sir John Donaldson MR (at p. 473) noted that the rule of practice dated from the days when bank accounts and savings were much rarer than they are today and maintenance orders were literally a hand (or pocket) to mouth matter. The philosophy underlying the rule must therefore have been that if the complainant waited a year to seek enforcement of the order, she did not need the money, or at least had managed well enough without it, and the husband might reasonably regard the liability as something which he could forget about. He emphasised that this was not to say that the rule had changed in modern times when a wife might reasonably live on her savings for a period and expect to be reimbursed by a single large payment. However, it did point to the fact "that the courts should take account of the extent to which the complainant has sought to assert her rights". In that case the order for maintenance had been made within twelve months of the commencement of enforcement proceedings but had been backdated. This was held to justify a departure from the usual rule so as to permit enforcement of arrears attributable to a period more than twelve months before the complaint for enforcement. In *Dickens* v *Pattison* [1985] FLR 610 it was held that the mere fact that the person liable to pay the maintenance is an irregular or reluctant payer is not an unusual circumstance justifying a departure from the rule.

Where an order under Part I of the Domestic Proceedings and Magistrates' Courts Act 1978 has been registered in the High Court it is specifically provided that payment of arrears due more than twelve months before enforcement proceedings are begun cannot be recovered without leave of the court (DPMCA 1978, s.32(4)). This provision places such orders on the same footing as other orders enforceable in the High Court or a county court (see Part 4, below). Arrears due under an order at the date of death of the person liable to make payments are not recoverable (*Re Bidie* [1949] Ch 121).

## (i) Recovery of payments

A magistrates' court has no general power to order repayment of sums already paid in view of changes in the circumstances of the parties (*Fildes* v *Simkin* [1960] P 70). Payment to the clerk in his capacity of collecting officer is equivalent to payment to the wife. The clerk must remit to the wife payments received and has no power to withhold such payments pending determination of an appeal (*Board* v *Board* [1981] The Times 29 June. See s.29(3) of the Domestic Proceedings and Magistrates' Courts Act 1978 for the powers of the court to order payment by a recipient where an order for periodical payments is discharged on appeal or the amount of the payments are reduced on appeal). However, where an order under ss.2(1), 6 or 7 of the Domestic Proceedings and Magistrates' Courts Act 1978 making provision for a spouse continues in force after the marriage is dissolved or annulled, provision is now made for the recovery of payments made under such an order, or provision in an order, after it has ceased to have effect on the remarriage of the recipient, in the mistaken belief that it still subsists (Domestic Proceedings and Magistrates Courts Act 1978, s.35). No action can be brought against the recipient for recovery of such sums as having been paid under a mistake of fact, but an application can be made by the person who has made the payments or his personal representatives for an order for repayment against the recipient or her personal representatives. Such an application cannot be made to a magistrates' court, but may be made in proceedings in the High Court or a county court for leave to enforce or the enforcement of payment of arrears under the order, and otherwise to a county court. (This need not be to a divorce county court. A county court has jurisdiction irrespective of the amount involved: s.35(6).) The court may order the recipient or her personal representatives to pay to the applicant a sum equal to the amount of the payments made after cessation of the order or, if it appears to the court that it would be unjust to make that order, it may order payment of such lesser sum as it thinks fit or dismiss the application.

## 4. Registration of maintenance orders

### (a) The scope of registration

The Maintenance Orders Act 1958 introduced provisions enabling maintenance orders made by the High Court or a county court to be registered in a magistrates' court, and maintenance orders made in a magistrates' court to be registered in the High Court. Once an order has been registered, the court where it is registered ("the court of registration") can enforce the order in all respects as if the order had been made in that court, and as long as the registration is in force the order cannot be enforced in the court by which it was made ("the original court") (s.3). The object of registration is to facilitate enforcement, though it also enables a person entitled under an order of the High Court or a county court to take advantage of the role of the magistrates' clerk as collecting officer. The expression "maintenance order" includes:

(a) an order for periodical or other payments made, or having effect as if made, under Part II of the Matrimonial Causes Act 1973;

(b) an order for maintenance or other payments to or in respect of a spouse or child being an order made under Part I of the Domestic Proceedings and Magistrates' Courts Act 1978;

(c) orders under ss.11B, 11C or 11D of the Guardianship of Minors Act 1971 or s. 2(3) or 2(4)A of the Guardianship Act 1973;

(d) orders under s.6 of the Family Law Reform Act 1969;

(e) orders under s.106 of the Social Security Administration Act 1992;

(f) orders registered under the Maintenance Orders Act 1950, Part II (see below);

(g) orders registered in a magistrates' court under Part I of the Maintenance Orders (Reciprocal Enforcement) Act 1972, or Part I of the Civil Jurisdiction and Judgments Act 1982 (see below);

(h) orders under Part III of the Matrimonial and Family Proceedings Act 1984.

(Administration of Justice Act 1970, s.27 and Sched. 8 as amended).

## (b) Procedure

A person entitled to receive payments under an order of the High Court or a county court may apply to the court by which the order was made for registration of that order in a magistrates' court and the original court may, if it thinks fit, grant the application (Maintenance Orders Act 1958 s.2(1)). If the application is granted and the original court is satisfied either at that time or within 14 days thereafter that no proceedings for enforcement of the order remain pending or in force, a certified copy of the order will be sent to the clerk of the magistrates' court acting for the petty sessions area in which the defendant appears to be. On receipt of the certified copy the clerk must register the order in that court. If at the expiration of 14 days, the proceedings for enforcement are still pending in the original court, the grant of the application for registration becomes void. Where an application has been granted, no proceedings for enforcement may be commenced before registration of the order or the expiration of 14 days from the grant of the application, whichever first occurs (*ibid.* s.2(2)). An attachment of earnings order ceases to have effect upon the grant of the application (Attachment of Earnings Act 1971, s.11).

A person entitled to receive payment under a magistrates' court order who considers that the order could be more effectively enforced if it were registered, may apply to the court by which the order was made for registration of that order in the High Court (Maintenance Orders Act 1958, s.2(3)). In contrast to the High Court and county courts which have always had a discretion, a magistrates' court has been bound to grant the application on being satisfied that at the time when the application was made an amount equal to not less than four payments in the case of an order for weekly payments, or not less than two payments in the case of other orders, was due and unpaid. However, this was changed by the Civil Jurisdiction and Judgments Act 1982 which gives a magistrates' court a discretion whether or not to grant the application (Sched. 11 Part I, para 2). Where a magistrates' court order provides both for the payment of a lump sum and for the making of periodical payments, the person entitled to receive a lump sum under the order who considers that so far as it relates to the lump sum, the order could be more effectively enforced if it were registered may apply to the court by which the order was made for the registration of the order so far as it relates to the lump sum. The court has a discretion to grant the application, and if it does then registration takes effect in relation to that part of the order as if it were a separate order (s.2(3A) and (3B) inserted by the Civil Jurisdiction and Judgments Act 1982, Sched. 11 Part I para 2).

If the application for registration is granted no proceedings for the enforcement of the order can be started before the registration takes place, and no warrant or other process for the enforcement of the order can be issued in consequence of enforcement proceedings begun before the grant of the application. Any warrant of commitment issued for the enforcement of the order ceases to have effect when the person in possession of the warrant is informed of the grant of the application unless the defendant has then already been detained in pursuance of the warrant. A certified copy of the order will be sent to the prescribed officer of the High Court if the original court is satisfied that no process for the enforcement of the order issued before the grant of the application remains in force (*ibid.* s.2(4)). On receipt of such a certified copy the officer must cause the order to be registered (*ibid.* s.2(5)). An attachment of earnings order ceases to have effect on the grant of an application (Attachment of Earnings Act 1971, s.11).

### (c) Effect of registration

Generally once an order has been registered it is enforceable in all respects as if it had been made by the court in which it is registered and not in any other way (*ibid.* s.3(1) and (4)). Thus it is provided that an order registered in a magistrates' court shall be enforceable as if it were a magistrates' court maintenance order (s.3(2) as amended).

Where a High Court or county court order is registered in a magistrates' court then if a means of payment order under s.1(7) of the Maintenance Enforcement Act 1991 has effect in relation to the order in question, it will continue to have effect after registration. In any other case, the magistrates' court must order that all payments to be made under the order in question (including any arrears accrued before registration) must be made to the clerk of the court or the clerk of any other magistrates' court (s.2(6ZA) inserted by Maintenance Enforcement Act 1991, Sched. 1 para. 7). Where proceedings are brought for the enforcement of an order of the High Court or a county court registered in a magistrates' court, then the court may vary the order by exercising one of its powers under s.59(3) of the Magistrates' Courts Act 1980 to make a means of payment order (Magistrates' Courts Act 1980, s.76(4), (5) and (6) as amended by Maintenance Enforcement Act 1991, Sched 1, para 8). Where a magistrates' court order is registered in the High Court, then if payments under the order are required to be made (otherwise than to the clerk of a magistrates' court) by standing order or similar means under s.59(6) of the Magistrates' Courts Act 1980, any order requiring payment by that method will continue to have effect after registration. Any order by virtue of which sums payable under the magistrates' court order are required to be paid to the clerk of a magistrates' court (whether or not by standing order or similar means) on behalf of the person entitled thereto will cease to have effect (s.2(6)).

### (d) Variation of orders

The general principle is that only the original court can vary, revoke, suspend or revive a registered order. However, a rate of payments specified by an order of the High Court or a county court registered in a magistrates' court can only be varied by a magistrates' court, which may exercise the same jurisdiction to vary any rate of payments as is exercisable by the original court (*ibid.* s.4(1) and (2)). This does not apply if, at the time of the application to vary, one of the parties to the order is not present in England (*ibid.* s.4(2)). This power to vary now includes a power to vary the order by exercising one of its powers to make a means of payment order under s.59(3) of the Magistrates' Courts Act 1980 if the court is satisfied that payment has not been made in accordance with the order (s.4(2A) inserted by Maintenance Enforcement Act 1991, Sched. 1 para 9. See 3(a) above for means of payment orders).

If it appears appropriate to the court to which an application is made for variation of a rate of payments specified by a registered order in view of these limitations or for any other reason, it should remit the application to the original court which must then deal with it as if it had not been registered (Maintenance Orders Act 1958, s.4(4). See *Brown* v *Brown* (1973) 3 Family Law 41, and *Gsell* v *Gsell* [1971] 1 WLR 225). An application to vary any provision of the order other than the rate of payments or for revocation of the order must, of course, be made to the original court. No application for any variation of a registered order can be made to any court while proceedings for any variation of the order are pending in any other court (s.4(6)). Where a magistrates' court varies, or refuses to vary, a registered order, an appeal lies to the High Court (s.4(7)).

Where a magistrates' court order (other than one made under Part I of the Maintenance Orders (Reciprocal Enforcement) Act 1972) is registered in the High Court, then the High Court may exercise the same powers in relation to that order as are exercisable under s.1 of the Maintenance Enforcement Act 1991 in relation to a qualifying periodical maintenance order (s.4A inserted by Maintenance Enforcement Act 1991, Sched. 1, para 10).

### (e) Cancellation of registration

If a person entitled to receive payments under a registered order wants the registration to be cancelled, he may give notice to that effect to the court of registration which must cancel the registration if it is satisfied (a) that no process for the enforcement of the registered order issued before the giving of the notice remains in force, and (b) in the case of an order registered in a magistrates' court, that no proceedings for the variation of the order are pending in a magistrates' court (s.5(1) and (4)). Once such notice has been given, no proceedings for the enforcement of the registered order can be begun before cancellation of the registration and no writ, warrant or other process for the enforcement of the order can be issued in consequence of any such proceedings begun before the notice is given. Where the order is registered in a magistrates' court, any warrant of commitment issued for the enforcement of the order ceases to have effect when the person in possession of the warrant is informed of the giving of the notice, unless the defendant has then already been detained in pursuance of the warrant (s.5(4)). An attachment of earnings order ceases to have effect upon the giving of a notice with a view to cancellation (s.11). For the effect of cancellation on the method of payment, see s.5(5) as substituted by Maintenance Enforcement Act 1991, Sched. 1, para 11. If the High Court or a county court varies or discharges an order registered in a magistrates' court, the registration may be cancelled by the original court (Maintenance Orders Act 1958, s.5(2)). If a magistrates' court varies or discharges an order registered in the High Court it must direct cancellation of the registration if there are no arrears to be recovered (*ibid.* s.5(3)). For the effect of cancellation on the method of payment, see s.5(6) as substituted by Maintenance Enforcement Act 1991, Sched. 1, para 11).

## 5. Enforcement of orders in and from the United Kingdom

### (a) Registration

A maintenance order made by the High Court, a county court, or a magistrates' court in England or Wales may be registered in a court in another part of the United

Kingdom with a view to its enforcement there. Similarly a maintenance order made in another part of the United Kingdom may be registered in a court in England or Wales (Maintenance Orders Act 1950, Part II).

The expression "maintenance order" includes for this purpose the following orders made by courts in England and Wales (*ibid.* s.16 as amended):

(a) orders made under ss.22, 23(1), (2) and (4) and 27 of the Matrimonial Causes Act 1973 and s.14 or 17 of the Matrimonial and Family Proceedings Act 1984;

(b) orders made under Part I of the Domestic Proceedings and Magistrates' Courts Act 1978;

(c) orders made under the Children Act 1989;

(d) orders made under s.106 of the Social Security Administration Act 1992.

### (b) Procedure

Application for registration of an order must be made to the court by which the order was made. If it appears that the person liable to make payments under the order resides in another part of the United Kingdom, and that it is convenient that the order shall be enforceable there, a certified copy of the order will be sent to the prescribed officer of an equivalent court in that part of the United Kingdom for registration. Application for registration may be made either by or on behalf of the person entitled to the payments under the order or, where the payments are made to or through an officer of the court, by that officer on the request of the person entitled to the payments. An order can be registered in only one court at any one time (Maintenance Orders Act 1950, s.17).

### (c) The effect of registration

Once an order has been registered in a court in any part of the United Kingdom it may be enforced in that part of the United Kingdom in all respects as if it had been made by that court and as if that court had jurisdiction to make it. It can then only be enforced in the court of registration, and no proceedings with respect to enforcement can be taken elsewhere (Maintenance Orders Act 1950, s.18 as amended by the Maintenance Enforcement Act 1991, Sched. 1, para. 3).

### (d) Variation and discharge of registered orders

Generally a registered order may be varied or discharged only by the court by which it was made and not by the court in which it is registered (Maintenance Orders Act 1950, s.21). However, where an order is registered in a court of summary jurisdiction, the rate of payments under the order may be varied only by that court and not by the court which made it. (Thus there is no power to suspend the operation of the order.) This is subject to the limitation that no such variation may impose liability on the person liable to make payments under the order in excess of the maximum rate (if any) in force in that part of the United Kingdom in which the order was made (Maintenance Orders Act 1950, s.22. No maximum rates are now prescribed in England and Wales. For the position in relation to the method of payment, see the amendments introduced by the Maintenance Enforcement Act 1991, Sched. 1 para 5). When an order is registered in a court of summary jurisdiction, provision is made whereby the person liable to make payments under the order may give evidence to the court of registration for transmission to the original court hearing an application for variation or discharge. Similarly, the person entitled to payments under the order may give evidence to the original court for transmission to the court of registration hearing an application for variation in the rate of payments under the order (*ibid.* s.22(5)).

Application for cancellation of registration must be made to the court of registration (*ibid.* s.24).

## 6. Enforcement of orders outside the United Kingdom and orders and claims made outside the United Kingdom

*(a) Enforcement under Maintenance Orders (Facilities for Enforcement) Act 1920 and the Maintenance Orders (Reciprocal Enforcement) Act 1972*

(i) Scope

Maintenance orders made by a court in England and Wales may be enforced in certain Commonwealth countries specified by Order in Council under the Maintenance Orders (Facilities for Enforcement) Act 1920, and orders made in those countries may be enforced in a magistrates' court in England and Wales. It has been noted in Chapter 16 that provision for the repeal of the 1920 Act has been made in the Maintenance Orders (Reciprocal Enforcement) Act 1972 (s.22(2)), but this has not yet been effected. Part I of the 1972 Act makes provision for the reciprocal enforcement of maintenance orders made in the United Kingdom and in countries which have been designated by Order in Council as "reciprocating" for the purpose of the Act. (See Reciprocal Enforcement of Maintenance Orders (Designation of Reciprocating Countries) Orders 1974 (SI 1974 No. 556), 1975 (SI 1975 No. 2187) 1979 (SI 1979 No. 115) and 1983 (SI 1983 No. 1125).) When a country has been designated as a "reciprocating country" under Part I of the 1972 Act an order has also been made revoking the application of the 1920 Act to that country. Accordingly, the 1920 Act still applies to those countries designated under that Act that have not been designated as "reciprocating countries" under the 1972 Act. The machinery of the 1920 Act is similar to that of Part I of the 1972 Act considered below, though the powers of the court are narrower in some respects. Thus in contrast to the position under s.9 of the 1972 Act an English magistrates' court has no power to vary an overseas order registered under the 1920 Act.

It should be noted that Part II of the 1972 Act provides only for the transmission of claims for maintenance between the United Kingdom and the countries to which the United Nations Convention on the Recovery Abroad of Maintenance (1956) applies and which are designated by Order in Council as "convention countries" (see Chapter 16). There is no provision for the transmission of an existing order to a convention country or by a convention country to the United Kingdom. However, s.40 of the 1972 Act authorises the application by Order in Council of the provisions of the Act, with such exceptions, adaptations and modifications specified in the Order, to other arrangements relating to orders made in favour of, or against, persons resident outside the United Kingdom. Orders made under s.40 in respect of arrangements between the United Kingdom and the Republic of Ireland (Reciprocal Enforcement of Maintenance Orders (Republic of Ireland) Orders 1974 (SI 1974 No. 2140) and 1979 (SI 1979 No. 131)), and the Hague Convention Countries (Reciprocal Enforcement of Maintenance Orders (Hague Convention Countries) Order 1979 (SI 1979 No. 1317), 1983 (SI 1983 No. 885), 1983 (SI 1983 No. 1523), 1987 (SI 1987 No. 1282) provide for the reciprocal enforcement of maintenance orders (see *R* v *Clerkenwell Magistrates' Court, ex p. Scharff* March 6, 1985, Lexis Enggen). The countries are Czechoslovakia, Finland, France, Norway, Portugal, Sweden, Switzerland, Turkey, West Germany.

In *Macaulay* v *Macaulay* [1991] 1 WLR 179 the Divisional Court had to consider article 6(5) of the Reciprocal Enforcement of Maintenance Orders (Republic of Ireland) Order 1974 which provides that "an order shall not be registered ... (c) if the order is irreconcilable with a judgment given in the United Kingdom in proceedings between the same parties." The wife had obtained an order for maintenance against her husband in the Republic of Ireland which was based on the husband's obligation to maintain his wife. The marriage was subsequently dissolved by an English decree of divorce and so brought an end to the obligation on which the Irish order was based. The order should not therefore be registered in England. This was consistent with the decision of the European Court in *Hoffman* v *Krieg* [1988] ECR 645 in relation to a similar provision in the Brussels Convention given effect by the Civil Jurisdiction and Judgments Act 1982. Booth J did not consider that any injustice or hardship was caused to the wife as a result. The wife could apply at any time for financial orders under the Matrimonial Causes Act 1973 when the fact that there might be arrears owing to her under the Irish order would be one of the circumstances of the case to which the court would have regard ([1991] 1 WLR 179 at p. 186).

(ii) Enforcement under Part I of the 1972 Act

Where the person liable to make payments under a maintenance order made by a court in England or Wales resides or has assets in a reciprocating country, the person entitled to the payments may apply for the order to be sent to that country for enforcement. Application must be made to the prescribed officer of the court which made the order, and if he is satisfied that the person liable is resident or has assets in the reciprocating country, a certified copy of the order will be sent to the Secretary of State with a view to being transmitted to the responsible authority in that country (s.2). Conversely, an order made in a reciprocating country may be registered in a court in England and Wales, and it may then be enforced as if it had been made by the court of registration and as if that court had jurisdiction to make it (s.6. For the powers of a magistrates' court in England and Wales to make an order in relation to the means of payment, see s.7 as amended by the Maintenance Enforcement Act 1991, Sched. 1, para 12).

A "maintenance order" for this purpose means an order (however described) of any of the following descriptions:
 (a) an order (including an affiliation order or an order consequent upon an affiliation order) which provides for the payment of a lump sum or the making of

periodical payments towards the maintenance of any person, being a person whom the person liable to make payments under the order is, according to the law applied in the place where the order was made, liable to maintain; and

(b) an affiliation order or order consequent upon an affiliation order, being an order which provides for the payment by a person adjudged, found or declared to be a child's father, of expenses incidental to the child's birth or, where the child has died, of his funeral expenses.

(s.21(1) as amended by the Civil Jurisdiction and Judgments Act 1982, Sched. 11, para. 4).

In the case of a maintenance order which has been varied, it means that order as varied. Under the provisions of the Act of 1920 a maintenance order does not include an affiliation order (s.10)

An order made by a court in England or Wales which has been transmitted to a reciprocating country may be varied or revoked by the court which made the order (ss.2(5) and 5(1)). However, where it proposes to vary the order by increasing the rate of payments, then, unless either (a) both parties appear, or (b) the applicant appears and the other party has been served, the order varying the order must be a provisional order (s.5(3)). A provisional order has no effect unless and until confirmed with or without alteration by a competent court in the reciprocating country (s.21(1)). Where a provisional order is made by a court in a reciprocating country varying an order made by a court in England or Wales, the latter court may confirm the variation with or without alteration, or not at all.

In *Armitage* v *Nanchen* (1983) 4 FLR 293 the Divisional Court held that a magistrates' court in the United Kingdom could only refuse to register an order of a foreign court if it had been obtained by fraud or similar delinquency, or if the foreign law concerned was so offensive to the conscience of the English court that it would constitute an infraction of the rules of natural justice. In the Scottish case of *Killen* v *Killen* (1981) SLT 77 it was said that the court was not entitled to act as a court of appeal from the decision of the foreign court, or to substitute its own law and practice for that of the foreign court, or to criticise the way in which the foreign court has applied its own law and practice to the facts of the case as it found them. However, it was open to the court, if satisfied that it had ascertained the truth of the relevant facts, to make an alteration on the basis that the foreign court had been labouring under a misapprehension or mistake or ignorance as to the relevant facts on which its decision was based. In that case the judge in the Ontario court had expressly recognised in his judgment that he had no precise information before him about the income and financial responsibilities of the husband who resided in Scotland. The Scottish court remitted the order in favour of the wife to the Ontario court to give the wife an opportunity of giving evidence about the husband's statements as to his liability to maintain her. The order in respect of the child was confirmed at the weekly rate of $30 instead of $40 on the basis that if the relevant facts as to the husband's means had been known to the court in Ontario, it was reasonable to assume that the lower figure would have been awarded in accordance with the law and practice of that court. The position is different when the court is deciding whether a provisional order of variation or revocation should be confirmed. The court must then proceed as if the application for variation or revocation of the order had been made to that court (s.5(6)). In *Horn* v *Horn* [1985] FLR 984 where the court refused to confirm a provisional order of the magistrates' court in Gibraltar varying an order of an English court, Wood J said that s.5 gave the English court a wide discretion and this was confirmed by the provisions of ss.13 and 14 relating to evidence. In that case the registrar had formed the view that the husband had not been totally frank in his evidence to the court in Gibraltar. (See also *Re McKee* [1976] The Times 13 July.)

## (b) Enforcement under the Civil Jurisdiction and Judgments Act 1982

The Civil Jurisdiction and Judgments Act 1982 gives effect in the United Kingdom to the Brussels Convention of 27 September 1968 on jurisdiction and the enforcement of judgments in civil and commercial matters (together with the Protocol of 3 June 1971 on the interpretation of the Convention by the European Court, and as amended by the Convention of 9 October 1978 providing for the accession of Denmark, the Republic of Ireland and the United Kingdom to the 1968 Convention and the 1971 Protocol). The Act was brought into force in 1986.

Article 31 of the Convention provides that a judgment in a contracting state and enforceable in that state shall be enforced in another contracting state when, on the application of any interested party, the order for the enforcement has been issued there. In the United Kingdom such a judgment is to be enforced in England and Wales, in Scotland or in Northern Ireland when, on the application of any interested party it has been registered for enforcement in that part of the United Kingdom. In England and Wales an application must be submitted to the High Court except in the case of a maintenance judgment when it must be submitted to a magistrates' court (Article 32). A judgment, other than a maintenance order, is, to the extent that its enforcement is authorised by the High Court, to be registered in the prescribed manner in that court. The judgment is then of the same force and effect and may be enforced in the same way as if it had originally been given by the High Court (s.4(1) and (3)). Similarly, a maintenance order once registered in a magistrates' court is of the same force and effect and enforceable in the same way as if it had been originally made by that court (s.5. See the amendments introduced by the Maintenance Enforcement Act 1991 Sched. 1, para. 21 in relation to the means of payment). The procedures are set out in the Magistrates' Courts (Civil Jurisdiction and Judgments Act 1982) Rules 1986 (SI 1986 No. 1962) and are similar to those applicable under the Maintenance Orders (Reciprocal Enforcement) Act 1972.

Although the Act clearly applies to the enforcement of maintenance orders, the scope of its application is not free from uncertainties. These arise partly from the absence of any satisfactory definition of a maintenance order in the Act and the Conventions, and partly from the provisions of Article 1 of the Convention. This provides, *inter alia,* that the Convention shall not apply to "(1) the status or legal capacity of natural persons, rights in property arising out of a matrimonial relationship, wills and succession." The distinction between "maintenance" which is within the Convention and matters relating to matrimonial property which are excluded from the scope of the Convention is not easy to draw, especially in the context of English law. The Official Report on the Convention (the Schlosser Report, O.J 1979, c.59) acknowledges the difficulties and discusses the distinction in some detail.

In *de Cavel* v *de Cavel (No. 1)* [1979] 2 CMLR 547 the European Court (at p. 558) held that the term "rights in property arising out of matrimonial relationship" includes not only property arrangements specifically and exclusively envisaged by certain national legal systems in the case of marriage, but also any proprietary relationship resulting directly from the matrimonial relationship or the dissolution thereof. Thus disputes relating to the assets of spouses in the course of proceedings for divorce may, depending on the circumstances, concern or be closely connected with:

(a) questions relating to the status of persons; or
(b) proprietary legal relationships between spouses resulting directly from the matrimonial relationship or its dissolution; or
(c) proprietary legal relations existing between them which have no connection with the marriage.

Whereas disputes of the third category fall within the scope of the Convention, those relating to the first two categories are excluded from it.

These considerations apply to measures relating to the property of spouses whether they are provisional or definitive in nature. As provisional protective measures relating to property, such as the freezing of assets, may serve to safeguard a variety of rights, their inclusion in the scope of the Convention is determined not by their own nature but by the nature of the rights which they serve to protect. In *de Cavel* the husband had obtained in divorce proceedings in France "protective measures" relating to certain property situated in Germany. These measures were excluded from the scope of the Convention and accordingly not enforceable in Germany. This approach was also adopted by the European Court in *C.H.W.* v *G.J.H.* [1983] 2 CMLR 125.

It seems that "maintenance" is not confined to periodical payments, but may extend to orders for lump sum payments. This view was taken in the Schlosser Report which defined maintenance in terms of financial support as compared with compensation for loss of marital status. In the judgment of the European Court in *de Cavel* v *de Cavel (No.2)* [1980] 3 CMLR 1 at p. 5 it is stated that "compensatory payments" provided for in s.270 *et seq.* of the French Civil Code were in the nature of maintenance, being concerned with financial obligations between former spouses after divorce and fixed on the basis of their respective needs and resources. In that case it was held that the orders of the French court providing for the making of monthly payments by the husband to the wife were enforceable as maintenance orders under the Convention. Unfortunately the position may not be so clear in relation to orders under the Matrimonial Causes Act 1973 where orders for lump sum payments and transfer of property orders may be concerned with the reallocation of property as well as with financial support.

It was also confirmed in *de Cavel* v *de Cavel (No.2)* that the Convention applies to maintenance awarded as ancillary relief in proceedings for divorce even though the divorce is excluded from the scope of the Convention as a matter relating to individual status. The court said (at p. 6) that ancillary claims come within the scope of the Convention according to the subject-matter with which they are concerned, and not according to the subject-matter involved in the principal claim.

Article 27(3) provides that a judgment shall not be recognised if it is irreconcilable with a judgment given in a dispute between the same parties in the State in which recognition is sought. The scope of this provision was considered by the European Court on a reference from the High Court of the Netherlands in *Hoffman* v *Krieg* [1988] ECR 645 where it was held that it was possible to plead that a German maintenance order was irreconcilable with a subsequent Netherlands decree of divorce and consequently no longer enforceable in the Netherlands. (See also *Macaulay* v *Macaulay* [1991] 1 WLR 179 where a similar provision in the Reciprocal Enforcement of Maintenance Orders (Republic of Ireland) Order 1974 was considered.)

# Chapter 23

# Anti-avoidance provisions

## 1. Applications under the Matrimonial Causes Act 1973

*(a) The problem and possible remedies*
A spouse may attempt to defeat a claim for financial provision or an adjustment of property rights under the Matrimonial Causes Act 1973 by reducing his financial resources and assets in the hope of persuading the court that he is unable to afford to make provision - either at all or, at any rate, beyond a certain level. In the same way he may seek to frustrate or, at any rate, impede the enforcement of an existing order.

The court has generally been able to counter the most obvious tactic, namely a deliberate reduction of income, by taking into account potential earning capacity in deciding the appropriate amount of maintenance (see Chapter 11). It has also been able to take into account the fact that a person who appears to have no income is being supported by a person to whom he has transferred the bulk of his assets (*Donaldson* v *Donaldson* [1958] 2 All ER 660). Where an order for maintenance had been made it also had power to restrain a disposition designed to frustrate the enforcement of that order (*Wright* v *Wright* [1954] 1 WLR 534). In 1958 the court was given power to restrain or set aside transfers of assets so as to preserve capital pending the making of an order (Matrimonial Causes (Property and Maintenance) Act 1958, s.2). The power to restrain and avoid dispositions by means of what are known as "avoidance of disposition orders" was widened by the Matrimonial Proceedings and Property Act 1970, and is now contained in s.37 of the Matrimonial Causes Act 1973. The provisions relating to such orders are considered in the next section.

If the conditions for the making of an avoidance of disposition order are not satisfied the court has an inherent jurisdiction to preserve specific assets which are the subject-matter of proceedings, pending determination of the issues involved. Thus the court may grant an injunction restraining the other party from removing liquid assets out of the jurisdiction pending a hearing. In *Roche* v *Roche* (1981) 11 Fam Law 243 the Court of Appeal upheld an order restraining the respondent husband from disposing of one-quarter of the proceeds of his claim for damages against two defendants for serious personal injuries. This decision was followed by Anthony Lincoln J in *Shipman* v *Shipman* [1991] 1 FLR 250. He took the view that *Roche* v *Roche* was not affected by the comments of Lord Hailsham LC in *Richards* v *Richards* [1984] AC 174 at p. 179 in relation to the inherent power of the court to grant injunctions in a rather different context. There had been no express disapproval of the decision in *Richards* v *Richards* and it was accordingly binding on the court. It had also been followed by Sheldon J in *Walker* v *Walker* (1983) 4 FLR 455. Accordingly Anthony Lincoln J upheld an order restraining the husband from disposing of or dealing with $300,000 or one half of his severance pay (whichever was the greater) pending the outcome of the wife's application for ancillary relief.

### (b) Avoidance of disposition orders

A person who brings proceedings for financial relief may apply for an "avoidance of disposition order" against the other party to the proceedings (Matrimonial Causes Act 1973, s.37(2)). Such an order may take one of three forms depending on the circumstances.

(1) If the court is satisfied that the other party is about to make any disposition or to transfer out of the jurisdiction or otherwise deal with any property with the intention of defeating the claim for financial relief, it may make such order as it thinks fit for restraining the other party from so doing or otherwise for protecting the claim. (See *Quartermain* v *Quartermain* (1974) 118 SJ 597. In *Ex p. Matthews* (1964) 108 SJ 749 the court had granted an injunction restraining an executor from sending to a husband resident abroad the share to which the husband was entitled under his mother's will. There is no reference to the court's statutory powers.) The court must be satisfied that a dealing in the property is about to take place and this is a question of fact. A "dealing" for this purpose means some positive act and does not cover a failure to deal with property (*Crittenden* v *Crittenden* [1990] 2 FLR 361 at pp. 365-366). The section makes no distinction between property which is easily disposable and property which is less easily disposable. It does not imply that the court must freeze a husband's freely disposable assets pending the determination of the wife's claim for financial provision. Thus, in *Smith* v *Smith* (1973) 117 SJ 525 the husband had lived for many years in the house which was part of the subject-matter of the application and there was no evidence that he was about to dispose of the house or the money which was also the subject-matter of the application. An order was refused. The court should not make an order for payment of the money in dispute to the applicant, especially on an *ex parte* application (see *Jackson* v *Jackson* (1979) 9 Fam Law 56).

(2) If the court is satisfied that the other party has made a disposition with the intention of defeating the claim for financial relief, and that if the disposition were set aside financial relief, or different financial relief, would be granted to the applicant, it may make an order setting aside the disposition.

Where the spouses had resumed cohabitation by the time the matter was considered by the court, there was no ground for financial relief being granted so that one of the statutory ingredients had ceased to exist and a disposition could not be set aside (*Chhokar* v *Chhokar* [1984] FLR 313).

(3) If the court is satisfied, in a case where an order for financial relief has been obtained by the applicant against the other party, that the latter has made a disposition with the intention of defeating the claim for financial relief, it may make an order setting aside the disposition.

Where the court has made an order under (2) or (3) setting aside a disposition it must give such consequential directions as it thinks fit for giving effect to the order (including directions requiring the making of any payments or the disposal of any property) (s.37(3)). In *Green* v *Green* [1981] 1 All ER 97 Eastham J held that the court's power to give consequential directions was restricted to giving directions requiring, for example, the repayment of any money which had been paid under the conveyance which had been set aside. It was not wide enough to enable the court to give directions such as those sought by the wife in that case, for setting aside or reducing a charge made by the transferee under a conveyance set aside under s.37. This would also deprive the chargee of the statutory defence in s.37(4) (see below). In fact the conveyance to the chargor in *Green* v *Green* could not be set aside under s.37 on the application of the wife (who had been a party to the conveyance).

Where the court declines to make an order setting aside the disposition of a property, it is doubtful whether the court can make an order in respect of the proceeds of sale of the property (*per* Butler-Sloss LJ in *Sherry* v *Sherry* [1991] 1 FLR 307 at p. 315). In *Sherry* v *Sherry* the disposition of one particular property could not be set aside because it had already been sold by the purchaser. The direction of the judge at first instance that the respondent husband pay the original proceeds of sale to the wife's solicitors was not part of the order made by the Court of Appeal.

*(c) Claims which may be protected*

An application for an avoidance of disposition order may be made in order to protect claims for the following financial relief (s.37(1)):

(1) maintenance pending suit;

(2) periodical payments, secured periodical payments, lump sum payments, transfers of property, settlements of property and variation of settlements, whether by a spouse or by, or for the benefit of, a child of the family, in proceedings for divorce, nullity or judicial separation;

(3) provision on the ground of failure to provide reasonable maintenance under s.27 of the Matrimonial Causes Act 1973;

(4) variation of existing orders for any of the foregoing (except an application to vary a secured periodical payments order after the death of the person liable to make the payments); and

(5) alteration of maintenance agreements.

*(d) Dispositions which may be restrained or set aside*

The term "disposition" includes any conveyance, assurance or gift of property of any description, whether made by an instrument or otherwise, but does not include any provision contained in a will or codicil (s.37(6)). In the recent case of *Shipman* v *Shipman* [1991] 1 FLR 250 at p.252 Anthony Lincoln J rejected the argument that a disposition for this purpose can only be to a third party. He accepted the view that if the husband in that case used the asset in question, namely severance pay, as a deposit on the purchase of a house or to maintain himself or to pay off existing debts, he would be disposing of the asset. He would "be 'dealing with' the money, an activity caught by the section". This appears to be at variance with the view expressed by Ormrod LJ in *Roche* v *Roche* (1981) 11 Fam Law 243 that: "The essence of s.37 is that it deals with dispositions made by a party to a third party. It does not deal with the situation of the husband (or wife, as the case may be) disposing of their assets in a way which would make it difficult for the other party to recover any sum awarded and make it difficult for the court to deal with the case." In both cases the court was, in any event, not satisfied that the necessary intention to defeat the wife's claim was present. No order was made under s.37 in either case, but an order was made under the court's inherent jurisdiction (see above).

In *H* v *H* and *W* v *Barclays Bank Ltd* (1980) 10 Fam Law 152 it was held that the act of paying in a cheque representing the net proceeds of sale of the husband's business into a bank account in the name of the business in partial reduction of an overdraft was not a disposition by the husband of personal funds. Although the cheque was made out to the husband it represented funds due to the creditors of the business.

Before the Matrimonial Proceedings and Property Act 1970 no disposition could be set aside if it had been made more than three years before the date of the application. This restriction no longer applies, though dispositions which had ceased to be liable to avoidance under the former provisions are safeguarded by a prohibition against applications with respect to dispositions made before 1 January 1968 (s.37(7)). A disposition may not be set aside if it was made for valuable consideration (other than marriage) to a person who, at the time of the disposition, acted in relation to it in good faith and without notice of any intention on the part of the other party to defeat a claim for financial relief (s.37(4)).

In *Sherry* v *Sherry* [1991] 1 FLR 307 one of the dispositions could not be set aside because the property had been sold by the purchaser to a second purchaser. However, Beldam LJ said (at p. 322) that if the first purchaser had been acting in collusion with the husband and had disposed of the property to a person with actual or constructive notice of the husband's intention, the court would have had to consider whether it could regard the subsequent disposition made by the purchaser as in reality made on the husband's behalf and so as a disposition by the husband which could be set aside. That was not the case in *Sherry* v *Sherry*.

The notice that is relevant in this context is notice of a "dishonest intent" on the part of the spouse who has made the disposition, and not notice of the applicant's interest, if any, in the asset disposed of, or of the applicant spouse's application for financial provision or transfer of property.

It has been noted earlier that in *Whittingham* v *Whittingham* [1979] Fam 9 it was held that a wife's claim for a transfer of property order was registrable as a pending land action under s.5(1)(a) of the Land Charges Act 1972 and therefore if not registered was not binding on a mortgagee bank. In the Court of Appeal it was conceded by the wife that on that basis (if that was so) her appeal against the refusal of Balcombe J to set aside the bank's mortgage failed. (At first instance Balcombe J had also found that the bank did not have constructive notice, at the time of the mortgage, of the husband's intention to defeat the wife's claim for ancillary relief.

However, this was not discussed in the Court of Appeal where Eveleigh LJ expressly left open the question of the relationship between s.37(4) and notice in s.199(1) of the Law of Property Act 1925. Stamp LJ stressed the advantage to the wife of registrability of her application (as was subsequently illustrated in *Perez-Adamson* v *Perez-Rivas* [1987] Fam 89) and said (at p. 21) that if her application was not registrable "... she is placed in the unenviable position of having to establish that a transaction which subsequently takes place by way of sale or mortgage is a reviewable disposition within s.37, involving litigation in which the good faith of the purchaser or mortgagee and the question of whether he had notice of the wife's intention fall to be considered". In any event the wife's application for financial relief may not be made until some time after the disposition which it is sought to set aside. This occurred in *Kemmis* v *Kemmis* [1988] 1 WLR 1307 where the Court of Appeal drew a clear distinction between protection of the wife's application by registration, which makes it binding on a subsequent purchaser or mortgagee, and notice of the husband's intention to defeat her claim which it is necessary to show if a disposition is to be set aside under s.37 where there has been no registration. Purchas LJ said (at p. 235) that "... if the bank had either actual or constructive notice of the husband's intention to prejudice the powers to make orders for financial relief, the court's powers under s.37 should not be frustrated by the failure to register a *lis pendens* by the wife. If this were so then other innocent parties such as dependent children would be affected through no fault of theirs. The laws, statutory and common law, relating to competing interests in land are, in my judgment, not directly imported into the powers given by s.37 of the 1973 Act".

The court did, however, accept that a third party might be affected by constructive notice, and referred to the principles of constructive notice in property law by way of analogy. It was emphasised that it is not enough to say that the third party disponee had failed to make such enquiries as ought reasonably to have been made. It is also not enough to say that if it had made such enquiries, it would not, or might not, have entered into the transaction. "The question is whether if it had made such enquiries, the intention of the husband to defeat the wife's claim would have come to its knowledge" (*per* Lloyd LJ at p. 1328). In *Kemmis* v *Kemmis* the judge had found that the mortgagee bank knew that the wife was in occupation of the mortgaged property and that the mortgagor husband was not. Applying the doctrine of constructive notice the mortgagee ought reasonably to have made enquiry of the wife, but the only form which the enquiry could reasonably have taken, said Nourse LJ, was to ask whether she claimed any, and if so what, right or interest adverse to the husband's proposed mortgage. She had no such interest and the Court of Appeal took the view that there was therefore no interest of which the mortgagee could have had constructive notice. Moreover, Nourse LJ said (at p. 1334) that although the husband had an intention to defeat a future claim by the wife for financial relief, "the wife's consequential right to have the mortgage restrained or set aside was ... of such an inchoate and evanescent nature as to make it incapable of existence for the purposes of the doctrine of constructive notice." Lloyd LJ asked whether, if enquiries had been made of the wife, she would have said anything more than that she had a beneficial interest in the property. Would she in 1980 (some three years before the divorce) have said anything to throw doubt on the husband's intentions?

He found it a difficult question but in the end "was not persuaded that such enquiries as the bank should have made in 1980 would, in 1980, have led to the bank discovering the husband's intention". (See p. 1328.)

In contrast, in *Sherry* v *Sherry* [1991] 1 FLR 307 the court found that a purchaser of several properties from the husband did have constructive notice of the husband's intention of defeating his wife's claim for financial relief. The search made by the solicitors acting for the purchaser in relation to some of the properties disclosed inhibitions registered in accordance with an injunction obtained by the wife restraining the husband from selling the properties. The purchases were completed on the strength of an order discharging the injunctions produced by the husband. The Court of Appeal held that the production of the order, while a factor which could be taken into account in deciding whether a bona fide purchaser had constructive notice of the husband's intention, was not overriding or of decisive weight. Beldam LJ said (at p. 322): "The mere fact that an asset is released from an injunction cannot be taken to imply that the party who formerly sought to restrain the disposition had abandoned all claims to an interest in the proceeds of sale".

The presence of the inhibitions had raised doubts in the mind of the solicitor and the purchaser, as a friend of the husband, knew in quite some detail of the matrimonial dispute between the husband and wife. A simple question to the wife's solicitors or to the solicitors acting for the husband in matrimonial matters would have made the position clear.

### (e) Property affected

An avoidance of disposition order can only be made in respect of property in which either or both of the parties to the marriage has or had a beneficial interest, either in possession or in reversion. Thus an order cannot be made in relation to a dealing with the property of a company in which the spouses, or one of them, have shares though it could be made in relation to the shares in such a company held by one of the spouses (*per* Dillon LJ in *Crittenden* v *Crittenden* [1990] 2 FLR 361 at p. 365).

In *Hamlin* v *Hamlin* [1985] 2 All ER 1037 it was held that the court may make an order restraining a respondent from disposing of property of any kind situated outside the jurisdiction. Such an order does not operate directly on the property but is directed to the respondent and if he or she is within the jurisdiction or otherwise amenable to the court's coercive powers there is no difficulty. If he or she is not, then different considerations arise (though in relation to property situated within the jurisdiction there are now also additional powers under s.37(3) Supreme Court Act 1981). There is a crucial difference between the jurisdiction of the court to make orders and the question whether the jurisdiction should in fact be exercised in a given case as a matter of discretion. In the exercise of their discretion English courts will not make orders which they cannot enforce. It follows that in relation to property situated abroad, even if the parties are present within the jurisdiction, the courts will in general not make any order whose effectiveness depends on its recognition or enforcement by the courts or other authorities abroad if the evidence shows that this would be denied. However, such matters are relevant to discretion and not to jurisdiction. In *Hamlin* the Court of Appeal held that the court did have power to grant an order under s.37(2)(a) that the husband be restrained from disposing of a

Anti-avoidance provisions

villa in Spain worth £50,000/£60,000, which was in the husband's name and consti-tuted virtually the only unmortgaged capital asset of the marriage. The husband intended to sell it to pay off debts of some £25,000, stating that this was necessary to avoid bankruptcy. The case was remitted to the county court for a decision on the merits.

*(f) The intention to defeat a claim*

The court must be satisfied that a disposition was made, or is about to be made, with the intention of defeating the applicant's claim for financial relief before it can make an order setting aside or restraining that disposition, as the case may be. It is provid-ed that any reference to defeating an applicant's claim for financial relief is a refer-ence to preventing financial relief from being granted to the applicant, or to the applicant for the benefit of a child of the family, or reducing the amount of any financial relief which might be so granted, or frustrating, or impeding the enforce-ment of any order which might be, or has been, made at the instance of the applicant (s.37(1)).

Where an application is made in respect of a disposition which took place within the preceding three years, and the court is satisfied that the disposition would have the effect of defeating the applicant's claim for financial relief, or, where an order for financial relief has already been obtained, has had that effect, there is a presump-tion that the disposition was made with the intention of defeating such a claim. There is a similar presumption where an application is made in respect of a disposi-tion which is about to take place, and the court is satisfied that the disposition would have the effect of defeating the applicant's claim for financial relief (s.37(5). See *Shipman* v *Shipman* [1991] 1 FLR 250 where the presumption raised by subs.(5) was rebutted on the evidence). On the other hand, although an application can now be made in respect of a disposition made more than three years before the date of the application, the onus is on the applicant to prove that such a disposition was made with the intention of defeating his or her claim for financial relief (s.37(5)).

The court is concerned with the subjective intention of the party against whom an order is sought. It is his state of mind which has to be investigated, not the conse-quence of his acts. However, in determining whether a spouse has or had the requi-site state of mind, a court may have regard to the natural consequences of his act. Generally the natural consequence of the disposition would not be enough by itself to support an inference of intention, but it would certainly be a factor to be taken into account in deciding whether or not to draw the inference of intention in any given case (*per* Lloyd LJ in *Kemmis* v *Kemmis* [1988] 1 WLR 1307 at p. 1326). In *Kemmis* v *Kemmis* Nourse LJ (at p. 1331) said that the intention of defeating a claim for financial provision did not have to be the spouse's sole or even his domi-nant intention. It was enough if it played a substantial part in his intentions as a whole. If it were otherwise, s.37(2) would fail to catch the case where a husband makes a disposition with the dominant intention of gratifying his mistress and only the subsidiary intention of defeating his wife's claim for financial relief.

In *K* v *K (Avoidance of Reviewable Disposition)* (1983) 4 FLR 31 the Court of Appeal took the view that the word "satisfied" should be given its ordinary meaning without the addition of any adverbial phrase or qualification such as "beyond reasonable doubt" or "on the balance of probability": see Ormrod LJ adopting statements made in *Blyth* v *Blyth* [1966] AC 643 by Lord Pearce at p. 672 and Lord Pearson at p. 676. In *Kemmis* v *Kemmis* Nourse LJ (at p. 1331) rejected a submission that the standard of proof was higher than proof on the balance of probabilities, though, since what had to be proved was not merely a dishonourable intention but a dishonest and fraudulent one, the evidence which was required to tip the balance had to be correspondingly more convincing.

## 2. Inheritance (Provision for Family and Dependants) Act 1975

*(a) The "net estate" from which provision can be ordered*
A person may also attempt to defeat a claim for financial provision out of his estate after his death by disposing of his property *inter vivos*. Provision under the Inheritance (Provision for Family and Dependants) Act 1975 can only be ordered out of the "net estate" of the deceased. This means, in the first place, "all property of which the deceased had power to dispose by his will (otherwise than by virtue of a special power of appointment) less the amount of his funeral, testamentary and administration expenses, debts and liabilities, including any inheritance tax payable out of his estate on his death" (Inheritance (Provision for Family and Dependants) Act 1975, s.25(1)). Under the previous legislation no other property was included. Thus the "net estate" did not include property disposed of *inter vivos* by the deceased (see *Re Carter* (1968) 112 SJ 136), property nominated by him, property which was the subject of a *donatio mortis causa* made by him, or the deceased's beneficial interest as a joint tenant which accrued automatically to the surviving joint tenant(s). The Act of 1975 has extended the definition of "net estate" to prevent these and other devices being used to avoid a claim under the Act. In some cases property is automatically made part of the "net estate" while in other cases an order of the court is necessary as outlined below.

*(b) Pension funds*
There remain certain assets which become available on a person's death which do not form part of his net estate for this purpose. This will usually be the case in relation to a death benefit payable under an occupational pension scheme of which the deceased was a member. If the deceased member's estate is entitled to payment of such a sum it will, of course, form part of his net estate. In the majority of cases payment of such a sum is likely to be in the discretion of the trustees of the pension fund. In these circumstances the payment will not form part of the net estate even though the deceased was entitled or required to nominate a beneficiary to whom the sum should be paid. The power of an employee member to dispose of the death benefit is usually strictly circumscribed. Thus in *Re Cairnes (deceased)* (1983) 4 FLR 225 the nomination could only be made in favour of certain classes of persons and had to be made on a special form. It also required the consent of the employer company, as did its revocation or alteration. Anthony Lincoln J concluded that the fund was in the power of the trustees, and that the employee had a contractual right enforceable against the trustees as to what they could do in disposing of the fund.

He himself could not dispose of or exercise any power relating to the fund. He could only name third parties to whom the trustees could dispose of the fund. The death benefit was not part of the net estate though it was acknowledged that the position might be different where the rules of the scheme were different. On the other hand, if there had been no effective nomination and no surviving widow, the death benefit would have passed to his personal representatives and would have formed part of the net estate.

Even though a payment from a pension fund does not form part of the net estate, the fact that it has been paid can be taken into account by the court. Thus, in *Re Crawford (deceased)* (1983) 4 FLR 273 on the application of the deceased's former wife the court had regard to the fact that the deceased's second wife had received a substantial lump sum as a result of the exercise of discretion by the trustees of a pension fund. This lump sum, together with the pensions received by the second wife and the children of the second marriage, were financial resources within s.3(1)(c) of the 1975 Act. (See also *Jessop* v *Jessop* [1992] 1 FLR 591.)

### (c) Nominated property
Money or property nominated by the deceased under any enactment is to be treated for the purposes of the 1975 Act as part of the net estate of the deceased (s.8(1)). In order to facilitate payment without delay a person who pays out money in accordance with the directions given in the nomination is not liable to the applicant for having done so, but the nominee is then liable to make the nominated sum available to meet a claim under the Act if the court so orders (after deducting therefrom any inheritance tax paid in respect of the nominated property). Section 8 applies only to statutory nominations and not to non-statutory nominations under private occupational pension schemes.

### (d) Donatio mortis causa
Where a sum of money or other property is received by a person as a *donatio mortis causa*, that sum of money or that property is to the extent of the value thereof at the date of the deceased's death, after deducting in either case any tax payable, to be automatically treated as part of the net estate of the deceased donor for the purposes of the 1975 Act (s.8(2)). A person who pays money or transfers property in order to give effect to a *donatio mortis causa* is protected from liability for having done so, but the donee is, of course, liable to make the subject-matter available if the court so orders.

### (e) Joint property
Where a deceased person was immediately before his death beneficially entitled to a joint tenancy of any property, his severable share in such property can now be made available under s.9 to meet an order for financial provision under the 1975 Act. It does not automatically form part of the "net estate" for this purpose, but where an application is made for an order for financial provision under s.2 of the Act, the court may order that the deceased's severable share of property of which immediately before his death he was a beneficial joint tenant shall, in whole or in part, be treated as part of the net estate of the deceased. An order of the court is, therefore,

necessary, and can only be made when an application for an order under s.2 is made within the period prescribed by s.4 for such applications, namely six months from the date on which representation with respect to the estate of the deceased was first taken out (see Chapter 21). Under s.4 the court has power to permit an application under s.2 to be made after that period has expired, but if it does so, no order can be made under s.9. Similarly, on an application under s.6 of the Act to vary an existing order no order can be made under s.9.

For the avoidance of doubt it is declared that for the purpose of s.9 there may be a joint tenancy of a chose in action (s.9(4)). This means that a joint bank account is within the scope of s.9. A person who acts in relation to the property concerned without taking into account the possibility that an order might be made under s.9 is protected (s.9(3)). This will protect a bank paying money to the surviving customer in accordance with the terms on which the account was held. This does not prevent an order being made against the surviving customer to whom the bank has paid money.

Although s.9 provides that an order can be made "for the purpose of facilitating the making of financial provision for the application", the court's discretion to treat the deceased's severable share as part of the "net estate" can and should be exercised at each stage of the consideration of an application under s.2. Thus the exercise of that discretion should not be deferred until the court is deciding what order should be made, but should be exercised when the court is dealing with the preliminary issue as to whether reasonable financial provision has been made for the applicant. In *Kourkgy* v *Lusher* (1983) 4 FLR 65 at p. 80 Wood J said: "If the court did not exercise its discretion at the earlier stage under s.3 the usefulness of s.9 would be seriously curtailed and the mischief at which I believe that section to be aimed, namely, hardship caused in some instances by the principle of survivorship, would not be met". He took the example of an application by a cohabitee who had two children by the deceased where the net estate without the severable share was worth £1,000, and the former matrimonial home vested in the joint names of the deceased and his wife was worth £300,000. If the house was too large for the widow and she could move into a smaller home also in joint names so that the larger home could be sold, and there were no children of the marriage, he would exercise his discretion to include the severable share. If the discretion was exercised "the value of the net estate would thus be increased from £1,000 to £160,000" (sic). This might make all the difference not only to facilitating the making of an order, but in deciding whether an order should be made, or whether the deceased had failed to make reasonable financial provision.

There are no specific principles to guide the court in deciding whether or not to exercise its discretion under s.9. In *Re Crawford* (1983) 4 FLR 273 at p. 280 Eastham J said that s.9 "contains everything which is necessary for the purpose of guiding the court in deciding whether or not to exercise its discretion and as to the appropriate amount in respect of which it ought to exercise its discretion ...". In that case he made an order that £35,000, being the deceased's half share in a lump sum placed by him in joint accounts, be treated as part of the net estate. This provided the whole of the lump sum which he ordered to be paid to the former wife - this order provided reasonable financial provision for her and left the provisions of the deceased's will largely unaffected so far as the beneficiaries were concerned. In *Jessop* v *Jessop* [1992] 1 FLR 591, the Court of Appeal ordered that the deceased's severable share in the property occupied by him and his cohabitee should be treated as part of his net estate to the extent of £10,000. The court took into account the fact that the cohabitee had received almost £40,000 from the deceased's pension fund, and so ordered payment of a lump sum of £10,000 to the widow. (See also *Re McBroom, (deceased)* [1992] 2 FLR 49 and *Powell* v *Osborne* [1993] 1 FLR 1001.)

### (f) Inter vivos dispositions

Where a person has made an application for financial provision under s.2 of the Act, he or she may apply for an order under s.10 against any person to whom, or for the benefit of whom, a disposition was made by the deceased less than six years before his death. Such an order will not provide for the disposition to be "set aside" as this might raise difficult problems where the subject-matter of the disposition has passed into the hands of third parties before the deceased's death (see the position under s.37 Matrimonial Causes Act 1973 above). Instead an order under s.10 may require the donee to provide money or other property out of which a claim for financial provision may be satisfied. It is, therefore, not necessary that the donee should still be the owner of, or still be entitled to the benefit of, the property disposed of in his favour, but his liability is limited to the amount of money given to him or paid for his benefit, or the value of the property given to him at the deceased's death or earlier disposal by him (s.10(3) and (4)).

An order under s.10 can be made only if the court is satisfied:

(a) that the disposition was made by the deceased with the intention of defeating an application for financial provision under the Act; and

(b) that full valuable consideration for the disposition was not given by the donee or by any other person; and

(c) that the exercise of the powers conferred by s.10 would facilitate the making of financial provision for the applicant under the Act.

The onus is always on the applicant to show that the disposition was made by the deceased with the intention of defeating an application for financial provision under the Act. There is no presumption as to the deceased's intention to defeat an application for financial provision similar to that which applies in applications under s.37 of the Matrimonial Causes Act 1973 in respect of dispositions within three years of the application. The intention will be established if the court is of opinion, on a balance of probabilities, that in making the disposition, it was the intention of the deceased (though not necessarily his sole intention) to prevent an order for financial provision being made under the Act, or to reduce the amount of the provision which might otherwise be granted by an order under the Act (s.12(1)).

In *Re Dawkins* [1986] 2 FLR 360 the deceased, a little over a year before his death, had transferred the house in which he lived with his second wife, to his daughter by his previous marriage. This rendered ineffective the gift to the wife of a life interest in the house under his existing will though in any event he subsequently made a will leaving all his estate to his daughter. More significantly, the transfer, by removing the principal asset from his estate, had the effect of making the estate insolvent at the time of his death. It was conceded that if the house had still formed part of his estate at his death then the disposition of his estate would not have been such as to make reasonable provision for his widow and that provision for her would have had to have been made. Bush J thought that when the deceased had sold the house to his daughter for £100 he may have been persuading himself that since the widow had released her life interest in her previous home to her sons for £5,000 then he ought to preserve his own house for the benefit of his daughter and perhaps eventually his grandson. Nevertheless, Bush J was satisfied that the transfer had been made with the intention, though not necessarily the sole intention, of preventing an order for financial provision being made under the Act, or reducing the amount of provision which might otherwise have been granted. He made an order under s.10 that the daughter provide from the proceeds of the house (which had been sold for £27,000) the sum of £10,000 which was the appropriate lump sum for the widow to receive. Valuable consideration for this purpose does not include marriage or a promise of marriage (s.25(1)).

A "disposition" for the purpose of s.10 is widely defined (s.10(7)). It does not include any provision in a will, for property so disposed of is already available to meet a claim for financial provision under the Act. Similarly, property which is the subject-matter of a nomination or a *donatio mortis causa* is already available to meet such a claim (s.8. See above) and such dispositions are also excluded from the ambit of s.10. It is also specifically provided that it does not include any appointment made *inter vivos* in the exercise of a special power of appointment. (It does include an appointment made *inter vivos* in exercise of a general power of appointment. For the position in relation to powers of appointment see (*h*) below.) Subject to this, a "disposition" includes "any payment of money (including the payment of a premium under a policy of assurance) and any conveyance, assurance, appointment or gift of property of any description whether made by an instrument or otherwise" (s.10(7)).

In *Clifford* v *Tanner* June 10, 1986 Lexis Enggen, a father had transferred the house in which he lived with his second wife to his daughter by a previous marriage. The daughter had covenanted, *inter alia*, to allow her stepmother to reside in the house after the death of her father, but shortly before his death the father executed a deed releasing his daughter from that covenant. The Court of Appeal held that the deed of release was a "disposition" within s.10 of the right released. That right to enforce the covenant was an asset belonging to the deceased. This was crucial since the original transfer had been made more than six years before the father's death and thus was outside the scope of the section (as were all dispositions made before the commencement of the Act on 1 April 1976 (s.10(8)).

An application for an order under s.10 can only be made initially by a person who has made an application for an order for financial provision under s.2 of the Act. However, once such a person has made an application, then the donee under the disposition so challenged (or any other applicant for an order under s.2) may seek an order under s.10 on the basis of any other disposition made by the deceased within six years of his death. The conditions to be satisfied, and the court's powers if they are satisfied, are then the same as in relation to the disposition challenged in the original application (s.10(5)).

The court has a discretion as to whether or not to exercise the powers given by s.10 and, if so, to what extent. In determining whether and in what manner to exercise its powers, the court is required to have regard to:

(i) the circumstances in which any disposition was made and any valuable consideration which was given in return;

(ii) the relationship, if any, of the donee to the deceased;

(iii) the conduct and financial resources of the donee; and

(iv) all the other circumstances of the case.

(s.10(6)).

In *Re Dawkins* [1986] 2 FLR 360 Bush J took into account that the transferee was the deceased's daughter, but said that the claims of a widow could not be subordinated to the claims of a daughter who was young, fit and capable of earning her own living and also had a certain amount of capital resource.

Where a court makes an order under s.10 it may give such consequential directions as it thinks fit for giving effect to the order or for securing a fair adjustment of the rights of the persons affected thereby (s.12(3)). Thus, where a donee is ordered to transfer a specific item of property, the court may order some payment to be made to the donee out of the net estate and make consequential adjustments of the rights of beneficiaries.

Where the donee dies, an application under s.10 may nevertheless be made or continued against his estate. However, once any property of the donee has been distributed by his personal representative, no order can be made in respect of that property. The personal representative who distributes any such property before he has notice of an application is relieved from liability for not taking into account the possibility of such an application being made. The liability of a person to whom property was disposed of as a trustee by the deceased is limited to such money or other property in his hands at the date of the order as consists of, or represents, or is derived from, the money or property originally transferred by the deceased (s.13(1)). The powers of the court under s.10 may be exercised against persons who are the trustees for the time being of a trust established by the deceased even though they are not the original trustees. They are similarly protected (s.13(3)). Moreover, a trustee is not liable for having distributed any money or other property in accordance with the terms of the trust on the ground that he ought to have taken into account the possibility that an application would be made under s.10 (s.13(2)). However, although trustees who have parted with property will be protected, the beneficiaries under the trust will still remain liable to provide money or property under s.10, for a donee includes a person to whom or *for whose benefit* the disposition was made. (But see doubts expressed in the House of Lords, HL Deb. Vol. 359, cols. 1085 and 1089.)

### (g) Contracts relating to the disposition of property

An applicant for financial provision under s.2 of the Act may apply for an order under s.11 in respect of a contract made by the deceased by which he agreed to leave by his will a sum of money or other property to any person, or by which he agreed that a sum of money or other property would be paid or transferred to any person out of his estate. (Such a contract does not prevent revocation of the will but revocation will be a breach of contract.) An application under s.11 cannot be made in the course of an application for variation under s.6. If any money has been paid or other property has been transferred to or for the benefit of the donee in accordance with the contract, the court may make an order directing the donee to provide, for the purpose of making financial provision under s.2, such sum of money or other property as may be specified in the order. If the money, or all of the money, has not been paid, or the property, or all the property, has not been transferred in accordance with the contract, the court may make an order directing the personal representatives not to make any payment or further payment, or transfer any property, or any further property, as the case may be, in accordance with the contract. Alternatively, they may make an order directing the personal representatives to make only such payment, or transfer such property, as may be specified in the order (s.11(2)).

The court can exercise its powers under s.11 only if it is satisfied:

(i)   that the contract was made by the deceased with the intention of defeating an application for financial provision under the Act;

(ii)  that when the contract was made full valuable consideration for the contract was not given or promised by the person with whom, or for the benefit of whom, the contract was made (the donee) or by any other person; and

(iii) that the exercise of the powers conferred by s.11 would facilitate the making of financial provision for the applicant under the Act.

(s.11(2)).

The necessary intention will be established if the court is of opinion that, on a a balance of probabilities, the intention of the deceased, or a substantial part of his intention, in making the contract was to defeat a claim for financial provision under the Act either wholly or in part (s.12(2)). Where no valuable consideration was given or promised for the contractual promise of the deceased, then there is a presumption that the deceased made the contract with the intention of defeating an application for financial provision under the Act. On the other hand, where valuable consideration was given, the onus is on the applicant to prove that the contract was entered into with the necessary intention, that is, that although valuable consideration was given it was not full valuable consideration. It is further specifically provided that the court may exercise the powers under s.11 in relation to any contract made by the deceased only to the extent that the court considers that the amount of any sum of money paid or to be paid, or the value of any property transferred or to be transferred in accordance with the contract exceeds the value given or to be given for that contract. For this purpose the court is to have regard to the value of the property at the date of the hearing (s.11(3)).

"Valuable consideration" does not include marriage or a promise of marriage (s.25(1)). It does include executory consideration other than a promise of marriage.

The powers of the court under s.11 are limited to contracts made after the commencement of the Act on 1 April 1976 (s.11(6)). Apart from this, the date of the contract is immaterial in the sense that it is subject to the provisions of s.11 however long before the date of death of the deceased it was made. The situation following a contract is different from that following a disposition *inter vivos*. In the case of a disposition *inter vivos* the deceased will generally have immediately divested himself of the property affected, whereas the deceased will have retained full enjoyment during his lifetime of the property affected by a contract. It was not, therefore, thought appropriate to limit the powers of the court to contracts made within six years before the death of the deceased in the way that the powers of the court under s.10 in relation to dispositions *inter vivos* are limited to dispositions made within such a period (see Law Com. No. 61, para 237).

The court has a discretion whether or not to exercise its powers under s.11 and also as to the extent to which they should be exercised. In exercising its discretion the court is required to have regard to the circumstances in which the contract was made; the relationship, if any, of the promisee under the contract to the deceased; the conduct and financial resources of the promisee; and all the other circumstances of the case (s.11(4)). If the court makes an order under s.11 the rights of any person to enforce that contract or to recover damages or to obtain other relief for the breach thereof, are subject to any adjustment made by the court, and survive only to such extent as is consistent with giving effect to the terms of the order (s.11(5)). The court is given a wide power to make consequential directions for giving effect to an order or for securing a fair adjustment of the rights of the persons affected thereby (s.12(3)). Thus a court which makes an order will also be able to give directions as to what contractual rights, if any, still survive, and as to how they shall be satisfied. Again, where the promisee under a contract is ordered to restore or renounce property which was to be transferred to him under the contract, the court may order a cash payment to be made to him out of the estate.

The court's powers under s.11 are exercisable against the estate of the promisee if he has died, but once property has been distributed by the personal representatives of the promisee no order under s.11 can be made in respect of that property (s.12(4)). There are provisions protecting personal representatives of the promisee and protecting and limiting the liability of persons to whom property has been transferred as trustees pursuant to the contract (see s.13). These are similar to those applicable in relation to the powers of the court under s.10 in respect of dispositions *inter vivos* though perhaps less likely to be needed in practice.

### (h) Property subject to a power of appointment

Property over which the deceased had a general power of appointment exercisable by will or by deed is part of the deceased's "net estate" for the purposes of the 1975 Act if it was exercised by will or was not exercised at all. Property over which the deceased had a general power of appointment exercisable by deed but not by will is part of the deceased's "net estate" for this purpose if he has made no appointment (s.25(1)). In these situations, therefore, the property affected is available automatically to meet a claim for financial provision. On the other hand, where the deceased made an appointment *inter vivos* in exercise of a general power, then such an appointment is a disposition within s.10 of the 1975 Act and can be made the basis of an order under that section. In such a case the property which is the subject-matter of the appointment is not automatically available to meet a claim under the Act, but the appointees can be ordered by the court to provide money or property in order to meet such a claim (see above). Property over which the deceased had a special power of appointment exercisable by will is not available to meet a claim for provision as part of the "net estate" of the deceased, and an appointment in exercise of a special power cannot be made the basis of an order under s.10 whether it was by deed or by will. The Act of 1975 provides no definition of a general or a special power for this purpose, but it is submitted that the approach should be that a power should be regarded as general if the donee can appoint in his own favour without the consent of any other person. The consent of trustees for this purpose might be regarded as a general power notwithstanding a requirement that the consent of the trustees of a settlement be obtained (see *Re Phillips* [1931] 1 Ch 347 at p. 354 for the position in relation to the availability of property to meet the donee's debts).

## 3. Insolvency Act 1986

It has been noted in Chapter 8 that under ss.423-425 of the Insolvency Act 1986 (replacing s.172 of the Law of Property Act 1925) where a person has entered into a transaction at an undervalue the court may make such order as it thinks fit for restoring the position to what it would have been if the transaction had not been entered into and for protecting the interests of persons who are victims of the transaction.

# Index